Management Information

Managing Information Technology in the Networked Enterprise

THIRD EDITION

Management Information Systems

Managing Information Technology in the Networked Enterprise

James A. O'Brien
College of Business Administration
Northern Arizona University

IRWIN

Chicago • Bogotá • Boston • Buenos Aires • Caracas
London • Madrid • Mexico City • Sydney • Toronto

Publisher:	Tom Casson
Senior sponsoring editor:	Rick Williamson
Developmental editor:	Christine Wright
Marketing manager:	Michelle Hudson
Project editor:	Jean Lou Hess
Production supervisor:	Lara Feinberg
Assistant manager, graphics	Charlene R. Perez
Designer:	Matthew Baldwin
Cover designer:	Matthew Baldwin
Cover illustrator:	Boris Lyubner
Photo research Coordinator:	Keri Johnson
Photo researcher:	Sarah Evertson, Image Quest
Art studio:	ElectraGraphics, Inc.
Compositor:	Better Graphics, Inc.
Typeface:	10/12 Berkeley Old Style
Printer:	Von Hoffmann Press, Inc.

**Times Mirror
Higher Education Group**

Library of Congress Cataloging-in-Publication Data

O'Brien, James A.
    Management information systems: managing information technology
in the networked enterprise/James A. O'Brien.—3rd ed.
        p.   cm.
    Includes index.
    ISBN 0-256-17354-0   ISBN 0-256-20688-0 (International students ed.)
    1. Management information systems.   2. Computer networks.
    I. Title.
    T58.6.027   1996
    658.4'038'011—dc20

95–38515
CIP

To all who read these words
May you love the Light within you and everyone and everything
And to Erika Hildegard Germain
May you always walk in beauty and dance in the Light

About the Author

James A. O'Brien is a professor of Computer Information Systems in the College of Business Administration at Northern Arizona University. He completed his undergraduate studies at the University of Hawaii and Gonzaga University and earned an M.S. and Ph.D. in Business Administration from the University of Oregon. He has been coordinator of the CIS area at Northern Arizona University, professor of Finance and Management Information Systems and chairman of the Department of Management at Eastern Washington University, and a visiting professor at the University of Alberta, the University of Hawaii, and Central Washington University.

Dr. O'Brien's business experience includes working in the Marketing Management Program of the IBM Corporation, as well as serving as a financial analyst for the General Electric Company. He is a graduate of General Electric's Financial Management Program. He has also served as an information systems consultant to several banks and computer services firms.

Jim's research interests lie in developing and testing basic conceptual frameworks used in information systems development and management. He has written eight books, including several that have been published in multiple editions, as well as in Dutch, French, or Japanese translations. He has also contributed to the field of information systems through the publication of many articles in business and academic journals, as well as through his participation in academic and industry associations in the field of information systems.

Preface

What are the new skills demanded of effective managers in the 1990s? Competence and comfort in handling information technology (IT) will be high on the list. . . .

    Business managers are moving from a tradition where they could avoid, delegate, or ignore decisions about IT to one where they cannot create a marketing, product, international, organizational, or financial plan that does not involve such decisions.[1]

Managers and Information Technology

As tomorrow's managers, entrepreneurs, or business specialists, business students need to know how to use and manage information technology in today's networked enterprises and global markets. In this new environment, they will rely on global networks of information systems to share ideas and information and work together over wide geographical and cultural distances. Fast communications across the enterprise and easy collaboration among work groups become vital keys to business success. And of course, information technology makes it all happen.

    This text is written as an introduction to information systems for the business students of today who will work in this dynamic environment. As tomorrow's business professionals, they will rely on interconnected networks of information systems for:

- End user collaboration, including communications and computing among end user work groups and teams.
- Enterprisewide computing, including communications and information processing for business operations, managerial decision making, and strategic advantage.

About the Text

This is the managerial and networked enterprise perspective that the third edition brings to the study of information systems. Of course, as in the second edition, this edition:

- Loads the text with real world cases and problems about real people and companies in the business world.
- Organizes the text around a simple five-level framework that emphasizes the IS knowledge a managerial end user needs to know.
- Distributes and integrates information systems foundation theory throughout the text instead of concentrating it in several early chapters.
- Places a major emphasis on the strategic role of information systems in providing competitive advantage, as well as on the operational and decision support roles of information technology.

[1]Peter Keen, *Shaping the Future: Business Design Through Information Technologies* (Cambridge: Harvard Business School Press, 1991), pp. 1, 236.

- Emphasizes how a systems approach to the problem-solving process can provide information system solutions to business problems.

This new third edition is a major revision that retains these important features, while significantly updating coverage of IS technology and its business and managerial applications. In addition, this edition includes a new chapter on the strategic use of IT for competitive advantage. Major revisions have been made to the organization of topics in many chapters, and new pedagogical components have been added to end-of-chapter materials. Finally, the third edition provides all new Real World Cases and Problems in every chapter.

This text is designed for use in undergraduate or introductory MBA courses in management information systems, which are required in many business administration or management programs as part of the *common body of knowledge* required of all business majors. Thus, this text treats the subject area known as information systems (IS), management information systems (MIS), or computer information systems (CIS) as a major functional area of business that is as important to management education as are the areas of accounting, finance, operations management, marketing, and human resource management.

This text is designed to support the attainment of **information system literacy** by students. That is, its objective is to build a basic understanding of the value and uses of information technology in information systems for business operations, managerial decision making, and strategic advantage. Although this text is not designed for courses in *computer literacy*, it does include a module entitled "Information Technology: A Managerial Overview." The four chapters of this module emphasize managerial implications of information technology. However, they do contain overviews of computer hardware, software, telecommunications, and database management that can be used as a refresher on such topics or to help remedy deficiencies in student computer literacy.

An Information Systems Framework

This text provides a teaching-learning resource that reduces the complexity of an introductory course in information systems by using a conceptual framework that organizes the knowledge needed by business students into five major areas:

- **Foundation concepts.** Basic information systems concepts and the operations, decision-making, and strategic roles of information systems (Chapters 1 and 2). Other behavioral, managerial, and technical concepts are presented where appropriate in other chapters.
- **Technology.** Major concepts, developments, and managerial implications involved in computer hardware, software, telecommunications technologies, and database management (Chapters 4, 5, 6, and 7). Other technologies used in computer-based information systems are discussed where appropriate in selected chapters.
- **Applications.** How information technology is used in modern information systems to support end user collaboration, enterprise operations, managerial decision making, strategic advantage, and artificial intelligence and expert systems (discussed in Chapters 8, 9, 10, 11, and 12).
- **Development.** Developing information system solutions to business problems using a systems approach to problem solving and application develop-

ment (presented in Chapter 3 and Appendix B and in other chapters when discussing development issues for major types of information systems).

- **Management.** The challenges and methods of managing information systems technologies, activities, and resources, including information resource management, global IT management, issues in planning and implementing change with IT, and security and ethical challenges (emphasized in each chapter, but discussed specifically in Chapters 13, 14, and 15).

This text makes extensive use of up-to-date "real world" case studies and problems. These are not fictional stories, but actual situations faced by business firms and other organizations as reported in current business and IS periodicals. This includes three real world case studies in each chapter that apply specifically to that chapter's contents, six real world problems provided at the end of every chapter, and seven major case studies found in Appendix A. In addition, each chapter contains several Application Exercises, including at least two hands-on spreadsheet or database software assignments in Chapters 2 through 14. The purpose of this variety of assignment options is to give instructors and students many opportunities to apply each chapter's material to real world situations, using managerial problem solving or end user development approaches.

Real World Cases, Problems, and Exercises

This text introduces students early on to (1) basic information system concepts, (2) a systems approach to problem solving, and (3) information systems development. This approach emphasizes that information system concepts, the systems approach, and the systems development process are fundamental interrelated concepts used by both end users and IS specialists to solve business problems.

Many students are better motiviated if they can be shown how to apply such concepts to business problem solving early in the course. Then they can learn how to identify, analyze, and propose possible information system solutions to a variety of simple business problems early in the course. So this text introduces students to a systems approach to problem solving (demonstrated with a business case study) in the first section of Chapter 3, while the second section introduces the systems development process as a way for end users to develop IS solutions to business problems. At the option of the instructor, the Application Exercises in Chapter 8 can be assigned to present end user development approaches to the use of spreadsheet and database software, while Appendix B can be assigned to provide coverage of systems development tools. This helps students to begin analyzing chapter cases and problems and completing hands-on exercises early in the course. Students will also be ready to analyze the case studies in Appendix A and any actual business situations that instructors may assign as class projects.

Developing Information System Solutions to Business Problems

MIS texts have traditionally lumped coverage of systems theory, information theory, decision theory, management theory, and organization theory into their first three or four chapters. Although this placement is conceptually natural and defensible, it devastates many students and frustrates their instructors. It's just too much theory, too early, for most students. Much of it is forgotten by the time they finally get to chapters that apply such theories to various information system applications.

Distributing and Integrating IS Theory

That's why this text distributes and integrates theory throughout the text, especially in chapters covering major information system applications. For example, important concepts from management and decision theory are discussed in the first section of Chapter 10, followed by coverage of management reporting, decision support, and executive information systems in the second section of that chapter. This method of organizing the text ties theoretical concepts more directly and naturally to their application to major types of information systems. It thus makes it easier for students to understand and remember such concepts, while providing a rationale for the importance of specific information systems applications and issues.

Strategic, International, and Ethical Dimensions

This text contains substantial text material and cases reflecting the strategic, international, and ethical dimensions of information systems. This can be found not only in Chapter 11, *Information Systems for Strategic Advantage*, in Chapter 13, *Managing IT: Enterprise and Global Management*, and in Chapter 15, *Managing IT: Security and Ethical Challenges*, but in all other chapters of the text. This is especially evident in many Real World Cases and Problems, such as GE Plastics, Abaco Grupo Financiero, Scotiabank, West American T-Shirt Company, Wal-Mart Stores, R. J. Reynolds, Tropicana Products, DHL Worldwide Express, PC Gifts and Flowers, Opticon Holding A/S, Capital One Financial, Nissan Motor Corp., Canada Trust, Levi Strauss & Co., Barclays Bank, Nestle, and Elf Atochem, ABB Asea Brown Boveri, the World Bank, Kevin Mitnick and Tsutomu Shimomura, David LaMacchia of MIT, Canter and Siegel, Johnson Controls, Credit Agricole-Lazard, and many, many others. These samples repeatedly demonstrate the strategic and ethical challenges of managing information technology for competitive advantage in global business markets and in the global information society in which we all live and work.

Modular Structure of the Text

The text is organized according to the five major areas of the framework for information systems knowledge mentioned earlier. Figure 1 illustrates how the text is organized into four modules and two appendices. Also, each chapter is organized into two distinct sections. This is done to avoid proliferation of chapters, as well as to provide better conceptual organization of the text and each chapter. This organization increases instructor flexibility in assigning course material since it structures the text into modular levels (i.e., modules, chapters, and sections) while reducing the number of chapters that need to be covered.

Each chapter starts with a Chapter Outline and Learning Objectives and ends with a Summary, Key Terms and Concepts, a Review Quiz tied directly to the Key Terms and Concepts, Discussion Questions, Real World Problems, Application Exercises, Review Quiz Answers, and Selected References. Real World Cases are also provided at the end of each section and chapter.

Module I: Foundations of Information Systems

The first module of this text is designed as a **core module** of foundation concepts. Once instructors have covered this module, they can assign any other module, depending on their pedagogical preferences. Chapter 1 stresses the importance of information systems and information technology in business, and introduces a framework of information systems knowledge needed by managerial end users. Chapter 2 introduces the generic components and properties of information systems, and how the major types of information systems support business operations, managerial decision making, and strategic advantage. Chapter 3 introduces a sys-

FIGURE 1
The modular organization of the text.

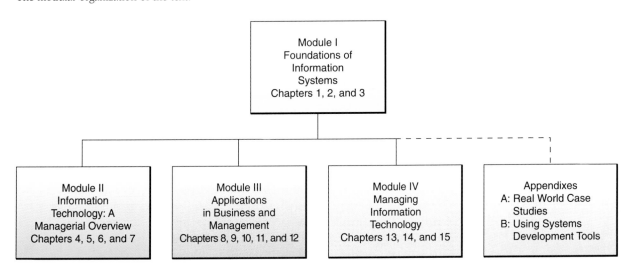

tems approach to business problem solving and then applies these concepts to the information systems development process from the viewpoint of a managerial end user.

Module II contains chapters on computer hardware (Chapter 4), software (Chapter 5), telecommunications (Chapter 6), and database management (Chapter 7). Its purpose is to give students an overview of the technology used in modern computer-based information systems and its implications for end user management. This material is consolidated in an independent module since students may have already covered some of these topics in an earlier course. Thus, instructors can selectively use the chapters and sections of this module, depending on the preparation of their students. This is especially useful in the case of the important topics of telecommunications and database management, in which many students, typically, have had only a brief exposure. Students need an adequate background in such topics in order to propose realistic information system solutions to business problems.

*Module II:
Information
Technology: A
Managerial Overview*

Module III contains five chapters that discuss the basic concepts and major applications of computer-based information systems. It emphasizes how information systems support end user productivity and the operations, managerial decision making, and competitive advantage of business firms and other organizations. Thus, it includes coverage of concepts and applications in end user computing and collaboration and office automation (Chapter 8), business information systems and transaction processing (Chapter 9), managerial reporting, decision support, and executive information systems (Chapter 10), information systems for strategic advantage (Chapter 11), and artificial intelligence, human information processing, and expert systems (Chapter 12).

*Module III:
Applications in
Business and
Management*

Module IV: Managing Information Technology

It is important that prospective managerial end users learn that although information technology can help them solve business problems, it also poses major managerial challenges. That is the focus of the three chapters of Module IV. The impact of information technology, the importance of information resource management, and the managerial implications of the global use of information technology are covered in Chapter 13. Chapter 14 discusses management issues in the planning and implementation of organizational change caused or enabled by IT. Chapter 15 explores the controls and safeguards needed to improve information system performance and security, as well as the ethical challenges posed by computer crime and other societal impacts of information technology.

Appendixes

Appendix A is a 39-page appendix containing seven major case studies which can be used at the option of the instructor. They describe problems and opportunities in business operations, managerial decision making, competitive advantage, or information systems management faced by actual computer-using firms and organizations. These cases can thus be used to integrate many of the concepts and applications discussed in the text. They are an additional method of giving students an opportunity to apply knowledge gained throughout the course to the development of information system solutions to business problems. Thus, these longer case studies can be used as the basis for class discussion or for term project assignments.

Appendix B offers optional coverage of systems development tools. This includes simple introductions to systems flowcharts, data flow diagrams, and entity relationship diagrams.

Summary of Changes

Besides providing all new Real World Cases and Problems, the third edition represents a major revision of chapter contents. Highlights of the changes made in the second-edition material are found in the following third-edition chapters:

Chapter 1: *Introduction to Information Systems in Business.*
Section II of this chapter is a new section that emphasizes the importance of IT in business with an overview of the impact of IT on business developments such as globalization, reengineering, and competitive advantage.

Chapter 2: *Fundamentals of Information Systems.*
Coverage of information system concepts and components, formerly in Chapter 1, has been revised and moved to Section I of this chapter, with an overview of the types and roles of information systems moved to Section II.

Chapter 3: *Solving Business Problems with Information Systems.*
The coverage of the systems approach in business problem solving in Section I has been thoroughly revised and combined with an analysis of a business case study formerly in Appendix B.

Chapter 4, 5: *Managerial Overview: Computer Hardware* and *Managerial Overview: Computer Software.*
Updated and reorganized coverage of computer hardware and software.

Chapter 6:   *Managerial Overview: Telecommunications.*
               A major revision and new topics such as open systems, client/server, the information superhighway, and business use of the Internet.

Chapter 7:   *Managerial Overview: Database Management.*
               Updated and reorganized coverage of the role of database management in managing organizational and end user data resources in Section I, and technical topics in database management in Section II.

Chapter 8:   *Information Systems for End User Computing and Collaboration.*
               This revised chapter emphasizes the importance of end user computing and office automation applications, including new material on end user collaboration, work group computing, and hypertext and multimedia applications.

Chapter 9:   *Information Systems for Business Operations.*
               Section I is a revision and consolidation of material on IS support of the functional areas of business formerly in Chapter 12. Section II contains revised material on EDI, EFT, and transaction processing systems.

Chapter 10:   *Information Systems for Managerial Decision Making and Support.*
               Substantial new material has been added on online analytical processing (OLAP) and decision support and executive information systems. Also, coverage of information quality and management information systems (information reporting systems), formerly in Chapter 9, has been consolidated into this chapter.

Chapter 11:   *Information Systems for Strategic Advantage.*
               Section I of this new chapter contains new and revised coverage of competitive strategy concepts, formerly in Chapter 2. Section II contains much new material on the strategic use of IT for business process reengineering, total quality management, agile competition, virtual corporations, and strategic use of the Internet.

Chapter 12:   *Information Systems and Artificial Intelligence Technologies.*
               Revised coverage of artificial intelligence and expert systems, and new material on case-based reasoning, neural networks, fuzzy logic, virtual reality, intelligent agents, and hybrid AI systems in business.

Chapter 13:   *Managing IT: Enterprise and Global Management.*
               Section I is a revision of managerial issues in IT, including management involvement in IS governance, trends in IS organization, and the managerial and organizational impact of IT. Section II contains much new and revised material on global IT management, formerly in Chapter 15, including cultural challenges, global company requirements, and global business/IT strategies.

Chapter 14:   *Managing IT: Planning and Implementing Change.*
               The focus and content of this chapter has been revised to stress planning and implementing change with IT. This includes new IS planning materials on competitive advantage, reach and range analysis, and the scenario approach added to Section I (formerly in Chapter 13). Section II contains new material on managing change caused by implementing new information technologies in an organization.

Chapter 15:   *Managing IT: Security and Ethical Challenges.*
Section I of this chapter contains new material on IS security and controls, and was formerly in Chapter 14. Section II contains new material on computer crime and ethical controversies on the Internet, as well as revised coverage of ethical and societal IT issues. Chapter 15 thus serves as a *capstone chapter* whose content provides an integrating and stimulating series of topics, Real World Cases and Problems, and Application Exercises for class discussion and assignments at the end of the course.

Appendix A: *Real World Case Studies.*
This optional appendix contains seven major case studies of computer-using firms. All of the case studies are new to this edition.

Appendix B: *Using Systems Development Tools.*
This optional appendix contains revised material on systems development tools, including new material on entity relationship diagrams.

Support Materials

The IRWIN Advantage Series is a collection of laboratory tutorials for the most popular microcomputer software packages available. There are over 30 lab manuals available, so you can choose any combination to accommodate your individual class needs.

A revised **software case book,** *Application Cases in MIS: Using Spreadsheet and Database Software,* second edition, by James N. Morgan, of Northern Arizona University, is available to supplement the hands-on exercises in this edition. This optional case book contains an extensive number of hands-on cases, many of which include a suggested approach for solving each case with a spreadsheet or database management software package to develop solutions for realistic business problems.

An **Instructor's Resource Manual,** revised by Margaret Edmunds, of Mount Allison University, is available to instructors upon adoption of the text. It contains instructional aids and suggestions, detailed annotated chapter outlines with instructional suggestions for use in lectures, answers to chapter questions, and problems and case study questions. A data/solutions disk is included for use with the spreadsheet and database exercises in the text. There are also several additional case studies and their solutions that do not appear in the text.

A set of 40 color **overhead transparencies** of line art from the book is available to adopters.

A **Transparency Masters** manual of line art from the book is available to adopters. In addition, there is a **presentation graphics disk** in Power Point that supplies a color slide show for each real world case and problem to support classroom discussion, as well as additional teaching tips and suggestions.

A **Test Bank,** which contains over 3,000 true-false, multiple choice, and fill-in-the-blank questions, has been revised by Margaret Edmunds, of Mount Allison University. It is available as a separate test manual and in computerized form on floppy disk for use with the Irwin Test Generator Program.

Acknowledgments

The author wishes to acknowledge the assistance of the following reviewers whose constructive criticism and suggestions helped invaluably in shaping the form and content of this text:

Linda J. Behrens, *University of Central Oklahoma*
William E. Burrows, *University of Washington*
Jane M. Carey, *Arizona State University-West*
Robert Golladay, *University of North Texas*
Betsy S. Hoppe, *Wake Forest University*
Christopher V. Jones, *Simon Fraser University*
Albert Kagan, *Arizona State University*
Jane M. Mackay, *Texas Christian University*
Dick Ricketts, *Lane Community College*

My thanks also go to James N. Morgan, of Northern Arizona University, who authored the software casebook that can be used with this text and developed most of the hands-on Application Exercises in the text, as well as the Data/Solutions disk in the Instructor's Resource Manual. Additional acknowledgments are owed to Margaret Edmunds, of Mount Allison University, who revised the Instructor's Resource Manual and the Test Bank.

Much credit should go to several individuals who played significant roles in this project. Thus, my thanks go to the editorial and production team at Irwin, especially Rick Williamson, senior sponsoring editor, Christine Wright, developmental editor, Jean Lou Hess, project editor, and Matthew Baldwin, designer. Their ideas and hard work were invaluable contributions to the successful completion of the project. Thanks also to Michele Allen whose word processing skills helped me meet many manuscript deadlines. The contributions of many authors, periodicals, and firms in the computer industry who contributed case material, ideas, illlustrations, and photographs used in this text are also thankfully acknowledged.

Acknowledging the Real World of Business

The unique contribution of over 200 business firms and other computer-using organizations that are the subject of the real world cases, problems, exercises, and case studies in each chapter is also gratefully acknowledged. The real-life situations faced by these firms and organizations provide the readers of this text with a valuable demonstration of the benefits and limitations of using information technology to support business operations, managerial decision making, and strategic advantage.

James A. O'Brien

Contents in Brief

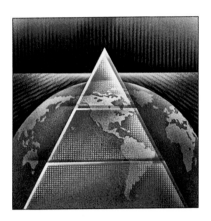

Contents

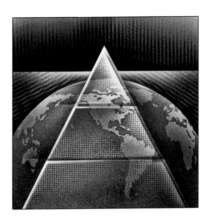

MODULE II
Information Technology: A Managerial Overview   105

Available as a supplement:

IRWIN
INFORMATION SYSTEMS VIDEO LIBRARY

Applications Oriented
CASE STUDIES from a Wide Variety of Businesses
10–12 Minutes in Length

Introduction to Information Systems
Explains how people, data, procedures, and technology unite to form an information system.

Connections: AT&T's Vision of the Future
Introduces students to a wide range of technology.

Information Systems in Human Resource Management
Demonstrates how Hewitt Associates uses information systems.

Manufacturing Systems
Explains how Nucor Steel uses CIM.

Information Systems in Marketing
Shows how Soft Ad and Navistar International use marketing databases.

Financial Management Information Systems
Demonstrates the impact of financial networks on global financial markets.

Corporate Training Systems
Shows how Allstate Insurance and United Airlines use IS for corporate training.

Interacting with Internet
Demonstrates how the Internet can improve world-wide communications.

Information Systems for the Retail Market
Shows how Spiegel uses CAD technology.

Multimedia Presentations
Shows how Stop & Shop, Mannington Mills, and IBM use CDI, CD-ROM, and other technologies.

Business Process Reengineering
Demonstrates the steps and stages of BPR at Caterpillar.

Client/Server Technology
Demonstrates a sophisticated client/server system called Marketing Information Machine (MIM).

Management Information Systems

Managing Information Technology in the Networked Enterprise

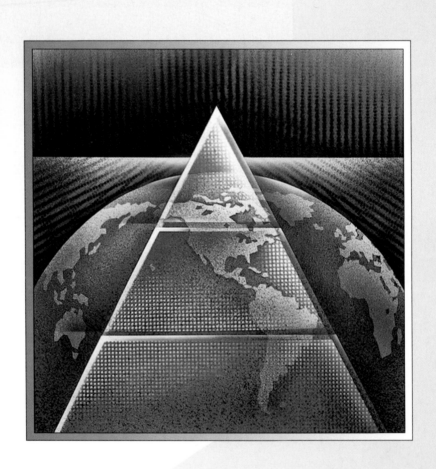

Foundations of Information Systems

Why study information systems? Why do businesses need information technology? What do you need to know about the use and management of information systems? How can you help develop information system solutions to business problems? The three chapters of Module I are designed to answer these fundamental questions about information systems.

Chapter 1, "Introduction to Information Systems in Business," introduces you to the importance of information systems knowledge for managerial end users, and some of the key issues in the business use of information technology.

Chapter 2, "Fundamentals of Information Systems," explains the conceptual system components and properties of information systems, and then provides an overview of the major roles and types of information systems for business operations, managerial decision making, and strategic advantage.

Chapter 3, "Solving Business Problems with Information Systems," presents a systematic approach to problem solving. It then introduces traditional and prototyping approaches to developing information system solutions to business problems.

Introduction to Information Systems in Business

CHAPTER OUTLINE

LEARNING OBJECTIVES

The purpose of this chapter is to give you an understanding of the importance of information systems by analyzing (1) how the field of information systems relates to managerial end users, and (2) the vital role of information technology in business.

Section I of this chapter introduces the field of information systems. It discusses the importance of the information systems field to business professionals and managers, and provides a framework for organizing a business end user's knowledge of information systems.

Section II emphasizes the vital role information systems play in business operations, managerial decision making, and strategic advantage. It spotlights how businesses are using information technology to meet the challenge of change by programs of globalization, business process reengineering, and agile competition.

After reading and studying this chapter, you should be able to:

1. Explain why knowledge of information systems is important for managerial end users and identify five areas of information systems knowledge they need.

2. Give examples to illustrate how information systems can help support a firm's business operations, managerial decision making, and strategic advantage.

3. Identify how businesses can use IT for strategic competitive advantage through programs of globalization, business process reengineering, and agile competition.

┌ **SECTION I**
│ **Why Study Information Systems?**

Why Information Systems Are Important

Why study **information systems?** That's the same as asking why anyone should study accounting, finance, operations management, marketing, human resource management, or any other major business function. Information systems have become a vital component of successful business firms and other organizations. They thus constitute an essential field of study in business administration and management. That's why most business majors must take a course in information systems. Since you probably intend to be a manager, entrepreneur, or business professional, it is just as important to have a basic understanding of information systems as it is to understand any other functional area in business.

Information System Resources and Technologies

An **information system** is an organized combination of people, hardware, software, communications networks, and data resources that collects, transforms, and disseminates information in an organization. See Figure 1.1. People have relied on information systems to communicate with each other using a variety of physical devices (hardware), information processing instructions (software), communications channels (networks), and stored data (data resources) since the dawn of civilization. Today's end users rely on many types of information systems (IS). They might include simple *manual* (paper-and-pencil) hardware devices and *informal* (word-of-mouth) communications channels. However, in this text, we will concentrate on *computer-based information systems* that use computer hardware and software, telecommunications networks, computer-based data management techniques, and other forms of **information technology** (IT) to transform data resources into a variety of information products. We will discuss this concept further in the next chapter and in the chapters of Module II on Information Technology.

An End User Perspective

Anyone who uses an information system or the information it produces is an **end user.** This usually applies to most people in an organization, as distinguished from the smaller number of people who are *information system specialists,* such as systems analysts or professional computer programmers. A *managerial end user* is a manager, entrepreneur, or managerial-level professional who personally uses information systems. So most managers are managerial end users. This book is written for potential managerial end users like you and other students of business administration and management.

Whatever your career will be, you can increase your opportunities for success by becoming a knowledgeable end user of information technology. Businesses and other organizations need people who can use networked computer workstations to enhance their own personal productivity and the productivity of their work groups, departments, and organizations. For example, you should be able to use word processing and electronic mail to communicate more effectively, spreadsheet packages to more effectively analyze decision situations, database management packages to provide better reports on organizational performance, and specialized business software to support your specific work activities. You should also be aware of the management problems and opportunities presented by the use of information technology, and how you can effectively confront such challenges. Then you can play a major role in seeing that information system resources are used efficiently and

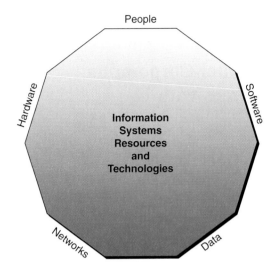

People

Hardware

Software

**Information
Systems
Resources
and
Technologies**

Networks

Data

FIGURE 1.1
Information systems use people,
hardware, software, communications networks, and data
management technologies to
collect, transform, and dissemi-
nate information in an
organization.

effectively to benefit your career goals and the goals of the business firms or other
organizations you may work for in the future.

Information systems play a vital role in the business success of an enterprise.
Information technology can provide the information a business needs for efficient
operations, effective management, and competitive advantage. However, if information systems do not properly support the strategic objectives, business operations, or
management needs of an enterprise, they can seriously damage its prospects for survival and success. So, the proper management of information systems is a major
challenge for managers. Thus, the information systems function represents:

- A major functional area of business that is as important to business success
  as the functions of accounting, finance, operations management, marketing,
  and human resource management.
- A major part of the resources of an enterprise and its cost of doing business,
  thus posing a major resource management challenge.
- An important factor affecting operational efficiency, employee productivity
  and morale, and customer service and satisfaction.
- A major source of information and support needed to promote effective decision making by managers.
- An important ingredient in developing competitive products and services
  that give an organization a strategic advantage in the global marketplace.
- A vital, dynamic, and challenging career opportunity for millions of men and
  women.

*An Enterprise
Perspective*

Let's take a moment to bring the real world into our discussion of the importance of
information systems. Read the Real World Case of Manor Care Inc. and Bechtel
Corporation on page 8. Then let's analyze it together.

**The Real World of
Information
Systems**

Manor Care Inc. and Bechtel Corporation: Managing Human Resources with IT

Information technology is helping many businesses reshape their human resource systems into something more effective and vital than just backroom record-keeping. A growing crop of "client/server" human resources (HR) packages is helping users replace old, inflexible, and frequently homegrown mainframe computer-based HR systems. *Client/server systems* rely on interconnected networks of end user microcomputer workstations (*clients*), networked to more powerful computers (*servers*) for sharing data, software, and hardware resources, and coordinating communications and computing among the users on the network.

Not long ago, it was common for human resources staffs to request a specific report from the information systems department and then wait days or weeks for it to be delivered. However, because of the ease-of-use and responsiveness of the new client/server software, users say they can now access and analyze data on a timely basis. The real plus is they can deliver better information more quickly to business managers to help them make decisions about issues such as employee promotions, cutbacks, reassignments, fringe benefits, or training requirements.

"That was the main thing—access to information," said Troy Albright, director of human resources administration and systems at Manor Care, Inc. The health management company in Silver Springs, Maryland, recently migrated from an outdated mainframe HR package to a client/server-based human resource management system from

PeopleSoft, Inc. "The level of expertise that was required by the old system meant that only about three employees out of 28,000 knew how to get information out of the old system," Albright said. Now, all human resource management specialists and managers can easily retrieve information they need.

Other users agree that client/server systems are critical because they provide more information faster and easier than older systems. "We had a system that just aged," said Bob Klumb, a manager in charge of human resources information systems at Bechtel Corp. in San Francisco. The engineering firm is migrating to an Oracle Corporation client/server-based human resource management system.

Bechtel's business is based on worldwide engineering projects, so "the movement of people, the training and the development of people are fairly mission-critical items," Klumb said. Unlike the old system, the Oracle software gives project managers more up-to-date information on employees to staff up and plan for projects.

CASE STUDY QUESTIONS

1. How important are computer-based human resource information systems to the success of Manor Care and Bechtel? Explain.

2. What major change in information technology occurred at these companies? What benefits resulted?

Source: Adapted from Rosemary Cafasso, "HR Staffs Recruit Client/Server Systems," *Computerworld,* January 16, 1995, p. 61. Copyright 1995 by Computerworld, Inc., Framingham, MA 01701—Reprinted from *Computerworld.*

Analyzing Manor Care and Bechtel

We can learn a lot about the importance of computers and information systems from the Real World Case of Manor Care and Bechtel.

Both Manor Care and Bechtel are using information technology to improve their management of human resources. They have replaced their older, unresponsive mainframe computer-based systems with new client/server systems that are quicker, more responsive, and easier to use. The mainframe-based software provided a limited amount of information that only a few skilled specialists could extract from the system. The new HR software was designed for end users at PC workstations connected to servers in client/server networks. It is thus a lot easier for HR staffers and managers to get the information they need.

Human resource data on employees can now be accessed and analyzed faster and easier by the HR staff of both companies. They can now deliver better information more quickly to help business managers make human resource management decisions. These HR decisions are "mission-critical"—that is, vital to the successful staffing of the worldwide engineering projects of Bechtel Corporation, for example.

Information is a basic resource in today's society. We are living in a **global information society**, with a global economy that is increasingly dependent on the creation, management, and distribution of information resources. People in many nations no longer live in agricultural societies, composed primarily of farmers, or even industrial societies, where a majority of the workforce consists of factory workers. Instead, the workforce in many nations consists primarily of workers in service occupations or **knowledge workers**, that is, people who spend most of their workday creating, using, and distributing information. See Figure 1.2.

Knowledge workers include executives, managers, and supervisors; professionals such as accountants, engineers, scientists, stockbrokers, and teachers; and staff personnel such as secretaries and clerical office personnel. Most of them are end users who make their living using information systems to create, distribute, manage, and use information resources. Thus, information systems help them manage the human, financial, material, energy, and other resources involved in their work responsibilities.

This brings up the question of what your responsibilities are in the ethical use of information technology. As a prospective managerial end user and knowledge worker, you should begin to think about what **ethical responsibilities** are generated by the use of information systems. For example, what uses of information technology might be considered improper or irresponsible to other individuals or to society? What is the proper use of an organization's information resources? What does it take to be a *responsible end user* of information technology and protect

A Global Information Society

FIGURE 1.2
Business end users are knowledge workers who are part of a global information society.

Charles Thatcher/Tony Stone Images.

yourself from computer crime? These are some of the questions that outline the ethical dimensions of information systems that we will discuss in this text.

Information and information systems, then, are valuable resources for knowledge workers, their organizations, and society. A major challenge for our global information society is to manage its information resources to benefit all members of society while meeting the strategic goals of organizations and nations. This means, for example, using information systems to find more efficient, profitable, and socially responsible ways of using the world's limited supplies of material, energy, and other resources. Since the information systems of so many organizations are interconnected by local, regional, and global telecommunications networks, knowledge workers can now access and distribute information and manage resources all over the world.

For these reasons, information systems play an increasingly vital role in our global economy, as many real world cases and problems in the text will demonstrate. For example, read the Real World Case on GE Plastics on page 11. Then let's analyze how it proves this point.

Analyzing GE Plastics

The marketing managers at GE Plastics asked themselves how they could better communicate with their worldwide base of customers. They knew that the pace of change in information technology had been rapid, as were the dynamic changes occurring in the global business environment. So they decided to try something new—establish a computer connection on the Internet for their customers. Now, over 12,000 times a month, customers and prospects from all over the world access their Internet database to inquire about GE Plastics products. They feel it definitely gives them a competitive advantage.

More and more businesses are establishing ways for their customers or prospects to communicate with them via computers and telecommunications networks. This may involve global telecommunications networks like the Internet, public information services like CompuServe, Prodigy, or America OnLine, or local and regional networks they establish themselves or with other businesses. This taps into new markets and prospective customers, as well as making it easier for many current customers to communicate and access information about a company's products and services.

Technological and Behavioral Dimensions of IS

Computer science, engineering, and mathematics are disciplines that contribute to the *technological* aspects of information systems in business. It is these disciplines, along with the information systems discipline, whose research drives developments in computer hardware, software, telecommunications, database management, and other information technologies. For example, much technological research and development focuses on designing better computer processors, operating system software, telecommunications network architectures, and new database structures.

Areas such as psychology, sociology, and political science, on the other hand, contribute to the *behavioral* aspects of information systems in organizations. The research findings of these behavioral disciplines and the discipline of information systems shed light on how individuals and organizations can effectively use and manage information technology. For example, research in psychology and sociology helps in the design of information technologies which support individual and group communications, decision making, and cooperative work. Some of the research

GE Plastics: Global Marketing on the Internet

GE Plastics, a $6 billion subsidiary of General Electric Co., began 1995 on the Internet with 1,500 pages of online data on its products for buyers and users around the world. "A year or so ago, we said to ourselves, `We haven't changed fundamentally the way we communicate with our customers for a long time,'" says Richard Pocock, general manager of marketing communications at GE Plastics. "And yet, the pace of change in information technology has been extreme. What are we missing?"

After considering a number of options such as CD-ROM, the company decided to establish a computer connection on the Internet, mostly because of its around-the-world and around-the-clock reach. One month after setting up an Internet computer server and product information database, GE Plastics was getting some 12,000 inquiries a month on its database from buyers and users all over the world looking for information about the company's products.

According to Pocock, GE customers worldwide can now get in minutes information that would have taken many days via a telephone call and "snail-mail" delivery. "I believe it definitely gives us a competitive advantage," he says.

Pocock admits it is too early to assess the costs and benefits of the new service, but he says he expects incremental costs to be offset by savings in the printing and distribution of paper products.

Pocock says that other GE Plastics marketing executives are also enthused about the long term marketing potential of the global "network of networks" and global "information superhighway" that the Internet has become. "It is only a matter of time before the Internet becomes a very dominant business-to-business communications tool," Pocock says. "We see this as an opportunity to establish a plastics community tied together via the Internet. We want to create a dialogue with a large community that's otherwise difficult to have."

CASE STUDY QUESTIONS

1. How important to GE Plastics is their Internet connection? Explain.

2. Could other types of businesses benefit from similar computer connections to regional or global telecommunications networks? Explain.

Source: Adapted from Gary Anthes, "Cruisin'," *Computerworld*, December 26, 1994/January 2, 1995, pp. 20–21. Copyright 1995 by Computerworld, Inc., Framingham, MA 01701—Reprinted from *Computerworld*.

drawn from political science, on the other hand, focuses on the politics and governance issues involved in managing the introduction and the use of information technology in organizations.

Both of these aspects, the technological and the behavioral, are important for business end users. That's because computer-based information systems, though heavily dependent on information technologies, are designed, operated, and used by people in a variety of organizational settings. Thus, the success of an information system should not be measured only by its *efficiency* in terms of minimizing costs, time, and the use of information resources. Success should also be measured by the *effectiveness* of the information technology in supporting and meeting the goals of end users and their work groups and organizations.

Figure 1.3 emphasizes this interplay of technological and behavioral components in a business enterprise [10]. In this sociotechnical enterprise model, a business is viewed as consisting of five basic behavioral and technological components. These are people and their cultures, organizational structures, management strategies, business processes, and information systems and technologies. These components interact with each other as the enterprise is subjected to influences from the external sociotechnological environment. For example, new development in information technology, workplace cultures, or marketplace competition could affect

FIGURE 1.3
A business enterprise consists of behavioral and technological components, including information systems and technologies, that interact within a sociotechnological environment.

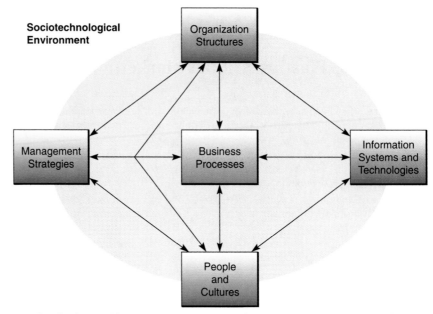

Source: Adapted and reprinted from Djoen Tan, "IT Management Plateaus: An Organizational Architecture for IS." *Information Systems Management* (New York: Averbach Publications) Winter 1995, p. 45. © 1995 Warren, Gorham & Lamont. Used with permission.

all five components of the business. The job of the organization's managers would be to ensure that adjustments are made to each basic component, including information systems and technologies, so that the goals of the enterprise and its people are accomplished [2, 10].

What Managerial End Users Need to Know

The real world examples of Manor Care, Bechtel, and GE Plastics should help convince you that managerial end users need to know how information systems can be employed successfully in a global business environment. That's why this text contains over 130 Real World Cases and Problems describing actual situations (not fictional stories) occurring in real companies and organizations throughout the world. Business firms and other organizations need people who can help them manage their information resources. Knowledgeable managerial end users can play a major role in *information resource management* (IRM). That is, they can learn to manage information system hardware, software, data, and information resources so they are used for the efficient operation, effective management, and strategic success of their organizations.

However, what exactly does a business end user need to know about information systems? The answers are as diverse and dynamic as the area itself. As we have just mentioned, the field of information systems, like other areas in management and business administration, is based on a variety of academic disciplines and encompasses a great amount of technological and behavioral knowledge. The IS field is constantly changing and expanding as dramatic technological developments and behavioral research findings push back the frontiers of this dynamic discipline.

Information Systems

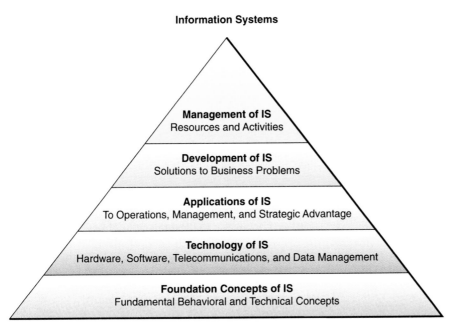

FIGURE 1.4
This framework outlines the major areas of information systems knowledge needed by managerial end users.

Because many chief executive officers, if not most, are resigned to techno-illiteracy, they depend on resident technologists—usually at the chief information officer level—for critical decisions that may make or break the company. Unfortunately, as much as CEOs are unfamiliar with information technology, the CIOs are unfamiliar with the core businesses that technology is intended to support [11].

That's the conclusion of Charles Wang, the chairman and CEO of Computer Associates International, a multibillion-dollar software company, after meeting with hundreds of CEOs throughout the world. So even top executives can feel overwhelmed by the complex technologies, abstract behavioral concepts, and specialized applications involved in the field of information systems. However, most managers and other end users do not have to absorb all of this knowledge. Figure 1.4 illustrates a useful conceptual framework that outlines what end users need to know about information systems. It emphasizes that you should concentrate your efforts in five areas of **knowledge:** foundation concepts, technology, applications, development, and management.

A Framework for Managerial End Users

What are information systems, and why are they important to end users and their organizations? In order to answer this question, you need to understand what the basic components and types of information systems are. This requires an understanding of some fundamental concepts in *general systems theory* and information processing. However, you should also appreciate the vital roles played by information systems in businesses and other organizations. For example, you should learn some fundamental behavioral and technical concepts that will help you understand how information systems can support the business operations, managerial decision making, and strategic advantage of business firms and other organizations. Chapters 1 and 2 and other chapters of the text support this area of knowledge.

Foundation Concepts

Technology

What should end users know about the technologies used in computer-based information systems? The answer to this question is that they should have an understanding of major concepts, developments, and management issues in **information technology**—that is, hardware, software, telecommunications, database management, and other information processing technologies. Technology is so dynamic in this field that a factual knowledge that concentrates on detailed characteristics and capabilities would soon be outdated. Instead, you should focus on generic capabilities, major developmental trends, and management challenges in the use of information systems technology. Chapters 4 through 7 of Module II along with other chapters of the text support this area of information systems knowledge.

Applications

In what ways can information systems assist end users and organizations in accomplishing their work activities and meeting their strategic objectives? Answering this question requires a knowledge of the major applications of information systems for end user activities and the operations, management, and competitive advantage of business firms and other organizations. You should gain a basic understanding of information systems concepts and applications in areas such as end user computing, office automation, transaction processing, the functional areas of business, management reporting, decision support, executive support, competitive advantage, and artificial intelligence. Chapters 8 to 12 of Module III support this learning objective.

Development

How should end users or information specialists develop information systems solutions to business problems? To answer this question, you should learn some fundamental problem-solving and developmental concepts. You should understand how methodologies such as the *systems approach,* the *systems development life cycle,* and *prototyping* can be used by end users and IS specialists to construct information systems applications that successfully meet end user and organizational needs. Chapter 3 of Module I helps you gain such knowledge and begin applying it to simple business problems. The goal of this chapter is to help you propose information systems solutions to business problems found in the case studies in each chapter, and in Appendix A, "Real World Case Studies." Other chapters in the text, as well as Appendix B, "Using Systems Development Tools," build on the content of Chapter 3. They provide additional information and examples of important systems development tools and considerations.

Management

How should business end users meet the major challenges they face in managing information technology in their organizations? Answering this question requires understanding what methods you can use to manage the resources, technologies, and activities of information systems. Developing and using information technology can be as difficult and costly as it is beneficial to a firm. Thus, you should understand concepts such as *information resource management, global IT management* and *information systems planning, implementation,* and *control* as well as important security and ethical challenges in information systems. Chapters 13, 14, and 15 of Module IV specifically cover these topics, but all of the chapters in the text emphasize the managerial challenges of information technology. Their goal is to help you develop a managerial perspective for dealing with the problems and opportunities presented by the use of information technology in today's dynamic global business environment.

SECTION II
Why Businesses Need Information Technology

Information technology is reshaping the basics of business. Customer service, operations, product and marketing strategies, and distribution are heavily, or sometimes even entirely, dependent on IT. The computers that support these functions can be found on the desk, on the shop floor, in the store, even in briefcases. Information technology, and its expense, have become an everyday part of business life [8].

Figure 1.5 illustrates the fundamental reasons for the use of information technology in business. Information systems perform three vital roles in any type of organization:

- Support of business operations.
- Support of managerial decision making.
- Support of strategic competitive advantage.

Let's take a retail store as an example to illustrate this important point. As a consumer, you have to deal regularly with the information systems that support business operations at the many retail stores where you shop. For example, most retail stores now use computer-based information systems to help them record customer purchases, keep track of inventory, pay employees, buy new merchandise, and evaluate sales trends. Store operations would grind to a halt without the support of such information systems. See Figures 1.6 and 1.7.

Information systems also help store managers make better decisions and attempt to gain a strategic competitive advantage. For example, decisions on what lines of merchandise need to be added or discontinued, or on what kind of investment they require, are typically made after an analysis provided by computer-based information systems. This not only supports the decision making of store managers but also helps them look for ways to gain an advantage over other retailers in the competition for customers.

For example, store managers might make a decision to install computerized touch-screen catalog ordering systems in all of their stores, tied in with computer-based Touch-Tone telephone ordering systems and a home computer shopping

The Roles of Information Systems

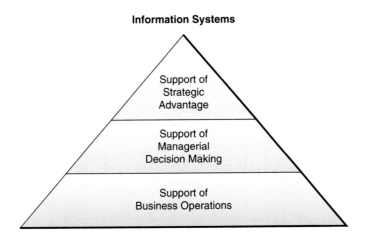

Information Systems

Support of Strategic Advantage

Support of Managerial Decision Making

Support of Business Operations

FIGURE 1.5
The three major roles of information systems. Information systems provide an organization with support for business operations, managerial decision making, and strategic advantage.

FIGURE 1.6
Waldenbooks bookstores
depend on computer-based
information systems to support
their business operations, managerial decision making, and
competitive advantage.

Robert Brenner/PhotoEdit.

FIGURE 1.7
Managers and employees at Waldenbooks bookstores depend on the hardware, software, telecommunications network, and
database resources of their computer-based information systems.

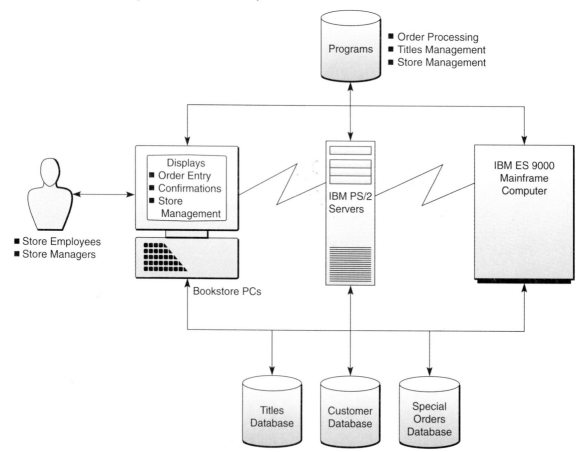

network. This might lure customers away from other stores, based on the ease of ordering merchandise provided by such computer-based information systems. Thus, strategic information systems can help provide strategic products and services that give a business organization a comparative advantage over its competitors.

The Winds of Change

Today's managers need all the help they can get. Their firms are being buffeted on all sides by strong, frequently shifting winds of change. Organizations' *strategic objectives* (chosen markets, product strategy, expected outcomes) and their *business processes* (such as research and development, production, cash-flow management, and order fulfillment) are undergoing significant and volatile changes, placing great pressure on firms and their managers [2].

The shifting winds of change in today's business environment have made information systems and information technology vital components that help keep an enterprise on target to meet its business goals. Information technology has become an indispensable ingredient in several strategic thrusts which businesses have initiated to meet the challenge of change. These include globalization, business process reengineering, agile competition, and using information technology for competitive advantage. They are a major reason why today's businesses need information technology. We will introduce these topics here and cover them in greater detail in later chapters.

Globalization

As we mentioned earlier, many companies are in the process of globalization; that is, becoming global enterprises. For example, businesses are expanding into global markets for their products and services, using global production facilities to manufacture or assemble products, raising money in global capital markets, forming alliances with global partners, and battling with global competitors for customers from all over the globe. Managing and accomplishing these strategic changes would be impossible without the global computing and telecommunications networks that are the central nervous system of today's global companies.

Figure 1.8 illustrates how information technology supports globalization. For example, global companies operate in a competitive environment in which networked computer systems make possible global markets that can instantly and cheaply process business transactions. So companies can now operate globally, sometimes by forming global business alliances with other organizations, including customers, suppliers, former competitors, consultants, and government agencies. Today's networked global corporation can collectively exploit many national market niches that would be too small for any one national company to service. They can also pool skills from many countries to work on projects that need workers with a variety of skills that cannot be found in any one country [1]. We will discuss managing global IT and its impact on global business operations further in Chapter 13.

Business Process Reengineering

When IT *substitutes* for human effort, it *automates* a task or process.
When IT *augments* human effort, it *informates* a task or process.
When IT *restructures*, it *transforms* a set of tasks or processes [2].

Information technology has been used by businesses for many years to automate tasks—from automated bookkeeping to automated manufacturing. More

FIGURE 1.8
How information technology can
support the globalization of
business.

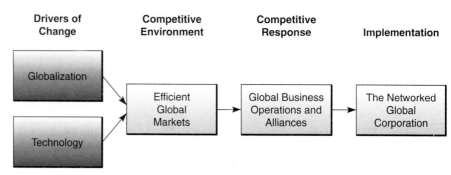

Source: Adapted and reprinted by permission of Harvard Business School Press from *Globalization, Technology, and Competition: The Fusion of Computers and Telecommunications in the 1990s* by Stephen Bradley, Jerry Hausman, and Richard Nolan. Boston: 1993, p. 4. Copyright © 1993 by the President and Fellows of Harvard College.

recently, businesses have used computer-based information systems to support the analysis, interpretation, and presentation of data to support business decision making. Using a spreadsheet package to analyze business alternatives is a common example of *informating* a business task.

However, **business process reengineering** (BPR) is an example of how information technology is being used to restructure work by transforming business processes. A business process is any set of activities designed to produce a specified output for a customer or market. New product development or the purchase of inventory are typical examples. Reengineering guru Michael Hammer defines reengineering as "the fundamental rethinking and radical redesign of business processes to achieve dramatic improvements, such as cost, quality, service, and speed" [6]. Thus, reengineering questions all assumptions about "the way we do business." It focuses on the *how* and *why* of a business process so major changes can be made in how work is accomplished. BPR thus moves far beyond mere cost cutting or automating a process to make marginal improvements [2]. See Figure 1.9.

Figure 1.10 illustrates how information technology was used to help reengineer several business processes at an agricultural chemical company. Notice that business processes at the individual, work group, and business unit levels can be changed by using information technologies to provide economic benefits. For example, the use of laptops for sales calls supported greater interaction between the individual salespeople and customers of an agricultural chemicals company, which resulted in significantly greater sales [3].

Agile Competition

Rapid, relentless, and uncertain change is the most unsettling marketplace reality that companies and people must cope with today. New products, even whole markets, appear, mutate, and disappear within shorter and shorter periods of time. The pace of innovation continues to quicken, and the direction of innovation is often unpredictable. Product variety has proliferated to a bewildering degree (Seiko markets 3,000 different watches; Philips sells more than 800 color TV models), and imitative competition is swift and profit-destroying [5].

Agile competition is the ability of a company to profitably operate in a competitive environment of continual and unpredictable changes in customer opportunities. An agile company can operate in markets with broader product ranges and shorter model lifetimes, and can process orders in arbitrary lot sizes. Agile companies depend heavily on information technology to give them the information pro-

- *Old rule:* Managers make all decisions.

  Information technology: Decision support tools (database access, modeling software).

  New rule: Decision making is part of everyone's job.

- *Old rule:* Only experts can perform complex work.

  Information technology: Expert systems.

  New rule: A generalist can do the work of an expert.

- *Old rule:* Information can appear in only one place at one time.

  Information technology: Shared databases.

  New rule: Information can appear simultaneously in as many places as it is needed.

- *Old rule:* Field personnel need offices where they can receive, store, retrieve, and transmit information.

  Information technology: Wireless data communication and portable computers.

  New rule: Field personnel can send and receive information wherever they are.

FIGURE 1.9
How information technology can help reengineer business processes.

Source: Adapted from Michael Hammer and James Champy. *Reengineering the Corporation: A Manifesto for Business Revolution* (New York, Harper Collins, 1993), pp. 92–96.

	IT Initiative	Process Changed	Business Benefit
Individual	Laptop System	Sales Call	Increased Sales
Work Group	Product Database	Product Distribution	Greater Customer Satisfaction
Business Unit	Product Management System	Channel Communications	Improved Competitive Position

FIGURE 1.10
How information technology reengineered business processes at several levels of a business.

Source: Adapted and reprinted by permission of Harvard Business School Press from *Process Innovation: Reengineering Work through Information Technology* by Thomas H. Davenport. Boston: 1993, p. 47. Copyright © 1993 by Ernst & Young.

cessing capability to treat masses of customers as individuals. This allows agile companies to offer individualized products while maintaining high volumes of production. Developments in computer hardware, software, and telecommunications networking technologies are making it possible for groups of companies to coordinate their geographically distributed capabilities into *virtual corporations* that can achieve significant competitive advantages [5].

Information technology is indispensable for companies wanting to be agile competitors. These companies need to have a "fast response" capability for identifying customer needs and responding to them quickly. This means, typically, using telecommunications, specialized software packages, and networked computer systems and databases to dramatically speed up market research, product development, production and distribution, order processing, and customer service. However, this

FIGURE 1.11
Many businesses are providing their employees with laptop computers to support their moves toward globalization, reengineering, agile competition, and competitive advantage.

Jon Feingersh/Uniphoto.

Stephen Agricola/Stock Boston.

Courtesy of IBM Corporation.

Tom Pantages.

quick response capability is accomplished in concert with a *total quality management* commitment to provide only the highest quality products and services to a company's customers [5]. Figures 1.11 and 1.12 show many examples of the use of networked laptop computers to gain a fast response capability.

Competitive Advantage

Using information technology for globalization, business process reengineering, and agile competition frequently results in the development of information systems that help give a company a **competitive advantage** in the marketplace. These *strategic information systems* use information technology to develop products, service, processes, and capabilities that give a business a strategic advantage over the competitive forces it faces in its industry. These forces include not only a firm's competitors; but also its customers and suppliers, potential new entrants into its industry, and companies offering substitutes for its products and services. Figure 1.13 illustrates that information technology can be used to implement competitive strategies to confront these competitive forces [2, 9]. These include:

- **Cost strategies:** Becoming a low-cost producer, lowering your customers' or suppliers' costs, or increasing the costs your competitors must pay to remain in the industry.

FIGURE 1.12
How companies in a variety of industries use networked laptop computers to gain a quick response capability.

Industry or Function	Application	Benefits
Marketing	Track status of promotions Identify purchase influencers and timing of decisions Prepare reports on site	Better information on sales activities Reports get done more quickly
Distribution	Bill of lading data and calculations Delivery and field sales data collection Enter and track parcel data	More timely information on field operations Better customer service
Field service	Remote access to parts catalog and availability Troubleshooting support Repair handbooks Scheduling and dispatching Service records Payment and receipt records	Better service to customer More efficient scheduling
Transportation	Airline and train schedules Reservations Rental car check-in and receipt generation Report graffiti and damage Monitor on-time performance	Convenience to customers Replaces paper forms and records More timely information
Financial services	Stock exchange floor trader support	More accurate records Reduces risk of fraud
Wholesale sales	Record sales results Send results to corporate mainframe Receive updates on product prices and availability	More accurate and timely information, both in the field and at corporate headquarters Eliminate unnecessary phone contacts Cuts paperwork
Retail sales	Capture sales and demographic data Update inventory data	Assess promotional results Tighter control over field operations
Insurance	Access corporate data for quotes Perform complex rate calculations	Quicker quotations to customers

Source: Adapted and reprinted from Louis Fried, "Information Security and Technology: Potential Threats and Solutions," *Information Systems Management* New York: Averbach Publications, Summer 1994, p. 61 © 1994 Warren, Gorham & Lamont. Used with permission.

- **Differentiation strategies:** Developing ways to differentiate your company's products or services from your competitors' so your customers perceive your products or services as having unique features or benefits.
- **Innovation strategies:** Introducing unique products or services, or making radical changes in your business processes that cause fundamental changes in the way business is conducted in your industry.
- **Growth strategies:** Significantly expanding your capacity to produce goods and services, expansion into global markets, diversifying into new products and services, or integrating into related products and services.
- **Alliance strategies:** Establishing new business linkages and alliances with your customers, suppliers, competitors, consultants, and others. These may

FIGURE 1.13
Businesses can develop competitive strategies to confront the competitive forces they face in the marketplace.

Competitive Forces

Competitive Strategies	Supplier	Customer	Competitor	New Entrant	Substitute
Differentiation					
Cost					
Innovation					
Growth					
Alliance					

FIGURE 1.14
Examples of the use of information technology to implement strategies for competitive advantage.

Strategy	Company	Strategic Information System	Business Benefit
Cost Leadership	Levitz Furniture Metropolitan Life Deere & Company	Centralized Buying Medical Care Monitoring Machine Tool Control	Cut Purchasing Cost Cut Medical Costs Cut Manufacturing Costs
Differentiation	Navistar Setco Industries Consolidated Freightways	Portable Computer-based Customer Needs Analysis Computer-aided Job Estimation Customer Online Shipment Tracking	Increase in Market Share Increase in Market Share Increase in Market Share
Innovation	Merrill Lynch Federal Express McKesson Corp.	Customer Cash Management Accounts Online Package Tracking and Flight Management Customer Order Entry and Merchandising	Market Leadership Market Leadership Market Leadership

include mergers, acquisitions, and joint ventures, or other marketing, manufacturing, or distribution agreements.

Figure 1.14 provides a variety of examples of how information technology has helped businesses gain competitive advantages [9]. We will discuss in greater detail the role of information technology in gaining strategic competitive advantages in Chapter 11.

Allstate Insurance and the AAA: Strategic Reengineering with IT

If you build it, they will come. At least that's what the insurance industry hopes for as it evaluates the information technology and expertise that deliver its insurance products to market. Figure 1.15 outlines the top 10 strategic business priorities of IS executives in the life insurance industry, which are echoed by similar surveys of the entire insurance industry.

Allstate Insurance Co. is a typical example. The property and casualty firm says it hopes to offer its 25 million customers better service and new insurance products more quickly as it moves to implement a "client/server computing" architecture, where computer workstations at employees' desks are networked to server computers in every office of the company. "We're going through a massive reinvention process" to reduce the company's product cycle times by putting networked computing power on every employees' desk, says John Klaas, vice president of education and training at Allstate in Northbrook, Illinois.

Across the board, the strategic importance of reengineering systems is clear. "When a competitor has a new insurance product out before we do, it represents millions of dollars in [potential revenue loss] per week," Klaas says. "Using information technology like new business software and client/server computing networks to cut our product cycle time is essential in staying ahead of our competition."

Of course, these new technologies are expected to reduce staffing despite cautious implementation. Staff cutbacks are a harsh reality as insurance agencies become more efficient,

yet remaining staff can expect new opportunities, analysts predict.

"We're contributing a significant amount of money to our retraining efforts in two major areas"—business problem-solving and client/server computing skills, says Mary Hepler, vice president of information and processing services at AAA Michigan. Hepler says she hopes strong business problem-solving skills will help her staff work closely with the leaders of the American Automobile Association's business units to revamp and improve computer-based business operations. Moreover, enhancing client/server computing skills will enable the company to retain some of its older, traditional "legacy" systems by improving employee access to the databases and information they need.

CASE STUDY QUESTIONS

1. How can information technology help Allstate reengineer its business processes and gain strategic advantages?

2. How will improving employee business problem-solving and client/server computing skills help the AAA's business performance?

3. What do the top 10 IS business priorities of the life insurance industry (Figure 1.15) reveal about the potential value of information technology in business?

Top IS business priorities:

1. Link information technology investment to business strategies.
2. Improve/enhance/reengineer current administration system.
3. Generate better management information.
4. Cost-justify information technology investment.
5. Integrate customer information.
6. Provide more effective technical support to field.
7. Introduce new technologies.
8. Replace current administration system.
9. Retrain information systems staff on new technologies.
10. Introduce rapid application development techniques.

FIGURE 1.15
The top ten IS business priorities in the life insurance industry.

Summary

■ **Why study information systems?** An understanding of the effective and responsible use and management of information systems is important for managers and other business knowledge workers in today's global information society. Information systems play a vital role in the efficient operations, effective management, and strategic success of businesses and other organizations that must operate in a global business environment. They must balance the technological capabilities of information technology with its behavioral effects on people and organizations to efficiently and effectively meet their strategic objectives. Thus, the field of information systems has become a major functional area of business administration.

■ **Why businesses need information technology.** Information systems perform three vital roles in business firms. That is, they support an organization's business operations, managerial decision making, and strategic advantage. Information technology has also become an indispensable ingredient in several major strategies that businesses are implementing to meet the challenges of a rapidly changing business environment. These include globalization, business process reengineering, agile competition, and using information technology for strategic competitive advantage.

Key Terms and Concepts

These are the key terms and concepts of this chapter. The page number of their first explanation is in parentheses.

1. Agile competition (18)
2. Business process reengineering (17)
3. Competitive advantage (20)
4. End user (6)
5. Global information society (9)
6. Globalization (17)
7. Information system (6)
8. Information technology (6)
9. Knowledge needed about information systems (12)
10. Knowledge workers (9)
11. Roles of information systems (15)
12. Technological and behavioral dimensions of information systems (10)

Review Quiz

Match one of the key terms and concepts listed above with one of the brief examples or definitions listed below. Look for the best fit for answers that seem to fit more than one key term or concept. Defend your choices.

____ 1. People who spend most of their workday creating, using, and distributing information.

____ 2. You should know some fundamental concepts about information systems and their technology, development, applications, and management.

____ 3. We are living in a global economy that is dependent on information.

____ 4. An organized combination of resources that collects, transforms, and disseminates information.

____ 5. Computer hardware and software, telecommunications, data management, and other technologies.

____ 6. Anyone who uses an information system or the information it produces.

____ 7. Efficient use of information technology can effectively support business relationships among end users and work groups.

____ 8. Information systems support an organization's business operations, managerial decision making, and strategic competitive advantage.

____ 9. Businesses are expanding into global markets and forming alliances with global partners.

____ 10. Some companies can operate profitably in a competitive environment of continual change.

____ 11. The fundamental rethinking and redesign of business operations.

____ 12. Using information technology to gain a strategic advantage over competitors.

Discussion Questions

1. Who is an end user? Is a business end user also a knowledge worker? Explain.

2. What are five major areas of information systems knowledge? How could a knowledge of these areas help a business end user?

3. Refer to the Real World Case on Manor Care and Bechtel in the chapter. What are client/server systems? What do you think are some of the benefits and limitations of client/server computing?

4. Refer to the Real World Case on GE Plastics in the chapter. Do you think an Internet connection gives them a strategic competitive advantage? Why or why not?

5. How can a manager demonstrate that he or she is a responsible end user of information systems? Give several examples.

6. How can information systems support a company's business operations, decision making by their managers, and give

them a competitive advantage? Give examples to illustrate your answer.

7. Refer to the Real World Case of Allstate Insurance and the AAA in the chapter. Which of the top 10 business priorities of the life insurance industry (Figure 1.15) is most important for a business? Explain your reasoning.

8. Refer to Real World Case on United Parcel Service in the chapter. Why do you think that CIO Frank Erbrick of UPS says that "nobody will be able to touch us by the year 2000". How could UPS outdistance competitors like FedEx, Airborne Express, and DHL?

9. How important is information technology to the globalization of a business? Use examples to illustrate your answer.

10. Can using information technology for business process reengineering help to make a company an agile competitor? Give an example to illustrate your answer.

Real World Problems

1. Mirage Resorts, Inc.: The Business Value of IT Investments

Las Vegas resorts spend lavishly on guest comforts and atmospherics. The theory: The more plush the accommodations, the more inclined people will be to gamble. The same normally doesn't go for business information systems. However, Mirage Resorts, Inc., a billion-dollar-plus resort holding company that manages the Mirage and other resorts, is betting that new computer systems can help deliver improved guest services. It also hopes to make managers and operations staffers more productive and help them make better, quicker decisions with nearly realtime access to enterprise data.

Last month, Mirage went live with a system to analyze product sales at the company's 50-plus gift shops. The goal: Help buyers and managers stock appropriate merchandise and receive quicker inventory turns. Sales data is analyzed on PCs running Microsoft's Excel. "Users can drill down, for example, to see what size of what T-shirt sold well in what color, in what store, sold by what vendor," said Walid Abu-Hadba, a Microsoft consultant involved with the project. Meanwhile, a new yield management system is enabling Mirage to maximize room occupancy and rates while matching guests' budgetary and travel needs. The system pulls

reservation data off a database, allowing management, for instance, to forecast the types of rate structures needed to keep the resorts near 100 percent occupancy. The 9-month-old system is already having an impact. "Management recently said the application resulted in a revenue increase of $5 million for 1994," said Julie Koentopp, IS project manager.

a. How has information technology improved business operations at Mirage Resorts?

b. Could other types of business benefit from similar types of IT applications? Give several examples.

Source: Adapted from Steve Alper, "Mirage Resorts to Client/Server," *Computerworld Client/Server Journal*, February 1995, p. 15. Copyright 1995 by Computerworld, Inc., Framingham, MA 01701—Reprinted from *Computerworld.*

2. Travelers Insurance Co.: Reengineering Case Management

A couple of years ago, case managers handling workers' compensation claims at Travelers Insurance's 50 or so remote sites where buried by paperwork. Rapid business growth made it increasingly difficult for case managers to provide detailed status reports on claims that the company's corporate clients demanded. It was also difficult to track the claim amounts as negotiations ensued. Case managers were typically college graduates handling the more complex identity claims where someone is out of work. "But they would usually hand off work to clerical people who had to interact with our accounting-based system," said Ron Calabrese, technical director in Travelers' PC Claim Systems Division. "If you went to a remote office, you could typically see a case manager with paper files for dozens of active claims spread over his or her desktop. They needed immediate access to those paper files to manage a claim to its full resolution."

Travelers' new, PC-based case management application is used by virtually all of the 1,600 case managers. IT integrates Travelers' OS/2-based workers' compensation application and Customer Service Information System with off-the-shelf Windows-based productivity applications. It allows case managers to view all these applications, side by side, on one screen. The application also generates a daily to-do list, calendar and tickler file, and lets a case manager quickly inventory a list of cases and sort those cases by number or employee.

The new system gives experienced case managers a clearer overall picture of an entire case and lets them track it. Also, case managers have discovered that they can more accurately track and analyze calls and uncover trends through customer questions, which helps them anticipate customer needs. In addition, each of the company's remote offices received a local database that lets case managers access essential information much more quickly. The net result is that case managers who handled 30-case workloads a couple of years ago now, typically, handle 100 cases.

a. In what ways has Travelers used IT to improve the productivity and responsiveness of case managers?

b. Is this an example of reengineering business processes? Explain.

Source: Adapted from Ed Scannell, "Travelers Reduces Risk of Claim Errors," *Computerworld,* February 13, 1995, p. 74. Copyright 1995 by Computerworld, Inc., Framingham, MA 01701—Reprinted from *Computerworld.*

3. Chase Manhattan Bank: Desktop Video for Global Competitive Advantage

While most of America was cheering football teams on Super Bowl Sunday, electricians and technicians here were racing the clock to wire the Chase Manhattan Bank's new high-tech trading floor with high-speed networking and on-demand video. By 7:30 A.M. on Jan. 30, 1995, 100M bit/sec. fiber-optic networks were in place and the available capacity on Chase's trading floor had shot up 20-fold, said Bill Schimoler, vice president of trading technology at Chase. That extra elbowroom on the data highway allows on-screen videoconferencing for the first time.

Video puts realtime data feeds into context. It allows brokers in New York to talk to one another about market conditions and about buy/sell stock recommendations. Chase traders also use videoconferencing rooms to speak with their counterparts worldwide. For example, a news tip that Chase transmits globally from its traders in New York to those in London can create profits—even before television

networks broadcast the tip widely. "If something breaks and we can get that word out on a global basis in a few seconds or a few minutes, that's a competitive advantage," said Rupi S. Puri, senior vice president of Chase's global trading operations and technology.

Chase decided two years ago to upgrade its trading floors in New York, London, and Tokyo to speed international communications. The cost of the New York upgrade alone was about $100 million. But the investment in advanced video applications, investment analysis programs and high-speed networks should pay off in significantly higher bank revenue. Last week, New York traders were using their video "windows," dialing up other New York colleagues by double-clicking on a menu of user names. "I've got the video option, and I'm watching CNBC and CNN," said Beniot Jadoul, a vice president for foreign exchange marketing. In all, there are nearly 900 Chase traders worldwide, each equipped with two Unix workstations: one for market data and another for applications. Chase's extra network capacity supports more applications, including Chase's Electronic Book of traders' investment positions, which is passed around the world as each global office heads home at night.

a. How might Chase's advanced video application give them a competitive advantage?

b. Could other types of businesses gain similar competitive advantages? Give several examples.

Source: Adapted from Jean Bozman, "Chase Manhattan Trades Up to High-speed Network," *Computerworld,* February 6, 1995, p. 6. Copyright 1995 by Computerworld, Inc., Framingham, MA 01701—Reprinted from *Computerworld.*

4. Gold's Gym Health Clubs: Computerizing Small Business

Gold's Gym health clubs, franchises of Power House Gym in Venezuela, needed to automate to improve profitability. So Caracas, Venezuela-based J. L. Sistemas, a software development firm, took on the task and created the Gym's Gold Health club management application. Designed to help manage their health clubs, Gym's Gold handles registration, invoicing, payroll, point-of-sale and reporting for each health club business. Gym's Gold uses a camera to photograph members, storing the photos in a database, and generating member ID cards. The system also includes an electronic cash drawer and an interface for controlling electrical doors.

Gym's Gold boasts a friendly graphical user interface that makes training easy. Franchise profitability has climbed thanks to:

- The system's tracking of cash receipts.
- Improvements in cash flow thanks to better tracking of revenues, members, instructors and costs.
- Reductions in paperwork and access to more accurate information.

Automation of processes brought order to the organization, freeing managers of paperwork so they could concentrate on marketing their health club services.

a. Can the benefits of IT for Gold's Gyms be gained by other small businesses? Give several examples.

b. How else would you use computers to improve the business success of a health club?

Source: "Reorganizing Business Innovation." Special Advertising Supplement, *Computerworld*, April 10, 1995, p. 9. Copyright 1995 by Computerworld, Inc., Framingham, MA 01701—Reprinted from *Computerworld.*

5. MCI Communications: Sales Force Automation

MCI Communications has kicked off the largest sales force automation project ever. The $60 million investment in mobile computing technology (using 5,000 IBM Think Pad 755CD multimedia notebook PCs at over $7,000 each) is designed to transform the $15 billion telecommunications giant into an information provider. Successfully executing the Field Automation project is so crucial to MCI that "I don't see how I'm going to be able to be effective without this two years from now," said Rick Ellenberger, the project's champion and senior vice president of worldwide sales for MCI's core Business Markets unit in Atlanta. MCI is so eager that the speed of its deployment schedule borders on hyperactive. After launching a pilot program in February, MCI put 4,700 notebooks into the field in April and expects to finish the rollout by mid-June of 1995.

By automating and networking the sales force, Ellenberger said MCI believes it can bring just-in-time manufacturing concepts to the information services world. For instance, giving salespeople online remote access to MCI's entire product information database will enable them to instantly respond to customer questions. What is more, online access to the MCI Library, an intelligent database, will link sales people with co-workers who can answer questions that they cannot. Also, by taking the best presentations and proposals from its top salespeople and making them available to the sales force in template form, MCI hopes to drive overall sales performance levels much higher.

Ellenberger said he championed the project because it gives the company both an opportunity to catapult itself into entirely new lines of business and the potential to change the way many businesses operate. MCI points to videoconferencing, document sharing, Internet access and other technology-driven products as its new revenue generators.

a. How can networked laptops improve MCI's productivity, agility, and competitive advantage?

b. Why do you think Rick Ellenberger says, "I don't see how I'm going to be effective without this two years from now?" Do you agree or disagree? Explain.

Source: Adapted from Michael Fitzgerald, "MCI Mobilizes Sales," *Computerworld*, April 10, 1995, pp. 1, 127. Copyright 1995 by Computerworld, Inc., Framingham, MA 01701—Reprinted from *Computerworld.*

6. Burlington Northern: Just-in-Time with IT

Having rounded the halfway point on a massive, enterprisewide information technology overhaul, Burlington Northern, Inc., has begun deploying systems that give the entire railroad—and some of its largest customers—realtime access to critical shipping and scheduling data. Late last month, the $5 billion company also threw the switch on a state-of-the-art network operations center in Fort Worth, Texas, where it is consolidating virtually all of its logistics operations and business processes. Driving both initiatives is a need to significantly bolster customer service and get maximum productivity from the railroad's 25,000 miles of track, 65,000 freight cars, and 2,500 locomotives.

"When we were delivering coal and grain, it didn't matter if we showed up on a Tuesday or a Wednesday," said Charlie Feld, Burlington's acting chief information officer. "But with the move to just-in-time, everything is much more customer-centered," he added. "We must deliver to tighter and tighter schedules."

To meet more precise delivery windows, Burlington is deploying a new locomotive tracking system and a second scheduling execution system. Both run under a three-tiered architecture of desktop OS/2-based PC workstations and Unix-based servers linked to a mainframe running IBM's MVS operating system, and a centralized DB2 database. A third computerized dispatching system runs on a Digital Equipment Alpha server tied into the railroad's network. Using this system, dispatchers at the Fort Worth operations center will control signals and switches for the entire railway. Taken together, the new enterprisewide systems replace several separate regional applications that formerly updated a central mainframe on a nightly and sometimes weekly basis. Feld estimates that about 65 percent of the 10,000 PC workstations have been installed so far. The reconstruction project is scheduled for completion in 1997. Feld would not disclose the cost of the project but said he expected it to pay for itself in one to two years.

a. How critical to its business success are Burlington Northern's new investments in information technology? Explain.

b. How do you think Burlington Northern's huge IT investment can "pay for itself in one or two years"?

Source: Adapted from Julia King, "IS Revamp on Track," *Computerworld*, April 10, 1995, pp. 1, 15. Copyright 1995 by Computerworld, Inc., Framingham, MA 01701—Reprinted from *Computerworld.*

Application Exercises

1. Auto Shack Stores

The president of Auto Shack Stores asked the following questions at a recent meeting of store managers and the vice president of information systems. Match each question with one of the major areas of information systems knowledge illustrated in Figure 1.4. Explain your choices.

a. How can we use information systems to support sales floor activities and store manager decision making and outhustle the competition?

b. How can we involve store managers in building such applications?

c. How can we use information technology to motivate our employees, please our customers, and build a close-knit organization?

d. What hardware, software, telecommunications, and database management resources do we need to support our goals?

e. How are we going to manage the hardware, software, people, and data resources of our information systems at the store and corporate level?

2. Western Chemical Corporation

Western Chemical Corporation is forming business alliances and building a global telecommunications network with other chemical companies throughout the world to offer their customers worldwide products and services. Western Chemical is in the midst of making fundamental changes to their computer-based systems to increase the efficiency of their business operations and their managers' ability to react quickly to changing business conditions.

Identify how each of the following uses of information technology is occurring in the activities of Western Chemical.

a. Agile competition.

b. Business process reengineering.

c. Globalization.

d. Strategic competitive advantage.

e. Support of managerial decision making.

Review Quiz Answers

1. *10*	4. *7*	7. *12*	10. *1*
2. *9*	5. *8*	8. *11*	11. *2*
3. *5*	6. *4*	9. *6*	12. *3*

Selected References

1. Bradley, Stephen; Jerry Hausman; and Richard Nolan. Eds *Globalization, Technology, and Competition: The Fusion of Computers and Telecommunications in the 1990s.* Boston: Harvard Business School Press, 1993.

2. Cash, James, Jr.; Robert Eccles; Nitin Nohria; and Richard Nolan. *Building the Information Age Organization: Structures, Control, and Information Technologies.* Burr Ridge, IL: Richard D. Irwin, 1994.

3. Davenport, Thomas. *Process Innovation: Reengineering Work Through Information Technology.* Boston: Harvard Business School Press, 1993.

4. Fried, Louis. "Information Security and Technology: Potential Threats and Solutions." *Information Systems Management,* Summer 1994.

5. Goldman, Steven; Roger Nagel; and Kenneth Preis. *Agile Competitors and Virtual Organizations: Strategies for Enriching the Customer.* New York: Van Nostrand Reinhold, 1995.

6. Hammer, Michael, and James Champy. *Reengineering the Corporation: A Manifesto for Business Revolution.* New York: HarperCollins, 1993.

7. Jacobson, Ivar; Maria Ericsson; and Agneta Jacobson. *The Object Advantage: Business Process Reengineering with Object Technology.* New York: The ACM Press, 1995.

8. Keen, Peter. *Shaping the Future: Business Design through Information Technology.* Cambridge: Harvard Business School Press, 1991.

9. Neumann, Seev. *Strategic Information Systems: Competition through Information Technologies.* New York: MacMillan College Publishing Co., 1994.

10. Tan, Djoen. "IT Management Plateaus: An Organizational Architecture for IS." *Information Systems Management,* Winter, 1995.

11. Wang, Charles. "Technology Disconnect—Real World Danger." *Computerworld,* September 19, 1994.

United Parcel Service: The Global Business Payoff of IT Investment

Technology leaders are made, not born. Just ask Frank Erbrick. In 1985, board members at Atlanta-based UPS concluded that the shipping company was lagging behind archrivals Federal Express Corp. and Roadway Services, Inc., in information technology.

Executives split. Some argued that "Big Brown" needed to pull itself into the technological age. Others noted UPS already had the best on-time record in the industry. And the new UPS CIO? "I was dragged in kicking and screaming," laughs Erbrick, a 33-year UPS veteran.

The rest is industry history. Led by Chairman Kent "Oz" Nelson, the world's largest package delivery service launched a five-year, $2 billion technology plan. The buildup was awesome. In 1985, UPS's information systems group comprised a mere 118 people and spent $40 million. Today's IS staff totals 4,000. Some other statistics:

- UPS delivers 3 billion packages a year to 200 countries and territories.
- Annual IS spending is $200 million.
- IS spending per employee is $635.
- Annual IS spending as percent of revenue is 1.02 percent.

Erbrick became a technology champion. His teams cranked dramatic firsts: In 1993, UPS created the first nationwide mobile data service, which linked 70 commercial carriers. A $180 million program placed handheld data collection computers in 53,000 vehicles. Last year, UPS became the first package deliverer to let customers use CompuServe and Prodigy to order services.

Has the investment paid off? Since 1985, UPS's annual sales have surged from $7.6 billion to $19.4 billion. Annual income climbed to $900 million, from $568 million. Technology also let UPS go global: It now delivers 3 billion packages a year to 200 countries and territories and employs 303,000.

It's difficult to say how much growth resulted from information technology. But there's no turning back. UPS budgeted another $1 billion for information technology between 1992 and 1997. And, Erbrick says, "we're going to exceed that."

Topping the new priority list is a new global customer automation system and worldwide deployment of the on-truck computers.

Next month, a revamped version of its Maxi-Ship package tracking system will reach 25,000 large customers. UPS says it will invest $100 million annually for the next few years on customer automation. By late 1996, Erbrick says, UPS will be able to provide realtime electronic data on each of the 12 million packages it will ship daily. UPS also hopes to create stronger electronic links with its 12 million customers.

Despite huge gains, the battle is not won. UPS trailed rivals DHL Worldwide Express and FedEx in Asia Pacific. Likewise, its UPS Worldwide Logistics subsidiary faces heavy competition for global distribution, warehousing, and inventory management business.

But the once hesitant Erbrick remains undaunted. "Nobody in the industry will be able to touch us by the year 2000."

CASE STUDY QUESTIONS

1. Has the "awesome" investment in information technology paid off for UPS? Explain.

2. Did UPS invest in IT to gain a competitive advantage or as a strategic necessity? Explain your reasoning.

3. What business advantages and limitations does UPS have compared to FedEx and DHL? How could IT make a difference in this competition?

Source: Joseph Maglitta "The Global 100: United Parcel Service." *Computerworld*, May 1, 1995, p. 15. Copyright 1995 by Computerworld, Inc., Framingham, MA 01701—Reprinted from *Computerworld*.

Fundamentals of Information Systems

CHAPTER OUTLINE

LEARNING OBJECTIVES

The purpose of this chapter is to give you an understanding of the roles played by information systems in organizations by analyzing (1) fundamental concepts used in the study of information systems, and (2) the operations and management support roles of information systems.

Section I introduces basic concepts about the components and types of information systems that are important for business end users.

Section II of this chapter presents an overview of the major operational and managerial support roles of information systems.

After reading and studying this chapter, you should be able to:

1. Identify and give examples of the components and functions of the generic concept of a system introduced in this chapter.

2. Identify and give examples of the components of real world information systems. Emphasize the concept that an information system uses people (end users and IS specialists), hardware (machines and media), and software (programs and procedures) as resources to perform input, processing, output, storage, and control activities that transform data resources into information products.

3. Give examples of how the roles of information systems have expanded to provide support for a firm's business operations, managerial decision making, and strategic advantage.

4. Identify three major types of operations support systems, and discuss how each supports the operations of a business.

5. Identify the major types of management support systems, and discuss how each supports the managers of an organization

SECTION I
Fundamental Information System Concepts

System concepts underlie the field of information systems. That's why this section shows you how generic system concepts apply to business firms and the components and activities of information systems. Understanding system concepts will help you understand many other concepts in the technology, applications, development, and management of information systems that we will cover in this text. For example, systems concepts help you understand:

- That computers are systems of information processing components.
- That business uses of computers are really interconnected business information systems.
- That developing ways to use computers in business includes designing the basic components of information systems.
- That managing information technology emphasizes the quality, business value, and security of an organization's information systems.

System Concepts

What is a system? A system can be simply defined as *a group of interrelated or interacting elements forming a unified whole.* Many examples of systems can be found in the physical and biological sciences, in modern technology, and in human society. Thus, we can talk of the physical system of the sun and its planets, the biological system of the human body, the technological system of an oil refinery, and the socioeconomic system of a business organization.

However, the following generic system concept provides a more appropriate framework for describing information systems:

A **system** is a group of interrelated components working together toward a common goal by accepting inputs and producing outputs in an organized transformation process.

Such a system (sometimes called a "dynamic system") has three basic interacting components or functions:

- **Input** involves capturing and assembling elements that enter the system to be processed. For example: raw materials, energy, data, and human effort must be secured and organized for processing.
- **Processing** involves transformation processes that convert input into output. Examples are a manufacturing process, the human breathing process, or mathematical calculations.
- **Output** involves transferring elements that have been produced by a transformation process to their ultimate destination. For example, finished products, human services, and management information must be transmitted to their human users.

EXAMPLE

A manufacturing system accepts raw materials as input and produces finished goods as output. An information system can be viewed as a system that accepts data resources as input and processes them into information products as output. See Figure 2.1.

FIGURE 2.1
This manufacturing system illustrates the generic components of many types of systems.

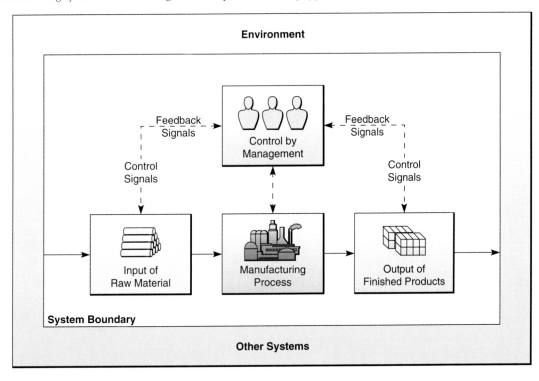

The systems concept can be made even more useful by including two additional components: feedback and control. A system with feedback and control components is sometimes called a cybernetic system, that is, a self-monitoring, self-regulating system.

Feedback and Control

- **Feedback** is data about the performance of a system. For example, data about sales performance is feedback to a sales manager.

- **Control** involves monitoring and evaluating feedback to determine whether a system is moving toward the achievement of its goal. The control function then makes necessary adjustments to a system's input and processing components to ensure that it produces proper output. For example, a sales manager exercises control when he or she reassigns salespersons to new sales territories after evaluating feedback about their sales performance.

Feedback is frequently included as part of the concept of the control function because it is such a necessary part of its operation. Figure 2.1 shows the relationship of feedback and control to the other components of a system. The flow of feedback data to the managerial control component and the resulting control signals to the other components are shown as dashed arrows. This emphasizes that the role of feedback and control is to ensure that other system components properly transform inputs into outputs so a system can achieve its goal.

┌─── EXAMPLE

A familiar example of a self-monitoring, self-regulating system is the thermo-stat-controlled heating system found in many homes, which automatically monitors and regulates itself to maintain a desired temperature. Another example is the human body, which can be regarded as a cybernetic system that automatically monitors and adjusts many of its functions, such as temperature, heartbeat, and breathing. A business also has many control activities. For example, computers may monitor and control manufacturing processes, accounting procedures help control financial systems, data entry displays provide control of data entry activities, and sales quotas and sales bonuses attempt to control sales performance.

Other System Characteristics

Figure 2.1 points out several other system characteristics that are important to a proper understanding of information systems. Note that a system does not exist in a vacuum; rather, it exists and functions in an **environment** containing other systems. If a system is one of the components of a larger system, it is called a **subsystem,** and the larger system is its environment. Also, a system is separated from its environment and other systems by its system *boundary.*

Several systems may share the same environment. Some of these systems may be connected to one another by means of a shared boundary, or **interface.** Figure 2.1 also illustrates the concept of an *open system,* which is a system that interacts with other systems in its environment. In this diagram, the system exchanges inputs and outputs with its environment. Thus, we could say that it is connected to its environment by input and output interfaces. Finally, if a system has the ability to change itself or its environment in order to survive, it is known as an *adaptive system.* Now let's look at the example suggested by Figure 2.2.

┌─── EXAMPLE

Organizations such as businesses and government agencies are good examples of the systems in society, which is their environment. Society contains a multitude of such systems, including individuals and their social, political, and economic institutions. Organizations themselves consist of many subsystems, such as departments, divisions, and other work groups. Organizations are examples of open systems, since they interface and interact with other systems in their environment. Finally, organizations are examples of adaptive systems, since they can modify themselves to meet the demands of a changing environment.

Components of an Information System

We are now ready to apply the systems concepts we have learned to help us better understand how an information system works. For example, we have said that an information system is a system that accepts data resources as input and processes them into information products as output. How does an information system accomplish this? What system components and activities are involved?

Figure 2.3 illustrates an **information system model** that expresses a fundamental conceptual framework for the major components and activities of information systems:

Stakeholders in the Business Environment

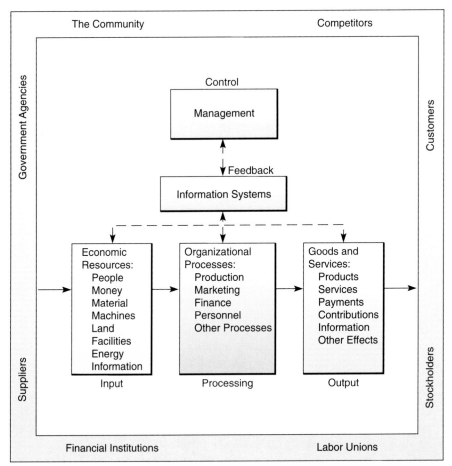

FIGURE 2.2
A business is an organizational system where *economic resources* (input) are transformed by various *organizational processes* (processing) into *goods and services* (output). Information systems provide information (feedback) on the operations of the system to *management* for the direction and maintenance of the system (control), as it exchanges inputs and outputs with its environment.

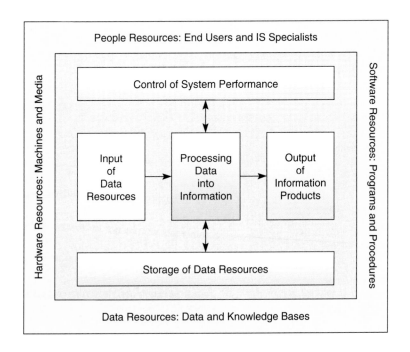

FIGURE 2.3
The components of an information system. All information systems use people, hardware, and software resources to perform input, processing, output, storage, and control activities that transform data resources into information products.

An **information system** uses the resources of people (end users and IS specialists), hardware (machines and media), and software (programs and procedures), to perform input, processing, output, storage, and control activities that convert data resources into information products.

This information system model highlights the relationships among the components and activities of information systems. It provides a framework that emphasizes four major concepts that can be applied to all types of information systems:

- People, hardware, software, and data are the four basic resources of information systems.
- People resources include end users and IS specialists, hardware resources consist of machines and media, software resources include both programs and procedures, and data resources can include data and knowledge bases.
- Data resources are transformed by information processing activities into a variety of information products for end users.
- Information processing consists of input, processing, output, storage, and control activities.

Information System Resources

Our basic IS model shows that an information system consists of four major resources: people, hardware, software, and data. Let's briefly discuss several basic concepts and examples of the roles these resources play as the fundamental components of information systems. You should be able to recognize these four components at work in any type of information system you encounter in the real world. Figure 2.4 outlines several examples of typical information system resources and products.

People Resources

People are required for the operation of all information systems. These **people resources** include *end users* and *IS specialists*.

- **End users** (also called users or clients) are people who use an information system or the information it produces. They can be accountants, salesper-

---

FIGURE 2.4
Examples of information system resources and products.

People Resources
   Specialists—systems analysts, programmers, and computer operators.

   End users—anyone else who uses information systems.
Hardware Resources
   Machines—computers, video monitors, magnetic disk drives, printers, and optical scanners.

   Media—floppy disks, magnetic tape, optical disks, plastic cards, and paper forms.
Software Resources
   Programs—operating system programs, spreadsheet programs, word processing programs, and payroll programs.

   Procedures—data entry procedures, error correction procedures, and paycheck distribution procedures.
Data Resources
   Product descriptions, customer records, employee files, and inventory databases.
Information Products
   Management reports and business documents using text and graphics displays, audio responses, and paper forms.

sons, engineers, clerks, customers, or managers. Most of us are information system end users.

- **IS specialists** are people who develop and operate information systems. They include systems analysts, programmers, computer operators, and other managerial, technical, and clerical IS personnel. Briefly, systems analysts design information systems based on the information requirements of end users; programmers prepare computer programs based on the specifications of systems analysts; and computer operators operate computer systems.

The concept of **hardware resources** includes all physical devices and materials used in information processing. Specifically, it includes not only **machines,** such as computers and calculators, but also all data **media,** that is, all tangible objects on which data is recorded from sheets of paper to magnetic disks. Examples of hardware in computer-based information systems are:

Hardware Resources

- *Computer systems,* which consist of central processing units (CPUs) and a variety of interconnected peripheral devices. Examples are large mainframe computer systems, minicomputers, and microcomputer systems.
- *Computer peripherals,* which are devices such as a keyboard or electronic mouse for input of data and commands, a video screen or printer for output of information, and magnetic or optical disks for storage of data resources.
- *Telecommunications networks,* which consist of computers, communications processors, and other devices interconnected by a variety of telecommunications media to provide computing power throughout an organization.

The concept of **software resources** includes all sets of information processing instructions. This generic concept of software includes not only the sets of operating instructions called **programs,** which direct and control computer hardware, but also the sets of information processing instructions needed by people, called **procedures.** So even information systems that don't use computers have a software resource component. The following are examples of software resources:

Software Resources

- *System software,* such as an *operating system* program, which controls and supports the operations of a computer system.
- *Application software,* which consists of programs that direct processing for a particular use of computers by end users. Examples are a sales analysis program, a payroll program, and a word processing program.
- *Procedures,* which are operating instructions for the people who will use an information system. Examples are instructions for filling out a paper form or using a software package.

Data is more than the raw material of information systems. The concept of data resources has been broadened by managers and information systems professionals. They realize that data constitute a valuable organizational resource. Thus, you should view data as **data resources** that must be managed effectively to benefit all end users in an organization.

Data Resources

Data can take many forms, including traditional *alphanumeric data,* composed of numbers and alphabetical and other characters that describe business transactions and other events and entities. *Text data,* consisting of sentences and paragraphs used in written communications, *image data,* such as graphic shapes and figures, and *audio data,* the human voice and other sounds, are also important forms of data.

FIGURE 2.5
Data versus information. Note that information is processed data placed in its proper context to give it value for specific end users.

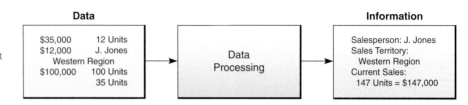

The data resources of information systems are typically organized into:

- **Databases,** which hold processed and organized data.
- **Knowledge bases,** which hold knowledge in a variety of forms such as facts and rules of inference about various subjects.

For example, data about sales transactions may be accumulated and stored in a sales database for subsequent processing, which yields daily, weekly, and monthly sales analysis reports for management. *Knowledge bases* are used by information systems called *expert systems* to give end users expert advice on specific subjects. We will explore these concepts further in later chapters.

Data versus Information

The word **data** is the plural of *datum,* though *data* is commonly used to represent both singular and plural forms. Data are raw facts or observations, typically about physical phenomena or business transactions. For example, a spacecraft launch or the sale of an automobile would generate a lot of data describing those events. More specifically, data are objective measurements of the *attributes* (the characteristics) of *entities* (such as people, places, things, and events).

EXAMPLE

A spacecraft launch generates vast amounts of data. Electronic transmissions of data *(telemetry)* from thousands of sensors are converted to numeric and text data by computers. Voice and image data are also captured through video and radio monitoring of the launch by mission controllers. Of course, buying a car or an airline ticket also produces a lot of data. Just think of the hundreds of facts needed to describe the characteristics of the car you want and its financing, or the details for even the simplest airline reservation.

The terms *data* and *information* are often used interchangeably. However, it is better to view data as raw material *resources* that are processed into finished information *products*. **Information** can then be defined as data that has been converted into a meaningful and useful context for specific end users. Thus, data is usually subjected to a "value-added" process (we call *data processing* or *information processing*) where (1) its form is aggregated, manipulated, and organized; (2) its content is analyzed and evaluated; and (3) it is placed in a proper context for a human user. So, you should view information as *processed data* placed in a context that gives it value for specific end users. See Figure 2.5.

Input
   Optical scanning of bar-coded tags on merchandise.
Processing
   Calculating employee pay, taxes, and other payroll deductions.
Output
   Producing reports and displays about sales performance.
Storage
   Maintaining records on customers, employees, and products.
Control
   Generating audible signals to indicate proper entry of sales data.

FIGURE 2.6
Business examples of the basic activities of information systems.

EXAMPLE

Names, quantities, and dollar amounts recorded on sales forms represent data about sales transactions. However, a sales manager may not regard these as information. Only after such facts are properly organized and manipulated can meaningful sales information be furnished, specifying, for example, the amount of sales by product type, sales territory, or salesperson.

Let's take a closer look now at each of the basic **information processing** (or **data processing**) activities that occur in information systems. You should be able to recognize input, processing, output, storage, and control activities taking place in any information system you are studying. Figure 2.6 lists business examples that illustrate each of these information system activities.

Information System Activities

Data about business transactions and other events must be captured and prepared for processing by **input** or *data entry* activities such as recording and editing. End users typically *record* data about transactions on some type of physical medium such as a paper form, or enter it directly into a computer system. This usually includes a variety of *editing* activities to ensure that they have recorded data correctly. Once entered, data may be transferred onto a *machine-readable* medium such as magnetic disk or tape, until needed for processing.

   For example, data about sales transactions can be recorded on *source documents* such as paper sales order forms. (A **source document** is the original formal record of a transaction.) Alternately, sales data could be captured by salespersons using computer keyboards or optical scanning devices who are visually prompted to enter data correctly by video displays. This provides them with a more convenient and efficient **user interface,** that is, methods of end user input and output with a computer system. Methods such as optical scanning and displays of menus, prompts, and fill-in-the-blanks formats make it easier for end users to enter data correctly into an information system.

Input of Data Resources

Data is typically manipulated by such activities as calculating, comparing, sorting, classifying, and summarizing. These **processing** activities organize, analyze, and manipulate data, thus converting it into information for end users. The quality of any data stored in an information system must also be *maintained* by a continual process of correcting and updating activities.

Processing of Data into Information

FIGURE 2.7
Common data elements. This is
a common method of organizing
stored data in information systems.

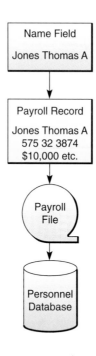

■ A **field** is a grouping of characters that represent a characteristic of a person, place, thing, or event. For example, an employee's *name field*.

■ A **record** is a collection of interrelated fields. For example, an employee's *payroll record* might consist of a name field, a social security number field, a department field, and a salary field.

■ A **file** is a collection of interrelated records. For example, a *payroll file* might consist of the payroll *records* of all employees of a firm.

■ A **database** is an integrated collection of interrelated records or files. For example, the *personnel database* of a business might contain payroll, personnel action, and employee skills files.

For example, data received about a purchase can be (1) *added* to a running total of sales results, (2) *compared* to a standard to determine eligibility for a sales discount, (3) *sorted* in numerical order based on product identification numbers, (4) *classified* into product categories (such as food and nonfood items), (5) *summarized* to provide a sales manager with information about various product categories, and, finally, (6) used to *update* sales records.

Output of Information Products

Information in various forms is transmitted to end users and made available to them in the **output** activity. The goal of information systems is the production of appropriate **information products** for end users. Common information products are *video displays, paper documents,* and *audio responses* that provide us with *messages, forms, reports, listings, graphics displays,* and so on. We routinely use the information provided by these products as we work in organizations and live in society. For example, a sales manager may view a video display to check on the performance of a salesperson, accept a computer-produced voice message by telephone, and receive a printout of monthly sales results.

Storage of Data Resources

Storage is a basic system component of information systems. Storage is the information system activity in which data and information are retained in an organized manner for later use. For example, just as written text material is organized into words, sentences, paragraphs, and documents, stored data is commonly organized into *fields, records, files,* and *databases.* This facilitates its later use in processing or its retrieval as output when needed by users of a system. These common *data elements* are shown in Figure 2.7.

Control of System Performance

An information system should produce feedback about its input, processing, output, and storage activities. This feedback must be monitored and evaluated to determine if the system is meeting established performance standards. Then appropriate system activities must be adjusted so that proper information products are produced for end users. These activities are known as **control.** For example, a manager may discover

Frank Herholdt/Tony Stone Images.

FIGURE 2.8
You should be able to recognize the basic components of any information systems you encounter in the real world.

that subtotals of sales amounts in a sales report do not add up to total sales. This might mean that data entry or processing procedures need to be corrected. Then changes would have to be made to ensure that all sales transactions would be properly captured and processed by a sales information system.

Recognizing Information Systems

There are many kinds of information systems in the real world. All of them use hardware, software, and people resources to transform data resources into information products. Some are simple *manual* information systems, where people use simple tools such as pencils and paper, or even machines such as calculators and typewriters. Others are **computer-based information systems** that rely on a variety of computer systems to accomplish their information processing activities.

It is important not to confuse our discussion of *information systems* with the concept of *computer systems*. As we will see in Chapter 4, a computer system is a group of interconnected hardware components that may take the form of a *microcomputer, minicomputer,* or large *mainframe* computer system. However, whether it sits on a desk or is one of many computers in a telecommunications network, a computer system still represents only the *hardware resources* component of a computer-based information system. As we have just seen, an information system also consists of people, software, and data resources.

As a managerial end user, you should be able to recognize the fundamental components of information systems you encounter in the real world. This means that you should be able to identify:

- The people, hardware, software, and data resources they use.
- The types of information products they produce.
- The way they perform input, processing, output, storage, and control activities.

This kind of understanding will help you be a better user, developer, and manager of information systems. And that, as we have pointed out in this chapter, is important to your future success as a manager, entrepreneur, or professional in business. See Figure 2.8.

FIGURE 2.9
An IS component matrix highlights the resources needed to accomplish activities that produce information products needed by end users.

Information System Activities	Hardware Resources		Software Resources		People Resources		Data Resources	Information Products
	Machines	Media	Programs	Procedures	Specialists	Users		
Input								
Processing								
Output								
Storage								
Control								

The IS Component Matrix

An **IS component matrix** can be used to document the components of an information system[6]. As shown in Figure 2.9, an IS component matrix views an information system as a matrix of resources, products, and activities. It highlights how the basic information systems activities of input, processing, output, storage, and control are accomplished, and how the use of people, hardware, and software resources supports the conversion of data resources into information products. An IS component matrix poses a fundamental question that should be answered by both end users and IS specialists: What resources are required to accomplish the activities that can produce the information products needed by end users?

Figure 2.10 illustrates the use of an IS component matrix to document the basic components of a sales processing system for a retail store. Note how it spotlights the activities needed, resources used, and products produced by this information system. Some cells are left blank because information for each cell may not be available or applicable. However, duplicate entries are also possible, because the same resources and products can be used to support several information system activities. Still, an IS component matrix serves its purpose by emphasizing the information system components used in a real world information system.

Analyzing the ShuttleExpress Information System

Read the Real World Case on ShuttleExpress on page 45. Then let's analyze the resources used, activities performed, and information products produced by their information systems. See Figure 2.11.

Figure 2.11 illustrates some of the components you might see in the ShuttleExpress information system. People resources include reservation agents, dispatchers, drivers, and managers who use the system. Hardware resources include machines such as the reservation and dispatcher PCs, the Digital Alpha server, and drivers' pagers as well as media such as magnetic disks. Software resources include reservations and trip-scheduling programs, the Access database management and Windows NT operating system programs, and the procedures followed by ShuttleExpress employees and managers. Data resources are contained in the customer, reservations, and scheduling data in the customer service database. Information products include video displays for data entry support, reservations information, and trip scheduling.

FIGURE 2.10
An example of an IS component matrix for a sales processing system at a retail store. Note how it emphasizes the basic activities needed, resources used, and products produced by this information system.

Information System Activities	Hardware Resources		Software Resources		People Resources		Data Resources	Information Products
	Machines	Media	Programs	Procedures	Specialists	Users		
Input	POS terminals	Bar tags mag stripe credit cards	Data entry program	Data entry procedures		Salesclerks Customers	Customer data Product data	Data entry displays
Processing	Mainframe computer		Sales processing program Sales analysis program	Sales transaction procedures	Computer operators	Salesclerks Managers	Customer inventory, and sales databases	Processing status displays
Output	POS terminals Management workstations	Paper reports and receipts	Report generator program Graphics programs	Output use and distribution procedures		Salesclerks Managers Customers		Sales analysis reports and displays Sales receipts
Storage	Magnetic disk drives	Magnetic disk packs	Database management program		Computer operators		Customer, inventory, and sales databases	
Control	POS terminals Management workstations	Paper documents and control reports	Performance monitor program Security monitor program	Correction procedures	Computer operators Control clerks	Salesclerks Managers Customers	Customer, inventory, and sales databases	Data entry displays Sales receipts Error displays and signals

FIGURE 2.11
Information system components in ShuttleExpress' computer-based information systems.

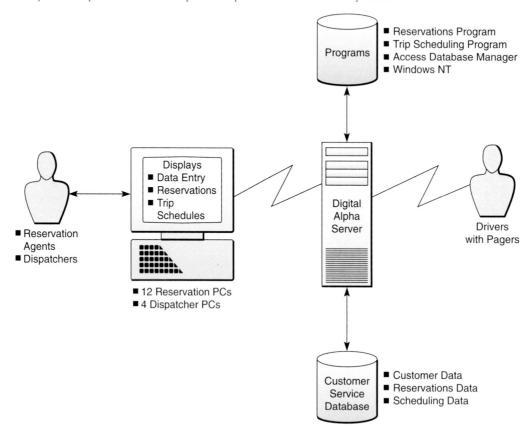

Customer reservations and dispatcher pickup data are entered into the system as input through the keyboards of the PCs. Processing is accomplished by PCs and the Digital Alpha server executing programs to accomplish reservation processing and trip scheduling. Output of information products produces video displays for data entry support, reservation information, and trip scheduling for dispatchers and drivers. Storage of data and software resources is provided by magnetic disk drives, on which are stored the customer service database, and reservations, trip-scheduling, database management, and operating system programs. Control is accomplished by ShuttleExpress' programs and procedures, which ensure quick and accurate customer service.

So you see, analyzing an information system to identify its basic components is not a difficult task. Just identify the resources that the information system uses, the information processing activities it performs, and the information products it produces. Then you will be better able to identify ways to improve these components, and thus the performance of the information system itself. That's a goal that every business end user should strive to attain.

REAL WORLD CASE

ShuttleExpress: From Manual to Computer-Based IS

Your trip to Seattle is nearly over. You've concluded your business and had your last cup of espresso and checked out of the hotel. All that remains is to catch the shuttle van to the airport and fly home. In what is sometimes still called the Jet City, a van ride to the airport is just about the last thing you might expect as having a high-tech component.

Two years ago, you would have been correct, but not today. Back then, the vans servicing customers of Seattle's ShuttleExpress were booked and dispatched using an entirely manual, paper-based system. Vans were tracked using a chalkboard and magnets to show each van's location on its routes.

"Sometimes the magnet designating a particular van got moved, and they missed the pickup so ShuttleExpress would have to call a cab at its own expense to take the customer to the airport", said Fred Taucher, chairman and chief executive officer of Corporate Computer, Inc.

The Seattle-based software development company replaced the chalkboard system with a computer-based system built on a network of PCs running the Microsoft Access database management package. The underlying network uses the Windows NT operating system.

The reservations system uses 12 NEC 486–based PCs networked to a Digital Equipment Alpha AXP server that has 128M bytes of RAM and four 1.2G-byte hard disks. There are four more NEC 486 PCs for the dispatch systems that can also double as reservation systems when it gets exceptionally busy.

For ShuttleExpress, which was founded in 1987, computerizing its reservations and van dispatch system went extremely smoothly, according to company officials. Most of the system was finished in about six months, ShuttleExpress officials said.

One of the secrets to the system's successful development and deployment process was that ShuttleExpress involved people who would have to use the system, said John Bartanen, one of the company's dispatchers. "I find it easy to use, and we can carry at least twice as many people today

as under the paper system," said Bartanen, who had no previous computer experience when the project started. "Everybody had an opportunity to get their input into it," said John Hagen, manager of ShuttleExpress's guest support center.

When the customer calls the reservations number, an agent enters all of the relevant information, including a customer's pickup location, his or her destination, and any special instructions into the customer service database. The reservations portion of the program calculates fares based on location and generates a reservation confirmation number. Many common pickup points are preprogrammed, along with directions for drivers. The dispatchers then take the reservations data and assign them to "trips," which consist of a set of pickups for a particular van during a specific time period. Once trips are scheduled, they are dispatched to each van. The Access database program is set up to automatically dial out to drivers' alphanumeric pagers and give them all of the particulars for each customer on the trip.

Since the system became operational, the company has handled more than 695,000 reservations. On average, about 1,500 passengers travel to and from the airport daily in ShuttleExpress vans, which number approximately 75.

"Routing the vans used to take eight hours, but now it's down to three hours, and where it used to take three dispatchers each shift, now it's down to two in the morning and one in the afternoon," Hagen said.

CASE STUDY QUESTIONS

1. What people, hardware, software, data resources, and information products do you recognize at ShuttleExpress?

2. What IS input, processing, output, storage, and control activities do you recognize in ShuttleExpress's systems?

3. How has the use of information technology benefitted ShuttleExpress?

Source: Adapted from Stuart Johnston, "Van Service Books Client/Server." *Computerworld*, April 17, 1995, p. 44. Copyright 1995 by Computerworld, Inc., Framingham, MA 01701—Reprinted from *Computerworld*..

SECTION II
Overview of Information Systems

The Expanding Roles of Information Systems

In Chapter 1, we stressed that information systems play three fundamental roles in the business success of an enterprise:

- Support of its business operations.
- Support of decision making by its managers.
- Support of its strategies for competitive advantage.

In this section, you will see that these vital roles are implemented by many different types of information systems. You will also see that the roles given to the information systems function have expanded significantly over the years. Figure 2.12 summarizes these changes.

Until the 1960s, the role of information systems was simple: transaction processing, record-keeping, accounting, and other *electronic data processing* (EDP) applications. Then another role was added, as the concept of *management information systems* (MIS) was conceived. This new role focused on providing managerial end users with predefined management reports that would give managers the information they needed for decision-making purposes.

By the 1970s, it was evident that the prespecified information products produced by such *management information systems* were not adequately meeting many of the decision-making needs of management. So the concept of *decision support systems* (DSS) was born. The new role for information systems was to provide managerial end users with ad hoc and interactive support of their decision-making processes. This support would be tailored to the unique decision-making styles of managers as they confronted specific types of problems in the real world.

FIGURE 2.12
The expanding roles of information systems. Note how the roles of computer-based information systems have expanded over time. Also, note the impact of these changes on the end users and managers of an organization.

Data Processing: 1950s–1960s
Electronic data processing systems
   Transaction processing, record-keeping, and traditional accounting applications
Management Reporting: 1960s–1970s
Management information systems
   Management reports for prespecified information to support decision making
Decision Support: 1970s–1980s
Decision support systems
   Interactive ad hoc support of the managerial decision-making process
Strategic and End User Support: 1980s–1990s
End user computing systems
   Direct computing support for end user productivity
Executive information systems
   Critical information for top management
Expert systems
   Knowledge-based expert advice for end users
Strategic information systems
   Strategic products and services for competitive advantage

In the 1980s, several new roles for information systems appeared. First, the rapid development of microcomputer processing power, application software packages, and telecommunication networks gave birth to the phenomenon of *end user computing*. Now, end users can use their own computing resources (and networks of workgroup and corporate resources) to support their job requirements, instead of waiting for the indirect support of corporate information services departments.

Next, it became evident that most top corporate executives did not directly use either the reports of management information systems or the analytical modeling capabilities of decision support systems, so the concept of *executive information systems* (EIS) was developed. These information systems attempt to give top executives an easy way to get the critical information they want, when they want it, tailored to the formats they prefer.

Third, breakthroughs were made in the development and application of artificial intelligence (AI) techniques to business information systems. *Expert systems* (ES) and other *knowledge-based systems* forged a new role for information systems. Today, expert systems can serve as consultants to users by providing expert advice in limited subject areas.

Finally, an important new role for information systems appeared in the 1980s and continues into the 1990s. This is the concept of a strategic role for information systems, sometimes called *strategic information systems* (SIS). In this concept, information systems are expected to play a direct role in achieving competitive advantages for a firm. This places a new responsibility on the information systems function of a business. No longer is IS merely an *information utility,* a service group providing information processing services to end user departments within the firm. Now it must become a *producer of information-based products and services* that earn profits for the firm and also give it a competitive advantage in the marketplace.

All these changes have increased the importance of the information systems function to the success of a firm. However, as we will see in this text, they also present new challenges to managers and end users to effectively capitalize on the potential benefits of information technology.

Operations and Management Classifications

Information systems perform important operational and managerial support roles in businesses and other organizations. Therefore, several types of information systems can be classified conceptually as either *operations* or *management* support systems. Figure 2.13 illustrates this conceptual classification of information systems. Information systems are categorized this way to spotlight the major roles each plays in the operations and management of a business.

Operations Support Systems

Information systems have always been needed to process data generated by and used in business operations. Such **operations support systems** (OSS) produce a variety of information products for internal and external use. However, they do not emphasize producing the specific information products that can best be used by managers. Further processing by management support systems is usually required. The role of a business firm's operations support systems is to efficiently process business transactions, control industrial processes, support office communications and

FIGURE 2.13

Operations and management classifications of information systems. Note how this conceptual overview emphasizes the main purpose of information systems that support business operations and managerial decision making.

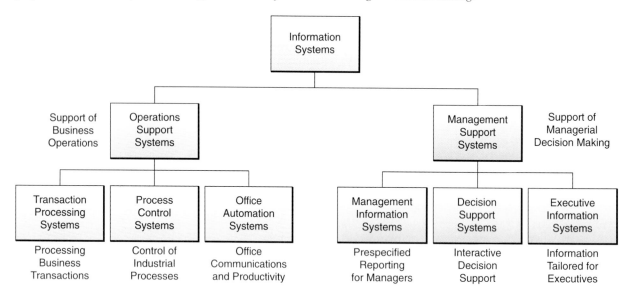

productivity, and update corporate databases. Figure 2.14 is an example of an operations support system. It illustrates the components and activities of a sales transaction processing system that captures sales transaction data, updates databases, and responds to end user inquiries.

Transaction Processing Systems

Operations support systems include the major category of **transaction processing systems** (TPS). Transaction processing systems record and process data resulting from business transactions. Typical examples are information systems that process sales, purchases, and inventory changes. The results of such processing are used to update customer, inventory, and other organizational databases. These databases then provide the data resources that can be processed and used by information reporting systems, decision support systems, and executive information systems.

Transaction processing systems also produce a variety of information products for internal or external use. For example, they produce customer statements, employee paychecks, sales receipts, purchase orders, dividend checks, tax forms, and financial statements. Transaction processing systems process transactions in two basic ways. In **batch processing,** transactions data is accumulated over a period of time and processed periodically. In **realtime** (or *online*) **processing,** data is processed immediately after a transaction occurs. For example, point-of-sale (POS) systems at retail stores may use electronic cash register terminals to capture and transmit sales data over telecommunications links to regional computer centers for immediate (realtime) or nightly (batch) processing. See Figure 2.15. We will discuss transaction processing systems in more detail in Chapter 9.

Process Control Systems

Operations support systems also make routine decisions that control operational processes. Examples are automatic inventory reorder decisions and production control decisions. This includes a category of information systems called **process control systems** (PCS), in which decisions adjusting a physical production process are

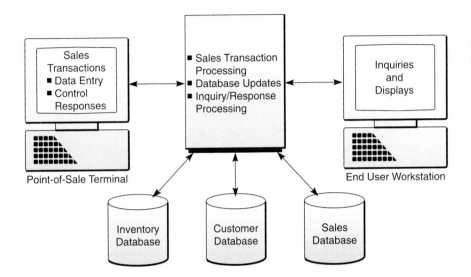

FIGURE 2.14
A sales transaction processing system is an example of an operations support system.

Mark Richards/Photo Edit.

FIGURE 2.15
This sales transaction processing system captures sales transactions data, updates databases, and responds to end user inquiries.

automatically made by computers. For example, petroleum refineries and the assembly lines of automated factories use such systems. They monitor a physical process, capture and process data detected by sensors, and make realtime adjustments to a process. We will discuss process control systems further in Chapter 9.

Another major role of operations support systems is the transformation of traditional manual office methods and paper communications media. **Office automation systems** (OAS) collect, process, store, and transmit information in the form of electronic office communications. These automated systems rely on text processing, telecommunications, and other information systems technologies to enhance office communications and productivity. For example, a business may use word processing for office correspondence, electronic mail to send and receive electronic messages, desktop publishing to produce a company newsletter, and teleconferencing to hold electronic meetings. We will discuss office automation systems in detail in Chapter 8.

Office Automation Systems

Management Support Systems

When information systems focus on providing information and support for effective decision making by managers, they can be called **management support systems** (MSS). Management support systems began when the concept of *management information systems* (MIS) originated in the 1960s. MIS became the byword (and the *buzz-word*) of almost all attempts to relate computer technology and systems theory to data processing in organizations. At that time, it became evident that computers were being applied to the solution of business problems in a piecemeal fashion, focusing almost entirely on the computerization of clerical and record-keeping tasks. The concept of management information systems was developed to counteract such *inefficient* development and *ineffective* use of computers. Though tarnished by early failures, the MIS concept is still recognized as vital to efficient and effective information systems in organizations for two major reasons:

- It emphasizes the **management orientation** of information technology in business. A major goal of computer-based information systems should be the support of *management decision making,* not merely the processing of data generated by business operations.
- It emphasizes that a **systems framework** should be used for organizing information systems applications. Business applications of information technology should be viewed as interrelated and integrated *computer-based information systems* and not as independent data processing jobs.

Figure 2.16 illustrates the relationship of management support systems and operations support systems to business operations and management. Management

FIGURE 2.16
The relationship of management support systems and operations support systems to business operations and the levels of management.

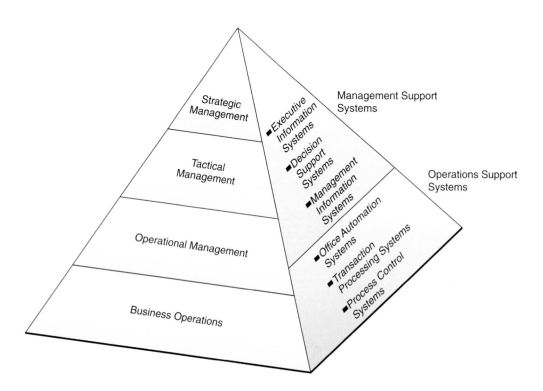

support systems support the decision-making needs of strategic (top) management, tactical (middle) management, and operating (supervisory) management. Operations support systems support the information processing requirements of the day-to-day operations of a business, as well as some lower-level operations management functions.

Providing information and support for management decision making by all levels of management (from top executives to middle managers to supervisors) is a complex task. Conceptually, several major types of information systems are needed to support a variety of managerial end user responsibilities: (1) management information systems, (2) decision support systems, and (3) executive information systems. Figure 2.17 illustrates some of the resources needed and information products produced by several types of management support systems.

Management information systems (MIS) are the most common form of management support systems. They provide managerial end users with information products that support much of their day-to-day decision-making needs. Management information systems provide a variety of reports and displays to management. The content of these information products are specified in advance by managers so that they contain information that managers need. Management information systems retrieve information about internal operations from databases that have been updated by transaction processing systems. They also obtain data about the business environment from external sources.

Information products provided to managers include displays and reports that can be furnished (1) on demand, (2) periodically, according to a predetermined schedule, or (3) whenever exceptional conditions occur. For example, sales managers could receive: (1) instantaneous visual displays at their workstations in response to requests for information about the sales of a particular product; (2)

Management Information Systems

FIGURE 2.17
The components and activities of management support systems. Note some of the resources needed to provide management reporting, decision support, strategic information, and expert advice to managerial end users.

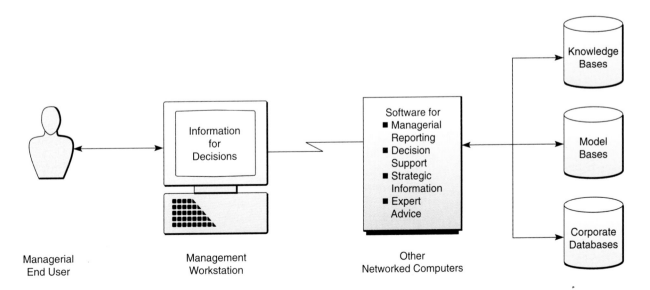

weekly sales analysis reports evaluating sales results by product, salesperson, and sales territory; or (3) reports produced automatically whenever a salesperson fails to produce sales results during a specified period. We will discuss management information systems further in Chapter 10.

Decision Support Systems

Decision support systems (DSS) are a natural progression from management information systems and transaction processing systems. Decision support systems are interactive, computer-based information systems that use decision models and specialized databases to assist the decision-making processes of managerial end users. Thus, they are different from transaction processing systems, which focus on processing the data generated by business transactions and operations, though they extract data from corporate databases maintained by TPS. They also differ from management information systems, which focus on providing managers with prespecified information (reports) that can be used to help them make more effective, structured types of decisions.

Instead, decision support systems provide managerial end users with information in an interactive session on an ad hoc (as needed) basis. A DSS provides managers with analytical modeling, data retrieval, and information presentation capabilities. Managers generate the information they need for more unstructured types of decisions in an interactive, computer-based process. For example, electronic spreadsheets and other decision support software allow a managerial end user to pose a series of what-if questions and receive interactive responses to such ad hoc requests for information.

Thus, information from a DSS differs from the prespecified responses generated by management information systems. When using a DSS, managers are exploring possible alternatives and receiving tentative information based on alternative sets of assumptions. Therefore, managerial end users do not have to specify their information needs in advance. Instead, a DSS interactively helps them find the information they need. Decision support systems are discussed further in Chapter 10.

Executive Information Systems

Executive information systems (EIS) are management support systems tailored to the strategic information needs of top and middle management. Top executives get the information they need from many sources, including letters, memos, periodicals, and reports produced manually as well as by computer systems. Other sources of executive information are meetings, telephone calls, and social activities. Thus, much of a top executive's information comes from noncomputer sources. Computer-generated information has not played a primary role in meeting many top executives' information needs.

The goal of computer-based executive information systems is to provide top and middle management with immediate and easy access to selective information about key factors that are critical to accomplishing a firm's strategic objectives. Therefore, EIS are easy to operate and understand. Graphics displays are used extensively, and immediate access to internal and external databases is provided. An EIS provides information about the current status and projected trends for key factors selected by top executives. EIS have become so popular in recent years that their use is spreading into the ranks of middle management. Executive information systems are discussed again in Chapter 10. See Figure 2.18.

Jon Riley/Tony Stone Images.

FIGURE 2.18
Management support systems provide information and decision support to managers at all levels of an organization.

Other Classifications of Information Systems

Several other categories of information systems provide more unique or broad classifications than those we have just mentioned. That's because these information systems can support either operations or management applications. For example, *expert systems* can provide expert advice for operational chores like equipment diagnostics or for managerial decisions such as loan portfolio management. Another example is *end user computing systems,* which provide direct hands-on support of end users for either operational or managerial applications. Finally, information systems which focus on operational and managerial applications in support of basic business functions such as accounting or marketing are known as *business information systems.*

Expert Systems

The frontiers of information systems are being affected by developments in **artificial intelligence** (AI). Artificial intelligence is an area of computer science whose long-range goal is to develop computers that can think, as well as see, hear, walk, talk, and feel. For example, AI projects involve developing natural computer interfaces, advanced industrial robots, and intelligent computer software. A major thrust is the development of computer functions normally associated with human intelligence, such as reasoning, learning, and problem solving. One of the most practical applications of AI is the development of **expert systems** (ES). An expert system is a *knowledge-based information system;* that is, it uses its knowledge about a specific area to act as an expert consultant to users. The components of an expert system are a knowledge base and software modules that perform inferences on the knowledge and offer answers to a user's questions. Expert systems are being used in many different fields, including medicine, engineering, the physical sciences, and business. For example, expert systems now help diagnose illnesses, search for minerals, analyze compounds, recommend repairs, and do financial planning. Expert systems can support either operations or management activities. We will discuss artificial intelligence and expert systems further in Chapter 12.

End User Computing Systems

End user computing systems are computer-based information systems that directly support both the operational and managerial applications of end users. You should think of end user computing primarily as the direct, hands-on use of computers by end users, instead of the indirect use provided by the hardware, software, and professional resources of an organization's information services department. In end user computing systems, end users typically use microcomputer workstations and a variety of software packages and databases for personal productivity, information retrieval, decision support, and applications development. For example, users may do word processing, send electronic mail, retrieve information from a database, manipulate an analytical model, or develop a new business application. We will discuss end user computing systems in Chapter 8.

Strategic Information Systems

The strategic role of information systems involves using information technology to develop products, services, and capabilities that give a company strategic advantages over the competitive forces it faces in the global marketplace. This creates **strategic information systems**, information systems that support or shape the competitive position and strategies of an enterprise. So a strategic information system can be any kind of information system (TPS, MIS, DSS, etc.) that helps an organization gain a competitive advantage, reduce a competitive disadvantage, or meet other strategic enterprise objectives. For example, as we saw in Chapter 1, online package tracking systems helped Federal Express gain market dominance, customer cash management account systems helped Merrill Lynch seize market leadership, and portable computer-based applications helped Navistar significantly increase their market share. We will discuss strategic information systems in detail in Chapter 11.

Business Information Systems

As a future managerial end user, it is important for you to realize that information systems directly support both operations and management activities in the business functions of accounting, finance, human resource management, marketing, and operations management. Such **business information systems** are needed by all business functions.

For example, marketing managers need information about sales performance and trends provided by marketing information systems. Financial managers need information concerning financing costs and investment returns provided by financial information systems. Production managers need information analyzing resource requirements and worker productivity provided by a variety of manufacturing information systems. Personnel managers need the information concerning employee compensation and professional development provided by human resource information systems. Thus, business information systems provide managers with a variety of information products to support their decision-making responsibilities in each of the functional areas of business. We will discuss these systems in more detail in Chapter 9.

Integrated Information Systems

It is also important to realize that information systems in the real world are, typically, integrated combinations of several types of information systems we have just mentioned. That's because conceptual classifications of information systems are designed to emphasize the many different roles of information systems. In practice, these roles are integrated into *composite* or *cross-functional* information systems that provide a variety of functions. Thus, most information systems are designed to produce information and support decision making for various levels of management and business functions, as well as do record-keeping and transaction processing chores.

Operations support systems process data generated by business operations. Major categories are:
- **Transaction processing systems** process data resulting from business transactions, update operational databases, and produce business documents.
- **Process control systems** monitor and control industrial processes.
- **Office automation systems** automate office procedures and enhance office communications and productivity.

Management support systems provide information and support needed for effective decision making by managers. Major categories are:
- **Management information systems** provide information in the form of prespecified reports and displays to managers.
- **Decision support systems** provide interactive ad hoc support for the decision-making process of managers.
- **Executive information systems** provide critical information tailored to the information needs of executives.

Other categories of information systems can support either operations, management, or strategic applications.
- **Expert systems** are knowledge-based systems that provide expert advice and act as expert consultants to users.
- **End user computing systems** support the direct, hands-on use of computers by end users for operational and managerial applications.
- **Business information systems** support the operational and managerial applications of the basic business functions of a firm.
- **Strategic information systems** provide a firm with strategic products, services, and capabilities for competitive advantage.

FIGURE 2.19
A summary of the major categories of information systems.

For example, a payroll system that processes employee time cards and produces employee paychecks is an operations support system. An information system that uses payroll data to produce labor analysis reports showing variances and trends in labor costs is a human resource management information system. However, in most cases, these functions are combined in an integrated payroll/labor analysis system.

Another example involves sales order/transaction processing, which is an operations support system, and sales analysis, which is a marketing management information system. However, these two systems are typically integrated in a business. Thus, a sales order processing system would collect and record sales transaction data and provide input to a sales analysis system, which produces reports for sales managers concerning sales performance.

So whenever you analyze a business information system, you will probably see that it provides information for a variety of managerial levels and business functions. Figure 2.19 summarizes the major categories of information systems we have discussed in this section.

Pizza Hut and KFC: Fast Food Information Systems

When Pizza Hut, Inc., opened its electronic storefront (http:"www.pizzahut.com) on the Internet's World-Wide Web last August, the project may have looked like information systems fiddling around while the Romano cheese burns. With corporate profits down 15 percent on the year, Pizza Hut's pilot—initially limited to residents of Santa Cruz, California—generated fewer than 10 orders per week. That barely covered the cost of the PC server, says Dan Cooke, vice president of MIS at Pizza Hut, a subsidiary of Pepsi-Co, Inc., in Purchase, New York. Yet Cooke sees the company's foray into cyberspace as a success, and Pizza Hut is readying plans for Internet ordering in other markets. "Our goal is to be wherever our customers are," he says.

Like its sister companies in PepsiCo's restaurant division, Taco Bell and KFC Corp., Pizza Hut is the world's no. 1 chain in its food specialty in revenue and is considered an information technology leader in the fast-food business. But profits at all three chains have cooled lately. As the chains fight to stay on top, IS will be under the gun to deliver systems that can bolster the company's financial performance.

As a result, finding—and retaining—customers worldwide has become the new mantra of corporate strategists at Wichita, Kansas–based Pizza Hut. According to Chief Operations Officer Pat Williamson, the company has been "operations driven" in the past. But today, Pizza Hut focuses less on wringing costs out of the system and more on keeping customers of its ubiquitous red-roofed restaurants and delivery services happy. "Our mission is 100 percent customer satisfaction," Williamson says.

For Cooke and his 200-member IS staff, the changing corporate strategy means IS must redirect many of its priorities. Like many major players in the fast-food industry, Pizza Hut has invested heavily in point-of-sale (POS) systems and in automating back-of-store operations—all in pursuit of the so-called paperless restaurant.

Most big chains today have systems that were developed in-house, such as KFC's manager's workstation and Pizza Hut's field management system. Each provides a suite of applications to assist store managers in business forecasting, inventory management, and human resources management. Such systems alert managers to potential problems and are networked with headquarters to enable the company to monitor individual store performance.

Across the fast-food industry, handheld, wireless order devices are showing up in many restaurants. To make POS systems more friendly to the largely part-time, high-turnover restaurant workforce, companies such as Park City Group in Park City, Utah, are building technology—artificial intelligence, wizards, and metaphor-based graphical user interfaces—into their retail management systems.

To get everyone in the company focused on increasing sales in its 2,900 company-owned stores, KFC is restructuring its reporting systems to track repeat business and other sales performance indicators, Cooke says. They help the company get more product across the counter. The system spots unusual orders, such as a chicken meal without a side dish, and prompts cashiers with a "suggested sell," an extra menu item that can complete the meal and pad the check in the process. This is a new frontier for many store managers, whose responsibility has traditionally been profits, not sales.

Staying focused will be a competitive necessity for all three chains in PepsiCo's restaurant division. As price pressures and changing consumer tastes spur Pizza Hut, KFC, and Taco Bell to refine their competitive recipes, IS managers will be expected to quickly deliver hot and value-priced applications that support them.

CASE STUDY QUESTIONS

1. What types of information systems do you recognize being used by Pizza Hut? Explain.

2. How do Pizza Hut's computer-based information systems support their business operations? Managerial decision making? Strategic advantage?

3. How could other types of business firms benefit from some of the systems used by Pizza Hut? Give several examples.

Source: Adapted from Brian McWilliams, "Coming Back for More," *Computerworld*, February 13, 1995, pp. 101–106. Copyright 1995 by Computerworld, Inc.,, Framingham, MA 01701—Reprinted from *Computerworld*.

Summary

- **System Concepts.** A system is a group of interrelated components working toward the attainment of a common goal by accepting inputs and producing outputs in an organized transformation process. Feedback is data about the performance of a system. Control is the component that monitors and evaluates feedback and makes any necessary adjustments to the input and processing components to ensure that proper output is produced.

- **Information System Concepts.** An information system uses the resources of hardware (machines and media), software (programs and procedures), and people (specialists and users) to perform input, processing, output, storage, and control activities that convert data resources into information products. Data is first collected and converted to a form that is suitable for processing (input). Then the data is manipulated and converted into information (processing), stored for future use (storage), or communicated to its ultimate user (output) according to correct processing procedures (control).

- **IS Resources and Products.** Hardware resources include machines and media used in information processing. Software resources include computerized instructions (programs) and

instructions for people (procedures). People resources include information systems specialists and users. Data resources include alphanumeric, text, image, video, audio, tactile, and sensor data. Information products produced by an information system can take a variety of forms, including paper reports, visual displays, documents, messages, graphics, and audio responses.

- **Categories of Information Systems.** Major conceptual categories of information systems include operations support systems, such as transaction processing systems, process control systems, and automated office systems, and management support systems, such as management information systems, decision support systems, and executive information systems. Other major categories are end user computing systems, expert systems, strategic information systems, and business function information systems. However, in the real world, these conceptual classifications are typically combined into integrated information systems which provide information and decision support for managers and also perform operational information processing activities. Refer to Figure 2.19 for a summary of the major categories of information systems.

Key Terms and Concepts

These are the key terms and concepts of this chapter. The page number of their first explanation is in parentheses.

1. Artificial intelligence (53)
2. Business information systems (54)
3. Classifications of information systems (47)
4. Computer-based information system (41)
5. Control (33)
6. Data (38)
7. Data or information processing (39)
8. Data resources (37)
9. Decision support systems (52)
10. End user computing systems (54)
11. Environment (34)
12. Executive information systems (54)
13. Expanding roles of information systems (46)
14. Expert systems (53)

15. Feedback (33)
16. Hardware resources (37)
  a. Machines
  b. Media
17. Information (38)
18. Information systems (36)
19. Information system activities (39)
  a. Input (39)
  b. Processing (39)
  c. Output (40)
  d. Storage (40)
  e. Control (40)
20. Information system resources (36)
21. Integrated information systems (54)
22. Interface (34)
23. IS component matrix (42)
24. Management information systems (51)

25. Management support systems (50)
26. Office automation systems (49)
27. Operations support systems (47)
28. People resources (36)
  a. IS specialists
  b. End users
29. Process control systems (48)
30. Software resources (37)
  a. Programs
  b. Procedures
31. Strategic information systems (54)
32. Subsystem (34)
33. System (32)
34. Transaction processing systems (48)

Review Quiz

Match one of the key terms and concepts listed above with one of the brief examples or definitions listed below. Look for the best fit for answers that seem to fit more than one key term or concept. Defend your choices.

_____ 1. A system that uses hardware, software, and people resources to perform information processing activities that transform data resources into information products for end users.

_____ 2. An information system that uses computers and their hardware and software.

_____ 3. Anyone who uses an information system or the information it produces.

_____ 4. Examples include jobs such as computer operators, programmers, and systems analysts.

_____ 5. A group of interrelated components working together toward the attainment of a common goal.

_____ 6. Data about a system's performance.

_____ 7. Making adjustments to a system's components so that it operates properly.

_____ 8. A shared boundary between systems.

_____ 9. Facts or observations.

_____ 10. Data that has been placed into a meaningful context for an end user.

_____ 11. The act of converting data into information.

_____ 12. Programs and procedures.

_____ 13. A set of instructions for a computer.

_____ 14. A set of instructions for people.

_____ 15. Machines and media.

_____ 16. Computers, disk drives, video monitors, and printers are examples.

_____ 17. Magnetic disks, optical disks, and paper forms are examples.

_____ 18. Using the keyboard of a computer to enter data.

_____ 19. Computing loan payments.

_____ 20. Printing a letter you wrote using a computer.

_____ 21. Saving a copy of the letter on a magnetic disk.

_____ 22. Having a sales receipt as proof of a purchase.

_____ 23. Information systems can be classified into operations, management, and other categories.

_____ 24. Information systems have evolved from a data processing orientation to the support of decision making, end users, and strategic initiatives.

_____ 25. Include transaction processing, process control, and office automation subsystems.

_____ 26. Handle routine information processing generated by business activities.

_____ 27. Control ongoing physical processes.

_____ 28. Provide electronic office communications.

_____ 29. Include management information, decision support, and executive information systems.

_____ 30. Provide information for managers in a variety of structured formats.

_____ 31. Provide ad hoc, interactive support for decision making.

_____ 32. Hopes to develop computers that can see, hear, walk, talk, feel, and think.

_____ 33. Serve as consultants to end users.

_____ 34. Provide direct computer support for the activities of end users.

_____ 35. Support the functional areas of business in an organization.

_____ 36. Perform traditional data processing activities and also provide information to the managers of an organization.

Discussion Questions

1. What software resources are required in a manual or mechanical (a noncomputerized) information system? Give several examples to illustrate your answer.

2. Identify several uses of the term *system* in the chapter. Why is this term so useful in the study of computers and information systems?

3. Refer to the Real World Case of ShuttleExpress in the chapter. Why did computerizing their reservation and scheduling operations go so smoothly? Is this typical? Explain.

4. Identify several types of data resources and information products mentioned in the chapter. What other examples can you think of?

5. What is the difference between a computer system and a computer-based information system? Give an example to illustrate your answer.

6. Refer to the Real World Case of Pizza Hut and KFC in the chapter. How are they using IT to increase sales? What do you think of such marketing strategies? Explain.

7. In what major ways have the roles of information systems expanded during the last 40 years?

8. Why are there so many conceptual classifications of information systems? Why are they typically integrated in the information systems found in the real world?

9. Refer to the Real World Case of Saks Fifth Avenue at the end of the chapter. Why does Saks have to "quickly spot the hot and dying trends"? How will SmartStream help store managers and buyers accomplish this?

10. How do decision support systems differ from management information systems and executive information systems in their support of a manager's decision making?

Real World Problems

1. Banco de A. Edwards: Banking Information Systems

As the banking market in Chile has become more competitive, Banco de A. Edwards sought ways to lower operational overhead while improving process times. Its solution, developed with Xerox Chile and Santiago-based Open Tek, is Banca Virtual, a new commercial banking platform from which the bank's executives have been able to better satisfy their clients' business banking needs. "Banca Virtual," comments project head Nicolas Roca, "allows our executives to have all client and product information on hand. It has a multientry point design that allows any specific function to be reached through product or action groupings."

Roca notes that Banca Virtual, which is used by 120 executives of the bank, "allows various simulations of the bank's loan and investment products, identifying the best option for the client as well as displaying the other alternatives. Banca Virtual has given our bank a competitive edge, allowing us to lower operational overhead and costs while improving process times. Banca Virtual is not simply a software solution, but a solution that has involved fundamental changes in the critical business processes of our bank."

a. Is Banca Virtual a management information system? A decision support system? Explain.

b. Why do you think a system like Banca Virtual has given Banco de A. Edwards a competitive edge?

Source: "Recognizing Business Innovation," Special Advertising Supplement, *Computerworld*, April 10, 1995, p.7. Copyright 1995 by Computerworld, Inc., Framingham, MA 01701—Reprinted from *Computerworld*.

2. Campbell Soup Company: Customer Services Information Systems

The recipe for their information systems overhaul will cost $30 million, but Campbell Soup Company executives said last week they expect a sweet reward: annual savings of more than $18 million. "This is the most aggressive project we've ever undertaken," said Harry Wallaesa, vice president of MIS at the Camden, New Jersey, food manufacturer. And he said he can beat his 18-month timetable for deployment. Wallaesa is referring to Project Compass, which kicked off a couple of months ago. Its charter is to streamline Campbell's customer service, order management and logistics systems across four business units in the United States and Canada by moving them off 25-year-old mainframes and onto a network of Unix servers and desktop and laptop PCs.

The biggest savings will come from "pulling together all the aspects of the business around a united order management and supply chain system," said Jane Biddle, a senior industry analyst at Benchmarking Partners in Cambridge, Massachusetts. She has been consulting with Campbell on the project for the past eight months. A reduction in paper processing and often-duplicated administrative steps will equate to faster and more accurate orders, she explained. By integrating their supply chain systems, the various units can move inventory more efficiently. And by more carefully managing promotions, the company can reduce selling costs, she added.

As part of the project, Campbell last week announced a $3.1 million contract with Industri-Matematik, in Tarrytown, New York, for its System ESS. ESS, which uses an Oracle database management system, is an integrated, Unix-based order management system that will run on Unix servers and PC clients. Campbell said it expects the new software platform to reduce the time it takes to process and validate a customer order from hours to minutes. The company is counting on more focused and better customer relationships. "More accurate transactions between ourselves and our customers mean more accurate invoicing and improved customer service," Wallaesa said. "That is, delivering what the customers want, when they want it, at the price they expect."

a. What types of information systems do you recognize in this case? Explain.

b. How will Project Compass "add an information component to the customer relationship?" What are the business benefits of this strategy?

Source: Ellis Booker, "Mmm, Mmm, Cost-Effective," *Computerworld*, January 23, 1995, p. 4. Copyright 1995 by Computerworld, Inc., Framingham, MA 01701—Reprinted from *Computerworld*.

3. San Bernardino County: Construction Management Information System

When San Bernardino County undertook a $463 million construction project, it was clear that only automation would keep the effort from being deluged in paperwork. "Without the Construction Project Management Information System," reports Evane Foster, program manager, "the project would generate five million documents." The county feared not only productivity losses and rising costs but also legal claims for compensation. Instead, the multimedia CPMIS integrates a 9,000-activity construction schedule, change order control, document management, workflow, office automation, labor tracking, field inspections and cost planning and control systems.

All types of construction documents are transmitted electronically, enabling the sharing of common data and the speeding up of construction management reporting and decision-making processes. Foster notes that the CPMIS encourages the project's 80 different contractors "to work in harmony to achieve a common objective. Sharing common data, access to a single electronic copy of contract documents monitoring response times and speeding up management, reporting, and decision-making processes encourages partnering."

a. What types of information systems are integrated in the Construction Project Management Information System? Explain.

b. What are the business benefits of CPMIS? Of the "partnering" that CPMIS encourages?

Source: "Recognizing Business Innovation," Special Advertising Supplement, *Computerworld*, April 10, 1995, p. 12. Copyright 1995 by Computerworld, Inc., Framingham, MA 01701—Reprinted from *Computerworld*.

4. Hertz Corporation: Wireless Information Systems

Hertz Corporation has been piloting a new wireless radio and pen computing system in five airports around the United States, including Boston's Logan International Airport and Hartsfield International Airport, in Atlanta. Hertz plans to have the wireless networks in more than 20 airports around the United States by the end of the year. "Wireless computing may be advanced for some companies, but it gives us a real competitive advantage," said David Merritt, a research and development project leader at Hertz in Oklahoma City. "We've had to work through a number of problems, but without a doubt the benefits outweigh the headaches," he said.

At these airports, Hertz courtesy bus drivers are equipped with Norand Corp. PenKey handheld computers and wireless modems, which they use to complete customer rental agreements. Then the drivers transmit the data to the airport terminal office over SMR (specialized mobile radio) wireless networks. The data is received by the Hertz office computer network, where hard-copy reservation agreements are generated and waiting for customers upon being dropped off.

a. What people, hardware, software, data resources, and information products do you recognize in this case?

b. What input, processing, output, storage, and control activities do you recognize in Hertz's wireless system? Which IS activities could you assume are also taking place?

Source: Michael Moeller, "Fortune 500 Ramps Up Wireless Net Projects," *PC Week*, March 27, 1995, pp. 1, 121. Reprinted from PC Week. Copyright © 1995 Ziff-Davis Publishing Company, L. P.

5. IST Incorporated: Field Service Information Systems

In a market the size of New York and Pennsylvania combined, it just doesn't pay to send a service technician out on the same job twice. Eliminating repeat service calls was a major problem for IST Incorporated, a 14-person management-consulting and systems-integration firm based in Casper, Wyoming. Technicians could spend a day driving across the state and into neighboring Colorado and Montana on a service call only to find they lacked the right piece of equipment or software needed for a repair, says IST President Bill Harms. In some instances, technicians holed up for a night in a hotel waiting for the proper equipment to arrive via overnight express service. Even proximate service calls frequently required trips back to IST's offices to fetch proper equipment, forcing IST to pay service reps to drive in circles. Then IST took a page from its own book, examined the way it operated, and found a way to use PCs to solve its problem: a field service tracking program from Open Systems Inc.

OSAS Field Service, a module of the Open Systems Accounting Software (OSAS) system, maintains a database of all the equipment installed at customer sites as well as a database of its service technicians' skills and training. When customers call with a service problem, OSAS Field Service tells IST what equipment to send on the call and which technician can best solve the problem. "We've turned a service call into a single, organized event rather than an event that at some points would take two or three days to accomplish," says Harms. OSAS Field Service streamlines the entire service-call process. Instead of tacking a service-call note on a technician's door, receptionists take detailed information from customers and enter it into a PC. The computer assigns the job to the most qualified technician available and generates a work order listing the customer's equipment and any recent repairs. "My technicians are being more efficient, so we're generating almost $20,000 a month more in technical service income with the same number of technicians," says Harms.

IST has even linked Field Service to work orders so that OSAS can track parts and reorder automatically when the levels fall below a predetermined amount. It's also tied to payroll so IST can evaluate technicians' performance and to customer accounts for use as a sales tool. "We give our customers a list of what we've done over the past quarter," says Harms. "We're also using it very effectively as a marketing tool saying, 'This piece of equipment is probably due to be replaced because it's costing you a lot of money and here's the documentation.'"

a. Which types of information systems can you recognize in OSAS Field Service? Explain.

b. What IS resources and IS activities do you recognize in this case? Document them in an IS component matrix as in Figure 2.10.

Source: Adapted from J. W. Huttig, "Oh Give Me a Home Where the Technicians

Roam," *PC Today,* February 1995, p. 56. PC Today, 120 W. Harvest Drive, Lincoln, NE 68521. For subscription information, please call 800-472-4100.

6. Amoco and Chevron USA: Management Support Systems

When Amoco production company's construction department realized its future depended on "its collective ability to quickly and effectively assess and exploit business opportunities," the firm began work on PETS, a networked client/server–oriented decision support system that links in-house and third-party applications with a database and an expert system. The business goal of PETS was to quickly and effectively evaluate opportunities and to stimulate more creativity and imagination in business deals. PETS was developed to help project evaluators quickly assess the factors and circumstances that have the largest impact on "the business deal." PETS accelerates and enhances the overall analysis and evaluation process by automating routine number crunching and business graphic and report generation. Team leader Michael Ruggiero reports that PETS has reduced time spent on gathering cost data, generating cost estimates, and documenting results by an estimated 60 percent.

Inaccurate and manually intensive information and out-of-date work processes were affecting Chevron USA's costs and its ability to react quickly to changing business conditions. The solution is Chevron land department's LIS, an enterprisewide land, lease, and contract management system that fully integrates digitally captured land map data, textual information, scanned images, and documents into a simple modular interface. Data (geopolitical, organizational and cross-reference) that was once managed manually is now automatically created by the system. Integrated scanning and E-mail have eliminated previous copying and mailing requirements. Now processes that used to take 75-plus days and 16 people are completed in hours with three people or less.

a. Which types of information systems are integrated in Amoco's PETS and Chevron's LIS systems? Explain.

b. What other types of businesses could benefit from systems like PETS and LIS? Give several examples.

Source: "Recognizing Business Innovation," Special Advertising Supplement, *Computerworld,* April 10, 1995, p. 8. Copyright 1995 by Computerworld, Inc., Framingham, MA 01701—Reprinted from *Computerworld.*

Application Exercises

1. Office Products Corporation

Office Products Corporation has an IBM AS/400 computer that runs almost around the clock. Over 10,000 customer orders a month flow through the system, drawing on a combined inventory of over 1,000 office products stocked at the company's warehouse. Over 60 personal computer workstations, many with printers, are installed at Office Products headquarters, and many of its dealers are connected by telecommunications links to the AS/400. Orders are received by phone or mail and entered into the system by order entry personnel at video display terminals, or they are entered directly by dealers who have installed terminals linked to Office Products. Entry of orders is assisted by formatted screens that help operators follow data entry procedures to enter required information into the system, where it is stored on the magnetic disks of the AS/400.

As the order is entered, the AS/400 checks the availability of ordered products, allocates the stock, and updates customer and product databases stored on the computer's magnetic disks. It then sends the order pick list to the warehouse printer, where it is used by warehouse personnel to fill the order. The company president has a PC workstation in her office, as do the controller, sales manager, inventory manager, and other executives. They use simple database management inquiry commands to get responses and reports concerning sales orders, customers, and inventory, and to review product demand and service trends.

Make an outline or prepare an IS component matrix (illustrated in Figures 2.9 and 2.10) to identify the information system components in Office Products' order processing system.

a. Identify the people, hardware, software, and data resources and the information products of this information system.

b. Identify the input, processing, output, storage, and control activities that occurred.

2. Western Chemical Corporation

Western Chemical uses telecommunications systems that connect its computers to those of its customers and suppliers to capture data about sales orders and purchases. This data is processed immediately, and inventory and other databases are updated. Word processing and electronic mail services are also provided. Data generated by a chemical refinery process are captured by sensors and processed by a computer that also suggests answers to a complex refinery problem posed by an engineer. Managerial end users receive reports on a periodic, exception, and demand basis, and use computers to interactively assess the possible results of alternative decisions. Finally, top management can access text summaries and graphics displays that identify key elements of organizational performance and compares them to industry and competitor performance.

Make an outline that identifies:

a. How information systems support (1) business operations,

(2) management decision making, and (3) strategic advantage at Western Chemical.

b. There are many different types of information systems at Western Chemical. Identify as many as you can in the preceding scenario. Refer to Figure 2.19 to help you. Explain the reasons for your choices.

3. Jefferson State University

Students in the College of Business Administration of Jefferson State University use its microcomputer lab for a variety of assignments. For example, a student may load a word processing program from a microcomputer's hard disk drive into main memory and then proceed to type a case study analysis. When the analysis is typed, edited, and properly formatted to an instructor's specifications, the student will save it on a floppy disk and print a copy on the microcomputer's printer. If the student tries to save the case study analysis using a file name he or she has already used for saving another document, the program will display a warning message and wait until it receives an additional command.

Make an outline or prepare an IS component matrix (illustrated in Figures 2.9 and 2.10) to identify the information system components in the preceding example.

a. Identify the people, hardware, software, and data resources and the information products of this information system.

b. Identify the input, processing, output, storage, and control activities that occurred.

4. Analyzing an Information System

Prepare an IS component matrix that summarizes the system activities, resources, and products of a manual or computerized information system with which you are familiar. For example, you could analyze your use of an information system such as a department store POS system, a supermarket checkout system, a university registration system, or a bank ATM system. Refer to Figures 2.9 and 2.10 to help you in your analysis of:

a. The people, hardware, software, and data resources and the information products of this information system.

b. The input, processing, output, storage, and control activities of the information system.

5. Al's Appliance City

The sales staff at Al's Appliance are paid on a commission basis. The amount of commission earned is based on two components. A standard commission of 2 percent is paid on all sales. An additional bonus is paid on sales of items that have been identified as "high-priority items." Generally, these are items that are overstocked. At the beginning of each week Al distributes to his sales staff a list of the high-priority items for that week and indicates the bonus percentage that will be paid for sales of those items. Al often varies this bonus percentage from week-to-week, as needed, to move overstocked items.

Because of the complexity and changing nature of the commission system used, commissions have always been hand calculated. Al's Appliance City uses a PC-based accounting package to handle its order processing. That package is used to produce weekly sales totals for each salesperson. The total dollar amount of all sales and the dollar amount of sales of high-priority items by each salesperson is reported. A listing of this data for the most recent week is shown below.

Al's Appliance City Weekly Sales Data

Salesperson	Total Sales	High Priority Sales
Caldwell, C.	$15,725	$4,250
Flowers, R.	18,240	5,340
Garrett, P.	17,835	3,890
Howard, M.	21,065	6,275
Johnson, A.	16,240	3,100
Lerner, V.	14,270	4,275
Masters, T.	23,500	6,950
Miller, J.	19,730	4,635
Sanderson, T.	12,040	2,830
Ward, W.	20,140	5,115

Al has requested that you create a spreadsheet for him that will allow him to calculate the total bonus owed each employee. The bonus rate for high-priority sales should appear on the spreadsheet as a parameter that Al can change when necessary.

a. Based on the sample data, create a spreadsheet to calculate the commission earned by each salesperson and total commissions earned. Assume a bonus rate for high-priority items of 3 percent. Get a printed listing of your results.

b. Suppose the bonus rate for high-priority items had been 5 percent. Change the bonus rate parameter on your spreadsheet and print a revised set of commissions.

c. What type of information system does this application represent? Explain your reasoning.

6. Monroe City School District

The Monroe City School District currently operates four high schools. Enrollment in three of these schools is significantly above their planned capacity. The school board will meet soon to examine proposals to alleviate overcrowding. The superintendent of the Monroe City School District has collected data showing planned capacity and actual enrollment for each high school over the past five years. These data are shown below.

Your task is to summarize these data in graphical form in a way that will highlight the nature of the problem for the school board members. Your graphs should give an overall picture of the problem and also allow more detailed examination of the situation faced by individual schools. The data you present should highlight the magnitude of the current problem but should also give the board members a feel for the historical trends that are at work.

Enrollment in Monroe City High Schools

School	Planned Capacity	Actual Enrollment by Year				
		1991	1992	1993	1994	1995
Washington	680	642	628	631	618	620
Jefferson	750	715	743	761	766	791
Lincoln	660	652	679	701	722	737
Roosevelt	900	830	848	887	934	986

a. Create a spreadsheet application incorporating the data shown. Perform any calculations on the raw data that are needed to generate useful information for graphic display. (For example, "enrollment as a percentage of capacity" or "enrollment minus capacity" might be an appropriate item for a graph. Also, you might want to base one or more graphs on totals across all of the schools.)

b. Create a set of graphs highlighting the information discussed above and get a printout of each graph.

c. What type of information system does this application represent? Explain your reasoning.

Review Quiz Answers

1. *18*
2. *4*
3. *28b*
4. *28a*
5. *33*
6. *15*
7. *5*
8. *22*
9. *6*
10. *17*
11. *7*
12. *30*
13. *30a*
14. *30b*
15. *16*
16. *16a*
17. *16b*
18. *19a*
19. *19b*
20. *19c*
21. *19d*
22. *19e*
23. *3*
24. *13*
25. *27*
26. *34*
27. *29*
28. *26*
29. *25*
30. *24*
31. *9*
32. *1*
33. *14*
34. *10*
35. *2*
36. *21*

Selected References

1. Cash, James, Jr.; Robert Eccles; Nitin Nohria; and Richard Nolan. *Building the Information Age Organization: Structure, Control, and Information Technologies,* Burr Ridge, IL: Richard D. Irwin, 1994.

2. Cash, James, Jr.; F. Warren McFarlan; James McKenney; and Lynda Applegate. *Corporate Information Systems Management.* 4th ed. Homewood, IL: Richard D. Irwin, 1995.

3. Davis, Gordon, and Margarethe Olson. *Management Information Systems: Conceptual Foundations, Structure, and Development.* 2nd ed. New York: McGraw-Hill, 1985.

4. Forgionne, Guisseppi. "Decision Technology Systems: A Step Toward Complete Decision Support." *Information Systems Management,* Fall 1991.

5. Neumann, Seev. *Strategic Information Systems: Competition Through Information Technologies.* New York: Macmillan College Publishing Co., 1994.

6. O'Brien, James, and Craig VanLengen. "Using an Information System Status Model for Systems Analysis and Design: A Missing Dimension." *Journal of Information Systems Education,* December 1988.

7. Sprague, Ralph, and Barbara NcNurlin, eds. *Information Systems Management in Practice.* 3rd ed. Englewood Cliffs, NJ: Prentice Hall, 1993.

8. Wand, Yair, and Ron Weber. "An Ontological Analysis of Some Information Systems Concepts." *Proceedings of the Ninth International Conference on Information Systems,* 1988.

Saks Fifth Avenue: Decision Support in Retailing

Upscale retailer Saks Fifth Avenue recently spent $5 million on Dun & Bradstreet (D&B) Software's SmartStream, a decision support client/server application; on 53 Hewlett-Packard HP9000 servers; and on consulting services. The systems, to be deployed enterprisewide, will initially be used by the Saks merchandise group, including buyers and store managers, to more quickly use customer data.

The new systems replace an in-house client/server data analysis system the retailer began working on in 1993. Saks built its own data access software with the C programming language and off-the-shelf tools such as Forrest & Trees from Trinzic Corp, in Palo Alto, California. This system was an improvement over the mainframe-only days. Then, staffers frequently waited a week for reports, and the resulting time lag made information much less useful. Yet by last year, Saks had determined that the system provided only limited access capabilities to analyze its Sybase databases, which contain data downloaded from mainframe systems.

The original client/server system simply required too much care and feeding to maintain, said Robert Ramsden, a Saks senior vice president and the retailer's chief information officer. Ramsden said Saks spent roughly $1 million on this project, and most of it—including Sun Microsystems workstations, Sybase databases and some in-house-designed software—will be reused in different projects.

A data analysis system is critical in retailing because it is so basic to tracking customer trends. The better the analysis system, the more quickly a retailer can track activity and take action such as shifting merchandise from one region to another, analysts said.

"Saks is a high-fashion, customer-intimate merchant," said Seth Dranz, a management consultant at the Waltham, Massachussetts, consulting and integration unit of Computer Sciences Corp. in El Segundo, California. "So they have to quickly spot the hot and dying trends." Kranz, a retail consultant who said he had worked on a Saks-related project on a previous consulting job at Coopers & Lybrand, explained that the company's current data analysis efforts, while not trailblazing, do put the store ahead of some other retailers.

Acknowledging the need for a better data analysis system, Ramsden's team shopped last year for a client/server package that could provide data access and analysis capabilities. Saks' mainframe software was from D&B Software, and it was already planning to convert to D&B Software's financial operations client/server software this year or next. So the team checked out SmartStream Decision Support Software, which also works with Sybase databases.

"What they were going to provide was the integration of all the data access tools, and having had the experience before, that looked very attractive," Ramsden said. The team began installing the D&B Software package late last year and will eventually replace both the outdated reporting capabilities of the mainframe software and the first client/server data access system.

IS is now building two systems, or "workbenches": one aimed at the merchandise group and the other at store managers. About 250 buyers and merchandise staffers have been trained on the merchant's workbench to date, Ramsden said. The buyers are now analyzing store data to help determine what would sell and how quickly it would move at individual stores.

CASE STUDY QUESTIONS

1. What information systems resources and activities do you recognize in this case?

2. Is SmartStream a decision support system? A management information system? Explain.

3. Is the use of a system like SmartStream critical for businesses other than retailers? Explain.

Solving Business Problems with Information Systems

CHAPTER OUTLINE

LEARNING OBJECTIVES

The purpose of this chapter is to give you an understanding of how end users can apply the systems approach to problem solving and the systems development process to develop information system solutions to business problems.

Section I of this chapter describes and gives examples of the steps involved in using a systems approach to solve business problems, including applying the systems approach to a case study example.

Section II describes and gives business examples of the activities involved and products produced in each of the stages of the information systems development cycle, including the use of computer-aided and prototyping approaches. After reading and studying this chapter, you should be able to:

1. Describe and give examples to illustrate each of the steps of the systems approach to problem solving and the information systems development cycle.

2. Explain how computer-aided systems engineering and prototyping have affected the process of information systems development for end users and information systems specialists.

3. Use the systems approach, the systems development cycle, and a model of information system components as problem-solving frameworks to help you propose information systems solutions to simple business problems.

SECTION I
A Systems Approach to Problem Solving

Suppose the chief executive of a firm where you are the sales manager asks you to find a better way to get information to the salespeople in your company. How would you start? What would you do? Would you just plunge ahead and hope you could come up with a reasonable solution? How would you know whether your solution was a good one for your company? Do you think there might be a systematic way to help you develop a good solution to your chief executive's request? There is. It's a problem-solving process called the **systems approach.**

The Systems Approach

The systems approach to problem solving uses a systems orientation to define problems and opportunities and develop solutions. As Figure 3.1 illustrates, studying a problem and formulating a solution involves the following interrelated activities:

1. Recognize and define a problem or opportunity in a systems context.
2. Develop and evaluate alternative system solutions.
3. Select the system solution that best meets your requirements.
4. Design the selected system solution so that it meets your requirements.
5. Implement and evaluate the success of the designed system.

FIGURE 3.1
The systems approach to problem solving. Note some of the activities involved in developing system solutions to business problems.

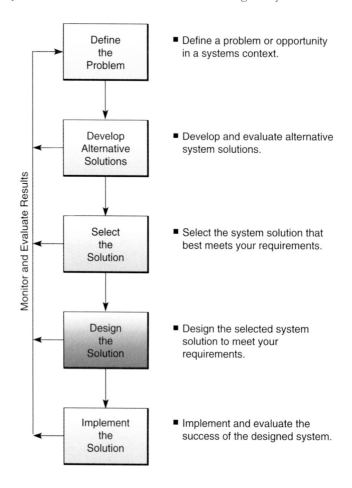

Let's now examine each step of the systems approach to problem solving to see how it can help you develop system solutions to business problems. Then we will apply the systems approach to a business case study example.

Defining Problems and Opportunities

Problems and opportunities are identified in the first step of the systems approach. A *problem* can be defined as a basic condition that is causing undesirable results. An *opportunity* is a basic condition that presents the potential for desirable results. *Symptoms* must be separated from *problems*. Symptoms are merely signals of an underlying cause or problem.

> **EXAMPLE**
>
> *Symptom:* Sales of a company's products are declining. *Problem:* Salespersons are losing orders because they cannot get current information on product prices and availability. *Opportunity:* We could increase sales significantly if salespersons could receive instant responses to requests for price quotations and product availability.

A Systems Context

Understanding a problem or opportunity in a **systems context** is one of the most important aspects of the systems approach. When you use a systems context, you try to find systems, subsystems, and components of systems in the situation you are studying. This ensures that important factors and their interrelationships are considered. This is known as having a *systemic* view of a situation. For example, the business organization or business process in which a problem or opportunity arises could be viewed as a system of input, processing, output, feedback, and control components. Then to understand a problem and solve it, you would determine if these basic system functions are being properly performed.

> **EXAMPLE:**
>
> The sales function of a business can be viewed as a system. You could then ask: Is poor sales performance (output) caused by inadequate selling effort (input), out-of-date sales procedures (processing), incorrect sales information (feedback), or inadequate sales management (control)? Figures 3.2 and 3.3 illustrate this concept.

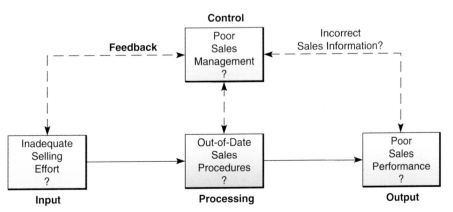

FIGURE 3.2
Evaluating the system components of a sales system.

FIGURE 3.3
You can better understand a sales problem or opportunity by identifying and evaluating the components of a sales system.

Jay Freis/The Image Bank.

Developing Alternative Solutions

There are usually several different ways to solve any problem or pursue any opportunity. Jumping immediately from problem definition to a single solution is not a good idea. It limits your options and robs you of the chance to consider the advantages and disadvantages of several alternatives. You also lose the chance to combine the best points of several alternative solutions.

Where do alternative solutions come from? Experience is a good source. The solutions that have worked, or at least been considered in the past, should be considered again. Another good source of solutions is the advice of others, including the recommendations of consultants and the suggestions of expert systems. You should also use your intuition and ingenuity to come up with a number of creative solutions. These could include what you think is an ideal solution. Then, more realistic alternatives that recognize the limited financial, personnel, and other resources of most organizations could be developed. Also, decision support software packages can be used to develop and manipulate financial, marketing, and other business operations. This *simulation* process can help you generate a variety of alternative solutions. Finally, don't forget that "doing nothing" about a problem or opportunity is a legitimate solution, with its own advantages and disadvantages. See Figure 3.4.

Evaluating Alternative Solutions

Once alternative solutions have been developed, they must be evaluated so that the best solution can be identified. The goal of evaluation is to determine how well each alternative solution meets your **business and personal requirements.** These requirements are key characteristics and capabilities that you feel are necessary for your personal or business success.

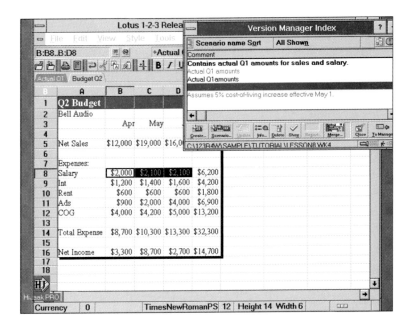

FIGURE 3.4
Using an electronic spreadsheet
package for what-if analysis can
generate alternative solutions.

EXAMPLE

If you were the sales manager of a company, you might develop very specific requirements for solving the sales-related information problems of your salespeople. You would probably insist that any computer-based solution for your salesforce be very reliable and easy to use. You might also require that any proposed solution have low start-up costs or have minimal operating costs compared to present sales processing methods.

Then you would develop **evaluation criteria** and determine how well each alternative solution meets these criteria. The criteria you develop will reflect your previously defined business and personal requirements. For example, you will probably develop criteria for such factors as start-up costs, operating costs, ease of use, and reliability.

Criteria may be ranked or weighted, based on their importance in meeting your requirements. For example, you might rank a criterion concerning operating costs higher than a criterion of ease of use. Finally, each alternative solution must be evaluated based on how well it meets your evaluation criteria. Figure 3.5 illustrates a simple example of the evaluation of two alternative solutions using several criteria.

Once all alternative solutions have been evaluated, you can begin the process of selecting the best solution. Alternative solutions can be compared to each other because they have been evaluated using the same criteria. For example, the two alternatives in Figure 3.5 can be screened and ranked and selected or rejected, based

Selecting the Best Solution

FIGURE 3.5

An example of evaluating alternative solutions. Note (1) the use of five weighted evaluations criteria, (2) the summary of each alternative's advantages and disadvantages, and (3) the use of scores for each criterion.

Criteria	Relative Weights	Alternative A: Sales Data Entry by Sales Reps Using Portable Computers Transmitting to the Data Center	Relative Score	Alternative B: Sales Data Entry by Optical Scanning of Forms Mailed to the Data Center by Sales Reps	Relative Score
Start-up costs	20	$1 million	12	$100,000	18
Operating costs	30	$100,000/year	25	$200,000/year	20
Ease of use	20	Good	16	Fair	12
Accuracy	20	Excellent	20	Fair	6
Reliability	10	Excellent	10	Excellent	10
Overall score	100		83		66
Summary of advantages/ benefits		Low operating costs, easy to use, accurate, and reliable		Low start-up cost and reliable	
Summary of disadvantages/ costs		High start-up cost		High operating costs, difficult to use, and not very accurate	

on individual criteria or overall scores. Then you could use the following decision rule:

> **EXAMPLE**
>
> Alternatives with a low accuracy evaluation (an accuracy score less than 10), or a low overall evaluation (an overall score less than 70) should be rejected. Therefore, alternative B for sales data entry is rejected, and alternative A, the use of laptop computers by sales reps, is selected.

Of course, it is possible that you might not select the top-ranked alternative. A lower-ranked solution could be chosen for a variety of other reasons. For example, unforeseen budget constraints, political developments, or legal challenges may disqualify your top choice. Or, all proposed alternatives could be rejected. In this case, new alternative solutions must be identified and evaluated. However, don't forget that the legitimate alternative of "doing nothing" could be selected as the best option.

Designing and Implementing a Solution

Once a solution has been selected, it must be designed and implemented. You may have to depend on other business end users and technical staff to help you develop *design specifications* and an *implementation plan*. Typically, design specifications might describe the detailed characteristics and capabilities of the people, hardware, software, and data resources and information system activities needed by a new system. An implementation plan specifies the resources, activities, and timing needed for proper implementation. For example, the following items might be included in the design specifications and implementation plan for a computer-based sales support system:

- Types and sources of computer hardware and software to be acquired.
- Operating procedures for the new sales system.
- Training of sales reps and other personnel.
- Conversion procedures and timetables for final implementation.

Postimplementation Review

The final step of the systems approach recognizes that an implemented solution can fail to solve the problem for which it was developed. The real world has a way of confounding even the most well-designed solutions. Therefore, the results of implementing a solution should be monitored and evaluated. This is called a **postimplementation review** process, since the success of a solution is reviewed after it is implemented. The focus of this step is to determine if the implemented solution has indeed helped the firm and selected subsystems meet their system objectives. If not, the systems approach assumes you will cycle back to a previous step and make another attempt to find a workable solution.

Using the Systems Approach

Now that we have discussed each step of the systems approach, let's apply it to the solution of a problem faced by a company in the world of business. Read the Case Study Example on p. 74, and then let's analyze it together, using the steps of the systems approach to problem solving.

Defining the Problem

Several symptoms make it obvious that a serious problem exists for Auto Shack Stores.

1. **Sales performance symptoms.** Sales are growing more slowly than in previous years, and at a slower rate than that of several major competitors. Sales performance is not meeting the firm's objective of increasing the growth rate of sales in order to increase its market share. Actual sales are not meeting annual sales forecasts.
2. **Selling floor symptoms.** Salespeople are spending too much time writing up sales transactions. They are not giving adequate service and selling effort to customers. Customers are not receiving prompt service and personal attention.
3. **Management symptoms.** Corporate and store managers are spending too much time obtaining necessary information, or they are making decisions based on inadequate information. Managers are not spending enough time on marketing, planning, and other duties.

Statement of the Problem

Managers, salespeople, and customers are being provided with inferior information products and services. The sales performance of the firm is crippled by slow processing of sales transactions, which limits salespeople's selling efforts and hurts customer service. Managers are not receiving the type of sales performance information they need, and they are spending too much time trying to acquire that information, which reduces the time spent on other management duties. For these reasons, the quality of marketing decisions and the company's sales performance have suffered.

A C A S E S T U D Y E X A M P L E

Auto Shack Stores: Solving a Business Problem

Auto Shack Stores is a chain of auto parts stores in Arizona, with headquarters in Phoenix. The firm has grown to 14 stores in just 10 years, and it offers a wide variety of automotive parts and accessories. Sales and profits have increased each year, but the rate of sales growth has failed to meet forecasts in the last three years. Early results for 1996 indicate that the rate of sales growth is continuing to drop, even with the addition of two new stores in 1995. Adding the new stores was the solution decided on by corporate management last year to reverse the trend in sales performance.

In recent meetings of corporate and store managers, the issue of computer use has been raised. Auto Shack uses computers for various information processing jobs, such as sales transactions processing, analysis of sales performance, employee payroll processing, and accounting applications. However, sales transactions by customers are still written up by salespeople. Also, corporate and store managers depend on daily sales analysis reports that contain information that is always several days old.

Most store managers see the installation of a company-wide network of point-of-sale (POS) systems as a key to reversing Auto Shack's sales trends. They believe using networks of POS terminals in each store would drastically shorten the time needed by a salesperson to write up a sale. This would not only improve customer service, it would free salespeople to sell to more customers. The managers call these the selling floor benefits of POS systems.

Another major point raised is that POS systems would allow immediate capture and processing of sales transaction data. Up-to-date sales performance information could then be made available to managers at personal computer workstations connected into the company's telecommunications network. This would provide the capability for information on sales performance to be tailored to each manager's information needs. Currently, managers have to depend on daily sales analysis reports that use the same report format. Too much of a manager's time is being used to generate sales performance information not provided by the system. Managers complain they don't have enough time to plan and support sales efforts unless they make decisions without enough information.

The president of Auto Shack has resisted previous proposals to automate the selling process. He knows automation would involve a large initial investment and resistance to the technology by some salespeople and managers. He fears the loss of salesperson/customer interactions. He also fears that managers will become too dependent on computers if they have them in their offices. However, the continued disappointing sales performance has softened his position. Also, the president realizes that POS systems have become commonplace in all types of retail stores. Auto Shack's major competitors have installed such systems, and their growth continues to outpace his own firm's. The company is failing to achieve its goal of increasing its share of the automotive parts market.

Statement of Business Requirements

Long-range planning sessions with the managers and a management consulting group identified a strategic role for information systems in the company. A long-range strategic plan was developed that stressed the need to use information systems technology to reduce the company's cost of doing business and to enhance the products and services the firm offers. Advanced POS systems were identified as one possible platform to support this role for information systems. Other possibilities include advanced systems in marketing, distribution, and a number of other areas. The plan also defines other business requirements to be met by new information systems. They are (1) support of personal selling, (2) tailoring of information to support managers' decision-making needs, and (3) integration and interconnectivity of information systems resources and applications to increase the company's efficiency and agility in the marketplace.

Note: In order to shorten this case study analysis, we will limit ourselves to two alternative solutions. However, several other solutions ranging between these two could be developed, especially if more data were given or more assumptions made.

Summary of Alternative Solutions

- **Solution 1:** Keep the current information system for sales processing and sales analysis. Hire more salespeople to provide better service to customers. Hire more staff assistants to relieve managers of sales information analysis duties.
- **Solution 2:** Develop a new information system using advanced POS technology. POS systems will allow sales transactions to be captured quickly, thus allowing salespeople to provide better customer service. The new system should also make it easy for managers to receive immediate responses to requests for sales information, tailored to their needs.

Advantages.

1. Low start-up costs for training of new personnel.
2. Simple, easy-to-use manual system for salespeople.
3. Increased sales expected due to more personal selling and service to customers by more salespeople.
4. Information tailored to managers by staff assistants should lead to better use of management time and improved decision making.

Evaluation of Alternative Solutions
Evaluation of Solution 1

Disadvantages.

1. High operating-cost increases due to hiring of new personnel.
2. Time-consuming sales transaction processing for salespersons.
3. Sales performance information will always be several days old.
4. Not capable of integration with advanced marketing, distribution, and other systems being planned.
5. Does not fit into the organization's plans to use information systems technology to reduce costs and enhance sales and service.

Advantages.

Evaluation of Solution 2

1. Relatively low operating costs for operations and maintenance.
2. Easy-to-use POS system using widely accepted, current technology.
3. Fast processing of sales transactions by salespeople using POS terminals.
4. Up-to-date sales performance information will be immediately available to managers.
5. Increased sales expected due to more personal selling and service to customers and better use of management time.
6. Information tailored to management, based on up-to-date data, and available on demand should lead to improved decision making.
7. Designed to be integrated with the advanced marketing, distribution, and other systems being planned.
8. Fits into the organization's plans to use information systems technology to reduce costs and enhance sales and service.

Disadvantages.

1. High start-up costs for hardware, software, and the development and implementation of the new system.
2. Reluctance to use POS technology by some salespeople and managers.

Rationale for the Selected Solution

Auto Shack Stores should develop a POS-based sales information system. It will allow fast processing of sales transaction by salespeople, while providing managers with timely information tailored to their needs. Salespeople will have more time for selling and service to customers, and managers will have more time for other managerial duties. The higher start-up cost is a reasonable price to pay for these benefits, and for the ability of the new POS network to be integrated with other advanced systems and with the firm's strategic plan for information systems.

Now the new POS system for Auto Shack Stores needs to be designed and implemented. That process will be illustrated in our discussion of information systems development in Section II.

Watkins Johnson Co.: Cost-Benefit Analysis for IT Decisions

The Watkins Johnson Co. faced a dilemma: Should it keep its homegrown, 25-year-old suite of financial applications? The mainframe-based, patched-over systems were straining to meet the needs of the $264 million electronics firms based in Palo Alto, California. And if the decision was made to replace them, would it be more effective to build a custom system in-house or buy one from a vendor that would require only minor modifications?

Thanks to a methodology developed by Robert Benson, a professor at the Center for the Study of Data Processing at Washington University in St. Louis, Watkins Johnson was able to make that decision successfully. So successfully, in fact, that the company will replace its traditional return on investment analysis methods for upcoming capital appropriations decisions with the same methodology that helped it make the move to client/server.

Benson labeled his methodology *information economics*. But Watkins Johnson first encountered it under the name *CB-90*—a name given to it by Oracle Corp., whose consulting group recommended it (along with several other return on investment techniques) to clients clamoring for a reliable benefits analysis formula. Although CB-90 originally stood for "cost-benefit analysis for the 90s," Perrone says Oracle now bills it as a "consensus-building" tool because it draws users into the process in a way that they simultaneously welcome and appreciate the contribution information technology makes to their jobs.

In-depth analysis prior to making a major capital investment is not unusual at Watkins Johnson. Every proposed capital expenditure must undergo a rigorous cost-benefit analysis that has been in place at the firm for years, says Bill Perrone, manager of internal controls, who oversees auditing functions at the firm.

But CB-90 "provided us with a lot more detail than our previous way of doing a capital expenditure analysis," Perrone says. Perrone was particularly impressed with CB-90's ability to roll the intangible benefits into the decision process logically. "That's something a traditional ROI can't do," he says.

The CB-90 method involves asking key users at the company to assess the tangible and intangible benefits of the application in question, as well as the risks involved. The application can either be installed or proposed; the methodology will demonstrate the value either way.

In this particular case, information planning manager Ed Abell knew he wanted to replace Watkins Johnson's IBM MVS financial systems. But beyond that, he was stumped. Abell debated whether to build his own system or go outside. When Oracle suggested the CB-90 methodology to determine how much value the software would provide, Abell thought there was little to lose by trying it.

The first step in CB-90 is to form a team of key users from the affected departments. Abell first asked financial "experts"—a combination of managers and staffers in such areas as credit and collections and cost accounting—to go over the proposed system. He asked them to formulate, feature by feature, the tangible and intangible benefits they expected if such a product were installed. These benefits were to be stated in business, not technical, terms.

A tangible benefit of the new accounting module, for example, would be the ability to send out payment-due letters faster. This would speed up collections on overdue accounts. An intangible benefit, one that would be difficult to assign a dollar value to, would be more accurate financial forecasting. On the other hand, a potential risk of the new system could be a lack of user acceptance for it.

At the end of this process, the team had thought of 13 tangible benefits, 5 intangible benefits, and six risks for installing the Oracle system, Abell says. Tangible benefits included reduced head count and reducing the accounts receivable cycle by two days. Intangible benefits included better control of departmental budgets, improved financial reporting to executives, and keeping on top of potential cash flow problems before the end-of-the-month closing. Risks included the system's inability to respond to quick changes in the manufacturing climate and employee resistance to any sort of change.

As a comparison analysis, the company similarly examined the impact of building a system from scratch. In that scenario, the company decided it could build its own system, but the time factor would delay tangible and intangible benefits alike.

Once these analyses were completed and compared side by side, it was easy for the company to decide to buy the Oracle software and modify it, Abell says.

CASE STUDY QUESTIONS

1. Could the CB-90 methodology be part of a systems approach to problem solving? Explain.
2. Why are end users involved in making an IT decision?
3. What cost-benefit analysis features make CB-90 attractive for helping to make business decisions?

┌─ SECTION II
◢ *Developing Information System Solutions*
└───

Developing information system solutions to business problems is a major responsibility of today's managers. They are responsible for proposing or developing new or improved information systems for their organizations. They must also frequently manage the development efforts of information systems specialists and other end users. This section builds on the problem-solving concepts in the previous section to show you how information system solutions that meet the business needs of end users and their organizations can be developed.

The Systems Development Cycle

When the systems approach to problem solving is applied to the development of information system solutions to business problems, it is called **information systems development** or *application development*. Most computer-based information systems are conceived, designed, and implemented using some form of systematic development process. In this process, end users and information specialists *design* information systems based on an *analysis* of the information requirements of an organization. Thus, a major part of this process is known as *systems analysis and design*. However, as Figure 3.6 shows, several other major activities are involved in a complete development cycle.

When the systems approach is applied to the development of information system solutions, a multistep process or cycle emerges. This is frequently called the systems development cycle, or **systems development life cycle** (SDLC). Figure 3.7 summarizes what goes on in each stage of the traditional *information systems development cycle,* which includes the steps of (1) investigation, (2) analysis, (3) design, (4) implementation, and (5) maintenance.

You should realize, however, that all of the activities involved are highly related and interdependent. Therefore, in actual practice, several developmental activities can occur at the same time. So, different parts of a development project can be at dif-

FIGURE 3.6
Developing information systems solutions to business problems is typically a multistep process or cycle.

ferent stages of the development cycle. In addition, analysts may recycle back at any time to repeat previous activities in order to modify and improve a system they are developing.

Finally, you should realize that developments such as computer-aided systems engineering (CASE), prototyping, and end user development are automating and changing some of the activities of information systems development. These developments are improving the quality of systems development and making it easier for IS professionals, while enabling more end users to develop their own systems. We will discuss them shortly. Now, let's take a look at each step of this development process.

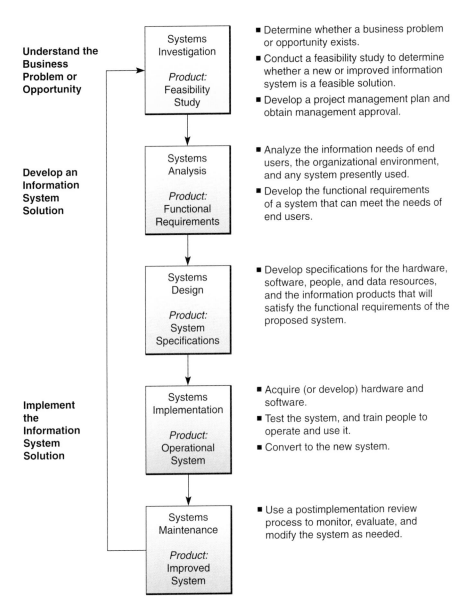

Understand the Business Problem or Opportunity

Systems Investigation

Product: Feasibility Study

- Determine whether a business problem or opportunity exists.
- Conduct a feasibility study to determine whether a new or improved information system is a feasible solution.
- Develop a project management plan and obtain management approval.

Develop an Information System Solution

Systems Analysis

Product: Functional Requirements

- Analyze the information needs of end users, the organizational environment, and any system presently used.
- Develop the functional requirements of a system that can meet the needs of end users.

Systems Design

Product: System Specifications

- Develop specifications for the hardware, software, people, and data resources, and the information products that will satisfy the functional requirements of the proposed system.

Implement the Information System Solution

Systems Implementation

Product: Operational System

- Acquire (or develop) hardware and software.
- Test the system, and train people to operate and use it.
- Convert to the new system.

Systems Maintenance

Product: Improved System

- Use a postimplementation review process to monitor, evaluate, and modify the system as needed.

FIGURE 3.7
The traditional information systems development cycle. Note how the five steps of the cycle are based on the stages of the systems approach. Also note the products that result from each step in the cycle.

Systems Investigation

Do we have a business problem (or opportunity)? What is causing the problem? Would a new or improved information system help solve the problem? What would be a *feasible* information system solution to our problem? These are the questions that have to be answered in the **systems investigation** stage—the first step in the systems development process. This stage includes the screening, selection, and preliminary study of proposed information system solutions to business problems.

Information Systems Planning

The investigation stage may involve the study of information systems development proposals generated by a formal **information systems planning** process, which we will discuss in Chapter 14. A formal information systems planning process that is part of the regular business planning process of the organization is highly desirable. There are, typically, many opportunities to use information systems to support an organization's end users and its business operations, management decision making, and strategic objectives. However, in the real world, end users, departments, and the organization itself have only limited amounts of human and financial resources to allocate to the development of new information systems, no matter how desirable they may be. Therefore, business and information systems planning helps to generate, screen, and select potential information systems for development.

Feasibility Studies

Because the process of developing a major information system can be costly, the systems investigation stage frequently requires a preliminary study called a **feasibility study.** A feasibility study is a preliminary study to investigate the information needs of prospective users and determine the resource requirements, costs, benefits, and feasibility of a proposed project. The methods of gathering information summarized in Figure 3.8 are used to collect data for a feasibility study. The findings of this study are usually formalized in a written report. It includes preliminary specifications and a developmental plan for the proposed system. This report is submitted to the management of the firm for its approval before development can begin. If management approves the recommendations of the feasibility study, the **systems analysis** stage can begin.

Cost/Benefit Analysis

Feasibility studies, typically, involve **cost/benefit analysis.** If costs and benefits can be quantified, they are called tangible; if not, they are called intangible. Examples of **tangible costs** are the costs of hardware and software, employee salaries, and other quantifiable costs needed to develop and implement an IS solution. **Intangible costs** are difficult to quantify; they include the loss of customer goodwill or employee morale caused by errors and disruptions arising from the installation of a new system.

FIGURE 3.8
Ways to gather information for systems development.

- Interviews with employees, customers, and managers.
- Questionnaires to appropriate end users in the organization.
- Personal observation or involvement in business operations.

- Examination of documents, reports, procedures manuals, and other documentation.
- Development, manipulation, and observation of a model of the business operations.

Tangible Benefits	Example
Increase in sales or profits	Development of computer-based products and services
Decrease in information processing costs	Elimination of unnecessary procedures and documents
Decrease in operating costs	Reduction in inventory carrying costs
Decrease in required investment	Decrease in inventory investment required
Increased operational ability and efficiency	Improvement in production ability and efficiency; for example, less spoilage, waste, and idle time

Intangible Benefits	Example
New or improved information availability	More timely and accurate information and new types of information
Improved abilities in computation and analysis	Analytical modeling
Improved customer service	More timely service response
Improved employee morale	Elimination of burdensome and boring job tasks
Improved management decision making	Better information and decision analysis
Improved competitive position	Systems which lock in customers and suppliers
Improved business and community image	Progressive image as perceived by customers, suppliers, and investors

FIGURE 3.9
Possible benefits of computer-based information systems, with examples. Note that an opposite result for each of these benefits would be a cost or disadvantage of computer-based information systems.

Tangible benefits are favorable results, such as the decrease in payroll costs caused by a reduction in personnel or a decrease in inventory carrying costs caused by a reduction in inventory. **Intangible benefits** are harder to estimate. Such benefits as better customer service or faster and more accurate information for management fall into this category. Figure 3.9 lists typical tangible and intangible benefits with examples. Possible tangible and intangible costs would be the opposite of each benefit shown.

The Feasibility of a System

The goal of feasibility studies is to evaluate alternative systems and to propose the most feasible and desirable systems for development. The feasibility of a proposed system can be evaluated in terms of four major categories, as illustrated in Figure 3.10.

The focus of **organizational feasibility** is on how well a proposed information system supports the objectives of the organization and its strategic plan for information systems. For example, projects that do not directly contribute to meeting an organization's strategic objectives are typically not funded. **Economic feasibility** is concerned with whether expected cost savings, increased revenue, increased profits, reductions in required investment, and other types of benefits will exceed the costs of developing and operating a proposed system. For example, if a project can't cover its development costs, it won't be approved, unless mandated by government

FIGURE 3.10
Organizational, economic, technical, and operational feasibility factors. Note that there is more to feasibility than cost savings or the availability of hardware and software.

Organizational Feasibility	Economic Feasibility
• How well the proposed system supports the strategic objectives of the organization	• Cost savings • Increased revenue • Decreased investment • Increased profits
Technical Feasibility	**Operational Feasibility**
• Hardware and software capability, reliability, and availability	• End user acceptance • Management support • Customer, supplier, and government requirements

FIGURE 3.11
Examples of how a feasibility study measured the feasibility of the POS system proposed for Auto Shack Stores.

Auto Shack Stores: POS Feasibility

The team of store managers and systems analysts from the information services department conducted a feasibility study of the POS options facing Auto Shack. The study team made personal observations of the sales processing system in action and interviewed managers, salespeople, and other employees. Based on a preliminary analysis of user requirements, the team proposed a new sales processing system. This new system features a telecommunications network of point-of-sale (POS) terminals and management workstations. Outlined below are several examples of feasibility factors that were determined for the new point-of-sale system. After reviewing the feasibility study, the top management of Auto Shack gave the go-ahead for the development of the new POS system.

Organizational Feasibility	Economic Feasibility
• How well the proposed system fits the store's plans for integrating sales, marketing and financial systems	• Savings in checkout costs • Increased sales revenue • Decreased investment in inventory • Increased profits
Technical Feasibility	**Operational Feasibility**
• Capability, reliability, and availability of POS hardware and software	• Acceptance of salespeople • Store management support • Customer acceptance

regulations or other considerations. **Technical feasibility** can be demonstrated if reliable hardware and software capable of meeting the needs of a proposed system can be acquired or developed by the business in the required time. Finally, **operational feasibility** is the willingness and ability of the management, employees, customers, suppliers, and others to operate, use, and support a proposed system. For example, if the software for a new system is too difficult to use, employees may make too many errors and avoid using it. Thus, it would fail to show operational feasibility. See Figure 3.11.

Systems Analysis

What is **systems analysis?** Whether you want to develop a new application quickly or are involved in a long-term project, you will need to perform several basic activities of systems analysis. Many of these activities are an extension of those used in conducting a feasibility study. Some of the same information-gathering methods are used, plus some new tools that we will discuss shortly. However, systems analysis is not a preliminary study. It is an in-depth study of end user information needs that produces **functional requirements** that are used as the basis for the design of a new information system. Systems analysis traditionally involves a detailed study of:

- The information needs of the organization and end users like yourself.
- The activities, resources, and products of any present information systems.
- The information system capabilities required to meet your information needs, and those of other end users.

Organizational Analysis

An **organizational analysis** is an important first step in systems analysis. How can you improve an information system if you know very little about the organizational environment in which that system is located? You can't. That's why you have to know something about the organization, its management structure, its people, its business activities, the environmental systems it must deal with, and its current information systems. You must know this information in more detail for the specific end user departments that will be affected by the new or improved information system being proposed. For example, you cannot design a new inventory control system for a chain of department stores until you learn a lot about the company and the types of business activities that affect its inventory.

Analysis of the Present System

Before you design a new system, it is important to study the system that will be improved or replaced (if there is one). You need to analyze how this system uses hardware, software, and people resources to convert data resources, such as transactions data, into information products, such as reports and displays. Then you should document how the information system activities of input, processing, output, storage, and control are accomplished. For example, you might note the format, timing, volume, and quality of input/output activities that provide *user interface* methods for interaction between end users and computers. Then, in the systems design stage, you can specify what the resources, products, and activities *should be* in the system you are designing. Figure 3.12 outlines the activities of the present sales processing system at Auto Shack Stores.

- When a customer wants to buy an auto part, a salesclerk writes up a sales order form. Recorded on this form is customer data, such as name, address, and account number, and product data, such as name, product number, and price. A copy of the sales order form is given to the customer as a receipt.

- Sales order forms are sent at the end of each day to the information services department. The next day they are entered into the computer system by data entry clerks using video terminals and stored on the mainframe computer's magnetic disk units.

- These daily sales transactions are used by a sales processing program to update a sales master file to reflect the sales for the day.

- Sales processing also involves the use of a sales analysis program to produce sales analysis reports that tell store managers the trends in sales for various types of auto parts.

FIGURE 3.12
An overview of the present sales processing system at Auto Shack Stores.

FIGURE 3.13
Functional requirements specify information system capabilities required to meet the information needs of users.

- **User interface requirements.** The input/output needs of end users that must be supported by the information system, including sources, formats, content, volume, and frequency of each type of input and output.
- **Processing requirements.** Activities required to convert input into output. Includes calculations, decision rules, and other processing operations, and capacity, throughput, turnaround time, and response time needed for processing activities.
- **Storage requirements.** Organization, content, and size of databases, types and frequency of updating and inquiries, and the length and rationale for record retention.
- **Control requirements.** Accuracy, validity, safety, security, and adaptability requirements for system input, processing, output, and storage functions.

FIGURE 3.14
Examples of functional requirements for a sales transaction processing system at Auto Shack Stores.

User Interface Requirements
Automatic entry of product data and easy-to-use data entry screens for salespeople.

Processing Requirements
Fast, automatic calculation of sales totals and sales taxes.

Storage Requirements
Fast retrieval and update of data from product, pricing, and customer databases.

Control Requirements
Signals for data entry errors and easy-to-read receipts for customers.

Functional Requirements Analysis

This step of systems analysis is one of the most difficult. You need to work with systems analysts and other end users to determine your specific information needs. For example, you need to determine what type of information you require; what its format, volume, and frequency should be; and what response times are necessary. Second, you must try to determine the information processing capabilities required for each system activity (input, processing, output, storage, control) to meet these information needs. Your main goal should be to identify what should be done, not how to do it. Finally, you should try to develop **functional requirements.** Functional requirements are end user information requirements that are not tied to the hardware, software, and people resources that end users presently use or might use in the new system. That is left to the design stage to determine. For example, Figure 3.13 outlines some of the key areas where functional requirements should be developed. Figure 3.14 shows examples of functional requirements for a sales transaction processing system at Auto Shack Stores.

Systems Design

Systems analysis describes *what* a system should do to meet the information needs of users. **Systems design** specifies *how* the system will accomplish this objective. Systems design consists of design activities that produce **system specifications** satisfying the functional requirements developed in the systems analysis stage. These specifications are used as the basis for software development, hardware acquisition,

- When a customer wishes to buy an auto part, the salesclerk enters customer and product data using an online POS terminal. The POS terminal has a keyboard for data entry and a video screen for display of input data, as well as data entry menus, prompts, and messages. POS terminals are connected in a telecommunications network to the store's mainframe computer, which uses a comprehensive sales transaction processing program.

- The POS terminal prints out a sales receipt for the customer that contains customer and product data and serves as a record of the transaction.

- The POS terminal transmits sales transaction data to the store's mainframe computer. This immediately updates the sales records in the company's database, which is stored on magnetic disk units.

- The computer performs sales analyses using the updated sales records in the company database. Afterward, sales performance information is available to corporate and store managers in a variety of report formats at their management workstations.

FIGURE 3.15
A design overview of the new point-of-sale system proposed for Auto Shack Stores.

FIGURE 3.16
Systems design can be viewed as the design of user interfaces, data, and processes.

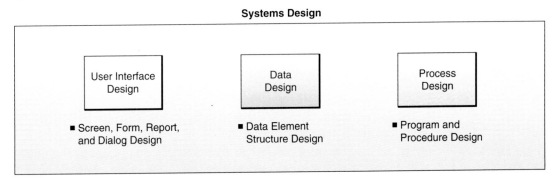

system testing, and other activities of the implementation stage. A variety of tools and methods which can be used for systems design are discussed in Appendix B at the back of this text. Figure 3.15 is a design overview of the new point-of-sale system proposed for Auto Shack Stores.

A useful way to look at systems design is illustrated in Figure 3.16. This concept focuses on three major products or *deliverables* that should result from the design stage. In this framework, systems design consists of three activities: **user interface, data, and process design.** This results in specifications for user interface methods and products, database structures, and processing and control procedures [1].

User Interface, Data, and Process Design

The user interface design activity focuses on designing the interactions between end users and computer systems. Designers concentrate on input/output methods and the conversion of data and information between human-readable and machine-readable forms. As we will see shortly, user interface design is frequently a *prototyping* process, where working models or *prototypes* of user interface methods are designed and modified with feedback from end users. Thus, user interface design produces

User Interface Design

FIGURE 3.17
System specifications specify the
details of a proposed information system.

- **User interface specifications:** The content, format, and sequence of user interface products and methods such as display screens, interactive dialogues, audio responses, forms, documents, and reports.
- **Database specifications:** Content, structure, distribution, and access, response, maintenance, and retention of databases.
- **Software specifications:** The required software package or programming specifications of the proposed system, including performance and control specifications.
- **Hardware and facilities specifications:** The physical and performance characteristics of the equipment and facilities required by the proposed system.
- **Personal specifications:** Job descriptions of persons who will operate the system.

detailed specifications for information products such as display screens, interactive user/computer dialogues (including the sequence or flow of dialogue), audio responses, forms, documents, and reports.

Data Design

The data design activity focuses on the design of the structure of databases and files to be used by a proposed information system. Data design frequently produces a *data dictionary*, which catalogs detailed descriptions of:

- The *attributes* or characteristics of the *entities* (objects, people, places, events) about which the proposed information system needs to maintain information.
- The relationships these entities have to each other.
- The specific data elements (databases, files, records, etc.) that need to be maintained for each entity tracked by the information system.
- The integrity rules that govern how each data element is specified and used in the information system.

Process Design

The process design activity focuses on the design of *software resources,* that is, the programs and procedures needed by the proposed information system. It concentrates on developing detailed specifications for the program modules that will have to be purchased as software packages or developed by custom programming. Thus, process design produces detailed program specifications and procedures needed to meet the user interface and data design specifications that are developed. Process design must also produce specifications that meet the functional control and performance requirements developed in the analysis stage.

System Specifications

The design of user interface methods and products, database structures, and processing and control procedures results in hardware, software, and personnel specifications for a proposed system. Systems analysts work with you so they can use your knowledge of your own work activities and their knowledge of computer-based systems to specify the design of a new or improved information system. The final design must specify what types of hardware resources (machines and media), software resources (programs and procedures), and people resources (end users and information systems staff) will be needed. It must specify how such resources will convert data resources (stored in files and databases they design) into information products (displays, responses, reports, and documents). These specifications are the

---

User Interface Specifications

Use handheld optical scanning wands to automatically capture product data on bar-coded tags. Use data entry screens with key data highlighted for better readability.

Database Specifications

Develop databases that use a relational structure to organize access to all necessary customer and merchandise data.

Software Specifications

Develop or acquire a sales processing program that can accept entry of optically scanned bar codes, retrieve necessary product data, and compute sales amounts in less than 0.5 seconds. Acquire a relational database management package to manage stored databases.

Hardware Specifications

Install POS terminals at each checkout station connected to a system of networked microcomputers in each store that are also connected to the corporate headquarters network.

Personnel Specifications

All hardware and software must be operable by regular store personnel. IS personnel should be available for hardware and software maintenance as needed.

FIGURE 3.18

Examples of system specifications for a new point-of-sale system at Auto Shack Stores.

final product of the systems design stage, and are called the **system specifications.** Figure 3.17 outlines some of the key characteristics that should be included in system specifications. Figure 3.18 shows examples of system specifications that could be developed for a point-of-sale system at Auto Shack Stores.

Implementation and Maintenance

Once a proposed information system has been designed, it must be implemented. The **systems implementation** stage involves hardware and software acquisition, software development, testing of programs and procedures, development of documentation, and variety of installation activities. It also involves the education and training of end users and specialists who will operate a new system. Finally, implementation involves converting from the use of a present system to the operation of a new or improved system. This may involve operating both new and old systems in *parallel* for a trial period, operation of a *pilot* system on a trial basis at one location, *phasing* in the new system one application or location at a time, or an immediate *cutover* to the new information system.

Systems maintenance involves the monitoring, evaluating, and modifying of a system to make desirable or necessary improvements. This may include a *postimplementation review* process to ensure that the newly implemented system meets the functional requirements established for it. Errors in the development of a system are corrected by the maintenance activity. Systems maintenance also includes making changes to tax computations in the payroll systems and tax-accounting systems of a business.

We will discuss the activities of the implementation process further in Chapter 14. For the present, you should realize that implementation can be a difficult and time-consuming process. However, it is vital in ensuring the success of any newly developed system. For even a well-designed system will fail if it is not properly implemented. Figure 3.19 outlines examples of activities that Auto Shack Stores might use to implement its new point-of-sale systems.

FIGURE 3.19
Examples of implementation
activities for Auto Shack's new
POS systems.

- Evaluate and acquire new hardware and software. Hardware includes computer systems, POS terminals, and telecommunications processors and network facilities. Software includes network management programs and POS transaction processing packages.

- Develop computer programs or make any necessary modifications to software packages that are acquired.

- Prepare training materials and documentation on how to operate the new POS system for managers and salespeople.

- Educate and train managers, salespeople, and information systems personnel to operate the new system.

- Test the system and make corrections until it operates properly.

- Convert to the new system on a phased store-by-store basis to minimize disruption. Use the first store converted as a pilot installation to help with testing and training.

- Perform a postimplementation audit within 30 days of each store's conversion to determine if the new POS systems are achieving their expected advantages.

Computer-Aided Systems Engineering

Major changes are occurring in the traditional process of systems development that we described in this chapter. That's because the SDLC process has often been too inflexible, time-consuming, and expensive. In many cases, end user requirements are defined early in the process, and then end users are locked out until the system is implemented. Also, the backlog of unfilled user requests has grown to two to five years in many companies. Therefore, a **computer-aided systems engineering** (CASE) process has emerged due to the availability of a variety of software packages for systems and software development. CASE (which also stands for **computer-aided software engineering**) involves using software packages, called CASE tools, to perform many of the activities of the systems development life cycle. For example, software packages are available to help do business planning, project management, user interface design, database design, and software development. Thus, CASE tools make a computer-aided systems development process possible. See Figure 3.20.

Using CASE Tools

Some of the capabilities of CASE tools are also found in the application development capabilities of end user software such as electronic spreadsheet and database management packages. That's why **end user development** has become a major category of end user computing. For example, end users, alone or working with systems analysts, can use the screen and report generators in database management packages to develop data entry screens or management reports. CASE tools also help automate the use of graphics tools such as flowcharts and data flow diagrams, which are described in Appendix B. See Figure 3.21.

Figure 3.22 emphasizes that CASE packages provide many computer-based tools for both the *front end* of the systems development life cycle (planning, analysis and design) and the *back end* of systems development (implementation and maintenance). Note than a *system repository* and systems developers such as programmers and systems analysts help integrate the use of tools at both ends of the development cycle. The system repository is a computerized database for all of the details of a system generated with other systems development tools. The repository helps to ensure consistency and compatibility in the design of the data elements, processes, user interface, and other aspects of the system being developed.

FIGURE 3.20

The components of CASE. This is an example of the CASE software tools and repositories in an integrated CASE product.

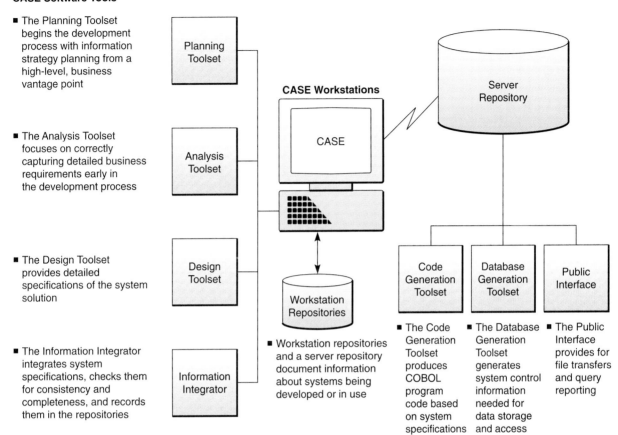

CASE Software Tools

- The Planning Toolset begins the development process with information strategy planning from a high-level, business vantage point

- The Analysis Toolset focuses on correctly capturing detailed business requirements early in the development process

- The Design Toolset provides detailed specifications of the system solution

- The Information Integrator integrates system specifications, checks them for consistency and completeness, and records them in the repositories

- Workstation repositories and a server repository document information about systems being developed or in use

- The Code Generation Toolset produces COBOL program code based on system specifications

- The Database Generation Toolset generates system control information needed for data storage and access

- The Public Interface provides for file transfers and query reporting

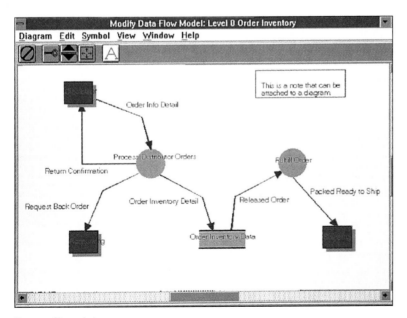

FIGURE 3.21

Displays of a CASE software package. The Excelerator package allows a system analyst to interactively develop system specifications, use a variety of analysis and design tools, and design the format of screens and reports.

Courtesy of Intersolv Inc.

FIGURE 3.22
The role of CASE tools. Note
their use in the stages of the systems development life cycle,
and the integrative role of
systems developers and system
repositories.

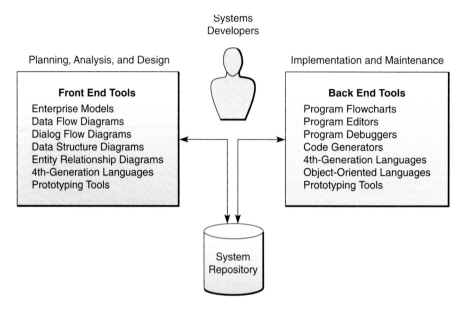

Integrated CASE tools (called I-CASE) are now available that can assist all of the stages of systems development. Some of these CASE tools support *joint application design* (JAD), where a group of systems analysts, programmers, and end users can jointly and interactively design new applications. Finally, if the development of new systems can be called *forward engineering,* some CASE tools support *backward engineering.* That is, they allow systems analysts to inspect the logic of a program code for old applications, and convert it automatically into more efficient programs that significantly improve system effectiveness.

Prototyping

Microcomputer workstations and a variety of CASE and other software packages allow the rapid development and testing of working models, or **prototypes,** of new applications in an interactive, iterative process involving both systems analysts and end users. **Prototyping** not only makes the development process faster and easier for systems analysts, especially for projects where end user requirements are hard to define, but it has opened up the application development process to end users. These developments are changing the roles of end users and information systems specialists in systems development.

The Prototyping Process

Prototyping can be used for both large and small applications. Typically, large systems still require using the traditional system development approach, but parts of such systems can frequently be prototyped. A prototype of an information system needed by an end user is developed quickly using a variety of application development packages. The prototype system is then repeatedly refined until it is acceptable to an end user.

As Figure 3.23 illustrates, prototyping is an iterative, interactive process that combines steps of the traditional systems development cycle. End users with sufficient experience with application development packages can do prototyping themselves. Alternatively, an end user can work with a systems analyst to develop a prototype system in a series of interactive sessions. For example, they could develop prototypes of management reports or data entry screens, such as the one illustrated in Figure 3.24. The prototype is usually modified several times until the end user

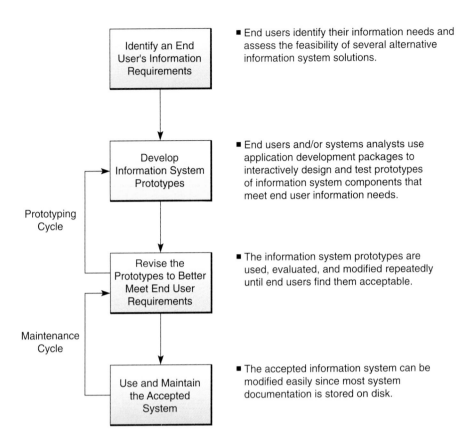

- End users identify their information needs and assess the feasibility of several alternative information system solutions.

- End users and/or systems analysts use application development packages to interactively design and test prototypes of information system components that meet end user information needs.

- The information system prototypes are used, evaluated, and modified repeatedly until end users find them acceptable.

- The accepted information system can be modified easily since most system documentation is stored on disk.

FIGURE 3.23
Application development using prototyping. Note how prototyping combines the steps of the traditional systems development cycle and changes the traditional roles of information systems specialists and end users.

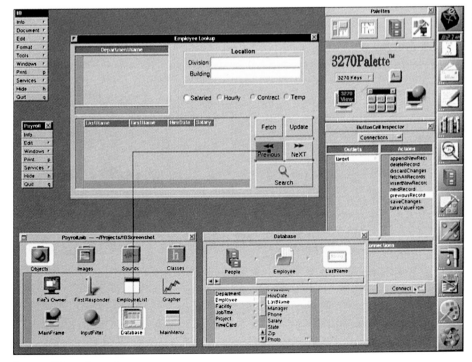

FIGURE 3.24
Using an application development package to design a prototype employee personnel record screen.

Courtesy of Quyen System, Inc.

finds it acceptable. Any program modules not directly developed by the CASE software can then be coded by programmers using conventional programming languages. The final version of the system is then turned over to the end user for operational use.

Checklist for End User Analysis and Design

Figure 3.25 outlines key questions you can use as a checklist to begin the process of analysis and design. Also included are answers that identify generic system components which are typically found in most computer-based information systems in business. Use this checklist as a tool to identify such components yourself in any information system you are studying. Then use it again as a source of design features you may want to suggest for a new or improved system.

FIGURE 3.25
A checklist for end user analysis and design.

Input of Data Resources

Question: How is data captured and prepared for processing? How should it be? What data resources are or should be captured?

Answers: Input data is frequently collected from *source documents* (such as payroll time cards) and converted to machine-sensible data by a *keyboarding* data entry process. Other input that may be captured directly by transaction terminals (such as point-of-sale terminals) using devices such as optical scanners. Input into the system typically consists of:

- **Transaction data.** *Example:* Data describing sales transactions is captured by a point-of-sale terminal.
- **Database adjustments.** *Example:* A change in a customer's credit limit, using an online terminal in the credit department or processing a "credit increase request form" mailed in by a customer.
- **Inquiries.** *Example:* What is the balance owed on a customer's account?
- **Output of other systems.** *Example:* The output of a sales transaction processing system includes data needed as input by an inventory control system to reflect transactions that change the amount of inventory on hand.

Processing of Data Resources

Question: How is data manipulated and transformed into information? How should it be? What processing alternatives should be considered?

Answers: Data resources are subjected to sorting, summarizing, calculating, and other manipulation activities. Processing alternatives include batch processing and realtime processing. *Examples:*

- Calculating employee payroll.
- Sorting employee record by employee number.
- Summarizing employees payroll costs.
- Realtime processing of sales data from point-of-sale terminals.
- Nightly batch processing of deposited checks by banks.

FIGURE 3.25
Concluded

Output of Information Products

Question: How is information communicated to users? How should it be? What **information products** are and should be produced?

Answers: Output typically takes the form of the following information products:

- **Reports.** *Example:* A sales analysis report outlining the sales made during a period by sales territory, product, and salesperson.
- **Documents.** *Example:* A paycheck or sales receipt.
- **Displays or responses.** *Example:* A video terminal displays the balance owed on a customer's account. The same information can be transmitted to a telephone by a computer audio-response unit.
- **Control listings.** *Example:* Each time an employee paycheck is printed, a line on a listing known as a payroll register is also printed and recorded on magnetic tape. This helps provide an *audit trail* for control purposes.
- **Input to other systems.** *Example:* Part of the output of a payroll system serves as input to a labor-cost accounting system and the general ledger system of the firm.

Storage of Data Resources

Question: How are **data resources** organized, stored, updated, and retrieved? How should they be?

Answers: Data resources are stored and organized into files and databases. This facilitates:

- Supplying data needed by the organization's information system applications. *Example:* The current credit balance of a customer is retrieved from a customer database by sales and accounting personnel.
- The updating of files and databases to reflect the occurrence of new business transactions. *Example:* A customer's credit balance is increased to reflect recent purchases on credit.

Control of System Performance

Question: How are input, processing, output, and storage activities monitored and controlled? How should they be? What control methods should be considered?

Answers: Input, processing, output, and storage activities must be controlled so that an information system produces proper information products and achieves its other objectives. Typical control methods include:

- **Input controls.** *Example:* Formatted data entry screens warn users if input data exceed specified parameters.
- **Processing controls.** Software may contain checkpoint routines that check the accuracy of intermediate results during processing.
- **Output controls.** *Example:* Computer users may check the accuracy of specified control totals in reports.
- **Storage controls.** *Example:* Databases may be protected by security programs that require proper identification and authorization codes by end users.

Garber Travel: The End User Development Role of IS

Rock Blanco typifies the new generation of business-savvy IS managers—long on strategic vision and short on staff. In the seven years he has been vice president of information technology at Garber Travel Services in Cambridge, Massachusetts, he has dismantled a mainframe-based, centralized IT operation, built a PC LAN and client/server infrastructure, farmed out applications development, outsourced basic services to American Airlines' SABRE system, and reduced the staff and IS cost by more than one-third.

Now the travel agency, with revenues in excess of $200 million, has an IS budget of less than $1 million, a stunning ratio for an information-dependent service company.

The downsizing moves give Blanco the opportunity to help end users and business units develop profitable products and services. "The key focus that IT had in the 1980s was personal productivity," he says. "In the 90s, the shift is to work group technology, which involves the management of enormous amounts of information from all different types of hosts and sources, and people working together in a network."

Helping users and department managers build their own reports and applications using data and a variety of groupware-enabled applications, such as Lotus Notes and Groupwise from Novell, is how Blanco views his role. "I see IS becoming more information brokers and/or information service bureaus," he explains. "It's not so much picking and designing end user applications, but assisting end users to

get information from various sources and organize and manage it. Our job is to provide that type of access to end users who are either in a work group environment, working from home, or wherever—the extended workgroup of today.

"That puts IS out of being the development shop of new applications as well as deciding on platforms and products. We want to keep our MIS department small so we view third parties as part of our team."

Small, but creative, Blanco has been working with business managers to develop a host of services for Garber's customers. The company has already developed a remote travel-information service that is accessed via various networks by any type of end user device. "In the future, the key will be distribution of information regardless of the interface into the network—it may be personal digital assistants, beepers, cellular phones or laptop computers," he predicts.

CASE STUDY QUESTIONS

1. How does Rock Blanco view the role of the IS organization at Garber Travel?
2. What are the roles of end users and third-party companies in application development at Garber?
3. Should other types of businesses adopt similar roles for their IS function? Explain.

Source: Larry Marion, "Garber Travel Arrives at Development Nirvana," Special Advertising Supplement, *Computerworld*, March 13, 1995, p. 9. Copyright 1995 by Computerworld, Inc., Framingham, MA 01701—Reprinted from *Computerworld*.

CHAPTER 3 *Solving Business Problems with Information Systems*

Summary

- **The Systems Approach.** Managerial end users can use a systems approach to help them develop information system solutions to business problems. The steps and activities of the systems approach are summarized in Figure 3.1.
- **The Systems Development Cycle.** End users and systems analysts should use a systems approach to help them develop information system solutions to business problems. This, typically, involves an information systems development cycle where IS specialists and end users conceive, design, and implement computer-based information systems. The stages,

activities, and products of the information systems development cycle are summarized in Figure 3.7.
- **CASE and Prototyping.** Major changes occurring in the traditional information systems development cycle include computer-aided systems engineering (CASE) software packages, which computerize and automate parts of the systems development process, and prototyping tools and methodologies, which promote an iterative, interactive process that develops prototypes of user interfaces and other information system components.

Key Terms and Concepts

These are the key terms and concepts of this chapter. The page number of their first explanation is given in parentheses.

1. Computer-aided systems engineering (88)
2. Cost/benefit analysis (80)
3. Economic feasibility (81)
4. Feasibility study (80)
5. Functional requirements (84)
6. Information systems planning (80)
7. Intangible
   a. Benefits (81)
   b. Costs (80)
8. Operational feasibility (82)
9. Organizational analysis (83)
10. Organizational feasibility (81)
11. Postimplementation review (73)
12. Problems versus symptoms (69)
13. Prototype (90)
14. Prototyping (90)
15. Systems analysis (83)
16. Systems approach (68)
17. Systems context (69)
18. Systems design (84)
19. Systems development life
cycle (78)
20. Systems implementation (87)
21. Systems investigation (80)
22. Systems maintenance (87)
23. System specifications (86)
24. Tangible
   a. Benefits (81)
   b. Costs (80)
25. Technical feasibility (82)
26. User interface, data, and process design (85)

Review Quiz

Match one of the key terms and concepts listed above with one of the brief examples or definitions listed below. Try to find the best fit for answers that seem to fit more than one term or concept. Defend your choices.

_____ 1. Using an organized sequence of activities to study a problem or opportunity in a systems context.

_____ 2. Declining sales is a symptom of an underlying problem.

_____ 3. Trying to find systems and components of systems in any situation you are studying.

_____ 4. Evaluating the success of a solution after it has been implemented.

_____ 5. Your evaluation shows that benefits outweigh costs for a proposed system.

_____ 6. The costs of acquiring computer hardware, software, and specialists.

_____ 7. Loss of customer goodwill caused by errors in a new system.

_____ 8. Increases in profits caused by a new system.

_____ 9. Improved employee morale caused by efficiency and effectiveness of a new system.

_____ 10. A multistep process to conceive, design, and implement an information system.

_____ 11. The first stage of the systems development cycle.

_____ 12. Determines the organizational, economic, technical, and operational feasibility of a proposed information system.

_____ 13. Cost savings and additional profits will exceed the investment required.

_____ 14. Reliable hardware and software are available to implement a proposed system.

_____ 15. Customers will not have trouble using a proposed system.

_____ 16. The proposed system supports the strategic plan of the business.

_____ 17. Studying in detail the information needs of users and any information systems presently used.

_____ 18. A detailed description of user information needs and the input, processing, output, storage, and control capabilities required to meet those needs.

_____ 19. The process that results in specifications for the hardware, software, people, and data resources and information products needed by a proposed system.

_____ 20. Systems design should focus on developing end user input/output methods, data structures, and programs and procedures.

_____ 21. A detailed description of the hardware, software, people, and data resources and information products required by a proposed system.

_____ 22. Acquiring hardware and software, testing and documenting a proposed system, and training people to use it.

_____ 23. Making improvements to an operations system.

_____ 24. Using software packages to computerize many of the activities in the systems development process.

_____ 25. A working model of an information system.

_____ 26. An interactive and iterative process of systems development.

Discussion Questions

1. Could you use the systems approach to problem solving as a way to solve a marketing problem? A financial problem? A human resource management problem? Explain.

2. Refer to the Real World Case of Watkins Johnson Co. in the chapter. Watkins Johnson plans to replace its traditional ROI methods for capital expenditures with the CB-90 methodology. Do you think this is a good idea? Explain.

3. Why have computer-aided systems development and prototyping methods become so popular? What are their limitations?

4. Refer to the Real World Case of Garber Travel Services in the chapter. Do you agree that a company's IS function should act more as information brokers and/or information service bureaus? Why or why not?

5. What applications software packages can be used by end users to help them do applications development? Give several examples.

6. Refer to the Real World Case of Abaco Grupo Financiero in the chapter. Is Abaco's use of Microsoft programming tools an example of computer-aided systems engineering? Explain.

7. How could computer-aided systems engineering be used in each step of the systems development cycle?

8. Does prototyping replace or supplement traditional information systems development? Explain.

9. Pick a task you would like to computerize. How could you use the steps of the systems approach as illustrated in Figure 3.1 to help you? Use examples to illustrate your answer.

10. Pick a task you would like to computerize. How could you use the steps of the information systems development cycle as illustrated in Figure 3.7 to help you? Use examples to illustrate your answer.

Real World Problems

1. Patricia Seybold Group: The New Application Development Methodology

Corporatewide productivity, not just IS productivity, is an overarching financial consideration that tilts the scales in favor of standardizing on more systems development tools rather than fewer ones. "IS should support whatever the users want because they will be more productive with the tools they picked," notes Mitch Kramer, contributing editor to the Boston-based consulting firm Patricia Seybold Group. The Seybold Group emphasizes that joint application development, rapid application development and other methods are IT-centric in a world that is quickly becoming line-of-business–centric. In this new environment,

the typical application development process looks like this:

- A few end users and line-of-business developers form a team to develop an application's specifications.
- Initial prototype schematic design developed.
- Schematic converted into simple point-and-click prototype using end user tools.
- A few screens and routine linkages are presented to users.
- After the team gets feedback from users, the prototype is reiterated.
- Further presentations and reiterations.
- Consultation with central IT developer/consultants to

identify potential improvements and conformance to existing standards.

- Prototype converted to finish application.
- User review and sign-off.
- Application loaded onto servers.

a. What are the roles of end users, IS developers, and computer-aided development tools in the methodology outlined above?

b. Do you think the application development process outlined in this case is a good methodology for developing computer-based business applications? Why or why not?

Source: Larry Marion, "Application Development in the Decentralized Enterprise," Special Advertising Supplement, *Computerworld,* March 13, 1995, p. 12. Copyright 1995 by Computerworld, Inc., Framingham, MA 01701—Reprinted from *Computerworld.*

2. Physical Software and Florida Power: End User Development Tools

Corporate developers are finding that new application development tools, such as the one recently introduced by ParcPlace Systems, make it easier to involve end users in business process reengineering projects. The tools also help developers design applications that more closely meet business needs. New users said ParcPlace's tool, called MethodWorks, is so straightforward that line-of-business users can use it to provide input during the early phases of application design. "When users are involved in the development process, you get software that fits the business better, that's the biggest payoff," said Joe Whitesell, president of Physical Software, Inc., in East Lansing, Michigan.

Whitesell is using MethodWorks on a consulting project at Florida Power & Light Co. in Juno Beach, Florida. He said he was surprised at the degree to which users are involved in application design at the utility. "The trend is toward users acting as developers because the tools are getting to the point where they are simple enough," he said. MethodWorks, in particular, was designed to "get way upstream in the software process," Whitesell said. The tool lets Whitesell take the Florida Power end users' plain English descriptions of what business task they need to accomplish with a piece of software and turn those descriptions into a more formal object model of the business process. Applications are then developed using VisualWorks, a Smalltalk programming environment from ParcPlace.

a. How are end users assisted in the application development process by tools such as MethodWorks?

b. What are the benefits of end user involvement in application development?

Source: Adapted from Elizabeth Heichler, "Object Tools Help Developers Leverage User Input," *Computerworld*, May 15, 1995, p. 15. Copyright 1995 by Computerworld, Inc., Framingham, MA 01701—Reprinted from *Computerworld.*

3. Bradlees, Inc.: Getting Requirements Right

Retailers have always equated success with location. But in today's ultracompetitive world, location has as much to do with optimal data placement as it does with walk-in traffic. So Northeast regional retailer Bradlees, Inc., decided it could no longer tolerate dislocated data. It began planning and it budgeted $35 million to exit its mainframe and build an enterprisewide, cross-functional, client/server system of networked PCs and powerful servers. However, lackluster 1994 results and a better appreciation of the costs and challenges involved in client/server computing is forcing the Braintree, Massachusetts-based company to decelerate its plan. In fact, management at the $1.9 billion retailer recently decided to upgrade—rather than purely maintain—mainframe applications.

Bradlees is forging ahead, though more slowly. The retailer is using Powersoft's PowerBuilder CASE tool to build a client/server promotion planning system that will tie together their buying, planning, and advertising departments. The decision support system is designed to alleviate the vast amount of paperwork required to plan what Bradlees would promote, when, at what price, and in what type of ad. The system will eventually enable some 300 networked Windows PC users to share data residing on a Unix-based Sybase database server.

"In hindsight, we took a rapid application development approach that was a little short-sighted," said Kevin Maloney, director of financial and store systems. "We jumped right into prototyping but should have stayed longer with defining requirements, scoping, and collecting data."

a. On which stages of the systems development process should Bradlees have spent more time?

b. Why do you think Bradlees decided to develop a decision support system for promotional planning as their first attempt at building a client/server system?

Source: Adapted from Alen Alper, "Bradlees Takes Stock of Client/Server," *Computerworld Client/Server Journal*, April 1995, p. 9. Copyright 1995 by Computerworld, Inc., Framingham, MA 01701—Reprinted from *Computerworld.*

4. The U.S. Department of Defense: Using the IEF CASE Tool

The computer-aided software engineering tool set offered by Logicon Inc. for the U.S. Department of Defense's Integrated-CASE program has an entrenched Defense Department competitor: Texas Instruments Inc.'s Information Engineering Facility (IEF). Consider one Army project, the Homes Operations Management (HOMES) program. When Chuck Rettew, HOMES chief, was offered a chance to run a pilot site for the I-CASE program last year, he politely declined. Rettew's staff at the Army Information Systems Software Development Center–Washington has been using Texas Instruments' IEF for more than two years and wasn't about to switch to Logicore, the CASE environment built by Logicon. "Why should I transition over to a new system that hasn't even proven itself?" Rettew said. "It takes too long to learn a whole new set of tools, and I've got something that's known to work." Rettew said IEF generates 100 percent of a program's code automatically, in several programming languages, and on any platform.

Since August 1992, the HOMES team has used IEF to reengineer and consolidate two complex housing management systems. The new systems are now running at 18 Army bases, with 80 more in line for deployment. Among other improvements, Rettew said he has seen a 60 percent reduction in the handling of data change requests. Besides the HOMES program, according to Texas Instruments, IEF is in use in 17 sites in the Army, Navy, and Air Force, as well as in the Joint Logistics Systems Center and the Defense Logistics, National Security, and Defense Information Systems agencies. As part of JLSC's Material Management Standard System Integration program, 500 software technicians will use IEF to reengineer 10 systems. The program manager, Lt. Col. Mike Taint, said IEF was selected over other CASE environments "because it covers the greatest span of the development life cycle, from process modeling to code generation."

a. What are the benefits of using IEF for the U.S. Department of Defense?

b. How does a CASE tool set like IEF support the stages of the systems development life cycle?

Source: Adapted from Paul Constance, "Will IEF Get An I-CASE Role?" *Government Computer News*, April 17, 1995, p. 58.

5. Paul Youngworth: Systems Development by Walking Around

I had developed an application that let users in finance allocate product expenses across selected transactions for that product. The results are used in month-end reporting. The old system involved a lot of manual effort; users would extract the transactions for selected products from a mainframe file, calculate the allocations and key the results back into a database. Allocating expenses to a handful of items could require manually entering hundreds of transactions and take four to five hours. The new system was designed to take advantage of a client/server environment to minimize data entry. It pulls transactions for each product from an Oracle database server and displays them in a graphical user interface on end user PCs. Users can then point and click to select the transactions they want to include in the allocation. With a click of the mouse, results are written back to the server.

After design, the application went through user testing without snags. However, it's the little things that can get you. We had designed an *exclude* button that lets financial users click on an item to exclude geographic regions when allocating expenses to a product. The button, a feature developers discussed with users during design, made it through testing without problems. Too bad this innocent little button caused data entry to come to a dead stop, leaving the user staring at the computer screen in confusion. I would never have known this feature was a showstopper if I hadn't spent an hour or so quietly observing users working with the system.

After observing several end users in action, I learned what the problem was. When they were testing the application, they were concentrating solely on the software, and the exclude button was no problem. But in the real world, there are deadlines to meet, phone calls to take, visitors asking for reports and three things to do at once. In the real world, when users click a check box to exclude a region, they want the data gone—at once—not after they find some namby-pamby button. I was amazed that I wouldn't have known about the problem if I hadn't watched the application in action. And it took a mere 15 seconds to fix a problem that had the potential to cause users to miss critical business deadlines.

Welcome to what I call "programming by walking around." I borrowed this phrase from the business concept of "management by walking around." In management by walking around, business executives visit suppliers, employees, and customers to see how the company's product is made and used. The goal is quality improvement. In my adaptation, programmers and systems analysts get up from their machines, leave their cubicles, and observe "customers" (users) using the "product" (the application). The goal is to improve the quality of applications based on hands-on observation. The exclude button incident underscored the fact that this type of observation on a system developer's part is absolutely essential to creating programs that work like users do.

Note: Paul Youngworth is a programmer/analyst at a Midwest-based manufacturing company.

a. What is "programming by walking around?" How is it related to "management by walking around?"

b. Is this case an example of a prototyping approach? Of end user involvement in systems development? Explain.

Source: Adapted from Paul Youngworth, "Being There," *Computerworld*, April 10, 1995, pp. 99-100. Copyright 1995 by Computerworld, Inc., Framingham, MA 01701—Reprinted from *Computerworld*.

6. Revlon and Bancone: Two Application Development Approaches

Cosmetics giant Revlon and BancOne represent two strikingly different approaches to the selection and use of application development tools. BancOne is a rigidly centralized bank holding company, with an IT subsidiary that supplies applications to 80 banks around the country. The more creative environment and culture of Revlon has led to a much more involved end user role.

a. What business or management reasons might cause Revlon and BancOne to have such different approaches to application development?

b. Which approach do you prefer? Why?

Source: Adapted from Larry Marion, "Application Development in the Decentralized Enterprise," Special Advertising Supplement, *Computerworld*, March 13, 1995, p. 16. Copyright 1995 by Computerworld, Inc., Framingham, MA 01701—Reprinted from *Computerworld*.

	Revlon	BancOne Services
IS executives	Gene Pinadella, SVP&CIO	Dale Terrell, EVP
User base	3,000	48,000
Size of programming staff	85	900
Corporate structure	Business units	Centralized
Application development	Business units, with IS standards and support	Centralized; "We don't want to support 50 different tools."
Architecture	SNA, NetWare, Unix	OS/2, NetWare, Unix
RDBMS	Oracle, DB/2	DB/2, Sybase, Oracle
Application standards	Canned applications with Visual Data	In evaluation
Software selection process	Power users at departments test IS nominations, report results to IS	Standard architecture, includes 2-3 choices per platform
Who decides?	MIS and end-user committee	IS Architecture council
Exception process	None	Various management-level approvals required and "occasionally followed."
Who develops applications?	"End users take development initiative—they are responsible for projects."	IS "is responsible for all company development," departments modify according to local needs using standard tools

Application Exercises

1. ABC Department Stores

The president of ABC Department Stores made several statement and asked several questions in a recent meeting of store management. Match each statement or question with one of the steps of the systems approach outlined in Figure 3.1. Explain your choices.

a. I think John's suggestion for a sale on small appliances might be the way to boost sales without raising costs or disturbing our sales staff.

b. Have any of you collected information that might help us understand the reasons for the recent drop in sales of small appliances in all of our stores?

c. Let's hear some suggestions for ways to turn around this situation quickly, but I want to know the good and bad points for any suggestions you make.

d. I want reports on how small appliance sales are going every day during our sale.

e. Let's cut prices 20 percent on small appliances next week as part of an "ABC Means Value" promotional campaign.

The president also asked the following questions of the vice president for information services. Match each question with one of the steps of the information systems development cycle outlined in Figure 3.7. Explain your choices.

f. What are the specific information needs of our store managers?

g. Will the recent changes in the tax laws require us to change our computer-based payroll system?

h. Is a new point-of-sale system a feasible solution to this store's problems?

i. Have our employees been trained to use this POS system?

j. What are the exact specifications for the hardware and software needed?

2. Village Inn Restaurants

Village Inn Restaurants is a national chain of coffee shop restaurants. Typically, a waitress takes your order on a paper form, inserts it into a small terminal connected to an in-store minicomputer, and enters appropriate data about your order. The computer produces a paper printout of your order in the kitchen for the cooks, calculates your bill, and prints the details of your order on the paper order form. This form is then returned to your table. When you are ready to leave, you give this form to the cashier, who keys data about your payment into a point-of-sale terminal. Data are stored on magnetic tape cassettes and mailed each week to corporate headquarters in Nashville, Tennessee.

Assume that some customers are complaining about slow service, which the cooks blame on incorrect orders by waitresses. Also assume that restaurant managers are complaining about the slow response by corporate management to changes in customer preferences. Use the concepts of the systems approach to answer the following questions.

a. What specific steps would you take to study this problem and propose a solution?

b. What are three questions you would ask in a systems study interview?

c. What do you think the problem(s) is (are)? Why?

d. What are two possible solutions you can think of? What are their advantages and disadvantages?

e. If you had to choose one solution, what would it be? Why did you choose it?

f. How would you implement your solution?

3. System Study Report

Study an information system described in a case study in this text or one used by an organization to which you have access. Use the systems approach to problem solving outlined in Figure 3.1 to help you identify any problems or opportunities, develop proposed solutions, and write up the results in a *systems study report*. Make a presentation to the class based on the results of your system study. Use the following outline as a table of contents for your report and the outline of your presentation. Use overhead transparencies to display key points of your analysis.

a. Introduction to the organization and information system. The name of the organization, what the organization does, and the type of information system studied.

b. Analysis of the current information system. Identify the following system components in your report. Prepare an IS component matrix (see Figures 2.9 and 2.10 on pages 42 and 43 to summarize the components of your information system. Use the checklist in Figure 3.25 to help you identify the components that are or should be part of this information system. You may also use a system flowchart, data flow diagram, or entity-relationship diagram (refer to Appendix B) to graphically illustrate your analysis.

   (1) Input, processing, output, storage, and control methods currently used.

   (2) Hardware, software, and people involved.

   (3) Data captured and information products produced.

   (4) Files and databases accessed and maintained.

c. Evaluation of the current information system.

   (1) Efficiency: Does it do the job right? Is the information system well organized? Inexpensive? Fast? Does it require minimum resources? Process large volumes of data, produce many information products?

   (2) Effectiveness: Does it do the right job? The way the end users want it done? Give them the information they need, the way they want it? Does it support the objectives of the organization?

d. Design and implementation of an information system proposal.

   (1) Do end users need a new system or just improvements? Why?

   (2) What exactly are you recommending they do?

   (3) Is it feasible? What are its benefits and costs?

   (4) What will it take to implement your recommendations?

4. Systems Maintenance at ABC Products

Modifying systems in response to user requests is a major aspect of systems maintenance for the Information Systems Department at ABC Products Company. Users can request changes to information systems by filling out a change request form. The change request form is a manual form. A copy of the form is sent to the group charged with maintenance responsibilities for the affected system.

Many users have complained of long response times to their change requests and lack of follow-up to ensure that the changes made are acceptable. To expedite the processing of change requests, ABC Products has decided to assign a user, you, authority and responsibility for coordinating the processing of change requests.

To better track the processing of change requests, you have decided to maintain a database file providing summary information about each change request. You will record the name of the user requesting the change, the date of the request, the name of the information system that is to be modified, the member of the maintenance team assigned to the request, and data about the status of work on the request. A request will be listed as IP (for in-process) when you assign it to a maintenance team. Once the changes have been completed, you are to be notified. At that point the status is changed to PA (for pending-approval). You then will notify the user who submitted the work request that he or she is to evaluate the changes. When the evaluation is completed, the changes are either accepted (status AC) or rejected (status RE). If changes are rejected, the user submits a new change request form describing further modifications that are required. Sample data for this file are shown in Figure 3.26.

a. Create a database file to store this information and enter the sample records shown.

b. Create and print a report categorized by maintenance team number and summarize the status of all change requests.

c. Perform and get printed listings of the following retrievals:

   (1) Retrieve all information for requests whose status is IP.

   (2) Retrieve the request number, request date, and status of all requests addressed to the Acct. Rec. system.

   (3) Retrieve a count of the number of change requests whose status is AC.

5. Assessing Vendor Service Performance at Morris Manufacturing

Morris Manufacturing Company purchases microcomputer hardware from a number of vendors. In order to do a better job of tracking the service performance of those suppliers, Morris Manufacturing surveys its employees annually to determine how satisfied they are with the service provided by these suppliers. Each employee who has microcomputer

Requesting User	Request ID. No.	Request Date	System Affected	Maint. Team Assigned	Completion Status
Davis, L.	7843	10/07/95	Payroll	PO3	AC
Evans, G.	7844	10/09/95	Acct. Rec.	PO2	RE
Morris, M.	7845	10/09/95	Inventory	PO1	PA
Allen J.	7846	10/12/95	Payroll	PO3	IP
Jones, P.	7857	10/28/95	Order Proc.	PO2	AC
Lewis, R.	7872	11/07/95	Inventory	PO1	AC
Evans, G.	7879	11/18/95	Acct. Rec.	PO2	IP
Norton, M.	7886	11/22/95	Inventory	PO1	IP
Powers, R.	7889	11/24/95	Payroll	PO3	IP

FIGURE 3.26
Sample change request records for ABC Products.

equipment is asked to rate the supplier of that equipment with respect to: (1) the *speed* with which they have responded to service requests and (2) the *quality* of the servicing provided. This information is to be stored in a database file. Sample ratings for a recent year are shown below.

a. Create a database file to store this information and enter the sample data shown.

b. Create a report that will show the average rating given to each supplier in each category. Get a printed listing of this report.

c. Perform the following data retrievals and produce printed listings of their results:
   (1) Retrieve a list of the names of all employees who provided ratings for the supplier CompStar.
   (2) Retrieve a count of the number of Quality ratings assigned a value of less than 6.

Sample of Microcomputer Hardware Supplier Ratings

Employee Name	Supplier Name	Speed Rating	Quality Rating
Jones, B.	CompStar	8	9
Bates, N.	PCs Are We	7	3
Adams, A.	CompStar	8	7
Morris, M.	PC Power	9	10
Lewis, J.	PCs Are We	8	5
Jarvis, M.	CompStar	7	9
Dandes, K.	PC Power	9	9
Thomas, R.	PC Power	8	10
Ward, M.	PCs Are We	8	5
Evans, J.	CompStar	6	8
Eads, M.	PC Power	9	9

Review Quiz Answers

1. *16*
2. *12*
3. *17*
4. *11*
5. *2*
6. *24b*
7. *7b*
8. *24a*
9. *7a*
10. *19*
11. *21*
12. *4*
13. *3*
14. *25*
15. *8*
16. *9*
17. *15*
18. *5*
19. *18*
20. *26*
21. *23*
22. *20*
23. *22*
24. *1*
25. *13*
26. *14*

Selected References

1. Andersen Consulting. *Foundations of Business Systems.* 2nd ed. Chicago: Dryden Press, 1992.

2. Banker, Rajiv, and Robert Kauffman. "Reuse and Productivity in Integrated Computer-Aided Software Engineering: An Empirical Study." *MIS Quarterly,* September 1991.

3. Burch, John. *Systems Analysis, Design and Implementation.* Boston: Boyd & Fraser, 1992.

4. Cerveny, Robert; Edward Garrity; and Lawrence Sanders. "A Problem-Solving Perspective on Systems Development." *Journal of Management Information Systems,* Spring 1990.

5. Cooprider, Jay, and John Henderson. "Technology-Process Fit: Perspectives on Achieving Prototyping Effectiveness." *Journal of Management Information Systems,* Winter 1990/91.

6. Forte, Gene, and Ronald Norman. "CASE: A Self Assessment By

the Software Engineering Community." *Communications of the ACM,* April 1992.

7. Hershey, Gerald, and Donna Kizzier. *Planning and Implementing End User Information Systems.* Dallas: South Western Publishing, 1992.

8. Keen, Peter. *Shaping the Future: Business Design Through Information Technology.* Boston: Harvard Business School Press, 1991.

9. Lederer, Albert, and Vijay Sethi. "Critical Dimensions of Information Systems Planning" *Decision Sciences Journal,* Winter 1991.

10. Orlikowsky, Wanda. "CASE Tools as Organizational Change: Investigating Incremental and Radical Changes in Systems Development." *MIS Quarterly,* September 1993.

11. Pei, Daniel, and Carmine Cutone. "Object-Oriented Analysis and Design." *Information Systems Management,* Winter 1995.

12. Rochester, Jack. "Re-engineering Existing Systems." *I/S Analyzer,* October 1991.

13. Vessey, Iris, and Robert Glass. "Applications-Based Methodologies: Development by Application Domain." *Information Systems Management,* Fall 1994.

14. Watson, Hugh, and Mark Frolick. "Determining Information Requirements for an EIS." *MIS Quarterly,* September 1993.

15. Whitten, Jeffrey; Lonnie Bentley; and Vic Barlow. *Systems Analysis and Design Methods.* 3rd ed. Homewood, IL: Richard D. Irwin, 1994.

REAL WORLD CASE

Abaco Grupo Financiero: Application Development for Competitive Advantage

Ever since the Mexican government announced the devaluation of the peso, the currency has fallen more than 50 percent against the U.S. dollar, and interest rates have skyrocketed by nearly 100 percent. To help insulate its loan customers from runaway inflation, Abaco Grupo Financiero recently began developing applications designed to let customers restructure their payments over longer periods of time.

For example, since late February, 70 programmers at the Monterrey, Mexico, bank have been using Microsoft Visual Basic, SQL Server and Visual C++ application development and programming tool kits to reengineer the consumer loan systems in order to protect clients from triple-digit interest rates.

"All Mexican financial institutions are trying to restructure their loan portfolios at this time, but the tools we're using give us the advantage of developing these applications very quickly," said Jorge Reyesvera, manager of research and development at Abasis, the bank's information technology arm. He said he expects the consumer loan applications to go live later this month.

Abaco's reliance on Microsoft's application development products is not new. When the bank was privatized in 1994, it inherited a handful of IBM 4361 mainframes and a few isolated Unix servers. To deliver information in a more timely fashion, the bank has invested $80 million since 1991 to develop a client/server technology infrastructure—an approach that has become common among Mexican banks—using Microsoft's application tools.

In contrast to their Third World setting, Mexican banks have developed fairly sophisticated information technology architectures, according to banking analysts. This is due in large part to the North American Free Trade Agreement (NAFTA), which has forced Mexican banks to develop products and services quickly in order to remain competitive with multinational banks that are now muscling in on their once-exclusive turf.

Before NAFTA, Mexican banks "existed in an insulated, regulated environment," said Deborah Williams, a technology analyst at The Tower Group, a Wellesley, Massachusetts, banking and technology consultancy. Mexican banks "are really under time pressure to get products to market," Williams said. So the use of computer-aided development to speed product development has become more critical than ever, she said.

For example, Abaco's first major postprivatization project was the development of a point-of-sale (POS) system that supports more than 140 types of financial transactions. Using Visual Basic, Visual C++ and SQL Server, Abasis developed a 55-teller Windows-based POS system in less than a year. It now runs at 200 branches on more than 1,000 teller PCs and is supported by a Sybase SQL Server database package that runs on a Hewlett-Packard HP9000 midsize computer.

Because the branch databases are connected to one another, Abaco and non-Abaco customers alike can cash checks and transfer account balances from the branch of their choice. The distributed POS system has helped the bank save more than $200,000 annually on mainframe maintenance costs since the last IBM mainframe was scuttled in March 1993. More importantly, the POS System has enabled Abaco to increase customer service levels and drive new business, Reyesvera said.

"In this competitive market, if we hadn't developed this POS system, we would have gone out of business," he said.

CASE STUDY QUESTIONS

1. Why are Abaco and other Mexican banks under time pressure to develop new computer-based banking systems?
2. How can Abaco develop new banking applications so quickly?
3. Could Abaco's IT strategy be implemented by other types of businesses? Explain.

Source: Adapted from Thomas Hoffman, "Bank Reengineers to Fight Mexican Inflation," *Computerworld*, April 3, 1995, p. 76. Copyright 1995 by Computerworld, Inc., Framingham, MA 01701—Reprinted from *Computerworld*.

M O D U L E **II**

Information Technology: A Managerial Overview

What challenges do information systems technologies pose for managerial end users? What basic knowledge should business end users possess about information technology? The four chapters of this module give you an overview of the major technologies used in modern computer-based information systems and their implications for end users and managers.

Chapter 4, "Managerial Overview: Computer Hardware," reviews micro, midrange, mainframe, and networked computer systems, and the major types of peripheral devices used for computer input, output, and storage by end users.

Chapter 5, "Managerial Overview: Computer Software," reviews the basic features and functions of major types of system and application software packages used to support traditional and end user computing.

Chapter 6, "Managerial Overview: Telecommunications," presents you with an overview of major trends, concepts, applications, and technical alternatives in telecommunications. It emphasizes the implications of telecommunications for managerial end users and the strategic success of organizations.

Chapter 7, "Managerial Overview: Database Management," emphasizes management of the data resources of computer-using organizations. It outlines the managerial implications of basic concepts and applications of database management in organizational information systems.

Managerial Overview: Computer Hardware

CHAPTER OUTLINE

LEARNING OBJECTIVES

The purpose of this chapter is to provide a managerial overview of computer hardware by reviewing the basic types of computer systems and the major types of computer peripheral devices used for input, output, and storage.

Section I of this chapter analyzes the basic functions, components, and major trends in computer systems. It then presents an overview of microcomputer, midrange, mainframe, and networked computer systems.

Section II surveys the major characteristics and functions of computer peripheral devices, including support of the user interface through visual and voice input/output methods, and the use of semiconductor memory, magnetic disks and tape, and optical disks to provide storage capabilities for computer systems.

After reading and studying this chapter, you should be able to:

1. Identify the components and functions of a computer system.
2. Outline the major differences and uses of microcomputers, midrange, mainframe, and networked computers.
3. Identify the major types and uses of computer peripherals for input, output, and storage.
4. Explain the benefits, limitations, and trends in major types of computer systems and peripheral devices.

┌─ S E C T I O N   I
Computer Systems: End User and Enterprise Computing

The Computer System Concept

Before we examine the major types of computers in use today, we should review what the term *computer system* means. A computer is more than a high-powered calculator, or a collection of electronic devices performing a variety of information processing chores. A computer is a **system**, an interrelated combination of components that performs the basic system functions of *input, processing, output, storage,* and *control,* thus providing end users with a powerful information processing tool. Understanding the computer as a **computer system** is vital to the effective use and management of computers. You should be able to visualize any computer this way, from a microcomputer like that shown in Figure 4.1 to a large computer system whose components are interconnected by a telecommunications network and spread throughout a building or geographic area.

Figure 4.2 illustrates that a computer is a system of hardware devices organized according to the following system functions:

- **Input.** The input devices of a computer system include keyboards, touch screens, pens, electronic "mice," optical scanners, and so on. They convert data into electronic *machine-readable* form for direct entry or through telecommunications links into a computer system.
- **Processing.** The *central processing unit* (CPU) is the main processing component of a computer system. (In microcomputers, it is the *main microprocessor.*) In particular, the *arithmetic-logic unit,* one of the CPU's major components, performs the arithmetic and logic functions required in computer processing.

FIGURE 4.1
A microcomputer is a system of computing components. This microcomputer system includes (1) a keyboard and mouse for input, (2) microprocessors and other circuitry in its main system unit for processing and control, (3) a video monitor and printer for output, and (4) memory chips and a built-in floppy disk drive and hard disk unit for storage.

John Curtis.

FIGURE 4.2

The computer system concept. A computer is a system of hardware components and functions.

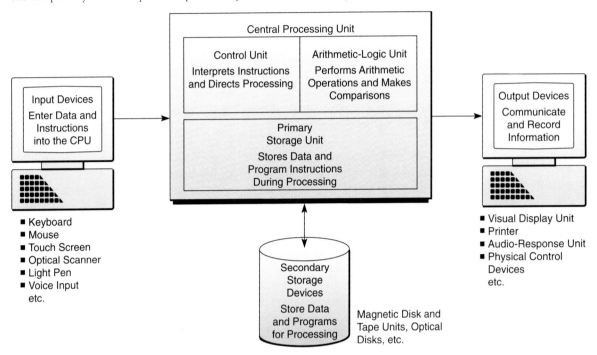

- **Output.** The output devices of a computer system include video display units, printers, audio response units, and so on. They convert electronic information produced by the computer system into *human-intelligible* form for presentation to end users.
- **Storage.** The storage function of a computer system takes place in the computer's *primary storage unit*, or *memory*, and in *secondary storage* devices such as magnetic disk and tape units. These devices store data and program instructions needed for processing.
- **Control.** The *control unit* of the CPU is the control component of a computer system. It interprets computer program instructions and transmits directions to the other components of the computer system.

Computer System Components

Let's take a closer look now at how each of these vital system functions is accomplished by the components of computer systems. Then we will discuss the major types of computer systems in use today.

The Central Processing Unit

The **central processing unit** is the most important hardware component of a computer system. It is also known as the CPU, the *central processor* or *instruction processor*, and the main microprocessor in a **microprocessor.** Conceptually, the CPU can be subdivided into two major subunits: the arithmetic-logic unit and the control unit. The CPU also includes specialized circuitry and devices such as *registers* for high-speed, temporary storage of instruction and data elements, and various subsidiary processors such as those for arithmetic operations, input/output, and telecommunications support. (Sometimes a computer's primary storage unit or memory is shown as part of a CPU.)

The **control unit** obtains instructions from those stored in the primary storage unit and interprets them. Then it transmits directions to the other components of the computer system, ordering them to perform required operations. The **arithmetic-logic unit** performs required arithmetic and comparison operations. A computer can make *logical* changes from one set of program instructions to another (e.g., overtime pay versus regular pay calculations) based on the results of comparisons made in the ALU during processing.

Multiple Processors

Many current computers, from microcomputers to large mainframes, use **multiple processors** for their processing functions. Instead of having one CPU with a single control unit and arithmetic-logic unit, the CPUs of these computers contain several types of processing units. Let's briefly look at the major types of such **multiprocessor** designs.

A **support processor** design relies on specialized microprocessors to help the main CPU perform a variety of functions. These microprocessors may be used for input/output, memory management, arithmetic computations, and telecommunications, thus freeing the main processor to do the primary job of executing program instructions. For example, many microcomputers rely on support microprocessors such as arithmetic co-processors, video display controllers, and magnetic disk controllers to reduce the process on their main microprocessors. A large computer may use support microprocessors called *channels* to control the movement of data between the CPU and input/output devices. Advanced microprocessor designs integrate the functions of several support processors on a single main microprocessor. See Figure 4.3.

A **coupled processor** design uses multiple CPUs or main microprocessors to do *multiprocessing,* that is, executing more than one instruction at the same time.

FIGURE 4.3
The Intel Pentium microprocessor contains over three million transistors and features dual-execution units and high-speed memory caches that give it a top processing speed of over 100 million instructions per second.

Courtesy of Intel Corporation.

Some configurations provide a *fault-tolerant* capability, since multiple CPUs provide a built-in backup to each other should one of them fail.

A **parallel processor** design uses a group of instruction processors to execute several program instructions at the same time. Sometimes, hundreds or thousands of processors are organized in clusters or networks in **massively parallel processor** (MPP) computers. Other parallel processor designs are based on simple models of the human brain called *neural networks*. All of these systems can execute many instructions at a time in *parallel*. This is a major departure from the traditional design of current computers, called the *Von Neumann design,* which executes instructions *serially* (one at a time). Though difficult to program, many experts consider parallel processor systems the key to providing artificial intelligence capabilities to fifth-generation computers.

Many advanced technical workstations and other computers rely on a processor design called RISC (reduced instruction set computer). This contrasts with most current computers which use CISC (complex instruction set computer) processors. RISC processor designs optimize a CPU's processing speed by using a smaller *instruction set*. That is, they use a smaller number of the basic *machine instructions* that a processor is capable of executing. By keeping the instruction set simpler than CISC processors and using more complex software, a RISC processor can reduce the time needed to execute program instructions. Thus, RISC processors like Digital Equipment's Alpha chip have become popular for computers such as network servers and technical workstations. Also, a new generation of powerful microcomputers is emerging that uses RISC microprocessors like the Power PC, codeveloped by Motorola, Apple, and IBM. See Figure 4.4.

RISC Processors

How fast are computer systems? Computer operating speeds that were formerly measured in **milliseconds** (thousandths of a second) are now being measured in the **microsecond** (millionth of a second) and **nanosecond** (billionth of a second) range, with **picosecond** (trillionth of a second) speed being attained by some computers. Such speeds seem almost incomprehensible. For example, an average person taking one step each nanosecond would circle the earth about 20 times in one second!

Many microcomputers and midrange computers, and most mainframe computers operate at nanosecond speeds and can thus process several *million instructions*

Computer Processing Speeds

Ed Kashi.

FIGURE 4.4
This Apple Power Macintosh relies on a Power PC microprocessor as its central processing unit.

FIGURE 4.5
A comparison of five generations of Intel microprocessors.

Intel Microprocessor	Bus Width (bits)	Register Size (bits)	Clock Speed (MHz)	MIPS
8088	8	8	5–8	0.33
80286	16	16	8–12	1.2
80386	32	32	16–33	2.5–6
80486	32	32	25–66	15–40
Pentium	64	64	66–100	112

per second (MIPS). Another measure of processing speed is *megahertz* (MHz), or millions of cycles per second. It is commonly called the *clock speed* of a microprocessor, since it is used to rate microprocessors by the speed of their timing circuits or internal clock. However, megahertz ratings can be misleading indicators of the effective processing speed of microprocessors as measured in MIPS and other measures. That's because processing speed depends on a variety of factors besides a microprocessor's clock speed. Important examples include the size of circuitry paths, or *busses,* that interconnect microprocessor components, the capacity of instruction processing *registers,* the use of high-speed memory *caches,* and the use of specialized microprocessors such as a *math co-processor* to do arithmetic calculations faster.

Note: *Registers* are small high-speed storage circuitry elements in a CPU used to temporarily store parts of an instruction or data element during the execution of an instruction. *Cache memory* is a high-speed temporary storage area in a CPU for storing parts of a program or data during computer processing.

For example, Intel's 80486 microprocessor, which has a cache memory and math coprocessor built into the chip, is rated at 20 to 40 MIPS. This is about twice the processing speed of the Intel 80386 microprocessor, even when both chips run at the same megahertz speeds. Just for comparison, Intel's Pentium microprocessor runs at 66 to 100 MHz and is rated at over 100 MIPS. Supercomputers have been clocked at more than 1,000 MIPS and perform arithmetic computations in billions of floating-point operations per second, or *gigaflops.* See Figure 4.5.

Primary and Secondary Storage

The **primary storage unit** (also called *main memory*) holds data and instructions between processing steps and supplies them to the control unit and arithmetic-logic unit during processing. All data and programs must be placed in memory before they can be used in processing.

The primary storage unit is also used to hold data and program instructions between processing steps, and after processing is completed but before output. In modern computers, the primary storage unit consists of microelectronic *semiconductor memory* chips. Most of memory is known as **RAM** (random access memory). The contents of these memory chips can be instantly changed to store new data. Other, more permanent memory chips are called **ROM** (read only memory).

Data and programs are also stored in **secondary storage devices,** such as magnetic disk and tape units, which greatly enlarge the storage capacities of computer systems. Also, since memory circuits typically lose their contents when electric power is turned off, most secondary storage media provide a more permanent type of storage. However, the contents of secondary storage devices cannot be processed without first being brought into the primary storage unit. Thus, external secondary storage devices play a supporting role to the primary storage unit of a computer system. For example, programs and files are typically stored until needed on magnetic floppy disks and hard disks on microcomputer systems, and on large magnetic tape disk and tape units on larger computer systems.

Data is processed and stored in a computer system through the presence or absence of electronic or magnetic signals in the computer's circuitry or in the media it uses. This is called a "two-state" or **binary representation,** of data since the computer and the media can exhibit only two possible states or conditions. For example, transistors and other semiconductor circuits are either in a conducting or nonconducting state. Media such as magnetic disks and tapes indicate these two states by having magnetized spots whose magnetic fields have one of two different directions, or polarities. This binary characteristic of computer circuitry and media is what makes the *binary number system* the basis for representing data in computers. Thus, for electronic circuits, the conducting (ON) state represents the number one, while the nonconducting (OFF) state represents the number zero. For magnetic media, the magnetic field of a magnetized spot in one direction represents a one, while magnetism in the other direction represents a zero.

The smallest element of data is called a **bit,** or binary digit, which can have a value of either zero or one. The capacity of memory chips is usually expressed in terms of bits. A **byte** is a basic grouping of bits that the computer operates as a single unit. Typically, it consists of eight bits and is used to represent one character of data in most computer coding schemes. Thus, the capacity of a computer's memory and secondary storage devices is usually expressed in terms of bytes. Computer codes such as ASCII (American Standard Code for Information Interchange) use various arrangements of bits to form bytes that represent the numbers zero through nine, the letters of the alphabet, and many other characters. See Figure 4.6.

Storage capacities are frequently measured in **kilobytes** (abbreviated as KB or K) or **megabytes** (abbreviated as MB or M). Although *kilo* means one thousand in the metric system, the computer industry uses K to represent 1,024 (or 2^{10}) storage

Computer Storage Capacities

Character	ASCII Code	Character	ASCII Code
0	00110000	I	01001001
1	00110001	J	01001010
2	00110010	K	01001011
3	00110011	L	01001100
4	00110100	M	01001101
5	00110101	N	01001110
6	00110110	O	01001111
7	00110111	P	01010000
8	00111000	Q	01010001
9	00111001	R	01010010
A	01000001	S	01010011
B	01000010	T	01010100
C	01000011	U	01010101
D	01000100	V	01010110
E	01000101	W	01010111
F	01000110	X	01011000
G	01000111	Y	01011001
H	01001000	Z	01011010

FIGURE 4.6
Examples of the ASCII computer code.

FIGURE 4.7
Computer storage capacity and speed elements.

Computer Time Elements	Storage Elements (approximate capacities)
Millisecond = One thousandth of a second Microsecond = One millionth of a second Nanosecond = One billionth of a second Picosecond = One trillionth of a second	Kilobyte = One thousand bytes Megabyte = One million bytes Gigabyte = One billion bytes Terabyte = One trillion bytes

positions. Therefore, a memory size of 640K, for example, is really 655,360 storage positions, rather than 640,000 positions. However, such differences are frequently disregarded in order to simplify descriptions of storage capacity. Thus, a megabyte is roughly 1 million bytes of storage, while a **gigabyte** is roughly 1 billion bytes and a **terabyte** represents about 1 trillion bytes. Typically, computer primary storage capacities now range from 4 to 64 megabytes for microcomputer memories to several gigabytes of memory for large mainframe computer systems. Magnetic disk capacities generally range from one to several megabytes for floppy disks, from over 200 megabytes to several gigabytes for hard disk drives, and over 500 megabytes for an optical disk. Mainframe magnetic disk units supply many gigabytes of online storage. Figure 4.7 summarizes these important **storage capacity elements.**

Types and Trends in Computers

As an informed business end user, it is important that you recognize several major trends in computer systems. These trends have developed in the past during each major stage, or **generation,** of computers, and they are expected to continue into the future. The first generation of computers began in the early 1950s; the second generation in the late 1950s; the third generation in the mid-1960s; and the fourth generation began in the 1970s and continues to the present. A fifth generation of computers is expected to develop by the end of the century. Figure 4.8 highlights trends in the characteristics and capabilities of computers. Notice that computers continue to become smaller, faster, more reliable, and less costly to purchase and maintain.

Computer Generations

First-generation computers (1951–1958) used hundreds or thousands of **vacuum tubes** for their processing and memory circuitry. These computers were quite large and generated enormous amounts of heat, and vacuum tubes had to be replaced frequently. Thus, they had large electrical power, air conditioning, and maintenance requirements. First-generation computers had main memories of only a few thousand characters and millisecond processing speeds. They used magnetic drums or tape for secondary storage and punched cards or paper tape as input and output media.

    Second-generation computers (1959–1963) used **transistors** and other *solid-state, semiconductor* devices that were wired to circuit boards. Transistorized circuits were much smaller and much more reliable, generated little heat, were less expensive, and required less power than vacuum tubes. Tiny *magnetic cores* were used for the computer's memory, or internal storage. Many second-generation computers had main memory capacities of less than a hundred kilobytes and microsecond processing speeds. Removable *magnetic disk packs* were introduced, and magnetic tape emerged as the major input, output, and secondary storage medium for large computer installations.

FIGURE 4.8
Major trends in computer characteristics and capabilities.

	First Generation	Second Generation	Third Generation	Fourth Generation	Fifth Generation
SIZE (Typical computers)	Room Size Mainframe	Closet Size Mainframe	Desk-Size Minicomputer	Desktop and Laptop Microcomputers	Credit Card-Size Micro?
CIRCUITRY	Vacuum tubes	Transistors	Integrated Semi-conductor Circuits	Large-Scale Integrated (LSI) Semi-Conductor Circuits	Very Large-Scale Integrated (VSLI) Superconductor Circuits?
DENSITY (Circuits per component)	One	Hundreds	Thousands	Hundreds of Thousands	Millions?
SPEED (Instructions/second)	Hundreds	Thousands	Millions	Tens of Millions	Billions?
RELIABILITY (Failure of circuits)	Hours	Days	Weeks	Months	Years?
MEMORY (Capacity in characters)	Thousands	Tens of Thousands	Hundreds of Thousands	Millions	Billions?
COST (Per million instructions)	$10	$1.00	$.10	$.001	$.0001?

Third-generation computers (1964–1979) began using **integrated circuits,** in which thousands of transistors and other circuit elements are etched on tiny chips of silicon. Main memory capacities of several megabytes and processing speeds of millions of instructions per second (MIPS) were achieved, and telecommunications capabilities became common. This made it possible for *operating system* programs to come into widespread use that automated and supervised the activities of many types of peripheral devices and processing of several programs at the same time, sometimes from networks of users at remote terminals. Integrated circuit technology also made possible the development and widespread use of small computers called **minicomputers** in the third computer generation.

Fourth-generation computers (1979 to the present) use LSI (large-scale integration) and VSLI (very-large-scale integration) technologies that cram hundreds of thousands or millions of transistors and other circuit elements on each chip. Main memory capacities ranging from a few megabytes to several gigabytes can be achieved by the memory chips that replaced magnetic core memories. LSI and VSLI technologies also allowed the development of **microprocessors,** in which all of the circuits of a CPU are contained on a single chip with processing speeds of millions of instructions per second. **Microcomputers,** which use in microprocessor CPUs and a variety of peripheral devices and easy-to-use software packages to form small personal computer systems (PCs) or networks of linked PCs, are a hallmark of the fourth generation of computing.

Computer Categories

Today's computer systems display striking differences as well as basic similarities. Differing end user needs and technological discoveries have resulted in the development of several major categories of computer systems with a variety of characteristics and capabilities. Thus, computer systems are typically classified as *microcomputers, midrange computers,* and *mainframe computers.* However, as Figure 4.9 illustrates, these are not precise classifications. For example, variations of these categories include *minicomputers, superminicomputers,* and *supercomputers.* Also, a variety of application categories, which describe major uses for various types of computers, are common. Examples are host computers, network servers, and technical workstations.

Such categories are attempts to describe the relative computing power provided by different *computing platforms,* or types of computers. Computers may differ in their processing speed and memory capacity, as well as in the number and capabilities of peripheral devices for input, output, and secondary storage they can support. However, you will find microcomputers that are more powerful than some midrange computers and midrange computers that are more powerful than some mainframe computers. So these computer classifications do overlap each other, as Figure 4.9 illustrates. In addition, experts continue to predict the merging or disappearance of several computer categories. For example, they argue that minicomputers and many mainframe computers are being made obsolete by the power and versatility of networks of microcomputer systems.

Computer manufacturers, typically, produce *families,* or product lines, of computers. So computer systems can have a variety of models with different processing speeds, memory capacities, and other capabilities. This allows manufacturers to provide a range of choices to customers, depending on their information processing needs. Most models in a family are compatible; that is, programs written for one

FIGURE 4.9
Computer system classifications. Note the overlap among the traditional and application categories of the three major classifications of computers.

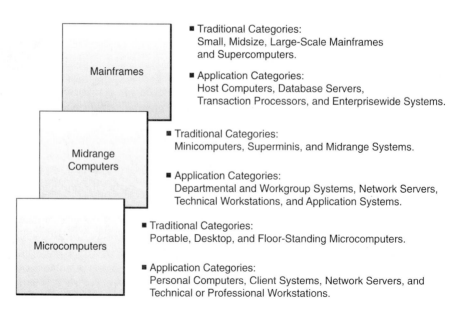

model can usually be run on other models of the same family with little or no change. This allows customers to move up (*migrate*) to larger models of the same computer product line as their needs grow.

Microcomputers are the smallest but most important category of computer systems for end users. A microcomputer is, typically, referred to as a *personal computer,* or PC. However, microcomputers have become much more than small computers used by individual persons. Their computing power now exceeds that of the mainframes of previous computer generations at a fraction of their cost. For this reason, they have become powerful *professional workstations* for use by end users in businesses and other organizations.

      Microcomputers come in a variety of sizes and shapes for a variety of purposes, as Figure 4.10 illustrates. Microcomputers categorized by size include *handheld, notebook, laptop, portable, desktop,* and *floor-standing* microcomputers. Or, based on their use, they include *home, personal, professional, workstation,* and *multiuser* computers

Microcomputer Systems

FIGURE 4.10
Examples of microcomputer systems.

Courtesy of Compaq Computer Corporation.
a. A local area network of microcomputer systems.

Hewlett Packard.
c. The microcomputer as a professional workstation.

Tom Tracy/The Stock Market.
b. The microcomputer as a technical workstation.

and special-purpose categories such as **personal digital assistants** (PDAs) or telecommunications *network servers*. However, the classifications of *desktop* versus *portable* are the most widely used distinctions. That is because most microcomputers are designed either to fit on top of an office desk, transforming it into an end user workstation, or to be conveniently carried by end users, such as by salespersons or consultants who do a lot of traveling.

Most microcomputers are single-user computers designed to support the work activities of a variety of end users. However, powerful **workstation computers** (*technical workstations*) are available that support applications with heavy mathematical computing and graphics display demands such as computer-aided design (CAD) in engineering, or investment and portfolio analysis in the securities industry. One of the fastest growing microcomputer application categories is **network servers**. They are usually more powerful microcomputers that coordinate telecommunications and resource sharing in local area networks (LANs) of interconnected microcomputers and other computer system devices.

Midrange Computer Systems

Midrange computers, also called **minicomputers**, are larger and more powerful than most microcomputers but are smaller and less powerful than most large mainframe computer systems. However, this is not a precise distinction. High-end models of microcomputer systems (*supermicros*) are more powerful than some midrange computers, while high-end models of midrange systems (superminis) are more powerful than some smaller models of mainframe computers. In addition, midrange systems cost less to buy and maintain than mainframe computers. They can function in ordinary operating environments, and do not need special air conditioning or electrical wiring. See Figure 4.11.

Midrange computers are being used for many business and scientific applications. They first became popular as *minicomputers* for scientific research, instrumentation systems, engineering analysis, and industrial process monitoring and control.

FIGURE 4.11
A midrange computer system, the HP 9000.

Courtesy of Hewlett Packard Company.

Minicomputers could easily handle such uses because these applications are narrow in scope and do not demand the processing versatility of mainframe systems. Thus, midrange computers serve as industrial process-control and manufacturing plant computers, and they play a major role in computer-aided manufacturing (CAM). They can also take the form of powerful *technical workstations* for computer-aided design (CAD) applications. Midrange computers are often used as *front-end* computers to help mainframe computers control data communications networks with large numbers of data entry terminals.

Midrange computers have also become popular as powerful *network servers* to help manage large interconnected local area networks that tie together many end user microcomputer workstations, and other computer devices in departments, offices, and other work sites. In addition, some midrange systems are used as departmental or office computers because they can provide large departments or offices more processing power and support more users at the same time than networked microcomputers.

Mainframe computers are large, powerful computers that are physically larger than micros and minis and usually have one or more central processors with faster instruction processing speeds. For example, they may be able to process from 10 million to 200 million instructions per second (MIPS). Mainframes have large primary storage capacities. For example, their main memory capacity can range from about 64 megabytes to several gigabytes of storage. Many mainframe models have the ability to service hundreds of users at once. For example, a single large mainframe can process hundreds of different programs and handle hundreds of different peripheral devices (terminals, disk and tape drives, printers, etc.) for hundreds of different users at the same time. See Figure 4.12.

Mainframe computers are designed to handle the information processing needs of major corporations and government agencies with many employees and

Mainframe Computer Systems

FIGURE 4.12
A large mainframe computer system, the IBM ES/9000.

Courtesy of International Business Machines Corporation.

customers or with complex computational problems. For example, large computers are necessary for organizations processing millions of transactions each day, such as major international banks, airlines, oil companies, and the national stock exchanges. They can also handle the processing of thousands of customer inquiries, employee paychecks, student registrations, sales transactions, and inventory changes, to give a few examples. Large mainframes can handle the great volume of complex calculations involved in scientific and engineering analyses and simulations of complex design projects, such as analyzing seismic data from oil field exploration, or designing aircraft. Mainframes are also becoming popular as *super servers* and corporate *database servers* for the large interconnected telecommunications networks of major corporations.

Supercomputer Systems

The term **supercomputer** has been coined to describe a category of extremely powerful mainframe computer systems specifically designed for high-speed numeric computation. A small number of large supercomputers are built each year for government research agencies, military defense systems, national weather forecasting agencies, large time-sharing networks, and major corporations.

The leading maker of supercomputers is Cray Research, along with NEC, Fugitsu, and a few others. These models can process hundreds of millions of instructions per second (MIPS). Expressed another way, they can perform arithmetic calculations at a speed of billions of floating-point operations per second (gigaflops). *Teraflop* (1 trillion floating-point operations per second) supercomputers, which use advanced *massively parallel* designs, are becoming available.

Purchase prices for large supercomputers are in the $5 million to $50 million range. However, the use of *massively parallel processing* (MPP) designs of thousands of interconnected microprocessors has spawned a breed of *minisupercomputers* with prices below $1 million. Thus, supercomputers continue to advance the state of the art for the entire computer industry.

Networked Computer Systems

Solitary computer systems are becoming a rarity in corporate computing. From the smallest microcomputer to the largest mainframe, computers are being *networked*, or interconnected by telecommunications links with other computer systems. This networked distribution of computer power throughout an organization is called **distributed processing.** It frequently takes the form of a **client/server** approach, with networks of end user microcomputers (*clients*) and network servers tied together, sometimes with midrange computers or mainframes acting as *superservers*. Networked computer systems allow end users and work groups to communicate electronically, and share the use of hardware, software, and data resources. For example, end users in an office **local area network** (LAN) of microcomputers can communicate with each other using electronic mail, work together on group projects, and share the use of software packages, laser printers, and work group databases. See Figure 4.13.

So, many computer systems consist of peripheral devices interconnected by communications links to one or more central processing units. Thus, networked computing depends on telecommunications. **Telecommunications,** or, more narrowly, *data communications,* is the use of networks of interconnected computers and peripheral devices to process and exchange data and information. Telecommunications networks use a variety of telecommunications media, hardware, and software to accomplish and control communications among computers and peripheral devices. For example, microcomputers rely on *modems* to convert

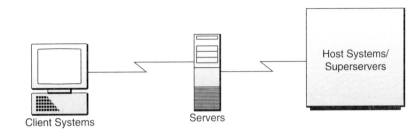

FIGURE 4.13
The computer systems in client/server computing.

- Types: PCs, Workstations, Macintoshes.
- Functions: Provide user interface, perform some/most processing on an application.

- Types: Supermicros, workstations, or midrange systems.
- Functions: Shared computation, application control, distributed databases.

- Types: Mainframes, superminicomputers.
- Functions: Central database control, security, directory management, heavy-duty processing.

Courtesy of Compaq Computer Corporation.

FIGURE 4.14
Networked microcomputers are replacing midrange computers and mainframes in many organizations.

data from digital to analog form and back, while *network operating system* programs control resource sharing and communications flow among computers and peripherals in a local area network. We will discuss telecommunications further in Chapter 6.

Networks of small computers have become a major alternative to the use of larger computer systems, as many organizations are **downsizing** their computing platforms. For example, a network of several midrange computers and many microcomputer workstations may replace a large mainframe computer system with many end user terminals. Alternately, networks of microcomputers can replace both minicomputers and mainframes in many organizations. Networked microcomputers have proven to be easier to install, use, and maintain, and provide a more efficient, flexible, lower-cost alternative to larger computer systems for many applications. See Figure 4.14.

Networked microcomputer systems are being used for jobs formerly given to large midrange or mainframe systems. Many LANs can easily handle the sharing of computing power, software, and databases that is required in time-sharing and resource-sharing applications. Networked computers also support *work group computing*. For example, end users in a work group can use their networked computers to communicate electronically and share data as they work together on joint projects. Finally, networked microcomputers are even being used for *transaction processing* applications. For example, some organizations are using networks of microcomputers to process thousands of daily credit card purchases, money transfers, credit checks, customer account inquiries, and other business transactions.

REAL WORLD CASE

 # The Darby Group: Switching to Distributed Systems

A few years ago, the outlook for medical products distributor The Darby Group Co. was a bit grim. Severe competition was driving down prices and shrinking profits in an already margin-thin business. The situation prompted Mike Ashkin, chief executive officer at the Westbury, New York, company, to launch a major technology renovation. His goal was to help the company deliver products and services faster and more efficiently as well as significantly reduce recurring costs.

One of those recurring costs was the company's aging network of mainframe and minicomputer systems. "It was always a chicken or egg thing in terms of either downsizing employees or downsizing the IS operation," Ashkin said. "We were sort of betting the company on this move."

That bet has paid off handsomely. In less than three years, Ashkin and his team have weaned Darby Group off a mishmash of host-based systems and software. The company now has a single mainframe that anchors a more standardized distributed platform that is better able to accommodate emerging technologies. One result has been a streamlining of the information systems operation.

In late 1991, Darby's IS operating environment consisted of IBM 3030, 4381, and 9370 mainframes and AS/400 minis running multiple operating systems; Digital Equipment minicomputers; a distributed network of AT&T servers; and Paradyne Data 100 network links connecting the company's dozen or so remote sites. There was not a LAN in the house, and the handful of PCs sat unconnected.

But during the last couple of years, all that has been sliced down to a single IBM 3090 mainframe. The company now has Microsoft Windows NT and Novell NetWare running on relatively low cost Intel-based servers connecting well over 1,000 PCs. The company has cut its IS expenses approximately 35 percent during the last three years and reduced annual IS labor costs by $250,000. "PCs have given my company a chance to have a bottom line. If not for those systems, we would not be profitable," Ashkin said.

Through this distributed systems approach, Darby moved its order-entry application from its IBM System 370 architecture machines to LAN-based systems. Within 18 months of making that decision, the firm had replaced almost all of its terminals with PCs and built a wide area network that connected all remote offices to the mainframe at headquarters.

This client/server approach has also allowed Darby to improve the efficiencies of the "returns" aspect of its generic drug business. Returns in the pharmaceuticals market are more complicated than in other businesses because of strict government regulations. Before the company proceeded with its distributed strategy, typically, it was a few weeks behind in processing returns. But since the company rolled its IBM 4381 out the door and rolled in a client/server system running Windows NT and SQL Server, those backlogs have been cut down to a day or two.

While Darby has aggressively moved forward with its distributed strategy, including putting LAN administrators in some of its remote sites, company officials do not see true decentralization of IS operations coming any time soon. In fact, they prefer to keep a tight grip on certain core IS functions, including application software development. "We used to have 100 people in IS, and now we have 70," said Neal Perlman, Darby's IS director. "We could accept a 30 percent reduction by eliminating anything that was redundant in the home office with remote sites. It is why you need to keep certain things centralized, even as you distribute other functions out."

In retrospect, what perhaps propelled Ashkin's aggressive vision of a distributed computing strategy was when his son Carl, now Darby's chief information officer, planted a PC on his father's desk just a few years ago. "I think he thought it was going to be a toy. But when he found out he could put a report on a laptop and distribute it to others—and not have to wait weeks for IS to help him—he got interested," Carl Ashkins said. "It never hurts you to have the CEO of the company really into information technology."

CASE STUDY QUESTIONS

1. Why did The Darby Group switch to a distributed computing approach?

2. Is the approach also an example of client/server computing? Explain.

3. Why do you think Darby continues to use a mainframe computer?

Source: Adapted from Ed Scannel, "Medical Company Goes Distriibuted," *Computerworld*, January 30, 1995, p. 42. Copyright 1995 by Computerworld, Inc., Framingham, MA 01701—Reprinted from *Computerworld*.

┌ **SECTION II**
│ *Computer Peripherals: Input, Output, and Storage*
│ *Technologies*

A computer is just a high-powered "processing box" without *peripherals*. **Peripherals** is the generic name given to all input, output, and secondary storage devices that are part of a computer system. Peripherals depend on direct connections or telecommunications links to the central processing unit of a computer system. Thus, all peripherals are **online** devices; that is, they are separate from, but can be electronically connected to and controlled by, a CPU. (This is the opposite of **offline** devices, which are separate from and not under the control of the CPU.) The major types of peripherals and media that can be part of a computer system are discussed in this section.

Input/Output Hardware Trends

There are many technologies for input and output at the *user interface* between computer systems and end users. Figure 4.15 shows you the major trends in input/output media and methods that have developed over four generations of computers and are expected to continue into a future fifth generation.

Figure 4.15 emphasizes that there is a major trend toward the increased use of a variety of **direct input/output devices** to provide a more natural user interface. More and more, data and instructions are entered into a computer system directly, through input devices such as keyboards, electronic mice, pens, touch screens, and optical scanning wands. These direct input/output devices drastically reduce the need for paper source documents and their conversion to machine-readable media. Direct output of information through video displays of text and graphics and voice response devices is increasingly becoming the dominant form of output for end users.

FIGURE 4.15
Input/output hardware trends. Note the trend toward direct input and output media and methods to provide a more natural user interface.

	First Generation	Second Generation	Third Generation	Fourth Generation	Fifth Generation?
INPUT MEDIA/ METHOD	Punched Cards Paper Tape	Punched Cards	Key to Tape/Disk	Keyboard Data Entry Direct Input Devices Optical Scanning	Speech Input Tactile Input
TREND: Towards Direct Input Devices that Are Easy to Use.					
OUTPUT MEDIA/ METHOD	Punched Cards Printed Reports	Punched Cards Printed Reports	Printed Reports Video Displays	Video Displays Audio Responses Printed Reports	Graphics Displays Voice Responses
TREND: Towards Direct Output Devices that Communicate Quickly and Clearly.					

The most common user interface method still involves a keyboard for entry of data and a video display screen for output to users. **Computer terminals** of various types are widely used for such input and output. Technically, any input/output device connected by telecommunications links to a computer is called a terminal. However, most terminals use a keyboard for input and a TV-like screen for visual output, and are called **visual** (or video) **display terminals** (VDTs) or CRT (cathode ray tube) terminals. They allow keyed-in data to be displayed and edited before entry into a computer system.

There is a trend away from *dumb terminals,* which have no processing capabilities themselves, toward **intelligent terminals,** which have their own microprocessors and memory circuits. Many intelligent terminals are really desktop or portable microcomputers used as telecommunications terminals to larger computers. Therefore, they can perform data entry and other information processing tasks independently. Another trend is the widespread use of **transaction terminals** in banks, retail stores, factories, and other work sites. Examples are automated teller machines (ATMs), factory production recorders, and retail point-of-sale (POS) terminals. These terminals use a variety of input/output methods to capture data from end users during a transaction and transmit it over telecommunications networks to a computer system for processing.

Computer Terminal Trends

Keyboards are the most widely used devices for entering data and text into computer systems. However, **pointing devices** are a better alternative for issuing commands, making choices, and responding to prompts displayed on your video screen. For example, pointing devices such as electronic mice and trackballs allow you to easily choose from menu selections and icon displays using *point-and-click* or *point-and-drag* methods. **Icons** are small figures that look like familiar devices, such as a file folder (for accessing a file), a wastebasket (for deleting a file), or scissors (for cut and paste operations), and so on. Using icons helps simplify computer use since they are easier to use with pointing devices than menus and other text-based displays. See Figure 4.16.

Pointing Devices

Sygma Photo News.

FIGURE 4.16
The keyboard and the mouse are the most widely used computer input devices.

FIGURE 4.17
The pointing stick is a popular pointing device for portable computers. Note that this multimedia laptop PC also includes a CD-ROM drive.

Courtesy of IBM Corporation.

The **electronic mouse** is a pointing device used to move the cursor on the screen, as well as to issue commands and make icon and menu selections. Some mice contain a roller ball, which moves the cursor in the direction the ball is rolled. Others use an optical sensing technology that recognizes points on a special pad. By moving the mouse on a desktop or pad, you can move the cursor onto an icon displayed on the screen. Pressing a button on the mouse begins the activity represented by the icon selected.

The **trackball** and the **pointing stick** are other pointing devices most often used in place of the mouse. A trackball is a stationary device related to the mouse. You turn a roller ball with only its top exposed outside its case to move the cursor on the screen. A pointing stick (also called a *trackpoint*) is a small buttonlike device, sometimes likened to the eraserhead of a pencil. It is usually centered one row above the space bar of a keyboard, about where the G, H, and B keys meet. The cursor moves in the direction of the pressure you place on the trackpoint. Trackballs and pointing sticks are easier to use than a mouse for portable computer users and are thus built in to many laptop computer keyboards. See Figure 4.17.

Touch-sensitive screens are devices that allow you to use a computer by touching the surface of its video display screen. Such screens emit a grid of infrared beams, sound waves, or a slight electric current, which is broken when the screen is touched. The computer senses the point in the grid where the break occurs and responds with an appropriate action. For example, you could indicate your selection on a menu display by just touching the screen next to that menu item.

Pen-Based Computing

End users can write or draw directly on a video screen or on other surfaces using a variety of penlike devices. One example is the **light pen.** This pen-shaped device uses photoelectric circuitry to enter data into the computer through a video screen. A user can write on the video display because the light-sensitive pen enables the computer to calculate the coordinates of the points on the screen touched by the light pen. A **graphics tablet** is a form of *digitizer* that allows you to draw or write on

FIGURE 4.18
This pen-based notebook computer recognizes handwriting on its display screen.

Courtesy of Compaq Computer Corporation.

its pressure-sensitive surface with a pen-shaped *stylus.* Your handwriting or drawing is digitized by the computer, accepted as input, and displayed on its video screen.

Light pen and graphics pad technologies are being used in a new generation of **pen-based** personal computers and personal digital assistants (PDAs) that recognize handwriting. These notebook PCs and PDAs are portable, tablet-style microcomputers that contain software that recognizes and digitizes handwriting, handprinting, and hand drawing. They have a pressure-sensitive layer like a graphics pad under their slatelike liquid crystal display (LCD) screen. So instead of writing on a paper form fastened to a clipboard, inspectors, field engineers, and other mobile workers can use a pen to enter handwritten data directly into a computer. See Figure 4.18.

Video Input/Output

Video and Multimedia Input

Video images can serve as input as well as output. For example, input from a TV receiver, camcorder, or VCR can be digitized and compressed for storage on magnetic or optical disks. Digitizing *snapshot* images can be done with an optical scanner. Digitizing *full motion* video images from camcorders and VCRs requires PCs that use technologies like *digital video interactive* (DVI). Equipping your PC with a DVI capability requires additional software, circuit boards, memory, and magnetic or optical disk capacity. This would give you a *multimedia development* capability. Then you could merge text, graphics, sound, and TV images to produce computer-generated video presentations. We will discuss multimedia technologies and applications further in Chapter 8. See Figure 4.19.

Video Output

Video displays are the most common type of computer output. Most video displays use a **cathode ray tube** (CRT) technology similar to the picture tubes used in home TV sets. Usually, the clarity of the display and the support of monochrome or color displays depend on the type of video monitor used and the graphics circuit board, or *video adapter,* installed in the microcomputer. These can provide a variety of graphics modes of increasing capability. A high level of clarity is especially important to support the more complex graphical displays of many current software packages. These packages provide a *graphical user interface* (GUI), which uses icons and a variety of screen images and typically splits the screen into multiple *window* displays.

FIGURE 4.19
This multimedia PC can help
you develop multimedia video
presentations.

Courtesy of IBM Corporation.

FIGURE 4.20
This laptop microcomputer features an LCD display and built-
in trackball.

Index Stock Photography, Inc.

Liquid crystal displays (LCDs), such as those used in electronic calculators
and watches, are also being used to display computer output. Their biggest use is to
provide a visual display capability for portable microcomputers and terminals.
Advances in technology have improved the clarity of such displays, which were formerly hard to see in bright sunlight and artificial light. LCD displays need significantly less electric current and provide a thin, flat display. Full-color LCD displays
are now available. See Figure 4.20.

Plasma display devices have replaced CRT devices in a limited number of
applications where a flat display is needed. Plasma displays are generated by electrically charged particles of gas (plasma) trapped between glass plates. Plasma display
units are significantly more expensive than CRT and LCD units. However, they use
less power, provide faster display speeds, and produce clearer displays that are easier to see from any angle and in any lighting conditions.

Courtesy of Hewlett Packard Company.

FIGURE 4.21
A laser printer produces high-quality printed output.

Printed Output

After video displays, printed output is the most common form of visual output for the user interface. Most computer systems use **printers** to produce permanent (hard copy) output in human-readable form. End users need printed output if they want copies of output to take away from the computer and to share with others. Hard copy output is also frequently needed for legal documentation. Thus, computers can usually produce printed reports and documents, such as sales invoices, payroll checks, and bank statements, as well as hard copy of graphics displays. **Plotters,** which draw graphics displays on paper, also produce printed paper output.

Many printers are **impact printers.** They form characters and other images on paper through the impact of a printing mechanism that presses a printing element (such as a print wheel or cylinder) and an inked ribbon or roller against the face of a sheet of paper. Multiple copies can be produced because the impact of the printing mechanism can transmit an image onto several layers of multiple copy forms. Popular impact printers for microcomputer systems use a **dot matrix** printing element, which consists of short print wires that form a character as a grouping or matrix of dots. Speeds of several hundred characters per second are attainable. Mainframe computer systems typically use high-speed line printers, which can print up to several thousand lines per minute. A moving metal chain or cylinder of characters is used as the printing element.

Nonimpact printers are quieter than impact printers, since the sound of a printing element being struck is eliminated. However, they do not produce multiple copies like impact printers. **Laser printers** and **ink jet printers** are examples of popular nonimpact printing methods for producing high-quality printed output. Laser printers allow companies to produce their own business forms, as well as formal reports and manuals. Such *desktop publishing* applications are discussed in Chapter 8. Laser printers for microcomputer systems have speeds from less than 5 to over 200 pages per minute. See Figure 4.21.

Voice Recognition and Response

Voice recognition and *voice response* promise to be the easiest method of providing a user interface for data entry and conversational computing, since speech is the easiest, most natural means of human communication. Voice input and output of data has now become technologically and economically feasible for a variety of applications. A voice recognition capability can be added to a microcomputer by acquiring a voice recognition circuit board and software for less than a thousand dollars. The circuit board contains a digital signal processor (DSP) microprocessor and other circuitry for voice recognition processing, and a vocabulary in ROM ranging from several hundred to over 30,000 words. For example, personal dictation systems for word processing (including a circuit board and software), are now available for under $1,000 for a 34,000 word vocabulary system. See Figure 4.22.

Voice recognition systems analyze and classify speech or vocal tract patterns and convert them into digital codes for entry into a computer system. Most voice recognition systems require "training" the computer to recognize a limited vocabulary of standard words for each user. Operators train the system to recognize their voices by repeating each word in the vocabulary about 10 times. Trained systems regularly achieve a 99 percent plus word recognition rate. Speaker-independent voice recognition systems, which allow a computer to understand a voice it has never heard before, are used in a limited number of applications.

Voice recognition devices are used in work situations where operators need to perform data entry without using their hands to key in data or instructions, or where it would provide faster and more accurate input. For example, voice recognition systems are being used by manufacturers for the inspection, inventory, and quality control of a variety of products, and by airlines and parcel delivery companies for voice-directed sorting of baggage and parcels. Voice recognition is also available for software packages like spreadsheets and database managers for voice input of data and commands. In addition, voice input for word processing is becoming a popular application of voice recognition technology.

Voice response devices range from mainframe *audio-response* units to *voice-messaging* minicomputers to *speech synthesizer* microprocessors. Speech microprocessors can be found in toys, calculators, appliances, automobiles, and a variety of other consumer, commercial, and industrial products.

Voice-messaging minicomputer and mainframe audio response units use voice-response software to verbally guide an operator through the steps of a task in many kinds of activities. They may also allow computers to respond to verbal and Touch-Tone input over the telephone. Examples of applications include computerized telephone call switching, telemarketing surveys, bank pay-by-phone bill-paying

FIGURE 4.22
Using voice recognition for word processing in a hospital patient care system.

Martin Schneider and Associates.

services, stock quotations services, university registration systems, and customer credit and account balance inquiries.

Optical and Magnetic Recognition

Optical Scanning

Optical scanning devices read text or graphics and convert them into digital input for a computer. They include **optical character recognition** (OCR) equipment that can read special-purpose characters and codes. Optical scanning of pages of text and graphics is especially popular in desktop publishing applications. Thus, optical scanning provides a method of direct input of data from source documents into a computer system.

There are many types of optical readers, but they all employ photoelectric devices to scan the characters being read. Reflected light patterns of the data are converted into electronic impulses, which are then accepted as input into the computer system. Devices can currently read many types of printing and graphics. Progress is continually being made in improving the reading ability of scanning equipment. See Figure 4.23.

OCR-based optical scanning systems are used extensively in the credit card billing operations of credit card companies, banks, and oil companies. They are also used to process utility bills, insurance premiums, airline tickets, and cash register machine tapes. OCR scanners are used to automatically sort mail, score tests, and process a wide variety of forms in business and government.

Optical scanning devices such as handheld **wands** are used to read data on merchandise tags and other media. This frequently involves reading *bar coding*, a code that utilizes bars to represent characters. Thus, Universal Product Code (UPC) bar coding on packages of food items and other products has become commonplace.

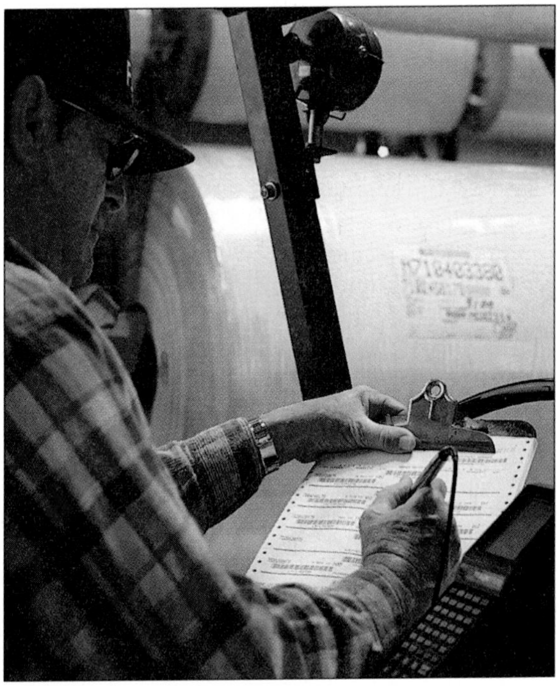

Jeff Zaruba/The Stock Market.

FIGURE 4.23
Using an optical scanning wand to read bar coding of product data in a warehouse shipping and receiving system.

For example, UPC bar coding is read by the automated checkout scanners found in many supermarkets. Supermarket scanners emit laser beams, which are reflected off a UPC bar code. The reflected image is converted to electronic impulses, which are sent to the in-store minicomputer, where they are matched with pricing information. Pricing information is returned to the terminal, visually displayed, and printed on a receipt.

Magnetic Data Entry

The computer systems of the banking industry can magnetically read checks and deposit slips using **magnetic ink character recognition** (MICR) technology. Computers can thus sort, tabulate, and post checks to the proper checking accounts. Such processing is possible because the identification numbers of the bank and the customer's account are preprinted on the bottom of the checks with an iron oxide-based ink. The first bank receiving a check after it has been written must encode the amount of the check in magnetic ink on the check's lower right-hand corner. The MICR system uses 14 characters (the 10 decimal digits and 4 special symbols) of a standardized design.

MICR characters can be either preprinted on documents or encoded on documents using a keyboard-operated machine called a *proof-inscriber*. Equipment known as MICR *reader-sorters* read a check by first magnetizing the magnetic ink characters and then sensing the signal induced by each character as it passes a reading head. In this way, data are electronically captured by the computer system. The check is then sorted by directing it into one of the pockets of the reader-sorter. Reader-sorters can read over 2,400 checks per minute, with a data transfer rate of over 3,000 characters per second. However, several large banks have begun replacing MICR technology with optical scanning systems.

Another familiar form of magnetic data entry is the **magnetic stripe** technology that helps computers read credit cards. The dark magnetic stripe on the back of credit and debit cards is the same iron oxide coating as on magnetic tape. Customer account numbers can be recorded on the stripe so it can be read by bank ATMs, credit card authorization terminals, and other *magnetic stripe readers*.

Storage Trends and Trade-Offs

Data and information need to be stored after input, during processing, and before output. Even today, many organizations still rely on paper documents stored in filing cabinets as a major form of storage media. However, computer-based information systems rely primarily on the memory circuits and secondary storage devices of computer systems to accomplish the storage function. Figure 4.24 illustrates major trends in primary and secondary storage methods. Continued developments in very-large-scale integration (VLSI), which packs millions of electronic circuit elements on tiny semiconductor memory chips, are responsible for a significant increase in the main memory capacity of computers. Secondary storage capacities are also expected to escalate into the billions and trillions of characters, due primarily to use of optical media.

There are many types of storage media and devices. Figure 4.25 illustrates the speed, capacity, and cost relationships of several alternative primary and secondary storage media. Note the cost/speed/capacity trade-offs as one moves from semiconductor memories to magnetic media, such as magnetic disks and tapes, to optical disks. High-speed storage media cost more per byte and provide lower capacities. Large-capacity storage media cost less per byte but are slower. This is why we have different kinds of storage media.

FIGURE 4.24
Major trends in primary and secondary storage methods.

	First Generation	Second Generation	Third Generation	Fourth Generation	Fifth Generation?
PRIMARY STORAGE	Magnetic Drum	Magnetic Core	Magnetic Core	LSI Semiconductor Memory	VLSI Semiconductor Memory
TREND: Towards Large Capacities Using Smaller Microelectronic Circuits.					
SECONDARY STORAGE	Magnetic Tape Magnetic Drum	Magnetic Tape Magnetic Disk	Magnetic Disk Magnetic Tape	Magnetic Disk Optical Disk	Optical Disk Magnetic Disk
TREND: Towards Massive Capacities Using Magnetic and Optical Media.					

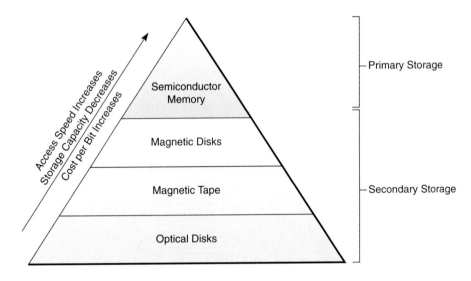

FIGURE 4.25
Storage media cost, speed, and capacity trade-offs. Note how cost increases with faster access speeds but decreases with increased capacity.

Note in Figure 4.25 that semiconductor memories are used mainly for primary storage, though they are finding increasing use as high-speed secondary storage devices. Magnetic disk and tape and optical disk devices, on the other hand, are used as secondary storage devices to greatly enlarge the storage capacity of computer systems. Also, since most primary storage circuits use RAM (random access memory) chips, which lose their contents when electrical power is interrupted, secondary storage devices provide a more permanent type of storage media for storage of data and programs.

Primary storage media such as semiconductor memory chips are called **direct access** or *random access memories* (RAM). Magnetic disk devices are frequently called *direct access storage devices* (DASD). On the other hand, media such as magnetic tapes are known as **sequential access** devices.

The terms *direct access* and *random access* describe the same concept. They mean that an element of data or instructions (such as a byte or word) can be directly stored and retrieved by selecting and using any of the locations on the storage media.

Direct and Sequential Access

FIGURE 4.26
Sequential versus direct access storage. Magnetic tape is a typical sequential access medium. Magnetic disks are typical direct access storage devices.

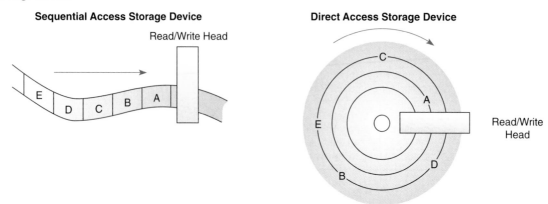

They also mean that each storage position (1) has a unique address and (2) can be individually accessed in approximately the same length of time without having to search through other storage positions. For example, each memory cell on a micro-electronic semiconductor RAM chip can be individually sensed or changed in the same length of time. Also any data record stored on a magnetic or optical disk can be accessed directly in approximately the same time period. See Figure 4.26.

Sequential access storage media such as magnetic tape do not have unique storage addresses that can be directly addressed. Instead, data must be stored and retrieved using a sequential or serial process. Data are recorded one after another in a predetermined sequence (such as in numeric order) on a storage medium. Locating an individual item of data requires searching much of the recorded data on the tape until the desired item is located.

Semiconductor Memory

The primary storage (main memory) of most modern computers consists of micro-electronic **semiconductor memory** circuits. Millions of storage circuits can be etched on large-scale integrated (LSI) silicon chips. *Memory chips* with capacities of 256K bits, 1 million bits (1 megabit), 4 megabits, and 16 megabits are now used in many computers.

Some of the major attractions of semiconductor memory are small size, great speed, shock and temperature resistance, and low cost due to mass production capabilities. One major disadvantage of most semiconductor memory is its **volatility.** Uninterrupted electric power must be supplied or the contents of memory will be lost. Therefore, emergency transfer to other devices or standby electrical power (through battery packs or emergency generators) is required if data are to be saved. Another alternative is to permanently "burn in" the contents of semiconductor devices so that they cannot be erased by a loss of power.

Thus, there are two basic types of semiconductor memory: **random access memory** (RAM) and **read only memory** (ROM).

- **RAM: random access memory.** These memory chips are the most widely used primary storage medium. Each memory position can be both sensed (read) and changed (written), so it is also called read/write memory. This is a volatile memory.
- **ROM: read only memory.** Nonvolatile random access memory chips are used for permanent storage. ROM can be read but not erased or overwritten. Frequently used control instructions in the control unit and programs in primary storage (such as parts of the operating system) can be permanently burned in to the storage cells during manufacture. This is sometimes called *firmware*. Variations include PROM (programmable read only memory) and EPROM (erasable programmable read only memory), which can be permanently or temporarily programmed after manufacture.

Semiconductor Secondary Storage

Semiconductor memory chips are being used as direct access primary and secondary storage media for both large and small computers. Plug-in memory circuit boards containing up to several megabytes of semiconductor memory chips (RAM cards) can be added to a microcomputer to increase its memory capacity. These provide additional primary storage, but they can also be used for secondary storage. A computer's operating system program can be instructed to treat part of RAM as if another disk drive has been added to the system. This provides a very-high-speed semiconductor secondary-storage capability, sometimes called a RAM *disk*. Semiconductor secondary storage devices also include removable credit-card-size "flash memory" RAM *cards*. They provide up to 40 megabytes of erasable direct access storage for some notebook or handheld PCs. Peripheral devices consisting of semiconductor memory chips are also marketed as high-speed alternatives to magnetic disk units for mainframe computers.

Magnetic Disk Storage

Magnetic disks are the most common form of secondary storage for modern computer systems. They provide fast access and high storage capacities at a reasonable cost. The two basic types of magnetic disk media are conventional (hard) metal disks and flexible (floppy) diskettes. Several types of magnetic disk peripherals are used as DASDs in both small and large computer systems. See Figure 4.27.

Magnetic disks are thin metal or plastic disks that are coated on both sides with an iron oxide recording material. Several disks may be mounted together in a vertical cylinder on a vertical shaft, which typically rotates the disks at speeds of 2,400 to 3,600 revolutions per minute (rpm). Electromagnetic read/write heads are positioned by access arms between the slightly separated disks to read and write data on concentric, circular **tracks.** Data is recorded on tracks in the form of tiny magnetized spots to form binary digits arranged in serial order in common computer codes. Thousands of bytes can be recorded on each track, and there are several hundred data tracks on each disk surface, each of which is subdivided into a number of **sectors.** See Figure 4.28.

Types of Magnetic Disks

There are several types of magnetic disk arrangements, including removable disk packs and cartridges as well as fixed disk units. The removable disk devices are popular because they can be used interchangeably in magnetic disk units and stored offline for convenience and security when not in use.

FIGURE 4.27
Magnetic disk media: A 3½-inch floppy disk and a hard magnetic disk drive.

Walter Bibikow/The Image Bank.   Courtesy of Quantum Corporation.

FIGURE 4.28
Characteristics of magnetic disks. Note especially the concepts of cylinders, tracks, and sectors.

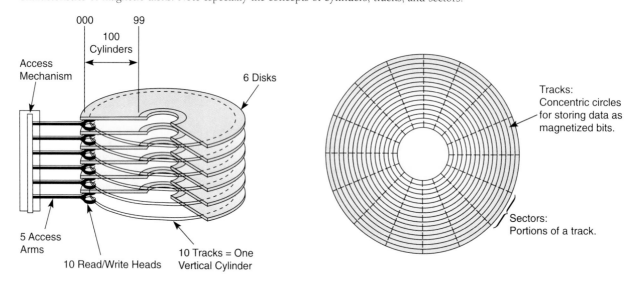

- **Floppy disks,** or magnetic *diskettes,* are disks that consist of polyester film covered with an iron oxide compound. A single disk is mounted and rotates freely inside a protective flexible or hard plastic jacket, which has access openings to accommodate the read/write head of a disk drive unit. The 3½-inch floppy disk, with capacities of 720 kilobytes and 1.44 or 2.8 megabytes, is rapidly replacing the older 5¼-inch size.

- **Hard disk drives** combine magnetic disks, access arms, and read/write heads into a sealed module. This allows higher speeds, greater data-recording densities, and closer tolerances within a sealed, more stable environment.

Fixed or removable *disk cartridge* versions are also available. Capacities of hard drives typically range from 120 megabytes to several gigabytes of storage.

- **RAID.** Large-capacity mainframe disk drives are being challenged by disk arrays of interconnected microcomputer hard disk drives to provide many gigabytes of online storage. Known as **RAID** (redundant arrays of independent disks), they combine from 6 to over 100 small hard disk drives and their control microprocessors into a single unit. RAID units provide large capacities with high access speeds since data is accessed in parallel over multiple paths from many disks. RAID units also provide a *fault tolerant* capability, since their redundant design offers multiple copies of data on several disks. If one disk fails, data can be recovered from backup copies automatically stored on other disks.

Magnetic tape is another widely used secondary storage medium. Data is recorded in the form of magnetized spots on the iron oxide coating of the plastic tape by the read/write heads of magnetic tape drives. Magnetic tape is usually subdivided into horizontal tracks to accommodate recording bits into common computer codes. Blank spaces, known as gaps, are used to separate individual data records and blocks of grouped records. These gaps are required to allow for such mechanical operations as the start/stop time of a magnetic tape unit. Most devices group records into blocks to conserve storage space instead of leaving gaps between each record.

    Magnetic tape comes in the form of tape reels and cartridges for mainframes and minicomputers, and small cassettes or cartridges for microcomputers. Mainframe magnetic cartridges are replacing tape reels and can hold over 200 megabytes. Small cartridges can store over 100 megabytes and are a popular means of providing backup capabilities for microcomputer hard disk drives.

Magnetic Tape Storage

Optical disks are a fast growing storage medium. Mainframe and midsize computer versions use 12-inch plastic disks with capacities of several gigabytes, with up to 20 disks held in "jukebox" drive units. The version for use with microcomputers is called **CD-ROM** (compact disk–read only memory). CD-ROM technology uses 12-centimeter (4.7-inch) compact disks (CDs) similar to those used in stereo music systems, and *CD-ROM drives* for microcomputer systems. Each disk can store over 600 megabytes. That's the equivalent of over 400 1.44 megabyte floppy disks or more than 300,000 double spaced pages of text. Data are recorded by using a laser to burn permanent microscopic pits in a spiral track on a master disk from which compact disks can be mass produced. Then CD-ROM disk drives use a laser device to read the binary codes formed by those pits. See Figure 4.29.

    Other optical disk technologies produce **WORM** (write once, read many) and **CD-R** (compact disk recordable) disks. This allows computers with the proper optical disk drive units to record their own data once on an optical disk, then be able to read it indefinitely. The major limitation of CD-ROM, CD-R, and WORM disks is that recorded data cannot be erased. However, **erasable optical disk** systems have now become available. This technology records and erases data by using a laser to heat a microscopic point of the disk's surface. In some versions, a magnetic coil changes the spot's reflective properties from one direction to another, thus recording a binary one or zero. A laser device can then read the binary codes on the disk by sensing the direction of reflected light.

Optical Disk Storage

FIGURE 4.29
CD-ROM disks can hold over 600 million characters of information.

David Pollack/The Stock Market.

FIGURE 4.30
A display screen from Compton's Multimedia Encyclopedia.

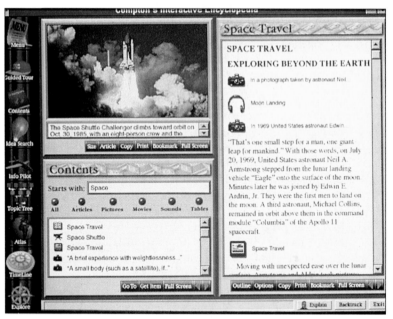

Courtesy of Compton's New Media, Inc.

One of the major uses of optical disks in mainframe and midrange systems is in *image processing,* where long-term *archival storage* of historical files of document images must be maintained. Financial institutions, among others, are using optical scanners to capture digitized document images and store them on WORM optical disks as an alternative to microfilm media. One of the major uses of CD-ROM disks is to provide companies with fast access to reference materials in a convenient, compact form. This includes catalogs, directories, manuals, periodical abstracts, part listings, and statistical databases of business and economic activity.

Interactive **multimedia applications** in business, education, and entertainment are another major use of CD-ROM disks. *Multimedia* is the use of a variety of media, including text and graphics displays, voice, music, and other audio, photographs, animation, and video segments. Multimedia has large storage requirements. For example, it takes one megabyte for a color picture, 2.4 megabytes for a four minute song, and over 1 gigabyte for a minute of full motion video, though this can be reduced by video compression technologies. Thus the large storage capacities of CD-ROM are a natural choice for computer video games, educational videos, multimedia encyclopedias, and advertising presentations. See Figure 4.30.

Thus, optical disks have emerged as a popular storage medium for image processing and multimedia applications, and they appear to be a promising alternative to magnetic disks and tape for very large (mass) storage capabilities for enterprise and end user computing systems. However, erasable optical technologies are still being perfected. Also, optical disk devices are significantly slower and more expensive (per byte of storage) than magnetic disk devices. So optical disk systems are not expected to displace magnetic disk technology in the near future.

Casino Software and Others: Profiles in Voice Recognition

PROFILE

Oliver Schubert, president and developer of Casino Software and Services, Las Vegas, Nevada.
Voice Recognition System: Self-designed Blackjack Survey Voice, based on DragonDictate.

Software designer Oliver Schubert knew it was a sure bet. While plenty of programs help a player win, he found none to help a casino spot "card counters," that is, gamblers who are illegally counting card activity. So he came up with the Blackjack Survey Voice program, based on DragonDictate software. His player evaluation program is straight out of a James Bond film.

Casinos regularly monitor activities at the blackjack tables through "eye-in-the-sky" cameras. In the past, a surveillance team would watch the action as cards were dealt, plays made, and bets wagered. "That was an ineffectual way to spot counters," says Schubert. "With our voice recognition program, casino workers can keep their eyes trained on the gamblers and speak the plays into the computer." The computer, using Schubert's software, analyzes the data on card players' actions and identifies card counters, whom the casinos can then legally bar. Already The Mirage, Treasure Island, Tropicana, and other top casinos are using this method of weeding out cardsharps.

PROFILE

Dave MacFarlane, retired software engineer, Honeywell Information Systems, Monroe, Connecticut.
Voice Recognition System: IBM Voice Type Dictation.

I'm in seventh heaven," says Dave MacFarlane, a quadriplegic who recently began using IBM Voice-Type Dictation. "It's liberating. It allows me to accomplish things that I never could before." Now he roams cyberspace, writes letters, pays his bills, and sends and receives faxes—tasks that were once difficult, if not impossible, to accomplish.

MacFarlane is a former Honeywell, Inc. product manager who retired 20 years ago after his battle with multiple sclerosis rendered him a quadriplegic. He has been using the OS/2-based system to run a computer bulletin board from his home in Monroe, Connecticut. MacFarlane, who has used a variety of speech recognition systems for the past 10 years, said IBM's VoiceType Dictation product is the best he has ever used. "For straight keyboard replacement, IBM's system is light-years ahead—and I'm no great fan of IBM," MacFarlane said. Unlike most speech recognition systems, which often have trouble understanding dialects, the IBM system can be trained to recognize user's accents and speaking patterns. Users must train the system to understand their pronunciations by reading a Mark Twain short story for 90 minutes. Each time the system is used thereafter, it continues to learn how to interpret the user's speech.

PROFILE

Dr. Carl Teplitz, chair and professor, Diagnostic Pathology and Laboratory Medicine, Beth Israel Medical Center, the Albert Einstein College of Medicine, New York.
Voice Recognition System: Kurzweil Pathology Product, Kurzweil Voice Path, and Kurzweil Voice for Windows.

Dr. Carl Teplitz, Beth Israel Medical Center's pathology chair, has been so delighted with Kurzweil's voice recognition program that soon his entire department—some 400 employees—will be using it. "Our hospital is incredibly busy," says Teplitz. "It's vital to return a diagnosis as quickly as possible. However rapid our pathologists were, it would take from two to three days to have a report transcribed."

Now the interval between the time that a doctor receives a specimen and the time the report is filed averages 18 hours. In addition, the program gives the pathologist complete and immediate control over what is dictated. "Pathologists are very compulsive people," explains Teplitz. "When they depend on other people, it's hard for them to get a report exactly as they like."

PROFILE

Darcy Readman, bankruptcy lawyer, Duncan & Craig Law Firm, Edmonton, Alberta, Canada.
Voice Recognition System: Intvox Communications' Law Talk, based on DragonDictate.

"Lawyers have a keyboard phobia," claims bankruptcy lawyer Darcy Readman. He should know. Until Readman discovered DragonDictate in 1991, he shunned computers. These days, Readman has become such a voice recognition software enthusiast that 10 partners in his firm have followed suit. "We were burning cash in Dictaphone costs," he says. "Nearly half our secretaries' time was taken up transcribing. Voice recognition frees them up to do more productive work."

CASE STUDY QUESTIONS

1. What are the benefits and limitations of voice recognition systems?

2. What are some other business applications of voice recognition? Give several examples.

3. Would you like to use a PC voice recognition system? Why or why not?

Source: Adapted from Thomas Hoffman, "IBM's Voice System Carves Out User Niche," *Computerworld*, November 21, 1994, p. 40. Copyright 1994 by Computerworld, inc., Framingham, MA 01701—Reprinted from *Computerworld*, and Daniel Tynian, "What You Say Is What You Get?" PC World, January 1995, pp. 148-160. Reprinted with the permission of *PC World*.

Summary

- **Computer Systems.** A computer is a system of information processing components that perform input, processing, output, storage, and control functions. Its hardware components include input and output devices, a central processing unit (CPU), and primary and secondary storage devices. The major functions and hardware in a computer system are summarized in Figure 4.2. Major types and trends in computer systems are summarized in Figures 4.8 and 4.9.

- **Microcomputer Systems.** Microcomputers are used as personal computers, professional workstations, technical workstations, and network servers. Microcomputers typically use a keyboard for input, a system unit containing the main microprocessor for processing and control, semiconductor RAM and ROM circuits for primary storage, floppy disk and hard disk drives for secondary storage, and a video display monitor and printer for output. A wide variety of other hardware devices are available, as are thousands of application software packages.

- **Other Computer Systems.** Midrange computers are general-purpose computers that are larger and more powerful than most microcomputers. They are used as powerful network servers and for many business data processing and scientific applications. Mainframe computers are larger and more powerful than most minicomputers. They are usually faster, have more memory capacity, and can support more input/output and secondary storage devices. They are designed to handle the information processing needs of organizations with government agencies with many customers and employees, or with complex computational problems. Supercomputers are a special category of extremely powerful mainframe computer systems designed for massive computational assignments.

- **Peripheral Devices.** Refer to Figures 4.31 and 4.32 for summaries of the functions, characteristics, advantages, and disadvantages of peripheral devices for input, output, and storage discussed in this chapter.

Peripheral Equipment	Media	Primary Functions	Major Advantages and/or Disadvantages
Video display terminals	None	Keyboard input and video output	Conventional and inexpensive, but limited display capacity and no hard copy
Printers	Paper	Printed output of paper reports and documents	Hard copy, but inconvenient and bulky; many printers are relatively slow
Pointing devices	None	Input by mouse, trackball, pointing stick, pen, touch screen, and graphics pad. Video output.	Input devices are easy to use and inexpensive, but may have limited applications and software support
Voice input/ output devices	None	Voice input and output	Easiest I/O but is slow, has limited vocabulary, and accuracy problems
Optical scanners	Paper documents	Direct input from written or printed documents	Direct input from paper documents, but some limitations on input format
Magnetic ink character recognition (MICR) readers	MICR paper documents	Direct input of MICR documents	Fast, high-reliability reading, but documents must be preprinted and the character set is limited

FIGURE 4.31
A summary of important input/output methods. Note especially the advantages and disadvantages of each method in providing hardware support of the user interface.

FIGURE 4.32
A summary of important computer storage methods. Note the advantages and disadvantages of each method.

Peripheral Equipment	Media	Primary Functions	Major Advantages and/or Disadvantages
Magnetic disk drive	Hard disk Disk pack Disk cartridge	Secondary storage (direct access) and input/output	Large capacity, fast, direct access storage device (DASD), but relatively expensive
Floppy disk drive	Magnetic diskette: 3½- and 5¼-inch diameters	Secondary storage (direct access) and input/output	Small, inexpensive, and convenient, but slower and smaller capacity than other DASDs
Magnetic tape drive	Magnetic tape reel and cartridge	Secondary storage (sequential access), input/output, and disk backup	Inexpensive, with a fast transfer rate, but only sequential access
Optical disk drive	Optical disk: CD-ROM, WORM, CD-R and erasable	Secondary storage (direct access) and archival storage	Large capacity, high-quality storage of data, text, and images. Primarily a read-only medium

Key Terms and Concepts

These are the key terms and concepts of this chapter. The page number of their first explanation is given in parentheses.

1. Arithmetic-logic unit (110)
2. Binary representation (113)
3. Cathode ray tube (127)
4. Central processing unit (109)
5. Client/server (120)
6. Computer system (108)
7. Computer terminals (125)
8. Control unit (110)
9. Direct access (133)
10. Direct input/output devices (124)
11. Distributed processing (120)
12. Downsizing (121)
13. Generations of computing (114)
14. Graphics tablet (126)
15. Icon (125)
16. Light pen (126)
17. Liquid crystal displays (128)
18. Local area network (120)
19. Magnetic disk storage (135)
   a. Floppy disk
   b. Hard disk
20. Magnetic ink character recognition (132)
21. Magnetic tape (137)
22. Mainframe computer (119)
23. Microcomputer (117)
24. Microprocessor (109)
25. Midrange computer (118)
26. Minicomputer (118)
27. Multimedia (138)
28. Multiple processors (110)
29. Network server (118)
30. Networked computer systems (120)
31. Offline (124)
32. Online (124)
33. Optical character recognition (131)
34. Optical disk storage (137)
   a. CD-ROM
   b. Erasable disks
   c. WORM disks
35. Optical scanning (131)
36. Pen-based computing (126)
37. Peripheral devices (124)
38. Plasma displays (128)
39. Plotters (129)
40. Pointing devices (125)
   a. Electronic mouse
   b. Pointing stick
   c. Trackball
41. Primary storage unit (112)
42. Printers (129)
43. Processing speeds (111)
44. Secondary storage device (112)
45. Semiconductor memory (134)
   a. RAM
   b. ROM
46. Sequential access (133)
47. Storage capacity elements (113)
   a. Bit
   b. Byte
   c. Kilobyte
   d. Megabyte
   e. Gigabyte
   f. Terabyte
48. Storage media trade-offs (132)

49. Supercomputer (120)
50. Time elements (111)
    a. Millisecond
    b. Microsecond
    c. Nanosecond
    d. Picosecond
51. Touch-sensitive screen (126)
52. Trends in computers (114)
53. Video input/output (127)
54. Voice recognition (130)
55. Voice response (130)
56. Volatility (134)
57. Wand (131)
58. Workstation (118)

Review Quiz

Match one of the key terms and concepts listed above with one of the brief examples or definitions listed below. Try to find the best fit for answers that seem to fit more than one term or concept. Defend your choices.

_____ 1. Computers will become smaller, faster, more reliable, easier to use, and less costly.

_____ 2. Major stages in the development of computers.

_____ 3. A computer is a combination of components that perform input, processing, output, storage, and control functions.

_____ 4. Contains the arithmetic-logic unit and control unit.

_____ 5. Performs computations and comparisons.

_____ 6. Interprets instructions and directs processing.

_____ 7. The memory of a computer.

_____ 8. Magnetic disks and tape and optical disks perform this function.

_____ 9. Capture data or communicate information without media.

_____ 10. Input/output and secondary storage devices for a computer system.

_____ 11. Connected to and controlled by a CPU.

_____ 12. Separate from and not controlled by a CPU.

_____ 13. Results from the presence or absence or change in direction of electric current, magnetic fields, or light rays in computer circuits and media.

_____ 14. The central processing unit of a microcomputer.

_____ 15. Can be a desktop or portable computer and a single- or multiuser unit.

_____ 16. A computer category between microcomputers and mainframes.

_____ 17. A computer that can handle the information processing needs of large organizations.

_____ 18. Dispersing networked computer power throughout an organization.

_____ 19. Many computer systems are now interconnected by telecommunications networks.

_____ 20. End user workstations are networked to server computers.

_____ 21. A computer with several CPUs is an example.

_____ 22. A computer that manages network communications and resources.

_____ 23. The most powerful type of computer.

_____ 24. A telecommunications network in an office or other worksite.

_____ 25. One billionth of a second.

_____ 26. Roughly one billion characters of storage.

_____ 27. Includes electronic mice, trackballs, and pointing sticks.

_____ 28. You can write on the pressure-sensitive LCD screen of notebook-size microcomputers with a pen.

_____ 29. Helps you "write" on a video screen with a light-sensitive pen.

_____ 30. Moving this along your desktop moves the cursor on the screen.

_____ 31. You can communicate with a computer by touching its display.

_____ 32. A peripheral device that digitizes data drawn on its pressure-sensitive surface.

_____ 33. Produces hard copy output such as paper documents and reports.

_____ 34. May use a mechanical arm with several pens to draw hard copy graphics output.

_____ 35. Promises to be the easiest, most natural way to communicate with computers.

_____ 36. Capturing data by processing light reflected from images.

_____ 37. Optical scanning of bar codes and other characters.

_____ 38. Bank check processing uses this technology.

_____ 39. Small figures are displayed to help you indicate activities to be performed.

_____ 40. A device with a keyboard and a video display connected to a computer is a typical example.

_____ 41. The most common video display technology.

_____ 42. Computer voice output.

_____ 43. Combining text, graphics, voice, and video in computer input and output.

_____ 44. A handheld device that reads bar coding.

_____ 45. Storage media cost, speed, and capacity differences.

_____ 46. You cannot erase the contents of these storage circuits.

_____ 47. The memory of most computers consist of these storage circuits.

_____ 48. The property that determines whether data is lost or retained when power fails.

_____ 49. Each position of storage can be accessed in approximately the same time.

_____ 50. Each position of storage can be accessed according to a predetermined order.

_____ 51. Microelectronic storage circuits on silicon chips.

_____ 52. Uses magnetic spots on metal or plastic disks.

_____ 53. Uses magnetic spots on plastic tape.

_____ 54. Uses a laser to read microscopic points on plastic disks.

Discussion Questions

1. Why is it important to think of a computer as a system instead of an information processing "box"?

2. What trends are occurring in the development and use of the major types of computer systems?

3. What is the difference between microcomputers used as professional or end user workstations and those used as workstation computers or technical workstations?

4. Refer to the Real World Case of the Darby Group. Why do you think CEO Mike Ashkin says that "PCs have given my company a chance to have a bottom line"?

5. Are networked computers making minicomputers and mainframe computers obsolete? Explain.

6. What are the benefits and limitations of parallel processors? RISC processors?

7. Refer to the Real World Case on Casino Software and others in the chapter. Why doesn't everyone use voice recognition to operate their computers?

8. Why are there so many types of peripheral devices for input and output? For secondary storage?

9. Refer to the Real World Case of CSX, Great Western, SUNY, and Santa Cruz County in the chapter. Do you see the role of mainframe computers increasing or decreasing in the years ahead? Explain.

10. What trends are occurring in the development and use of peripheral devices? Why are these trends occurring?

Real World Problems

1. Trimac Transportation: Client/Server Computing in Business

Trimac Transportation in Calgary, Alberta, is a major trucking company specializing in bulk highway hauling of cement, chemicals, and other cargo across North America. The company has more than 1,700 trucks, nearly 4,000 trailers and tankers, and 2,900 employees. With more than 100 branches in Canada and the United States, Trimac has a large computing requirement for dispatching, tracking, and processing financial applications. Since 1993 they have successfully migrated their information technology department away from mainframes and minicomputers to Pentium-based PCs on a companywide local area network/wide area network system.

Joe Strathern, information technology coordinator for Trimac Transportation, says that about four years ago the company started looking at ways to replace the old mainframe-based financial computing environment. They found a

financial software vendor who could supply about 90 percent of their requirements, which included 24-hour wide area network access dialup capability to the corporate office from many of their remote sites, ensuring that all users on the wide area network had access to all data, and installing a companywide computing system with acceptable growth potential. They decided to modify the system, in-house, for additional needs.

John Henderson, director of financial systems development, says, "Today, we have 15 ALR Pentium processor-based servers and approximately 300 client Intel processor-based PCs." The clients run DOS and Windows, and are used for standard office automation processing (accounting, word processing, database); dispatching, tracking, and operations tasks. Popular software packages, such as Microsoft Office and other productivity programs, are used. All client PCs contain at least a 200MB hard drive and 8MB of random access memory (RAM). The servers (file and database) use the NetWare network operating system from Novell. They include from 1GB to 14GB of hard disk space and from 64MB to 96MB of RAM. "The Pentium processor PCs and the client/server LAN methodology together have provided Trimac Transportation with the opportunity to distribute applications to our branch offices, allowing them to be more active in managing their business—something we couldn't easily do before," says Henderson.

a. What is client/server computing?

b. What are the benefits of client/server computing for Trimac?

Source: Adapted from Ron Levine, "Company Keeps on Truckin' with Pentium Network," *PC Today*, March 1995, p. 41.

2. U.S. Naval Sea Systems Command: Moving to Client/Server Systems

The U.S. Naval Sea Systems Command (Navsea) is steaming full speed ahead into client/server waters, and 26 mainframes are walking the plank. Navsea is also throwing to the sharks dozens of minicomputers running proprietary operating systems and taking on board workstations, servers, database management systems, and networks built to open system standards. Navsea is halfway through a five-year, $131 million information systems modernization project and is laying down an infrastructure that it says will reduce IS costs by $81 million a year. "My boss said to me, 'Figure out how to reduce the information technology budget by 25 percent,'" said John Rivers, manager of the Navsea Information Management Improvement Program. "We had to reduce unit costs. If we were delivering a function for $1, we had to deliver it for 75 cents. Those were our marching orders."

From the shipyard in Bremerton, Washington, to the Naval Surface Warfare Center in Panama City, Florida, machines from Unisys, Data General, Honeywell, and Control Data are giving way to client/server LANs populated by Sun Microsystems and Hewlett-Packard servers, and PC and Macintosh clients. The HP servers run database management systems from Oracle and the Sun machines are fitted with DBMSs from Sybase. The LANs run Banyan Systems VINES or Novell NetWare network operating systems.

The biggest challenge in the megaproject has not been dealing with the technology but persuading users and technicians to adopt new ways of thinking about computing, Johnson said. "Some people have dug in and refused," he said. "Some mainframes are still sitting out there acting as great big printers." Nevertheless, the move to open systems has proved itself, Rivers said. "We've shown that standards although not perfect, do work." He said that while it might take eight months to move an application from a Honeywell mainframe to the Sun/Oracle environment, that same application could be ported from Sun/Oracle to HP/Sybase in a couple of weeks. "We've also shown that in this environment, the move to graphical user interfaces or Windows interfaces is a lot easier, and managers really want that now," Rivers said.

a. What are the advantages of moving to client/server systems for Navsea?

b. Why do you think "some people have dug in and refused" to move? What could be done to lessen such resistance?

Source: Adapted from Gary Anthes, "Naval Command Sails to Client/Server," *Computerworld*, April 17, 1995, p. 73. Copyright 1995 by Computerworld, Inc., Framingham, MA 01701—Reprinted from *Computerworld*.

3. Mervyn's, Wal-Mart, and Others: Multiprocessor Computer Systems

Whether you are a regional business or a $70 billion national chain, you will likely have a symmetrical multiprocessing (SMP) system or massively parallel processing (MPP) system in your future. Take Mervyn's department stores, for example. Facing intense competition from Wal-Mart Stores, Inc., and Kmart Corp., this West Coast clothing and home furnishings retailer decided to build a decision-support system to keep its inventory in step with sales. Mary McCormick, technology director at the 288-store chain based in Hayward, California, invested more than $4 million in a 12-processor Sequent Symmetry SMP server running the Oracle database management system. The system fields complex queries against 750G bytes of data. With it, store buyers and inventory managers minimize inventory by tracking what is selling, what isn't selling, and what to mark up or down and what to shift. Few Mervyn's executives debate whether the $4.4 billion chain would be operating at its present strength if they had passed up the SMP system, a junior version of the MPP system that Wal-Mart uses for its 2,729 retail outlets. Indeed, McCormick didn't even need a cost-benefit analysis for the SMP Investment. "It was a strategic decision" that top management agreed was necessary to stay competitive, she says.

In many cases, the SMP/MPP users represent leaders in their fields: American Express has its customer analysis system on a Thinking Machines CM-5; American Airlines and Allstate Insurance have ticket-pricing and insurance processing, respectively, on IBM System 390 parallel mainframes; Ameritech operates its telephone usage tracking system on a Tandem Computers Himalaya/NonStop SQL; Chrysler uses a Cray Research Torus 3D for its automotive design system; Prudential Securities uses an Intel Paragon for running-stock-trading systems; and ING Bank in Amsterdam uses an NCuba 2/Oracle system to run a customer information system for stocks and other investments.

Although prices are coming down, massively parallel systems tend to be more expensive than SMP systems. One reason is that they require high-capacity buses to allow their distributed processors and distributed memories to exchange data and synchronize updates. They also require closely coordinated disk systems and more staff expertise. SMP machines, on the other hand, tend to have fewer processors (typically 4 to 16) sharing a common pool of memory, with an independent task running on each processor. A few simple commands designating processor assignments divides the workload via a job scheduler system utility. So McCormick says she thinks Mervyn's gets more for its money with SMP than it would with MPP because of its lower administrative costs. However, for a vigorous competitor such as Wal-Mart, its AT&T Global Information Solutions 3600 system which uses 476 Intel I486 microprocessors, yields big advantages in return for its greater expense. For example, a query that might tie up an SMP system for days or an IBM mainframe for a week can run on an MPP system in minutes or hours.

a. What are the major differences between SMP and MPP computer systems?

b. Why do businesses like Mervyn's, Wal-Mart, and others use such machines?

Source: Adapted from Charles Babcock, "Into the Mainstream," MPP & SMP Special Report, *Computerworld*, March 27, 1995, pp. 1-3. Copyright 1995 by Computerworld, Inc., Framingham, MA 01701—Reprinted from *Computerworld*.

4. ITT Hartford: The Challenge of Pen Computing

ITT Hartford Insurance Group in Hartford, Connecticut, began looking into pen-based computing in 1989 only to encounter various waves of immature technology, incomplete vendor offerings and high expectations from users. The company has survived those challenges and expects to outfit all of its 342 risk control workers with pen-based systems this year. Previously, risk control workers were not automated. Their work—helping large purchases of insurance reduce potential liability—was done manually. Wayne P. Warwick, director of systems development and loss control, and manager of the $2.5 million project, said the long delay involved several factors, including the following:

- Underpowered pen hardware and poorly designed software that focused on handwriting recognition.
- Problems deciding how best to use the technology.
- A major enterprise infrastructure shift at ITT Hartford that affected the potential for the project's rollout.

ITT Hartford uses the Stylistic 500 pen-based system from Fujitsu Personal Systems. Each employee gets a monitor and an external keyboard, and each loss control employee gets a software suite that includes Microsoft Office, Lotus CC:Mail, Delrina WinFax Pro, and Aba Software Inkwriter. Shiva LANRover-E is used for connectivity.

ITT Hartford's project is the type of undertaking pen-based technology was supposed to serve when it was touted as the hottest thing since sliced bread and before it turned into burned toast. "It's a 'check the boxes, don't work with handwriting' application and it's the world's most expensive yellow pad" of paper, Warwick joked. But it will pay for itself in reduced clerical costs, he added. With computers, risk control reps eliminate the need to dictate reports to stenographers. "What we're buying right now is improved communications," Warwick said.

a. What are the benefits of pen computing for ITT Hartford?

b. Why have pen computing applications in business taken so long to develop?

Source: Adapted from Michael Fitzgerald, "ITT Hartford Puts Pen To Work," *Computerworld*, March 6, 1995, p. 28. Copyright 1995 by Computerworld, Inc., Framingham, MA 01701—Reprinted from *Computerworld*.

5. The Chicago Board Options Exchange: Touch-screen Versus Handheld PCs

One of the greatest challenges financial exchanges have faced in the move to automation is how not to upset the cultural heritage of the trading pits. Some floor brokers at a variety of futures and options exchanges have argued defiantly against the deployment of handheld systems for order execution. They say these systems threaten the traditional open outcry market where market makers and brokers execute trades via hand and verbal signals. The Chicago Board Options Exchange (CBOE) seems to have struck a balance between its rich tradition and computerization. CBOE, the world's largest options marketplace, has rolled out 18 touch-screen systems to floor brokers in an effort to speed order processing while protecting the open outcry market.

CBOE has cut the time it takes for a broker to execute an order in the trading pits from 20 minutes to less than 2 minutes. That reduction is due to a $4 million project called the public automated routing system (PAR), which was designed to allow brokers to enter customer orders on touch-screen PCs from Trinitech Systems. Once a broker logs on to a Trinitech PC and places an order, the information is routed over a LAN to an IBM RS/6000 server. The data then passes to an Amdahl 1400E mainframe, where the orders are processed and sent to the originating brokerage and customer for confirmation.

Gerald O'Connell, senior vice president of the exchange's systems division says: "We already use handheld systems for our market makers, but brokers seem to favor the point-and-shoot touch-screen systems since it's one of the fastest ways to get information out of the pit." CBOE plans to roll out a total of 100 touch-screen PCs across its trading floor, he added. One of the biggest advantages of the touch-screen systems versus the former paper-based order process is that it enables floor brokers to place orders at the market price their customers desire before the market changes: There is no longer a time lag between order execution and confirmation. Even though PAR automates the ordering process, it gives floor brokers a screen image of the paper tickets they have become accustomed to using.

Still, there are some trade-offs between the use of touch-screen and handheld systems in the financial markets. Although handheld vendors have not yet agreed on the communications frequencies needed to ensure secure transmissions—the mobile devices do provide traders and brokers with a higher level of flexibility. "If a broker has to wander 15 feet to use a touch-screen, they might miss something that another broker might be picking up on," said Karen Scherberger, research director in the applications center at Gartner Group.

a. What are the advantages and limitations of using touch-screen versus handheld PCs in financial markets?

b. What other input/output technologies might also be used? Explain.

Source: Adapted from Thomas Hoffman, "Chicago Exchange Maintains Tradition," *Computerworld,* March 20, 1995, p. 41. Copyright 1995 by Computerworld, Inc., Framingham, MA 01701—Reprinted from *Computerworld.*

6. MCI Communications: Multimedia CD-ROM Notebook PCs

When notebook computer makers started building CD-ROM drives into their products, most observers thought the devices would appeal only to a select few users. But at MCI Communications Corp., the built-in CD-ROM drive was a major component of a massive sales force automation project requiring over 5,000 notebook PCs for its sales reps. Three of the four notebook PCs MCI considered had built-in CD-ROM drives. These included the eventual winner, the IBM ThinkPad 755CD, as well as the Panasonic V41 and the Toshiba Satellite 2150 CD.

Driving the move to CD-ROM technology was MCI's shifting corporate emphasis. As it came to market with products such as Network MCI Business, the company recognized that its focus was as much on software and services as it was on telecommunications—and the new emphasis demanded new technology. As its focus shifted, MCI realized that its salespeople were not well equipped to sell technology, said Rahim Shah, senior project manager at MCI.

So MCI specified CD-ROM drives in their notebook PC for several reasons:

- To improve its average sales pitch by allowing salespeople to use full motion multimedia presentations on CD-ROM.
- To eliminate the need for sales representatives to carry paper documents of product information.
- To make training more accessible and user-driven through the use of custom CD-ROM training applications.

a. Why did a change in MCI's business focus require notebook PCs with CD-ROM for their sales staff?

b. What other business occupations could benefit from similar systems?

Source: Adapted from Michael Fitzgerald, "MCI Improves Productivity with CD-ROM Technology," *Computerworld,* April 24, 1995, p. 43. Copyright 1995 by Computerworld, Inc., Framingham, MA 01701—Reprinted from *Computerworld.*

Application Exercises

1. Input Alternatives

Which method of input would you recommend for the following activities? Explain your choices. Refer to Figure 4.31 to help you.

a. Entering data from printed questionnaires.

b. Entering data from telephone surveys.

c. Entering data from bank checks.

d. Entering data from merchandise tags.

e. Entering data from engineering drawings.

2. Output Alternatives

Which method of output would you recommend for the following information products? Explain your choices. Refer to Figure 4.31 to help you.

a. Visual displays for portable microcomputers.

b. Legal documents.

c. Engineering drawings.

d. Financial results for top executives.

e. Responses for telephone transactions.

3. Storage Alternatives

Indicate which secondary storage medium you would use for each of the following storage tasks. Select from the choices on the right, using Figure 4.32 to help you.

a. Primary storage.   1. Magnetic hard disk

b. Large capacity, permanent storage   2. Floppy disk

c. Large capacity, fast direct access   3. Magnetic tape

d. Large files for occasional processing   4. Semiconductor memory

e. Inexpensive, portable direct access   5. Optical disk

4. Selecting a Computer Hardware Supplier

Your department is in the process of acquiring a number of microcomputer systems. A purchase of seven PC systems and two laser printers is planned. All seven PCs are to have SVGA color monitors. Four of the PCs should have 125 megabyte hard disks, while the other three will require 250 megabyte hard disks. You have been assigned the task of getting bids from three local suppliers of computer equipment and developing estimates of the cost of acquiring the needed equipment from each supplier. All items are to be purchased from a single supplier; no splitting of the order is allowed. Assume that the prices quoted by each supplier are as shown below, where the price shown is for a single unit of the component indicated.

Unit Price of System Components from Alternative Suppliers

Component	Supplier		
	ACME Systems	ACE Computers	Orange PC Palace
PC systems unit with keyboard	$ 785	$ 760	$ 810
SVGA color monitor	260	265	250
Hard disk upgrade to:			
125 megabytes	60	65	70
250 megabytes	145	155	160
Laser printer	1,190	1,210	1,185

a. Prepare a spreadsheet comparing the costs of acquiring this equipment from each of the three alternative suppliers.

b. (1) Based on cost alone, which supplier would you recommend?

   (2) If you were actually making a recommendation about this type of purchase, what factors, in addition to cost, would you want to consider?

c. Suppose your boss decided to modify the order by purchasing five laser printer units rather than the two originally planned. Modify your spreadsheet to reflect this change. Would this affect your recommendation?

5. Microcomputers at ABC Company

ABC Company has many microcomputers assigned to employees in various departments. You have been assigned the task of keeping track of your department's inventory of microcomputers. You need to keep records identifying each microcomputer system by its ID number, which employee the system is assigned to, the manufacturer's name, and the type of processor chip it uses. Data for the systems currently in use are shown in the following figure.

Lists of Microcomputers Assigned to Department Members

Identification Number	Manufacturer's Name	Processor Type	Employee Name
V673829	Vale	386	Barnes, V.
PX289476	Honeydale	486	Smith, W.
RT87931	Fast Systems	8088	Evan, D.
V510293	Vale	486	Powers, B.
LV692013	PC Powers	386	Morris, H.
V938124	Vale	286	Owens, M.
PX347923	Honeydale	486	Adams, A.
RV30129	Fast Systems	386	Jarvis, J.

a. Using a database management software package, create a database file to store this information. Then enter the appropriate data for the microcomputer systems listed in the figure.

b. Create and print a simple report showing all of the information for each system, sorted in alphabetical order by the name of the employee to whom the system is assigned.

c. Using the data retrieval capabilities of your database software, perform the following retrievals:

   (1) Retrieve the ID# and EMP__Name for all systems manufactured by Vale.

   (2) Retrieve a count of the number of systems with a 486 processor.

   (3) Retrieve all information recorded for the system assigned to Smith, W.

Review Quiz Answers

1.	52	15.	23	29.	16	43.	7
2.	13	16.	25	30.	40a	44.	57
3.	6	17.	22	31.	51	45.	48
4.	4	18.	11	32.	14	46.	45b
5.	1	19.	30	33.	42	47.	45a
6.	8	20.	5	34.	39	48.	56
7.	41	21.	28	35.	54	49.	9
8.	44	22.	29	36.	35	50.	46
9.	10	23.	49	37.	33	51.	45
10.	37	24.	18	38.	20	52.	19
11.	32	25.	50c	39.	15	53.	21
12.	31	26.	47e	40.	7	54.	34
13.	2	27.	40	41.	3		
14.	24	28.	36	42.	55		

Selected References

1. *Computerworld, Datamation, PC Week, PC Magazine,* and *PC World.* (Examples of good sources for current information on computer systems hardware and other developments in information systems technology.)

2. Datapro Corporation. *Datapro Reports.* (Series of regular, detailed reports on selected computer systems hardware.)

CSX, Great Western, SUNY, and Santa Cruz County: The Mainframe's New Role

One of the dreams of the client/server revolution was that off-loading application processing from host systems to PC networks would allow users to reduce their dependence on mainframes. Well, dream on.

It turns out that client/server systems do little to rein in mainframe workloads. So say information systems executives at several companies that continue to store corporate data on IBM System/390 mainframes as they head down the off-loading path.

Spreading powerful and user-friendly PCs around a company and letting them access mainframe databases can increase demands on big iron, the IS officials said. With PCs pulling down much greater amounts of data than terminals ever could, mainframes have more than enough work to keep them busy, even if their host processing role has been diminished, they explained.

"Dumb terminals can fit maybe 1,500 or 2,000 characters on a screen, but a single PC can ask for half of a database, so the mainframe activity that it can generate is pretty significant," said Doug Underhill, a technical specialist in the IS unit at CSX Corp., a railroad company in Richmond, Virginia.

CSX has started implementing an OS/2-based geographic information system that tracks the status of freight trains as they travel on the railroad. It plans to move more tasks to PCs in the next 12 to 18 months, Underhill said. However, data will still be stored centrally, and early indications are that the consumption of mainframe processing cycles will continue to increase. Reducing mainframe usage through off-loading "is probably only true if you don't ever expect PCs to come back and speak to it again," Underhill noted.

Even distributing data to smaller servers may not stem mainframe growth if batch processing is still done on a System/390. Charlie Burns, an analyst at Gartner Group, Inc. in Stamford, Connecticut, said he has seen cases where nightly batch workloads have shot up as much as 50 percent due to the strain put on the mainframe as it pulls the required data out of client/server systems.

"IS people are worrying about having to buy a new mainframe just to handle their batch processing," Burns said. "They don't know how to go and explain that to their management." The increased user productivity made possible by PCs "doesn't come for free," Burns said. "Most customers are looking at an increased mainframe workload no matter what they do."

"I haven't found that you off-load a whole lot," agreed Bill Neuser, director of capacity planning and support at Great Western Bank in Northridge, California. "The mainframe doesn't do it all now, but still does more work." Great Western installed LANs in its branch offices to process retail transactions locally, but all data is still uploaded to the mainframe and then made available for downloading on a companywide basis. "All we see is our back-office processors running a lot hotter than they used to," Neuser said. The bank plans to upgrade its System/390 this year. "Client/server ain't saving anybody anything," Neuser said grimly.

Luther Perry, information services director for the county of Santa Cruz, California, traded in his old water-cooled IBM 3090 Model 200S mainframe that he had bought used several years ago. This January, the county installed a spanking new four-processor, IBM 9672 model R41 mainframe and a pair of IBM's equally new air-cooled 90G-byte Ramac magnetic disk arrays. The new mainframe features CMOS (composite metal oxide semiconductor) circuitry, which drastically reduces cooling and space requirements. The switch to IBM's CMOS-based mainframe technology yielded the following savings for the county of Santa Cruz:

- Monthly hardware maintenance costs dropped from more than $8,000 to about $1,000.
- Energy consumption fell by roughly 90 percent.
- Floor space requirements reduced to one-tenth of previous amount.

The State University of New York (SUNY), has been migrating to client/server computing during the past several years, said Charles Blunt, associate vice chancellor for information technology systems. Still, the mainframe serves a valuable function. It remains a good central repository for some applications, especially "heavy-duty transaction processing." And the mainframe is being used increasingly as a network server, he added.

CASE STUDY QUESTIONS

1. What is the new role of mainframe computers?

2. Why can PCs increase the need for mainframe systems?

3. What are the benefits of recent improvements in mainframe technologies?

Source: Adapted from Craig Steadman, "Big Iron Awakens," *Computerworld*, December 26, 1994/January 2, 1995, pp. 1, 7; Neal Weinberg, "Users Parry with Big Iron," *Computerworld*, February 6, 1995, pp. 73, 76; and Craig Steadman, "Small Shops Objects of IBM's Desire," *Computerworld*, March 27, 1995, p. 78. Copyright 1995 by Computerworld, Inc., Framingham, MA 01701—Reprinted from *Computerworld*.

Managerial Overview: Computer Software

CHAPTER OUTLINE

C H A P T E R

5

LEARNING OBJECTIVES

The purpose of this chapter is to give you an overview of computer software by analyzing the functions, benefits, and limitations of major types of system and application software packages.

Section I of this chapter presents an overview of software types and trends and summarizes the major features and functions of operating systems and other system software including programming languages.

Section II surveys the major types of software available for end user computing applications, with an emphasis on microcomputer productivity software. Included are word processing, electronic spreadsheet, database management, telecommunications, graphics, and integrated packages.

After reading and studying this chapter, you should be able to:

1. Describe two major trends occurring in computer software.
2. Identify several major types of system and application software.
3. Outline the functions of operating systems and operating environments.
4. Describe the role of database management systems, telecommunications monitors, and programming language translator programs.
5. Explain the difference between machine, assembler, high-level, fourth-generation, and object-oriented languages.
6. Identify and explain the purpose of several popular microcomputer software packages for end user computing.

┌─ **SECTION I**
▌ *System Software: Computer*
   System Management

Introduction to Software

This chapter presents an overview of the major types of software you will depend on as you work with computers. It discusses their characteristics and purposes and gives examples of their uses. Information systems depend on software resources to help end users use computer hardware to transform data resources into a variety of information products. Software is needed to accomplish the input, processing, output, storage, and control activities of information systems. As we said in Chapter 1, computer software is typically classified into two major types of programs:

- **System software.** Programs that manage and support the resources and operations of a computer system as it performs various information processing tasks.
- **Application software.** Programs that direct the performance of a particular use, or *application,* of computers to meet the information processing needs of end users.

Let's begin our analysis of software by looking at an overview of the major types and functions of software available to computer users, shown in Figure 5.1.

FIGURE 5.1

An overview of computer software. Note the major types and examples of system and application software.

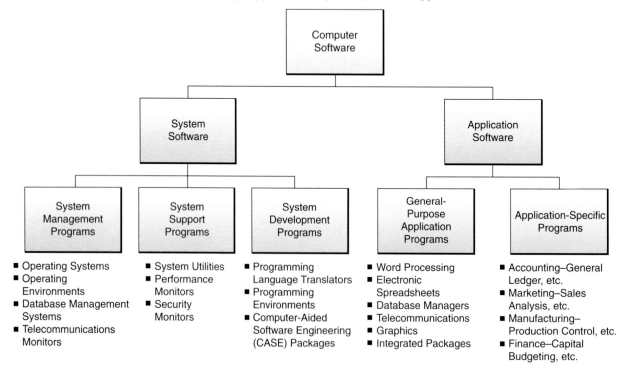

This figure summarizes the major categories of system and application software we will discuss in this chapter. Of course, this is a conceptual illustration. The types of software you will encounter depend primarily on the manufacturer and the model of the computer you use and, second, on what additional software is acquired to increase your computer's performance or to accomplish specific tasks for you and other end users.

Figure 5.2 emphasizes two major **software trends** important to managerial end users. First, there is a trend away from custom-designed one-of-a-kind programs developed by the professional programmers or end users of an organization. Instead, the trend is toward the use of off-the-shelf software packages acquired by end users from software vendors. This trend accelerated with the development of relatively inexpensive and easy-to-use productivity software packages for microcomputers, and it continues to grow, even for minicomputer and mainframe users.

Software Trends

      Second, there is a major trend away from (1) technical, machine-specific programming languages using binary-based or symbolic codes, and (2) *procedural languages,* which use brief statements and mathematical expressions to specify the sequence of instructions a computer must perform. Instead, the trend is toward *nonprocedural, natural languages* that are closer to human conversation. This trend has accelerated with the creation of easy-to-use, nonprocedural *fourth-generation languages* (4GLs). It continues to grow as developments in graphics and artificial intelligence produce natural language and *graphical user interfaces* that make software packages easier to use.

      In addition, expert system modules and other artificial intelligence features are being built into a new generation of **expert-assisted software** packages. For example, many spreadsheet, database management, and graphics packages now provide *intelligent help* features. Sometimes called *wizards,* they help you perform common software functions like graphing parts of a spreadsheet or generating reports from a database. Other software packages use capabilities called *intelligent agents* to perform activities based on instructions from a user. For example, an electronic mail package could use an intelligent agent capability to organize, send, and screen E-mail messages for you. See Figure 5.3.

FIGURE 5.2
Trends in computer software. The trend in software is toward multipurpose, expert-assisted packages with natural language and graphical user interfaces.

	FIRST GENERATION	SECOND GENERATION	THIRD GENERATION	FOURTH GENERATION	FIFTH GENERATION?
Trend: Toward Conversational Natural Programming Languages.					
Software Trends	User-Written Programs Machine Languages	Packaged Programs Symbolic Languages	Operating Systems High-Level Languages	Database Management Systems Fourth-Generation Languages Microcomputer Packages	Natural Languages Multipurpose Graphic-Interface Expert-Assisted Packages
Trend: Toward Easy-to-Use Multipurpose Application Packages.					

FIGURE 5.3
This software package provides
intelligent help features called
wizards.

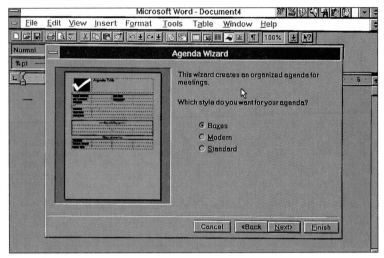

Sarah Evertson/Courtesy of Microsoft Corporation.

FIGURE 5.4
The system and application software interface between end
users and computer hardware.

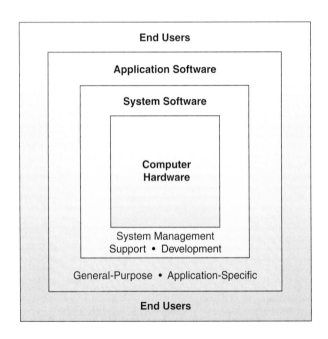

These major trends seem to be converging to produce a "fifth generation" of
powerful, multipurpose, expert-assisted software packages with natural language
and graphical interfaces for end users.

System Software Overview

System software consists of programs that manage and support a computer system
and its information processing activities. These programs serve as a vital *software
interface* between computer system hardware and the application programs of end
users. See Figure 5.4. Note that such programs can be grouped into three major
functional categories:

- **System management programs.** Programs that manage the hardware, software, and data resources of the computer system during its execution of the various information processing jobs of users. The most important system management programs are operating systems and operating environments, followed by telecommunications monitors and database management systems.

- **System support programs.** Programs that support the operations and management of a computer system by providing a variety of support services. Major support programs are system utilities, performance monitors, and security monitors.

- **System development programs.** Programs that help users develop information system programs and procedures and prepare user programs for computer processing. Major development programs are language translators, programming tools, and CASE (computer-aided software engineering) packages.

Operating Systems

The most important system software package for any computer is its **operating system.** An operating system is an integrated system of programs that manages the operations of the CPU, controls the input/output and storage resources and activities of the computer system, and provides various support services as the computer executes the application programs of users.

The primary purpose of an operating system is to maximize the productivity of a computer system by operating it in the most efficient manner. An operating system minimizes the amount of human intervention required during processing. It helps your application programs perform common operations such as entering data, saving and retrieving files, and printing or displaying output. If you have any hands-on experience on a computer, you know that the operating system must be loaded and activated before you can accomplish other tasks. This emphasizes the fact that operating systems are the most indispensable component of the software interface between users and the hardware of their computer systems.

Operating System Functions

An operating system performs five basic functions in the operation of a computer system: providing a user interface, resource management, task management, file management, and utilities and support services. See Figure 5.5.

The User Interface

The **user interface** is the part of the operating system that allows you to communicate with it so you can load programs, access files, and accomplish other tasks. Three main types of user interfaces are the *command-driven, menu-driven,* and *graphical user interfaces.* The trend in user interfaces for operating systems, operating environments, and other software is moving away from the entry of brief end user commands, or even the selection of choices from menus of options. Instead, the trend is toward an easy-to-use **graphical user interface** (GUI), which uses icons, bars, buttons, boxes, and other images. GUIs rely on pointing devices like the electronic mouse to make selections that help you get things done. See Figure 5.6.

Operating Environments

The user interfaces of operating systems are typically enhanced by the use of **operating environments.** Examples include the graphical user interface of Microsoft Windows 95 and the Workplace Shell in IBM's OS/2 Warp, or add-on packages for Microsoft DOS such as Windows 3.1 and Desqview. Operating environments

FIGURE 5.5
The basic functions of an operating system include a user interface, resource management, task management, file management, and utilities and other functions.

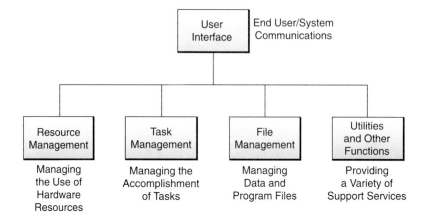

FIGURE 5.6
The graphical user interface of Microsoft's Windows 95 operating system.

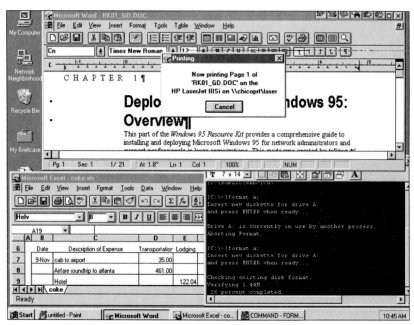

Courtesy of Computer World and Microsoft Corporation.

enhance the user interface by adding a graphical user interface between end users, the operating system, and their application programs. These packages serve as a *shell* to interconnect several separate application packages so that they can communicate and work together and share common data files. Operating environment packages provide icon displays and support the use of an electronic mouse or other pointing devices. They also allow the output of several programs to be displayed at the same time in multiple windows. Finally, several of these packages support some type of *multitasking,* where several programs or tasks can be processed at the same time.

Resource Management

An operating system uses a variety of **resource management** programs to manage the hardware resources of a computer system, including its CPU, memory, secondary storage devices, and input/output peripherals. For example, memory management programs keep track of where data and programs are stored. They may also subdivide memory into a number of sections and swap parts of programs and data between memory and magnetic disks or other secondary storage devices. This can provide a computer system with a **virtual memory** capability that is significantly larger than the real memory capacity of its primary storage unit. So, a computer with a virtual memory capability can process larger programs and greater amounts of data than the capacity of its memory circuits would normally allow.

An operating system contains **file management** programs that control the creation, deletion, and access of files of data and programs. File management also involves keeping track of the physical location of files on magnetic disks and other secondary storage devices. So operating systems maintain directories of information about the location and characteristics of files stored on a computer system's secondary storage devices.

File Management

The **task management** programs of an operating system manage the accomplishment of the computing tasks of end users. They give each task a slice of a CPU's time and interrupt the CPU operations to substitute other tasks. Task management may involve a **multitasking** capability where several computing tasks can occur at the same time. Multitasking may take the form of *multiprogramming,* where the CPU can process the tasks of several programs at the same time, or *time-sharing,* where the computing tasks of several users can be processed at the same time. The efficiency of multitasking operations depends on the processing power of a CPU and the virtual memory and multitasking capabilities of the operating system it uses.

Task Management

New microcomputer operating systems and most minicomputer and mainframe operating systems provide a multitasking capability. With multitasking, end users can do two or more operations (e.g., keyboarding and printing) or applications (e.g., word processing and financial analysis) *concurrently,* that is, at the same time. Multitasking on microcomputers has also been made possible by the development of more powerful microprocessors (like the Intel 80486) and their ability to directly address much larger memory capacities (up to 4 gigabytes). This allows an operating system to subdivide primary storage into several large partitions, each of which can be used by a different application program.

In effect, a single computer can act as if it were several computers, or *virtual machines,* since each application program is running independently at the same time. The number of programs that can be run concurrently depends on the amount of memory that is available and the amount of processing each job demands. That's because a microprocessor (or CPU) can become overloaded with too many jobs and provide unacceptably slow response times. However, if memory and processing capacities are adequate, multitasking allows end users to easily switch from one application to another, share data files among applications, and process some applications in a background mode. Typically, background tasks include large printing jobs, extensive mathematical computation, or unattended telecommunications sessions. See Figure 5.7.

MS-DOS (Microsoft Disk Operating System), along with the Windows operating environment, has been the most widely used microcomputer operating system. It is a single-user, single-tasking operating system, but was given a graphical user interface and limited multitasking capabilities by combining it with Microsoft Windows. Microsoft began replacing its DOS/Windows combination in 1995 with the **Windows 95** operating system. Windows 95 is an advanced operating system

Popular Operating Systems

FIGURE 5.7
Multitasking with OS/2 Warp.
Note how OS/2 Warp enables this
end user to do word processing,
page makeup, and video editing
operations concurrently.

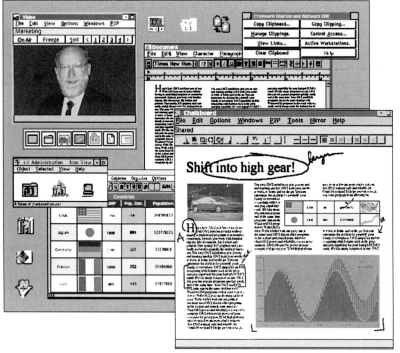

Courtesy of IBM Corporation.

featuring a graphical user interface, true multitasking, networking, multimedia, and many other capabilities. Microsoft introduced another operating system, **Windows NT** (New Technology) in 1993. Windows NT is a powerful multitasking, multiuser network operating system that is being installed on network servers to manage local area networks with high-performance computing requirements.

OS/2 (Operating System/2) is a microcomputer operating system from IBM. Its latest version, **OS/2 Warp,** was introduced in 1994 and provides a graphical user interface, multitasking, virtual memory, telecommunications, and many other capabilities. **UNIX** was originally developed by AT&T, but now is also offered by other vendors, including Solaris by Sun Microsystems, AIX by IBM, and Xenix by Microsoft. Unix is a multitasking, multiuser, network-managing operating system whose *portability* allows it to run on mainframes, midrange computers, and microcomputers. Unix is a popular choice for network servers in many client/server computing networks. **The Macintosh System** is an operating system from Apple for Macintosh microcomputers. Now in version 7.5, The System has a popular graphical user interface as well as multitasking and virtual memory capabilities. See Figure 5.8.

Database Management Systems

In mainframe and midrange computer systems, a **database management system** (DBMS) is viewed as a system software package that controls the development, use, and maintenance of the databases of computer-using organizations. A DBMS program helps organizations use their integrated collections of data records and files known as databases. It allows different user application programs to easily access the same database. For example, a DBMS makes it easy for an employee database to be

FIGURE 5.8
A comparison of popular operating systems.

Operating System	MS-DOS	OS/2 Warp	Windows 95	Macintosh System 7.5	Windows NT	UNIX
Developer	Microsoft	IBM	Microsoft	Apple	Microsoft	AT&T, Sun, IBM, Etc.
Primary Market	PCs	PCs	PCs	Macintoshes	Servers	Workstations Servers Midsize Mainframes
Primary Micro-processors	Intel	Intel Power PC	Intel	Motorola Power PC	Intel Alpha	Many
GUI		X	X	X	X	X
Single User	X	X	X	X		
Multitasking		X	X	X	X	X
Virtual Memory		X	X	X	X	X
Networking		X	X	X	X	X
Multiuser					X	X
Network Management					X	X

accessed by payroll, employee benefits, and other human resource programs. A DBMS also simplifies the process of retrieving information from databases in the form of displays and reports. Instead of having to write computer programs to extract information, end users can ask simple questions in a *query language.* Thus, many DBMS packages provide *fourth-generation languages* (4GLs) and other application development features. Examples of popular mainframe and midrange packages are DB2, by IBM, and Oracle, by Oracle Corporation. We will explore the use of database management packages in information systems in Chapter 7.

Telecommunications Monitors

Modern information systems rely heavily on telecommunications networks to provide electronic communication links between end user workstations, other computer systems, and an organization's databases. This requires system software called **telecommunications monitors.** These programs are used by the main computer in a network (called the host), or in telecommunications control computers such as *front-end processors* and *network servers.* Telecommunications monitors and similar programs perform such functions as connecting or disconnecting communication links between computers and terminals, automatically checking terminals for input/output activity, assigning priorities to data communications requests from terminals, and detecting and correcting transmission errors. Thus, they control and support the data communications activities occurring in a telecommunications network. We will discuss communications software in more detail in Chapter 6.

System Support Programs

System support programs are a category of software that performs routine support functions for the users of a computer system. **Utility programs,** or *utilities,* are an important example. These programs perform miscellaneous *housekeeping* and file conversion functions. For example, *sort programs* are important utility programs that perform the sorting operations on data required in many information processing applications. Utility programs also clear primary storage, load programs, record the contents of primary storage, and convert files of data from one storage medium to another, such as from tape to disk. Many of the operating system commands used with microcomputers and other computer systems provide users with utility programs and routines for a variety of chores.

Other system support programs include performance monitors and security monitors. **Performance monitors** are programs that monitor the performance and usage of computer systems to help its efficient use. **Security monitors** are packages that monitor and control the use of computer systems and provide warning messages and record evidence of unauthorized use of computer resources. These packages will be discussed further in Chapters 13 and 15.

Programming Languages

A proper understanding of computer software requires a basic knowledge of **programming languages.** A programming language allows a programmer or end user to develop the sets of instructions that constitute a computer program. To be a knowledgeable end user, you should know the basic categories of programming languages. Many different programming languages have been developed, each with its own unique vocabulary, grammar, and uses. Programming languages can be grouped into the five major categories shown in Figure 5.9.

Machine Languages

Machine languages (or *first-generation languages*) are the most basic level of programming languages. In the early stages of computer development, all program instructions had to be written using binary codes unique to each computer. This type of programming involves the difficult task of writing instructions in the form of strings of binary digits (ones and zeros) or other number systems. Programmers must have a detailed knowledge of the internal operations of the specific type of CPU they are using. They must write long series of detailed instructions to accomplish even simple processing tasks. Programming in machine language requires specifying the storage locations for every instruction and item of data used. Instructions must

FIGURE 5.9
Major categories of programming languages.

Object-Oriented Languages: Use combinations of objects
Fourth-Generation Languages: Use natural and nonprocedural statements
High-Level Languages: Use brief statements or arithmetic notation
Assembler Languages: Use symbolic coded instructions
Machine Languages: Use binary coded instructions

Machine Language 1010 11001 1011 11010 1100 11011	High-Level Languages BASIC: X = Y + Z COBOL: COMPUTE X = Y + Z
Assembler Language LOD Y ADD Z STR X	Fourth-Generation Language SUM THE FOLLOWING NUMBERS

FIGURE 5.10
Examples of four levels of programming languages. These programming language instructions might be used to compute the sum of two numbers as expressed by the formula $X = Y + Z$.

be included for every switch and indicator used by the program. These requirements make machine language programming a difficult and error-prone task. A machine language program to add two numbers together in the CPU of a specific computer and store the result might take the form shown in Figure 5.10.

Assembler languages (or *second-generation languages*) are the next level of programming languages. They were developed to reduce the difficulties in writing machine language programs. The use of assembler languages requires language translator programs called *assemblers,* which allow a computer to convert the instructions of such languages into machine instructions. Assembler languages are frequently called *symbolic languages,* because symbols are used to represent operation codes and storage locations. Convenient alphabetic abbreviations called *mnemonics* (memory aids) and other symbols are used to represent operation codes, storage locations, and data elements. For example, the computation $X = Y + Z$ in an assembler language might take the form shown in Figure 5.10.

Assembler Languages

In an assembler language, alphabetic abbreviations that are easier to remember are used in place of the actual numeric addresses of the data. This greatly simplifies programming, since the programmer does not need to know the exact storage locations of data and instructions. However, assembler language is still *machine oriented,* because assembler language instructions correspond closely to the machine language instructions of the particular computer model being used. Also, note that each assembler instruction corresponds to a single machine instruction, and that the same number of instructions are required in both illustrations.

Advantages and Disadvantages

Assembler languages are still widely used as a method of programming a computer in a machine-oriented language. Most computer manufacturers provide an assembler language that reflects the unique machine language instruction set of a particular line of computers. This feature is particularly desirable to *system programmers,* who program systems software (as opposed to *applications programmers,* who program applications software), since it provides them with greater control and flexibility in designing a program for a particular computer. They can then produce more *efficient* software—that is, programs that require a minimum of instructions, storage, and CPU time to perform a specific processing assignment.

High-level languages (or *third-generation languages*) use instructions, which are called statements, that closely resemble human language or the standard notation of mathematics. Individual high-level language statements are actually *macroinstructions*; that is, each individual statement generates several machine instructions when

High-Level Languages

translated into machine language by high-level language translator programs called *compilers* or *interpreters*. The use of macroinstructions is also common in fourth-generation languages and software packages such as spreadsheet and database management programs. High-level language statements resemble the phrases or mathematical expressions required to express the problem or procedure being programmed. The *syntax* (vocabulary, punctuation, and grammatical rules) and the *semantics* (meanings) of such statements do not reflect the internal code of any particular computer. For example, the computation $X = Y + Z$ would be programmed in the high-level languages of BASIC and COBOL as shown in Figure 5.10.

Advantages and Disadvantages

A high-level language is obviously easier to learn and understand than an assembler language. Also, high-level languages have less-rigid rules, forms, and syntaxes, so the potential for error is reduced. However, high-level language programs are usually less efficient than assembler language programs and require a greater amount of computer time for translation into machine instructions. Since most high-level languages are machine-independent, programs written in a high-level language do not have to be reprogrammed when a new computer is installed, and computer programmers do not have to learn a new language for each computer they program. Figure 5.11 highlights some of the major high-level languages in use today. Note that the most widely used languages include COBOL for business application programs, BASIC for microcomputer end users, and FORTRAN for scientific and engineering applications.

Fourth-Generation Languages

The term **fourth-generation language** is used to describe a variety of programming languages that are more nonprocedural and conversational than prior languages. These languages are called fourth-generation languages (4GLs) to differentiate them from machine languages (first generation), assembler languages (second generation), and high-level languages (third generation). It should be noted that some industry observers have begun to use the term *fifth-generation language* to describe languages using artificial intelligence techniques to accomplish results for users.

Most fourth-generation languages are **nonprocedural languages** that encourage users and programmers to specify the results they want, while the computer

FIGURE 5.11
Highlights of several important high-level languages. Note the differences in the characteristics and purposes of each language.

Ada: Named after Augusta Ada Bryon, considered the world's first computer programmer. Developed for the U.S. Department of Defense as a standard "high-order language" to replace COBOL and FORTRAN.

BASIC: (Beginner's All-Purpose Symbolic Instruction Code). A simple procedure-oriented language used for end user programming.

C: A mid-level structured language developed as part of the UNIX operating system. It resembles a machine-independent assembler language and is presently popular for system software programming and development of application software packages.

COBOL: (COmmon Business Oriented Language). Designed as an Englishlike language specifically for business data processing. It is the most widely used programming language for business applications.

FORTRAN: (FORmula TRANslation). The oldest of the popular high-level languages. It is still the most widely used programming language for scientific and engineering applications.

Pascal: Named after Blaise Pascal. Developed specifically to incorporate structured programming concepts.

determines the *sequence of instructions* that will accomplish those results. Users and programmers no longer have to spend a lot of time developing the sequence of instructions the computer must follow to achieve a result. Thus, fourth-generation languages have helped simplify the programming process. **Natural languages** are 4GLs that are very close to English or other human languages. Research and development activity in artificial intelligence (AI) is developing programming languages that are as easy to use as ordinary conversation in one's native tongue. In Figure 5.12, INTELLECT, a natural language 4GL, is compared to using 3GLs BASIC, Pascal, and COBOL to program a simple average exam score task.

FIGURE 5.12
Comparing a natural 4GL with third-generation languages. Note how brief, nonprocedural, and conversational INTELLECT is compared to BASIC, Pascal, and COBOL to accomplish the same task.

INTELLECT 4GL WHAT ARE THE AVERAGE EXAM SCORES FOR STUDENTS IN MIS 200?	**BASIC** 10 REM AVERAGE EXAM SCORE PROGRAM 20 LET COUNTER = 0 30 LET TOTAL = 0 40 OPEN "STUDDATA" FOR INPUT AS #1 50 INPUT #1, SCORE 60 WHILE SCORE <> 9999 70 LET COUNTER = COUNTER + 1 80 LET TOTAL = TOTAL + SCORE 90 INPUT #1, SCORE 100 WEND 110 LET AVERAGE = TOTAL/COUNTER 120 PRINT "AVERAGE SCORE IS", AVERAGE 130 END

COBOL (Procedure Division)
PROCEDURE DIVISION.
MAIN.
    PERFORM INITIALIZATION.
    PERFORM PROCESS-RECORDS UNTIL END-OF-FILE.
    PERFORM END-OF-JOB.
INITIALIZATION.
    OPEN INPUT IN-FILE.
    OPEN OUTPUT OUT-FILE.
    PERFORM READ-RECORD.
PROCESS-RECORDS.
    ADD SCORES TO STORE-SCORE.
    ADD 1 TO STORE-NUMBER.
    MOVE NAME-IN TO NAME-OUT.
    MOVE SCORE TO SCORE-OUT.
    WRITE OUT-REC FROM PRINTER-LINE
        AFTER ADVANCING 1.
    PERFORM READ-RECORD.
END-OF-JOB.
    DIVIDE STORE-NUMBER INTO STORE-SCORE GIVING
        AVERAGE.
    WRITE OUT-REC FROM AVERAGE-LINE
        AFTER ADVANCING 2 LINES.
    CLOSE IN-FILE.
    CLOSE OUT-FILE.
    STOP RUN.
READ-RECORD.
    READ IN-FILE
        AT END MOVE "Y" TO EOF-FLAG.
	Pascal
	PROGRAM averagescore {infile, outfile}
	VAR score, sum, average, count: real;
	    infile, outfile: text;
	BEGIN
	    sum. = 0.0, count. 0.0;
	    REPEAT
	        read{infile,score};
	        sum: = sum + score;
	        count: = count + 1.0
	    UNTIL eof{infile};
	    average: = sum/count;
	    write{outfile. 'Average score is', average}
	END.

Advantages and Disadvantages

There are major differences in the ease of use and technical sophistication of 4GL products. For instance, INTELLECT and CLOUT are natural query languages that impose no rigid grammatical rules, while SQL and FOCUS require concise structured statements. However, the ease of use of 4GLs is gained at the expense of some loss in flexibility. It is frequently difficult for an end user to override some of the pre-specified formats or procedures of 4GL. Also, the machine language code generated by a program developed by a 4GL is frequently much less efficient (in terms of processing speed and amount of storage capacity needed) than a program written in a language like COBOL. Major failures have been reported in some large transaction processing applications programmed in a 4GL. These applications were unable to provide reasonable response times when faced with a large amount of realtime transaction processing and end user inquiries. However, 4GLs have shown great success in end user and departmental applications that do not have a high volume of transaction processing.

Object-Oriented Languages

Object-oriented programming (OOP) languages have been around since Xerox developed Smalltalk in the 1960s. However, object-oriented languages have become a major tool of software development. Briefly, while most other programming languages separate data elements from the procedures or actions that will be performed upon them, OOP languages tie them together into *objects*. Thus, an object consists of data and the actions that can be performed on the data. For example, an object could be a set of data about a bank customer's savings account, and the operations (such as interest calculations) that might be performed upon the data. Or, an object could be data in graphic form such as a video display window, plus the display actions that might be used upon it. See Figure 5.13.

In procedural languages, a program consists of procedures to perform actions on each data element. However, in object-oriented systems, objects tell other objects to perform actions on themselves. For example, to open a window on a computer

FIGURE 5.13
An example of a bank savings account object. This object consists of data about a customer's account balance and the basic operations that can be performed on that data.

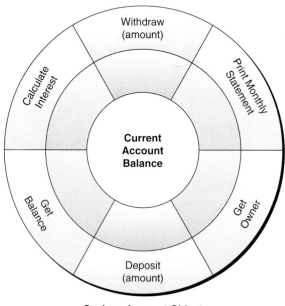

Savings Account Object

video display, a window object could be sent a message to open by a beginning menu object and it will appear on the screen. That's because the window object contains the program code for opening itself.

Object-oriented languages like Visual Basic and C++ are easier to use and more efficient for programming the graphics-oriented user interfaces required by many applications. Also, once objects are programmed, they are reusable. Therefore, reusability of objects is a major benefit of object-oriented programming. For example, programmers can construct a user interface for a new program by assembling standard objects such as windows, bars, boxes, buttons, and icons. Therefore, most object-oriented programming packages provide a GUI that supports a "point and click," "drag and drop" visual assembly of objects known as *visual programming*. Figure 5.14 shows a display of the Visual Basic object-oriented programming environment. Object-oriented technology is discussed further in the coverage of object-oriented databases in Chapter 7.

Language translators (or *language processors*) are programs that translate other programs into machine language instruction codes the computer can execute. They also help programmers write programs by providing program creation and editing facilities. Computer programs consist of sets of instructions written in programming languages, such as BASIC, COBOL, or Pascal, which must be translated by a *compilation* process into the computer's own machine language before they can be processed, or *executed*, by the CPU.

Programming language translator programs are known by a variety of names. An **assembler** translates the symbolic instruction codes of programs written in an assembler language into machine language instructions, while a **compiler** translates high-level language statements. An **interpreter** is a special type of compiler that translates and executes each program statement one at a time, instead of first producing a complete machine language program, like compilers and assemblers do.

Language Translator Programs

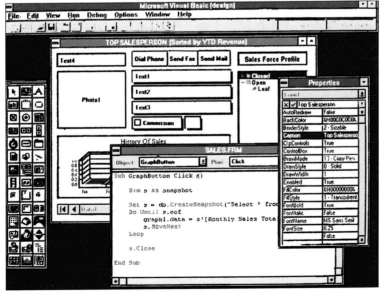

FIGURE 5.14
Using the Visual Basic object-oriented programming package.

Courtesy of Microsoft Corporation.

FIGURE 5.15
The language translation process. A program must be translated into machine language before it can be executed by a computer.

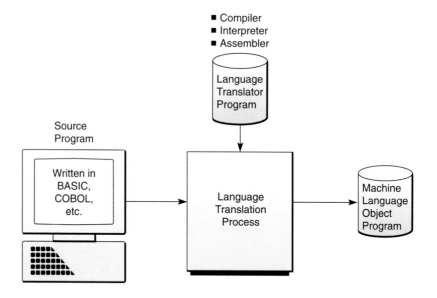

Figure 5.15 illustrates the typical language translation process. A program written in a language such as BASIC or COBOL is called a *source program.* When the source program is translated into machine language, it is called the *object program,* which can then be executed by a computer.

Programming Tools

Many language translator programs are enhanced by a *graphical programming interface* and a variety of built-in capabilities or add-on packages. Language translators have always provided some editing and diagnostic capabilities to identify programming errors or bugs. However, many language translator programs now include powerful graphics-oriented *editors* and *debuggers.* These programs help programmers identify and avoid errors while they are programming. Such **programming tools** provide a computer-aided programming *environment* or *workbench.* Their goal is to decrease the drudgery of programming while increasing the efficiency and productivity of programmers. Other programming tools include diagramming packages, code generators, libraries of reusable objects and program code, and prototyping tools. Many of these same tools are part of the *toolkit* provided by computer-aided software engineering (CASE) packages. See Figure 5.16.

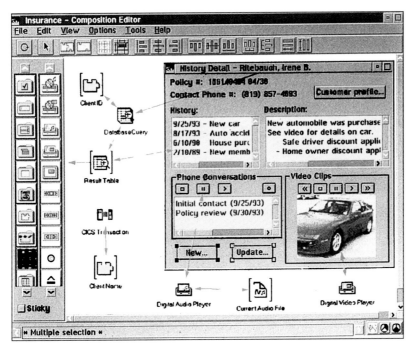

Courtesy of IBM Corporation.

FIGURE 5.16
Using the graphical programming interface of Visual Age, IBM's object-oriented programming tool.

Bank South and Huntington Bancshares: Choosing Operating Systems

The war may be over in the rest of the world, but the battle over PC operating systems has just begun in the banking industry. Currently, more than half of the top 50 U.S. banks are running their retail operations on IBM's OS/2 operating system. Those banks include KeyCorp in Cleveland, First Union Corp. in Charlotte, North Carolina, and Barnett Banks, Inc., in Jacksonville, Florida. Now, a familiar competitor, Microsoft Corp., has begun making inroads into what has traditionally been IBM's turf.

But even though Microsoft recently landed several significant Windows NT contracts—including ones with Bank South Corp. in Atlanta and Centura Banks, Inc., in Rocky Mount, North Carolina—the future of the market, according to banking watchers and players, will likely depend on how the industry receives Microsoft's Windows 95 environment.

"Windows NT is a larger system than OS/2 and is more adaptable to running a server than a client PC," said Bob Landry, a technology analyst at The Tower Group, a financial services and technology consultancy. "OS/2 is sized very nicely to support branch banking," Landry added, "but it will depend on whether Windows 95, which will be sized competitively with OS/2, can meet the performance and reliability objectives in a mission-critical environment."

Most banking executives interviewed said they chose the operating environment for their retail operations based on the branch automation package selected. For example, when Bank South recently decided to upgrade its 145 branch locations from a DOS-based IBM branch banking environment, it selected Unisys's Financial Business Architecture (FBA) Navigator application system. After choosing FBA, the bank had three operating systems to pick from: Windows NT, Unisys's CTOS, and Unix. They chose Windows NT.

"We were not going to Unix or CTOS. We already had a lot of Windows experience here, and even though OS/2 currently has a leg up in the banking world, everybody's writing for Windows," said Al Schulman, an information services project manager at Bank South, which has $6.9 billion in assets. Indeed, most of the leading branch banking packages originally written for OS/2—such as Argo Data

Resources' BankPro—have been or are being rewritten for Windows.

Yet many banks that have opted for an OS/2-led branch banking approach have done so for compelling reasons—and not just because IBM is the preeminent technology provider to the industry. For example, Huntington Bancshares, Inc., in Columbus, Ohio, began installing Argo's BankPro on IBM OS/2 LANs at its 350 branches four years ago in an effort to provide its tellers and customer services representatives with a more sales- and services-oriented culture.

Huntington Bancshares recently recommitted to OS/2 as part of a three-year effort beginning next month to upgrade nearly 2,000 IBM PS/2 workstations and servers to Intel Pentium-based machines. The reason is OS/2's ability to do robust multitasking at the workstation level, according to Rick Sellers, president of Huntington Service Co. in Columbus, the bank's operations and technology arm.

"Windows doesn't stand up to OS/2 in multitasking, and we have put so much functionality on our banking applications that it would bring Windows to its knees," Sellers said. Even though Windows and Windows NT would have worked in Huntington Bancshares' branch environment, Sellers said the Microsoft systems would have been too slow to allow its customer representatives to leverage multitasking for cross-selling opportunities.

But for all of the debate between OS/2, Windows NT, and Windows 95 in the banking arena, market dominance may well hinge on future industry developments. In the next 5 to 10 years, as electronic home banking pervades the market, banks will have to employ operating systems that can easily handle the many online applications that will be involved.

CASE STUDY QUESTIONS

1. Why do many banks use the OS/2 operating system?

2. Why are some banks choosing Windows NT as their operating system?

3. Why is choosing an operating system an important business decision?

Source: Adapted from Thomas Hoffman, "Banks Form Front Line in Battle for Operating System Dominance," *Computerworld*, February 27, 1995, p. 45. Copyright 1995 by Computerworld, Inc., Framingham, MA 01701—Reprinted from *Computerworld*.

SECTION II
Applications Software: End User Applications

Application software consists of programs that direct computers to perform specific information processing activities for end users. These programs are called *application packages* because they direct the processing required for a particular use, or *application,* that end users want accomplished. Thousands of application packages are available because there are thousands of different jobs end users want computers to do. The use of personal computers has multiplied the growth of such programs.

Figure 5.1 showed that application software includes a variety of programs that can be subdivided into *general-purpose* and *application-specific* categories. **General-purpose application programs** are programs that perform common information processing jobs for end users. For example, word processing programs, spreadsheet programs, database management programs, integrated packages, and graphics programs are popular with microcomputer users for home, education, business, scientific, and many other purposes. Because they significantly increase the productivity of end users, they are also known as *productivity packages.* We will briefly explain some of the most popular types of such packages in this section.

Thousands of application software packages are available to support specific applications of end users. Major categories of such **application-specific programs** are:

- **Business application programs.** Programs that accomplish the information processing tasks of important business functions or industry requirements. Examples of such business functions and their corresponding applications are accounting (general ledger), marketing (sales analysis), finance (capital budgeting), manufacturing (material requirements planning), operations management (inventory control), and human resource management (employee benefits analysis).
- **Scientific application programs.** Programs that perform information processing tasks for the natural, physical, social, and behavioral sciences; and for mathematics, engineering, and all other areas involved in scientific research, experimentation, and development. Some broad application categories include scientific analysis, engineering design, and monitoring of experiments.
- **Other application programs.** There are so many other application areas of computers that we lump them all into this category. Thus, we can talk of computer applications in education, entertainment, music, art, law enforcement, medicine, and so on. Some specific examples are computer-assisted instruction programs in education, video game programs in entertainment, and computer-generated music and art programs.

Word processing packages are programs that computerize the creation, editing, and printing of *documents* (such as letters, memos, and reports) by electronically processing *text data* (words, phrases, sentences, and paragraphs). Thus, word processing is an important application of *office automation,* which we will discuss in

Application Software for End Users

General-Purpose Programs

Application-Specific Programs

Word Processing Packages

FIGURE 5.17
Using the Microsoft Word for
Windows' word processing
package.

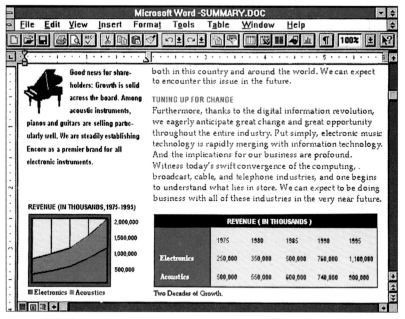

Courtesy of IBM Corporation.

Chapter 8. Figure 5.17 illustrates the use of a popular word processing package. With word processing packages such as WordPerfect and Microsoft Word, end users can:

- Use a computer to create and edit a document and have each line of text automatically adjusted to fit prespecified margins.
- Move to any point in a document and add, delete, or change words, sentences, or paragraphs.
- Move a block of text from one part of a document to another and insert standard text from another document file.
- Check a document for spelling or grammatical errors and selectively change all occurrences of a particular word or phrase.
- Store a document as a document file on a magnetic disk, retrieve it any time, and print it according to a variety of predesigned formats.

Many word processing packages provide advanced features or can be upgraded with supplementary packages. One example is a *spelling checker* program, which uses built-in dictionaries to identify and correct spelling errors in a document. Another is a *thesaurus program,* which helps you find a better choice of words to express ideas. *Grammar* and *style checker* programs can be used to identify and correct grammar and punctuation errors, as well as to suggest possible improvements in your writing style. Another text productivity tool is an *idea processor* or *outliner* program. It helps you organize and outline your thoughts before you prepare a document or develop a presentation. Also popular is a *mail-merge* program, which can automatically merge the names and addresses in a mailing list file with letters and other documents. Finally, many word processing programs are able to support a limited amount of *desktop publishing* activity. As we will discuss in Chapter 8, this allows end users to merge text, graphics, and other illustrations on each page to produce documents that look professionally published.

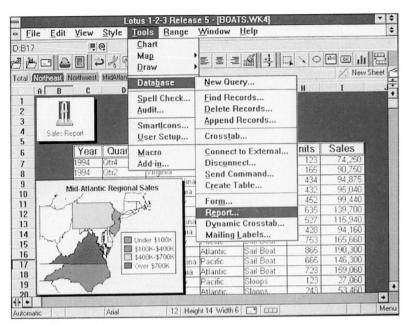

Courtesy of Lotus Development Corporation.

FIGURE 5.18
Using an electronic spreadsheet. The Lotus 1-2-3 for Windows spreadsheet allows you to work with multiple related spreadsheets and graphics.

Electronic Spreadsheet Packages

Electronic spreadsheet packages are application programs used for analysis, planning, and modeling. They provide an electronic replacement for more traditional tools such as paper worksheets, pencils, and calculators. They generate an electronic spreadsheet, which is a worksheet of rows and columns stored in the computer's memory and displayed on its video screen. You use the computer's keyboard to enter data and relationships (formulas) into the worksheet. In response to your input, the computer performs necessary calculations based on the relationships you defined in the spreadsheet. Results are immediately displayed for you to see. See Figure 5.18.

What-If Analysis

An electronic spreadsheet package creates a *spreadsheet model* of the mathematical and other relationships within a particular business activity. It can thus be used to record and analyze past and present activity. It can also be used as a decision support tool to help you answer *what-if questions* you may have. For example, "**What** would happen to net profit **if** advertising expense increased by 10 percent?" To answer this question, you would simply change the advertising expense formula on an income statement worksheet. The affected figures would be recalculated, producing a new net profit figure. You would then have a better insight into whether advertising expense should be increased. The use of electronic spreadsheets for such decision support will be discussed further in Chapter 10.

Once an electronic spreadsheet has been developed, it can be stored for later use or printed out as a report. Popular electronic spreadsheet packages for microcomputers include Lotus 1-2-3, Excel, and Quattro Pro. Mainframe and minicomputer users can also use the electronic spreadsheet modules of products such as Lotus 1-2-3M and Focus. Special-purpose spreadsheet models called *templates* are available for most spreadsheet packages. These worksheets are developed for many applications; such as tax accounting or real estate investment.

FIGURE 5.19
Using a DBMS package. Note how the Microsoft Access database management package lets you easily obtain information from a customer order database.

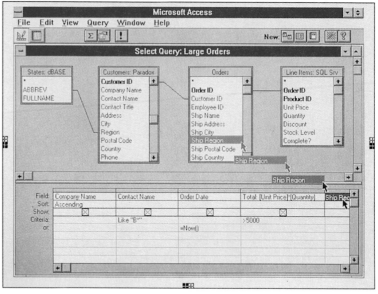

Courtesy of Microsoft Corporation.

Database Management Packages

Microcomputer versions of database management programs have become so popular that they are now viewed as general-purpose *application software* packages like word processing and spreadsheet packages. **Database management packages** such as Access, by Microsoft, or Approach, by Lotus Development, allow end users to set up databases of files and records on their personal computer systems and quickly store data and retrieve information. As Figure 5.19 illustrates, most DBMS packages can perform four primary tasks:

- **Database development.** Define and organize the content, relationships, and structure of the data needed to build a database.
- **Database interrogation.** Access the data in a database for information retrieval and report generation. End users can selectively retrieve and display information and produce printed reports and documents.
- **Database maintenance.** Add, delete, update, correct, and protect the data in a database.
- **Application development.** Develop prototypes of data entry screens, queries, forms, reports, and labels for a proposed application. Or use a 4GL or application generator to develop program codes.

Telecommunications Packages

Telecommunications software **packages** for microcomputers are also viewed as general-purpose application packages for end users. These packages can connect a microcomputer equipped with a modem to public and private networks. However, communications control packages such as Procomm Plus, Crosstalk, and Kermit are being challenged by the networking capabilities of operating systems like Windows 95 and OS/2 Warp, and by the telecommunications software provided by public information services like Prodigy, CompuServe, and America Online.

Telecommunications software is also available from many other sources, including Internet access providers, electronic mail software vendors, and

Courtesy of Attachmate Corporation.

FIGURE 5.20
Using the Crosstalk telecommunications package to transfer files on the Internet.

fax/modem suppliers. All of these packages help your microcomputer act as an *intelligent terminal* so it can transmit, receive, and store messages, information, and files of data and programs. For example, files of data and programs can be downloaded from a host computer to a microcomputer and stored on a disk. Or files can be *uploaded* from the microcomputer to a host computer. Some programs even allow files to be transferred automatically between unattended computer systems.

Telecommunications packages for microcomputers are fairly easy to use. Once you load the program, you are usually provided with a display that asks you to set communications *parameters* (transmission speed and mode, type of parity, etc.). Then you dial the computer system or network you want or have it done automatically for you. Most networks will provide you with a series of prompts or menus to guide you in sending or receiving messages, information, and files. See Figure 5.20.

Graphics Packages

Graphics packages convert numeric data into graphics displays such as line charts, bar graphs, and pie charts. Many other types of presentation graphics displays are possible. *Draw* and *paint* graphics packages support freehand drawing, while desktop publishing programs provide predrawn *clip art* graphics for insertion into documents. Images are displayed on your video monitor or copies can be made on your system printer or plotter. Not only are such graphic displays easier to comprehend and communicate than numeric data, but multiple-color displays can more easily emphasize strategic differences and trends in the data. Presentation graphics have proved to be much more effective than tabular presentations of numeric data for reporting and communicating in management reports or in presentations to groups of people.

Presentation graphics can be produced by graphics packages, such as Harvard Graphics and Lotus Freelance for microcomputers, and SAS Graph and Tell-A-Graph for minicomputers and mainframes, or by the graphics modules of electronic spreadsheets or integrated packages. To use such packages, typically, you select the

FIGURE 5.21
Using the Lotus Freelance
graphics package.

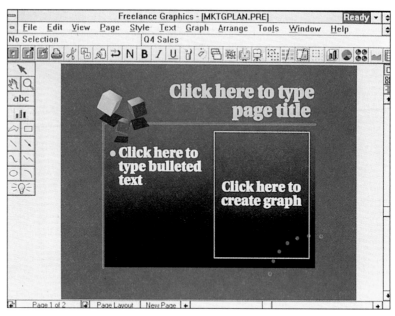

Courtesy of Lotus Development Corporation.

type of graph you want and enter the categories of data you want plotted. This is done in response to prompts displayed on your screen, or you can highlight the data you want graphed. The graphics program then analyzes the file of data you specify and generates the requested graphics. See Figure 5.21.

Integrated Packages and Software Suites

Integrated packages combine the abilities of several general-purpose applications in one program. Integrated packages were developed to solve the problems caused by the inability of individual programs to communicate and work together with common files of data. However, integrated packages typically reduce the functions they provide, and may compromise on the speed, power, and flexibility of some of their functions in order to achieve integration. Therefore, software vendors are now offering **software suites,** which combine several individual packages that share a common graphical interface and are designed to easily transfer data between them.

Examples of popular integrated packages are Microsoft Works, Lotus Works, and IBM Works. Examples of popular software suites are Lotus Smart Suite, Microsoft Office, and WordPerfect's Perfect Office. For example, the Microsoft Office suite consists of the Microsoft Word word processing package, Excel spreadsheet, Access database manager, and the Powerpoint graphics package. Such packages combine the functions of general-purpose application software such as electronic spreadsheets, word processing, graphics, database management, and data communications. Thus, you can process the same file of data with one package, moving from one function to the other by selecting a few icons on your video display. See Figure 5.22.

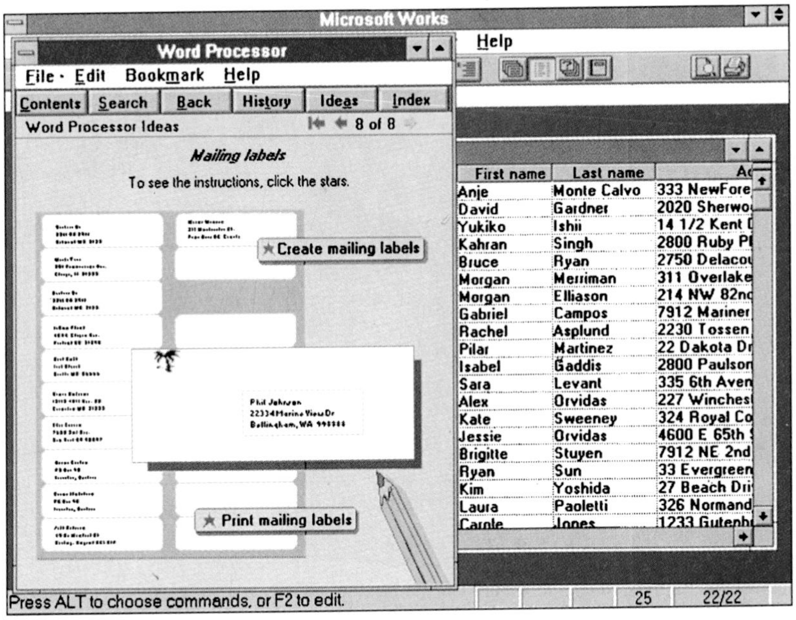

Courtesy of Microsoft Corporation.

FIGURE 5.22
Using the Microsoft Works integrated package. It provides word processing, spreadsheet, file management, telecommunications, and graphics capabilities in one package.

We could spend a lot more time discussing the many application packages available to end users for use on mainframes, minicomputers, and microcomputers. Microcomputer application packages support managerial, professional, and business uses such as decision support, accounting, project management, investment analysis, and desktop publishing. Still other packages support end users by helping them organize random pieces of information and accomplish routine tasks, or support applications such as personal finance, home management, entertainment, education, and information services. These and other software packages are discussed in upcoming chapters on telecommunications, database management, end user computing, office automation, decision support, expert systems, and other information systems.

Other End User Packages

National Benefit Resources: Choosing End User Software

Paul Friedman is vice president at National Benefit Resources (NBR), a medical care financing and information provider in Minneapolis. The company wanted to move from WordPerfect and Lotus 1-2-3 for DOS, to Windows-based end user productivity software. So Friedman's staff compared the three major office suites. Here's what they found.

Word Processors

Although Friedman preferred AmiPro for its speed and proficiency, his employees favored Word. They liked the way the screen looked. They felt comfortable, he says. Its major drawback was that it lacked a conversion filter for AmiPro. The users felt WordPerfect for Windows was so different from the DOS version that it was like learning a new product, so they were willing to change.

In terms of conversion costs the word processors were all equally as difficult, says Friedman. "The WordPerfect macros did not convert well. We had a lot of work ahead of us no matter which way we went."

Spreadsheets

Again all three candidates proved capable. Friedman ranked Excel, Quattro Pro, and 1-2-3 in that order, but again his users differed. "They were not comfortable with Excel," he says. "They wanted the ability to bring up an old menu by hitting the slash key."

To convert NBR's existing spreadsheets Friedman found two winners, 1-2-3 and Quattro Pro. Neither required many macros to be redone. The additional cost and time of having to convert all those was a negative for Excel, he says.

Presentations

Friedman's staff also uses presentation products heavily. In this category, says Friedman, "The Lotus freelance graphics package was the clear winner. Microsoft PowerPoint was a very, very distant second." WordPerfect's graphic offering fell short. He adds, "We were remarkably unimpressed with that package."

Databases

Since data confidentiality and integrity are critical for medical records, Friedman didn't even evaluate the suites' database management capabilities. "We're a FoxPro shop," he explains. "Our users are quite comfortable doing their own ad hoc queries in Fox."

Friedman believes this mirrors the position of other businesses, which already have vertical or custom-built solutions for their data processing problems. This may suggest why end user database management packages are just now expanding in the PC market.

Groupware

Friedman's users, like those at many companies, are completely networked. They already use E-mail to send messages and route files. So Friedman saw little use for the groupware modules in the suites. "We played with it a little and the universal response was, 'Who cares?'"

He says that all the word processors and spreadsheets allow you to attach notes. In Word for instance, "You can stick comments in that don't print or do print as you want, and everybody's comments come up in a different color, etc. What more do you need?"

Integration

Similarly, Friedman's staff was not swayed by connectivity features. "None of the users around here could care less whether they get the spreadsheet information that they need into their word processing document by OLE 2.0 or DDE. They don't see much difference in the way they do it now and the way they used to do it in WordPerfect 5.1.

"It's a little cuter now," he added, "but no one raved" at the ability to edit a spreadsheet live within a document.

And the Winner Is

"With this mixed bag," says Friedman, "we made the decision that none of the suites worked for us. We have decided to basically bite the bullet and spend a little more on software." Friedman's group will standardize on Word, 1-2-3, and Freelance Graphics. Friedman still saves money by purchasing Lotus SmartSuite, not loading Ami Pro, and buying Word separately.

"I think it needs to be emphasized," he concludes, "that too many people might take a look at the surface advantages of buying a suite, rather than buying the best specific application for their specific environment. I don't think that the cost savings are that significant. I think those are easily outweighed by other factors."

CASE STUDY QUESTIONS

1. Why do you think NBR switched to Windows-based application software?

2. Do you agree with the software choices made by NBR's end users? Why or why not?

3. Why didn't NBR choose a software suite? Do you agree with their reasoning? Why or why not?

Source: Adapted from Robert Schmidt, "Buying a Software Bundle: How Suite It Is," *PC Today*, January 1995, p. 27. PC Today, 120 W. Harvest Drive, Lincoln, NE 68521.

Summary

- **Software.** Computer software consists of two major types of programs: (1) system software, which controls and supports the operations of a computer system as it performs various information processing tasks, and (2) application software, which directs the performance of a particular use, or application, of computers to meet the information processing needs of users. Refer to Figure 5.1 for an overview of the major types of software.

- **System Software.** System software can be subdivided into system management programs, system support programs, and system development programs. System management programs manage the hardware, software, and data resources of a computer system during its execution of information processing jobs. Major system management programs are operating systems, operating environments, database management systems, and communications monitors. System support programs support the operations, management, and users of computer systems by providing a variety of support services. Major support programs are system utilities, performance monitors, and security monitors. System development programs help users develop information processing programs and procedures and prepare user programs for computer processing. Major development programs are language translators, programming editors and debuggers, code generators, and CASE tools.

- **Operating Systems.** An operating system is an integrated system of programs that supervises the operation of the CPU, controls the input/output storage functions of the computer system, and provides various support services. An operating system performs five basic functions: (1) a user interface for communication with users and operators, (2) resource management for managing the hardware resources of a computer system, (3) file management for managing files of data and programs, (4) task management for managing the tasks a computer must accomplish, and (5) utilities and other functions that provide miscellaneous support services.

- **Other System Software.** Operating environment programs add a graphical user interface to an operating system and may provide multitasking capabilities. Database management systems control the development, integration, and maintenance of databases. Telecommunications monitors control and support the telecommunication activities among the computers and terminals in a telecommunications network. Utilities are programs that perform routine computing functions, such as sorting data or copying files, as part of an operating system or as a separate package.

- **Programming Languages.** Programming languages are a major category of system software. They require the use of language translator programs to convert programming language instructions into machine language instruction codes. The four major levels of programming languages are machine languages, assembler languages, high-level languages, and fourth-generation languages. High-level languages such as BASIC and COBOL have been the most widely used programming languages for business applications. However, natural, nonprocedural fourth-generation languages, including object-oriented languages, are also widely used.

- **Application Software.** Application software includes a variety of programs that can be segregated into general-purpose, business, scientific, and other application-specific categories. General-purpose application programs perform common information processing jobs for end users. Examples are word processing, electronic spreadsheet, database management, telecommunications, and graphics programs. Business application programs accomplish information processing tasks that support specific business functions or industry requirements.

Key Terms and Concepts

These are the key terms and concepts of this chapter. The page number of their first explanation is given in parentheses.

1. Application software (169)
2. Application-specific programs (169)
3. Assembler language (161)
4. Database management package (158, 172)
5. Electronic spreadsheet package (171)
6. File management (157)
7. Fourth-generation language (162)
8. General-purpose application programs (169)
9. Graphical user interface (155)
10. Graphics package (173)
11. High-level language (161)
12. Integrated package (174)
13. Language translator program (165)
14. Machine language (160)
15. Multitasking (157)
16. Natural language (163)
17. Nonprocedural language (162)
18. Object-oriented language (164)
19. Operating environment package (155)
20. Operating system (155)
21. Programming tools (166)
22. Resource management (156)
23. Software suites (174)

24. System management programs (155)
25. System software (154)
26. System support programs (155)
27. Task management (157)
28. Telecommunications package (159, 172)

29. Trends in software (153)
30. User interface (155)
31. Utility programs (160)
32. Virtual memory (157)
33. Word processing package (169)

Review Quiz

Match one of the key terms and concepts listed above with one of the brief examples or definitions listed below. Try to find the best fit for answers that seem to fit more than one term or concept. Defend your choices.

____ 1. Programs that manage and support the operations of computers.

____ 2. Programs that direct the performance of a specific use of computers.

____ 3. An integrated system of programs that manages the operations of a computer system.

____ 4. Managing the processing of tasks in a computer system.

____ 5. Managing the use of CPU time, primary and secondary storage, and input/output devices.

____ 6. Managing the input/output, storage, and retrieval of files.

____ 7. The function that provides a means of communication between end users and an operating system.

____ 8. The use of icons, bars, buttons, and other image displays to help you get things done.

____ 9. Provides a greater memory capability than a computer's actual memory capacity.

____ 10. Serves as an end user graphics-based interface that integrates the use of the operating system and application programs.

____ 11. Manages and supports the maintenance and retrieval of data stored in databases.

____ 12. Manages and supports telecommunications in a network.

____ 13. Translates high-level instructions into machine language instructions.

____ 14. Performs housekeeping chores for a computer system.

____ 15. A category of application software that performs common information processing tasks for end users.

____ 16. Allows you to create and edit documents.

____ 17. Software available for the specific applications of end users in business, science, and other fields.

____ 18. Creates and displays a worksheet for analysis.

____ 19. Produces line, bar, and pie charts and other displays.

____ 20. A program that performs several general-purpose applications in one package.

____ 21. A group of individual general-purpose application packages that work easily together.

____ 22. Uses instructions in the form of coded strings of ones and zeros.

____ 23. Uses instructions consisting of symbols representing operation codes and storage locations.

____ 24. Uses instructions called statements that resemble human language or the standard notation of mathematics.

____ 25. Might take the form of query languages and report generators.

____ 26. Languages that tie together data and the actions that will be performed upon the data.

____ 27. You don't have to tell the computer how to do something, just what result you want.

____ 28. As easy to use as one's native tongue.

____ 29. Performing two or more operations or applications at the same time.

____ 30. Includes programming editors, debuggers, code generators and object libraries.

____ 31. Toward powerful, integrated, general-purpose, expert-assisted packages with easy-to-use graphic and natural language interfaces.

Discussion Questions

1. What major trends are occurring in software? What capabilities do you expect to see in future software packages?

2. How do the differences between system software and application software affect you as an end user?

3. Refer to the Real World Case on Bank South and Huntington Bancshares in the chapter. Why could future developments in electronic home banking affect the banking industry's choice of operating systems?

4. Why is an operating system necessary? That is, why can't an end user just load an application program in a computer and start computing?

5. Which type of user interface do you prefer: command-driven, menu-driven, or graphical user interface? Explain why.

6. Refer to the Real World Case on National Benefit Resources in the chapter. Why weren't NBR's users impressed with the groupware and integration capabilities of the software they reviewed?

7. What capabilities does a multitasking virtual memory operating system give to a business end user?

8. Should a managerial end user know how to use a programming language to develop custom programs? Explain.

9. Refer to the Real World Case on Curtice-Burns Foods in the chapter. Why do you think William DiPaulo chose a software suite instead of an integrated package?

10. Which application software packages are the most important for a managerial end user to know how to use? Explain the reasons for your choices.

Real World Problems

1. Purina Mills and Occidental Chemical: Spreadsheets and Databases

Though users may be happy with spreadsheet features, they are finding other uses for the product beyond its basic functions. More and more, spreadsheets are providing users with a familiar interface to perform complicated database-related tasks. Purina Mills, in St. Louis, uses spreadsheets as the interface to move data residing in an IBM RS/6000 to PC-based financial analysts. Senior business analyst Peter Willbrock used SAS Institute's database structure and tools to create a report writing and analysis application that lets users get this data in their spreadsheets. "We are not asking users to change the way they do things," Wellbrock noted. "And at the same time we can extend the life of some of our older systems."

"People are reluctant to step outside the familiar interface," said John McIntyre, program manager for business intelligence software at SAS. "It is the interface of choice for an entire generation of computer users whose entrance and understanding of how a computer works is framed by the spreadsheet." For example, using Excel and Sinper Corp.'s TM/1 online analytical processing software, employees at Occidental Chemical Corp., in Dallas, review the corporate database to see where product lines could be consolidated. Jim Bell, manager of manufacturing systems, said TM/1 is used to slice and dice the data, while Excel is used as the database front end and report writer. Bell noted that while spreadsheets do offer data modeling, the features are limited to small data models and do not support client/server architectures. But as simple databases, spreadsheets are easier to use than some database programs, many users find.

a. How are spreadsheet packages being used for database related tasks?

b. Why do people use spreadsheets instead of database management packages for such tasks? Do you agree with their reasoning? Why or why not?

Source: Adapted from Tim Ovellette, "Spreadsheets Mature into Sophisticated Business Tool," *Computerworld*, April 3, 1995, pp. 41, 50.

2. Enterprise Rent-A-Car: OS/2 and Application Software

Enterprise Rent-A-Car, the St. Louis-based vehicle rental and leasing operation, employs 1,000 IBM PS/2s running OS/2 at its 30 rental offices across the United States. These PCs are linked by local area networks and share data via a satellite network with 18 AS/400 midrange systems installed at the home office. Enterprise first chose OS/2 when it began automating its car-rental operations beyond its installed piecemeal DOS setup. "We decided against Microsoft Windows because we felt we needed the communications capabilities that OS/2 gave us, as well as the ability to run multiple applications concurrently," said Jim Miller, manager of Enterprise's PC department.

Enterprise runs a mix of off-the-shelf and custom-built OS/2 applications. Agents use Lotus' SmartSuite and Symantec's Activity Control Technology contact manager, along with Borland's Paradox and IBM's DB2 database managers. Enterprise also runs the Shapeware Windows-based Visio drawing program via OS/2's Win-OS2 subsystem, Miller said.

Enterprise agents have access to a custom communications utility programmed into PC Car-Book from Chrome Data Corp. The communications utility allows the agents to select the car that meets a customer's specifications and instantaneously compute costs. "We can provide information on customers, vehicles, transactions, and historical data, all of which are in our AS/400 databases," Miller said. The utility program also allows agents to use the PC Car-Book output to develop proposals for customers. The program translates the PC Car-Book data to the AS/400s, transmits it, and prints the output in a report format.

a. Why did Enterprise choose OS/2 over DOS/Windows as their operating system?

b. Did choosing OS/2 limit Enterprise's use of the application software they needed? Why or why not?

Source: Adapted from Mary Jo Foley, "OS/2 Drives Enterprise Rent-A-Car," *PCWeek*, March 27, 1995, pp. 27, 30. Reprinted from *PCWeek* Copyright © 1995 Ziff-Davis Publishing Company, L. P.

3. First Albany Corporation: Spreadsheets for Work Groups

With the success of its Notes groupware package, Lotus sees a work-group future for spreadsheets. "Industry has made the individual more productive. The return on investment will be when we can deliver a tool that can help people do more as part of the team process," said Jeff Anderholm, director of spreadsheet marketing at Lotus. For example, First Albany Corp. is leveraging Notes and 1-2-3 to help deliver timely investment analysis to its customers. Prior to the marriage of the two applications, investment reports lacked consistency and were time-consuming to prepare, according to Barry McCurdy, senior vice president and director at the Albany, New York, firm.

Information on the past and future financial performance of profiled companies is maintained as projections in a spreadsheet. Certain cells are made part of the Notes databases and serve as the basis for the investment reports which are created through Notes Field Exchange. Analysts can import updated information and spreadsheet analysis directly into the report so they can spend more time on the report narrative instead of performing data entry. "Now it takes 15 seconds instead of a half hour," McCurdy said. "The analysts can do their write-ups instead of entering numbers that are already old into the report."

a. How is First Albany supporting work group use of spreadsheets?

b. What benefits have resulted?

Source: Adapted from Tim Ovellette, "Spreadsheest Mature into Sophisticated Business Tool," *Computerworld*, April 3, 1995, p. 41. Copyright 1995 by Computerworld, Inc., Framingham, MA 01701—Reprinted from *Computerworld*.

4. DuPont and Others: Software Quality Problems

Calling the software "very, very buggy and very slow," the DuPont Co. is yanking the latest release of Microsoft Office off thousands of Macintoshes and reinstalling an earlier version. DuPont's dramatic action highlights the growing tension between vendors and users about the newest releases of desktop software. Many users say software today is more buggy and poorly supported than it was a few years ago. For example, reliability and performance issues are precisely what drove DuPont back to an earlier, more stable version.

"Microsoft Office on the Mac is a disaster," said David Pensak, principal consultant for advanced computing technology at the Wilmington, Delaware-based chemical giant. Pensak supports users in the company's research units. Even worse, he said last week, Microsoft is three months late with a promised maintenance release that is supposed to fix some bugs. However, Pensak noted that quality problems are hardly the province of any one vendor. "I am quite unhappy with the way prices are falling," he said. "To compete on hardware price, the system vendors cut their margins to the bone and then can't afford to do a really good job on software. It's happening across the industry."

"It shocks me how many bugs are still in Windows," said Robert Chambers, a software developer at Healthsource South Carolina, Inc., in Charleston. "It's amazing how tolerant users have become with an operating system you can count on crashing once or twice a day." "Overall, the quality of software has gone downhill," said James Hafen, a programmer/analyst at Megahertz Corp. in Salt Lake City. "When WordPerfect 6 for Windows came out, it was such a resource hog and had so many problems we brought in Microsoft Word, and now 70 percent of the company has converted to Word."

But it is impossible for vendors to test software on every possible user configuration, said Scott Winkler, vice president of operating systems research at Gartner Group, Inc. "No matter how hard a vendor tries to simulate everything that can occur, the only way to really find out is in the real world, sometimes long after the beta test." But not all users buy that argument. "I'm getting very upset with vendors that say, 'OK, let's do a beta,'" Pensick said. "What that means is, 'We're going to let our customers find the bugs; then we'll fix them.'"

a. What are some typical software quality problems?

b. Why are they occurring? What can be done about it?

Source: Adapted from Gary Anthes and William Brandel, "Quality Questioned," *Computerworld*, April 24, 1995, pp. 1, 14. Copyright 1995 by Computerworld, Inc., Framingham, MA 01701—Reprinted from *Computerworld*.

5. Sprint Corporation: Moving to Object-Oriented Development

Two years into its move to object-oriented programming, Sprint Corp. has reduced development time and increased the amount of code it can reuse. When Sprint set out on its object-oriented odyssey, its goals were to build a set of object code components that could be used across a variety of different applications and help provide a consistent look and feel across the business, according to Liz LaValley, assistant vice president of business systems development at the telecommunications services company. The move to objects has also helped Sprint roll out new services more quickly, LaValley said. Its Sprint Sense flat-rate calling plan, launched in January, was "rolled out in three weeks," she said. Sprint's development cycle had been 40 weeks, but it has gradually decreased during the past couple of years as developers have been able to reuse more code.

Sprint chose the Fusion methodology from Hewlett-Packard to provide some discipline for its object-oriented move, explained John Strand, director of technology planning and integration at Sprint's Network Design and Engineering Group in Overland Park, Kansas. The network management applications being built by Strand's group are large and must be distributed, and he is finding that tools to support distributed object-oriented design are still fairly weak. Another problem area, Strand said, is the lack of "open, published" interfaces to object-oriented development tools. "That is hampering us, so we're pushing vendors to provide us with interfaces to their systems so we can integrate them into our environment," he said. Strand's group is primarily using C++ but has also begun using Smalltalk to build graphical user interfaces. He would like to see better integration between the two languages. "And we'd all like to get fully automatic code generation, but that's still a ways away," he added.

a. Why is Sprint moving to object-oriented development?

b. What limitations are they experiencing?

Source: Adapted from Elizabeth Heichler, "Object Moves at Sprint," *Computerworld*, March 20, 1995, p. 73. Copyright 1995 by Computerworld, Inc., Framingham, MA 01701—Reprinted from *Computerworld*.

6. Grant Thornton LLP: Beyond Windows and Mac Interfaces

Today's graphical interface software is darn good at letting PC users get at and fiddle with data. So how come end user productivity isn't through the corporate roof by now? One answer lies in questioning the obvious: the Windows and Macintosh interfaces found on the majority of software today, which may have stunted the imaginations of some interface designers, according to Craig Lashmet, manager of the advanced technologies group at Chicago consultancy Grant Thornton LLP. For example, a large Chicago-area retailer signed on Grant Thornton last year to learn how to "think beyond the confines of Windows," Lashmet said. The retailer, like most user companies embracing structured usability concepts, did not want to be named for fear of tipping off competitors about what it hopes will be pivotal business advantages. The company is striving to make customer service data as accessible to users as possible. One of its goals, for example, is to make information never more than one mouse click away, Lashmet said.

Such single-click thinking can lead to innovation, he said. Take active icons: Instead of building an application where all icons continuously sit on a screen, Grant Thornton is helping the retailer create icons that pop up only under certain circumstances. A wrench, for example, will appear when system maintenance needs to be scheduled. Interfaces in the not-so-distant future are expected to carry more of these active icons, along with color-coded data, pictures, and far fewer row-and-column-style constructs because the human eye can pick up information faster than fingers can type and click. Some skeptics might doubt that a five-second savings of meander time on a single screen in an application means much. But Rick Poston, human factors team leader at IBM's AIX division in Austin, Texas, painted this picture:

Assume that 200 workers, each paid $15 an hour, access that screen once every 10 minutes during a typical day. The company ends up paying $1 per day per worker for that five seconds of lost screen-navigation time. Over the course of a year (with no vacation or holiday time), say goodbye to approximately $52,000. And that is just for a single screen in a single application. Get the picture?

a. Why are some businesses dissatisfied with the Windows and Macintosh interfaces on their software?

b. What alternatives are they exploring? What do they hope to gain?

Source: Adapted from Kim Nash, "New Age Interfaces," *Computerworld Client/Server Journal*, June 1995, p. 48.

Application Exercises

1. ABC Department Stores

ABC Department Stores would like to acquire software to do the following tasks. Identify what software packages they need.

a. Support telecommunications among their end users.

b .Control access and use of the hardware, software, and data resources of the system.

c. Monitor and record how the system resources are being used.

d. Make it easier to update and integrate their databases.

e. Add a graphical user interface and multitasking capabilities to their microcomputer operating systems.

f. Type correspondence and reports.

g. Analyze rows and columns of figures.

h. Develop line, bar, and pie charts.

2. Evaluating Software Packages

Have you used one of the software packages mentioned in this chapter?

a. Briefly describe the advantages and disadvantages of one of the packages you have used so far.

b. How would such a package help you in a present or future job situation?

c. How would you improve the package you used?

3. Morris Manufacturing Company: Spreadsheet Analysis

Susan Sanders is the assistant manager of the personnel department of Morris Manufacturing Company. She has been given the responsibility of selecting a copy machine for her office. After some preliminary research, she determines that there are three copiers available that will serve the needs of her office: the Canica 12000, the Duplicon Plus, and the Repro 882. Each of these copiers is available on an annual-lease basis. For each copier there is a fixed lease fee, plus some additional expenses that are proportional to the number of copies produced. The expected costs of each copier are as follows:

Canica 12000—This copier leases for $2,500 for the year. There is a charge of 1/2 cent per copy for service and maintenance of this copier. Paper and expendable copier supplies are expected to cost 2.5 cents per copy. This copier will handle all types of jobs automatically.

Duplicon Plus—This copier leases for $3,200 per year. Service and maintenance are included in the lease cost. Paper and expendable copier supplies are expected to cost 2.3 cents per copy. This copier will handle all types of jobs automatically.

Repro 882—This copier leases for $1,900 for the year. Service and maintenance cost $50 per hour, and it is expected that one hour of maintenance will be needed for each 7,500 copies made. Paper and expendable copier supplies are expected to cost 2.8 cents per copy. This copier has limited sorting features. The need for manual sorting is expected to require one hour of additional labor for each 3,000 copies made, at an average rate of $9.50 per hour.

Last year Susan's office made 68,000 copies. The number of copies needed this year is unknown and could range from the same level as last year to as much as 50 percent higher. Susan wants to be able to see how the costs of the copiers will compare if the number of copies is the same as last year, and if the number of copies is 25 percent or 50 percent higher than last year.

a. Create a spreadsheet that will let Susan compare the costs of the three alternative copiers and will let her see how changes in the number of copies affect these costs. Make a printout of your spreadsheet showing the costs for each copier if the number of copies is the same as last year.

b. Do what-if analysis. That is, analyze what would happen if the number of copies were 25 percent or 50 percent higher than last year. Print out the spreadsheets that result from these changes.

c. After discussions with several users, Susan finds that they have needed an hour of service for every 5,000 copies made. Make this adjustment on your spreadsheet and get a printout showing how this affects the relative cost of the copiers.

d. Based on the information in this case, which copier would you recommend? Why?

4. Software Training at ABC Company

ABC Company has recently purchased microcomputers for use by all office staff. All employees in your department are to be trained in the use of various software packages. Training is available for DOS, word processing, spreadsheet, and database management software. Each employee must complete a total of at least 16 hours of training but is free to choose the type of training to meet his or her own needs. Training is offered by your organization's information center. Employees are responsible for scheduling their own training.

You have been assigned the task of keeping track of the training records of employees in your department. Each time an employee in your department attends a training session, you are notified of the employee's name, the type of training, and the number of hours. The training received by your department's employee to date is shown below. Assume that you have been maintaining this data in handwritten form but now wish to create a spreadsheet to maintain this information and record all future changes.

ABC Company Software Training History

Employee Name	DOS	Word Processing	Spreadsheet	Database
Allen, D.	2	0	4	0
Barnett, S.	0	4	0	0
Davis, J.	4	0	0	4
Evans, W.	2	4	0	0
Forbes, M.	2	0	4	4
Grant, V.	0	0	0	0
Jenkins, J.	3	6	0	0
Milton, J.	0	4	4	0
Price, T.	2	0	4	4
Travis, B.	0	4	4	0

a. Using spreadsheet software, create an application to store the information shown below. Your spreadsheet should also indicate the total hours of training for each employee and the total amount of training (across all employees in your department) in each type of software. Print a copy of this spreadsheet.

b. You receive word from the information center that the following additional training has been completed: Davis, J., spreadsheet, four hours; Evans, W., DOS, two hours; and Forbes, M., word processing, six hours. Post the information to your spreadsheet and then print an updated copy of your spreadsheet.

Review Quiz Answers

1. 25	9. 32	17. 2	25. 7
2. 1	10. 19	18. 5	26. 18
3. 20	11. 4	19. 10	27. 17
4. 26	12. 28	20. 12	28. 16
5. 22	13. 13	21. 23	29. 15
6. 6	14. 31	22. 14	30. 21
7. 30	15. 8	23. 3	31. 29
8. 9	16. 33	24. 11	

Selected References

1. *Business Software Review, Computerworld, PC Magazine, PC Week,* and *Software Digest.* (Examples of good sources of current information on computer software packages.)

2. Datapro Corporation. *Datapro Reports.* (Series of regular detailed reports on selected software packages).

3. Ezzel, Ben. "Windows NT: The Power Under the Hood." *PC Magazine,* June 15, 1993.

4. Jacobsen, Ivar; Maria Ericsson; and Agenta Jacobsen. *The Object Advantage: Business Process Reengineering with Object Technology.* New York: ACM Press, 1995.

5. Simon, Barry. "Painless Programming." *Windows Sources,* June 1993.

6. Slitz, John. "Object Technology Profiles." Supplement to *Computerworld,* June, 1994.

7. Special OS/2 Warp Edition, *Personal Systems,* January, 1995.

8. "The CW Guide to Operating Systems." *Computerworld,* April 24, 1995.

William DiPaulo of Curtice-Burns Foods: The Case for Software Suites

At Curtice-Burns Foods, Inc., in Rochester, New York, we make our information systems decisions not on technical or emotional biases but by answering the question, "Is this the best business decision?" Because the food industry is extremely competitive, I'm thrilled when I can offer technology that will not only increase employee productivity but also require less support and be more cost-effective than other options.

We began selective user testing of the Microsoft Office suite nine months ago, and started a formal rollout to corporate headquarters two months ago. We're converting a 45-person Novell NetWare LAN from DOS, Lotus 1-2-3, and WordPerfect to Windows for Workgroups using Microsoft's Office. We'll be rolling out suites to our divisions across the country as business needs dictate.

Purchase price is the most obvious advantage suites offer. If you buy your suite at the competitive upgrade cost—and most people do—you will spend one-half or one-third of what you would on individual "best-of-breed" packages. Although these savings are significant, we've found that software's initial purchase price accounts for only about 20 percent of the cost of ownership. Support accounts for the remaining 80 percent. We believe suites will dramatically reduce support costs by eliminating application configuration and integration problems, as well as problems associated with dealing with multiple vendors.

When it comes to integration, suites have a big advantage. Suite applications share a common look and feel. They share common spell checkers and grammar and charting tools. This makes end users more comfortable and translates directly into reduced training and support costs.

In addition to large cost savings, better integration, simplified and cost-efficient support, and reduced training time, suites offer the strength of a single-vendor relationship, ease of upgrade management, and version control. When you upgrade your suite, you upgrade all applications and versions in it.

Our productivity increases have been impressive so far.

One executive secretary who used to support four people under our DOS-based multivendor system now supports nine people using Office. The suite enables her to share applications by dragging and dropping between them, reducing the need to input redundant information. We used to go to an outside company to produce our presentations; now the secretary can create these in-house using Microsoft's PowerPoint. Microsoft's Mail lets her electronically route documents she used to copy, print, and deliver manually.

Historically, discrepancies between a suite application and the market-leading best-of-breed application in a particular area were significant. Today, for 95 percent of business users, applications features tend to be equitable from an overall functional standpoint. Given this equity, *best-of-breed* becomes a misnomer. Office application choice has really become a support issue, and companies can no longer afford to support unlimited flavors of business applications.

As our computing environment gets more complex, including the move to a client/server setup, the ability to keep the PC software platform stable is of the utmost importance. Frankly, as systems professionals, we have enough to worry about without arguing about business applications. Thanks to suites, users don't have to worry about their business applications and can focus on their business needs.

Note: William DiPaulo is corporate network manager at Curtice-Burns Foods, Inc.

CASE STUDY QUESTIONS

1. What are the advantages and disadvantages of software suites?

2. Why does DiPaulo say that suites increase office productivity?

3. If cost was not a factor, would you choose several "best-of-breed" packages or a software suite?

Source: Adapted from Terry Brewster and William DiPaulo, "Best of Breed Apps vs. Suites," *Computerworld*, April 24, 1995, p. 121–22. Copyright 1995 by Computerworld, Inc., Framingham, MA 01701—Reprinted from *Computerworld*.

Managerial Overview: Telecommunications

CHAPTER OUTLINE

LEARNING OBJECTIVES

The purpose of this chapter is to give you an introduction to important telecommunications concepts needed by business end users.

Section I discusses basic trends and functions of the telecommunications networks that are vital to the operations and management of today's global business enterprise.

Section II reviews some of the major technical characteristics of telecommunications networks needed for a basic understanding of this technology by managerial end users.

After reading and studying this chapter, you should be able to:

1. Identify the basic components, functions, and types of telecommunications networks.

2. Identify several major developments and trends in the industries, technology, and applications of telecommunications.

3. Explain the functions of major types of telecommunications network hardware, software, and media.

Why Telecommunications is Important

Empower a business with a network that spans every location, and that organization can operate more efficiently and more creatively. By electronically linking workers, a network enables all employees to work together as efficiently as if they were in the same work group. A network allows people to make decisions based on the most current information; they don't have to rely on a report that was generated yesterday. This leads to better decisions and higher productivity. Propelled by the right corporate philosophy, an enterprisewide network can help even a monolithic corporation act like an agile start-up company [17].

End users need to communicate electronically to succeed in today's global information society. Managers, end users, and their organizations need to electronically exchange data and information with other end users, customers, suppliers, and other organizations. Only through the use of telecommunications can they perform their work activities, manage organizational resources, and compete successfully in today's fast-changing global economy. Thus, many organizations today could not survive without interconnected *networks* of computers to service the information processing and communications needs of their end users. As a managerial end user, you will thus be expected to make or participate in decisions regarding a great variety of telecommunications options. That's why we need to study the applications, technology, and managerial implications of telecommunications. See Figure 6.1.

Telecommunications is the sending of information in any form (e.g., voice, data, text, and images) from one place to another using electronic or light-emitting media. *Data communications* is a more specific term that describes the transmitting and receiving of data over communication links between one or more computer systems and a variety of input/output terminals. The terms *teleprocessing, telematics,* and

FIGURE 6.1
Telecommunications networks are a vital part of today's businesses.

Courtesy of Seth Resnick © 1992.

telephony may also be used since they reflect the integration of computer-based information processing with telecommunications and telephone technologies. However, all forms of telecommunications now rely heavily on computers and computerized devices. For this reason, the broader term *telecommunications* can be used as a synonym for data communications activities. Therefore, in this text, we will use these terms interchangeably.

Telecommunications networks provide invaluable capabilities to an organization and its end users. For example, some networks enable work groups to communicate electronically and share hardware, software, and data resources. Other networks let a company process sales transactions immediately from many remote locations, exchange business documents electronically with its customers and suppliers, or remotely monitor and control production processes. Telecommunications networks can also interconnect the computer systems of a business so their computing power can be shared by end users throughout an enterprise. And, of course, telecommunications networks enhance collaboration and communication among individuals both inside and outside an organization.

Figure 6.2 emphasizes the many possible applications of telecommunications. It groups a large number of telecommunications applications into the major categories of electronic communications systems, electronic meeting systems, and business process systems. Also note that these applications can be supported by several major types of telecommunications architectures. We will discuss these architectures in this chapter, and the end user and enterprise applications of telecommunications in Chapters 8 and 9.

Applications of Telecommunications

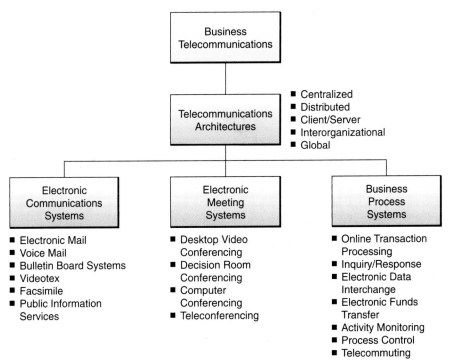

FIGURE 6.2
Applications of telecommunications. Note the major categories and types of applications supported by telecommunications networks.

Trends in Telecommunications

Major trends occurring in the field of telecommunications have a significant impact on management decisions in this area. Informed managerial end users should thus be aware of major trends in telecommunications industries, technologies, and applications that significantly increase the decision alternatives confronting their organizations. See Figure 6.3.

Industry Trends

The competitive arena for telecommunications service has changed dramatically in the United States, from a few government-regulated monopolies to many fiercely competitive suppliers of telecommunications services. With the breakup of AT&T and the Bell System in 1984, local and global telecommunications networks and services became available from a variety of large and small telecommunications companies. Hundreds of companies now offer businesses and end users a choice of everything from long-distance telephone services and access to communications satellite channels, to mobile radio and cellular phone services. Public information network services such as electronic mail, bulletin board systems, and commercial data banks are other examples. Thus, the services and vendor options available to meet a company's telecommunications needs have increased significantly, as has a manager's decision-making alternatives.

Technology Trends

Digital technology will make the phones we use today seem like two cans joined by a string. Within perhaps four years, we will see cellular service that costs almost as little to use as the corner phone booth, handheld communicators that will let us scribble notes with an electronic stylus and zap them wirelessly anywhere on earth, and networks that will automatically deliver our calls to the people we want to reach, wherever they happen to be. Travelers will commune with the office network as fully and easily as if they were sitting at their desks; workers with computers will commingle video, voice, data, and images on a single line as they seamlessly collaborate with faraway colleages [12].

Telecommunications is being revolutionized by a change from analog to digital network technologies. Telecommunications has always depended on voice-oriented analog transmission systems designed to transmit the variable electrical

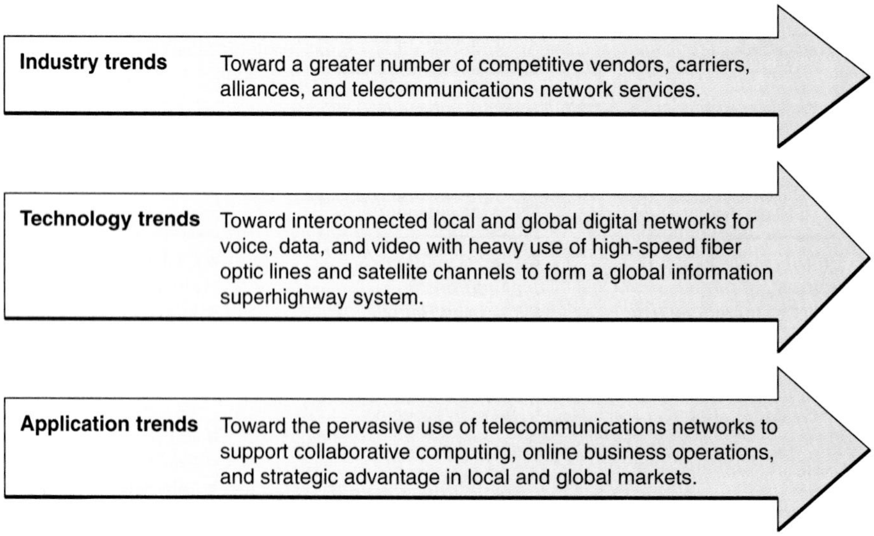

FIGURE 6.3
Major trends in telecommunications.

Industry trends	Toward a greater number of competitive vendors, carriers, alliances, and telecommunications network services.
Technology trends	Toward interconnected local and global digital networks for voice, data, and video with heavy use of high-speed fiber optic lines and satellite channels to form a global information superhighway system.
Application trends	Toward the pervasive use of telecommunications networks to support collaborative computing, online business operations, and strategic advantage in local and global markets.

frequencies generated by the sound waves of the human voice. However, local and global telecommunications networks are rapidly converting to digital transmission technologies, which transmit information in the form of discrete pulses, as computers do. This provides (1) significantly higher transmission speeds, (2) the movement of larger amounts of information, (3) greater economy, and (4) much lower error rates than analog systems. In addition, digital technologies, including ISDN (Integrated Services Digital Network), will allow telecommunications networks to carry multiple types of communications (data, voice, video) on the same circuits.

Another major trend in telecommunications technology is a change in communications media. Many telecommunications networks are switching from copper wire-based media (such as coaxial cable) and land-based microwave relay systems to fiber optic lines and communications satellite transmissions. Fiber optic transmission, which uses pulses of laser-generated light, offers significant advantages in terms of reduced size and installation effort, vastly greater communication capacity, much faster transmission speeds, and freedom from electrical interference. Satellite transmission offers significant advantages in speed and capacity for organizations that need to transmit massive quantities of data over global networks. These trends in technology give organizations more alternatives in overcoming the limitations of their present telecommunications systems.

Open Systems

Clearly, the direction of the computer field today is toward "increased connectivity"— where any computer in an organization, from mainframe to micro, can communicate with any other one. There are a lot of technical hurdles to overcome before reaching this goal. But there are also some key management decisions and policies that can help ease the task [16].

Another major telecommunications trend is toward easier access by end users to the computing resource of interconnected networks. This trend is based on both industry and technical moves toward building networks based on an *open systems* architecture. **Open systems** are information systems that use common standards for hardware, software, applications, and networking. Open systems create a computing environment that is open to easy access by end users and their networked computer systems. Open systems provide greater *connectivity,* that is, the ability of networked computers and other devices to easily access and communicate with each other and share information. An open systems architecture also provides a high degree of network *interoperability.* That is, open systems enable the many different applications of end users to be accomplished using the different varieties of computer systems, software packages, and databases provided by a variety of interconnected networks. Sometimes, software known as *middleware* may be used to help diverse systems work together. Network architectures like the Open Systems Interconnection (OSI) model of the International Standards Organization promote open, flexible, and efficient standards for the development of open telecommunications networks.

Application Trends

The changes in telecommunications industries and technologies just mentioned are causing a significant change in the business use of telecommunications. The trend toward more vendors, services, advanced technologies, and open systems dramatically increases the number of feasible applications. Thus, telecommunications is playing a more important role in support of the operations, management, and strategic objectives of both large and small companies. An organization's telecommunications function is no longer relegated to office telephone systems, long-distance calling arrangements, and a limited amount of data communications with corporate mainframes. Instead, it has become an integral part of local and global networks of computers which are used to cut costs, improve the collaboration of work groups, develop online operational processes, share resources, lock in customers and suppliers, and develop new products and services. This makes telecommunications a more complex and important decision area for businesses which must increasingly compete in both domestic and global markets.

The Information Superhighway

The trend toward open, high-speed, digital networks with fiber optic and satellite links has made the concept of an **information superhighway** technically possible, and has captured the interest of both business and government. In this concept, local, regional, nationwide, and global networks will be integrated into a vast "network of networks." The information superhighway system would connect individuals, households, businesses, government agencies, libraries, universities, and all other institutions and would support interactive voice, data, video, and multimedia communications. See Figure 6.4.

As championed by then Senator and now Vice President Albert Gore, the information superhighway could provide a National Information Infrastructure (NII) and economic network that would be the equivalent in its economic impact of the transcontinental railway and interstate highway systems combined. Critics question whether the potential benefits of the superhighway would be worth its cost [6]. The proposed national data highway system would be a massive undertaking, costing hundreds of billions of dollars and taking several decades to construct. For a example, government estimates of the investment cost include investment by private industry of $2 trillion, with the government investing $200 billion over 10–50 years [5].

Why build such a superhighway network? Proponents argue that the information superhighway (or *infobahn*) would create a national information infrastructure that would dramatically increase business efficiency and competitiveness by improving economic communications, collaboration, and information gathering. For example, the information superhighway could use electronic mail, videoconferencing,

FIGURE 6.4
Overview of the information superhighway.

- **Names:** Information superhighway, national data highway, infobahn, national information infrastructure.
- **Purpose:** Create a national telecommunications infrastructure of interconnected local, regional, and global networks to support all economic, societal, and individual telecommunications.
- **Participants:** All individuals, households, businesses, government agencies, libraries, schools, universities, and other institutions.
- **Communications:** Interactive voice, video, data, and multimedia telecommunications.
- **Examples:** Universal electronic mail, video conferencing, electronic data interchange, interactive home shopping, education, entertainment, and all forms of online, realtime computing.
- **Builders:** Private industry (telecommunications companies, entertainment companies, publishing companies, etc.) and the federal government.
- **Cost and time estimates:** From hundreds of billions to several trillions of dollars, over 10 to 50 years.

and electronic databank services to enable businesses throughout the country to build products faster through an electronic collaboration in the product design process. Or the highway could support an interactive video home shopping and entertainment system that could revolutionize the retailing and entertainment industries [5]. In any event, the information superhighway promises to have a major impact on developments in telecommunications and on our nation's economic and social life in the years to come.

A Telecommunications Network Model

Before we discuss the use and management of telecommunications, we should understand the basic components of a *telecommunications* network. Generally, a *communications network* is any arrangement where a *sender* transmits a *message* to a *receiver* over a *channel* consisting of some type of *medium.* Figure 6.5 illustrates a simple conceptual model of a **telecommunications network,** which shows that it consists of five basic categories of components:

- **Terminals,** such as networked microcomputer workstations or video terminals. Of course, any input/output device that uses telecommunications networks to transmit or receive data is a terminal, including telephones, office equipment, and the *transaction terminals* discussed in Chapter 4.
- **Telecommunications processors,** which support data transmission and reception between terminals and computers. These devices, such as *modems* and *front-end processors,* perform a variety of control and support functions in a telecommunications network. For example, they convert data from digital to analog and back, code and decode data, and control the accuracy and efficiency of the communications flow between computers and terminals in a telecommunications network.
- **Telecommunications channels and media** over which data are transmitted and received. Telecommunications *channels* use combinations of *media,* such as copper wires, coaxial cables, fiber optic cables, microwave systems, and communications satellites, to interconnect the other components of a telecommunications network.

FIGURE 6.5
The five basic components in a telecommunications network: (1) terminals, (2) telecommunications processors, (3) telecommunications channels and media, (4) computers, and (5) telecommunications software.

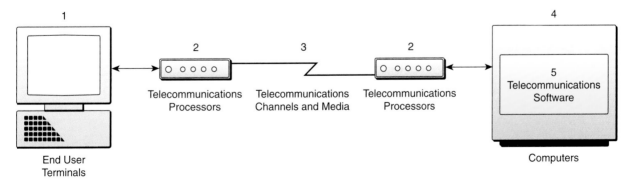

- **Computers** of all sizes and types are interconnected by telecommunications networks so that they can carry out their information processing assignments. For example, a mainframe computer may serve as a *host computer* for a large network, assisted by a minicomputer serving as a *front-end processor,* while a microcomputer may act as a *network server* for a small network of microcomputer workstations.

- **Telecommunications control software** consists of programs that control telecommunications activities and manage the functions of telecommunications networks. Examples include *telecommunications monitors* for mainframe host computers, *network operating systems* for microcomputer network servers, and *communications packages* for microcomputers.

No matter how large and complex real-world telecommunications networks may appear to be, these five basic categories of components must be at work to support an organization's telecommunications activities. This framework can thus be used to help you understand the various types of telecommunications networks in use today.

Types of Telecommunications Networks

There are many different types of telecommunications networks. However, from an end user's point of view, there are two basic types: *wide area* and *local area* networks.

Wide Area Networks

Telecommunications networks covering a large geographic area are called *remote networks, long-distance networks,* or, more popularly, **wide area networks** (WANs). Networks that cover a large city or metropolitan area (*metropolitan area networks*) can also be included in this category. Such large networks have become a necessity for carrying out the day-to-day activities of many business and government organizations and their end users. Thus, WANs are used by manufacturing firms, banks, retailers, distributors, transportation companies, and government agencies to transmit and receive information among their employees, customers, suppliers, and other organizations across cities, regions, countries, or the world. Figure 6.6 illustrates an example of a global wide area network for a major multinational corporation.

Local Area Networks

Local area networks (LANs) connect computers and other information processing devices within a limited physical area, such as an office, a building, manufacturing plant, or other work site. LANs have become commonplace in many organizations for providing telecommunications network capabilities that link end users in offices, departments, and other work groups.

LANs use a variety of telecommunications media, such as ordinary telephone wiring, coaxial cable, or even wireless radio systems to interconnect microcomputer workstations and computer peripherals. To communicate over the network, each PC must have a circuit board installed called a *network interface card.* Most LANs use a powerful microcomputer having a large hard disk capacity, called a *file server* or **network server,** that contains a **network operating system** program that controls telecommunications and the use of network resources. For example, it distributes copies of common data files and software packages to the other microcomputers in the network and controls access to laser printers and other network peripherals. See Figure 6.7.

LANs allow end users in a work group to communicate electronically; share hardware, software, and data resources; and pool their efforts when working on

FIGURE 6.6
The wide area network (WAN) of Falconbridge Limited interconnects a variety of local area networks (LANs).

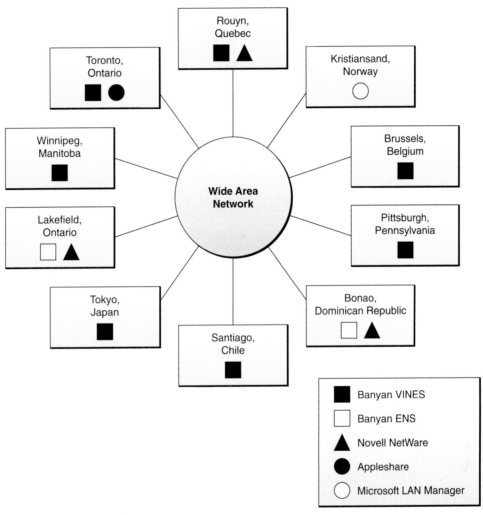

Source: Courtesy of Banyan Systems Incorporated.

group projects. For example, a project team of end users whose microcomputer workstations are interconnected by a LAN can send each other *electronic mail* messages and share the use of laser printers and hard magnetic disk units, copies of electronic spreadsheets or word processing documents, and project databases. LANs have thus become a more popular alternative for end user and work group computing than the use of terminals connected to larger computers.

Most local area networks are eventually connected to other LANs or wide area networks to create **internetworks.** That's because end users need to communicate with the workstations of colleagues on other LANs, or to access the computing resources and databases at other company locations or at other organizations. This frequently takes the form of *client/server* networks, where end user microcomputer workstations (*clients*) are connected to LAN *servers* and interconnected to other LANs and

Internetworks

FIGURE 6.7
A local area network (LAN). Note how this LAN allows users to share hardware, software, and data resources.

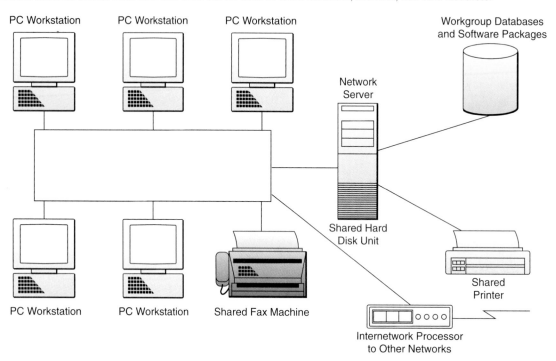

their servers, or to WANs and their mainframe *superservers.* Local area networks rely on **internetwork processors,** such as *bridges, routers, hubs,* or *gateways,* to make *internetworking* connections to other LANs and wide area networks.

The goal of such internetwork architectures is to create a seamless "network of networks" within each organization and between organizations that have business relationships. Such networks are designed to be open systems, whose connectivity provides easy access and interoperability among its interconnected workstations, computers, computer-based devices, databases, and other networks. Many companies, universities, and other organizations are creating such internetwork structures. Figure 6.8 is an example of an internetwork architecture.

Client Server Computing

Client/server technology promises many things to many people: to end users, easier access to corporate and external data; to managers, dramatically lower costs for processing; to programmers, reduced maintenance; to corporate planners, an infrastructure that enables business processes to be reengineered for strategic benefits. Whether client/server lives up to these promises will depend in large part on how carefully it is planned for, and how intelligently policies are put forth to manage it [13].

Client/server computing has become the model for a new *information architecture* that will take enterprisewide computing into the 21st century. We introduced client/server networks in Chapter 4, in our discussion of networked computer systems. Computing power has rapidly become distributed and interconnected throughout many organizations through networks of all types of computers. More

FIGURE 6.8
An example of the internetwork architecture of South Boston Savings Bank.

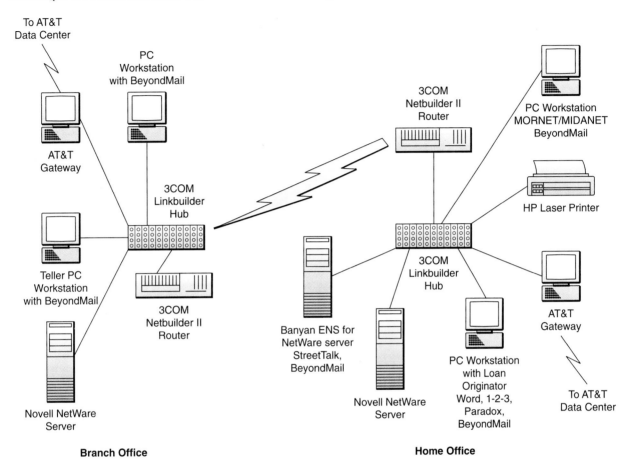

Branch Office

Home Office

Source: Courtesy of Banyan Systems Incorporated.

and more, networked computer systems are taking the form of client/server networks. In a client/server network, end user microcomputer workstations are the **clients.** They are interconnected by local area networks and share application processing with LAN **servers,** which also manage the networks. These local area networks may also be interconnected to other LANs and wide area networks of client workstations and servers. See Figures 6.9 and 6.10.

With client/server computing, end users at client LAN workstations can handle a broad range of information processing tasks. They can thus perform some or most of the processing of their business applications. This includes data entry and other user interface activities, inquiry response, transaction processing, updating databases, generating reports, and providing decision support. LAN servers can share application processing, manage work group collaboration, and control common hardware, software, and databases. Thus, data can be completely processed locally, where most input and output (and errors and problems) must be handled anyway, while still providing access to the workstations and servers in other networks. This provides computer processing more tailored to the needs of end users

FIGURE 6.9
Client/server networks enable cooperative processing among end user workstations and network servers.

Courtesy of Hewlett-Packard Company.

and increases information processing efficiency and effectiveness as users become more responsible for their own applications systems.

Client/server computing also lets large central-site computers handle those jobs they can do best, such as high-volume transaction processing, communications network security and control, and maintenance and control of large corporate databases. User clients at local sites can access these *superservers* to receive corporatewide management information or transmit summary transaction data reflecting local site activities.

Distributed Processing

Client/server computing is the latest form of **distributed processing.** In *distributed processing,* information processing activities in an organization are accomplished by using a network of computers interconnected by telecommunications links instead of relying on one large *centralized* computer facility or on the *decentralized* operation of several independent computers. For example, a distributed processing network may consist of mainframes, minicomputers, and microcomputers, dispersed over a wide geographic area and interconnected by wide area networks. Or it may take the form of a client/server network of end user workstations and network servers distributed within user departments in interconnected local area networks.

Cooperative Processing

Client/server computing may also involve **cooperative processing.** Cooperative processing allows the various types of computers in a distributed processing network to share the processing of parts of an end user's application. Application software packages are available which have common user interfaces and functions so they can

FIGURE 6.10

A client/server model for distributed and cooperative processing. Note the functions performed by different types of computers acting as clients, servers, and superservers for the Westland Group; a Wisconsin banking and insurance company.

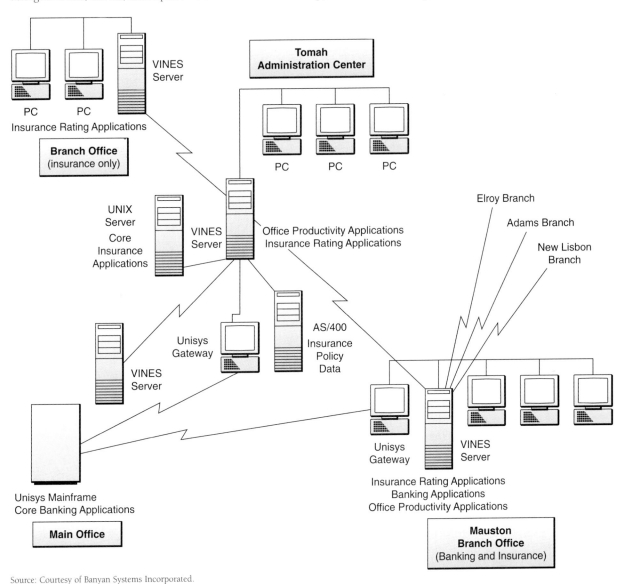

Source: Courtesy of Banyan Systems Incorporated.

operate consistently on networks of micro, mini, and mainframe computer systems. For example, an end user could use a spreadsheet package provided to his or her microcomputer workstations by a local area network server to perform financial analysis on databases managed by a corporate mainframe.

Many of the applications of telecommunications we have just mentioned can be classified as **interorganizational networks.** As Figure 6.11 illustrates, such networks link a company's wide area and local area networks to the networks of its customers,

Interorganizational Networks

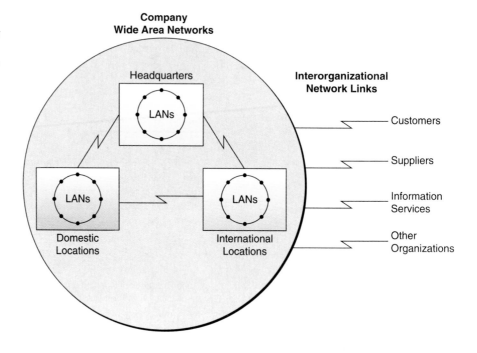

suppliers, information service providers, and other organizations. For example, you can think of a computerized account inquiry system for access by customers as an example of an interorganizational network. So is the use of electronic document interchange, which links the computers of a company with its suppliers and customers. Accessing information services such as Dow-Jones News Retrieval or the data banks of government agencies for information about market and economic conditions is another example. Electronic funds transfer applications also depend on interorganizational networks established among banks, businesses, employees, customers, and suppliers.

Thus, the business use of telecommunications has moved beyond the boundaries of work groups and the organization. Now many business firms have extended their telecommunications networks to their customers and suppliers, both domestically and internationally. As we will see in Chapter 11, such *interorganizational systems* build new strategic business relationships and alliances with those *stakeholders* in an attempt to increase and lock in their business, while locking out competitors. Also, transaction processing costs are frequently reduced, and the quality of service increases. In addition, the availability of external information about industry, market, economic, and political developments provides better information for managerial decision making. Because of these benefits, the trend toward increased connectivity between the networks of an organization and its external stakeholders is expected to continue.

The Internet

The Internet is the largest "network of networks" today, and the closest model we have to the information superhighway of tomorrow. The Internet (the Net) is a rapidly growing global web of thousands of business, educational, and research networks connecting millions of computers and their users in over 100 countries to

■ **E-mail:** Exchange electronic mail with millions of Internet users.

■ **Usenet:** Post messages on bulletin board systems formed by thousands of special interest discussion groups.

■ **Internet Relay Chat:** Hold realtime conversations with Internet users around the world on hundreds of discussion channels.

■ **File Transfer Protocol (FTP):** Download data files, programs, reports, articles, magazines, books, pictures, sounds, and other types of files from thousands of sources to your computer system.

■ **Telenet:** Log on to and use thousands of Internet computer systems around the world.

■ **World Wide Web:** Point and click your way to thousands of hyperlinked Internet sites and resources using graphical browser software like Mosaic and Netscape.

FIGURE 6.12
Important telecommunications services on the Internet.

each other. The Internet evolved from a research and development network (ARPANET) established in 1969 by the U.S. Defense Department to enable corporate, academic, and government researchers to communicate with E-mail and share data and computing resources. The Net doesn't have a central computer system or telecommunications center. Instead each message sent has an address code so any computer in the network can forward it to its destination [8, 9].

The Internet doesn't have a headquarters or governing body. The Internet society in Reston, Virginia, is a volunteer group of individual and corporate members who promote use of the Internet and the development of new communications standards or *protocols*. These common standards are the key to the free flow of messages among the widely different computers and networks in the system. The Internet is growing rapidly. For example, the Internet more than doubled in size in 1993, and again in 1994, growing to over 5 million host computer networks and over 20 million users in early 1995. The monthly rate of growth of the Internet was estimated at between 7 to 10 percent per month. One of Internet's founders, Vinton Cerf, expects the Internet to eventually interconnect over 1 billion networks [1, 2].

The most popular Internet application is E-mail. Internet E-mail is fast, faster than many public networks. Messages usually arrive in seconds or a few minutes, anywhere in the world. And Internet E-mail messages can take the form of data, text, fax, and video files. The Internet also supports bulletin board systems formed by thousands of special interest groups. Anyone can post messages on thousands of topics for interested users to read. Other popular applications include accessing files and databases from libraries and thousands of organizations, logging on to other computers in the network, and holding realtime conversations with other Internet users. See Figure 6.12.

Business on the Internet

No discussion of the business applications of telecommunications would be complete today without mention of the Internet. From small businesses to blue chip companies like General Electric, IBM, Merrill Lynch, Motorola, and Xerox, business use of the Internet has expanded rapidly. By 1995, over 1.5 million of the host networks on the Internet belonged to businesses or their research labs [2, 16]. Businesses are connecting their networks to the Internet for several reasons. One is the ease of worldwide communications and collaboration through Internet's global

E-mail and bulletin board systems. Another reason is the access to a vast range of information provided by the networks on the Internet.

But businesses are also connecting to the Internet because it represents the wave of the future in business telecommunications. Internet expert Mary Cronin, of Boston College, says that "the most compelling argument for connecting is that the Internet is the biggest and earliest manifestation of the way business is going to be conducted from now on. Networked information and communication are the standard for the future" [4]. For businesses, the information superhighway may be years away, but the Internet is available now.

Many businesses use the Internet primarily as a way to send E-mail messages to colleagues anywhere in the world. For example, IBM employees used the Internet to exchange 580,000 messages with outsiders in just one month [16]. Businesses also rely on the Internet to support worldwide collaboration among their employees and consultants, customers, and suppliers. They use the Internet to link their workstations together to form *virtual work groups* to work on joint projects such as product development, marketing campaigns, and scientific research.

Another major business use of the Internet is gathering information. You can make online searches for information in a variety of ways. Hundreds of library catalogues from university libraries to the Library of Congress are available, as are electronic versions of numerous academic and industry journals. You can also access hundreds of databases, downloading everything from the latest satellite weather photos from NASA to world almanac excerpts from the U.S. Central Intelligence Agency. You can also sit in electronically on thousands of computer conferences, work sessions, E-mail exchanges, and bulletin board postings run by the members of thousands of Internet special-interest groups. Or you could place yourself on the E-mail mailing list of any Internet special interest group, industry association, business, or government agency in which you have an interest.

Getting to any of the vast array of information used to be difficult. However, a variety of software packages have been developed to make navigating the Internet easier. For example, you could use a program called Gopher to check the White House server, which contains the President's schedule for today. Or you could use your mouse and programs like Mosaic or Netscape to point and click your way through a network of multimedia Internet information sources called the World Wide Web. Gopher and Mosaic are distributed free to any Internet user who requests them [2, 22]. See Figure 6.13.

Other uses of the Internet are developing as companies investigate its business potential. For example many companies view the millions of members of the Internet as a vast market of potential customers. Thus, they have developed *home page* sites on the World Wide Web that provide multimedia versions of advertising, press releases, new product demonstrations, product catalogues, and shopping malls. However, early attempts by some direct mail companies met with almost unanimous resistance, so companies are now being more selective in their approaches and offerings [15]. Still, the Internet is viewed by many companies as an electronic highway on which to test drive their business strategies for the information superhighway of the future.

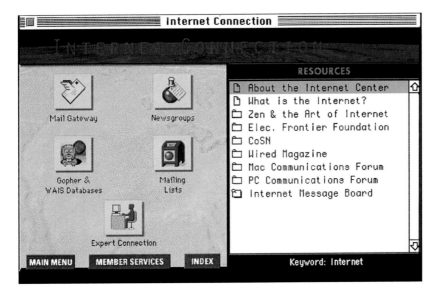

Courtesy of America OnLine, Inc.

FIGURE 6.13
You can access the Internet through the Internet Connection options of America OnLine.

West American T-Shirt Co.: Entrepreneurship on the Internet

Dave Asprey used to peddle T-shirts the old-fashioned way—by selling them at outdoor fairs. Then in early 1994, the 22-year-old computer major at California State University discovered the Internet. Soon Asprey was posting enticing descriptions of his shirts and their coffee-inspired designs on a newsgroup (an Internet discussion group) dedicated to people addicted to the pleasures of caffeine. Now, Asprey, president of West American T-shirt Co. in Manteca, California, is selling hundreds of T-shirts a month to customers all over the world and raking in thousands of dollars in sales.

"It won't make anyone a millionaire," says Asprey, who's planning to create specially designed T-shirts targeted at members of other Internet newsgroups, "but for a very small business like mine, the Internet is great."

Asprey's Internet strategy was simple yet effective—and best of all, it wasn't expensive. Asprey had access to the Internet and plenty of time to read postings (notices) on newsgroups, allowing him to study the market before diving in. Two newsgroups that particularly appealed to him were *alt.flame.roommate* (a bulletin board for college students who hate their roommates) and the aforementioned *alt.drugs.caffeine*. One day, Asprey spotted a note from a newsgroup member describing a cool T-shirt that he'd purchased and saw an opportunity to start peddling his own company's T-shirts online.

Asprey also customized his product. Instead of trying to sell his existing stock on the Internet, he created a custom shirt designed to appeal to the alt.drugs.caffeine members. "I posted a note stating that an unofficial alt.drugs.caffeine shirt was available—even though it doesn't say the name anywhere on it," Asprey recalls.

The way Asprey sees it, "The Internet is a guerrilla marketer's paradise. People automatically sort themselves into categories far more detailed than the average consumer survey could ever do."

Most important, he used the soft sell. Rather than blitz the Internet with junk E-mail—a practice universally condemned on the Internet as "spamming"—Asprey posted tasteful yet appealing descriptions of his T-shirts. His postings also included a disclaimer at the bottom apologizing to anyone who might be offended by his use of the Internet for commercial purposes.

"I don't sell the shirts," Asprey says. "I describe the product and tell the newsgroup members to E-mail me." Instead of setting up a mail reflector to zap out brochures automatically, Asprey responded to every E-mail message personally.

Finally, Asprey did more than simply post T-shirt advertisements online—he became an active member of the group. "I post regularly to the group with coffee stories such as 'this is the proper way to froth milk for your espresso,'" he says.

The bottom line: "I made more from Internet posts in two months than I had made locally in six months, and I shipped shirts to eight countries," says Asprey, who has pocketed roughly $2,000 in profits so far on a monthly $50 investment. "Most of the orders I've had came with nice letters—people thanking me for making the shirt available. I should also say," Asprey adds, "that I've never been even lightly flamed [receiving highly critical E-mail or BBS messages] for advertising on the Net."

This entrepreneur's approach may not work for every business; it's probably impractical for, say, a large corporation that's geared toward marketing to millions of people at a time instead of selling products one to one. On the other hand, it's a marketing strategy that may just work—for entrepreneurs willing to invest the time to master the nuances of Internet culture.

CASE STUDY QUESTIONS

1. Why has Dave Asprey been a business success on the Internet?

2. Why does he say that "the Internet is a guerrilla marketers' paradise"?

3. What other types of business ventures do you think would be a success on the Internet? Why?

Source: Adapted from Rosalind Resnick "Coffee and Tees," *Home Office Computing,* February 1995, p. 64. Reprinted by permission from *Home Office Computing* magazine © 1995.

┌─ **SECTION II**
│ *Technical Telecommunications Alternatives*
└

Telecommunications is a highly technical, rapidly changing field of information systems technology. Most end users do not need a detailed knowledge of its technical characteristics. However, it is important that you understand some of the important characteristics of the basic components of telecommunications networks. This understanding will help you participate effectively in decision making regarding telecommunications alternatives. Figure 6.14 outlines key telecommunications network components and alternatives. Remember, a basic understanding and appreciation, not a detailed knowledge, is sufficient for most business end users.

Telecommunications Alternatives

Telecommunications channels (also called communications *lines* or *links*) are the means by which data and other forms of communications are transmitted between the sending and receiving devices in a telecommunications network. A telecommunications channel makes use of a variety of **telecommunications media.** These include twisted-pair wire, coaxial cables, and fiber optic cables, all of which physically link the devices in a network. Also included are terrestrial microwave, communications satellites, cellular and LAN radio, all of which use microwave and other radio waves, and infrared systems, which use infrared light to transmit and receive data. Figure 6.15 illustrates some of the major types of media used in modern telecommunications networks.

Telecommunications Media

Ordinary telephone wire, consisting of copper wire twisted into pairs (*twisted-pair wire* is the most widely used media for telecommunications). These lines are used in established communications networks throughout the world for both voice and data transmission. Thus, twisted-pair wiring is used extensively in home and office telephone systems and many local area networks and wide area networks. See Figure 6.16.

Twisted-Pair Wire

Network Component	Examples of Alternatives
Media	Twisted-pair wire, coaxial cable, fiber optics, microwave radio, communications satellites, cellular and LAN radio, infrared
Processors	Modems, multiplexers, bridges, routers, hubs, gateways, front-end processors, private branch exchanges
Software	Telecommunications monitors, telecommunications access programs, network operating systems, end user communications packages
Channels	Analog/digital, switched/nonswitched, transmission speed, circuit/message/packet switching, simplex/duplex, asynchronous/synchronous
Topology/architecture	Point-to-point, multidrop, star/ring/bus, OSI, ISDN

FIGURE 6.14
Key telecommunications network components and alternatives.

FIGURE 6.15

An example of the telecommunications media in a telecommunications channel. Note the use of telecommunications satellite, earth stations with dish antennas, microwave links, fiber optic and coaxial cable, and a wireless LAN.

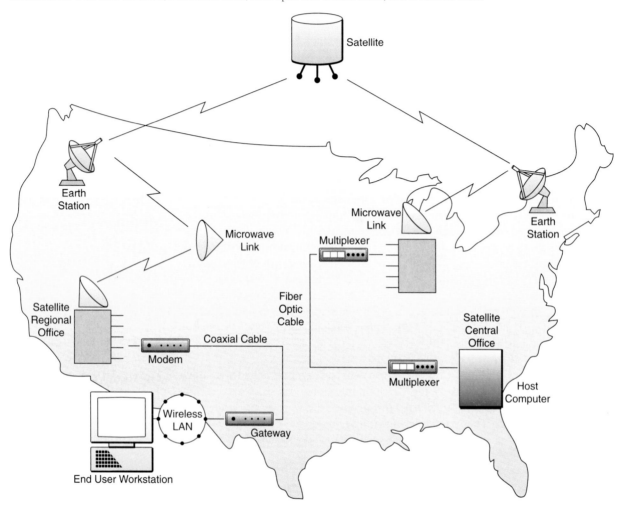

Coaxial Cable

Coaxial cable consists of a sturdy copper or aluminum wire wrapped with spacers to insulate and protect it. The cable's cover and insulation minimize interference and distortion of the signals the cable carries. Groups of coaxial cables may be bundled together in a big cable for ease of installation. These high-quality lines can be placed underground and laid on the floors of lakes and oceans. They allow high-speed data transmission and are used instead of twisted-pair wire lines in high-service metropolitan areas, for cable TV systems, and for short-distance connection of computers and peripheral devices. Coaxial cables are also used extensively in office buildings and other work sites for local area networks.

Fiber Optics

Fiber optics uses cables consisting of one or more hair-thin filaments of glass fiber wrapped in a protective jacket. They can conduct light pulses generated by lasers at transmission rates as high as 30 billion bits per second. This is about 60 times greater than coaxial cable and 3,000 times better than twisted-pair wire lines. Fiber

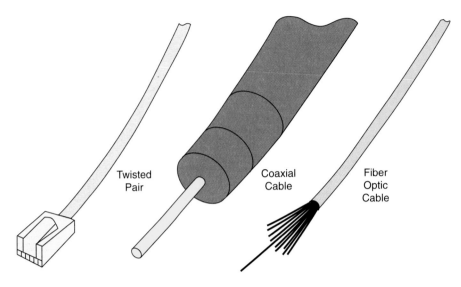

FIGURE 6.16
Telecommunications wire and cable alternatives.

Twisted Pair

Coaxial Cable

Fiber Optic Cable

optic cables provide substantial size and weight reductions as well as increased speed and greater carrying capacity. A half-inch-diameter fiber optic cable can carry up to 50,000 channels, compared to about 5,500 channels for a standard coaxial cable.

Fiber optic cables are not affected by and do not generate electromagnetic radiation; therefore, multiple fibers can be placed in the same cable. Fiber optic cables have a minimal need for repeaters for signal retransmissions, unlike electrical wire media. Fiber optics also has a much lower data error rate than other media and is harder to tap than electrical wire and cable. The biggest disadvantage of fiber optics has been the difficulty of splicing the cable to make connections, though this is also a security advantage that limits line tapping. However, new splicing techniques have made it easier to splice fiber cables. Fiber optic cables have already been installed in many parts of the United States, and they are expected to replace other communications media in many applications in the near future.

Terrestrial Microwave

Terrestrial microwave involves earthbound microwave systems which transmit high-speed radio signals in a line-of-sight path between relay stations spaced approximately 30 miles apart. Microwave antennas are usually placed on top of buildings, towers, hills, and mountain peaks, and they are a familiar sight in many sections of the country. They are still a popular medium for both long-distance and metropolitan area networks.

Communications Satellites

An important telecommunications medium is the use of **communications satellites** for microwave transmission. There are several dozen communications satellites from several nations placed into stationary *geosynchronous* orbits approximately 22,000 miles above the equator. Satellites are powered by solar panels and can transmit microwave signals at a rate of several hundred million bits per second. They serve as relay stations for communication signals transmitted from *earth* stations. Earth stations use *dish antennas* to beam microwave signals to the satellites, which amplify and retransmit the signals to other earth stations thousands of miles away.

While communications satellites were used initially for voice and video transmission, they are now also used for high-speed transmission of large volumes of data. Because of time delays caused by the great distances involved, they are not suitable for interactive, realtime processing. Communications satellite systems are operated by several firms, including AT&T, Western Union, American Satellite Company, and Intellsat, an international consortium of over 100 nations. Many large corporations and other users have developed networks of small satellite dish antennas known as VSAT (very-small-aperture terminal) to connect their distant work areas. These satellite networks are also called *bypass networks* because firms are bypassing the regular communications networks provided by communications carriers.

Cellular Radio

Cellular radio is the radio communications technology that makes cellular phones possible. It divides a metropolitan area into a honeycomb of cells. This greatly increases the number of frequencies and users that can take advantage of mobile phone service. Each cell has its own low-power transmitter, rather than having one high-powered radio transmitter to serve an entire city. This significantly increases the number of radio frequencies available for mobile phone service. However, this technology requires a central computer and other communications equipment to coordinate and control the transmissions of thousands of mobile phone users as they drive from one cell to another.

Cellular radio has become an important communications medium for mobile voice and data communications. For example, Federal Express uses cellular radio for data communications with terminals in each of its thousands of delivery vans as part of its competitive edge. The integration of cellular and other mobile radio technologies is expected to accelerate in the next few years. This will provide a full range of mobile computing capabilities to laptop computer users [25].

Wireless LANs

Wiring an office or a building for a local area network is often a difficult and costly task. Older buildings frequently do not have conduits for coaxial cables or additional twisted-pair wire, and the conduits in newer buildings may not have enough room to pull additional wiring through. Repairing mistakes and damages to wiring is often difficult and costly, as are major relocations of LAN workstations and other components.

One increasingly popular solution to such problems is installing a **wireless LAN**, using one of several wireless technologies. One example is **LAN radio**, which uses radio transmissions to interconnect LAN components. LAN radio may involve a high-frequency radio technology similar to cellular radio, or a low-frequency radio technology called *spread spectrum*. The other wireless LAN technology is called **infrared**, because it uses beams of infrared light to establish network links between LAN components. See Figure 6.17.

Obviously, a wireless LAN eliminates or greatly reduces the need for wires and cables, thus making a LAN easier to set up, relocate, and maintain. However, current wireless technologies have higher initial costs and other limitations. For example, an infrared LAN transmits faster than radio LANs but is limited to line-of-sight arrangements to a maximum of about 80 feet between components. High-frequency radio LANs do not need line-of-sight links, but are limited to 40 to 70 feet between components in enclosed areas. Spread spectrum radio LANs can penetrate masonry walls and link components from 100 to 200 feet away in enclosed areas, but are more subject to receiving or generating radio interference. However, even with these limitations, the use of wireless LAN technologies is expected to increase significantly [3].

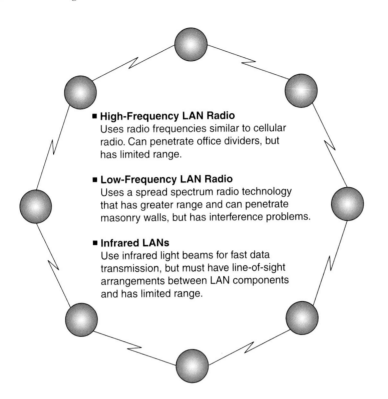

FIGURE 6.17
Three competing wireless LAN technologies. Note the benefits and limitations of each.

- **High-Frequency LAN Radio**
  Uses radio frequencies similar to cellular radio. Can penetrate office dividers, but has limited range.

- **Low-Frequency LAN Radio**
  Uses a spread spectrum radio technology that has greater range and can penetrate masonry walls, but has interference problems.

- **Infrared LANs**
  Use infrared light beams for fast data transmission, but must have line-of-sight arrangements between LAN components and has limited range.

Telecommunications channels for wide area networks can be owned by an organization or provided by other companies. In the United States, several companies have traditionally used a variety of communications media to create networks that can provide a broad range of communications services.

These **common carriers** provide the wide area communications networks used by most computer-using firms and individuals. They have traditionally been authorized by government agencies to provide a selected number of communication services to the public. Examples are the former Bell operating companies, General Telephone and Electronics, Western Union, and many independent telephone companies. Some common carriers specialize in selling long-distance voice and digital data communications services in high-density areas of the country and the world. Examples of such specialized carriers are AT&T Long Distance, ITT World Communications, Southern Pacific Communications, U.S. Sprint, and MCI Communications.

Common carriers can provide an organization needing the data communications capabilities of a wide area telecommunications network with several options. For example, an organization could use regular, voice-grade, direct-distance dialing (DDD), which is more expensive, slower, and less reliable than other options due to delays caused by excessive communications traffic and the noise of voice-switching circuits. Or it could sign up for a wide area telephone service (WATS) and pay a monthly fee and a per hour fee for use of a set amount of telephone line capacity. This would be cheaper for an organization with a lot of communications activity, but it would have the same reliability problem as DDD.

Telecommunications Carriers

Common Carriers

A company could lease its own communications lines (called *leased lines*) from telephone companies and be guaranteed exclusive use of a low-noise, fast communications channel. However, this is an expensive alternative that is economically feasible only for large corporations and government agencies with massive data communications needs. Another expensive option is the use of a company that provides communications satellite services. Or an organization could build a *bypass* system, in which it installs its own dish antennas and bypasses the common carrier networks and transmits directly to communications satellites. Once again, this is a more expensive alternative attractive only to organizations with a high volume of data communications.

Value-Added Carriers

Other major communications carriers are companies called **value-added carriers.** These are third-party vendors who lease communications lines from common carriers and offer communications services to customers. Typically, messages from customers are transmitted in groupings called packets, via *packet-switching* networks. However, the networks of such carriers are known as *value-added networks* (VANs), because they add value to their leased communications lines by using communications hardware and software and their expertise to provide not only packet switching but other data communication services. Value-added networks also take over the responsibility for the management of the network, thus relieving their customers of the technical problems inherent in long-distance communications.

Value-added carriers offer their customers, or *subscribers,* high-quality, relatively low-cost service in return for a membership fee and usage charges based on the amount of communications activity accomplished. By spreading the cost of leasing the lines among many subscribers and using the capacity of the lines intensively, they are able to sell their services at attractive prices and still make a profit. Examples of value-added companies are GTE Telenet, General Electric's Mark Net, and Compunet by CompuServe. These VANs have become so popular that common carriers such as the Bell operating companies, AT&T, MCI, and Western Union and large corporations such as IBM and RCA now offer VAN services.

Telecommunications Processors

Telecommunications processors such as modems, multiplexers, bridges, front-end processors, and other devices perform a variety of support functions between the terminals and computers in a telecommunications network. Let's take a look at some of these devices and their functions. See Figure 6.18.

FIGURE 6.18
A summary of important communications processors.

- **Modem:** Serves as a telecommunications interface for personal computers and converts transmissions from digital to analog and back.
- **Multiplexer:** Allows a single communications channel to carry simultaneous data transmissions from many terminals.
- **Internetwork processor:** Includes bridges, routers, hubs, and gateways which interconnect a local area network with other local and wide area networks.
- **Private branch exchange:** Switches external and internal voice and data transmissions over telephone lines within an office or other work area.
- **Front-end processor:** Handles data communications control and network management functions for a larger computer.

FIGURE 6.19
Modems perform a modulation-demodulation process that converts digital signals to analog and back.

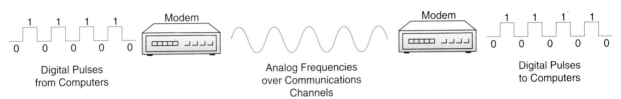

Digital Pulses
from Computers

Analog Frequencies
over Communications
Channels

Digital Pulses
to Computers

Modems

Modems are the most common type of communications processor. They convert the *digital* signals from a computer or transmission terminal at one end of a communications link into analog frequencies, which can be transmitted over ordinary telephone lines. A modem at the other end of the communications line converts the transmitted data back into digital form at a receiving terminal. This process is known as *modulation* and *demodulation*, and the word *modem* is a combined abbreviation of those two words. Modems come in several forms, including small stand-alone units, plug-in circuit boards, and microelectric modem chips. Many modems also support a variety of telecommunications interface functions, such as transmission error control, automatic dialing and answering, and a faxing capability.

Modems are used because ordinary telephone networks were primarily designed to handle continuous analog signals (electromagnetic frequencies), such as those generated by the human voice over the telephone. Since data from computers are in digital form (voltage pulses), devices are necessary to convert digital signals into appropriate analog transmission frequencies and vice versa. However, *digital communications networks* that transmit only digital signals and do not need analog/digital conversion are becoming commonplace. Since most modems also perform a variety of telecommunications support functions, modems may still be needed in digital networks. See Figure 6.19.

Multiplexers

A **multiplexer** is a communications processor that allows a single communications channel to carry simultaneous data transmissions from many terminals. Thus, a single communications line can be shared by several terminals. Typically, a multiplexer merges the transmissions of several terminals at one end of a communications channel, while a similar unit separates the individual transmissions at the receiving end.

This is accomplished in two basic ways. In *frequency division multiplexing* (FDM), a multiplexer effectively divides a high-speed channel into multiple slow-speed channels. In *time division muliplexing* (TDM), the multiplexer divides the time each terminal can use the high-speed line into very short time slots, or time frames. The most advanced and popular type of multiplexer is the *statistical time division multiplexer,* most commonly referred to as a statistical multiplexer. Instead of giving all terminals equal time slots, it dynamically allocates time slots only to active terminals according to priorities assigned by a telecommunications manager.

Internetwork Processors

As we have previously mentioned, many local area networks are interconnected by **internetwork processors** such as *bridges, routers, hubs,* or *gateways* to other LANs or wide area networks. A *bridge* is a communications processor that connects two similar LANs, that is, LANs based on the same network standards or *protocols*. A *router* is a communications processor that connects LANs to networks based on different protocols. A *hub* is a *port switching* communications processor. Advanced versions of hubs provide automatic switching among connections called *ports* for shared access to a network's resources. LAN workstations, servers, printers, and other LAN resources are connected to ports, as are bridges and routers provided by the hub to other LANs and WANs. Networks that use different communications architectures are interconnected by using a communications processor called a *gateway*. All these devices are essential to providing connectivity and easy access between the multiple LANs within an organization and the wide area networks connecting them to other company locations and organizations.

Private Branch Exchange

The **private branch exchange** (PBX) is a communications processor that serves as a switching device between the telephone lines within a work area and the local telephone company's main telephone lines, or *trunks*. PBXs can be as small as a telephone or as large as a minicomputer. They not only route telephone calls within an office but also provide other services, such as automatic forwarding of calls, conference calling, and least-cost routing of long-distance calls. Some PBX models can control communications among the terminals, computers, and other information processing devices in local area networks in offices and other work areas. Other PBXs can integrate the switching of voice, data, and images in *integrated services digital networks* (ISDN) that we will be discussing shortly.

Front-End Processors

A **front-end processor** is typically a minicomputer dedicated to handling the data communications control functions for large mainframe **host computers.** For example, a front-end processor uses telecommunications control programs to provide temporary buffer storage, data coding and decoding, error detection, recovery, and the recording, interpreting, and processing of control information (such as characters that indicate the beginning and end of a message). It can also poll remote terminals to determine if they have a message to send or if they are ready to receive a message.

A front-end processor also has other, more advanced responsibilities. It controls access to a network and allows only authorized users to use the system, assigns priorities to messages, logs all data communications activity, computes statistics on network activity, and routes and reroutes messages among alternative communication links. Thus, the front-end processor can relieve the host computer of its data communications control functions so it can concentrate on its other information processing chores.

Telecommunications Software

Software is a vital component of all telecommunications networks. **Telecommunications control software** includes programs stored in the host computer as well as programs in front-end computers and other communications processors. Such software controls and supports the communications occurring in a telecommunications network. For example, telecommunications software packages for mainframe-based wide area networks are frequently called telecommunications monitors or *teleprocessing (TP) monitors*. CICS (Customer Identification Control System) for IBM mainframes is a typical example. Local area networks rely on software called **network operating systems,** such as Novell NetWare or Microsoft LAN Manager. Many communications software packages are also available for microcomputers, as we discussed in Chapter 5. See Figure 6.20.

Matthew Bonkoski/Stock Boston.

FIGURE 6.20
This display of a telecommunications monitor shows the status of local area and wide area networks.

Common Software Functions

Telecommunications software packages provide a variety of communications support services. The number and type of terminals, computers, communications processors, and communications activities involved determine the capabilities of the program required. However, several major functions are commonly provided by telecommunications packages.

Access Control

This function establishes the connections between terminals and computers in a network. The software works with a communications processor (such as a modem) to connect and disconnect communications links and establish communications parameters such as transmission speed, mode, and direction. Access control may also involve automatic telephone dialing and redialing, logging on and off with appropriate account numbers and security codes, and automatic answering of telephone calls from another computer. Many communications packages include a *script language* which allows you to develop programs to customize access control, such as accessing other computers at night or while you are away.

Transmission Control

This function allows computers and terminals to send and receive commands, messages, data, and programs. Some error checking and correction of data transmissions may also be provided. Data and programs are usually transmitted in the form of files, so this activity is frequently called *file transfer.*

Network Management

This function manages communications in a telecommunications network. Software such as LAN network operating systems and WAN telecommunications monitors determines transmission priorities; routes (switches) messages, polls, and terminals in the network; and forms waiting lines (*queues*) of transmission requests. It also logs statistics of network activity and the use of network resources by end user workstations.

Error Control

This function involves detection and correction of transmission errors. Errors are usually caused by distortions in the communications channel, such as line noise and power surges. Communications software and processors control errors in transmission by several methods, including *parity checking*. Parity checking involves determining whether there is an odd or even number of *binary one digits* in a character being transmitted or received. Besides parity bits, additional *control codes* are usually added to the message itself. These specify such information as the destination of the data, their priority, and the beginning and end of the message, plus additional error detecting and correcting information. Most error correction methods involve retransmissions. A signal is sent back to the computer or terminal to retransmit the previous message.

Security Management

This function protects a communications network from unauthorized access. Network operating systems or other security programs restrict access to data files and other computing resources in LANs and other types of networks. This restriction usually involves control procedures that limit access to all or parts of a network by various categories of users, as determined by the *network manager* or *administrator* of the network. Automatic disconnection and callback procedures may also be used. Data transmissions can also be protected by coding techniques called **encryption**. Data is scrambled into a coded form before transmission and decoded upon arrival.

Telecommunications Network Topologies

There are several basic types of network **topologies**, or structures, in telecommunications networks. The two simplest are *point-to-point* lines and *multidrop* lines. When point-to-point lines are used, each terminal is connected by its own line to a computer system. When multidrop lines are used, several terminals share each data communications line to a computer. Obviously point-to-point lines are more expensive than multidrop lines: All of the communications capacity and equipment of a communications line is being used by a single terminal. Therefore, point-to-point lines are used only if there will be continuous communications between a computer and a terminal or other computer system. A multidrop line decreases communications costs, because each line is shared by many terminals. Communications processors such as multiplexers and concentrators help many terminals share the same line. See Figure 6.21.

Star, Ring, and Bus Networks

Figure 6.22 illustrates three basic topologies used in wide area and local area telecommunications networks. A **star network** ties end user computers to a central computer. In a **ring network** local computer processors are tied together in a ring on a more equal basis. A **bus network** is a network in which local processors share the same bus, or communications channel. In many cases, star networks take the form of hierarchical networks. In hierarchical networks, a large headquarters computer at the top of the company's hierarchy is connected to medium-size computers at the divisional level, which are connected to small computers at the departmental or work group level. A variation of the ring network is the *mesh* network. This uses direct communications lines to connect some or all of the computers in the ring to each other. Another variation is the tree network, which joins several bus networks together.

Multidrop Lines   **Point-to-Point Lines**

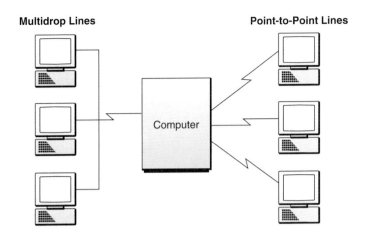

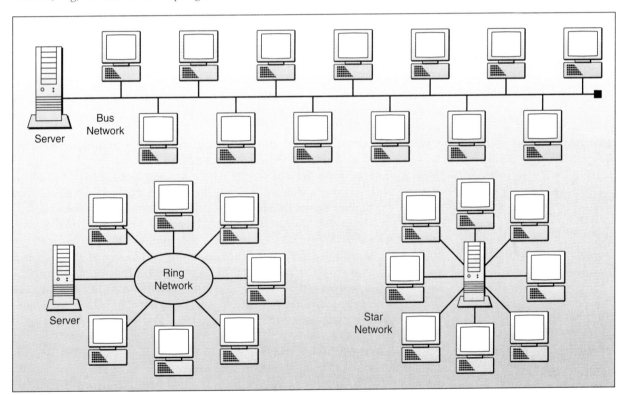

FIGURE 6.21
Multidrop lines allow terminals
to share a communications line.
Point-to-point lines provide a
separate communications line
for each terminal.

FIGURE 6.22
The star, ring, and bus network topologies.

In most cases, distributed processing systems use a combination of star, ring, and bus approaches. Obviously, the star network is more centralized, while ring and bus networks have a more decentralized approach. However, this is not always the case. For example, the central computer in a star configuration may be acting only as a **switch,** or message-switching computer, that handles the data communications between autonomous local computers.

Star, ring, and bus networks differ in their performances, reliabilities, and costs. A pure star network is considered less reliable than a ring network, since the other computers in the star are heavily dependent on the central host computer. If it fails, there is no backup processing and communications capability, and the local computers will be cut off from the corporate headquarters and from each other. Therefore, it is essential that the host computer be highly reliable. Having some type of *multiprocessor architecture* to provide a *fault tolerant* capability is a common solution.

Star network variations are common because they can support the *chain-of-command* and hierarchical structures of most organizations. Ring and bus networks are most common in local area networks. Ring networks are considered more reliable and less costly for the type of communications in such networks. If one computer in the ring goes down, the other computers can continue to process their own work as well as to communicate with each other.

Network Architectures and Protocols

Until quite recently, there was a lack of sufficient standards for the interfaces between the hardware, software, and communications channels of data communication networks. For this reason, it is quite common to find a lack of compatibility between the data communications hardware and software of different manufacturers. This situation has hampered the use of data communications, increased its costs, and reduced its efficiency and effectiveness. In response, computer manufacturers and national and international organizations have developed standards called *protocols* and master plans called *network architectures* to support the development of advanced data communications networks.

Protocols

A **protocol** is a standard set of rules and procedures for the control of communications in a network. However, these standards may be limited to just one manufacturer's equipment, or to just one type of data communications. Part of the goal of communications network architectures is to create more standardization and compatibility among communications protocols. One example of a protocol is a standard for the physical characteristics of the cables and connectors between terminals, computers, modems, and communications lines. Other examples are the protocols that establish the communications control information needed for *handshaking,* which is the process of exchanging predetermined signals and characters to establish a telecommunications session between terminals and computers. Other protocols deal with control of data transmission reception in a network, switching techniques, internetwork connections, and so on.

Network Architectures

The goal of **network architectures** is to promote an open, simple, flexible, and efficient telecommunications environment. This is accomplished by the use of standard protocols, standard communications hardware and software interfaces, and the design of a standard multilevel interface between end users and computer systems.

The OSI Model and Other Architectures

The International Standards Organization (ISO) has developed a seven-layer Open Systems Interconnection (OSI) model to serve as a standard model for network architectures. By dividing data communications functions into seven distinct layers, the ISO hopes to promote the development of modular network architectures. This would assist the development, operation, and maintenance of large telecommunications networks. Figure 6.23 illustrates the functions of the seven levels of the OSI model architecture.

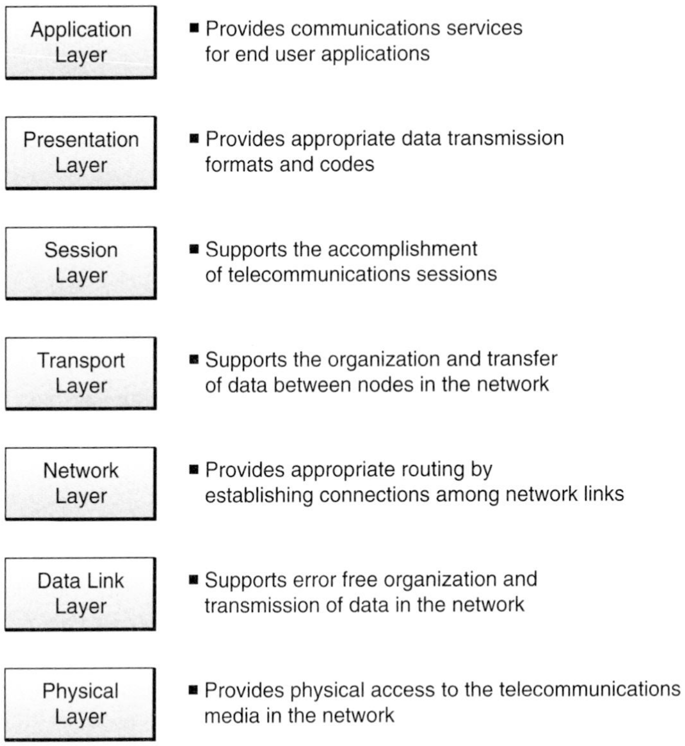

| Application Layer | ▪ Provides communications services for end user applications |

| Presentation Layer | ▪ Provides appropriate data transmission formats and codes |

| Session Layer | ▪ Supports the accomplishment of telecommunications sessions |

| Transport Layer | ▪ Supports the organization and transfer of data between nodes in the network |

| Network Layer | ▪ Provides appropriate routing by establishing connections among network links |

| Data Link Layer | ▪ Supports error free organization and transmission of data in the network |

| Physical Layer | ▪ Provides physical access to the telecommunications media in the network |

FIGURE 6.23
The seven layers of the OSI communications network architecture. The OSI model is recognized as an international standard for telecommunications networks.

Examples of network architectures include IBM's System Network Architecture (SNA) and DECnet by the Digital Equipment Corporation. An important suite of protocols that has become so widely used that it is equivalent to a network architecture is the Internet's Transmission Control Protocol/Internet Protocol known as TCP/IP. Another example is the local area network architecture for automated factories sponsored by General Motors and other manufacturers called the Manufacturing Automation Protocol (MAP).

Related to the development of network architectures is the development of a set of standards for ISDN, the Integrated Services Digital Network. This is a set of international standards needed to establish public and private digital telecommunications networks capable of handling voice, data, image, and video communications throughout the world. Many communications carriers and corporations are developing, testing, and installing ISDN networks.

ISDN promises to revolutionize telecommunications and networking. If ISDN is fully implemented, voice, video, and data transmissions would be available through your telephone company and the normal twisted-pair telephone wiring of your office or home just by plugging your computer or *videophone* into a telephone wall socket. So ISDN will enable end users to enjoy multimedia computing and communications. However, much more development work remains to be done by communications carriers, computer manufacturers, and end user organizations. ISDN's technology must still be perfected, costs must become competitive, and organizations must learn how to use this new communications service. Only then will the promise of ISDN become a reality.

Integrated Services Digital Network

Communications Channel Characteristics

The communication capabilities of telecommunication channels can be classified by *bandwidth.* This is the frequency range of the channel, which determines the channel's maximum transmission rate. Data transmission rates are typically measured in bits per second (BPS). This is sometimes referred to as the *baud* rate, though baud is more correctly a measure of signal changes in a transmission line.

Transmission Speed

Voiceband, or low-speed analog, channels are typically used for transmission rates from 300 to 9,600 BPS, but can now handle up to 1 million BPS (MBPS). They are usually unshielded twisted-pair lines commonly used for voice communications, but are also used for data communications by microcomputers, video terminals, and fax machines. *Medium-band,* or medium-speed, channels use shielded twisted-pair lines for transmission speeds from 9,600 BPS up to 10 MBPS.

Broadband, or high-speed digital, channels allow transmission rates at specific intervals from 256,000 BPS to several billion BPS. Typically, they use microwave, fiber optics, or satellite transmission. Examples are 1.54 million BPS for TI communications channels developed by AT&T and up to 100 MBPS for satellite channels used by many large private communications networks. See Figure 6.24.

Transmission Mode

The two modes of transmitting data are called *asynchronous* and *synchronous* transmission. Asynchronous transmission transmits one character at a time, with each character preceded by a *start bit* and followed by a *stop bit.* Asynchronous transmission is normally used for low-speed transmission at rates below 2,400 BPS. Synchronous transmission transmits groups of characters at a time, with the beginning and end of a character determined by the timing circuitry of a communications processor. Synchronous transmission is normally used for high-speed transmission exceeding 2,400 BPS.

Switching Alternatives

Regular telephone service relies on *circuit switching,* in which a circuit is opened to establish a link between a sender and receiver that remains open until the communication session is completed. In *message switching,* a message is transmitted a block at a time from one switching device to another. This method is sometimes called store-and-forward transmission because messages may be temporarily stored by the switching device before being retransmitted.

Packet switching involves subdividing communications messages into groups called packets. For example, many packets are 128 characters long. The packet switching network is typically operated by a value-added carrier who uses comput-

FIGURE 6.24
Examples of telecommunications transmission speeds.

Media	Maximum Speeds
Twisted pair—unshielded	1 MBPS
Twisted pair—shielded	10 MBPS
Coaxial cable—baseband	264 MBPS
Coaxial cable—broadband	550 MBPS
Terrestrial microwave	100 MBPS
Satellite microwave	100 MBPS
LAN radio	3.3 MBPS
Infrared LAN	4 MBPS
Fiber optic cable	30 GBPS

MBPS = million BPS or megabits per second.   GBPS = billion BPS or gigabits per second.

ers and other communications processors to control the packet switching process and transmit the packets of various users over its leased lines.

Many packet switching networks are *X.25 networks*. The X.25 protocol is an international set of standards governing the operations of widely used, but relatively slow packet switching networks. *Frame relay* is another popular packet switching protocol. Frame relay is considerably faster than X.25, and is better able to handle the heavy telecommunications traffic of interconnected local area networks within a company's wide area network. ATM (*asynchronous transfer mode*) is an emerging high capacity packet switching technology based on the broadband ISDN (B-ISDN) international protocol. ATM networks are being developed by companies who need its fast, high capacity multimedia capabilities for voice, video, and data communications among their internetworked end users.

How can terminals and other devices access and share a network to transmit and receive data? As Figure 6.25 indicates, a variety of *access methods* are used to provide this capacity. In the *polling* approach, a host computer or communications processor polls (contacts) each terminal in sequence to determine which terminals have messages to send. The sequence in which the terminals are polled is based on the communications traffic expected from each terminal. Thus, the transmission of each terminal is based on a roll call of each terminal on the line. Polling can be an effective method because the speed of mainframe and communications processors computers allows them to poll and control transmissions by many terminals sharing the same line, especially if typical communications consist of brief messages and inquiries.

In the *contention approach*, line use is on a first-come, first-served basis, where a terminal can transmit data if the line is not in use, but it must wait if it is busy. One way to make contention work is a widely used method called *carrier-sense multiple access with collision detection* (CSMA/CD). This requires a terminal or other device to continually monitor the network and send a message only if it senses the network is not in use. If a collision is detected, the terminal must stop transmission, wait until the network is clear, and try again. This access method is used by the Ethernet standard for local area networks.

Another widely used method in local area networks is *token passing*. A token is a special signal code sent around the network. If a terminal or other device wants to transmit a message, it must wait for the token to come by, examine it to see if it is in use, and pass it on or use the token to help route its message to its destination on the network. After transmission is completed, the token is returned to the network by the receiving terminal if it is not needed. This access method is used in all *token ring* local area networks, the Datapoint and MAP *token bus* networks, and the high-speed fiber optic–based token ring LAN standard known as Fiber-Distributed Data Interface or FDDI.

Access Methods

- **Polling.** A communications processor conducts a roll call of the terminals in a network to determine if they have messages to send.
- **Contention.** Terminals send messages on the network on a first-come, first-served basis.
- **Token passing.** Terminals use an electronic signal code, or *token*, to send messages that are passed on to the appropriate terminal in the network.

FIGURE 6.25
Common telecommunications access methods.

Wal-Mart Stores: From Satellite to Land-Based Telecommunications

Mike Fitzgerel, director of communications technology at Wal-Mart Stores, Inc., is on a mission to build the best point-of-sale and transaction processing systems in the world. To succeed, Fitzgerel is literally bringing his wide area network down to earth, deploying an international frame-relay network in place of a nine-year-old very small aperture terminal (VSAT) communication satellite-based installation. The new data network will slash credit card and check authorization transaction times from several seconds to less than a second, although Fitzgerel guards the exact rate and anticipated savings as a corporate secret. However, with 10 million credit card transactions per month, it's safe to say the overhaul will translate into significant savings.

"We do everything with an eye toward customer service and to make us the price leader in the industry," Fitzgerel says. "Frame relay is just one more piece that makes us more efficient and helps control our costs."

But the benefits of moving to a router-based frame-relay network are far broader than just cost savings. Network throughput is projected to be four to five times greater with the new setup. And the move will enable Wal-Mart to embrace interactive processing across the wide area network and in its thousands of stores in North America, paving the way for wholesale changes in the company's in-store network strategy.

Wal-Mart currently uses proprietary IBM Token-Ring LANs to interconnect cash register terminals and other POS devices with in-store computers. The retailer plans to migrate to faster Ethernet LANs which will speed in-store handling of credit card and check authorization traffic.

The new LANs will also let Wal-Mart shop for greater savings on equipment. The network interface cards Wal-Mart uses from IBM, for instance, cost nearly double that of Ethernet cards today. With between 30 and 80 networked registers per store and more than 2,000 stores in the United States alone, hardware savings accumulate rapidly.

The network changes underscore a philosophy, embodied in one of the late founder Sam Walton's corporate rules: "Control your expenses better than your competition."

Wal-Mart has operated its VSAT network for just under a decade. But soon after the company's acquisition of the Woolco Canada chain in March 1994, it was faced with a decision about how to communicate with the new stores. Frame-relay technology emerged as the clear choice.

The primary drivers were a reduction in the cost of frame-relay service, and the improved response times and throughput gains we could achieve with today's land-based fiber optic lines and digital networks, compared to our satellite setup, Fitzgerel says.

Wal-Mart recently completed its Canadian network roll-out, installing Advanced Computer Communications (ACC) Amazon routers into 120 stores that are linked into Unitel's frame-relay network and then traffic routed back to the company's Bentonville, Arkansas, headquarters. In the United States, Wal-Mart has introduced Amazon routers into 200 stores and plans to have the routers and frame-relay up and running in 1,000 stores by year-end, Fitzgerel says. The goal is to eventually deploy a router in all of the company's 2,119 domestic stores that warrant frame-relay connections.

"There are areas that won't have economical digital service for quite some time," Fitzgerel says. Wal-Mart will continue to operate its satellite network to reach remote store locations and to pipe video and music to all of its stores.

Although Wal-Mart won't let on about its exact plans, Fitzgerel talks about tighter integration between store applications and POS systems. The company has already forged close ties to inventory and sales applications; as data flows out of stores, inventory is adjusted and orders are triggered automatically.

"Our goal is to have constantly flowing data between our home office and our stores," Fitzgerel says. "We want information on what it takes to replenish the stores and keep them well stocked for customers."

CASE STUDY QUESTIONS

1. What telecommunications network components and functions (see Figure 6.14) are mentioned in this case?

2. What land-based telecommunications technologies are involved? What are their advantages over satellite technologies?

3. What business reasons are causing Wal-Mart to switch from satellite to land-based networks?

Source: Adapted from Charles Bruno, "Wal-Mart Casts Wide Router Net," *Network World*, March 27, 1995, pp. 69, 73, 106. Copyright 1995 by Network World, Inc., Framingham, MA 01701—Reprinted from *Network World*.

Summary

- **Telecommunications Trends.** The information systems of many organizations depend on telecommunications networks to service the communications and information processing needs of their end users. Telecommunications has entered a competitive environment with many vendors, carriers, and services. Telecommunications technology is moving toward integrated digital networks for voice, data, and video, and the pervasive use of the technology to build global networks, like the Internet, that form information superhighways to support business operations, managerial decision making, and strategic advantage in a global economy.

- **Telecommunications Networks.** The major components of a telecommunications network are (1) terminals, (2) telecommunications processors, (3) communications channels and media, (4) computers, and (5) telecommunications control software. There are two basic types of telecommunications networks: wide area networks (WANs) and local area networks (LANs). WANs cover a wide geographic area, while LANs interconnect end user workstations and other devices at local work sites.

- **Client/Server Computing.** Telecommunications networks are being used to support client/server computing as organizations move away from centralized mainframe-based networks. In client/server networks, end user microcomputer workstations (clients) are interconnected within a local area network whose hardware, software, and database resources are managed by a LAN server. Application processing may be shared among clients and servers within a LAN, or by interconnections with clients and servers in other LANs and wide area networks in a cooperative processing approach.

- **Network Alternatives.** Key telecommunications network alternatives and components are summarized in Figure 6.14 for telecommunications media, processors, software, channels, and network architectures. A basic understanding of these major alternatives will help managerial end users participate effectively in decisions involving telecommunications issues. Telecommunications processors include modems, multiplexers, and various devices to help enhance the capacity and efficiency of telecommunications channels. Telecommunications channels include such media as twisted-pair wire, coaxial cables, fiber optic cables, terrestrial microwave, communications satellites, cellular and LAN radio, and infrared systems. Use of public communications channels is provided by companies called common carriers and value-added carriers who offer a variety of telecommunication services. Telecommunications software consists of a variety of programs that control and support the communications occurring in a telecommunications network.

Key Terms and Concepts

These are the key terms and concepts of this chapter. The page number of their first explanation is in parentheses.

1. Applications of Telecommunications (189)
2. Business use of the Internet (201)
3. Cellular radio (208)
4. Client/server computing (196)
5. Coaxial cable (206)
6. Common carriers (209)
7. Communications satellites (207)
8. Cooperative processing (198)
9. Distributed processing (198)
10. Fiber optic cables (206)
11. Front-end processors (212)
12. Host computer (194)
13. Information superhighway (192)
14. The Internet (200)
15. Internetworks (195)
16. Internetwork processors (211)
17. Interorganizational networks (199)
18. Local area network (194)
19. Modem (211)
20. Multiplexer (211)
21. Network operating system (194)
22. Network server (194)
23. Open systems (191)
24. Private branch exchange (212)
25. Protocol (216)
26. Telecommunications channels and media (193)
27. Telecommunications control software (212)
28. Telecommunications network (193)
   a. Architecture (216)
   b. Components (193)
   c. Topology (214)
29. Telecommunications processors (210)
30. Trends in telecommunications (190)
31. Value-added carriers (210)
32. Wide area network (194)
33. Wireless LANs (208)

Review Quiz

Match one of the key terms and concepts listed above with one of the brief examples or definitions listed below. Try to find the best fit for answers that seem to fit more than one term or concept. Defend your choices.

____ 1. Fundamental changes have occurred in the competitive environment, the technology, and the applications of telecommunications.

____ 2. Includes terminals, telecommunications processors, channels and media, computers, and control software.

____ 3. A communications network covering a large geographic area.

____ 4. A communications network in an office, a building, or other work site.

____ 5. Provide a variety of communications networks and services.

____ 6. They lease lines from common carriers and offer telecommunications services.

____ 7. Includes coaxial cable, microwave, fiber optics, and satellites.

____ 8. A communications media that uses pulses of laser light in glass fibers.

____ 9. Supports mobile data communications in urban areas.

____ 10. Includes modems, multiplexers, and front-end processors.

____ 11. Includes programs for control of communications access, transmission, networks, errors, and security.

____ 12. A common communications processor for microcomputers.

____ 13. Helps a communications channel carry simultaneous data transmissions from many terminals.

____ 14. The main computer in a data communications network.

____ 15. A minicomputer dedicated to handling communications functions for a mainframe.

____ 16. A computer that handles resource sharing and telecommunications in a local area network.

____ 17. Handles the switching of both voice and data in an office.

____ 18. The software that manages a local area network.

____ 19. A standard, multilevel interface to promote compatibility among telecommunications networks.

____ 20. A standard set of rules and procedures for control of communications in a network.

____ 21. Information systems with common standards that provide easy access to end users and their networked computer systems.

____ 22. Interconnected networks need communications processors such as bridges, routers, hubs, and gateways.

____ 23. Most networks are connected to other local area or wide area networks.

____ 24. A global network of millions of business, government, educational, and research networks, computer systems, and end users.

____ 25. A proposed national network of interconnected local, regional, and global networks that would support interactive voice, data, video, and multimedia communications.

____ 26. Telecommunications can support a wide range of business uses.

____ 27. Using the Internet for corporate communications, information retrieval, collaborative computing, and marketing.

____ 28. End user workstations are tied to LAN servers to share application processing.

____ 29. Computers at central and local sites interconnected by a network.

____ 30. Networked computers sharing the processing of parts of an end user's applications.

____ 31. Telecommunications networks interconnect an organization with its customers and suppliers.

Discussion Questions

1. Some people argue that one can no longer separate telecommunications from computing in business. Do you agree or disagree? Why?

2. Why have local area networks become so popular? What management problems are posed by the use of LANs?

3. Telecommunications is much too technical an area for managerial end users, and should be left to telecommunications specialists. Do you agree? Why or why not?

4. What examples can you give that trends in telecommunications include: (*a*) more telecommunications providers, (*b*) a greater variety of telecommunications services, and (*c*) an increased use of telecommunications applications in business?

5. What are the benefits and limitations of the following telecommunications technologies: (*a*) fiber optics, (*b*) communications satellites, (*c*) wireless LANs, and (*d*) ISDN?

6. Refer to the Real World Case on West American T-Shirt Co. in the chapter. What is the role of "Internet culture" in Dave Asprey's success? Is this culture changing? Explain.

7. Refer to the Real World Case on Wal-Mart Stores in the chapter. Should other businesses consider moving from satellite to land-based networks? Explain.

8. Why is there a trend toward open systems in computing and telecommunications?

9. How realistic is the concept of a national information superhighway? How valuable would the superhighway be for consumers, business, and the nation's economy?

10. What is the Internet's business significance, compared to commercial networks like America OnLine, CompuServe, and Prodigy?

Real World Problems

1. Fidelity, FedEx, and Capital One: Internet Web Sites

Hundreds of corporate World Wide Web sites (home pages) have been added to the Internet in recent months, but a surprising number lack any kind of interactive features. Some do not even allow visitors to send E-mail messages to corporate sponsors. Happily, some standout corporate Web pages exist that demonstrate what can be accomplished. Three companies, in particular, have put up home pages that let Web surfers do some interesting tasks. These include Fidelity Investments Co. in Boston, FedEx Corp. in Memphis, and Capital One, Inc., in Richmond, Virginia.

The Fidelity home page (http://www.fid.inv.com) contains information about Fidelity and its services, including information about 160 mutual funds. The interactive component is a form-based worksheet for calculating savings needs for a college fund. According to Iang Jeon, director of electronic marketing, the application was developed in-house and runs on a Sun Microsystems server. However, "users are clamoring for investment transactions across the 'net," Jeon said. He said Fidelity plans to wait until Internet security protocols have stabilized and the Securities and Exchange Commission (SEC) has given its blessing.

Capital One's home page (http://www.capital1.com) accepts online applications for Visa credit cards. The forms-based system runs on secure servers from Netscape. For its part, FedEx's home page (http://www.fedex.com) has been active since last year. Initially, this site was a tame "placeholder page," conceded Robert G. Hamilton, manager of information services marketing. Recently, FedEx created an interface between the Web page and its 12-year-old Powership, a PC-based package-tracking service. Now, Internet users can track FedEx packages as well. FedEx's home page server, a Netsite Commerce Server from Netscape Communications, receives roughly 16,000 hits a day.

a. What services do Fidelity, FedEx, and Capital One offer at their Internet Web sites?

b. What range of services should a business offer on the World Wide Web? Explain.

Source: Adapted from Ellis Booker, "Firms Pilot Interactive Web Pages," *Computerworld*, April 3, 1995, p. 64. Copyright 1995 by Computerworld, Inc., Framingham, MA 01701—Reprinted from *Computerworld*.

2. Holiday Inn Worldwide: Virtual LANs and Switching Hubs

One day recently, a user on Holiday Inn Worldwide, Inc.'s network decided to install, on his own, a Hewlett-Packard LaserJet printer on a network card configured for Apple Computer's AppleTalk. Once up and running, the printer promptly began broadcasting its presence to whatever AppleTalk stations were on the company's global computing network. If the printer had been connected just to its own LAN, all would have been well. However, Holiday Inn uses switching hubs and routers to connect its 1,700 worldwide LAN sites into "one virtual community" of thousands of "virtual LANs," where users can interconnect anywhere they have access rights, said Ed Boggs, senior network analyst at the Atlanta-based hotel chain. As a result, the printer's broadcasts were traveling all over the world, causing traffic jams on local and wide area circuits where bandwidth was scarce, he added. Once alerted to the problem, Boggs used a series of network management tools to analyze the problem, identify the LAN location and the offending device, and, finally, call up the user and request him to take the HP printer offline.

Virtual LANs are the latest attempt by the network industry to help corporate customers keep pace with the exploding demands of client/server installations. More powerful workstations, a growing user population and increasingly bandwidth-hungry applications such as multimedia are all contributing to this explosion. "Our paradigm is changing" from a group of users sharing access on individual LANs to virtual LANs consisting of user groups across multiple, interconnected physical LAN segments, said Chuck Rush, global networking manager at McDonald's Corp.

Virtual LANs use a new breed of internetwork processor, the *switching hub*. The switching hub's big plus is its ability to support virtual networks of users and devices that must communicate often and rapidly, independent of the actual physical structure of the network. For example, a company might set up physical LANs on each of its floors, then use the switching hub's software to define virtual LAN groups of users from any floor that share the same access control address and can therefore communicate quickly and efficiently over the network. This is particularly important for supporting work group computing, so users and applications can communicate freely, irrespective of their network location.

a. What are virtual LANs? What is the role of switching hubs?

b. Do virtual LANs make business sense? Should companies implement virtual LAN networks? Explain.

Source: Adapted from Elizabeth Horwitt, "Firing On All Cylinders," *Computerworld Client/Server Journal,* April 1995, pp. 35–36. Copyright 1995 by Computerworld, Inc., Framingham, MA 01701—Reprinted from *Computerworld.*

3. Campbell & Co.: Home-to-Office ISDN

High-bandwidth connections aren't just for computer jockeys. Looking for high-speed home-to-office links, securities traders in Towson, Maryland, picked ISDN lines for the job. And at the investment management firm Campbell & Company, speed was the primary concern. Traders at this 40-person firm do their financial modeling in the uncommon NeXTStep operating system environment because they like its object-oriented features and its high-end graphics. Several key employees have NeXT computer workstations at home for immediate, 24-hour access to the company network. The home-to-office links also provide convenient backups, with employees taking critical data off-site each night.

Senior Vice President of Research Andy Wernsdorfer handled the project. The company didn't want the expense of leased lines, but Wernsdorfer knew that tariffs had been lowered on ISDN, making it affordable. At 28.8 kilobits per second (Kbps), even high-speed modems can't match the data transfer rate of ISDN, which ranges from 64 Kbps to 128 Kbps. "We did a rough, break-even computation, and the story was that with about four simultaneous users we could break even using ISDN," says Wernsdorfer. With more users, ISDN presented significant savings.

As for equipment, the network server at Campbell & Co. needed a bridge to communicate with the central office. For that job, Wernsdorfer purchased a Network Express router. The home offices needed remote ISDN bridges as well. These modem-sized devices connect to an Ethernet card and the ISDN line. The ISDN equipment wasn't cheap, and several homes needed to have new phone lines laid. Nevertheless, ISDN was much less expensive than running dedicated lines, says Wernsdorfer. "For no greater dollars we got the higher speed, the higher throughput—all that stuff, and it fit our vision of having a high-speed network that extended beyond the boundaries of the office into our homes, our off-site offices."

a. What telecommunications network components and functions (see Figure 6.5) are mentioned in this case?

b. What other types of businesses might benefit from switching to ISDN? Explain.

Source: Adapted from Marti Remington, "Trading on High Bandwidth," *PC Today,* January 1995, p. 52.

4. Carnival Cruise Lines: Satellite Network Banking

Carnival Cruise Lines had it all—casinos, Caribbean ports of call, and Kathie Lee. The only thing missing was cash. Until recently, ships from Miami-based Carnival Corp. were cashless because there was no live data link between a floating automated teller machine (ATM) thousands of miles off shore and a host bank. But Carnival became the first cruise line to provide shipboard ATMs last month when it began bouncing data off a satellite to Bank Atlantic in Fort Lauderdale, Florida.

Douglas Eney, director of MIS at Carnival, said he took advantage of a satellite connection that the cruise line set up two years ago to carry digitized voice data from ship to shore so passengers could call friends and family. The 64K-byte satellite link is a dedicated connection that accommodates eight voice lines and one data link, Eney said. Each ship in the Carnival line is set up as a network with a Sun Microsystems SPARCstation 10 server. Using a router from Cisco Systems, Eney can funnel data packets from all 12 cruise ships through the satellite link. And because the open line was already there, Carnival does not have to pay extra to move the data.

Chris Klein, Florida-based marketing representative at the ATM division of AT&T Global Information Solutions in Dayton, Ohio, which sold Carnival the ATM machines, pointed out that 65 percent of cruise-goers run out of cash on the fifth day of a seven-day cruise. That means activity at the casino drops, the crew loses out on tips and people have to worry about getting their cars out of the lot without money in their pockets. "It created ill will," Klein said. According to Carnival, ATMs are now located on the promenade decks of the *Ecstasy* and the *Sensation.* The response has been so positive that the company is placing ATMs on the rest of its ships.

a. What telecommunications network components and functions (see Figure 6.5) are mentioned in this case?

b. What is the business value of Carnival's satellite network?

Source: Neal Weinberg, "Satellite Links Let Cash Flow out to Sea." *Computerworld,* May 8, 1995, p. 56. Copyright 1995 by Computerworld, Inc., Framingham, MA 01701—Reprinted from *Computerworld.*

5. Philadelphia Gas Works: Wireless Networks

A small miracle is unfolding at Philadelphia Gas Works: The problem-plagued, $800 million-a-year municipal utility is ahead of schedule on a massive customer service project involving the installation of more that 500,000 radio frequency-based meter readers, according to Tom Kuczynski, manager of IS at Philadelphia Gas Works (PGW). PGW is heading into the new year having equipped 90,000 residences with wireless meter readers. During the next six years, the utility will install about 560,000 of the devices, which will be read electronically on a drive-by basis by PGW staffers using radio equipment and PCs mounted in vans. With the wireless system, customer and route information stored on an IBM 3090 mainframe will be downloaded to the meter reading software. At day's end, meter readings will then be uploaded to the mainframe and posted to PGW's main customer information database.

Improving customer services—now much maligned by ratepayers—and cutting costs are the main goals of the $63 million wireless project. PGW estimates the system will more than pay for itself, saving the company about $13 million annually beginning in 2002. The company projects additional cost savings of $105 million during the next 10 years. A good chunk of the savings will derive from the fact that the utility will no longer need to enter customers' homes to read meters. Currently, PGW's "can't get in" rate is about 55 percent. The utility sends estimated bills, which must later be corrected, to these customers. "With automatic meter reading, virtually all of our billing will be based on actual usage," said Joseph G. Horan, senior vice president and chief operating officer at PGW. "We can begin to realize cost savings, and customers will no longer have to be concerned about rearranging their personal schedules to accommodate the meter reader."

PGW's electronic meter-reading project is among several wireless projects now under way in the utility industry. Boston Edison Co. and Wisconsin Power & Light Co. are also implementing electronic meter-reading using Metricom, Inc.'s Utilinet network. Other utilities, including Pacific Gas & Electric Co. and Southern California Edison Co., are using the Utilinet wireless data network to automate power distribution and voltage control.

a. What telecommunications network components and functions (see Figure 6.5) do you recognize in this case?

b. Why are electric utilities implementing wireless networks?

Source: Adapted from Julia King, "Practicality of Wireless Applications Grows." *Computerworld,* January 16, 1995, p. 53. Copyright 1995 by Computerworld, Inc., Framingham, MA 01701—Reprinted from *Computerworld.*

6. Bergan Mercy and Others: IS Online on the Internet

If his department's access to the online services' technical and vendor forums were cut off tomorrow, it would "severely hamper our network upgrades across the board," said Fred Hegner, director of application development at Bergan Mercy Health System, Inc., in Dallas. At Bergan, as at many other companies, information systems staffers are increasingly tapping into online networks like CompuServe and the Internet as a place to fetch software patches from vendors or to monitor discussion forums on the latest technical developments on myriad computing and networking subjects.

Using the 'net to search for employees is also a growing trend. For example, one IS manager hit on a way to resolve some of his technical issues and scout new talent at the same time. He posts especially thorny technical problems in the relevant Usenet discussion groups and watches for the best replies, then sends them an E-mail message. One of the key uses of Internet E-mail at Jacobs Engineering group in Pasadena, California, says Jim LoSasso, vice president of IS, is contact with suppliers and potential customers. "We request pricing information and get back replies very quickly," he said. The company also collects weekly work bids from the government, "which we pass along to the salespeople."

Next to exchanging electronic mail and monitoring technical chats, by far the most popular application of online networks in IS groups involves downloading software patches from vendors. At Ore-Ida Foods, Inc., in Boise, Idaho, for example, "all our upgrades for Apple software products come via Internet file transfer protocol," said Scott Robertson, an information technology strategist at Ore-Ida.

a. How do IS groups use the Internet and other online networks?

b. How do you envision people in other business areas (marketing, finance, etc.) using these networks?

Source: Adapted from Ellis Booker, "IS Staffs Take the Online Plunge," *Computerworld,* May 15, 1995, p. 59. Copyright 1995 by Computerworld, Inc., Framingham, MA 01701—Reprinted from *Computerworld.*

Application Exercises

1. Hands-on Internet for Business Advantage

Learn to use the Internet to access online business information that can give you a competitive advantage. Each of the services listed below has a site or E-mail address that will take you there or help you get more information. Make sure you honor uppercase and lowercase letters when keying in these addresses—Internet addresses are case-sensitive!

a. If the address for the service takes the form http://www.xxx.yyy, the site is a *home page* on the World Wide Web. Use a Web browser program such as Mosaic or Netscape to visit these sites.

b. If the address takes the form of gopher.xxx.yyy, use Xgopher, WinGopher, or other gopher software to access that site.

c. If you see an E-mail address such as info@xxx.com, simply send E-mail to the Internet address to get an automatic reply.

d. Send a short E-mail message to your instructor's Internet or other E-mail address summarizing something you learned when visiting one or more of the Internet sites in this exercise.

e. Prepare a one- or two-page summary of specific information gained from several of the following Internet sites which would help you start or expand a business, analyze an investment opportunity, or choose a business career.

Internet Business Center

Visit this clearinghouse of current information on what companies are doing on the Internet and learn how you can conduct business on the 'net more effectively. Free.
Web: http://tig.com/IBC/idx.html

Best Markets Reports

Here you'll find information and analysis of markets, including apparel, auto parts and service equipment, software, electrical power systems, laboratory scientific equipment, telecommunications equipment, and so on. Free.
Web: gopher://una.hh.lib.umich.edu/11/ebb/bmr

Gopher: una.hh.lib.umich.edu (choose "ebb" then "BMR").

Netsearch

Netsearch is a powerful database that helps you locate potential customers and contacts using the Web. You can use keywords to search for companies or even list your own company in the Netsearch database. Free.
WEB: http://www.afs.net/netsearch

Quotecom

The Quotecom server offers a wide variety of financial data. Offerings include free stock, commodity, and mutual fund quotes, Standard & Poor's Stock Guide, Hoover company profiles, European market data, BusinessWire news reports, and Freese-Notis weather reports. Some basic services are free, others require a subscription.
Web address: http://www.quote.com
E-mail address: info@quote.com

Infoseek

This makes searching the Internet fast, easy, and fun. You can access a large, up-to-date index of Web sites, Usenet news, computer periodicals, news wires, company profiles, and movie and book reviews. Enter a plain English query, and Infoseek will find the information for you in seconds. Free trial, subscription-based.
Web: http://www.city.net

City Net

This is a comprehensive international guide to communities around the world. City Net provides easy access to timely information on travel, entertainment, and local business, plus government and community services for all regions of the world. Free.
Web: http://www.city.net

Lycos and Webcrawler

Check out these Web search engines that can help you find people, places, and things on the Web. By periodically traversing the Web, these services attempt to build comprehensive indices for the content of thousands of Internet sites. Each does a slightly different type of indexing so try both. Free.
Web: http://lycos.es.cmu.edu
Web: http://webcrawler.cs.washington.edu/WebCrawler

Source: Adapted from Lori Dix, Kathie Gow, and Bob Rankin. "Cyberland: The Internet Game for Information and Business Professionals. *Computerworld,* April 17, 1995, pp 102–103.Copyright 1995 by Computerworld, Inc., Framingham, MA 01701—Reprinted from *Computerworld.*

2. Identifying Telecommunications Components and Media
Apply the telecommunications network model illustrated in Figure 6.5 to the telecommunications network of a business, university, or other organization you know that uses telecommunications. Do a short report which outlines the following:
a. Identifies as many of the five basic components of a telecommunications network that might exist in this particular network. Make assumptions about the network if necessary.
b. Describe how almost all of the communication media illustrated in Figure 6.15 could be used in this network.

3. Visiting Corporate Internet Web Sites
Visit the Internet World Wide Web sites (home pages) of Fidelity Investments in Boston, Federal Express in Memphis, and Capital One in Richmond, Virginia, as described in Real World Problem 1 of this chapter on page 223.
a. Use the Fidelity Investment home page (http://www.fid.inv.com) to look up information on Fidelity and its mutual funds. Then fill out the worksheet form for calculating savings needed for a college fund, and print it out on your system printer.
b. Visit the FedEx home page (http://www.fedex.com) to review information on FedEx and its services. You would need a copy of their Powership package and a FedEx account number and package tracking number to check the status of a shipment. So just print out a screenful of information on FedEx services to document your visit.
c. Use Capital One's home page (http://www.capital1.com) to find out information about Capital One's banking and financial services. Then fill out and print out the application form for a Visa card offered by Capital One. Don't submit the application to Capital (you can cancel the session any time) unless you are really interested in applying for their Visa card!

4. Morris Manufacturing Examines Communications Costs
Until recently, the volume of long-distance communication at Morris Manufacturing Company has been quite small. For this reason, Morris has always used traditional direct-distance dialing service for all of its long-distance communication. However, the cost of long-distance service at Morris Manufacturing has increased sharply in recent years. There are several likely reasons for this. Morris has recently opened

up a second plant in another state, and there is a substantial and expanding volume of both voice and data communications between the two plants. Also, Morris has begun to market its products aggressively through the sales staff making on-site visits to potential customers. The sales staff members use telephone credit cards to call the home office with orders and inquiries while in the field. In addition, customers who have service agreements with Morris Manufacturing can call the company collect when they need repair or servicing.

You have been asked to take a look at Morris Manufacturing's long-distance communications expenses over the past three years. You are to prepare materials to present to an executive committee that will highlight recent trends in Morris's long-distance communications costs. You are also to recommend any needed changes in the way Morris Manufacturing purchases its long-distance communications services.

By examining records, you have been able to obtain the estimates shown below. These figures indicate long-distance communications expenses by category for the past three years.

Morris Manufacturing Long Distance Expenses by Category of Call

Type of Call	1993	1994	1995
Outgoing calls:			
Plant-to-plant voice	$13,275	$17,650	$26,840
Plant-to-plant data	8,625	18,430	33,715
Other outgoing calls	17,235	16,430	14,270
Incoming calls charged to Morris:			
Credit card calls from employees	5,320	9,840	14,280
College calls from customers	7,260	7,415	7,300

a. Using spreadsheet software, create a spreadsheet application that will allow you to print reports and graphs highlighting trends in Morris's long-distance communications costs.

b. What changes in their long-distance communications services would you recommend that Morris Manufacturing consider?

5. ABC Products Buys a LAN

ABC Products Company has decided to purchase a small network of microcomputers for the use of its office staff. ABC buys all of its computing equipment from local suppliers who have agreed to give ABC a substantial discount on its purchases. You have been asked to determine the minimum configuration of the network and then develop estimates of the cost of acquiring this network. Your estimate is to include the cost of installation and two years of service by the vendor. You determine that the proposed network will need one high-capacity PC to act as the file server for the network and five additional PCs to serve as network stations. In addition, one laser printer will be attached to the file server unit and will serve the printing needs of all of the network's users. Each of the six PCs will need to be equipped with a network communications card.

You have been asked to solicit pricing information from the two local firms and to prepare a spreadsheet comparing their costs. Since installation and servicing are included, this order cannot be split between the two vendors. The prices quoted by the two vendors are as shown below. The prices of all hardware items are on a per-unit basis. The service contract cost is expressed as a percentage of the costs of all hardware items. The installation and software costs are overall costs for the entire network.

Price Quotes for Network Components by Vendor

	Vendor	
Item	CompuStore	Computers Are Us
Hardware:		
File Server PC unit	$2,240	$2,305
Participant PC unit	1,245	1,265
Laser printer	1,350	1,335
Network communications card	280	275
Two-year service contract (% of total hardware cost)	25%	20%
Installation	$1,200	$1,100
Network software (six-station license)	2,475	2,500

a. Prepare a spreadsheet comparing the costs of acquiring this network from each of the two alternative suppliers.

b. Based upon cost alone, which of the two suppliers would you select?

c. If you were actually making a recommendation about this type of purchase, what factors, in addition to cost, would you want to consider?

Review Quiz Answers

1. 30	9. 3	17. 24	25. 13
2. 28b	10. 29	18. 21	26. 1
3. 32	11. 27	19. 28a	27. 2
4. 18	12. 19	20. 25	28. 4
5. 6	13. 20	21. 23	29. 9
6 31	14. 12	22. 16	30. 8
7. 26	15. 11	23. 15	31. 17
8. 10	16. 22	24. 14	

Selected References

1. Anthes, Gary. "In Depth: Interview with Vinton Cerf." *Computerworld,* February 7, 1994.
2. Booker, Ellis. "A Tangled Web." *Computerworld Client/Server Journal,* April 1995.
3. Cats-Baril, William, and Tawfik Jelassi. "The French Videotex System Minitel: A Successful Implementation of a National Information Technology Infrastructure." *MIS Quarterly,* March 1994.
4. Cronin, Mary. *Doing More Business on the Internet.* New York: Van Nostrand Reinhold, 1995.
5. Eliot, Lance. "Data Highway Needs Fuzzy Look." *Expert,* January 1994.
6. Friend, David. "Client/Server vs. Cooperative Processing: Two Downsizing Topologies Compared." *Information Systems Management,* Summer 1994.
7. Gilder, George. "Into the Telecosm." *Harvard Business Review,* March/April 1991.
8. Gleason, Tim. "The Information Hypeway." *Oregon Quarterly,* Spring, 1994.
9. Green, James Harry. *The Irwin Handbook of Telecommunications.* 2nd. ed. Burr Ridge, IL; Richard D. Irwin, 1992
10. Keen, Peter. *Shaping the Future: Business Design through Information Technology.* Boston: Harvard Business School Press, 1991.
11. Kehoe, Brandan. *Zen and the Art of the Internet: A Beginners Guide.* 3rd. ed. Englewood Cliffs, NJ.: Prentice Hall, 1994.
12. Kupfer, Andrew. "The Future of the Phone Companies." *Fortune,* October 3, 1994.
13. Martin, E. Wainright; Daniel DeHayes; Jeffrey Hoffer; and William Perkins. *Managing Information Technology: What Managers Need to Know.* 2nd ed. New York: MacMillan, 1994.
14. O'Mara, Brendan. "Information Superhighway. *Online Access,* Internet Special Issue, April 1994.
15. Roche, Edward M. *Telecommunications and Business Strategy.* Chicago: Dryden Press, 1994.
16. Rochester, Jack, ed. "Plans and Policies for Client/Server Technology." *I/S Analyzer,* April 1992.
17. Schnaidt, Patricia. *Enterprise-wide Networking.* Carmel, IN: SAMS Publishing, 1992.
18. Sherman, Stratford. "Will the Information Highway Be the Death of Retailing?" *Fortune,* April 18, 1994.
19. Sprague, Ralph, Jr., and Barbara McNurlin. *Information Systems Management in Practice.* 3rd ed. Englewood Cliffs, NJ: Prentice Hall, 1993.
20. Stallings, William, and Richard Van Slyke. *Business Data Communications.* 2nd. ed. New York: Macmillan, 1994.
21. Stamper, David. *Business Data Communications.* 3rd. ed. Redwood City: Benjamin Cummings Publishing Co., 1992.
22. Tetzelli, Rick. "The Internet and Your Business." *Fortune,* March 7, 1994.
23. Von Schilling, Peter, and John Levis. "Distributed Computing Environments: Process and Organization Issues." *Information Systems Management,* Spring 1995.
24. Wrobel, Leo. "Developing Information Highways." *Information Systems Management,* Spring 1995.
25. Yankee Group. "White Paper: Wireless Communications." *Computerworld,* November 14, 1994.

REAL WORLD CASE

R.J. Reynolds: Rebuilding a Global Network

R. J. Reynolds Tobacco International, Inc. (RJR), wanted to replace the star-configured computer network it used to support operations around the world with a much larger and faster mesh network, but didn't want to divert resources from its main line of business—selling tobacco.

So rather than attempt to deal with post, telegraph, and telephone administrations in 35 countries, it hired Eunetcom—a joint venture of France Telecom and Deutsche Telekom AG. As of last week, 12 of the 60 sites RJR wants to connect were up and running, including RJR headquarters in Winston-Salem, North Carolina.

The new network will be anchored by hubs here and in Geneva, Hong Kong, and Cologne, Germany. Trunks between hubs operate at 256K bit/sec, while all other network links are at least 64K bit/sec. The existing net employs everything from 9.6K to 64K bit/sec lines.

"We wanted to move that up to something that was highly reliable—basically the same across the world," said Robert Wimmer, vice president and chief information officer for RJR.

Hugues Ferreboeuf, Eunetcom marketing director, said his organization has set up a technical, legal, and financial team to carry out the project. The team is developing relations for the first time with about half the countries in which RJR wants to network, he said. "In some sites, we have to find local subcontractors, mainly for first-level maintenance of equipment, sometimes for housing the equipment. We may not have our own buildings right there," Ferreboeuf said.

To establish reliable links to Kazakhstan, Romania, and Russia, Eunetcom is using very small aperture terminal (VSAT) links that avoid the local loop, he said.

Bill Sommers, RJR's director of technical services, said that since the project started in January, Eunetcom has met schedules with two exceptions. In Ukraine, RJR had to get involved in hiring a crew to mount a VSAT dish on the roof of a building. To avoid that in the future, RJR staff will arrive on site for testing one week after Eunetcom declares a site ready, Sommers said. And establishing service in Armavir, Russia, had to be delayed because the city sits near the Chechen Republic, which is at war with Russia.

By the end of the year, the RJR network should link its worldwide LANs, some of which are token rings and some Ethernet.

The technical challenge is integrating VSAT, X.25, and frame-relay on the main "backbone" net and letting each LAN talk to the others seamlessly, Ferreboeuf said.

Much of that work is being done by RJR itself, Sommers said. RJR is configuring routers under simulated network conditions and forwarding the configuration parameters to Eunetcom for use in the actual net.

CASE STUDY QUESTIONS

1. What telecommunications network components and functions (as illustrated in Figure 6.14) are mentioned in this case? Refer back to the chapter for any terms you do not understand.

2. What business reasons are behind RJR's network rebuilding decision?

3. What unique challenges arise in building a global network?

Source: Adapted from Tim Greene, "Tobacco Giant Works with Eunetcom to Link 60 Sites," *Network World*, April 3, 1995, p. 22. Copyright 1995 by Network World, Inc., Framinggham, MA 01701—Reprinted from *Network World*.

Managerial Overview: Database Management

CHAPTER OUTLINE

LEARNING OBJECTIVES

The purpose of this chapter is to give you an understanding of how data resources are managed in information systems by analyzing the managerial implications of basic concepts and applications of database management.

Section I of this chapter introduces the concept of data resource management and stresses the advantages of the database management approach. It also stresses the role of database management system software and the database administration function. Finally, it outlines several major managerial considerations of data resource management.

Section II surveys some of the more technical concepts in database management, including basic concepts of database organization, development, and access.

After reading and studying this chapter, you should be able to:

1. Explain the importance of data resource management and how it is implemented by methods such as database administration, data administration, and data planning.

2. Outline the advantages of the database management approach.

3. Explain the functions of database management software in terms of end users and database management applications.

4. Provide examples to illustrate each of the following concepts:

   a. Logical data elements.

   b. Fundamental database structures.

   c. Major types of databases.

   d. Database development.

┌ S E C T I O N I
◢ *A Manager's View of Database Management*

Data Resource Management

Data is a vital organizational resource, which needs to be managed like other important business assets. Most organizations could not survive or succeed without quality data about their internal operations and external environment.

> Organizations are under tremendous pressure to provide better quality decision-making information in forms easy to access and manipulate. Business users are reacting to their own mission-critical needs for better information due to rapidly changing, increasingly volatile and competitive markets, as well as ever-shortening product life cycles [13].

That's why organizations and their managers need to practice **data resource management**—a managerial activity that applies information systems technology and management tools to the task of managing an organization's data resources to meet the information needs of business users. This chapter will show you the managerial implications of using database management technologies and methods to manage an organization's data assets to meet the information requirements of a business. We will also introduce the concepts of database administration, data administration, and data planning, which are part of the data resource management function. See Figure 7.1.

Foundation Data Concepts

Before we go any further, let's review some fundamental concepts about how data is organized in information systems. As we first mentioned in Chapter 1, a hierarchy of several levels of data has been devised that differentiates between different groupings, or *elements,* of data. Thus, data may be logically organized into **characters, fields, records, files,** and **databases,** just as writing can be organized in letters, words, sentences, paragraphs, and documents. Examples of these **logical data elements** are shown in Figure 7.2.

Character

The most basic logical data element is the **character,** which consists of a single alphabetic, numeric, or other symbol. One might argue that the *bit* or *byte* is a more elementary data element, but remember that those terms refer to the *physical* storage

FIGURE 7.1
Managing data as organizational assets is an important focus for today's managers.

Reinhold Speigler.

elements provided by the computer hardware, discussed in Chapter 4. From a user's point of view (that is, from a *logical* as opposed to a *physical* or *hardware* view of data), a character is the most basic element of data that can be observed and manipulated.

The next higher level of data is the **field,** or *data item.* A field consists of a grouping of characters. For example, the grouping of alphabetic characters in a person's name forms a *name field,* and the grouping of numbers in a sales amount forms a sales *amount field.* Specifically, a data field represents an **attribute** (a characteristic or quality) of some **entity** (object, person, place, or event). For example, an employee's salary is an attribute that is a typical data field used to describe an entity who is an employee of a business.

Field

Related fields of data are grouped to form a **record.** Thus, a record represents a collection of attributes that describe an entity. An example is the payroll record for a person, which consists of data fields such as the person's name, social security number, and rate of pay. *Fixed-length* records contain a fixed number of fixed-length data fields. *Variable-length* records contain a variable number of fields and field lengths.

Record

A group of related records is known as a data **file,** or *table.* Thus, an *employee file* would contain the records of the employees of a firm. Files are frequently classified by the application for which they are primarily used, such as a *payroll file* or an *inventory file.* Files are also classified by their permanence, for example, a payroll *master file* versus a payroll *weekly transaction file.* A **transaction file,** therefore, would contain records of all transactions occurring during a period and would be used periodically to update the permanent records contained in a **master file.** A *history file* is an obsolete transaction or master file retained for backup purposes or for long-term historical storage called *archival storage.*

File

FIGURE 7.2

Examples of the logical data elements in information systems. Note especially the examples of how data fields, records, files, and databases are related.

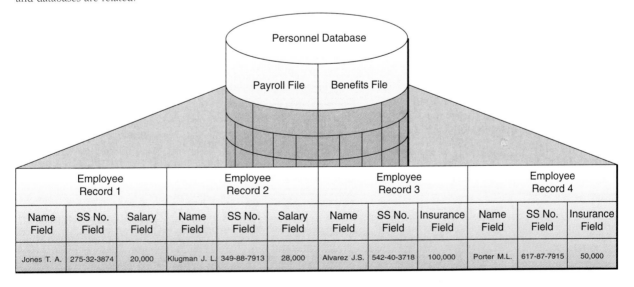

FIGURE 7.3
A personnel database consolidates data formerly kept in separate files.

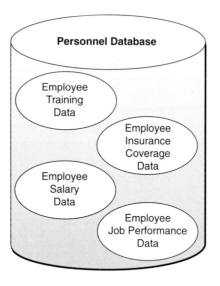

Database

A **database** is an integrated collection of logically related records or files. A database consolidates records previously stored in separate files into a common pool of data records that provides data for many applications. The data stored in a database is independent of the application programs using it and of the type of secondary storage devices on which it is stored. For example, a personnel database consolidates data formerly segregated in separate files such as payroll files, personnel action files, and employee skills files. See Figure 7.3.

The Database Management Approach

The development of *databases* and *database management software* is the foundation of modern methods of managing organizational data. In the **database management approach,** data records are consolidated into databases that can be accessed by many different application programs. In addition, an important software package called a *database management system* (DBMS) serves as a software interface between users and databases. This helps users easily access the records in a database. Thus, database management involves the use of database management software to control how databases are created, interrogated, and maintained to provide information needed by end users and their organizations.

For example, customer records and other common types of data are needed for several different applications in banking, such as check processing, automated teller systems, bank credit cards, savings accounts, and installment loan accounting. This data can be consolidated into a common *customer database,* rather than being kept in separate files for each of those applications. See Figure 7.4.

Thus, the database management approach involves three basic activities:

- Updating and maintaining common databases to reflect new business transactions and other events requiring changes to an organization's records.

- Providing information needed for each end user's application by using application programs that share the data in common databases. This sharing of data is supported by the common software interface provided by a *database management system* package. Thus, end users and programmers do not have to know where or how data are physically stored.

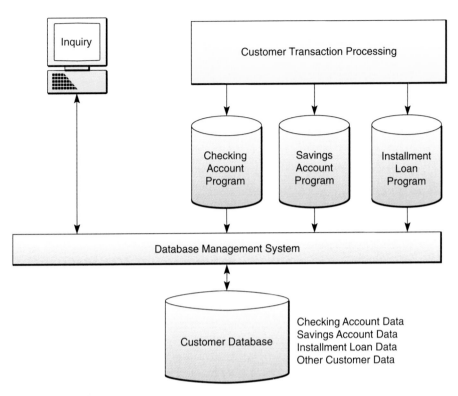

FIGURE 7.4
An example of a database management approach in a banking information system. Note how the savings, checking, and installment loan programs use a database management system to share a customer database. Note also that the DBMS allows a user to make a direct, ad hoc interrogation of the database without using application programs.

▪ Providing an inquiry/response and reporting capability through a DBMS package so that end users can easily interrogate databases, generate reports, and receive quick responses to their ad hoc requests for information.

Using Database Management Software

Let's take a closer look at the capabilities provided by database management software. A **database management system** (DBMS) is a set of computer programs that controls the creation, maintenance, and use of the databases of an organization and its end users. As we said in Chapter 5, database management packages are available for micro, mini, and mainframe computer systems. The four major DBMS uses are illustrated in Figure 7.5. Let's take a look at each of them now.

Database Development

Database management packages allow end users to easily develop the databases they need. However, a DBMS allows organizations to place control of organizationwide database development in the hands of **database administrators** (DBAs) and other specialists. This improves the integrity and security of organizational databases. The database administrator uses a *data definition language* (DDL) to develop and specify the data contents, relationships, and structure of each database, and to modify these database specifications when necessary. Such information is cataloged and stored in a database of data definitions and specifications called a *data dictionary,* which is maintained by the DBA. We will discuss database development further in Section II of this chapter.

The Data Dictionary

Data dictionaries have become a major tool of database administration. A **data dictionary** is a computer-based catalog or directory containing *metadata,* that is, data about data. A data dictionary includes a software component to manage a database

FIGURE 7.5

The four major uses of a DBMS package are database development, database interrogation, database maintenance, and application development.

- Database Development
- Database Interrogation
- Database Maintenance
- Application Development

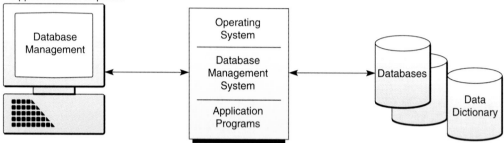

of *data definitions*, that is, metadata about the structure, data elements, and other characteristics of an organization's databases. For example, it contains the names and descriptions of all types of data records and their interrelationships, as well as information outlining requirements for end users' access, use of application programs, and database maintenance and security. See Figure 7.6.

Data dictionaries can be queried by the database administrator to report the status of any aspect of a firm's metadata. The administrator can then make changes to the definitions of selected data elements. Some *active* (versus *passive*) data dictionaries automatically enforce standard data element definitions whenever end users and application programs use a DBMS to access an organization's databases. For example, an active data dictionary would not allow a data entry program to use a nonstandard definition of a customer record, nor would it allow a data entry operator to enter a name of a customer that exceeded the defined size of that data element.

Database Interrogation

End users can use a DBMS by asking for information from a database using a *query language* or a *report generator.* They can receive an immediate response in the form of video displays or printed reports. No difficult programming is required. This **database interrogation** capability is a major benefit to ordinary end users. The **query language** feature lets you easily obtain immediate responses to ad hoc inquiries: you merely key in a few short inquiries. The **report generator** feature allows you to quickly specify a report format for information you want presented as a report. Figure 7.7 illustrates the use of a DBMS report generator.

SQL and QBE

SQL, or Structured Query Language, is a query language found in many database management packages. The basic form of an SQL query is:

SELECT . . . FROM . . . WHERE . . .

After SELECT you list the data fields you want retrieved. After FROM you list the files or tables from which the data must be retrieved. After WHERE you specify conditions that limit the search to only those data records in which you are interested. For example, suppose a financial manager wanted to retrieve the names, social

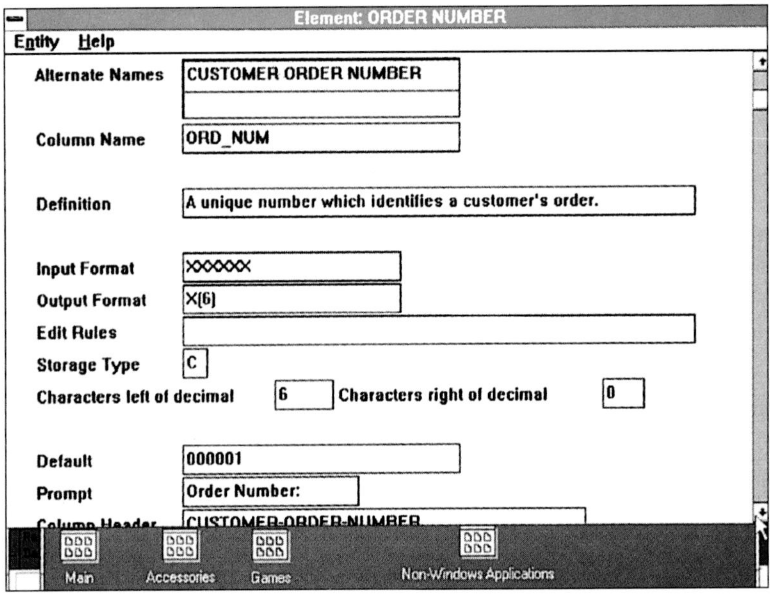

Courtesy Intersolv Inc.

FIGURE 7.6
A display of part of the information in a data dictionary for a customer order number data element.

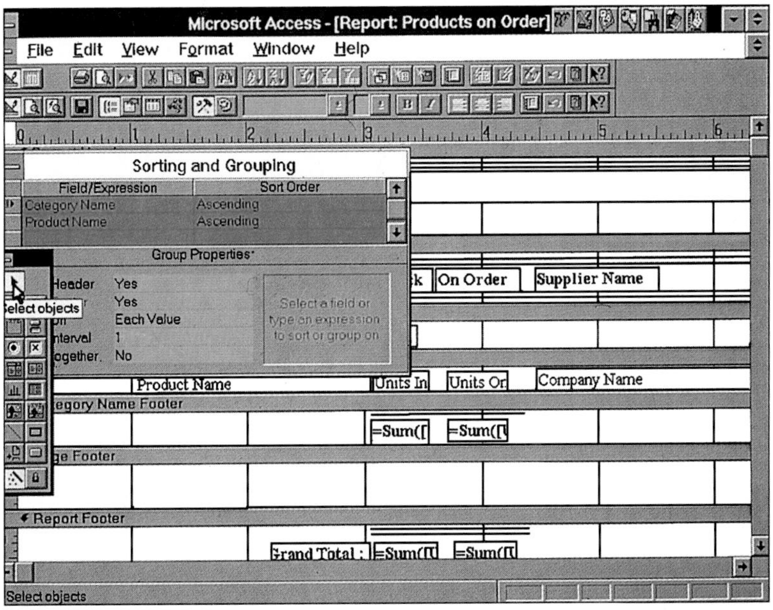

Sarah Evertson/Courtesy of Microsoft Corporation.

FIGURE 7.7
Using the report generator of Microsoft Access to produce an inventory report.

security numbers, departments, and salaries of all employees who are financial analysts from the employee and payroll files in the company's *human resources* database. Then he or she might use the SQL query shown in Figure 7.8 to display such information.

Another query language found in many database management packages is QBE, or *query by example.* QBE is a popular query language because its "point-and-

FIGURE 7.8
Using SQL (Structured Query Language) and QBE (Query By Example) to retrieve information about a company's financial analysts.

SQL Query
SELECT NAME, SSNO, DEPARTMENT, SALARY
FROM EMPLOYEE, PAYROLL
WHERE EMPLOYEE.SSNO = PAYROLL.SSNO
AND CLASSIFICATION = "FINANCIAL ANALYST"

QBE Query
EMPLOYEE ──┬─NAME─┬─ SSNO ─┬─ DEPARTMENT ──┬──
           ‖✓   ‖✓   ‖✓   ‖

PAYROLL─┬─ SSNO ─┬─ CLASSIFICATION ─┬─ SALARY ─┬──
        ‖   ‖ FINANCIAL ANALYST ‖   ‖
        ‖✓   ‖   ‖✓

click" capabilities make it easier for end users than SQL. This method displays boxes for each of the data fields in one or more files. You then use your keyboard or mouse to fill in, click on, query, or check boxes to indicate which information you want. For example, a QBE query that would retrieve information similar to the previous SQL query is shown in Figure 7.8.

Graphical and Natural Queries

Many end users (and IS professionals) have difficulty correctly phrasing SQL and other database language queries. So most end user's database management packages offer GUI (graphical user interface) point-and-click methods, which are easier to use. See Figure 7.9. Other packages are available that use **natural language** query statements that are similar to conversational English (or other languages). See Figure 7.10.

Database Maintenance

The databases of an organization need to be updated continually to reflect new business transactions and other events. Other miscellaneous changes must also be made to ensure accuracy of the data in the databases. This **database maintenance** process is accomplished by transaction processing programs and other end user application packages, with the support of the DBMS. End users and information specialists can also employ various *utilities* provided by a DBMS for database maintenance.

Application Development

DBMS packages play a major role in **application development.** A DBMS makes the job of application programmers easier, since they do not have to develop detailed data-handling procedures using a conventional programming language (a host language, such as COBOL) every time they write a program. Instead, they can include *data manipulation language* (DML) statements in their application programs, which let the DBMS perform necessary data-handling activities. Programmers can also use the internal programming language provided by many DBMS packages or a built-in application generator to develop complete application programs.

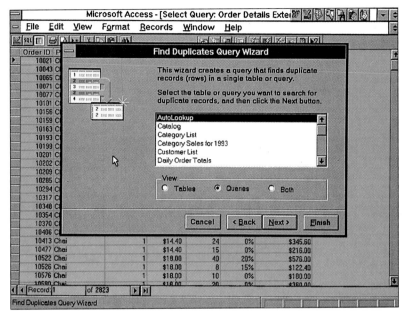

FIGURE 7.9
Using the Query Wizard of the Microsoft Access database management package to develop a query using a graphical point-and-click process.

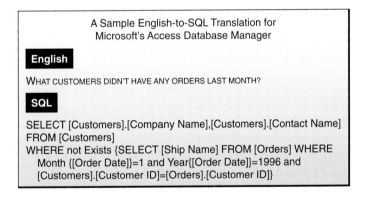

FIGURE 7.10
Comparing a natural language query with a SQL query.

Source: Adapted from Kim Nash, "Wizard Turns English into Database Language, *Computerworld,* February 20, 1995, p. 116. Copyright 1995 by Computerworld, Inc., Framingham, MA 01701—Reprinted from *Computerworld.*

Types of Databases

The growth of distributed processing, end user computing, and decision support and executive information systems has caused the development of several major **types of databases.** Figure 7.11 illustrates six major types of databases that may be found in computer-using organizations.

- **Operational databases.** These databases store detailed data needed to support the operations of the entire organization. They are also called *subject area databases* (SADB), *transaction databases,* and *production databases.* Examples are a customer database, personnel database, inventory database, and other databases containing data generated by business operations.

FIGURE 7.11
Examples of the major types of databases used by organizations and end users.

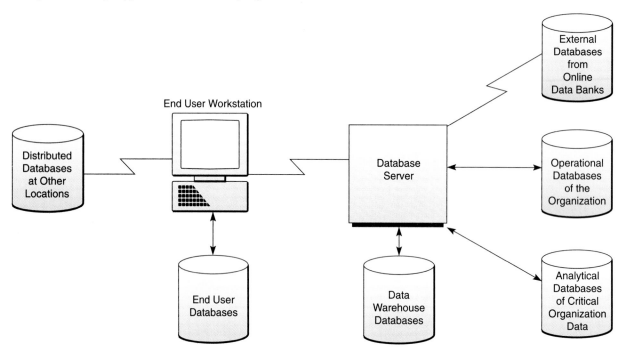

- **Analytical databases.** These databases store data and information extracted from selected operational and external databases. They consist of summarized data and information most needed by an organization's managers and other end users. Analytical databases are also called *management databases* or *information databases.* They may also be called multidimensional databases, since they frequently use a multidimensional database structure to organize data. These are the databases accessed by the *online analytical processing* (OLAP) systems, decision support systems, and executive information systems we will discuss in Chapter 10 [2, 4].
- **Data warehouse databases.** A *data warehouse* stores data from current and previous years that has been extracted from the various operational and management databases of an organization. It is a central source of data that has been standardized and integrated so it can be used by managers and other end user professionals throughout an organization. For example, a major use of data warehouse databases is *pattern processing,* where operational data is processed to identify key factors and trends in historical patterns of business activity [9, 13].
- **Distributed databases.** These are databases of local work groups and departments at regional offices, branch offices, manufacturing plants, and other work sites. These databases can include segments of both common operational and common user databases, as well as data generated and used only at a user's own site. Ensuring that all of the data in an organization's distributed databases are consistently and concurrently updated is a major consideration of data resource management.

FIGURE 7.12
Examples of the information available in the online databases of commercial information services.

Dow Jones Information Service.
Provides statistical data banks on stock market and other financial market activity, and on all corporations listed on the New York and American stock exchanges, plus 800 selected other companies. Its Dow Jones News/Retrieval system provides bibliographic data banks on business, financial, and general news from *The Wall Street Journal, Barron's,* the Dow Jones News Service, The Associated Press, Wall Street Week, and the 21-volume American Academic Encyclopedia.

Mead Data Central.
Its bibliographical data bank *Lexis* provides legal research information, such as case law, court decisions, federal regulations, and legal articles. *Nexis* provides a full text bibliographic database of over 100 newspapers, magazines, newsletters, news services, government documents, and so on. It includes full text and abstracts from the *New York Times* and the complete 29-volume Encyclopædia Britannica.

Lockheed Information Systems.
Its DIALOG system offers over 75 different data banks in agriculture, business, economics, education, energy, engineering, environment, foundations, general news publications, government, international business, patents, pharmaceuticals, science, and social sciences.

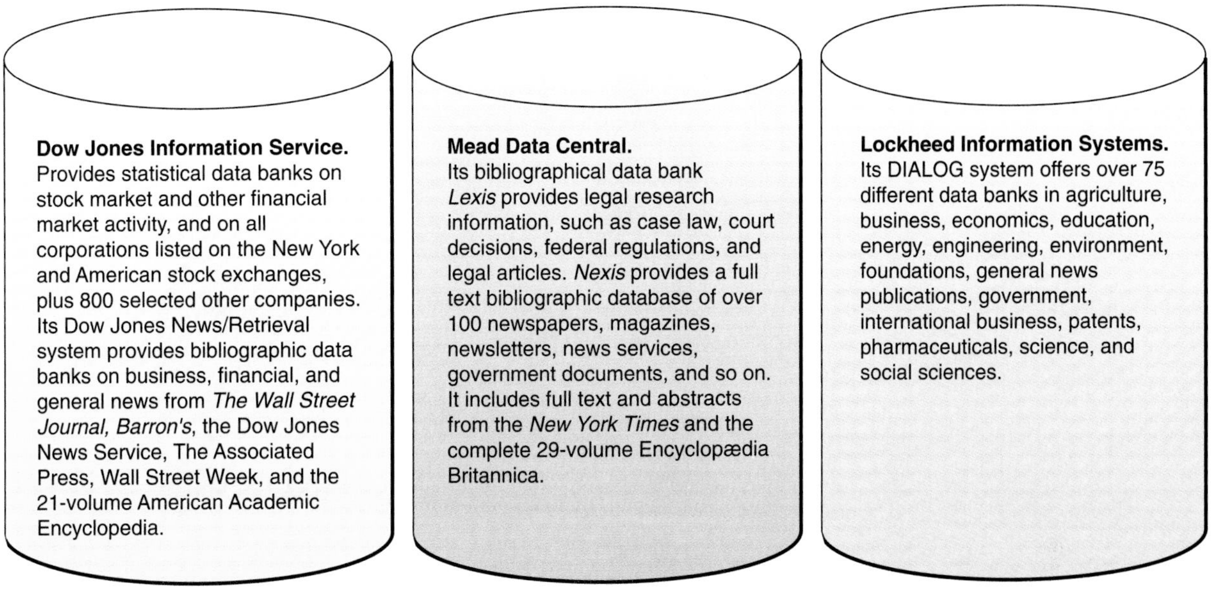

- **End user databases.** These databases consist of a variety of data files developed by end users at their workstations. For example, users may have their own electronic copies of documents they generated with word processing packages or received by electronic mail. Or they may have their own data files generated from using spreadsheet and DBMS packages.

- **External databases**. Access to external, privately owned *online databases* or *data banks* is available for a fee to end users and organizations from commercial information services. Data is available in the form of statistics on economic and demographic activity from *statistical* data banks. Or you can receive abstracts from hundreds of newspapers, magazines, and other periodicals from *bibliographic* data banks. See Figure 7.12.

Text Databases

Text databases are a natural outgrowth of the use of computers to create and store documents electronically. Thus, online database services store bibliographic information such as publications in large text databases. Text databases are also available on CD-ROM optical disks for use with microcomputer systems. Major corporations and government agencies have developed large text databases containing documents of all kinds. They use *text database management systems* software to help create, store, search, retrieve, modify, and assemble documents and other information stored as text data in such databases. Microcomputer versions of this software have been developed to help users manage their own text databases on CD-ROM disks.

Image and Multimedia Databases

Up to this point, we have discussed databases that hold data in traditional alphanumeric records and files or as documents in text databases. But a wide variety of images can also be stored electronically in **image databases** or **multimedia databases.** For example, *electronic encyclopedias* are available on CD-ROM disks that store thousands of photographs and many animated video sequences as digitized

FIGURE 7.13
CD-ROM disks can hold image
and multimedia databases.

Scott Goodwin.

images, along with thousands of pages of text. The main appeal of image databases for business users is in *document image processing*. Thousands of pages of business documents, such as customer correspondence, purchase orders and invoices, as well as sales catalogs and service manuals, can be optically scanned and stored as document images on a single optical disk. Image database management software allows employees in many companies to quickly retrieve and display documents from image databases holding millions of pages of document images. Workers can view and modify documents at their workstations and electronically route them to the workstations of other end users in the organization. See Figure 7.13.

Managerial Considerations for Data Resource Management

Managerial end users should view data as an important resource that they must learn to manage properly to ensure the success and survival of their organizations. But this is easier said than done.

Database management is an important application of information systems technology to the management of a firm's data resources. However, other major data resource management efforts are needed in order to offset some of the problems that can result from the use of a database management approach. Those are (1) database administration, (2) data planning, and (3) data administration. See Figure 7.14.

Benefits and Limitations of Database Management

The database management approach provides managerial end users with several important benefits. Database management reduces the duplication of data and integrates data so that they can be accessed by multiple programs and users. Programs are not dependent on the format of the data and the type of secondary storage hardware being used. Users are provided with an inquiry/response and reporting capability that allows them to easily obtain information they need without having to

FIGURE 7.14

Data resource management includes database administration, data planning, and data administration activities.

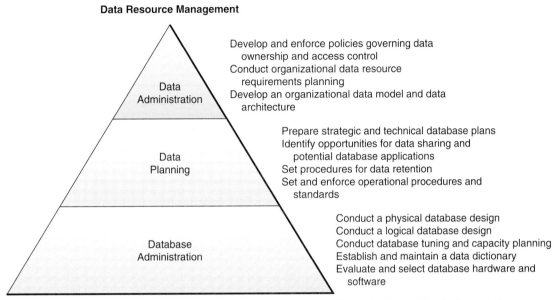

Data Resource Management

Data Administration
- Develop and enforce policies governing data ownership and access control
- Conduct organizational data resource requirements planning
- Develop an organizational data model and data architecture

Data Planning
- Prepare strategic and technical database plans
- Identify opportunities for data sharing and potential database applications
- Set procedures for data retention
- Set and enforce operational procedures and standards

Database Administration
- Conduct a physical database design
- Conduct a logical database design
- Conduct database tuning and capacity planning
- Establish and maintain a data dictionary
- Evaluate and select database hardware and software

Source: Adapted from Varun Grover, and James Teng. "How Effective is Data Resource Management? Reassessing Strategic Objectives," *Journal of Information Systems Management* (New York: Averbach Publications) Summer 1991, pp. 19–20. © 1991 Warren, Gorham & Lanant. Used with permission.

write computer programs. Computer programming is simplified, because programs are not dependent on either the logical format of the data or their physical storage location. Finally, the integrity and security of the data stored in databases can be increased, since access to data and modification of the database are controlled by database management system software, a data dictionary, and a database administrator function.

The limitations of database management arise from its increased technological complexity. Thus, a database management approach can pose problems in data resource management. Developing a large database and installing a DBMS can be difficult and expensive. More hardware capability is required, since storage requirements for the organization's data, overhead control data, and the DBMS programs are greater. Longer processing times may result from high-volume transaction processing applications since an extra layer of software (the DBMS) exists between application programs and the operating system. Finally, if an organization relies on centralized databases, its vulnerability to errors, fraud, and failures is increased. Yet problems of inconsistency of data can arise if a distributed database approach is used. Therefore, the security and integrity of an organization's databases are major concerns of an organization's data resource management effort.

Database administration is an important data resource management function responsible for the proper use of database management technology. Database administration has more operational and technical responsibilities than other data resource management functions. These include responsibilities for developing and maintaining the organization's data dictionary, designing and monitoring the performance of databases, and enforcing standards for database use and security. Database

Database Administration

administrators work with systems analysts, programmers, and end users to provide their expertise to major systems development projects.

Data Planning

Data planning is a corporate planning and analysis function that focuses on data resource management. It includes the responsibility for developing an overall *data architecture* for the firm's data resources that ties in with the firm's strategic mission and plans, and the objectives and processes of its business units. Data planning is thus a major component of an organization's strategic planning process. It shows that an organization has made a formal commitment to long-range planning for the strategic use and management of its data resources. In the next section we will discuss how data planning is also an important first step in developing databases for an organization.

Data Administration

Data administration is another vital data resource management function. It involves the establishment and enforcement of policies and procedures for managing data as a strategic corporate resource. This means that the collection, storage, and dissemination of all types of data are administered in such a way that data become a standardized resource available to all end users in the organization. Thus, a data administrator must learn to work with the diverse business units and work groups in an organization, many of whom are uncomfortable with any attempt to dictate the use of "their data."

Data administration typically is an organizationwide managerial function without the operational and technical focus of database administration. Its focus is the planning and control of data in support of an organization's business functions and strategic business objectives. A major thrust of data administration, therefore, is the establishment of a data planning activity for the organization. Data administration may also include responsibility for developing policies and setting standards for corporate database design, processing, and security arrangements, and for selecting database management and data dictionary software.

Tropicana Products: Multidimensional Databases for Competitive Advantage

Enlightened organizations are tapping a variety of database technologies to aid and abet the gathering and analysis of business-critical data. Many companies are rigging up so-called business intelligence systems that enable PC users networked across the enterprise to access and analyze key sales, marketing, and trends data.

The tools of the trade vary according to the company and its installed base of technology. These systems often distribute intelligence, processing, and data across a variety of platforms. For instance, data from mainframe production systems can be extracted via middleware software to populate data warehouse and multidimensional and/or distributed databases for further analysis and/or business modeling. Take Tropicana Products, for example.

Tropicana's year-end promotional strategy wasn't tasting quite right. So the $1.3 billion juice producer started sniffing around for a more effective campaign. But before it could put the squeeze on customers, the company needed better business intelligence on the impact different types of promotional campaigns might have on consumer buying habits.

Yet Tropicana's mainframe-based decision support system plainly wasn't delivering that type of juicy information. "It wasn't that we were losing money," explained Steve Goodfriend, business development manager for the Eastern division of the Bradenton, Florida-based fruit juice giant. "But it wasn't as much of a winner as we thought, and we weren't quite sure why."

One reason could have been that it often took days to gauge how effective a campaign had—or hadn't—been. And if a promotion had not been successful, time-consuming analysis translated into missed opportunities for both the juice maker and its retailers.

Time for a fresher way to run the numbers to develop a more effective campaign. Enter a multidimensional, client/server database management system called Accumate Enterprise that Tropicana had recently purchased from Cambridge, Massachusetts-based Kenan Technologies, Inc.

The system was built to analyze purchasing patterns by extracting order and promotional campaign data residing on the mainframe and placing the data in a multidimensional database residing on a server.

Tropicana picked one retailer to test its approach. In a matter of three weeks, Goodfriend and crew were able to carefully scrutinize historical data on biweekly buying patterns over a three-year period at that retail chain's stores throughout Florida.

The result was one heck of a happy new year for Tropicana—and its retailer. With the client/server analysis as its guide, Tropicana trashed its 12-week, one-coupon-per-day campaign and substituted a two-week, three-time promotion during that time span. The change brought a 20 percent profit increase and a 33 percent revenue increase.

Even the grocery chain, which Goodfriend declined to identify, experienced a 22 percent profit increase due to increased juice sales. Fully juiced, Tropicana is currently using its newfangled approach at other chains across the United States.

"It's now part of the company's culture," Goodfriend said. "The client/server system did the analysis much more quickly and with greater accuracy, so we were much more confident in the results. We might have reached the same conclusion with our previous system, although I can't even imagine how long it would have taken, but we certainly wouldn't have changed as quickly." Or as smartly.

CASE STUDY QUESTIONS

1. What is a multidimensional database? What is its business purpose?

2. How is Tropicana benefitting from the use of its client/server multidimensional database management system?

3. Why do you think the previous mainframe database system did not provide better business decision support?

Source: Adapted from Willie Schatz, "When Data Is Not Enough," *Computerworld Client/Server Journal*, April 1995, pp. 25–26. Copyright 1995 by Computerworld, Inc., Framingham, MA 01701—Reprinted from *Computerworld*.

┌─ **S E C T I O N   II**
▟ *Technical Foundations of Database Management*

Just imagine how difficult it would be to get any information from an information system if data were stored in an unorganized way, or if there was no systematic way to retrieve it. Therefore, in all information systems, data resources must be organized and structured in some logical manner so that they can be accessed easily, processed efficiently, retrieved quickly, and managed effectively. Thus, *data structures* and *access methods* ranging from simple to complex have been devised to efficiently organize and access data stored by information systems. In this section, we will explore these concepts, as well as more technical concepts of database management.

Database Structures

The relationships among the many individual records stored in databases are based on one of several logical *data structures* or *models*. Database management system packages are designed to use a specific data structure to provide end users with quick, easy access to information stored in databases. Five fundamental database structures are the *hierarchical, network, relational, object-oriented,* and *multidimensional* models. Simplified illustrations of the first three database structures are shown in Figure 7.15.

Hierarchical Structure

Early mainframe DBMS packages used the **hierarchical** structure, in which the relationships between records form a *hierarchy* or treelike structure. In the traditional hierarchical model, all records are dependent and arranged in multilevel structures, consisting of one *root* record and any number of *subordinate* levels. Thus, all of the relationships among records are *one-to-many,* since each data element is related only to one element above it. The data element or record at the highest level of the hierarchy (the department data element in this illustration) is called the *root* element. Any data element can be accessed by moving progressively downward from a root and along the *branches* of the tree until the desired record (for example, the employee data element) is located.

Network Structure

The **network** structure can represent more complex logical relationships, and is still used by many mainframe DBMS packages. It allows *many-to-many* relationships among records—that is, the network model can access a data element by following one of several paths, because any data element or record can be related to any number of other data elements. For example, in Figure 7.15, departmental records can be related to more than one employee record, and employee records can be related to more than one project record. Thus, one could locate all employee records for a particular department, or all project records related to a particular employee.

Relational Structure

The **relational** model has become the most popular of the three database structures. It is used by most microcomputer DBMS packages, as well as many minicomputer and mainframe systems. In the relational model, all data elements within the database are viewed as being stored in the form of simple **tables.** Figure 7.15 illustrates the relational database model with two tables representing some of the relationships among departmental and employee records. Other tables, or *relations,* for this organization's database might represent the data element relationships among projects, divisions, product lines, and so on. Database management system packages

HIERARCHICAL STRUCTURE

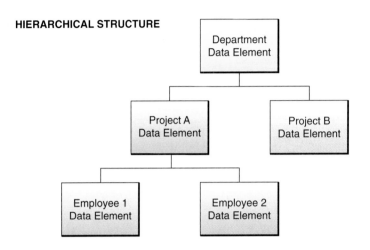

NETWORK STRUCTURE

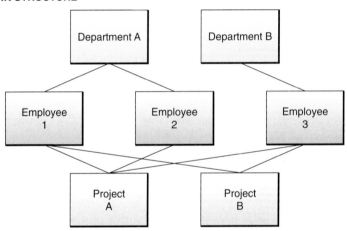

RELATIONAL STRUCTURE

Department Table

Deptno	Dname	Dloc	Dmgr
Dept A			
Dept B			
Dept C			

Employee Table

Empno	Ename	Etitle	Esalary	Deptno
Emp 1				Dept A
Emp 2				Dept A
Emp 3				Dept B
Emp 4				Dept B
Emp 5				Dept C
Emp 6				Dept B

FIGURE 7.15
Examples of three fundamental
database structures. They represent three basic ways to develop
and express the relationships
among the data elements in a
database.

based on the relational model can link data elements from various tables to provide information to users. For example, a DBMS package could retrieve and display an employee's name and salary from the employee table in Figure 7.15, and the name of his or her department from the department table, by using their common department number field (Deptno) to link or *join* the two tables.

FIGURE 7.16
The checking and savings account objects can inherit common attributes and operations from the bank account object.

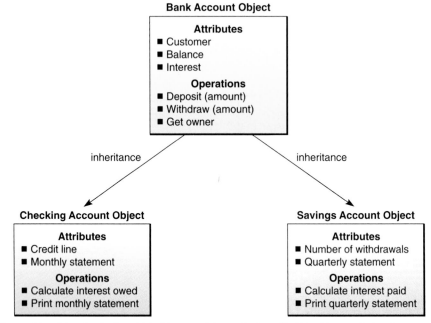

Source: Adapted from Ivar Jacobsen, Maria Ericsson, and Ageneta Jacobsen. *The Object Advantage: Business Process Reengineering with Object Technology* (New York: ACM Press, 1995), p. 65.

Object-Oriented Structure

Other database models are being developed to provide capabilities missing from the hierarchical, network, and relational structures. One example is the **object-oriented** database model. We introduced the concept of objects when we discussed *object-oriented programming* in Chapter 5. As Figure 7.16 illustrates, an **object** consists of data values describing the attributes of an entity, plus the operations that can be performed upon the data. This capability is called *encapsulation,* and it allows the object-oriented model to better handle more complex types of data (graphics, pictures, voice, text) than other database structures. The object-oriented model also supports *inheritance;* that is, new objects can be automatically created by replicating some or all of the characteristics of one or more *parent objects.* Thus, in Figure 7.16, the checking and savings account objects can both inherit the common attributes and operations of the parent bank account object. Such capabilities have made object-oriented database management systems (OODBMS) popular in computer-aided design (CAD) and similar applications. For example, they allow designers to develop product designs, store them as objects in an object-oriented database, and replicate and modify them to create new product designs.

Multidimensional Structure

The **multidimensional** database model uses multidimensional structures to store data and relationships between data. You can visualize multidimensional structures as cubes of data—and cubes within cubes of data. Each side of the cube is considered a dimension of the data. Figure 7.17 is an example that shows that each dimension can represent a different category, such as product type, region, sales channel, and time. Each cell within the multidimensional structure contains aggregated data related to elements along each of the dimensions. For example, a single cell may contain the total sales for a product in a region for a specific sales channel in a single

FIGURE 7.17
An example of the different dimensions of a multidimensional database.

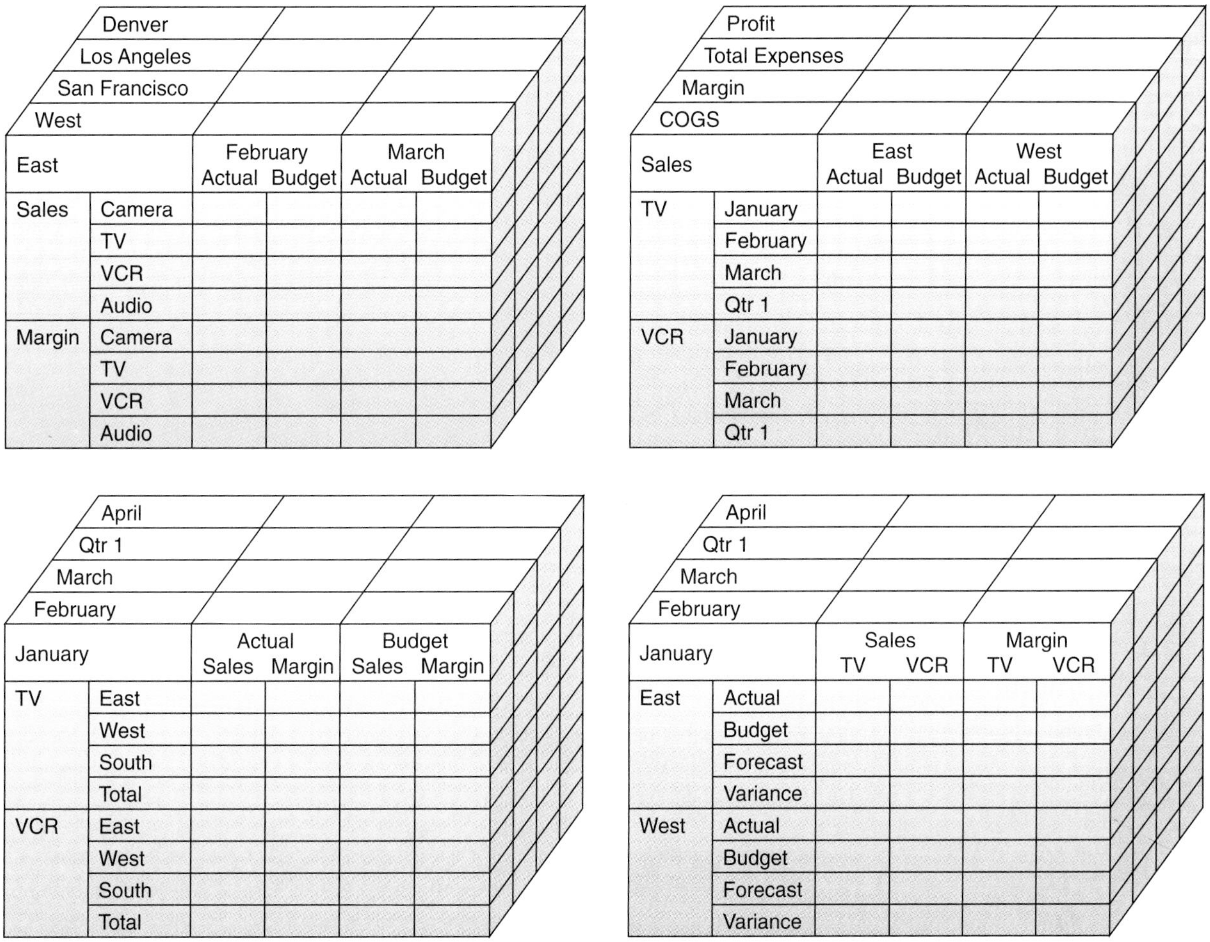

Source: Adapted from Richard Finkelstein, *Understanding the Need for On-Line Analytical Servers.* Ann Arbor, MI., *Arbor Software Corporation,* 1994, p. 9.

month. A major benefit of multidimensional databases is that they are a compact and easy-to-understand way to visualize and manipulate data elements that have many interrelationships. So multidimensional databases have become the most popular database structure for the *analytical databases* that support *online analytical processing* (OLAP) applications, in which fast answers to complex business queries are expected. We will discuss OLAP applications in Chapter 10.

The hierarchical data structure is a natural model for the databases used for many of the structured, routine types of transaction processing characteristic of many business operations. Data for many of these operations can easily be represented by groups of records in a hierarchical relationship. However, there are many cases where information is needed about records that do not have hierarchical relationships. For example, it is obvious that, in some organizations, employees from more than one department can work on more than one project (see Figure 7.15). A

Evaluation of Database Structures

network data structure could easily handle this many-to-many relationship. It is thus more flexible than the hierarchical structure in support of databases for many types of business operations. However, like the hierarchical structure, because its relationships must be specified in advance, the network model cannot easily handle ad hoc requests for information.

Relational databases, on the other hand, allow an end user to easily receive information in response to ad hoc requests. That's because not all of the relationships between the data elements in a relationally organized database need to be specified when the database is created. Database management software (such as Oracle, DB2, Access, and Approach) create new tables of data relationships using parts of the data from several tables. Thus, relational databases are easier for programmers to work with and easier to maintain than the hierarchical and network models.

The major limitation of the relational model is that database management systems based on it cannot process large amounts of business transactions as quickly and efficiently as those based on the hierarchical and network models, in which all data relationships are prespecified. However, this performance gap is narrowing with the development of advanced relational DBMS software. The use of database management software based on the object-oriented and multidimensional models is growing steadily, but these technologies are still not developed fully enough for widespread use in most business information systems.

Database Development

Developing small, personal databases is relatively easy using microcomputer database management packages. See Figure 7.18. However, developing a large database can be a complex task. In many companies, developing and managing large corporate databases is the primary responsibility of the database administrator and database design analysts. They work with end users and systems analysts to deter-

FIGURE 7.18
Creating a database with Microsoft Access. This display shows how a customer record is created and added to the Customers table that is part of a company database.

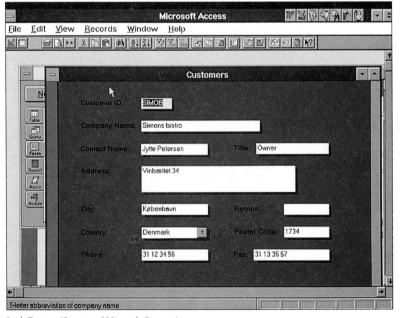

Sarah Evertson/Courtesy of Microsoft Corporation.

mine (1) what data definitions should be included in the database and (2) what structure or relationships should exist among the data elements.

As Figure 7.19 illustrates, database development may start with a top-down **data planning** process. Database administrators and designers work with corporate and end user management to develop an *enterprise model* that defines the basic business processes of the enterprise. Then they define the information needs of end users in a business process, such as the purchasing/receiving process that all businesses have [16].

Next, end users must identify the key data elements that are needed to perform their specific business activities. This frequently involves developing *entity relationship diagrams* (ERDs) that model the relationships among the many entities involved in business processes. For example, Figure 7.20 illustrates some of the relationships in a purchasing/receiving system. End users and database designers could use ERD models to identify what supplier and product data are necessary in the purchasing/receiving process. These *user views* are a major part of a **data modeling**

Data Planning and Database Design

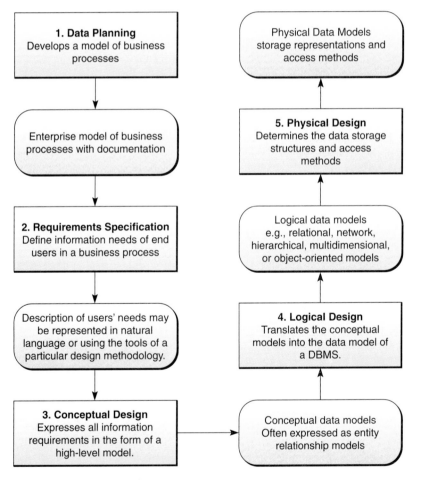

Source: Adapted from Veda Storey and Robert Goldstein, "Knowledge-Based Approaches to Database Design," *MIS Quarterly*, March 1993, p. 26. Reprinted with permission from the *MIS Quarterly*. Copyright 1993 by the Society for Information Management and the Management Information Systems Research Center at the University of Minnesota.

FIGURE 7.19
Database development involves data planning and database design activities. Data models that support business processes are used to develop databases that meet the information needs of users.

FIGURE 7.20
This entity relationship diagram
illustrates some of the relationships among entities in a pur-
chasing/receiving system.

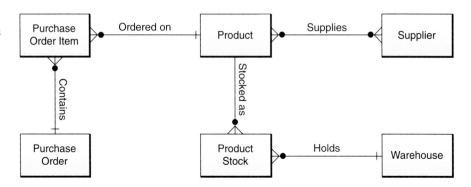

process where the relationships between data elements are identified. Each data model defines the logical relationships among the data elements needed to support a basic business process. For example, can a supplier provide more than one type of product to us? Can a customer have more than one type of account with us? Can an employee have several pay rates or be assigned to several project work groups? Answering such questions will identify data relationships that have to be represented in a data model that supports a business process.

These data models then serve as logical frameworks (called *schemas* and *subschemas*) on which to base the *physical design* of databases and the development of application programs to support the business processes of the organization. A schema is an overall logical view of the relationships between data in a database, while the *subschema* is a logical view of the data relationships needed to support specific end user application programs that will access that database.

Remember that data models represent *logical views* of the data and relationships of the database. Physical database design takes a *physical* view of the data (also called the *internal* view) which describes how data is to be physically arranged, stored, and accessed on the magnetic disks and other secondary storage devices of a computer system. For example, Figure 7.21 shows these different database views and the software interface of a bank database processing system.

Accessing Files and Databases

Databases and files are stored on various types of storage media and are organized in a variety of ways to make it easier to access the data records they contain. In database and file maintenance, records have to be continually added, deleted, or updated to reflect business transactions. Data must also be accessed so information can be produced in response to end user requests. Thus, efficient access to data is important.

· *Key Fields*

That's why all data records usually contain one or more identification fields, or keys, that identify the record so it can be located. For example, the social security number of a person is often used as a *primary* **key field** that uniquely identifies the data records of individuals in student, employee, and customer files and databases. Other methods can be used to identify and link data records stored in several different database files. For example, hierarchical and network databases may use *pointer fields*. These are fields within a record that indicate (point to) the location of another record that is related to it in the same file, or in another file. Hierarchical and net-

FIGURE 7.21
Examples of the logical and physical database views and the software interface of a database processing system in banking.

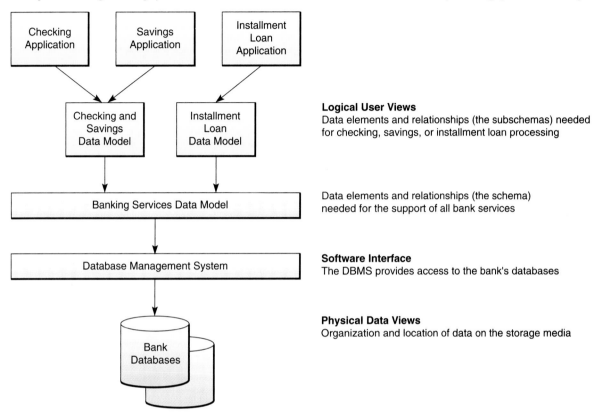

Logical User Views
Data elements and relationships (the subschemas) needed for checking, savings, or installment loan processing

Data elements and relationships (the schema) needed for the support of all bank services

Software Interface
The DBMS provides access to the bank's databases

Physical Data Views
Organization and location of data on the storage media

work database management systems use this method to link records so they can retrieve information from several different database files.

Relational database management packages use primary keys to link records. Each table (file) in a relational database must contain a primary key. This field (or fields) uniquely identifies each record in a file and must also be found in other related files. For example, in Figure 7.15, department number (Deptno) is the primary key in the Department table and is also a field in the Employee table. As we mentioned earlier, a relational database management package could easily provide you with information from both tables to *join* the tables and retrieve the information you want. See Figure 7.22.

One of the basic ways to access data is to use a **sequential organization,** in which records are physically stored in a specified order according to a key field in each record. For example, payroll records could be placed in a payroll file in a numerical order based on employee social security numbers. **Sequential access** is fast and efficient when dealing with large volumes of data that need to be processed periodically. However, it requires that all new transactions be sorted into the proper sequence for *sequential access processing.* Also, most of the database or file may have to be searched to locate, store, or modify even a small number of data records. Thus, this method is too slow to handle applications requiring immediate updating or responses.

Sequential Organization and Access

FIGURE 7.22

Joining the Employee and Department tables in a relational database allows you to selectively access data in both tables at the same time.

Department Table

Deptno	Dname	Dloc	Dmgr
Dept A			
Dept B			
Dept C			

Employee Table

Empno	Ename	Etitle	Esalary	Deptno
Emp 1				Dept A
Emp 2				Dept A
Emp 3				Dept B
Emp 4				Dept B
Emp 5				Dept C
Emp 6				Dept B

Direct Organization and Access

When using **direct access** methods, records do not have to be arranged in any particular sequence on storage media. However, the computer must keep track of the storage location of each record using a variety of **direct organization** methods so that data can be retrieved when needed. New transactions data do not have to be sorted, and processing that requires immediate responses or updating is easily handled. There are a number of ways to directly access records in the direct organization method. Let's take a look at three widely used methods to accomplish such *direct access processing*.

One common technique of direct access is called **key transformation.** This method performs an arithmetic computation on a key field of record (such as a product number or social security number) and uses the number that results from that calculation as an address to store and access that record. Thus, the process is called *key transformation* because an arithmetic operation is applied to a key field to transform it into the storage location address of a record. Another direct access method used to store and locate records involves the use of an **index** of record keys and related storage addresses. A new data record is stored at the next available location, and its key and address are placed in an index. The computer uses this index whenever it must access a record.

In the **indexed sequential access method** (ISAM), records are physically stored in a sequential order on a magnetic disk or other direct access storage device based on the key field of each record. In addition, each file contains an index that references one or more key fields of each data record to its storage location address. Thus, an individual record can be directly located by using its key fields to search and locate its address in the file index, just as you can locate key topics in this book by looking them up in its index. As a result, if a few records must be processed quickly, the file index is used to directly access the record needed. However, when large numbers of records must be processed periodically, the sequential organization provided by this method is used. For example, processing the weekly payroll for employees or producing monthly statements for customers would be done using sequential access processing of the records in the file or database.

REAL WORLD CASE

DHL Worldwide Express: Data Warehouses for Business Analysis

DHL Worldwide Express, the world's leading international express delivery service, moves hundreds of thousands of packages through 14 major international hubs every day, servicing customers in more than 220 countries. That makes data management a critical issue for DHL.

Adding to the challenge is the fact that DHL operates as a completely decentralized organization. Operations in each of its regions and countries are independent and each implements its own IT services based on global standards and infrastructure.

This decentralized data environment made worldwide reporting and analysis a challenge. Files from 188 costing areas in a variety of formats had to be painstakingly reconciled and merged to build a single view of all the information.

In addition, corporate customers depend on DHL to track their costs and service levels, because the diffusion of shipping activity across offices and departments makes it difficult for them to do so on their own. Customers expect DHL to be able to give them a precise accounting of how they've spent their money and what they've received in return.

But without a data warehouse, that type of report was the one package DHL couldn't easily deliver overnight.

Impetus for the data warehousing project was initially created by a request for an integrated information system at DHL's Worldwide Coordination Centre in Brussels, Belgium. Discussions with users pointed up the diverse ways different people wanted to correlate and view data. Both this need to slice data in different ways and the fact that the global IT team couldn't dictate any changes in the way each region and country ran its own operations led to the decision to build a data warehouse.

"We had to take the data as it was provided to us and work with that," says Dee Copelan, a member of the team that spearheaded the data warehousing project at DHL Systems in Burlingame, California. Copelan found that bringing in business managers added an extra dimension to the project. "They were the ones who could look beyond the way things were and tell us what they'd really like to see," she says.

Copelan cautions against the urge to do too much, though. "We originally planned to integrate data from five applications into the warehouse," she says, adding that they eventually scaled the first phase down to two applications. Copelan says that the integration of data from the two applications—marketing and costing—provided plenty of benefits.

She also feels confident that the flexibility of DHL's data warehousing approach will let them add other data sources incrementally as required. "With a data warehouse, it's more important to show results quickly and then respond to user feedback," she says. Copelan sees data warehousing as providing useful diagnostics because it helps make data logically consistent. "It really highlights problems in the corporate information environment, such as when different groups define terms differently," she says.

For DHL, data warehousing means that reports based on data from worldwide operations can now be generated in hours instead of days. And since users don't have to spend their time cleaning up data and massaging files, they can now address the kind of in-depth business analysis that delivers real value to the organization. What it means for DHL is that it can now better correlate information about cost and revenue variables in different countries and take appropriate action.

Perhaps most importantly, global account managers can now present their customers and prospects with accurate, good-looking reports in a timely fashion. "That ability alone goes a long way to justifying the cost of the project," says Copelan. "We've provided a new marketing tool to help DHL land and keep the global customers we're targeting."

CASE STUDY QUESTIONS

1. How does a data warehouse differ from other types of databases?

2. Why did DHL need a data warehouse? What benefits have resulted?

3. What challenges did DHL face in building its data warehouse? What lessons were learned that could help other businesses?

Summary

- **Data Resource Management.** Data resource management is a managerial activity that applies information systems technology and management tools to the task of managing an organization's data resources. It includes the database administration function which focuses on developing and maintaining standards and controls for an organization's databases. Data administration, however, focuses on the planning and control of data to support business functions and strategic organizational objectives. This includes a data planning effort that focuses on developing an overall data architecture for a firm's data resources.

- **Database Management.** The database management approach affects the storage and processing of data. The data needed by different applications is consolidated and integrated into several common databases, instead of being stored in many independent data files. Also, the database management approach emphasizes updating and maintaining common databases, having users' application programs share the data in the database, and providing a reporting and an inquiry/response capability so end users can easily receive reports and quick responses to requests for information.

- **Database Software.** Database management systems are software packages that simplify the creation, use, and maintenance of databases. They provide software tools so end users, programmers, and database administrators can create and modify databases, interrogate a database, generate reports, do application development, and perform database maintenance.

- **Types of Databases.** Several types of databases are used by computer-using organizations, including central, distributed, end user, management, data warehouse, and online databases. Text databases consist of data in text form, while image databases contain digitized images of documents, photographs, and other visual media. Special database management software is used to catalog and index such databases for quick retrieval of text and images of documents or other forms of information.

- **Database Development.** The development of databases can be easily accomplished using microcomputer database management packages for small end user applications. However, the development of large corporate databases requires a top-down data planning effort. This may involve developing enterprise and entity relationship models, subject area databases, and data models that reflect the logical data elements and relationships needed to support the operation and management of the basic business processes of the organization.

- **Data Organization and Access.** Data must be organized in some logical manner on physical storage devices so that it can be efficiently processed. For this reason, data is commonly organized into logical data elements such as characters, fields, records, files, and databases. Database structures, such as the hierarchical, network, relational, and object-oriented models, are used to organize the relationships among the data records stored in databases. Databases and files can be organized in either a sequential or direct manner and can be accessed and maintained by either sequential access or direct access processing methods.

Key Terms and Concepts

These are the key terms and concepts of this chapter. The page number of their first explanation is in parentheses.

1. Data administration (244)
2. Data dictionary (235)
3. Data modeling (251)
4. Data planning (244)
5. Data resource management (232)
6. Database administration (243)
7. Database administrator (235)
8. Database management approach (234)
9. Database management system (235)
10. Database structures (246)
    a. Hierarchical (246)
    b. Network (246)
    c. Multidimensional (248)
    d. Object-oriented (248)
    e. Relational (246)
11. Database and file access (252)
    a. Direct (254)
    b. Sequential (253)
12. DBMS uses (235)
    a. Application development (238)
    b. Database development (250)
    c. Database interrogation (236)
    d. Database maintenance (238)
13. Key field (252)
14. Logical data elements (232)
    a. Character (232)
    b. Field (233)
    c. Record (233)
    d. File (233)
    e. Database (234)
15. Query language (236)
16. Report generator (236)
17. Types of databases (239)
    a. Analytical (240)
    b. Distributed (240)
    c. End user (241)
    d. External (241)
    e. Image (241)
    f. Data warehouse (240)
    g. Multimedia (241)
    h. Operational (239)
    i. Text (241)

Review Quiz

Match one of the key terms and concepts listed above with one of the brief examples or definitions listed below. Try to find the best fit for answers that seem to fit more than one term or concept. Defend your choices.

___ 1. The use of integrated collections of data records and files for data storage and processing.

___ 2. A DBMS allows you to create, interrogate, and maintain a database, create reports, and develop application programs.

___ 3. A specialist in charge of the databases of an organization.

___ 4. This DBMS feature allows users to easily interrogate a database.

___ 5. Defines and catalogs the data elements and data relationships in an organization's database.

___ 6. Helps you specify and produce reports from a database.

___ 7. The main software package that supports a database management approach.

___ 8. Databases are dispersed throughout an organization.

___ 9. Your own personal databases.

___ 10. Databases of documents.

___ 11. Applies information systems technology and management tools to the management of an organization's data resources.

___ 12. Developing databases and maintaining standards and controls for an organization's databases.

___ 13. The planning and control of data to support organizational objectives.

___ 14. A top-down effort that ties database development to the support of basic business processes.

___ 15. Developing conceptual views of the relationships among data in a database.

___ 16. A customer's name.

___ 17. A customer's name, address, and account balance.

___ 18. The names, addresses, and account balances of all of your customers.

___ 19. An integrated collection of all of the data about your customers.

___ 20. An identification field in a record.

___ 21. A treelike structure of records in a database.

___ 22. A tabular structure of records in a database.

___ 23. Records are stored as cubes within cubes in a database.

___ 24. Transactions are sorted in ascending order by social security number before processing.

___ 25. Unsorted transactions can be used to immediately update a database.

___ 26. Databases that support the major business processes of an organization.

___ 27. A centralized and integrated database of current and historical data about an organization.

___ 28. Databases provided by online information services.

___ 29. Databases that store data as text, images, sound, and video.

Discussion Questions

1. Organizations could not survive or succeed without quality data about their internal operations and external environment. Do you agree? What examples can you give to defend your position?

2. If data is an important resource and asset to a firm, it must be managed properly. What role does database management and data administration play in managing data?

3. What are the advantages of the database management approaches to managing an organization's data resources? Give examples to illustrate your answer.

4. Refer to the Real World Case on Tropicana Products in the chapter. How can database technologies help create "business intelligence systems"?

5. What is a database management system? What functions does it enable end users and IS professionals to accomplish?

6. Databases of information about a firm's internal operations were formerly the only databases that were considered to be important to a business. What other kinds of databases are there? What is their importance to end users and their organizations?

7. Refer to the Real World Case on DHL Worldwide Express in the chapter. Why can't organizations get the benefits of a data warehouse by accessing the data in their traditional company databases?

8. Why has the relational database model become more

important than the hierarchical and network structures? Why do you think object-oriented database models are gaining in popularity?

9. Why would developing an organization's database require a data planning effort that was part of a strategic planning process of an organization?

10. Refer to the Real World Case on Time Warner and FedEx in the chapter. Mohammad Fahim of Time Warner says that "I've seen systems that cannot be changed—period." What does he mean? Do you agree? Why or why not?

Real World Problems

1. Scotiabank: Object-Oriented Database Applications

Two years ago, no one at Scotiabank had built an object, nevermind written a Smalltalk application for an object-oriented database. But today, that is just what developers at the 1,200-branch Toronto-based bank are doing. This week, Scotiabank plans to start user acceptance testing of an object-oriented deposit processing application designed to help new customers choose savings accounts. The module is one of four that made up an object-oriented banking sales and services system at Scotiabank, which operates branches in Canada and 45 other countries. The new system will keep demographic information on individual and commercial customers and help salespeople target investment, loan, and other bank products to individuals. Today, that is done largely via text-based applications or paper and pencil "and the common sense of our employees," said Drew Brown, manager of systems development at the bank.

The project also marks the first time databases will reside at local branches at all. Scotiabank standardized on object-oriented database management systems from Versant Object Technology. By putting database smarts at each branch, Scotiabank is shooting for more customizable applications. For example, not all branches offer the same loan, investment and other programs, so applications could be modified to reflect those differences, Brown said. Local databases also mean that each location can keep detailed data relevant to its community, passing along only the appropriate summary information to corporate headquarters. "Today everything comes up to the host, and that's just a waste of time and resources," Brown said.

a. Why would Scotiabank develop object-oriented banking applications and databases?

b. Why did they distribute these databases to each branch?

Source: Adapted from Kim Nash, "Toronto Bank Rolls into Object Mode," *Computerworld*, March 6, 1995, p. 69. Copyright 1995 by Computerworld, Inc., Framingham, MA 01701—Reprinted from *Computerworld*.

2. McKesson Corporation: Using Very Large Data Warehouses

Very large databases (VLDB)—storehouses of several hundred gigabytes or a few terabytes of data—are starting to arrive on Unix-based computers thanks to a combination of key hardware and software advances. Most Unix-based VLDBs are used for data warehousing, where a subset of the no-longer-live production data is downloaded to executives or marketers, for example, who use it to make assumptions and decisions.

Indeed, it is today's craze for data warehousing—the technology hula hoop of the 1990s—that will result in Unix users' pushing the outer limits of database size, according to Richard Winter, an analyst at The Winter Corp., a consulting firm in Cambridge, Massachusetts. Retailers are becoming detailers, Winter said, referring to the voracious appetite among grocery stores, clothing chains, discounters, and other consumer-oriented companies to find out why people buy what and when. "That's really just a series of sophisticated database queries on very large amounts of data," he said.

For McKesson Corp., one of the largest health and beauty products companies in the world, VLDB had to mesh with production data already stored on Oracle databases, said Tracy Currie, director of Unix computing at McKesson. The $13 billion San Francisco-based company plans to cut over from its old data warehouse, which is based on proprietary database software from Tandem Computers, Currie said. If all goes well, the system will track the 120,000 products, 30,000 clients, and 4,000 suppliers that account for McKesson's $33 million-a-day business, he explained.

a. Why is data warehousing so popular today?

b. How will McKesson benefit from its use of a new VLDB data warehouse?

Source: Adapted from Kim Nash, "Unix Databases Handling Larger Loads," *Computerworld*, May 8, 1995, p. 67. Copyright 1995 by Computerworld, Inc., Framingham, MA 01701—Reprinted from *Computerworld*.

3. Sikorsky Aircraft: Relational/Object Databases

The definition of *computer document* is changing to represent a container of text, images, graphics, audio, and video. For example, XyVision's Patiance Document Manager software lets users produce and store documents made up of text, images, and graphics to paper, CD-ROM, and networks. The information is stored in a relational database in the form of *binary large objects* or BLOBS. And information about the objects themselves is stored in system-generated or user-defined relational tables.

At Sikorsky Aircraft in Stamford, Connecticut, maintenance manuals can now be created on CD-ROM from the same information used for paper manuals at no additional cost. "We are moving away from publishing to managing information and leveraging that information and historical data to create new products and variations of products that we would never have been able to do before," said Rich Welch, director of technical support services at Sikorsky.

Sikorsky has about 750,000 pages of data in Parlance Document Manager right now, Welch said. The company has four core helicopter products, but numerous small variations and options create many different product lines, he said. "In the old system we had to replicate and recopy all that information," he said. "We wanted to break things into modules, because we were selling more and more derivative products, but it was costing more and more to publish this information."

a. How can multimedia documents be stored and managed by a relational DBMS?

b. How is Sikorsky Aircraft benefiting from the use of relational document management?

Source: Adapted from Tim Ouellette, "Document Management Gets a New Look," *Computerworld*, May 15, 1995, p. 49. Copyright 1995 by Computerworld, Inc., Framingham, MA 01701—Reprinted from *Computerworld*.

4. MCI Communications: Client/Server Data Warehouse

A client/server data warehouse has helped boost the odds in MCI's favor. Two years ago, the $10 billion Washington-based telecommunications company instituted a corporate systems reengineering program. Its Colorado Springs-based Systems Engineering Division was given the honor of executing the program for the company's operational systems. MCI's mantra: Give its sales and marketing folks enough ammunition to help the company retain current customers and attract new ones by getting them to disconnect from AT&T Corp. and Sprint Corp.

Before moving to a client/server database architecture, sales and marketing specialists would often wait days or weeks before one of 17 IBM ES/9000 mainframes responded to their query. That delay often left them feeling helpless, hopeless, and furious. Meanwhile, some customers and prospects, tired of waiting for answers, hung up on MCI. But by installing Sybase's System 10.2 relational database on Unix servers located at its four data centers in Sacramento, California, Rockville, Maryland, Perryman, Maryland, and North Royalton, Ohio, late last year, MCI has created a data warehouse that extracts all relevant sales and marketing information from the mainframe for easy access and manipulation. Using sophisticated front-end query tools, personnel on PCs anywhere across MCI's fully wired enterprise can now request data pertinent to closing a sale. Answers arrive back in minutes instead of in days.

a. What is the business incentive for developing a data warehouse?

b. How is MCI benefiting from the use of a client/server data warehouse?

Source: Adapted from Willie Schatz, "When Data Is Not Enough," *Computerworld Client/Server Journal*, April 1995, pp. 25–27. Copyright 1995 by Computerworld, Inc., Framingham, MA 01701—Reprinted from *Computerworld*.

5. R. R. Donnelley & Sons: E-Mail and Database Management

Chicago-based publisher R. R. Donnelley & Sons, Inc., has joined a growing number of users exploiting tighter links between databases and electronic mail systems to speed deployment of distributed applications. They are developing a multimedia publishing system that will be used by the company's clients and employees. It will exploit tight links between several E-mail systems and Oracle's document management and database management products. "Our intention is to use E-mail to support transaction processing as it pertains to publishing," said Donna Kmetz, product manager for Donnelley. "In a traditional document management system, any piece of mail might have a document attached to it. We're storing those documents in our standard database," she said.

As such, users will be able to retrieve documents, text and images from databases and route them around the organization or deliver them to clients via E-mail or by fax. Since the data is stored in a database managed by an Oracle DBMS, the company will be able to make quick queries to determine the whereabouts of data, according to Kmetz. This will help them more quickly fulfill customers' requests for particular information, she said. The application will also be integrated with an Internet browser so that users can retrieve information from the Internet, route it by E-mail to others in the organization, and store it in the database, Kmetz said.

a. What are the business benefits of linking E-mail systems with database management systems?

b. How is R. R. Donnelley going to implement an E-mail/database system? What benefits do they expect?

Source: Adapted from Barb Cole, "The Union of E-Mail and DBMS," *Network World*, April 10, 1995, pp. 1, 85.

6. Clemson University and Einstein Healthcare: English to SQL

English Wizard is a database utility that works with PC applications such as single-user databases, spreadsheets, and report writers (refer back to Figure 7.10 for an example). It translates English to various forms of SQL, the most common query language for talking to relational databases. "You don't have to know a lick of SQL, really, which means almost no training time for end users," said James Bradshaw, a director of database administration at Clemson University in Clemson, South Carolina. "You don't have to forget everything you always knew," he said. The college has tested English Wizard for four months to access an Oracle data warehousing database and a CA-IDMA mainframe database. Two hundred to 300 users across Clemson's campus use English Wizard to query and analyze information on student enrollment data, finances, purchasing and other topics, Bradshaw said.

Larry Harris, founder and president of Linguistic

Technology, which developed English Wizard, has roots in artificial intelligence. In 1975, he cofounded AICorp, which made a mainframe-based natural query language called Intellect. Most of English Wizard's 40 beta test sites are also Intellect users. English Wizard includes a data dictionary, a DOS file of English words and their meanings in different contexts. The product also translates complicated database functions such as "subselects" and "having" clauses.

Albert Einstein Healthcare Foundation has tested the Access version of the product for the past few months and plans to roll it out to end users "as soon as possible," said John Mastronardo, information center manager at the foun-

dation in Philadelphia. Accounting clerks and medical personnel will be able to pull down mainframe patient and payroll data without requesting special reports from Einstein's information systems department, Mastronardo said. "We think it will be a time-saver for a lot of people," he added.

a. Why is there a need for a query language like English Wizard?

b. How are Clemson and Einstein going to use and benefit from this product?

Source: Adapted from Kim Nash, "Wizard Turns English into Database Language," *Computerworld,* February 20, 1994, p. 116. Copyright 1995 by Computerworld, Inc., Framingham, MA 01701—Reprinted from *Computerworld.*

Application Exercises

1. End User Database Development.

Use a database management software package to create a Student Exam Scores file to store the set of sample data shown below. Each student record includes the student's name, social security number, gender, and grades for three exams.

Sample Student Exam Scores

Name	Soc. Sec. #	Gender	Exam 1	Exam 2	Exam 3
Bevins, M.	386-27-1894	Female	88	84	91
Davidson, P.	684-76-9013	Male	72	79	74
Gorton, A.	713-23-9870	Male	93	90	94
Jones, J.	593-94-7826	Female	57	63	61
Miller, G.	774-92-6927	Female	96	94	98
Perkins, P.	657-83-6204	Male	53	59	64
Shaw, J.	546-68-0632	Female	76	74	79

a. Create the student exam scores file, enter the data records for the seven students shown below, and get a printed listing of the Student Exam Scores file.

b. Edit the Student Exam Scores file by changing at least two exam scores and add at least one new student record. Choose any values you want for these changes and additions. When you have completed these changes, get another printed listing of the Student Exam Scores file.

c. Retrieve a printed listing of all students whose score on the first exam was 85 or higher.

d. Create and print a report showing the exam scores and total points earned by students aggregated into male and female categories.

2. Baxter Lawn Products Company

John Davis is in charge of the assembly department at Baxter Lawn Products Company. The company produces wheelbarrows, and John's department is responsible for the final assembly of the wheelbarrows and their packing for shipment. Two identical assembly lines are used, and each line is

Week#: 14

Shift	Line	Mon.	Tue.	Wed.	Thur.	Fri.	Total
Day	A	1426	1602	1574	1611	1538	
Day	B	1507	1564	1533	1498	1551	
Eve.	A	1588	1602	1618	1574	1498	
Eve.	B	1528	1517	1563	1548	1502	

Week#: 15

Shift	Line	Mon.	Tue.	Wed.	Thur.	Fri.	Total
Day	A	1523	1584	1593	1602	1577	
Day	B	1569	1602	1566	1592	1599	
Eve.	A	1558	1581	1583	1599	1563	
Eve.	B	1523	1543	1576	1567	1507	

Week#: 16

Shift	Line	Mon.	Tue.	Wed.	Thur.	Fri.	Total
Day	A	1498	1583	1569	1593	1573	
Day	B	1538	1592	1607	1572	1584	
Eve.	A	1611	1619	1607	1593	1592	
Eve.	B	1558	1538	1547	1539	1503	

operated on two shifts daily. The total number of units assembled is reported to upper management on a weekly basis. This information is collected on a daily basis by each shift's supervisor and recorded on a simple paper form like those shown above. At the end of the week, John adds up the daily figures and reports only a single weekly total, which is recorded in the organization's database and used by upper management.

In recent weeks, output of the assembly department has declined. When John discussed these problems with the shift supervisors and some of the assembly line workers, he found considerable disagreement about where the problems lay. Each shift and production line seemed to feel that another shift or line was responsible, and some workers specifically suggested that there were problems with the condition of workers and their performance on the Monday day shift and the Friday evening shift.

John decided to create his own database file to determine where the problems lay and to track performance on a day-to-day basis for each line. He plans to enter a record every week for each line of each shift, showing the output for that line for each day of the week. Each record will have the following variables: Week#, Line, Shift, Mon out, Tue out, Wed out, Thur out, Fri out and, Tot out.

a. Use a database package to create a database to store this data, enter the data, and check it for accuracy.

b. Create one or more reports providing comparisons of the performance of each line and shift and showing how production on each shift varied over the days of the week.

Review Quiz Answers

1.	8	9.	17c	17.	14c	25.	11a
2.	12	10.	17i	18.	14d	26.	17h
3.	7	11.	5	19.	14e	27.	17f
4.	15	12.	6	20.	13	28.	17d
5.	2	13.	1	21.	10a	29.	17g
6.	16	14.	4	22.	10e		
7.	9	15.	3	23.	10c		
8.	17b	16.	14b	24.	11b		

Selected References

1. Ahrens, Judith, and Chetan Sankar. "Tailoring Database Training for End Users." *MIS Quarterly,* December 1993.
2. Babcock, Charles. "OLAP Leads Way to Post-Relational Era." *Computerworld,* November 21, 1994.
3. Bruegger, Dave, and Sooun Lee. "Distributed Database Systems: Accessing Data more Efficiently." *Information Systems Management,* Spring 1995.
4. Cafasso, Rosemary. "Multidimensional DB on Comeback Trail." *Computerworld,* October 24, 1994.
5. Chan, Hock Chuan; Kee Wei Kwock; and Keng Leng Siau. "User-Database Interface: The Effect of Abstraction Levels on Query Performance." *MIS Quarterly,* December 1993.
6. Courtney, James, and David Paradice. *Database Systems for Management.* 2nd ed. Homewood, IL: Richard D. Irwin, 1992.
7. Grover, Varun, and James Teng. "How Effective Is Data Resource Management? Reassessing Strategic Objectives." *Journal of Information Systems Management,* Summer 1991.
8. Jacobsen, Ivar; Maria Ericsson; and Ageneta Jacobsen. *The Object Advantage: Business Process Reengineering with Object Technology.* New York: ACM Press. 1995.
9. Jenkings, Avery. "Warehouse Woes." *In Depth: Computerworld,* February 6, 1995.
10. Kroenke, David. *Database Processing: Fundamentals, Design, Implementation.* New York, MacMillan, 1992.
11. Nash, Kim. "Wizard Turns English into Database Language." *Computerworld,* February 20, 1995.
12. Pei, Daniel, and Carmine Cutone. "Object-Oriented Analysis and Design: Realism or Impressionism." *Information Systems Management,* Winter 1995.
13. "Shedding Light on Data Warehousing for More Informed Business Solutions." *Special Advertising Supplement, Computerworld,* February 13, 1995.
14. Slitz, John. "Object Technology Profiles." *Special Advertising Supplement, Computerworld,* June 13, 1994.
15. Smith, Lavica. "Developers Eye Object Databases," *PC Week,* February 15, 1993.
16. Storey, Veda, and Robert Goldstein. "Knowledge-Based Approaches to Database Design." *MIS Quarterly,* March 1993.
17. Tasker, Daniel. "Object Lesson." *Computerworld,* April 22, 1991.
18. Spiegler, Israel. "Toward a Unified View of Data: Bridging Data Structure and Content." *Information Systems Management,* Spring 1995.
19. Wylder, John. "The Network as the Enterprise Database." *Information Systems Management,* Spring 1995.

Time Warner and FedEx: Building Databases and Systems with Business Objects

Business objects are building blocks representing business actors, events, and processes such as customers, new store openings, and order fulfillment. They are, in essence, cousins of technology objects such as windows or data structures.

A small but growing number of companies, such as Fidelity Investment Co., US West, Inc., FedEx Corp., General Electric Co., and others, are embracing the concept. They're using business objects to model processes and systems in reengineering projects or to help analyze how their business works so they can build better databases and information systems.

Business objects include the behaviors, procedures, and attributes associated with the object. For example, a customer object includes attributes such as address, credit history, and behaviors like placing an order or paying an invoice. Business object models include not only the objects themselves but the interactions between them.

Early adopters say business objects offer several benefits:

- Faster and cheaper delivery of new systems and simplified maintenance of older applications.

- Tighter links between software and databases, and business processes and functions.

- Better consistency and easier integration of applications due to their reusable nature.

- Good suitability to distributed environments.

Time Warner

Mohammad Fahim came to Time Warner Communications a year ago for a daunting assignment: Develop all the software applications for a start-up local telephone company that would provide service to 40 locations around the country. Fahim knew that to accomplish this feat he would need an approach that would let him develop systems quickly and make continual changes to business processes. His choice: business objects.

Fahim says the ability to easily change how business is done is especially key in a new organization. Business processes are likely to evolve as the company grows and gains real-life experience, he notes, and computer systems must keep pace. "I have seen too many systems that are just too

brittle," says Fahim, director of information systems and services at the Denver-based cable television division of Time Warner, Inc. "I've seen systems that cannot be changed—period."

Pioneers such as Time Warner, which began its development efforts in May 1994, are plowing ahead. Time Warner rolled out its first business object systems—order management and trouble management—in Rochester, New York, late last year and in New York City last month.

Systems will be extended to other cities as local telephone service is turned on, Fahim says. Other systems under development included service provisioning, network monitoring, and billing.

His group plans to bring out dozens of systems during a three-year period. About 60 people, including 50 employees of CresSoft, Inc., a systems integrator in Englewood, Colorado, are working full-time to develop the systems.

The architecture for the new system comprises Sun Microsystems SPARC 2000 servers running Unix and Sybase System 10.2 relational database management system. The clients include SPARC 1000 workstations and Intel Pentium-based PCs.

To develop the objects, the group is using an object-oriented development tool called Visual Works from Parc Place Systems, Inc., in Sunnyvale, California.

FedEx

FedEx was attracted to business objects as a reengineering tool. In 1991 the parcel carrier began a massive project to reengineer its core air and ground operations. The goal was to prepare for a gradual move away from a centralized distribution system, explains Frank Ginett, a senior technical fellow at FedEx.

Under the old system, all packages were routed through Memphis. With the decentralized approach, packages travel through regional hubs. That meant moving from a centralized mainframe environment to a distributed client/server approach. "You want to have more of your resources closer to the customer," Ginett says.

The project involved several business processes, including aircraft scheduling, aircraft maintenance, crew scheduling, weather tracking, volume prediction, courier

Source: Adapted form Linda Wilson, "New Foundations," *Computerworld*, May 1, 1995, pp. 113–114. Copyright 1995 by Computerworld, Inc., Framingham, MA 01701—Reprinted from *Computerworld*.

scheduling, courier routing, and planning and dispatch.

To reengineer the systems, FedEx began with a traditional data model, which was converted to a business object model. From there, the company developed specific applications around so-called process scenarios.

For example, each flight leg, such as Memphis to St. Louis, is a business object. A regional crew-scheduling system, then, includes only those flight legs occurring in that region. But those flight leg objects will also appear in other systems, such as aircraft maintenance.

So far, FedEx has installed the new Unix-based distributed systems to numerous locations in Memphis. It also introduced several of the systems to regional hubs in Indianapolis, Dallas, and Japan. Although there are no plans to do so, IS is prepared to distribute systems to hubs in Newark, New Jersey; Oakland, California; Los Angeles; Dallas; and Brussels, Belgium.

CASE STUDY QUESTIONS

1. Why did Time Warner use business objects to develop new business systems?

2. How did FedEx implement business objects technology?

3. What are the benefits and limitations of using business objects?

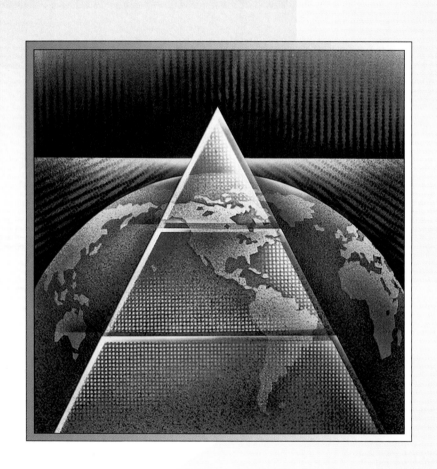

Applications in Business and Management

How are information systems used to support end user computing, business operations, managerial decision making, and strategic advantage? The five chapters of this module show you how such applications are accomplished in modern organizations.

Chapter 8, "Information Systems for End User Computing and Collaboration," discusses the resource requirements and managerial challenges of end user and work group computing applications. It also discusses the benefits and limitations of major types of office automation information systems.

Chapter 9, "Information Systems for Business Operations," describes how information systems support the business functions of marketing, manufacturing, human resource management, accounting, and finance. It also shows the various ways that information systems support the processing of transactions generated by business operations.

Chapter 10, "Information Systems for Managerial Decision Making and Support," shows how management information systems, decision support systems, and executive information systems have been developed and applied to business decision-making situations faced by managers.

Chapter 11, "Information Systems for Strategic Advantage," introduces fundamental concepts of strategic advantage through information technology, and illustrates strategic applications of information systems that can gain competitive advantages for an organization.

Chapter 12, "Information Systems and Artificial Intelligence Technologies," shows how artificial intelligence and expert systems are being used to support business operations and management.

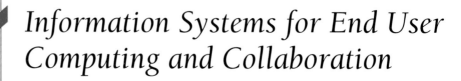

Information Systems for End User Computing and Collaboration

CHAPTER OUTLINE

LEARNING OBJECTIVES

The purpose of this chapter is to give you an understanding of the role played in organizations by information systems in end user computing and office automation.

Section I of this chapter explores the reasons for end user computing and work group computing and analyzes the resources needed to accomplish major end user computing applications. It also discusses the role of information centers, as well as the potential risks of end user computing and the resulting challenges posed to managerial end users.

Section II describes the major types of information systems that fall under the office automation umbrella. The benefits and limitations of such systems to end users are also emphasized.

After reading and studying this chapter, you should be able to:

1. Discuss the reasons for the growth of end user computing and collaboration.
2. Identify the major components and resources needed to support end user computing.
3. Identify and give examples for each of the major application categories of end user and work group computing.
4. Give examples of several risks in end user computing and possible managerial solutions to reduce such risks.
5. Discuss the purposes and activities of the major types of office automation systems.
6. Identify several types of electronic office communications and their benefits for end users.
7. Discuss the benefits and limitations of office automation systems.

┌─ **S E C T I O N   I**
▌ *End User Computing and Collaboration*
└───────────────────────────────────────

End User Computing

The days of relying primarily on information systems professionals to meet our information processing needs are over. Most organizations can't keep up with the information demands of their end users. So today's knowledge workers use networked microcomputers as professional workstations to get the information they need to accomplish their jobs successfully. That's what **end user computing** is all about. It's the direct, hands-on use of computers by end users, instead of the indirect use provided by the hardware, software, and professional resources of an organization's information services department. This doesn't mean that end users don't rely on IS resources. However, in end user computing, an information services department plays only a supportive role to an end user's own computing resources and efforts.

Why has end user computing grown? Because information services departments have shown that they cannot keep up with the information demands of end users. Remember the process of systems development we discussed in Chapter 3? Developing computer-based information system solutions for users by teams of systems analysts and programmers is costly and time-consuming. Thus, many organizations estimate they have a backlog of unfilled user requests for information systems development of two to five years. This backlog includes the development of new applications as well as the changes made to improve existing information systems in the systems maintenance activity. To make matters worse, the backlog discourages users from making additional requests for systems development. Experts estimate that this creates a *hidden backlog* of unsubmitted requests that is even greater than the apparent backlog of formal user requests.

Another major reason for the growth of end user computing lies in the dramatic improvements in the capabilities and availability of computer hardware, software, and networks. The development of networked microcomputers has brought computing power down to the departmental, work group, and individual levels. Also, software packages for end users for all types of applications have proliferated and improved in their power and ease of use. These improvements have made computer hardware, software, and networks affordable and attractive to many individuals and organizations. These developments are reinforced by the growing familiarity of many end users with computers, caused by their longtime and widespread use in schools, businesses, and other organizations. Thus, end users are able to turn to the direct use of information technology to solve their information processing problems.

End User Collaboration

The cooperation of individuals produces the finest end results, yet balancing cooperation and individualism is a never-ending challenge. The 1980s delivered a revolution in work and computing: the personal computer freed workers to compute independently. The information systems revolution of the 1990s is the local area network. Networks encourage people to work individually while fostering cooperation among them [15].

Most of us have to interact with others to get things done. And as you can see, information technology is changing the way we work. Telecommunications networks enable us to *collaborate:* to share resources, communicate ideas, and coordinate our

Tim Brown/Tony Stone Images.

FIGURE 8.1
Information technology enhances
end user collaboration.

efforts as members of the many formal and informal *work groups* that make up today's organizations. For example, the members of many office work groups depend on local area networks to communicate with electronic mail and share hardware devices, software packages, and work group databases. At large multinational corporations, work groups use global telecommunications networks to communicate with and coordinate the activities of their counterparts at various overseas locations. Thus in this chapter, we will explore the many types of applications that enhance the communications and coordination, and thus the collaboration of end user work groups and their organizations. See Figure 8.1.

Components of an End User Computing System

It is important to think of end user computing in an information system context. Figure 8.2 shows the resource components and application outputs of an end user computing system. It illustrates the major categories of end user computing applications, and the hardware, software, people, and data resources required. As you can see, end user computing systems are microcomputer-based information systems that directly support both the operational and managerial applications of end users.

Figure 8.2 also shows that many end users do not rely solely on their own microcomputer workstations, software packages, and databases. They can also rely on the support of software packages, databases, and computer systems at the work group, departmental, and corporate levels. In addition, many organizations provide *information centers* as another source of support for end user computing. Information center specialists serve as consultants to users who need assistance in their computing efforts. In this way, organizations hope to improve the efficiency and effectiveness of end user computing.

FIGURE 8.2

An end user computing system. Note the major categories of end user computing applications and the hardware, software, people, and data resources required.

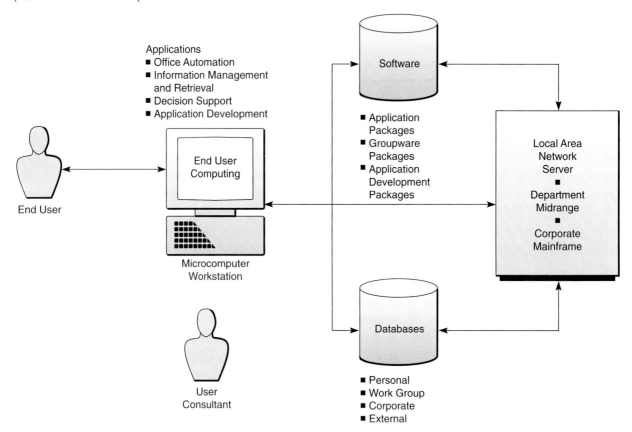

Resources for End User Computing

Figure 8.2 emphasizes that hardware, software, people, and data resources are needed for end user computing. Let's briefly consider each of these resources.

Hardware Resources: End User Workstations

The hardware resources for end user computing consist primarily of microcomputer workstations. Microcomputer systems (including their peripheral devices) provide the information processing capabilities needed for most user applications. Though dumb terminals connected to minicomputers or mainframes are sometimes used, they are rapidly being replaced by microcomputers with telecommunications capabilities. Therefore, as Figure 8.2 shows, microcomputer workstations may be tied by telecommunications links to other workstations in a local area network, with a more powerful microcomputer operating as a network server. Or they may be connected to larger networks, using departmental minicomputers or corporate mainframes as hosts. These computer systems (1) help control communications in the network including serving as gateways between networks, (2) oversee the sharing of software packages and databases among the workstations in the network, and (3) perform time-sharing processing services for jobs that are too big for the workstations to handle.

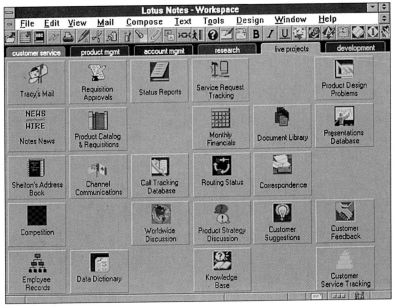

Courtesy of Lotus Development Corporation.

FIGURE 8.3
Lotus Notes is a popular group-ware package. Notice how it organizes end user activities to support end user collaboration.

Software Resources: End User Packages

Application software packages for microcomputer systems are the primary software resources needed for end user computing. These include general-purpose *productivity packages* for word processing, electronic spreadsheets, database and information management, graphics, data communications, and integrated packages, as discussed in Chapter 5. Other software resources include packages for *office automation* applications such as desktop publishing, electronic mail, and office support services. We will discuss such packages in Section II of this chapter. Of course, many other types of application software can be used, depending on the business needs of end users.

Groupware is a fast-growing category of software for end user computing. Groupware is *collaboration software,* that is, software that helps work groups of end users work together to accomplish group assignments. Typically, this includes software for applications like electronic mail, joint word processing and spreadsheet analysis, file sharing, computer conferencing, scheduling meetings, project management, and so on. See Figure 8.3.

Application development packages are another major category of software resources shown in Figure 8.2. This includes fourth-generation languages and other application development packages. As discussed in Chapter 5, 4GL packages allow users to specify what information they want, rather than how the computer system should do it. Major categories of 4GLs include natural and structured query languages, such as Intellect and SQL, and the report generators found in many spreadsheet programs, integrated packages, database management systems, and decision support system packages. Such tools allow end users to make ad hoc inquiries and generate their own reports. The application generators found in database management and other application development packages are also included in this category. These packages provide *visual programming* tools that allow experienced end users to interactively develop their own application programs, instead of relying on professional systems analysts and programmers.

Data Resources: Multiple Databases

Figure 8.2 emphasizes that end user computing relies on several major types of databases introduced in Chapter 7. Personal databases are created and maintained by end users to support their individual professional activities. For example, personal databases may have files of correspondence created by word processing or spreadsheets created by electronic spreadsheet packages. End users may also have access to work group and corporate databases through telecommunications network links. This allows end users to transfer data files among themselves and work group and corporate offices. Finally, end users can use the telecommunications capabilities of their workstations to access external databases. This allows them to access a wealth of economic and other types of information from the data banks of commercial information services.

People Resources: The Information Center

Figure 8.2 emphasizes that many organizations have made a major commitment of human resources to end user computing. This commitment may take the form of an **information center,** which is an organizational unit that supports the end users in an organization. The information center's biggest contribution to end user computing is a staff of user consultants consisting of systems analysts, programmers, and technicians. Their primary role is to educate and assist users in the effective use of microcomputer systems and their many software packages. They also work as consultants to end users to help them develop new applications using a variety of application development tools.

An **information center** is an organizational subunit that provides hardware, software, and people support to end users in an organization. Typically, it has been part of an organization's information services department, but it can also be found in individual end user departments. The concept of providing support facilities for end user computing has grown so popular that it has become a major factor in organizational computing. In recent years, many organizations have distributed responsibility for end user support to their business units and have abolished their centralized information centers. Instead, they have established **user liaison** or **user consultant** positions within each business unit to support end users' computing activities. However, information centers still play a major role in end user support [21]. Most information centers provide:

- **Hardware support** for end users who need it by providing the use of microcomputers, intelligent terminals, advanced graphic terminals, high-speed printers, plotters, and so on.
- **Software support** by offering the temporary use of advanced software packages for application development, desktop publishing, presentation graphics, database management, and so on.
- **People support** by a staff of end user consultants, systems analysts, and programmers who are trained to educate and help end users apply their own hardware and software resources to improve the efficiency and effectiveness of their work activities.

The Role of the Information Center

What do information centers do? Information centers provide a variety of services, depending on the type and size of the organization and the age and mission of each center [17]. Figure 8.4 summarizes many of the services provided by information centers. As you can see, most of the services can be categorized as dealing with end user education and training, assistance with applications development,

Basic Services	Enhanced Services
▪ Computer literacy education	▪ Development of telecommunications software
▪ Training on use of products	▪ Data administration
▪ Hardware/software sharing	▪ Installing and testing new software product releases
▪ Application consulting	
▪ Help center with hotline telephone service	▪ Maintenance of PC equipment
▪ Hardware/software evaluation	▪ Project management for user-development projects
▪ Hardware and software standards	▪ Quality assurance of user-written software
▪ Support for standard products	
▪ Security support	▪ Prototype development for end users

FIGURE 8.4
Information center services.
Note the variety of services that
may be provided.

Source: Adapted and reprinted by permission, Barbara C. McNurlin and Ralph H. Sprague, Jr., *Information Systems Management in Practice*, 2nd ed. (Englewood Cliffs, NJ: Prentice Hall, 1989), pp. 328–29.

hardware/software sharing and evaluation, or the development of administrative control methods for end user applications.

End User Computing Applications

Figure 8.2 listed four major categories of **end user computing applications:** (1) office automation, (2) information management and retrieval, (3) decision support, and (4) application development. These categories define what end users do when they do their own computing. Let's take a brief look at what's involved in each of them.

Office Automation

Office automation (OA) applications are a major category of end user computing, since much end user and work group computing takes place in office settings. Office automation will be discussed in detail in Section II of this chapter. OA applications enhance end user productivity and communications within work groups, organizations, and with external contacts such as customers and suppliers. This, typically, involves applications such as word processing, electronic mail, desktop publishing, and presentation graphics. For example, you could compose a business letter using word processing, send electronic messages to colleagues using electronic mail, and prepare graphic displays for a formal presentation using the hardware and software capabilities of your microcomputer workstation.

Information Management and Retrieval Applications

End users are inundated with data and information that must be organized, stored, and retrieved. Thus, one major application of end user computing is the use of database management packages to manage the creation, access, and maintenance of databases and files. In Chapter 5, we discussed how DBMS packages help end users create data files and databases to store data and retrieve information. The query languages and report generators of such packages allow end users to retrieve information from personal, work group, corporate, and external databases. Query languages allow simple inquiries to be made quickly and easily by end users. Report generators help end users prepare reports that extract, manipulate, and display information in a variety of formats. In Chapter 7, we saw how end users can make inquiries using a query language like SQL or QBE and receive immediate displays of information.

An example of a personal
information manager (PIM).
Notice some of the of ways
that information is recorded
and presented by Lotus
Organizer.

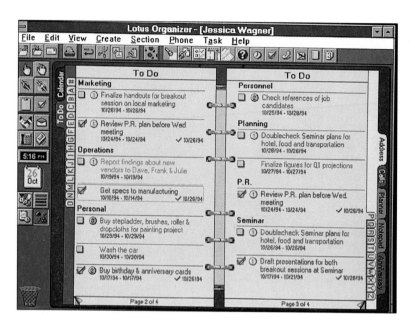

Courtesy of Lotus Development Corporation.

Another software package used for information management and retrieval is
the **personal information manager** (PIM). These packages help end users store,
organize, and retrieve text and numerical data in the form of notes, lists, clippings,
tables, memos, letters, reports, and so on. For example, information can be entered
randomly about people, companies, deadlines, appointments, meetings, projects,
and financial results. The PIM package will automatically organize such data with
minimal instructions from the end user. Then portions of the stored information can
be retrieved in any order, and in a variety of forms, depending on the relationships
established among pieces of data by the software and the user. For example, information can be retrieved as a list of appointments, meetings, or other things to do;
the timetable for a project; or a display of key facts and financial data about a competitor [18]. See Figure 8.5.

In Chapter 10, we will discuss how an executive information system (EIS)
enables end users who are corporate executives to easily retrieve information tailored
to their strategic information needs. So end user computing allows managerial end
users at all levels to bypass the periodic reporting process of traditional information
system applications. Instead, they can receive directly at their workstations much of
the information they need.

*Decision Support
Applications*

Software packages such as electronic spreadsheets, integrated packages, and other
decision support system (DSS) software allow end users to build and manipulate
analytical models of business activities. End users can thus create their own **decision
support** systems with the use of such tools and the variety of databases previously
mentioned. As we will discuss in Chapter 10, this allows end users to pose *what-if*
questions by entering different alternatives into a spreadsheet or other model. They
can then see the results displayed immediately on their workstation screens.

Thus, managerial end users can use an interactive modeling process to analyze
alternatives and help them make or recommend decisions. Besides spreadsheet pro-

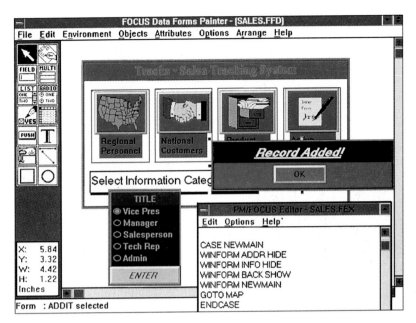

FIGURE 8.6
Using PC/Focus for end user application development, such as developing this sales tracking system.

Courtesy of Information Builders, Inc.

grams, a variety of 4GL products and financial, statistical, and mathematical analysis packages can be used by end users for decision support applications. This includes *group decision support system* (GDSS) software that enhances the joint decision making of work groups and other organizational units.

Another major category of end user computing is the development of new or improved computer applications by users. That is, end users can develop new or improved ways to perform their jobs without the direct involvement of professional systems analysts. Users themselves can accomplish the steps of the traditional or prototyping methods of information systems development discussed in Chapter 3. The primary reasons for this phenomenon are the application development capabilities of electronic spreadsheet, database management, and other microcomputer software packages. These software resources make it easier for end users to develop their own computer-based information systems. See Figure 8.6. Figures 8.29 and 8.32 in the *Application Exercises* at the end of the chapter outline the basic activities of the database and spreadsheet application development process for end users.

End User Application Development

Work is fundamentally social. Most activity, and certainly its meaning, arises in a context of cooperation [12].

Much of end user computing is a group effort known as **work group computing.** More formal terms include *computer-supported collaboration* (CSC), *computer-based systems for collaborative work* (CSCW), or *collaborative work support systems* (CWSS). But no matter what you call it, the fact is that end users are now using computers, software, and telecommunications networks to communicate and coordinate with each other about work assignments. For example, members of an office sales team may use interconnected local area networks and *groupware* software packages to communicate with electronic mail and jointly do the word processing, spreadsheet analysis, and report generation needed to accomplish a particular sales

Work Group Computing

FIGURE 8.7
Much of end user computing is
a work group effort.

Tim Brown/Tony Stone Images.

presentation assignment. Or they may use networked workstations in a *decision room* and *electronic meeting systems* (EMS) or *group decision support systems* (GDSS) software to help them make better group decisions at a project planning meeting. See Figure 8.7.

Electronic Work Groups

There are many types of work groups, each with its own work styles, agendas, and computing needs. A **work group** can be defined as two or more people working together on the same task or assignment. Thus, a work group can be as small as 2 persons or as large as 30 or more people. Work groups can be as formal and structured as a traditional office or department dedicated to one type of business activity—an *Accounts Payable Department,* for example. Or they can be as informal and unstructured as an ad hoc task force whose members work for different organizations in different parts of the world—the planning committee for a major international conference, for example.

Therefore, the members of a work group don't have to work in the same physical location. They can be members of a *virtual work group,* that is, one whose mem-

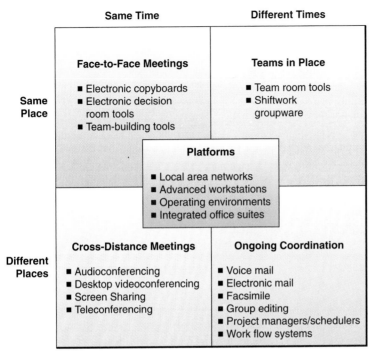

Same Time   **Different Times**

Same Place

Face-to-Face Meetings

- Electronic copyboards
- Electronic decision room tools
- Team-building tools

Teams in Place

- Team room tools
- Shiftwork groupware

Platforms

- Local area networks
- Advanced workstations
- Operating environments
- Integrated office suites

Different Places

Cross-Distance Meetings

- Audioconferencing
- Desktop videoconferencing
- Screen Sharing
- Teleconferencing

Ongoing Coordination

- Voice mail
- Electronic mail
- Facsimile
- Group editing
- Project managers/schedulers
- Work flow systems

Source: Adapted from Ralph Sprague and Barbara McNurlin, eds., *Information Systems Management in Practice, 3rd ed.* (Englewood Cliffs, NJ: Prentice Hall, 1993), p. 416.

FIGURE 8.8
Groupware is collaboration software that uses a variety of software tools to support work activities and foster cooperation among work group members at the same or different times and places.

bers are united by the tasks on which they are collaborating, not by geography or membership in a larger organization. In sociology and cultural anthropology, these work groups are called *social fields*—semiautonomous and self-regulating associations of people with their own work agendas, rules, relationships, and norms of behavior. Work group computing makes *electronic social fields* possible. Computers, groupware, and telecommunications allow end users to work together without regard to time constraints, physical location, or organizational boundaries [14].

Figure 8.8 shows that groupware is designed to make communication and coordination of work group activities, and cooperation among end users significantly easier, no matter where the members of the work group are located. So, though groupware packages provide a variety of software tools that can accomplish many important jobs, the work group cooperation and coordination they make possible is their key feature. That's why groupware is also known as *collaboration software*. It helps the members of a work group collaborate on group projects, at the same or different times and at the same or different places. So groupware provides some of the office automation, information management and retrieval, decision support, and application development tools work groups need to accomplish specific work assignments.

    Figure 8.9 outlines the major types of work group computing applications that may be supported by groupware packages. Some groupware packages support only one of these application areas, while others attempt to integrate several applications in one groupware package. For example, some software packages may be used

The Role of Groupware

FIGURE 8.9
Applications of groupware for
work group computing.

- **Electronic Messaging.** Sending electronic messages to work group members using electronic mail, voice mail, bulletin board systems, facsimile, and desktop videoconferencing.
- **Electronic Meetings.** Holding electronic meetings of work groups using computer conferencing and teleconferencing, and group decision support systems.
- **Scheduling Management.** Scheduling work group appointments and meetings using electronic calendars and appointment books.
- **Task and Project Management.** Managing work group tasks and projects by project scheduling, resource allocation, tracking, reminding, and record-keeping.
- **Document Creating and Management.** Joint work group editing and annotation of documents. Electronic filing, retrieval, and routing of documents to work group members.
- **Data Management.** Managing the storage and retrieval of work group data files and databases.
- **Decision Support.** Joint work group spreadsheet development and analysis. Using other types of group decision software.

primarily for document retrieval, while Lotus Notes, a top-selling groupware package, supports E-mail, document management, computer conferencing, and many other functions.

Management Implications of End User Computing

Managers face significant challenges in managing end user computing in their organizations. Managing the hardware, software, people, and data resources of end user computing systems is a major challenge. Workstations, computers, telecommunications networks, and software packages must be evaluated, budgeted for, and acquired. End users must be properly trained and assisted. The integrity and security of the databases that are created and available to end users must be ensured. Finally, the applications end users develop and implement must be evaluated for their efficiency and effectiveness in meeting the objectives of the business. Figure 8.10 illustrates some of the managerial challenges of end user computing.

So managing end user computing is not an easy job. However, it is a responsibility shared by every managerial end user, as well as by the management of an organization's information systems function. Business firms, typically, make a variety of organizational, policy, and procedural arrangements to support and control end user computing. Previously mentioned was the creation of information centers with user consultants in the business units of a company. Organizations also develop formal and informal methods to deal with data resource management, application development, and acquisition of end user computing resources.

The creation and access of data resources by end users makes the integrity and security of end user and corporate databases a major concern of data resource management. For example, passwords and other safeguards for proper access to sensitive corporate data must be developed. Also, end user databases extracted from corporate databases may become out-of-date or incorrect if they are not properly updated and maintained. So policies such as automatic monitoring and updating of work-group databases may be implemented.

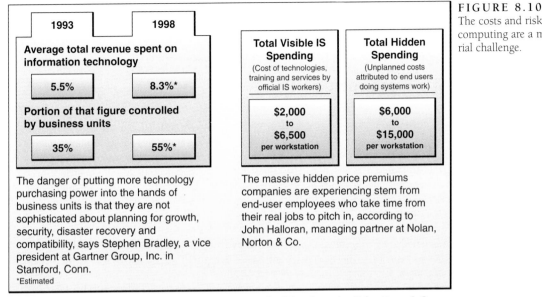

FIGURE 8.10
The costs and risks of end user computing are a major managerial challenge.

Source: Gartner Group, Inc., Stamford, CT (left chart); 1993 Survey of End User Computing, Nolan, Norton & Co. (right chart) adapted from Alice Laplante, "In Depth: End-User Invasion," *Computerworld,* July 18, 1994, p. 98. Copyright 1994 by Computerworld, Inc., Framingham, MA 01701—Reprinted from *Computerworld.*

Application development guidelines for end user computing encourage end users to develop the information systems they need to do their jobs. However, end users may have to demonstrate that their system is well documented with built-in controls that make efficient use of computing resources and does not threaten the integrity of the company's databases. Information center consultants and employees with user liaison responsibilities in the business units are a common way that companies use to help end users develop applications that meet such standards.

Managing end user computing also requires the development of policies and procedures concerning hardware and software acquisition by end users. So corporate or business unit guidelines regulating the cost and types of hardware and software end users can purchase are common. What managers are trying to do is to control the costs of end user computing and avoid proliferation of hardware and software, while ensuring compatibility with the organization's computing and telecommunications networks.

REAL WORLD CASE

McDonnell-Douglas and Chase Manhattan: Collaborative Computing

It would enable the most brilliant minds in the company to work together, regardless of where those minds reside. It is the answer to white-collar productivity, flexible team-based corporations, and flat management structures. No obstacle—not geography, not time differences, not sick days, not acts of God—can stand in its way. What is this miracle cure? Collaborative computing. Or so some think.

Many executives are drawing up grand plans to get their organizations communicating and cooperating both internally and with outside customers and suppliers, whether through workflow, document management, electronic mail, videoconferencing, just plain Lotus Notes, or (often) some combination thereof.

McDonnell-Douglas

"You don't want to bite off too much," says Joe Aubuchon, enterprise program manager of information systems at aerospace firm McDonnell-Douglas Corp. in St. Louis. Aubuchon wants to develop a collaborative environment because, he said, it reflects the way people work.

Groupware looks to be a safe first step. Aubuchon is replacing the current Microsoft Mail system with Novell GroupWise on 10,000 to 12,000 desktop PCs and Macintoshes. GroupWise is an integrated product that offers users one point of access for multiple types of data, including E-mail, Internet, and X400 messages; faxes; calendar items; and voice messaging.

Down the road, Aubuchon is planning to use Collabra Share, a group discussion package from Collabra Software. Novell and Collabra recently inked a pact to integrate Collabra Share into GroupWise.

Chase Manhattan

Myles Trachtenberg, vice president of distributed technology services at the Chase Manhattan Bank NA, in New York, said Chase plans to use not one but three different conferencing systems—plus Network Notes, a joint project between Lotus and AT&T—to meet its collaborative goal: to "extend the enterprise out to the customer" and make all forms of collaboration as simple as picking up the telephone. "It will appear to the customer that there's one system."

The $114 billion asset institution is partway there. The key, Trachtenberg said, is to create a "core platform" that tolerates differences in the technology running on top of it. "We may have someone within corporate finance who needs to talk to the London trading desk in conjunction with a customer in their office. There should be no question that they can select the location from a menu, click on it, and it connects," Trachtenberg said.

So why three different systems? Because of different customer needs. Executives use 15 to 17 frames/sec. room-based conferencing systems from PictureTel Corp. to consult with global customers. For private banking customers, nothing but 30 frames/sec. will do, so Intel's ProShare will likely be used.

Chase securities traders, on the other hand, keep tabs on one another using a dedicated phone line–based videoconferencing system from Uni-Data and Communications. The system is used by traders on two floors of the New York headquarters building as well as between London and New York.

Using groupware, Chase is similarly able to transcend geographical boundaries. Each of the bank's many business areas—the trading floor, corporate finance, private banking, and wholesale/retail banking—is supported by international teams of experts who develop best practices approaches to business problems by sharing documents and data using Lotus's Notes. "Notes is a strategic platform that we're using to enable workflow across geographies and environments," Trachtenberg said.

CASE STUDY QUESTIONS

1. What categories of end user computing applications and resources do you recognize in this example? Refer to Figure 8.2 to help you.

2. How does McDonnell-Douglas's use of Novell GroupWise computing support collaboration among its end users? What other technologies could they use?

3. How does Chase support collaborative computing? What business benefits does it provide?

Source: Adapted from Richard Adhikari, "All Together Now," *Computerworld Client/Server Journal,* June 1995, pp. 19–22. Copyright 1995 by Computerworld, Inc., Framingham, MA 01701—Reprinted from *Computerworld.*

SECTION II
Office Automation Systems

Office automation (OA) has changed the equipment and work habits of today's end users and work groups. Of course, none of us would like to work in an office where all information processing activities are done manually or mechanically. So the *mechanized office* has given way to the *automated office*. Investment in networks of computer-based workstations and other automated equipment is transforming traditional manual office methods and paper communications media. This transformation has resulted in the development of automated systems that rely on electronic collaboration and communication networks, text processing, image processing, and other information technologies.

Introduction

Office automation systems are telecommunications-based information systems that collect, process, store, and distribute electronic messages, documents, and other forms of communications among individuals, work groups, and organizations. Such systems can improve the collaboration and productivity of end users and work groups by significantly reducing the time and effort needed to produce, distribute, and share business communications. Figure 8.11 outlines major office automation systems.

One way people interact is by meeting together. Meetings can be supported by equipping conference rooms with computers and sophisticated software. Alternatively, videoconferencing and desktop conferencing enable people to meet without physically moving. Another way people interact is by speaking, which computers support with voice mail and voice annotation. People interact by writing, supported by collaborative writing tools and electronic mail applications. Electronic bulletin boards and newsgroups support broader communications [11].

Electronic Communications Systems

Electronic communications systems are the central nervous systems of today's organizations. *Electronic mail, voice mail, bulletin board systems,* and *facsimile* allow organizations to send messages in text, video, or voice form or transmit copies

FIGURE 8.11
An overview of office automation systems.

Office Automation Systems				
Electronic Publishing Systems	**Electronic Communications Systems**	**Electronic Collaboration Systems**	**Image Processing Systems**	**Office Management Systems**
■ Word Processing ■ Desktop Publishing ■ Copying Systems	■ Electronic Mail ■ Voice Mail ■ Facsimile ■ Desktop Videoconferencing	■ Electronic Meeting Systems ■ Collaborative Work Systems ■ Teleconferencing ■ Telecommuting	■ Electronic Document Management ■ Other Image Processing ■ Presentation Graphics ■ Multimedia Systems	■ Electronic Office Accessories ■ Electronic Scheduling ■ Task Management

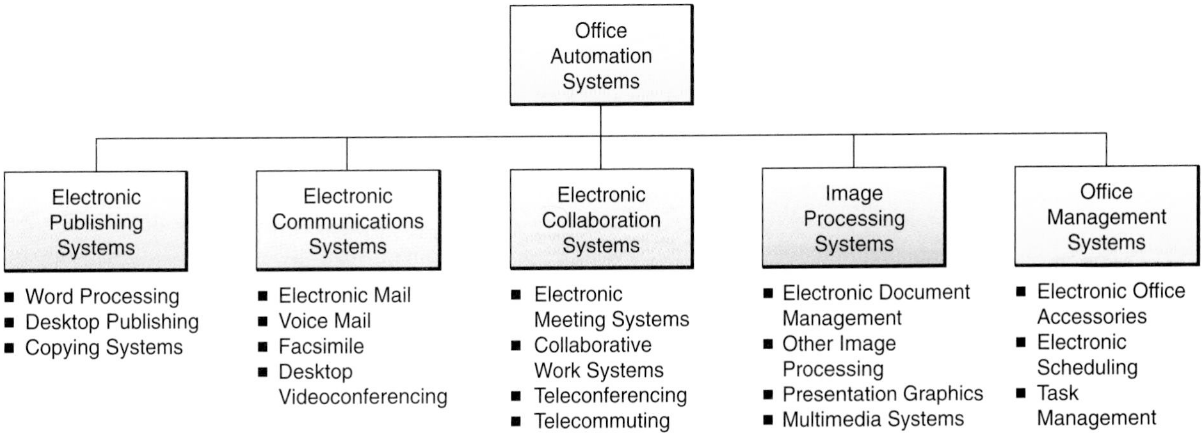

FIGURE 8.12
A summary of electronic communications systems.

- **Electronic Mail.** Using telecommunications networks to transmit, store, and distribute electronic text messages among the computer workstations of end users. (May also include audio, video, and image media.)
- **Voice Mail.** Using the telephone system and a voice mail computer to transmit, store, and distribute digitized voice messages among end users.
- **Bulletin Board Systems.** A service offered by public information networks or the networks of businesses and other organizations in which electronic messages and data, programs, and other types of files can be stored by end users for other end users to read or copy.
- **Videotex.** An interactive video service provided by cable TV or telephone networks.
- **Facsimile.** Using the telephone system to transmit images of documents and reproduce them on paper at a receiving station.

of documents and do it in seconds, not hours or days. Such systems transmit and distribute text and images in electronic form over telecommunications networks. This enhances the communications and coordination among work groups and organizations. Electronic communications systems help reduce the flow of paper messages, letters, memos, documents, and reports that floods our present interoffice and postal systems. However, in many cases, this paper flood has become an electronic one. For example, some end users routinely send unsolicited copies of E-mail to many of their colleagues, instead of being more selective in their E-mail messaging. Figure 8.12 summarizes electronic communications systems.

Electronic Mail

Electronic mail has changed the way people work and communicate. Millions of end users now depend on electronic mail (E-mail) to send and receive electronic messages. You can send E-mail to anyone else on your network for storage in their *electronic mailboxes* on magnetic disk drives. Whenever they are ready, they can read their electronic mail by displaying it on the video screens at their workstations. So, with only a few minutes of effort (and a few microseconds of transmission), a message to one or many individuals can be composed, sent, and received.

Many organizations and work groups now depend on E-mail packages and their wide and local area networks for electronic mail. As we mentioned in Chapter 6, the Internet has become the E-mail network of choice for millions of networked end users. Communications companies such as GTE, TELENET, and MCI also offer such services, as do personal computer networks such as CompuServe, GEnie, and Prodigy, many of which provide access to the Internet for E-mail. Figure 8.13 shows a video display provided by an electronic mail package.

Many E-mail packages can route messages to multiple end users based on predefined mailing lists and provide password security, automatic message forwarding, and remote user access. They also may allow you to store messages in *folders* with provisions for adding attachments to message files. Other E-mail packages may allow you to edit and send graphics as well as text, and provide bulletin board and computer conferencing capabilities. Finally, some E-mail packages can automatically filter and sort incoming messages (even news items from online services such as Dow Jones News/Retrieval Service) and route them to appropriate user mailboxes and folders [6].

Voice Mail

Another variation of electronic mail is **voice mail** (also called *voice store-and-forward*) where digitized voice messages, rather than electronic text, are used. In this method,

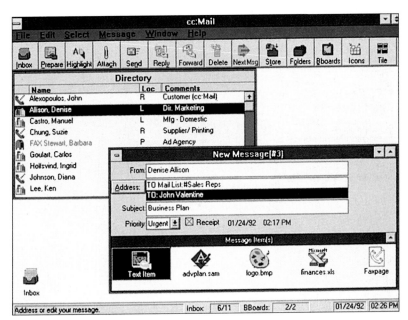

Courtesy of Lotus Development Corporation.

FIGURE 8.13
Using an electronic mail package.

you first dial the number of the voice mail service. In some secure systems, you may be asked to enter an identification code. Once you are accepted, you dial the voice mail number of the person you wish to contact and speak your message. Your analog message is digitized and stored on the magnetic disk devices of the voice mail computer system. Whenever you want to hear your voice mail, you simply dial your mailbox and listen to the stored message, which the computer converts back into analog voice form.

Bulletin Board Systems

Bulletin board systems (BBS) are a popular telecommunications service provided by the Internet, public information services, and thousands of business firms, organizations, and user groups. An electronic bulletin board system allows you to post public or private messages that other end users can read by accessing the BBS with their computers. Establishing a small BBS for a business is not that difficult. Minimum requirements are a microcomputer with a hard disk drive, custom or packaged BBS software, modem, and a telephone line.

Bulletin board systems serve as a central location to post and pick up messages or upload and download data files or programs 24 hours a day. A BBS helps end users ask questions, get advice, locate and share information, and get in touch with other end users. Thus, internal company bulletin board systems are being used by many business firms as a convenient, low-cost way to enhance the flow of information among their employees, while an external BBS helps them keep in touch with their customers and suppliers.

Public Information Services

Public information services are another major category of telecommunications applications. The Internet provides a wealth of information for free, while companies such as CompuServe, GEnie, and Prodigy offer a variety of information services for a fee to anyone. Gaining access to these services is easy if you have a personal computer equipped with a modem and a communications software package. They offer such services as electronic mail, bulletin board systems, financial market information, airline reservations, use of software packages for personal computing,

FIGURE 8.14
A menu of internet services
provided by CompuServe.

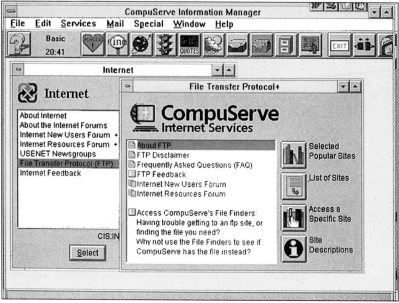

Courtesy of CompuServe Corporation.

electronic games, home banking and shopping, news/sports/weather information, and access to a variety of specialized data banks as discussed in Chapter 7. See Figures 8.14 and 8.15.

Videotex

Another way end users can get information using an information services network is **videotex**. Videotex is a computer-based interactive information service provided over phone lines or cable TV channels to access and selectively view text and graphics. End users can select specific video displays of data and information, such as electronic Yellow Pages and personal bank checking account registers. Thus, you can use a special terminal, intelligent TV set, or personal computer to do banking and shopping electronically. Videotex is widely used in France, where the Teletel system (popularly known as Minitel) has over 6 million subscribers and 20,000 services, and handles over 2 billion calls a year [2]. Many companies tried pilot programs of videotex services in the 1980s, but most efforts failed to generate sufficient consumer interest. Videotex services are currently available from several sources, including personal computer networks such as Prodigy, a joint venture of IBM and Sears, and the CompuServe Bank-at-Home and Shop-at-Home services. Several large companies like Viacom and Time Warner have started major pilot programs for new interactive video services. These programs are spurred by the desire to capitalize on the business potential of the future information superhighway [14].

Facsimile

Facsimile (fax) is not a new office telecommunications service. However, advances in digital imaging technology and microelectronics have caused a sharp drop in prices and a significant increase in capabilities. As a consequence, sales of fax machines have skyrocketed in the last few years, and faxing has become a commonplace business term. Facsimile allows you to transmit images of important documents over telephone or other telecommunication links. Thus, "long-distance copying" might be an appropriate nickname for this telecommunications process.

Usually, a fax machine at one office location transmits to a fax machine at another location, with both units connected to high-speed modems. Transmission

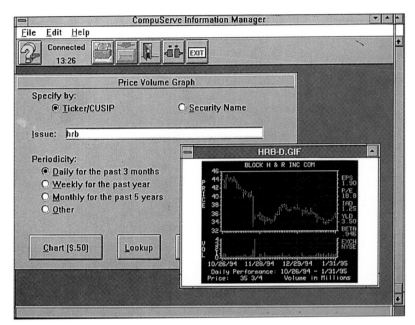

Courtesy of CompuServe Corporation.

FIGURE 8.15
Stock market information provided by CompuServe.

Jon Feingersh/The Stock Market.

FIGURE 8.16
Fax machines and PCs with fax modems have become a common and important component of telecommunications networks.

speeds for digital office fax machines range from one to four pages per minute, with quality equivalent to an office copier. However, facsimile circuit boards and fax modems are also available for microcomputers. Installing a fax board or fax modem and using a fax software package allows a personal computer to transmit copies of word processing, spreadsheet, and other files to fax machines anywhere. Thus, fax machines can now become remote dial-up printers for microcomputer systems. See Figure 8.16.

Electronic Meeting Systems

Why do people have to spend travel time and money to attend meetings away from their normal work locations? They don't have to if they use several types of **electronic meeting systems** (EMS), a growing method of electronic office telecommunications. Electronic meeting systems involve the use of video and audio communications to allow conferences and meetings to be held with participants who may be scattered across a room, a building, a country, or the globe. Reducing the need to travel to and from meetings should save employee time, increase productivity, and reduce travel expenses and energy consumption.

Electronic meeting systems are also being promoted as a form of *group decision support systems* (GDSS). Since EMS software can encourage, organize, and prioritize ideas from meeting participants, they promote more efficient and effective decision making by groups of people [10]. We will explore group decision support systems in Chapter 10.

There are several variations of electronic meeting systems, as summarized in Figure 8.17. In some versions, participants at remote sites key in their presentations and responses whenever convenient from their online terminals or workstations connected to a central conference computer. Since not all participants have to do this at the same time, this form of EMS is called *computer conferencing* and is like a form of interactive electronic mail. Group decision support systems for small groups may use a network of workstations and large-screen projection in a *decision room*. Both of these forms of electronic meeting systems provide computer and video facilities for their participants. Direct **desktop videoconferencing** between the workstations of end users is another promising development. The convenience of desktop videoconferencing promises to significantly enhance collaboration among the members of workgroups. See Figure 8.18.

Teleconferencing

Teleconferencing is an important form of EMS. Sessions are held in real time, with major participants being televised while participants at remote sites usually take part with voice input of questions and responses. See Figure 8.19. Teleconferencing can also consist of using closed-circuit television to reach multiple small groups, instead of using television broadcasting to reach large groups at multiple sites.

Several major communications carriers and hotel chains now offer teleconferencing services for such events as sales meetings, new product announcements, and employee education and training. However, organizations have found that teleconferencing and some forms of EMS are not as effective as face-to-face meetings, especially when important participants are not trained in how to communicate using these systems. Also, the cost of providing some electronic meeting services and facilities can be substantial and make EMS not as cost-effective as traditional meetings.

FIGURE 8.17
Major categories of electronic meeting systems.

- **Computer Conferencing.** Using online terminals and workstations to conduct conferences among participants at remote sites over a period of time, without the use of interactive video.
- **Desktop Videoconferencing.** Using appropriately equipped end user workstations to hold two-way interactive video conferences.
- **Decision Room Conferencing.** Using a meeting room with a network of workstations and large-screen video projection to hold meetings.
- **Teleconferencing.** Using interactive video telecommunications to hold conferences among many participants at remote sites.

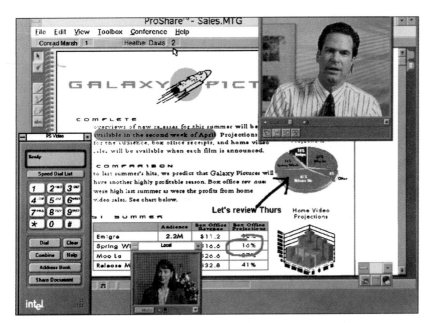

FIGURE 8.18
Using desktop videoconferencing. This is an example of using Intel's ProShare system for two-way interactive videoconferencing.

Courtesy of Intel Corporation.

FIGURE 8.19
Teleconferencing in action.

Matthew Berkowski/Stock Boston.

Telecommuting is the use of telecommunications by workers to replace commuting to work from their homes. It is also used to describe the use of telecommunications to carry on work activities from temporary locations other than offices and homes. Some people refer to telecommuting as the creation of *virtual offices*. Workers use a computer terminal or microcomputer with telecommunications capability to access

Telecommuting

their company's computer network and databases. Telecommuting workers and their colleagues also use electronic mail or voice mail to communicate with each other about job assignments.

Telecommuting is becoming a significant work alternative at major corporations and a common approach for many independent professionals. It seems to be most attractive to people whose jobs involve a lot of individual work, such as programmers, systems analysts, writers, consultants, and so on. It is especially helpful for handicapped persons and working parents of young children. Telecommuting is also being promoted as a way to conserve resources that would have been used to commute to work by cars and other means of transportation. However, studies have shown that telecommuting is not appropriate for many jobs and people. Productivity and job satisfaction seem to suffer unless workers spend several days each week at the office or other work sites with their colleagues. So telecommuting is considered only a temporary or partial work alternative for many knowledge workers [9].

Electronic Publishing Systems

Electronic publishing systems have transformed today's office into an in-house publisher of business documents. *Word processing* and *desktop publishing* are the information technologies that give the modern workplace electronic publishing capabilities. **Word processing** was the first, and is still the most common, office automation application. Word processing is the use of computer systems to create, edit, revise, and print text material. As we mentioned in Chapter 5, word processing involves manipulating **text data** (characters, words, sentences, and paragraphs) to produce information products in the form of **documents** (letters, memos, forms, and reports).

Desktop Publishing

One of the major applications in office automation is **desktop publishing.** Organizations can use desktop publishing systems to produce their own printed materials. They can design and print their own newsletters, brochures, manuals, and books with several type styles, graphics, and colors on each page. What constitutes a desktop publishing system? Minimum hardware and software requirements include:

- A personal computer with a hard disk.
- A laser printer or other printer capable of high-quality graphics.
- Software that can do word processing, graphics, and page makeup.

Word processing packages and **page composition** packages are used, typically, to do word processing, graphics, and page makeup functions. For higher-quality printing, end users need to invest in a more powerful computer with advanced graphic capabilities, a more expensive graphics and page makeup package with more extensive features, and a laser or other printer with a greater variety of capabilities.

How does desktop publishing work? Here are the major steps in the process.

1. Prepare your text and illustrations with a word processing program and a graphics package. Use an optical scanner to input text and graphics from other sources. You can also use files of **clip art,** predrawn graphic illustrations provided by your software or available from other sources.

2. Use the page composition program to develop the format of each page. This is where desktop publishing departs from standard word processing and graphics. Your video screen becomes an *electronic pasteup board* with rulers, column guides, and other page design aids.

Richard Pasley.

FIGURE 8.20
Desktop publishing in action.
The video display shows the use
of page makeup software to
produce a newsletter on a laser
printer.

3. Now merge the text and illustrations into the page format you designed. The page composition software will automatically move excess text to another column or page and help size and place illustrations and headings. Most page composition packages provide WYSIWYG (What You See Is What You Get) displays so you can see what the finished document will actually look like.

4. When the pages on the screen look the way you want them, you can store them electronically on your hard disk, then print them on a laser printer or other printer to produce the finished printed material. See Figure 8.20.

Many word processing packages now provide limited desktop publishing features. However, the desktop publishing process is not as easy as it sounds for the casual end user. Projects involving complex layouts require experience, skill, and a knowledge of graphics design techniques. However, advances in software have made the job easier in terms of ease of use and helping end users do a better job of graphics design. For example, predesigned forms for various types of printed material (called *templates* or *style sheets*) are frequently provided by many software packages.

Image Processing

Image processing is another fast-growing area of office automation. It allows end users to electronically capture, store, process, and retrieve images of documents that may include numeric data, text, handwriting, graphics, and photographs. **Electronic document management** (EDM) is based on image processing technology. However, it views a document as "something that has been authored for human comprehension." Thus, an electronic document is not just an electronic image of traditional documents as described earlier. It may also take the form of a digitized "voice note" attached to an electronic mail message, or electronic images for a color graphics presentation [6, 21].

FIGURE 8.21
An image processing
system.

Courtesy of IBM Corporation.

Electronic document management may interface with other electronic document preparation systems such as word processing, desktop publishing, electronic mail, and voice mail. However, one of the fastest growing application areas is *transaction document image processing*. Documents such as customer correspondence, sales orders, invoices, application forms, and service requests are captured electronically and routed to end users throughout the organization for processing. For example, a customer application form for a bank loan can be captured by optical scanning, indexed by the image database management system, stored on optical disk drives, electronically routed to various end user workstations for editing and financial and credit analysis, and then rerouted to a loan officer's workstation where the loan application decision is made. Such image processing and document management systems have shown productivity improvements of 20 to 25 percent, as well as significant cost savings [3, 11]. See Figure 8.21.

Computer Graphics

Which type of output would you rather see: columns of numbers or a graphics display of the same information? Most people find it difficult to quickly and accurately comprehend numerical or statistical data that is presented in a purely numerical form (such as rows or columns of numbers). That is why, typically, presentation graphics methods, such as charts and graphs, are used in technical reports and business meetings. As we mentioned in Chapter 5, microcomputer and graphics software packages give end users a variety of computer graphics capabilities, ranging from computer-aided design to computer art to presentation graphics. Graphics can be presented as video displays, printed material, transparencies, and color slides. Computer-based presentations containing many different graphics display screens are common, and the use of multimedia presentations with sound, animation, and video clips is growing. See Figure 8.22.

Computer graphics has been used for many years in design applications called computer-aided design (CAD). Engineers use CAD to design complex mechanical and electronic products and physical structures. Architects use CAD to

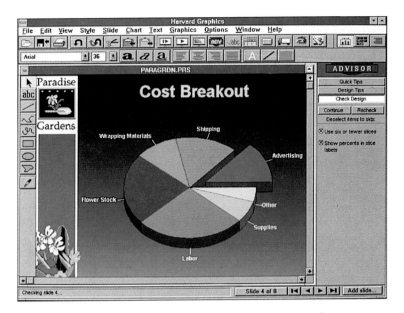

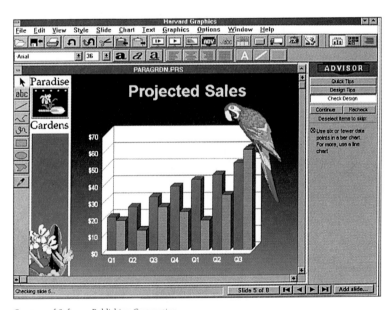

Courtesy of Software Publishing Corporation.

FIGURE 8.22
Presentation graphics displays. Note the use of color, line and bar graphs, three-dimensional graphics, and other graphics images.

help them design buildings, work spaces, and other environments. Computer graphics also assists researchers in analyzing volumes of data and process control technicians in monitoring industrial processes.

The goal of **presentation graphics** is to provide information in a graphical form that helps end users and managers understand business proposals and performance and make better decisions about them. This includes the use of line and bar graphs, pie

Presentation Graphics

charts, and pictorial charts using a variety of symbols. So instead of being overwhelmed by large amounts of computer-produced data, graphics displays can assist managers in analyzing and interpreting information presented to them.

Presentation graphics does not totally replace reports and displays of numbers and text material. Such methods are still needed to present the detailed information that many applications require. However, presentation graphics is becoming the usual method of presenting business information in reports, meetings, and other business presentations. That's because trends, problems, and opportunities hidden in data are easier to spot and communicate when using graphics displays. For example, presentation graphics makes it easier for a marketing manager to see complex market trends and communicate potential market problems and opportunities to the members of a sales team.

Multimedia Presentations

Information technology is enabling **multimedia presentations** for training employees, educating customers, making sales presentations, and adding impact to other business presentations. Business multimedia goes far beyond traditional forms of numeric, text, and graphics presentations. Multimedia methods of presentation give end users information in a variety of media, including text and graphics displays, voice and other digitized audio, photographs, and video clips. However, many multimedia systems go beyond one-way information presentations. They allow end users to select the form and content of the information presented and browse through the information in a random way, instead of being tied to the sequential access of information. Let's take a closer look now at the information technologies that make multimedia possible. See Figure 8.23.

FIGURE 8.23
An example of a multimedia business presentation.

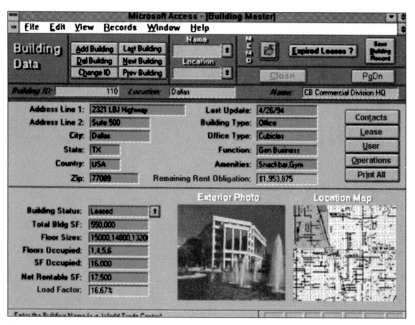

Courtesy of Computerworld.

Figure 8.24 outlines the basic hardware and software requirements of a typical microcomputer system that enables you to create, as well as enjoy multimedia presentations. Of course, owners of low cost *multimedia PCs* marketed for home use do not need *authoring software* or high-powered hardware capabilities in order to enjoy multimedia games and other entertainment and educational multimedia products.

But if you want to create your own multimedia productions, you will have to spend several thousand dollars to put together a high-performance multimedia system. As Figure 8.24 shows, this includes CD-ROM players, stereo speakers, high-resolution color graphics monitors, sound boards, video capture boards, a high-performance microprocessor, at least 16 megabytes of RAM, and over 300 megabytes of hard disk capacity. Software such as authoring tools, and programs for image editing and graphics creation can add several thousand more dollars to the startup costs of your multimedia authoring system [19].

Multimedia Hardware and Software

Hypertext and hypermedia are foundation technologies for multimedia presentations. **Hypertext** is a methodology for the construction and interactive use of text databases. By definition, hypertext contains only text and a limited amount of graphics. **Hypermedia** are electronic documents that contain multiple forms of media, including text, graphics, video, and so on. A hypertext or hypermedia document is a body of text of any size in electronic form that is indexed so that it can be quickly searched by the reader. For example, if you highlight a term on a hypermedia

Hypertext and Hypermedia

FIGURE 8.24
What you need to create multimedia productions.

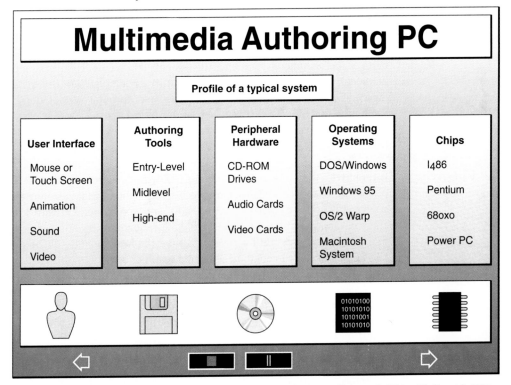

Source: Adapted from Elizabeth Wood, "Multimedia Comes Down to Earth," *Computerworld,* August 1, 1994, p. 71. Copyright 1994 by Computerworld, Inc., Framingham, MA 01701—Reprinted from *Computerworld.*

FIGURE 8.25
A display of a popular hyper-
text/hypermedia development
package, which uses the
Hypertext Markup Language
(HTML) to develop Hyperlinked
documents.

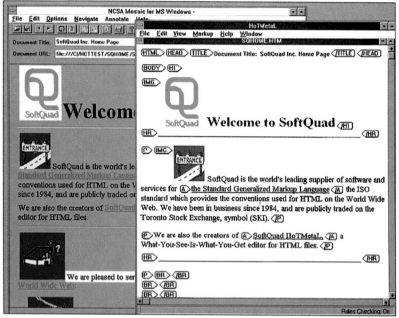

Courtesy of SoftQuad Inc.

document displayed on your computer video screen and press a key, the computer could instantly bring up a display of a passage of text and graphics related to that term. Once you finished viewing that pop-up display, you could return to what you were reading originally, or jump to another part of the document instantly.

Hypertext and hypermedia are developed using specialized programming languages like *Hypertext Markup Language* (HTML), which create *hyperlinks* to other parts of the document, or to other documents and media. Hypertext and hypermedia documents can thus be programmed to let a reader *navigate* through a multimedia database by following a chain of hyperlinks through various documents. The *home pages* on the World Wide Web of the Internet are a popular example of this technology. Thus, the use of hypertext and hypermedia provides an environment for online interactive presentations of multimedia. See Figure 8.25.

Interactive Video

Interactive video is another important multimedia technology that integrates computer and video technologies. Using technologies like digital video interactive (DVI) allows end users to digitally capture, edit, and combine video with text, pictures, and sound into multimedia business and educational presentations. For example, an interactive video session for training airline flight attendants can be produced on CD-ROM disks. It can combine animated graphics displays of different airplane configurations, presentation graphics of airline statistics, lists of major topics and facts, video clips of flight attendants working on various airplanes, and various announcements and sounds helpful in managing emergencies. Figure 8.26 summarizes many of the technologies that are used to create multimedia presentations.

Office Management Systems

Office management systems are an important category of office automation systems. They include electronic calendars, tickler files, electronic mail directories, schedulers, and task management systems. They provide computer-based support

---

Multimedia Technologies

- **Authoring Language.** A high-level computer programming facility with English language commands specifically designed to implement multimedia applications.

- **Compact Disk Interactive.** A multimedia standard proposed by Philips Corp. A specification to read data from a CD containing audio, image, graphics, and computer data.

- **Compressed Audio.** A method of digitally encoding and decoding several seconds of voice-quality audio per single videodisc frame. This increases the storage capability to several hours of audio per videodisc.

- **Computer Edit System.** A video editing system controlled by a computer and interfaced to several playback and record machines. This type of system is capable of making precise frame-accurate edits.

- **Digital Audio.** A technique that stores audio as a series of numbers.

- **Digital Video Interactive.** This technology compresses video images and, in its latest version, can produce animated scenes at 30 frames per second. The current compression ratio is 160-to-1.

- **Interactive Video.** The convergence of video and computer technology. A user has control over a coordinated video program and computer program through the user's actions, choices, and decisions, which affect how the program unfolds.

- **Musical Instrument Digital Interface.** Serial data transmission protocol for transporting musical information between compatible electronic musical devices.

- **Sound Board.** An add-in card with software that captures and plays back sound or music.

- **Storyboard:**
  1. A visualization of the order of a piece, using representative frames from each shot or sequence to show a visual skeleton of the piece.
  2. Documentation for video production that contains the audio script and a complete description of the visual content often in the form of pictures or sketches.

- **Video Capture Card.** An add-in card that digitizes analog video from a VCR, video camera, or still-image camera. Video can be digitized as a single frame or multiple frames per second to produce full-motion video.

FIGURE 8.26
Technologies for multimedia production and presentation.

Source: Elizabeth Wood, "Multimedia Comes Down to Earth," *Computerworld*, August 1, 1994, p. 70. Copyright 1994 by Computerworld, Inc., Framingham, MA 01701—Reprinted from *Computerworld*.

services to managers and other office professionals to help them organize their work activities. Office management software computerizes manual methods of planning such as paper calendars, appointment books, directories, file folders, memos, and notes. Microcomputer users can get some of the benefits of office management systems by using *desktop accessory* and *personal information manager* packages. **Groupware** packages are also available which enable members of work groups on local area networks to share a variety of office services; thus, office management systems can help end users and work groups organize routine office tasks.

For example, you could enter the date and time of a meeting into an electronic calendar. An electronic tickler file will automatically remind you of important events. Electronic schedulers use the electronic calendars of several people to help you schedule meetings and other activities with them. Desktop accessories provide features such as a calculator, notepad, alarm clock, phone directory, and appointment book that pop up in a window on the display screen of your workstation at the touch of a key. Electronic mail directories help you contact people easily. And electronic

FIGURE 8.27
Using an office management system for task management.

Courtesy of IBM Corporation.

task management packages help you plan a series of related activities so that scheduled results are accomplished on time. Figure 8.27 shows the use of an office management system.

Management Implications of Office Automation

Office automation systems help end users achieve the benefits of (1) more cost-effective communications and (2) more *time-effective* communications than traditional
written and telephone communications methods. For example, electronic mail and
facsimile systems are designed to minimize *information float* and *telephone tag*.
Information float is the time (at least several days) when a written letter or other
document is in transit between the sender and receiver, and thus unavailable for any
action or response. **Telephone tag** is the process of (1) repeatedly calling people, (2)
finding them unavailable, (3) leaving messages, and (4) finding out later you were
unavailable when they finally returned your calls.

Electronic mail, voice mail, and facsimile systems can also eliminate the effects
of mail that is lost in transit or phone lines that are frequently busy. They can also
reduce the costs of labor, materials, and postage for office communications (from
more than $5 for a written message to less than 50 cents for an electronic message
is one estimate). Also, the amount of time wasted in regular phone calls can be
reduced (by one-third, according to another estimate) [3, 20].

Of course, these advantages are not acquired without some negative effects.
First, the cost of automated office hardware is significantly higher than the equipment it replaces. The ease of use and lack of security of many office automation systems have also caused problems. Inefficient and unauthorized use of electronic mail,
voice mail, and facsimile services can significantly impair office productivity. One
example is sending copies of electronic mail messages to people who do not need or
want them. Another is "junk fax"—receiving unauthorized advertisements and unre-
quested documents that disrupt the normal use of office fax machines. Programs of
employee education and policies that stress efficient use of OA services are a natural
solution for such problems. Software which monitors and protects against improper
use of OA systems is another controversial but fast growing alternative.

Consolidated Edison, L.A. Water, and Others: Telecommuting to Work

If the organization is getting flatter, it's also getting more spread out. Some people are working from home, on the road, or from a neighborhood office center that spares them a long commute. Information systems managers will be called on to support these new work patterns.

At Consolidated Edison in New York, three customer service representatives now handle their regular duties—responding to customer phone calls and correspondence—from home. IBM's CallPath computer-integrated telephony software routes customer calls to the telecommuters, while correspondence is delivered by imaging and workflow software. In essence, the telecommuter links up to the company LAN and fetches the next available task, said Ed Glister, senior project manager in the customer operations unit. The only differences between in-house and remote users are remote users have ISDN connections and larger PC hard disks to hold more software, he said.

Nancy Muehter, administrator of the telecommuting project at the Los Angeles Metropolitan Water District, says that the water district has 50 to 60 workers telecommuting an average of one day a week, making use of Compaq 486-based laptops, modems, and home fax machines. Another 20 to 30 district workers would like to telecommute. Muehter's goal is to get 200 of the district's 2,000 employees to telecommute, a figure that helps the district meet Southern California's air quality regulations. Rule 1501, for example, requires all companies with 100 employees or more to plan a reduction in total worker trips to cut air pollution.

Much of the success of the water district program hinges on training workers. They get the exact same software on both their desktops and laptops. They have to be taught how to connect to the central office, access mainframe databases, and maintain security. "The benefits are not free. You have to spend some money to reap the rewards," Muehter notes.

Only two workers so far have been removed from the program because telecommuting led to problems in doing their jobs, she says. Another dropped out because he didn't like telecommuting. The early participants have been workers who were already computer users—lawyers, programmers, and engineers.

Principal Financial Group is a financial services firm in Des Moines, Iowa. "Like any other company perk, the alternate work hours plan is an additional benefit that accrues over time for eligible employees," says Leslie Packham, technology development analyst, pension business unit.

- An estimated 500 out of 6,500 eligible employees have at some time worked from home.

- Users can dial in remotely to their office desktops using specially configured versions of Symantec's PCAnywhere software. To get into the corporate LAN, a user's access request is routed to a communications server that identifies and verifies the request.

- The communications server is operated by corporate auditing and control.

- In addition to identifying themselves to the server, users must pass redundant security checks to gain system access.

Miles Corp., a division of the German firm Bayer AG, is a conglomerate based in Pittsburgh. "I see an emphasis on mobility. A lot of the orders we are placing right now are for notebooks and laptops with a lot of horsepower, larger hard disks, and full software suites," says James Baehr, manager, communications, technical procurement and services.

- No formal telecommunicating policy is in place yet. So far the company has worked on a case-by-case basis. When an employee is on maternity leave or disabled, Miles makes arrangements for that employee to work from home.

- Miles looks for licensing agreements that let company software be used at home, provided another copy is not in use at the same time.

- Security is ensured by requiring remote users to input matching parts of a precoded algorithm.

CASE STUDY QUESTIONS

1. What are some of the benefits and challenges of telecommuting?

2. When should organizations support telecommuting?

3. What technologies are needed to support telecommuting?

Source: Adapted from Jaikumar Vijayan, "Home Alone," *Computerworld*, December 26, 1994/January 2, 1995, p. 67; Mitch Betts, "Workers Slow to Accept Telecommuting," *Computerworld*, February 20, 1995, p. 97; and Charles Babcock, "Telecommuting: The Future Is Now," *Computerworld*, March 13, 1995, p.8. Copyright 1995 by Computerworld, Inc., Framingham, MA 01701—Reprinted from *Computerworld*.

Summary

- **End User Computing.** End user computing is the direct, hands-on use of computers by end users to perform the information processing needed to accomplish their work activities. End user computing has grown dramatically because information services have been unable to keep up with the information processing requests of users. Also, improvements in microcomputer hardware, software, and networking capabilities have made end user computing attractive, affordable, and effective for today's organizations. Major application areas of end user computing include office automation, information management and retrieval, decision support, and application development.

- **End User Computing Systems.** End user computing should be viewed as systems of hardware, software, people, and data resources. Hardware resources include microcomputer workstations, local area network servers, departmental minicomputers, and corporate mainframes. Software resources consist of application packages, groupware packages, and application development packages. People resources include end users and information center and other user consultants. Data resources include personal, work group, corporate, and external databases.

- **Work Group Computing.** Much of end user computing is a collaborative effort known as work group computing. End users are using networked computers and groupware packages to collaborate on work assignments without regard to time constraints, physical location, or organizational boundaries. Groupware packages can accomplish many applications, as summarized in Figure 8.9. However, the key features of such collaboration software are the work group communications and coordination that it makes possible.

- **Office Automation.** Office automation systems include electronic communications and collaboration systems, text processing, image processing, and other information technologies to develop computer-based information systems that collect, store, and transmit electronic messages, documents, and other forms of communications. Office automation systems include word processing, desktop publishing, graphics and multimedia presentations, electronic mail, voice mail, facsimile, image processing, electronic meeting systems, and office management systems.

Key Terms and Concepts

These are the key terms and concepts of this chapter. The page number of their first explanation is in parentheses.

1. Bulletin board systems (283)
2. Computer graphics (290)
3. Desktop publishing (288)
4. Desktop videoconferencing (286)
5. Document (288)
6. Electronic document management (289)
7. Electronic mail (282)
8. Electronic meeting systems (286)
9. End user collaboration (268)
10. End user computing (268)
    a. Rationale (268)
    b. Management implications (278)
    c. Resources (270)
11. End user computing applications (273)
    a. Office automation (273)

    b. Information management and retrieval (273)
    c. Decision support (274)
    d. Application development (275)
12. Facsimile (284)
13. Groupware (271, 277)
14. Hypermedia (293)
15. Hypertext (293)
16. Image processing (289)
17. Information center (272)
18. Information float (296)
19. Interactive video (294)
20. Multimedia presentations (292)
21. Office automation (281)
    a. Management implications (296)
    b. Types of systems (281)
22. Office management systems (294)

23. Personal information manager (274)
24. Presentation graphics (291)
25. Public information services (283)
26. Telecommuting (287)
27. Teleconferencing (286)
28. Telephone tag (296)
29. Text data (288)
30. User consultant (272)
31. Videotex (284)
32. Voice mail (282)
33. Word processing (288)
34. Work group (276)
35. Work group computing (275)

Review Quiz

Match one of the key terms and concepts listed above with one of the brief examples or definitions listed below. Try to find the best fit for answers that seem to fit more than one term or concept. Defend your choices.

___ 1. The direct, hands-on use of computers by users.

___ 2. End user applications frequently lack adequate controls.

___ 3. Examples are microcomputer workstations, application packages, information center consultants, and external databases.

___ 4. Using your workstation to prepare documents and communicate with your colleagues.

___ 5. Managing databases and generating reports.

___ 6. Using an electronic spreadsheet for what-if analysis.

___ 7. Developing new ways to use computers to perform jobs for you.

___ 8. Software that helps people collaborate on group work assignments.

___ 9. Members of an organization and its business partners communicate and coordinate on joint projects.

___ 10. Members of a work group share computer resources to jointly accomplish work assignments.

___ 11. Organizations have established these end user support groups.

___ 12. Automates office work activities and communications, but may disrupt traditional work roles.

___ 13. Includes word processing, desktop publishing, electronic mail, and teleconferencing.

___ 14. Text data is manipulated and documents are produced.

___ 15. Characters, words, sentences, and paragraphs.

___ 16. Letters, memos, forms, and reports.

___ 17. Users can produce their own brochures and manuals.

___ 18. Includes computer-aided design, presentation graphics, and computer art.

___ 19. Easier to understand than columns of numbers.

___ 20. Presenting information in a variety of forms of media.

___ 21. Helps you interactively browse through a text database.

___ 22. A multimedia form of hypertext technology.

___ 23. Allows end users to capture video and sound for computer-based presentations.

___ 24. Use your workstation to send and receive messages.

___ 25. Use your telephone as an electronic message terminal.

___ 26. The time a document is in transit between sender and receiver.

___ 27. You and the person you want to contact repeatedly miss each other's phone calls.

___ 28. Transmitting images of documents electronically.

___ 29. Saves travel time and money spent on meetings.

___ 30. Realtime televised electronic meetings at remote sites.

___ 31. Using telecommunications so you can work at home.

___ 32. End users can electronically capture, store, process, and retrieve images.

___ 33. Customer correspondence and sales orders can be optically captured and routed to end users for processing.

___ 34. Helps end users store information in a variety of forms and retrieve it in many different ways.

___ 35. Integrates calculator, calendar, address book, notepad, and other functions.

___ 36. Provides a variety of office automation services such as electronic calendars and meeting scheduling.

___ 37. End users can post public or private messages for other computer users.

___ 38. They specialize in providing a range of computing and communications services to microcomputer users.

___ 39. An interactive information service for home computers.

___ 40. Interactive video communications between end user workstations.

Discussion Questions

1. What developments are responsible for the growth of end user computing? Do you expect this growth to continue? Explain.

2. What changes do you expect in the future in the types of hardware, software, people, and data resources typically used in end user computing systems? In the four major application areas of end user computing?

3. Refer to the Real World Case on McDonnell-Douglas and Chase Manhattan in the chapter. What do you think are the top information technologies that promote collaborative computing? Explain your choices.

4. Why is work group computing becoming an increasingly important form of end user computing? What is the role of groupware in supporting this trend?

5. Why do you think some organizations are closing their information centers and distributing end user support to departments and other business units?

6. Refer to the Real World Case on Consolidated Edison and L.A. Water in the chapter. Would you like to be a telecommuter? Why or why not?

7. If you were a manager, how would you manage some of the risks of end user computing?

8. What office automation developments are moving us toward a "virtual" office? What circumstances inhibit movement in that direction?

9. How will the growth of graphics and multimedia presentations affect the information presentation preferences of managers? Explain.

10. Would you like to take part in electronic meetings such as teleconferences? Would you like to telecommute to work? Why or why not?

Real World Problems

1. Opticon Holding A/S: Organizing for Collaboration

Some would argue that technology is a secondary issue when it comes to true collaboration. More important, these people would say, is demolishing traditional corporate structure. Nowhere is this more true than at Danish hearing-aid manufacturer Opticon Holding A/S, in Copenhagen. In 1991, the 87-year-old firm was in the red, despite having only a 10 percent share of the worldwide hearing-aid market. That was before it became what President Lars Kolind calls a "spaghetti organization." Kolind used a carrot-and-stick approach to change Opticon. He told staffers to toe the line or else. He then had them form little groups, stepped back and let the enthusiasm flow.

Today, there are no formal departments. Instead, fluid work groups are created for projects, and staffers are expected to perform more than one function. Opticon's headquarters is a fully open room with an array of drawerless desks, mobile telephones, and PCs running office, engineering and other applications. Everyone, including managers, has a wheeled trolly with hanging files. There is also no paper or electronic correspondence. Kolind insists on face-to-face communication to keep things informal. Mail is scanned into a document work flow/imaging system from Recognition International, and then routed automatically using HP's NewWave software to staffers' E-mail boxes. Except for some files pertaining only to management, all documents in the repository are generally available.

The openness paid off when employees, searching for new projects, found plans for the first fully automatic hearing aid, invented at Opticon in the mid-80s. This helped turn Opticon's fortunes around. The company hammered out a new product, its Multi-Focus hearing aid, and put it on the market in less than four months—by the end of 1991. "This process of production and marketing would normally take two years," said Information Technology Coordinator Torben Petersen. By 1993, sales had improved by 19 percent and gross profits by 25 percent. Profit margins increased from 5.8 percent in 1992 to 12.9 percent in 1993, while administrative expenses remained unchanged.

a. How does Opticon's organization structure and use of IT promote collaboration?

b. Why would this new environment dramatically improve Opticon's business performance?

Source: Adapted from Richard Adhikari, "All Together Now," *Computerworld Client/Server Journal,* June 1995, p. 20. Copyright 1995 by Computerworld, Inc., Framingham, MA 01701—Reprinted from *Computerworld.*

2. Piper-Jaffrey and Georgia-Pacific: Outsourcing End User Support

Unwilling to shell out millions to build top-notch end user support organizations in-house, an increasing number of companies are *outsourcing* these services by enlisting outside providers for one-stop care of PC hardware and software. As part of the bargain, many information systems executives are finally getting a grip on out-of-control PC life cycle costs, which Gartner Group has estimated at $40,000 per desktop over five years. Procter & Gamble Co., in Cincinnati, Georgia-Pacific Corp., in Atlanta, and Piper-Jaffrey, Inc., a large regional brokerage firm in Minneapolis, have all recently signed fixed-rate, multiyear desktop support contracts. The services furnished under the deals include hardware and software installation and upgrades, asset inventory and management, LAN and electronic-mail administration, and centralized help desk support.

Piper-Jaffrey's contract with Entex Information Services "involves everything from soup to nuts," said David Collins, the brokerage's director of emerging technologies. As a result, he said, "it gives us a lot of leverage to negotiate service levels and costs." At Piper-Jaffrey, Entex built into its fixed-rate price "the cost of all services plus the cost of technology upgrades," Collins said. The arrangement should yield more predictable and lower costs than the brokerage's previous arrangements with multiple vendors.

Jim Carter, director of utility management services at Georgia-Pacific, says that Georgia-Pacific would have needed to hire "hundreds of people" to furnish desktop services to its 52,000 employees located at more than 500 sites nationwide. Instead, it recently hammered out a multiyear contract with General Electric Technology Management Services to provide the paper company with a whole range of desktop services at a fixed price. "Because it's a multiyear arrangement, we're able to predict our expenses with quite a bit of certainty," Carter noted. "We're also adding services we didn't previously have. Comparing what it would have cost us to staff up to provide them versus what we are going to be paying to GE represents a savings of hundreds of thousands of dollars each year."

a. How do Piper-Jaffrey and Georgia-Pacific benefit from outsourcing their end user support services?

b. Why couldn't their own IS organizations provide such support?

Source: Adapted from Julie King, "PC Pains Get Fixed-Price Remedy," *Computerworld*, January 16, 1995, pp. 1–14. Copyright 1995 by Computerworld, Inc., Framingham, MA 01701—Reprinted from *Computerworld*.

3. Johnson Controls and Carrier Corp.: Desktop Videoconferencing

Andrew Drummond did not let cynicism get in his way of installing desktop videoconferencing at Johnson Controls, Inc., in Plymouth, Michigan. At least not for very long. "If you'd asked me about desktop videoconferencing six months ago, I would have said it wouldn't be ready for another year or two," said Drummond, a LAN manager at the automotive seat manufacturer. That was then. Today, 15 Johnson sites participate in international training, technical support and even software distribution via Intel's ProShare desktop videoconferencing system. Johnson Controls is one of a small and slowly growing number of true believers. For those companies, desktop videoconferencing applications are spreading like wildfire even though this is still a high-cost technology.

"This stuff pays back in a matter of months," said Ken Pawiak, marketing communications manager at Carrier Corp., a subsidiary of United Technologies Corp. in East Hartford, Connecticut. A key to cost justification is that "you can milk this to do anything you want," Pawiak said. Originally, Carrier thought desktop videoconferencing would help it with training and remote technical support. But prod-

uct designers soon wanted a piece of the action, and managers realized it would help them better conduct financial reviews. This is how an 8-system pilot in August turned into a 60-system rollout earlier this month, with AT&T and its Vistium videoconferencing system the vendor and system of choice. Bottom-line benefits, Pawiak said, include cost and time savings as well as increased productivity and efficiency.

And soft benefits figure in strongly as well. "It gives a personal touch to the business," Pawiak said. For instance, why do United Technologies managers need to see one another during financial reviews? Why not just use data collaboration to share spreadsheets? "It's human nature," Pawiak said. "You've got to look someone in the eye if you're cutting their budget by 50 percent or asking them what happened with a particular customer."

a. How do Johnson Controls and Carrier Corp. use desktop videoconferencing?

b. What are some of the benefits and limitations of this technology?

Source: Adapted from Mary Brandel, "Videoconferencing Slowly Goes Desktop," *Computerworld*, February 20, 1995, pp. 81, 85. Copyright 1995 by Computerworld, Inc., Framingham, MA 01701—Reprinted from *Computerworld*.

4. Ogden Projects: Document Imaging Systems

For a company that manages 28 waste-to-energy facilities throughout North America, Ogden Projects sure had a lot to learn about conservation. That is because the $700 million subsidiary of New York services giant Ogden Corp. used to store all of its purchase orders, invoices, and other back-office accounting documents from its energy plants in a mountain of paper files at a records retention warehouse in Newark, New Jersey. But that has all changed with the recent installation of a document imaging system designed to streamline the flow of documents among Ogden Projects' facilities, which are as far-flung as Dartmouth, Nova Scotia, to its headquarters in Fairfield, New Jersey. When the company broke ground for its newest facility in Montgomery County, Maryland, in 1993, "We estimated our paper flow at 2 million pieces a year and counting," said Donald F. Warga, a manager of systems and programming at the unit. "Obviously, we had to find a better way to manage our internal paper flow."

Ogden Projects already had a computerized accounts payable system in place, but that merely tracked the paperwork manually—a tall order for a unit that handles more than 50,000 claims a year from as many as 12,000 vendors. So in June 1993, Ogden Projects installed an imaging system. The system, which cost approximately $500,000, includes an IBM Optical Library Data Server and Kodak High-Volume Image Link Scanner. The hardware, which runs off of Ogden Projects' AS/400 midsize computer, is operated using IBM's Image Plus/400 software.

"I think it's wonderful," said Jayne Gorab, an accounts payable clerk who is linked to the system through an IBM

OS/2 gateway. "It's so much easier to sit at your desk and retrieve files on your computer screen than to get them from the file room." In the past, Gorab said, it took her up to half an hour to locate an invoice in the file room and copy the necessary information. Now that those invoices are scanned and made available to users online the next business day, she can key in the invoice numbers to access a file within seconds.

a. What is document imaging? Why did Ogden Projects need an imaging system?

b. How does an imaging system help improve employee productivity and effectiveness?

Source: Adapted from Thomas Hoffman, "Waste-To-Energy Firm Uses Imaging to Dam Paper Tide," *Computerworld,* January 30, 1995, pp. 57, 61. Copyright 1995 by Computerworld, Inc., Framingham, MA 01701—Reprinted from *Computerworld.*

5. Ann Salmon of the NMMRA: Scheduling Meetings Electronically

Our PC support manager gave a demo of Campbell Services' OnTime for Networks, which would allow both the CEO and the secretary to use a calendar at the same time. The CEO was sufficiently impressed to buy the $1,770 25-user package practically on the spot. Because ours is a benign dictatorship, everyone switched to OnTime. However, I sat skeptically on the sidelines, clinging to my Franklin Planner. Though I was a fluent computer user, I dreaded not having my manual planner tucked under my arm. I also hated the idea of others looking at my personal schedule. Meanwhile, OnTime for Networks was catching on around the office. Our network administrator had installed it so the calendar appeared as soon as we turned on our computers. When I saw I was being scheduled for meetings, I'd dutifully copy the information into my Franklin Planner. But I soon realized I was duplicating my effort.

I decided to swallow my pride and learn the program, which turned out to be a simple matter. To my relief, I found I had worried needlessly about my privacy. Although I can see the times when others aren't available, I can't see *what* they're doing unless they make the information public. Now I spend my time doing real work instead of scheduling meetings. Rather than playing phone tag, I click on an icon to access people's calendars or to see the times conference rooms are reserved. I can see a list of people on the network and select those whose schedules I want to view. To see when they have free time, I just click OK to display all the calendars in a grid.

To send a request for a meeting, I click on Add Group Message and type the message in a dialog box; I can add a personal note as well. Then I go into the Category list and select Meeting or Appointment; a button gives me a list of all the personnel on the network, from which I select the people I want to invite. When I click on OK, OnTime sends out the meeting request message to my colleagues.

Note: Ann Salmon is the human resources manager of the New Mexico Medical Review Association (NMMRA).

a. What are the benefits of an electronic calendar and meeting scheduler?

b. Why was Ann Salmon reluctant to use the new system? Is such reluctance typical when a new IT system is introduced? Explain.

Source: Adapted from Ann Salmon, "The Never Ending Schedule." *PC World,* March 1995, pp. 39–40. Reprinted with permission of PC World.

6. Chevron Corporation: Collaboration through Discussion Databases

As the novelty of electronic mail wears off in some companies, users are starting to demand the next evolutionary step—information sharing. Chevron Corp. in San Francisco is trying to meet its employees' needs by taking them into the information age. One of the ways it is doing so is through a discussion database technology that gives staff a forum for exchanging ideas and information. Along the way, the company hopes to reap many benefits, such as reduced travel costs, a logical order to group discussion and a common forum for sharing best practices. "We saw that groupware could change the way organizations work," said George Alameda, information technology manager at Chevron U.S.A. Production Co., in Houston. "People could be on very diverse teams and spread out geographically. Through the use of E-mail, it became intuitive to share information and manage the information environment that E-mail was giving us."

The transition to a discussion database started in August of last year, said Jonathan Simon, a systems analyst in Houston. In October, Simon started evaluating Collabra Software's Share 1.0. In November, he negotiated an agreement with the company. This agreement was followed by an aggressive pilot program, with 250 users, in the beginning of January. Users in five states shared information on a variety of subjects. These included groups such as the gas integration team, which shared information with teams at different sites; facilities engineering; and quality improvement, which tried to leverage best practices.

But "the real problem for us was not application development by sharing information and sharing it faster than the competitors," Simon said. The real problem, as in many similar cases, was cultural. "We stirred up a lot of concerns by doing this pilot. However, on the whole, people have been very receptive. The more remote people are, the more enthusiastic they've been. It almost seems to be a function of how far they are." Simon said. That is because it is often hard for remote employees to find the expertise they need on a particular subject locally. In the larger offices, it may not be all that important.

a. What is a discussion database? How is it related to E-mail?

b. How could a discussion database like Chevron's promote end user collaboration? How else could it benefit Chevron?

Source: Adapted from Suruchi Mohan, "Chevron Plants to Keep People Talking," *Computerworld,* April 24, 1995, pp. 53, 57. Copyright 1995 by Computerworld, Inc., Framingham, MA 01701—Reprinted from *Computerworld.*

Application Exercises

1. End User Office Automation

Match one of the following office automation systems with the examples listed below:

a. Desktop publishing
b. Electronic mail
c. Office management systems
d. Teleconferencing
e. Voice mail

f. Word processing
g. Image processing
h. Facsimile
i. Electronic meetings
j. Desktop videoconferencing

___ 1. Composing, editing, and printing a letter to a customer.

___ 2. Producing a company newsletter with text and graphics.

___ 3. Being prompted that you have scheduled a meeting.

___ 4. Visually displaying messages that have been sent to you.

___ 5. Listening to a computer-generated message from an associate.

___ 6. Participating in a companywide TV workshop.

___ 7. Conducting a meeting where all participants use computers.

___ 8. Sending a copy of a letter electronically using the telephone system.

___ 9. Optically capturing and using document images instead of paper documents.

___ 10. Using video communications with colleagues at their workstations.

2. End User Database Development at ABC Company

ABC Company has seen rapid expansion in employee use of public information services and electronic bulletin board systems. You have been asked to develop a database to keep track of employee connections to CompuServe, the Dow Jones News/Retrieval Service, and the Internet.

This database should be designed to serve a variety of purposes. It will be used to track trends in the use of the various services across the various departments of the company and to identify individual employees participating in them. The company also desires to promote effective use of these services by developing user groups. The database will be used to develop user lists for each service, which can serve as mailing lists for newsletters and can be distributed to the users to promote the development of informal communication among the users of each service.

Develop a database to track employee users based on this description and the sample data shown in Figure 8.28. Refer to Figure 8.29 which outlines the basic activities of the end user database development process.

a. Develop an appropriate structure for a database file to store the necessary information, implement that structure, and enter the sample data shown.

Employee Name	Department	Office No.	Compu-Serve User	Dow Jones IS User	Internet Address
Davis, Sue	Marketing	C-217	Yes	Yes	SD@ABC.HQ.COM
Jones, AL	Accounting	B-111	No	Yes	
Lewis, Bob	R&D	A-247	Yes	No	BL@ABC.VAX.COM
Evans, Ann	Accounting	B-214	Yes	No	AEV@ABC.HQ.COM
Smith, Eve	Accounting	B-129	No	Yes	
Adams, Ed	R&D	A-269	Yes	Yes	ADAMS@ABC.VAX.COM
Dahl Art	Marketing	C-309	No	Yes	ART@ABC.HQ.COM
Towns, Jan	Marketing	C-104	No	No	
Vest, Ben	Accounting	B-119	No	Yes	BV@ABC.HQ.COM
Morris, Ed	Marketing	C-107	Yes	No	
James, Tim	Marketing	C-322	Yes	Yes	TJ@ABC.HQ.COM

FIGURE 8.28
Sample of employee users of external information services.

FIGURE 8.29
The basic activities of the end user database development process.

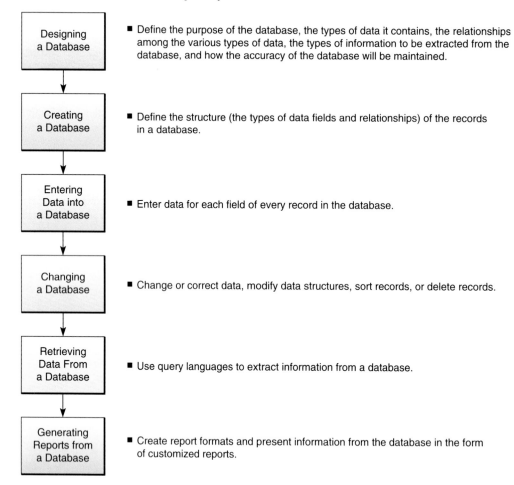

Designing a Database	▪ Define the purpose of the database, the types of data it contains, the relationships among the various types of data, the types of information to be extracted from the database, and how the accuracy of the database will be maintained.
Creating a Database	▪ Define the structure (the types of data fields and relationships) of the records in a database.
Entering Data into a Database	▪ Enter data for each field of every record in the database.
Changing a Database	▪ Change or correct data, modify data structures, sort records, or delete records.
Retrieving Data From a Database	▪ Use query languages to extract information from a database.
Generating Reports from a Database	▪ Create report formats and present information from the database in the form of customized reports.

b. Prepare a listing showing the number of employees, by department, participating in each service.

c. Prepare a summary listing of all employees connected to the Internet. This report should be suitable for distribution to the employees as an index of Internet users. It should be sorted by department and should show the Internet address, as well as the office address of each participating employee.

3. End User Spreadsheet Development at Cantel Cuisine

Cantel Cuisine is a regional producer of fresh pasta which is kept refrigerated and sold as a gourmet item in supermarkets. Cantel operates in Los Angeles and in San Francisco and has a production facility and office complex in each city. Cantel has always used standard long-distance service for phone calls between the two offices. However, management has noticed that there is a high volume of calls between the offices and wants to investigate the feasibility of leasing a line to connect the Los Angeles office with the San Francisco office. You have been asked to do a cost analysis comparing the current Direct Distance Dialing service with the costs of a leased line.

You are able to find the following information about call volumes and costs:

a. Cantel operates seven days a week. On an average day, there are 18 daytime calls and 12 calls during the evening or night. The calls last an average of six minutes. All calls

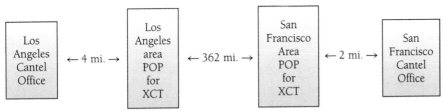

FIGURE 8.30
Distances between Cantel's offices.

	Fixed Charge	Distance Charge (per mile)
0 to 3 miles	$ 78.25	$8.50
4 to 10 miles	$ 83.50	$6.75

XCT Monthly Lease Rates

	Fixed Charge	Distance Charge (per mile)
0 to 100 miles	$134.00	$ .75
100 to 500 miles	$209.00	$ .55

FIGURE 8.31
Coastal Bell monthly lease rates for Los Angeles and San Francisco.

made on the weekend (Saturday and Sunday) are charged at the evening/night rate. There are 22 working days and 8 weekend days in a typical month.

b. The charges for Direct Distance Dialing phone service are as follows:

	Day Rate	Evening/Night/ Weekend Rate
First minute	$.16	$.09
Each additional minute	$.14	$.07

c. For a leased line, several components are needed. Circuits must be leased from the local phone company covering the distances from each Cantel office to the nearest point of presence (POP) of the long-distance carrier. Then a circuit must be leased from the long-distance carrier to connect those two points. Let's assume that the local phone company is Coastal Bell and the long-distance carrier is XCT. The lease charges have a fixed component and a component that varies with distance. The distances involved and rates charged are as shown in Figures 8.30 and 8.31.

d. Based upon the information provided, develop a spreadsheet application comparing the costs of the two alternatives. Refer to Figure 8.32 which outlines the basic activities of the spreadsheet application development process. Which alternative would you recommend?

FIGURE 8.32
The basic activities of the spreadsheet application development process.

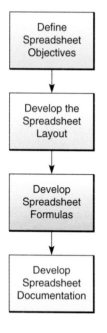

■ What information and decision support should be provided by the spreadsheet?

■ What should be the column and row headings of the spreadsheet? What other spreadsheet areas need to be specified?

■ What mathematical relationships need to be expressed as formulas in the spreadsheet? What built-in spreadsheet functions can be used to perform spreadsheet calculations?

■ What information about spreadsheet objectives, assumptions, values, and control measures needs to be documented?

Review Quiz Answers

1. 10	11. 17	21. 15	31. 26
2. 10b	12. 21a	22. 14	32. 16
3. 10c	13. 21b	23. 19	33. 6
4. 11a	14. 33	24. 7	34. 23
5. 11b	15. 29	25. 32	35. 3
6. 11c	16. 5	26. 18	36. 22
7. 11d	17. 3	27. 28	37. 1
8. 13	18. 2	28. 12	38. 25
9. 9	19. 24	29. 8	39. 31
10. 35	20. 20	30. 33	40. 4

Selected References

1. Amoroso, Donald, and Paul Cheney. "Testing a Causal Model of End User Application Effectiveness." *Journal of Management Information Systems,* Summer 1991.

2. Cats-Baril, William, and Tawfik Jelassi. "The French Videotex System Minitel: A Successful Implementation of a National Information Technology Infrastructure." *MIS Quarterly,* March 1994.

3. Carlson, Patricia Ann, and Michael Slave. "Hypertext Tools for Knowledge Workers: The Next Frontier: Tools that Teach." *Information Systems Management,* Spring 1992.

4. Chidambaram, Laku, and Beth Jones. "Impact on Communication Medium and Computer Support on Group Perceptions and Performance: A Comparison of Face-to-Face and Dispersed Meetings." *MIS Quarterly,* December 1993.

5. Doll, William, and Gholamreza Torkzadeh. "A Congruence Construct for User Involvement." *Decision Science Journal,* Spring 1991.

6. Groupware: The Team Approach." Supplement to *PC Week,* October 14, 1991.

7. Hershey, Gerald, and Donna Kizzier. *Planning and Implementing End User Information Systems.* Cincinnati: SouthWestern, 1992.

8. Karten, Naomi. "Standards for User-Driven Applications Development." *Information Systems Management,* Summer 1991.

9. Kling, Rob. "Cooperation, Coordination and Control in Computer Supported Work." *Communications of the ACM,* December 1991.

10. Kyng, Morten. "Designing for Cooperation: Cooperating in Design." *Communications of the ACM,* December 1991.

11. Lasher, Donald; Blake Ives; and Sirkka Jarvenpaa. "USAA-IBM Partnership in Information Technology: Managing the Image Project." *MIS Quarterly,* December 1991.

12. Lee, Allen. "Electronic Mail As a Medium for Rich Communications: An Empirical Investigation Using Hermeneutic Interpretation." *MIS Quarterly,* June, 1994.

13. Nunamaker, Jay; Alan Dennis; Joseph Valacich; Douglas Vogel; and Joey George. "Electronic Meeting Systems to Support Group Work." *Communications of the ACM,* July 1991.

14. Perin, Constance. "Electronic Social Fields in Bureaucracies." *Communications of the ACM,* December 1991.

15. Schnaidt, Partricia. *Enterprisewide Networking.* Carmel, IN: SAMS Publishing, 1992.

16. Sprague, Ralph, and Barbara McNurlin, eds. *Information Systems Management in Practice.* 3rd ed. Englewood Cliffs, NJ: Prentice Hall, 1993.

17. Tayntor, Christing. "New Challenges or the End of EUC?" *Information Systems Management,* Summer 1994.

18. Vessey, Iris, and Ajay Paul Sravanapudi. "CASE Tools as Collaborative Support Technologies." *Communications of the ACM,* January 1995.

19. Wood, Elizabeth. "Multimedia Comes Down to Earth," *Computerworld,* August 1, 1994.

20. Zigurs, Ilze, and Kenneth Kozar. "An Exploratory Study of Roles and Computer-Supported Groups." *MIS Quarterly,* September 1994.

Chiat/Day, IBM, and Others: The Virtual Office

Even in Venice, California, with its bizarre assortment of skaters, body builders, and seminude exhibitionists crowding the famous boardwalk, the building at 340 Main Street is an attention grabber. The three-story edifice, headquarters of the Chiat/Day advertising agency, is wrapped in brick beams and topped by a concrete slab, and its entrance is straddled by a pair of 100-ft.-tall black binoculars. Inside, the building is even more remarkable. Gone are the choice corner offices where agency executives once held forth, the cubicles once occupied by their secretaries, the once ubiquitous rows of filing cabinets. Executive chairs have been replaced by couches, business phones by the portable, flip-top variety. The only spaces left that employees can call their own are the red, green, blue, and black high school–style lockers where they stow their personal belongings. Unanchored, workers move about wherever their business takes them. Given the choice of working where they please, nearly half of the staff telecommutes, whether from home or from the road, keeping in touch by pages, cellular phone, fax, computer, and modem.

Welcome to the virtual office, a glimpse into the information age, which promises to change the way business does business. Some 3 million employees of U.S. companies already telecommute, performing all or part of their work away from their offices, and their numbers are increasing some 20 percent every year. The trend is likely to accelerate with the arrival of newer, more user-friendly technology designed specifically for mobile employees—or road warriors, as they are called. The impact could be profound, and not necessarily all for the good. For one thing, managers and workers will have to make difficult psychological and social adjustments. For another, restructuring is sure to produce some unexpected costs, both financial and managerial.

The transition at Chiat/Day, which announced plans in January to merge with TBWA International, was abrupt; just six months to transform the workplace from conventional to virtual. Now, employees who choose to go to the office on any given day stop at a "concierge's desk" in the lobby to pick up laptop computers and portable phones, which can be programmed with any employee's extension. The workers then head for any one of a dozen or so living room–like settings in a large, red-carpeted open area, plug into nearby modem jacks, and get cracking. For the occasional meetings of working groups, several "strategic business units" (conference rooms) have been set aside, but they are practically the only enclosed spaces.

Other than personal stationary and files stashed in each employee's private locker, paper has all but vanished. Faxes and memos show up on personal computer screens, and messages are left on voice mail. Documents once stored in filing cabinets are available only electronically on any of several computer terminals conveniently scattered around the premises. Clients can selectively tap into the firm's computer system to view advertising strategies and even critique new concepts.

Though perhaps not with the flair of Chiat/Day, other big companies are also experimenting with the virtual office. IBM, at which mobility is mandatory for more than 13,000 sales, marketing, technology, and administrative staff members, has outfitted these employees with PCs, printers, and fax-modems, enabling them to work away from its central offices. The computer giant's Denver operation, for example, was able to reduce its office space from nine floors to four, and it projects savings of $6 million over five years.

Ernst & Young, the nation's second biggest accounting firm, is in the process of eliminating 50 percent of its total U.S. office space by converting most E&Y accountants and consultants into part-time telecommuters who must literally make reservations to use the remaining offices. Under a system known as *hoteling*, E&Y employees in need of space must book at least one day in advance. Each office is equipped with the necessary hardware—as well as room for a few personal belongings, like portable pictures of the family. A similar switch to telecommuting and hoteling by the Chicago staff of industry leader Arthur Andersen & Co. enabled the firm to reduce the number of individual offices by nearly 100, saving more than $1 million annually.

Converting to the virtual office can be costly, however. At the CKS Group, a Cupertino, California, advertising agency, about a quarter of the agency's 160 employees work elsewhere, using the cellular phones, pagers, and PDAs (personal digital assistants) supplied by CKS to help them keep in touch. Not only does the firm pay half the purchase price for a staff member's home computer, but new technology is costing CKS an additional $10,000 to $15,000 per

Source: David Bjerklie, Patrick Cole, and Dan Cray, "Age of the Road Warrior," Special Issue: "Welcome to Cyberspace," *Time*, Spring 1995, pp. 38–40.

employee each year. CKS president Mark Kvammi estimates that technology expenditures amount to about $2 million every year. And the technology keeps getting more sophisticated. Last fall, for example, AT&T introduced PersonaLink Services, a package of communications software that facilitates computer, phone, fax, and paging functions in handheld personal communicators such as Sony's Magic Link and Motorola's Envoy; soon the AT&T interface will provide expanded wireless connectivity and be usable almost anywhere but underwater.

In the rush to embrace virtual-office technology, some managers may not be giving enough consideration to the psychological impact of the change. Executives who have labored for years to win such corporate status symbols as secretaries and luxurious corner offices are reluctant to shed their hard-won perks. Ambitious junior managers, mindful of the old adage "Out of sight, out of mind," resist spending too much time away from headquarters. For employees whose social life revolves largely around their co-workers, the transition can be wrenching. Some complain that their creativity, stimulated in part by informal corridor chatting or lunches with fellow employees, has been dampened. Even at Chiat/Day the metamorphosis has not been easy. "A lot of people left," admits Tony Stern, the firm's creative director. "'It isn't what I want' they said. "'It's too hard for me.'"

But technology that takes personal interaction away can also make up for it in new forms. At the New York City office of Chase Manhattan's Private Bank, Executive Vice President James Zeigon is able, with the click of his computer mouse, to dial his London and San Francisco branches and within five seconds conduct a "face-to-face" meeting with two colleagues thousands of miles apart. Using an advanced teleconferencing system from Avistar, the Chase bankers get consistently sharp video images in sync with clear sound and smooth movement. Their system allows for the on-screen display of documents as well as people from up to four locations at the same time. The cost per seat for such systems currently ranges from $2,000 to $5,000 but it could decline, say analysts, to $500 during the next two years.

The combination of plummeting costs and soaring sophistication in communications technology is changing the nature of business competition. Newfound access to vast libraries of digitized data, combined with the means to communicate cheaply and rapidly, has given small firms tools that until recently were available only to big corporations. Properly wired, so-called mom-and-pop enterprises now have the wherewithal to compete without overhead costs to weigh them down. Conversely, many big companies are finding it harder and harder to justify large proprietary staffs. To compete effectively with small rivals, many large companies have begun replacing those staffs with new digital gadgets in a process Bell Labs Nobel laureate Arno Penzias calls "the hollowing out of corporations."

"What we're going to see over the coming two decades is the devolution of many large corporations," says Peter Schwartz, president of Global Business Network, a cyberage research and consulting firm. Case in point, IBM. In the same massive restructuring that is bringing virtual offices and high-tech gadgetry to every level of its business, Big Blue has slashed its workforce by more than 170,000 jobs since its employment peak in the late 1980s. Many of these erstwhile employees have set up shop on their own, often doing business on a contract basis for IBM itself. Thoroughly armed with the modern weaponry of the road warrior, they—like the telecommuters at Chiat/Day—are among the forerunners of employment in the information age.

CASE STUDY QUESTIONS

1. Would you like to work in Chiat/Day's virtual office?
2. What are some of the things IBM, CKS, and Chase Manhattan are doing to promote virtual offices?
3. How is the growth of virtual offices affecting organiations and their employees?

Information Systems
for Business Operations

CHAPTER OUTLINE

LEARNING OBJECTIVES

The purpose of this chapter is to give you an understanding of how information systems support the information needs of the functional areas in business and the processing of business transactions.

Section I discusses information systems in marketing, manufacturing, and human resource management, and the most widely used types of accounting information systems, as well as information systems needed for the effective financial management of a firm.

Section II of this chapter outlines the major functions of transaction processing systems. It also discusses major changes taking place in transaction processing, as well as the advantages and disadvantages of major types of transaction processing systems.

After reading and studying this chapter, you should be able to:

1. Give examples of how information systems support the business functions of accounting, finance, human resource management, marketing, and production and operations management.

2. Identify the major activities of transaction processing systems, and give examples of how they support the operations of a business.

3. Identify the advantages and disadvantages of traditional data entry versus source data automation, and batch processing versus realtime processing.

4. Provide business examples that demonstrate the benefits and limitations of electronic data interchange and online transaction processing systems.

┌─ SECTION I
⬛ *Business Information Systems*
└─

IS in Business

There are as many ways to use information systems in business as there are business activities to be performed, business problems to be solved, and business opportunities to be pursued. As a prospective managerial end user, you should have a general understanding of the major ways information systems are used to support each of the **functions of business.** We will use the term **business information systems** to describe a variety of types of information systems (transaction processing, information reporting, decision support, etc.) that support a business function such as accounting, finance, marketing, or human resource management. Thus, applications of information systems in the functional areas of business are called *accounting information systems, marketing information systems, human resource information systems,* and so on. See Figure 9.1.

As a business end user, you should also have a *specific* understanding of how information systems affect a particular business function—marketing, for example— or a particular industry (e.g., banking) that is directly related to your career objectives. For example, someone whose career objective is a marketing position in banking should have a basic understanding of how information systems are used in banking and how they support the marketing activities of banks and other firms.

Cross-Functional Information Systems

Figure 9.1 illustrates how information systems can be grouped into business function categories. Information systems in this section will be analyzed according to the

FIGURE 9.1
Examples of business information systems. Note how they support the major functional areas of business.

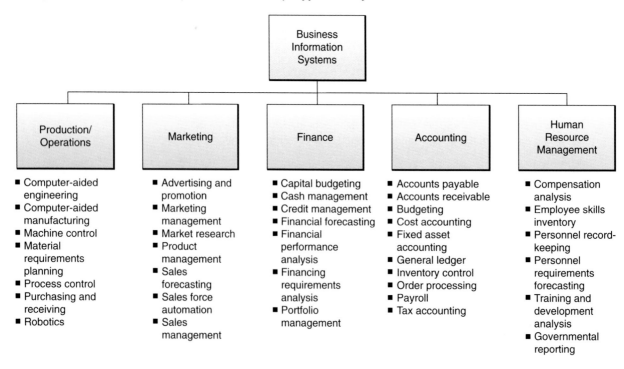

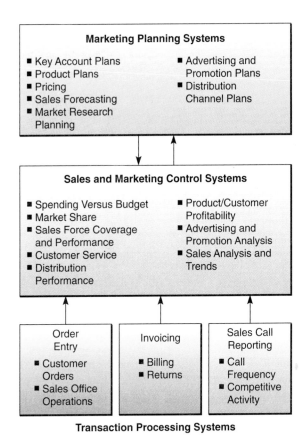

FIGURE 9.2
Marketing information systems provide information for the planning and control of major components of the marketing function.

business function they support to give you an appreciation of the variety of business information systems that both small and large business firms may use. However, as we emphasized in Chapter 2, information systems in the real world, typically, are integrated combinations of functional information systems. There is a strong emphasis in many organizations to develop such *composite* or **cross-functional information systems.** These organizations view cross-functional information systems as a strategic way to share information resources and improve the efficiency and effectiveness of a business, thus helping it attain its strategic objectives.

Marketing Information Systems

The business function of **marketing** is concerned with the planning, promotion, and sale of existing products in existing markets, and the development of new products and new markets to better serve present and potential customers. Thus, marketing performs a vital function in the operation of a business enterprise. Business firms have increasingly turned to computers to help them perform vital marketing functions in the face of the rapid changes of today's environment. Computers have been a catalyst in the development of **marketing information systems,** which integrate the information flows required by many marketing activities.

Figure 9.2 illustrates how marketing information systems provide information for planning, control, and transaction processing in the marketing function. Strategic, tactical, and operational information systems assist marketing managers in product planning, pricing decisions, advertising and sales promotion strategies and expenditures, forecasting market potential for new and present products, and deter-

FIGURE 9.3
Examples of important computer-based information systems
in marketing.

- **Sales Management**
  Plan, monitor, and support the performance of salespeople and sales of products and services.
- **Sales Force Automation**
  Automate the recording and reporting of sales activity by salespeople and the communications and sales support from sales management.
- **Product Management**
  Plan, monitor, and support the performance of products, product lines, and brands.
- **Advertising and Promotion**
  Help select media and promotional methods and control and evaluate advertising and promotion results.
- **Sales Forecasting**
  Produce short- and long-range sales forecasts.
- **Market Research**
  Collect and analyze internal and external data on market variables, developments, and trends.
- **Marketing Management**
  Develop marketing strategies and plans based on corporate goals and market research and sales activity data, and monitor and support marketing activities.

mining channels of distribution. Control reporting systems support the efforts of marketing managers to control the efficiency and effectiveness of the selling and distribution of products and services. Analytical reports provide information on a firm's actual performance versus planned marketing objectives. Figure 9.3 summarizes several important ways that computer-based information systems could be used to support the marketing function.

Sales Management

Sales managers must plan, monitor, and support the performance of the salespeople in their organizations. So in most firms, computer-based systems produce sales analysis reports (such as that shown in Figure 9.4), which analyze sales by product, product line, customer, type of customer, salesperson, and sales territory. Such reports help marketing managers monitor the sales performance of products and salespeople and help them develop sales support programs to improve sales results.

Sales Force Automation

However, sales analysis is only one aspect of the use of computers for sales management and support. Increasingly, computer-based information systems are providing the basis for **sales force automation.** In many companies, the sales force is being outfitted with laptop computers, handheld PCs, or even pen-based tablet computers. This not only increases the personal productivity of salespeople, but dramatically speeds up the capture and analysis of sales data from the field to marketing managers at company headquarters. In return, it allows marketing and sales management to improve the support they provide to their salespeople. Therefore, many companies are viewing sales force automation as a way to gain a strategic advantage in sales productivity and marketing responsiveness.

For example, salespeople use their PCs to record sales data as they make their calls on customers and prospects during the day. Then each night sales reps in the field can connect their computers by modem and telephone links to the mainframe computer at company headquarters and upload information on sales orders, sales calls, and other sales statistics, as well as send electronic mail messages and other

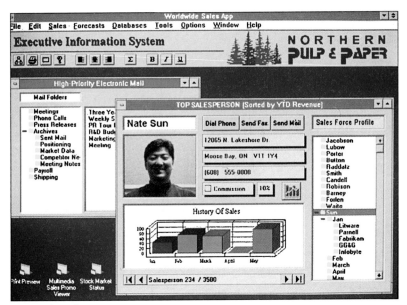

FIGURE 9.4
An example of a sales analysis display produced by an executive information system.

Courtesy of Comshare, Inc.

queries. In return, the host computer may download product availability data, *prospect lists* of information on good sales prospects, E-mail messages, and other sales support information.

Advertising and Promotion

Marketing managers need information to help them achieve sales objectives at the lowest possible costs for advertising and promotion. Computers use market research information and promotion models to help (1) select media and promotional methods, (2) allocate financial resources, and (3) control and evaluate results of various advertising and promotion campaigns. For example, Figure 9.5 illustrates the INFOSCAN system of Information Resources Incorporated (IRI). It tracks the sales of over 800,000 products by their universal product code (UPC) to over 70,000 U.S. households at over 2,400 retail stores. INFOSCAN measures the effect of promotional tactics such as price discounts, coupon offers, and point-of-purchase (POP) promotions. Then INFOSCAN's computer-based marketing models produce forecasts and other analyses of marketing strategy [11].

Product Management

Product managers need information to plan and control the performances of specific products, product lines, and brands. Computers can help provide price, revenue, cost, and growth information for existing products and new product development. Information and analysis for pricing decisions is a major function of this system. Information is also needed on the manufacturing and distribution resources proposed products will require. Computer-based models may be used to evaluate the performances of current products and the prospects for success of proposed products.

Sales Forecasting

The basic functions of sales forecasting can be grouped into the two categories of short-range forecasting and long-range forecasting. Short-range forecasting deals with forecasts of sales for periods up to one year, whereas long-range forecasting is

FIGURE 9.5
INFOSCAN analyzes the
effect of promotional devices
on the sales of over 800,000
products.

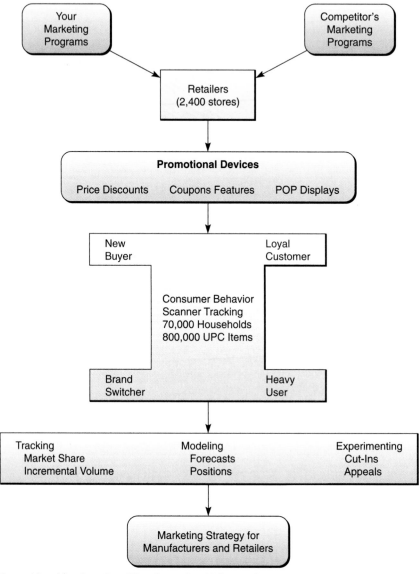

FIGURE 9.5
INFOSCAN analyzes the
effect of promotional devices
on the sales of over 800,000
products.

Source: Adapted from James Jiang, "Using Scanner Data," *Information Systems Management,* Winter 1995, p. 62.

concerned with sales forecasts for a year or more into the future. Marketing managers use systems like INFOSCAN (Figure 9.5) to capture market research data, historical sales data, and promotion plans, and to manipulate statistical forecasting models to generate short-range and long-range sales forecasts.

Market Research

The market research information system provides marketing intelligence to help managers make more effective marketing decisions. It also provides marketing managers with information to help them plan and control the market research projects of the firm. As the INFOSCAN system in Figure 9.5 illustrates, computers help the market research activity collect, analyze, and maintain an enormous amount of information on a wide variety of market variables that are subject to continual change. This includes information on customers, prospects, consumers, and competitors. Market, economic, and demographic trends are also analyzed. Data can be purchased in computer-readable form from external sources, or computers can help gather data through telemarketing and computer-aided telephone interviewing techniques. Finally, statistical analysis software packages help managers analyze market research data and spot important marketing trends.

Marketing managers use computer-based information systems to develop short-and long-range plans outlining product sales, profit, and growth objectives. They also provide feedback and analysis concerning performance-versus-plan for each area of marketing. Computer-based marketing models in decision support systems and expert systems are also being used to investigate the effects of alternative marketing plans. In addition, the fast capture of sales and marketing data by sales force automation systems helps marketing management respond faster to market shifts and sales performance trends and develop more timely marketing strategies.

Marketing Management

Manufacturing information systems support the **production/operations** function, which includes all activities concerned with the planning and control of the processes that produce goods or services. Thus, the production/operations function is concerned with the management of the *operational systems* of all business firms. Planning and control information systems are used for operations management and transaction processing, and are needed by *all* firms that must plan, monitor, and control inventories, purchases, and the flow of goods and services. Therefore, firms such as transportation companies, wholesalers, retailers, financial institutions, and service companies must use production/operations information systems to plan and control their operations. In this section, we will concentrate on computer-based manufacturing applications to illustrate information systems that support the production/operations function. See Figure 9.6.

Manufacturing Information Systems

Computer-based manufacturing information systems use several major techniques to support **computer-integrated manufacturing** (CIM). CIM is an overall concept that stresses that the goals of computer use in factory automation must be to:

Computer-Integrated Manufacturing

- **Simplify** (reengineer) production processes, product designs, and factory organization as a vital foundation to automation and integration.
- **Automate** production processes and the business functions that support them with computers and robots.
- **Integrate** all production and support processes using computers and telecommunications networks [2].

Thus, computers are simplifying, automating, and integrating many of the activities needed to produce products of all kinds. For example, computers are used to help engineers design better products using both *computer-aided engineering* (CAE) and *computer-aided design* (CAD), and better production processes with *computer-aiding processing planning* (CAPP). They are also used to help plan the types of material needed in the production process, which is called *material requirements planning* (MRP), and to integrate MRP with production scheduling and shop floor control, which is known as *manufacturing resource planning* (MRPII). *Computer-aided manufacturing* (CAM) may be used to help manufacture products. This could be

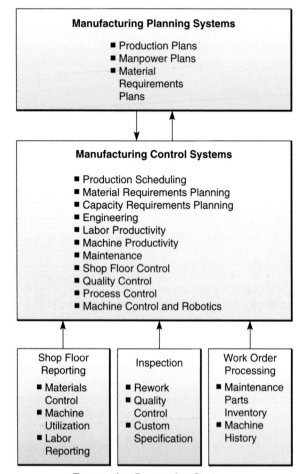

accomplished by monitoring and controlling the production process in a factory (*shop floor control*) or by directly controlling a physical process (*process control*), a machine tool (*machine control*), or a machine with some humanlike capabilities (robots). See Figures 9.7 and 9.8.

Some of the benefits of computer integrated manufacturing systems are:

- Increased efficiency through work simplification and automation, better production schedule planning, and better balancing of production workload to production capacity.

- Improved utilization of production facilities, higher productivity, and better quality control resulting from continuous monitoring, feedback, and control of factory operations, equipment, and robots.

- Reduced investment in production inventories and facilities through work simplification, just-in-time inventory policies, and better planning and control of production and finished goods requirements.

- Improved customer service by drastically reducing out-of-stock situations and producing high-quality products that better meet customer requirements.

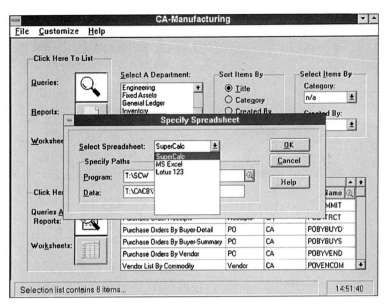

Courtesy of Computer Associates, Inc.

FIGURE 9.7
A display of a manufacturing resource planning package.

- **Computer-Aided Design**
  Create, simulate, and evaluate models of products and manufacturing processes.

- **Computer-Aided Manufacturing**
  Use computers and robots to fabricate, assemble, and package products.

- **Factory Management**
  Plan and control production runs, coordinate incoming orders and raw material requests, oversee cost, and quality assurance programs.

- **Quality Management**
  Evaluate product and process specifications, test incoming materials and outgoing products, test production processes in progress, and design quality assurance programs.

- **Logistics**
  Purchase and receive materials, control and distribute materials, and control inventory and shipping of products.

- **Maintenance**
  Monitor and adjust machinery and processes, perform diagnostics, and do corrective and preventive maintenance.

FIGURE 9.8
Examples of computer-based systems in manufacturing.

Process control is the use of computers to control an ongoing physical process. Process control computers are used to control physical processes in petroleum refineries, cement plants, steel mills, chemical plants, food product manufacturing plants, pulp and paper mills, electric power plants, and so on. Many process control computers are special-purpose minicomputer systems. A process control computer system requires the use of special sensing devices that measure physical phenomena such as temperature or pressure changes. These continuous physical measurements

Process Control

Michael Rosenfeld/Tony Stone Images.

are converted to digital form by analog-to-digital converters and relayed to computers for processing.

Process control software uses mathematical models to analyze the data generated by the ongoing process and compare them to standards or forecasts of required results. Then the computer directs the control of the process by adjusting control devices such as thermostats, valves, switches, and so on. The process control systems also provides messages and displays about the status of the process. So a human operator can take appropriate measures to control the process. In addition, periodic and on-demand reports analyzing the performance of the production process can be produced. Personal computers have become a popular method of analyzing and reporting process control data. See Figure 9.9.

Machine Control

Machine control is the use of a computer to control the actions of a machine. This is also popularly called *numerical control.* The control of machine tools in factories is a typical numerical control application, though it also refers to the control of typesetting machines, weaving machines, and other industrial machinery.

Numerical control computer programs for machine tools convert geometric data from engineering drawings and machining instructions from process planning into a numerical code of commands that control the actions of a machine tool. Machine control may involve the use of special-purpose microcomputers called programmable logic controllers (PLCs). These devices operate one or more machines according to the directions of a numerical control program. Specially equipped personal computers that can withstand a factory environment are being used to develop and install numerical control programs in PLCs. They are also used to analyze production data furnished by the PLCs. This analysis helps engineers fine-tune machine tool performance.

Robotics

An important development in machine control and computer-aided manufacturing is the creation of smart machines and robots. These devices directly control their own activities with the aid of microcomputers. **Robotics** is the technology of building and using machines (robots) with computer intelligence and computer-controlled humanlike physical capabilities (dexterity, movement, vision, etc.). Robotics has also become a major thrust of research and development efforts in the field of artificial intelligence.

Robots are used as "steel-collar" workers to increase productivity and cut costs. For example, one robot regularly assembles compressor valves with 12 parts at the

Tony Stone Images.

FIGURE 9.10
This robot consists of a computer-controlled robotic arm assembly, which prints electronic circuits on computer circuit boards.

rate of 320 units per hour, which is 10 times the rate of human workers. Robots are also particularly valuable for hazardous areas or work activities. Robots follow programs loaded into separate or on-board special-purpose microcomputers. Input is received from visual and/or tactile sensors, processed by the microcomputer, and translated into movements of the robot. Typically, this involves moving its "arms" and "hands" to pick up and load items or perform some other work assignment such as painting, drilling, or welding. Robotics developments are expected to make robots more intelligent, flexible, and mobile by improving their computing, visual, tactile, and navigational capabilities [16]. See Figure 9.10.

Manufacturing engineers use **computer-aided engineering** to simulate, analyze, and evaluate the models of product designs they have developed using **computer-aided design** methods. Powerful *engineering workstations* with enhanced graphics and computational capabilities are used to analyze and design products and manufacturing facilities. Products are designed according to product specifications determined in cooperation with the product design efforts of marketing research and product development specialists. One of the final outputs of this design process is the *bill of materials* (specification of all required materials) used by the MRP application. The engineering subsystem is frequently responsible for determining standards for product quality (i.e., *quality assurance*). It also is responsible for the design of the

Computer-Aided Engineering

Mathew Borkoski/Folio.

production processes needed to manufacture the products it designs. This function depends heavily on the use of computers to perform the necessary analysis and design, and it is known as *computer-aided process planning*.

Computer-aided design packages and engineering workstations are the software and hardware resources that make computer-aided engineering possible. Engineers use these high-powered computing and advanced graphics workstations for the design and testing of products, facilities, and processes. Input is by light pen, joystick, or keyboard, with the CAD package refining an engineer's initial drawings. Output is in two- or three-dimensional **computer graphics** that can be rotated to display all sides of the object being designed. The engineer can zoom in for close-up views of a specific part and even make parts of the product appear to move as they would in normal operation. The design can then be converted into a finished mathematical model of the product. This is used as the basis for production specifications and machine tool programs. See Figure 9.11.

Human Resource Information Systems

The **human resource management** (or personnel) function involves the recruitment, placement, evaluation, compensation, and development of the employees of an organization. Originally, businesses used computer-based information systems to (1) produce paychecks and payroll reports, (2) maintain personnel records, and (3) analyze the use of personnel in business operations. Many firms have gone beyond these traditional functions and have developed **human resource information systems** (HRIS), which also support (1) recruitment, selection, and hiring, (2) job placement, (3) performance appraisals, (4) employee benefits analysis, (5) training and development, and (6) health, safety, and security. See Figure 9.12.

Human resource information systems support the concept of *human resource management*. This business function emphasizes (1) *planning* to meet the personnel needs of the business, (2) *development* of employees to their full potential, and (3)

FIGURE 9.12

Human resource information systems support the strategic, tactical, and operational use of the human resources of an organization.

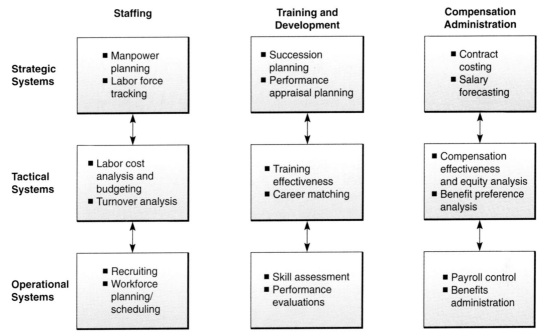

control of all personnel policies and programs. The goal of human resource management is the effective and efficient use of the human resources of a company. The major applications and objectives of information systems in human resource management are summarized in Figure 9.13.

Staffing

These information systems record and track human resources within a company to maximize their use. For example, a *personnel record-keeping* system keeps track of additions, deletions, and other changes to the records in a personnel database. Changes in job assignments and compensation, or hirings and terminations, are examples of information that would be used to update the personnel database. Another example is an *employee skills inventory* system, which uses the employee skills data from a personnel database to locate employees within a company who have the skills required for specific assignments and projects.

A final example is doing *personnel requirements forecasting* to assure a business of an adequate supply of high-quality human resources. This application provides information required for forecasts of personnel requirements in each major employment category for various company departments or for new projects and other ventures being planned by management. Such long-range planning may use a computer-based simulation model to evaluate alternative plans for recruitment, reassignment, or retraining programs.

Training and Development

Information systems help human resource managers plan and monitor employee recruitment, training, and development programs by analyzing the success history of present programs. They also analyze the career development status of each

FIGURE 9.13
Examples of the objectives of
human resource information
systems.

- **Flexible Compensation Administration**
  Contain benefits costs, while offering benefits program choices
- **Benefits Administration**
  Cost-effective plan administration
- **Compensation Management**
  Salary planning and budget impact analysis
- **Payroll Administration**
  Accurate, timely payroll with controls
- **Personnel Management.**
  Instant access to employee information
- **Defined Contributions**
  Provide pre-tax benefits to employees and employer
- **Position Control**
  Manage the mix of job positions in your organization
- **Historical Record-Keeping**
  Perform point-in-time and trend analysis to assist in legislative compliance and
  compensation planning
- **Recruiting and Applicant Tracking**
  Identify and attract qualified candidates
- **Career Development**
  Match employee skills to employer needs, to provide organizational flexibility
- **Pension Administration**
  Reduce administration costs for retirement planning

employee to determine whether development methods such as training programs
and periodic performance appraisals should be recommended. Computer-based
training programs and appraisals of employee job performance are available to help
support this area of human resource management. See Figure 9.14.

*Compensation
Analysis*

Information systems can help analyze the range and distribution of employee compensation (wages, salaries, incentive payments, and fringe benefits) within a company and make comparisons with compensation paid by similar firms or with
various economic indicators. This information is useful for planning changes in
compensation, especially if negotiations with labor unions are involved. It helps
keep the compensation of a company competitive and equitable, while controlling
compensation costs.

*Governmental
Reporting*

Nowadays, reporting to government agencies is a major responsibility of human
resource management. So organizations use computer-based information systems to
keep track of the statistics and produce reports required by a variety of government
laws and regulations. For example, in the United States, statistics on employee
recruitment and hiring must be collected for possible use in Equal Employment
Opportunity Commission (EEOC) hearings; statistics for employee health, workplace hazards, accidents, and safety procedures must be reported to the
Occupational Safety Health Administration (OSHA); and statistics on the use of hazardous materials must be reported to the Environmental Protection Agency (EPA).

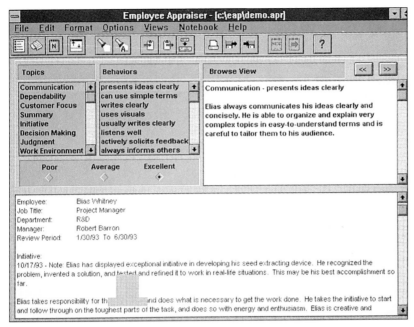

© Sarah Evertson.

FIGURE 9.14
An example of a performance evaluation display. Note how this employee's behavior on the job is being evaluated.

Software packages to collect and report such statistics are available from a variety of software vendors.

Accounting Information Systems

Accounting information systems are the oldest and most widely used information systems in business. They record and report business transactions and other economic events. Accounting information systems are based on the double-entry bookkeeping concept, which is hundreds of years old, and other, more recent accounting concepts such as responsibility accounting and profitability accounting. Computer-based accounting systems record and report the flow of funds through an organization on a historical basis and produce important financial statements such as balance sheets and income statements. Such systems also produce forecasts of future conditions such as projected financial statements and financial budgets. A firm's financial performance is measured against such forecasts by other analytical accounting reports.

Operational accounting systems emphasize legal and historical record-keeping and the production of accurate financial statements. Typically, these systems include transaction processing systems such as order processing, inventory control, accounts receivable, accounts payable, payroll, and general ledger systems. *Management accounting systems* focus on the planning and control of business operations. They emphasize cost accounting reports, the development of financial budgets and projected financial statements, and analytical reports comparing actual to forecasted performance.

Figure 9.15 illustrates the interrelationships of several important accounting information systems commonly computerized by both large and small businesses. Many accounting software packages are available for these applications. Let's briefly

FIGURE 9.15

Important accounting information systems for transaction processing and financial reporting. Note how they are related to each other in terms of input and output flows.

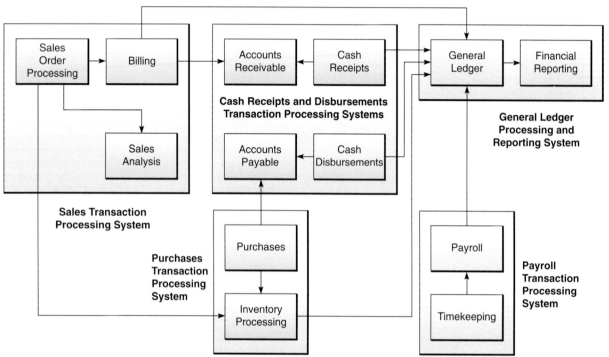

Source: Adapted from Joseph J. Wilkinson, *Accounting Information Systems: Essential Concepts and Applications.* Copyright © 1989 by John Wiley & Sons, Inc. Reprinted by permission of John Wiley & Sons, Inc.

review how several of these systems support the operations and management of a business firm. Figure 9.16 summarizes the purpose of six common, but important, accounting information systems.

Order Processing

Order processing, or *sales order processing,* is an important transaction processing system which captures and processes customer orders and produces invoices for customers and data needed for sales analysis and inventory control. In many firms, it also keeps track of the status of customer orders until goods are delivered. Computer-based sales order processing systems provide a fast, accurate, and efficient method of recording and screening customer orders and sales transactions. They also provide inventory control systems with information on accepted orders so they can be filled as quickly as possible. Figure 9.17 is an example of an invoicing display of an integrated accounting package.

Inventory Control

Inventory control systems process data reflecting changes to items in inventory. Once data about customer orders is received from an order processing system, a computer-based inventory control system records changes to inventory levels and prepares appropriate shipping documents. Then it may notify managers about items that need reordering and provide them with a variety of inventory status reports. Computer-based inventory control systems thus help a business provide high-quality service to customers while minimizing investment in inventory and inventory carrying costs.

- **Order Processing**
  Captures and processes customer orders and produces customer invoices.

- **Inventory Control**
  Processes data reflecting changes in inventory and provides shipping and reorder information.

- **Accounts Receivable**
  Records amounts owed by customers and produces monthly customer statements and credit management reports.

- **Accounts Payable**
  Records purchases from, amounts owed to, and payments to suppliers, and produces cash management reports.

- **Payroll**
  Records employee work and compensation data and produces paychecks and other payroll documents and reports.

- **General Ledger**
  Consolidates data from other accounting systems and produces the periodic financial statements and reports of the business.

FIGURE 9.16
A summary of six widely used accounting information systems.

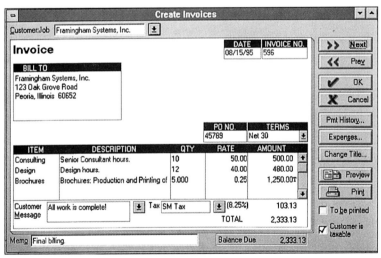

Courtesy of Intuit, Inc.

FIGURE 9.17
An example of an invoice display of a popular accounting software package, Quickbooks, by Intuit.

Accounts Receivable

Accounts receivable systems keep records of amounts owed by customers from data generated by customer purchases and payments. They produce monthly customer statements and credit management reports, as illustrated in Figure 9.15. Computer-based accounts receivable systems stimulate prompt customer payments by preparing accurate and timely invoices and monthly statements to credit customers. They provide managers with reports to help them control the amount of credit extended and the collection of money owed. This activity helps to maximize profitable credit sales while minimizing losses from bad debts.

Accounts Payable

Accounts payable systems keep track of data concerning purchases from and payments to suppliers. They prepare checks in payment of outstanding invoices and produce cash management reports. Computer-based accounts payable systems help ensure prompt and accurate payment of suppliers to maintain good relationships, ensure a good credit standing, and secure any discounts offered for prompt payment. They provide tight financial control over all cash disbursements of the business. They also provide management with information needed for the analysis of payments, expenses, purchases, employee expense accounts, and cash requirements.

Payroll

Payroll systems receive and maintain data from employee time cards and other work records. They produce paychecks and other documents such as earning statements, payroll reports, and labor analysis reports. Other reports are also prepared for management and government agencies. Computer-based payroll systems help businesses make prompt and accurate payments to their employees, as well as reports to management, employees, and government agencies concerning earnings, taxes, and other deductions. They may also provide management with reports analyzing labor costs and productivity.

General Ledger

General ledger systems consolidate data received from accounts receivable, accounts payable, payroll, and other accounting information systems. At the end of each accounting period, they "close the books" of a business and produce the general ledger trial balance, the income statement and balance sheet of the firm, and various income and expense reports for management. Computer-based general ledger systems help businesses accomplish these accounting tasks in an accurate and timely manner. They, typically, provide better financial controls and management reports and involve fewer personnel and lower costs than manual accounting methods.

Financial Information Systems

Computer-based **financial information systems** support financial managers in decisions concerning (1) the financing of a business and (2) the allocation and control of financial resources within a business. Major financial information system categories include cash and securities management, capital budgeting, financial forecasting, and financial planning. Accounting information systems are frequently included as a vital category of financial information systems. Figure 9.18 illustrates that the financial manager of a business may rely on a variety of financial planning, reporting, and transaction processing information systems to make financing, investment, and accounting decisions. Let's take a brief look at the functions of these computer-based financial systems. Figure 9.19 summarizes examples of important financial information systems.

Cash and Securities Management

Information systems collect information on all cash receipts and disbursements within a company on a realtime or periodic basis. Such information allows businesses to deposit or invest excess funds more quickly, and thus increase the income generated by deposited or invested funds. These systems also produce daily, weekly, or monthly forecasts of cash receipts or disbursements (cash flow forecasts), which are used to spot future cash deficits or surpluses. Mathematical models are frequently used to determine optimal cash collection programs and to determine alternative financing or investment strategies for dealing with forecasted cash deficits or surpluses.

Many businesses invest their excess cash in short-term marketable securities (such as U.S. Treasury bills, commercial paper, or certificates of deposit) so that investment income may be earned until the funds are required. The portfolio of such

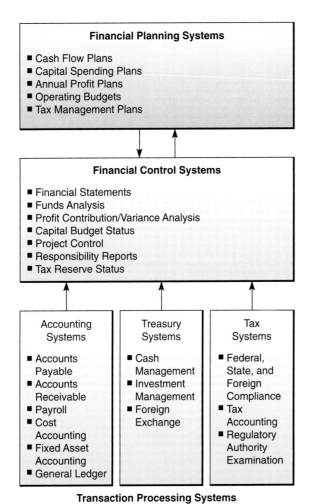

Financial Planning Systems

- Cash Flow Plans
- Capital Spending Plans
- Annual Profit Plans
- Operating Budgets
- Tax Management Plans

Financial Control Systems

- Financial Statements
- Funds Analysis
- Profit Contribution/Variance Analysis
- Capital Budget Status
- Project Control
- Responsibility Reports
- Tax Reserve Status

Accounting Systems

- Accounts Payable
- Accounts Receivable
- Payroll
- Cost Accounting
- Fixed Asset Accounting
- General Ledger

Treasury Systems

- Cash Management
- Investment Management
- Foreign Exchange

Tax Systems

- Federal, State, and Foreign Compliance
- Tax Accounting
- Regulatory Authority Examination

Transaction Processing Systems

FIGURE 9.18
Financial planning, reporting, and transaction processing information systems support decisions concerning the financing and the allocation and control of funds within a business.

- **Cash and Securities Management**
  Record data and produce forecasts of cash receipts and disbursements and manage investment in short-term securities.

- **Capital Budgeting**
  Evaluate the profitability and financial impact of proposed capital expenditures.

- **Financial Forecasting**
  Forecast business and economic trends and financial developments.

- **Financial Planning**
  Evaluate the present and projected financial performance and financing needs of the business.

FIGURE 9.19
Examples of important financial information systems.

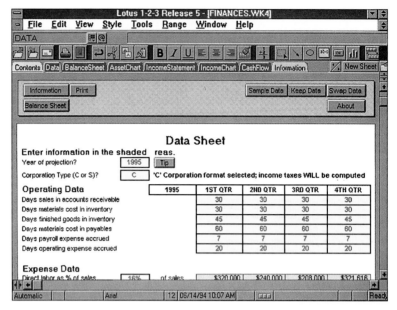

Courtesy of Lotus Development Corporation.

securities can be managed by portfolio management software. It helps a financial manager make buying, selling, or holding decisions for each type of security so that the optimum mix of securities is developed that minimizes risk and maximizes investment income.

Capital Budgeting

The capital budgeting process involves evaluating the profitability and financial impact of proposed capital expenditures. Long-term expenditure proposals for plants and equipment can be analyzed using a variety of techniques incorporating present value analysis of expected cash flows and probability analysis of risk. This application makes heavy use of spreadsheet models that are designed for corporate financial planning.

Financial Forecasting

A business must make financial and other forecasts of economic trends. A variety of statistical forecasting packages provide analytical techniques that result in economic or financial forecasts of national and local economic conditions, wage levels, price levels, and interest rates. This forecasting may involve the use of data about the external business environment obtained from proprietary financial and demographic data banks provided by the information services described in Chapter 8.

Financial Planning

Financial planning systems use **financial planning models** to evaluate the present and projected financial performance of a business or of one of its divisions or subsidiaries. They also help determine the financing needs of a business and analyze alternative methods of financing the business. Information concerning the economic situation, business operations, types of financing available, interest rates, and stock and bond prices are used to develop an optimal financing plan for the business. Electronic spreadsheet packages and DSS generators are frequently used to build and manipulate these models. Answers to what-if and goal-seeking questions can be explored as financial analysts and managers evaluate their financing and investment alternatives. Figure 9.20 displays an example of projected operating data generated by an electronic spreadsheet as part of a financial planning process.

R E A L   W O R L D   C A S E

Continental Insurance and Northrup Grumman: Skills Asset Management

Just as many large companies have lost track of how many and what kind of PCs they own, they are also in the dark about who knows what in their organizations. As a result, managers say, companies are hiring employees with skills that are redundant with those of existing staffers.

The lack of necessary information has also made assembling project teams costly and time-consuming. Moreover, employees are often being trained with little regard for how their new skills will be put to use in their companies.

Take Continental Insurance Corp. in Neptune, New Jersey. Until about 18 months ago, the company required all 1,700 of its IS staffers to take 10 days of training annually. "But we were filling the requirements without knowing if the training was actually being used on the job," said Barbara Strugala, assistant vice president of information technology.

Today, by contrast, Continental Insurance provides just-in-time training as projects come up. The company also now has concrete information on which skills it will require a year from now and what kind of training it needs to provide to bring employees up to speed on those skills.

What has made the difference is automated skills asset management systems, which more and more large companies are implementing to cut costs and keep closer tabs on evershifting skills requirements and resources.

In addition to SkillView Technologies, Inc., Hampstead, New Hampshire, companies with systems on the market include Bensu, Inc., in San Francisco, and People Sciences, Inc., in Maplewood, New Jersey. All three companies offer stand-alone PC-based software as well as client/server–based versions.

Northrup Grumman's Data Systems and Services Division uses Bensu's system to track not only what skills its staffers have but which ones the company needs as it steadily moves forward with distributed technologies. All that information is entered into an Oracle skills inventory database, which the Bensu system analyzes to identify gaps.

Using the system, managers can quickly locate people with the skills they require as well as develop the right training programs.

"As we flatten the organization, we have managers responsible for between 25 and 30 people, all of whom are geographically dispersed. This works as an online management tool to quickly find the people with the right skills," said Howard Cook, manager of skills and training.

In addition to defining skills needed for individual positions, skills inventory systems also function as performance assessment and career development tools for individual IS staffers. The People Sciences system, for instance, gives staffers online access to managers' assessments of their skills, plus a list of which of the 150 core competencies are necessary to move into other jobs. The system also provides training information, including online course registration and a summary of job postings and descriptions.

One point on which experts disagree is where IS skills management systems should fit within the company. Howard Cook is emphatic that IS groups should maintain their own skills management systems. "The reason is because human resource organizations typically don't understand technical skill requirements," he said. "They think bridges and routers are something you drive over, that C++ is something teachers give out, and that Unix are employees of a harem."

CASE STUDY QUESTIONS

1. What are the business benefits of skills asset management systems to Continental Insurance?

2. How do such systems help Northrup Grumman improve human resource management?

3. Do you agree with Howard Cook that IS groups should maintain their own skills management systems? Why or why not?

Source: Adapted from Julia King, "Packages Help Managers Figure Out Who Does What," *Computerworld*, April 24, 1995, pp. 91, 98. Copyright 1995 by Computerworld, Inc., Framingham, MA 017101—Reprinted from Computerworld.

Transaction Processing

Transaction processing systems (TPS) are information systems that process data resulting from the occurrence of business transactions. Figure 9.21 illustrates this concept. **Transactions** are events that occur as part of doing business, such as sales, purchases, deposits, withdrawals, refunds, and payments. Think, for example, of the data generated whenever a business sells something to a customer on credit. Data about the customer, product, salesperson, store, and so on, must be captured and processed. This in turn causes additional transactions, such as credit checks, customer billing, inventory changes, and increases in accounts receivable balances, which generate even more data. Thus, transaction processing activities are needed to capture and process such data, or the operations of a business would grind to a halt. Therefore, transaction processing systems play a vital role in supporting the operations of an organization.

Strategic TPS

However, remember that transaction processing systems can play strategic roles in gaining competitive advantages for a business. For example, many firms have developed *interorganizational* transaction processing systems that tie them electronically to their customers or suppliers with telecommunications network links. *Electronic data interchange* (EDI) systems (which exchange electronic copies of transaction documents) are an important example that we will discuss in this chapter. Many companies have also found that *realtime* or *online* transaction processing (OLTP) systems, which capture and process transactions immediately, can help them provide superior service to customers. This capability *adds value* to their products and services, and thus gives them an important way to differentiate themselves from their competitors [7, 9].

The Transaction Processing Cycle

Transaction processing systems capture and process data describing business transactions. Then they update organizational files and databases, and produce a variety of information products for internal and external use. You should think of these activities as a cycle of basic transaction processing activities. As Figure 9.22 illustrates, in the **transaction processing cycle,** systems go through a five-stage cycle of (1) data entry activities, (2) transaction processing activities, (3) file and database processing activities, (4) document and report generation, and (5) inquiry processing activities.

The Data Entry Process

The input activity in transaction processing systems involves a **data entry** process. In this process, data is captured or collected by recording, coding, and editing activities. Data may then be converted to a form that can be entered into a computer system. Data entry activities have always been a bottleneck in the use of computers for transaction processing. It has always been a problem getting data into computers accurately and quickly enough to match their awesome processing speeds. Thus, traditional *manual* methods of data entry that make heavy use of *data media* are being replaced by *direct automated* methods. These methods are more efficient and reliable and are known as *source data automation*. Let's take a look at both types of data entry. See Figure 9.23.

FIGURE 9.21
The role of transaction processing systems in a business. Note how business transactions such as sales to customers and purchases from suppliers are generated by the physical operations systems of this manufacturing firm. Documents describing such transactions are subsequently processed by the firm's transaction processing systems, resulting in updated databases and a variety of information products.

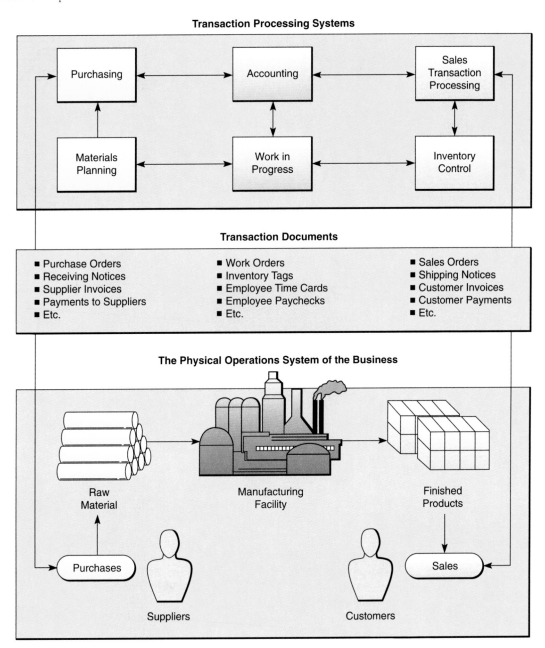

FIGURE 9.22
The transaction processing cycle. Note that transaction processing systems use a five-stage cycle of data entry, transaction processing, database maintenance, document and report generation, and inquiry processing activities.

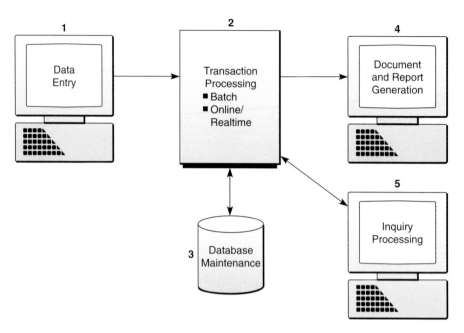

FIGURE 9.23
Traditional computer-based data entry involves keying data from source documents into a computer system.

Richard Pasley.

Traditional Data Entry

Traditional data entry methods, typically, rely on the end users of an information system to capture data on **source documents** such as purchase orders, payroll time sheets, and sales order forms. These source documents are then usually accumulated into batches and transferred to data processing professionals specializing in data entry. Periodically, the source documents are entered into a computer system. This is accomplished, typically, by employees or data entry specialists who must enter the data using the keyboards of data entry terminals or PCs.

It should not be surprising to discover that there has been a major shift away from traditional data entry. First, it requires too many activities, people, and data media. Second, it results in high costs and increases the potential for errors.

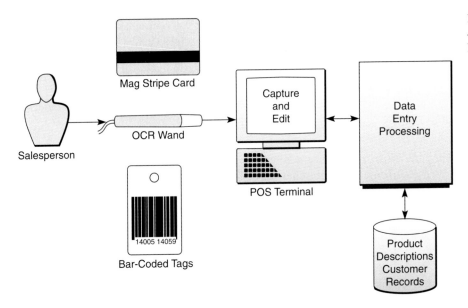

FIGURE 9.24
An automated data entry example: Sales transaction processing.

Therefore, the response of both users and the computer industry has been to move toward *source data automation.*

The use of automated methods of data entry is known as **source data automation.** Several methods have been developed to accomplish this automation, though very few completely automate the data entry process. They are all based on trying to reduce or eliminate many of the activities, people, and data media required by traditional data entry methods. Figure 9.24 is an example of source data automation. Notice that this sales transaction processing system:

*Source Data
Automation*

- Captures data *as early as possible* after a transaction or other event occurs by using POS terminals.
- Captures transaction data *as close as possible* to the source that generates the data. Salespersons at POS terminals capture and edit data right on the sales floor.
- Captures data by using *machine-readable media* initially (bar-coded tags and magnetic (mag) stripe credit cards), instead of preparing written source documents.
- Captures data that rarely changes by *prerecording* it on machine-readable media, or by storing it in the computer system.
- Captures data directly *without the use of data media* by optical scanning of bar code packaging.

The example in Figure 9.24 reveals some of the many types of devices used in source data automation. These include *transaction terminals,* such as POS terminals and automated teller machines (ATMs), and *optical character recognition* (OCR) devices, such as optical scanning wands and grocery checkout scanners. Many other input/output devices and telecommunications technologies discussed in Chapters 4 and 6 also play a role in source data automation. These include the use of PCs with cash drawers as intelligent POS terminals, portable digital radio terminals and pen-based tablet PCs for remote data entry, or touch screens and voice recognition systems for data entry. Organizations may also use local area networks of microcomputer workstations to accomplish data entry activities at regional centers, and then upload the data to corporate mainframes for further processing. Other organizations depend on LANs of networked PCs to accomplish their transaction processing activities [9].

Electronic Data Interchange

The ultimate in source data automation in many transaction processing systems is called **electronic data interchange,** or EDI. This involves the electronic transmission of business transaction data over telecommunications links between the computers of *trading partners* (organizations and their customers and suppliers). Data representing a variety of business *transaction documents* (such as purchase orders, invoices, requests for quotations, and shipping notices) are electronically transmitted using standard document message formats. Thus, EDI is an example of the almost complete automation of the data entry process.

Formatted transaction data is transmitted over telecommunications links directly between computers, without paper documents or human intervention. Besides direct network links between the computers of trading partners, third-party services are widely used. Value-added telecommunications carriers like GE Information Services, IBM, Control Data, and McDonnell Douglas offer EDI services, including an *electronic mailbox* for EDI documents [3, 16]. If necessary, EDI software is used to convert a company's own document formats into standardized EDI formats as specified by various industry and international protocols.

Figure 9.25 is an example of EDI in action. In this example, Motorola Codex has EDI links with its supplier, Texas Instruments, for the exchange of a variety of electronic transaction documents. In addition, it "closes the loop" by using *electronic funds transfer* (EFT) links to its banks so it can make electronic payments to its supplier [18].

Benefits of EDI

EDI eliminates the printing, mailing, checking, and handling by employees of numerous multiple-copy forms of business documents. Also, since standard document formats are used, the delays caused by mail or telephone communication between businesses to verify what a document means are drastically reduced. Some of the benefits of EDI that result are reductions in paper, postage, and labor costs; faster flow of transactions; reductions in errors; increases in productivity; support of just-in-time (JIT) inventory policies; reductions in inventory levels; and better customer service. For example, decreases of 25 to 50 percent in the total time it takes to receive, process, package, and ship customer orders are reported. Annual savings of $300 million in the grocery industry and $12 billion in the textile industry are expected. RCA expects the cost of processing a purchase order to drop from $50 to $4, and EDI is estimated to save $200 per automobile in the auto industry [16].

However, EDI is more than a way to increase efficiency, cut costs, and provide better service. In many industries, it has become an absolute business requirement. EDI is now a *strategic application* of information systems in many industries, where the message is "link up or lose out." Or, as Edward Lucente, IBM vice president, says: "Doing business without EDI will soon be like trying to do business without a tele-

Electronic Documents

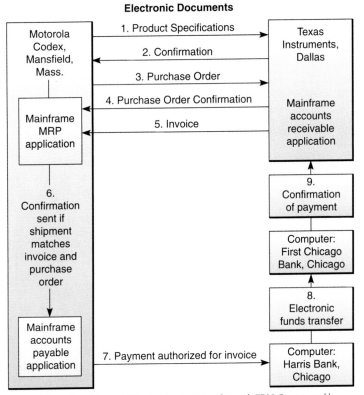

Source: Adapted from Clinton Wilder, "Codex Goes Paperless with EDI," *Computerworld, January 13, 1992, p. 6. Copyright © 1992 by* ComputerWorld, Inc., Framingham, MA 01701. Reprinted with permission of Computerworld.

FIGURE 9.25
An example of EDI. Motorola Codex uses EDI links to its supplier, Texas Instruments, for the exchange of business documents. Codex also makes electronic funds transfers to its banks to pay its suppliers.

phone. No EDI, no business." General Motors proved that point when it made EDI a requirement for thousands of its suppliers, as did the U.S. Department of Defense. Experts predict that, by the end of the decade, over one-third of all business documents will involve EDI. Thus, EDI promises to revolutionize data entry in many transaction processing systems while promoting strategic relationships between industry trading partners [3, 16].

Electronic funds transfer (EFT) systems are a major form of transaction processing systems in banking and retailing industries. EFT systems use source data automation technologies to capture and process money and credit transfers between banks and businesses and their customers. For example, bank telecommunications networks support teller terminals at all branch offices and automated teller machines (ATMs) at locations throughout a city or region. Also supported are pay-by-phone services, which allow bank customers to use their telephones as computer terminals to electronically pay bills. In addition, bank wide area networks may connect POS terminals in retail stores to bank EFT systems. This makes it possible for you to use a credit card or debit card to instantly pay for gas, groceries, or other purchases at participating retail outlets. See Figure 9.26.

Electronic Funds Transfer

FIGURE 9.26
Banks use networks of ATM terminals to provide convenient electronic funds transfer services.

Courtesy of IBM Corporation.

Batch Processing

Transaction processing systems process data in two basic ways: (1) **batch processing**, where transactions data is accumulated over a period of time and processed periodically, and (2) **realtime processing** (also called *online processing*), where data is processed immediately after a transaction occurs. Transaction processing systems still make heavy use of batch processing. However, the use of realtime processing is growing, and it is expected to eventually become the primary form of transaction processing.

Batch Processing Activities

In **batch processing**, transactions data are accumulated over a period of time and processed periodically. Batch processing usually involves:

- Gathering *source documents* originated by business transactions, such as sales orders and invoices, into groups called *batches*.
- Recording transaction data on some type of input medium, such as magnetic disks or magnetic tape.
- Sorting the transactions in a *transaction file* in the same sequence as the records in a sequential *master file*.
- Processing transaction data and creating an updated master file and a variety of *documents* (such as customer invoices and paychecks) and reports.
- Capturing and storing batches of transaction data at remote sites, and then transmitting them periodically to a central computer for processing. This is known as *remote job entry,* or RJE.

In batch processing, not only are the transaction data for a particular application accumulated into batches, but a number of different transaction processing jobs are run (processed) periodically (daily, weekly, monthly). The rationale for batch processing is that the grouping of data and the periodic processing of jobs uses computer system resources more efficiently, compared to allowing data and jobs to be

FIGURE 9.27
A batch processing system example. Batches of deposited checks are accumulated and processed daily in the banking industry.

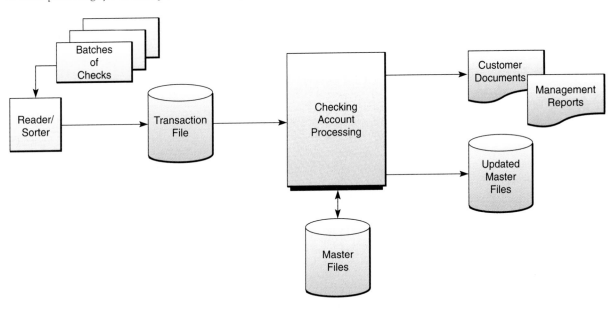

processed in an unorganized, random manner. Of course, this efficiency, economy, and control are accomplished by sacrificing the immediate processing of data for end users.

> **EXAMPLE**
> In a typical example of batch processing, the banking industry usually accumulates all checks deposited during the day into batches for processing each evening. Thus, customer bank balances are updated on a daily basis and many management reports are produced daily. Figure 9.27 illustrates a batch processing system where transaction data in the form of batches of deposited checks are captured each day by MICR reader/sorters, which read the data recorded in magnetic ink on the bottom of each check. This transaction data is then processed to update customer and other databases and produce a variety of customer documents and management reports.

Advantages and Disadvantages

Batch processing is an economical method when large volumes of transactions data must be processed. It is ideally suited for many applications where it is not necessary to update databases as transactions occur, and where documents and reports are required only at scheduled intervals. For example, customer statements may be prepared on a monthly basis, whereas payroll processing might be done on a weekly basis.

However, batch processing has some real disadvantages. Master files are frequently out-of-date between scheduled processing, as are the periodic scheduled reports that are produced. Also, immediate updated responses to inquiries cannot be made. For these reasons, more and more computer applications use realtime

FIGURE 9.28
Batch versus realtime processing. Note the major differences.

Characteristic	Batch Processing	Realtime Processing
Processing of transactions	Transaction data is recorded, accumulated into batches, sorted, and processed periodically	Transaction data is processed as generated
File update	When batch is processed	When transaction is processed
Response time/turnaround time	Several hours or days after batches are submitted for processing	A few seconds after each transaction is captured

processing systems. However, batch processing systems are still widely used, and some of their disadvantages are overcome by using realtime processing for some transaction processing functions, such as data entry or inquiry processing.

Realtime Processing

In transaction processing systems, a **realtime processing** capability allows transaction data to be processed immediately after they are generated and can provide immediate output to end users. Full-fledged realtime systems for transaction processing are popularly called **online transaction processing** (OLTP) systems. Transaction data are processed as soon as they are originated or recorded, without waiting to accumulate batches of data. Data are fed directly into the computer system from online terminals, without being sorted, and they are always stored online in direct access files. Files and databases are always up-to-date since they are updated whenever data are originated, regardless of its frequency. Responses to end users' inquiries are immediate, since information stored on direct access devices can be retrieved almost instantaneously. Realtime processing depends on wide area and local area networks to provide telecommunications links between transaction terminals, workstations, and other computers. A summary of the important capabilities differentiating batch processing and realtime processing is shown in Figure 9.28

> **EXAMPLE**
> An example of a realtime sales transaction processing system is shown in Figure 9.29. Note how POS terminals are connected by telecommunications links to a computer for immediate entry of sales data and control responses (such as customer credit verification). The customer, product, and sales databases are stored on online direct access devices (typically, magnetic disk drives) and can be updated immediately to reflect sales transactions. Finally, an inquiry processing capability and telecommunication links to employee workstations allow them to make inquiries and display responses concerning customers, sales activity, inventory status, and so on.

Fault Tolerant Processing

Many airlines, banks, telephone companies, and other organizations depend on **fault tolerant systems** to protect themselves against failure of their strategic online transaction processing applications. For example, airline reservation systems and bank electronic funds transfer systems use fault tolerant computers that provide a

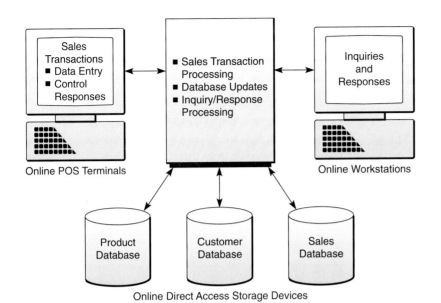

Online POS Terminals

Online Workstations

Online Direct Access Storage Devices

FIGURE 9.29
Example of a realtime sales processing system. Note that sales transaction processing, inquiries and responses, and database updates are accomplished immediately using online devices.

Courtesy of IBM Corporation.

FIGURE 9.30
These securities traders in the Morgan Stanley trading room in Hong Kong depend on fault tolerant transaction processing systems.

nonstop realtime transaction processing capability that allows them to continue operating even if parts of the system fail. As we mentioned in Chapter 4, fault tolerant computers may use a multiprocessor design of several coupled CPUs or a parallel processor design of many networked microprocessors to provide a built-in backup capability in case one or more processors fail. In addition, fault tolerant computers have redundant memory units, disk drives, and other devices, as well as duplicate copies of software, including, in some cases, redundant operating systems [11]. See Figure 9.30.

Advantages and Disadvantages

Realtime processing provides immediate updating of files and immediate responses to user inquiries. Realtime processing is particularly important for applications where a high frequency of changes must be made to a file during a short time to keep it updated. Only the specific records affected by transactions or inquiries need to be processed, and several files can be processed or updated concurrently.

Realtime processing has its disadvantages. Because of the online, direct-access nature of realtime processing, special precautions must be taken to protect the contents of databases. Thus, many realtime systems use magnetic tape files as *control logs* (to record all transactions made) or as *backup files* (by periodically making a magnetic tape copy of a file). Also, more controls have to be built into the software and processing procedures to protect against unauthorized access or the accidental destruction of data. In addition, organizations with critical OLTP applications have to pay a high cost premium for the security of fault tolerant computer systems. Thus, the many advantages of realtime processing must be balanced with the extra costs and security precautions that are necessary. However, many computer-using firms are willing to pay this price for the speed, efficiency, and superior service that realtime processing provides.

Database Maintenance

Database maintenance is a major activity of transaction processing systems. An organization's databases must be maintained by its transaction processing systems so that they are always correct and up to date. Therefore, transaction processing systems update the corporate databases of an organization to reflect changes resulting from day-to-day business transactions. For example, credit sales made to customers will cause customer account balances to be increased and the amount of inventory on hand to be decreased. Database maintenance ensures that these and other changes are reflected in the data records stored in the company's databases.

In addition, transaction processing systems process data resulting from miscellaneous adjustments to the records in a file or database. For example, name and address changes may have to be made to customer records, and tax withholding changes may have to be made to employee payroll records. Thus, one of the major functions of transaction processing systems is to update and make changes to an organization's corporate databases. These databases then provide the data resources that can be processed and used by information reporting systems, decision support systems, and executive information systems.

Document and Report Generation

The final stage in the transaction processing cycle is the generation of information products such as documents and reports. Figure 9.31 illustrates several examples. Documents produced by transaction processing systems are called **transaction documents**.

There are several major types of such documents:

- **Action documents.** These are documents that initiate actions or transactions on the part of their recipient. For example, a purchase order authorizes a purchase from a supplier, and a paycheck authorizes a bank to pay an employee.
- **Information documents.** These documents relate, confirm, or prove to their recipients that transactions have occurred. Examples are sales receipts, sales order confirmations, customer invoices and statements, and credit

FIGURE 9.31

Examples of information products produced by transaction processing systems. Transaction documents such as customer statements must be prepared and mailed to customers on a monthly basis. The cash requirements register is a control listing that lists the checks that must be prepared in payment of amounts owed to vendors.

STATEMENT OF CUSTOMER ACCOUNT

LANG CORPORATION

CUSTOMER NO. 554386

HITTON CORPORATION
138 MARSHALL DR.
PO BOX 851
LONG PORT, CA 94134

DATE 9/30/--

DATE MO	DY	YR	INVOICE NUMBER	REFERENCE NUMBER	DESCRIPTION	AMOUNT
09	08	--	185163		PRIOR BALANCE	$7,565.46
09	10	--	075126		INVOICE	1,685.91
					PAYMENT	1,865.00CR
09	15	--		091531	LC ADJUSTMENT	13.00CR
09	30	--			LATE CHARGES	8.00

CURRENT AMOUNT	30 DAYS	60 DAYS & OVER	BALANCE DUE
$1,693.91	$696.46		$2,390.37

KRAUSZ MANUFACTURING COMPANY
ACCOUNTS PAYABLE

KRAUSZ

CASH REQUIREMENTS REGISTER

DATE APR 12 19

VENDOR	VENDOR NUMBER	DUE DATE	INVOICE AMOUNT	DISCOUNT	CHECK AMOUNT
SOLVAY GEN SUP	1016	4/16	$ 773.30	$ 15.47	$ 757.83
ROCHESTER PR CO	1021	4/16	1,620.18	32.40	1,587.78
CALABRIA CONT	1049	4/16	143.65	2.87	140.78
ONONDAGA STL CO	1077	4/16	5,982.82	119.66	5,863.16
BLACK & NICHOLS	1103	4/16	14.25	.71	13.54
AUSTERHOLZ INC	1240	4/16	624.77	12.50	612.27
AUSTERHOLZ INC	1240	4/16	1,833.19	36.66	1,796.53
CHRISTIE & CO	1366	4/16	745.54		754.54
WILSON & WILSON	2231	4/16	2,936.12	58.72	2,877.40
CLAR. HIGGINS	2590	4/16	1,000.00		1,000.00
HONOUR BROS	3101	4/16	97.36	1.95	95.41
BASTIANI & SON	3112	4/16	3,580.85	71.62	3,509.23
DRJ WIRE CO	3164	4/16	256.90	5.14	251.76
HASTING-WHITE	3258	4/16	1,144.42	22.89	1,121.53
DARONO ART MET	3427	4/16	32.75	.66	32.09
DARONO ART MET	3427	4/16	127.52	2.55	124.97
DARONO ART MET	3427	4/16	96.60	1.93	94.67

rejection notices. Information documents can be used as control documents, since they document the fact that a transaction has occurred.

- **Turnaround documents.** Some types of transaction documents are designed to be read by magnetic or optical scanning equipment. Forms produced in this manner are known as turnaround documents because they are designed to be returned to the sender. For example, many computer-printed invoices consist of a turnaround portion, which is returned by a customer along with his or her payment. The turnaround document can then be automatically processed by optical scanning devices. Thus, turnaround documents combine the functions of an action document (the turnaround portion) and an information document (the receipt portion).

Transaction processing systems also produce several types of reports and displays designed to document and monitor the results of business transactions occurring or processed during a specific time period. They are not specifically tailored for management use, though they may be used by managers. Such reports can provide an audit trail for transaction control purposes. Examples are:

- **Control listings.** These are detailed reports that describe each transaction occurring during a period. They are also called *transaction logs*. For example, a listing known as a payroll register lists every paycheck printed on a specified payday by a payroll system.

- **Edit reports.** These are reports that describe errors detected during processing. For example, invalid account numbers, missing data, and incorrect control totals would be presented in edit reports.

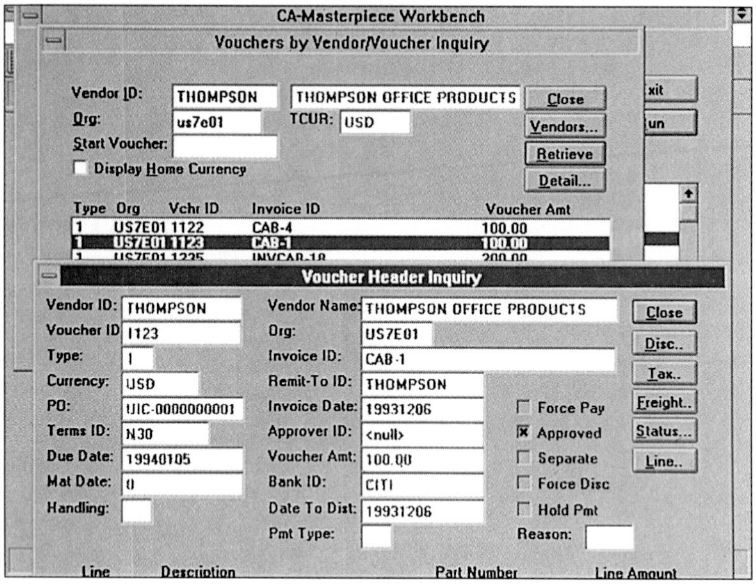

FIGURE 9.32
A vendor and voucher inquiry
display provided by a transaction
processing system.

Courtesy of Computer Associates, Inc.

- **Accounting statements.** These are reports that legally document the financial performance or status of a business. Examples are general ledger summaries, statements of cash flow, balance sheets, and income statements.

Inquiry Processing

Transaction processing and information reporting systems frequently support the realtime interrogation of online files and databases by end users. As we have previously mentioned, this **inquiry processing** capability can be provided by either batch or realtime processing. End users at workstations in wide area and local area networks can use database management query languages to make inquiries and receive responses concerning the results of transaction activity. Typically, responses are displayed in a variety of prespecified formats or *screens*. For example, employees can check on the status of a sales order, the balance in an account, or the amount of stock in inventory and receive immediate responses at their workstations. Or managers can receive responses and reports on demand concerning the performance of their employees, work groups, or departments. See Figure 9.32.

REAL WORLD CASE

 PC Gifts and Flowers: Selling versus Marketing on the Internet

If anybody knows how to make a buck in cyberspace, it's Bill Tobin. Last year, the president of Stamford, Connecticut-based PC Gifts and Flowers rang up more than $4 million in sales by peddling bouquets on Prodigy, a commercial online service with more than two million members.

But Tobin has yet to taste what he considers to be success on the Internet. Although his World Wide Web site (http://www.pcgifts.ibm.com) typically gets 24,000 to 30,000 hits a day, Tobin is chalking up fewer than 200 orders a month—a small fraction of the more than 150,000 orders a year he gets via Prodigy. While Tobin has big plans for expanding his business on the Internet, he won't consider it "a commercial environment" until his Web site generates $10 million to $15 million in annual sales. "Until then it's an experiment," he says.

For all the hype about Internet commerce, the reality is that Internet shopping is not yet ready for prime time. The Internet is great for marketing (depending on the audience you're trying to reach), but it's far less effective in generating direct sales.

Despite all the cybermalls and storefronts popping up on the Web these days, very few businesses are making big money selling goods and services on the Internet. More bouquets are sold by Prodigy's PC flowers every day than on all the Internet cybermalls combined—despite the fact that the Internet has more than 15 times as many users.

One of the reasons for PC Flowers' success on Prodigy is that the service is promoted on the welcome screen that Prodigy members see when they log on. Click on a colorful picture of a bouquet and you're instantly transported to an online shopping area where placing your order and completing the transaction is as easy as typing in your credit card number and hitting the Send button. On the Internet, you either have to know the location of an Internet flower shop or perform a keyword search using a utility like Lycos or WebCrawler.

Despite the many obstacles, companies are streaming onto the Internet in record numbers to cash in on what they see as one of the world's largest and fastest growing markets. Some companies are going it alone, while others are setting up shop in cybermalls.

For now, the Internet's real advantage isn't cost, it's presence. Combined with print, radio, television, direct mail, and telemarketing, the Internet can be a powerful tool,

allowing businesses to get their messages to a worldwide audience. By posting a brochure and other marketing information on the Web, they can show potential customers much more about their company and its products than they can in a quarter-page newspaper ad or a 30-second TV spot.

Meanwhile, merchants and technology companies are working together to forge solutions to make the Internet a more viable commercial environment for everyone. For example, Tobin has partnered with IBM to set up a Web site for PC Gifts and Flowers. To enhance his presence on the Web, Tobin has forged links with cybermalls such as MecklerWeb and Open Market as well as with Prodigy, which recently rolled out its new Web browser. He says he pays a 5 percent sales commission to each cybermall or online service that sends him business.

"I'm going to have 150 sites on the Web pointing to us within the next six months," Tobin proclaims. "On the Internet, you don't own that right like you do on an online service."

But Tobin isn't planning to stop there. To keep shoppers coming back, he has created a searchable database on his server that tells people everything they ever wanted to know about roses." Later on, Tobin says, he plans to add "communities of interest" about gardening, cooking, sports, and other topics. By the end of the year, Tobin plans to add a virtual guide who meets shoppers at the door and helps them select products and services.

"A lot of companies are just going on the Web for public relations reasons," Tobin states. "Nobody knows where they are, and nobody will ever find them. Unless you have all the pieces of the puzzle, don't go on the Web because you're just wasting your time."

CASE STUDY QUESTIONS

1. What steps of the transaction processing cycle are involved in placing an order with PCFlowers on Prodigy? On the Internet? Make any assumptions needed to supplement the information in the case.

2. Why do you think PCFlowers gets less than 200 orders a month, while getting 25,000 to 30,000 hits a day on the Internet?

3. Why do you think the Internet is "great for marketing...but far less effective in generating direct sales"?

Source: Adapted from Rosalind Resnick, "Business Is Good, Not," *Internet World,* June 1995, pp. 71–73.

Summary

- **IS in Business.** Business information systems support the functional areas of business (marketing, production/operations, accounting, finance, and human resource management) through a wide variety of computer-based operational and management information systems.

- **Marketing.** Marketing information systems provide information for the planning and control of the marketing function. Marketing planning information assists marketing managers in product planning, pricing decisions, planning advertising and sales promotion strategies and expenditures, forecasting the market potential for new and present products, and determining channels of distribution. Marketing control information supports the efforts of management to control the efficiency and effectiveness of the selling and distribution of products and services. The major types of marketing information systems are sales management, sales force automation, product management, advertising and promotion, sales forecasting, market research, and market management systems.

- **Manufacturing.** Computer-based manufacturing information systems use several major subsystems to achieve computer-aided manufacturing (CAM). Computers are automating many of the activities needed to produce products in manufacturing industries. For example, computer-aided design (CAD) systems help engineers design products. Then material requirements planning (MRP) systems help plan the types of material needed in the production process. Finally, computers may be used to manufacture products on the factory floor by directly controlling a physical process (process control), a machine tool (numerical control), or machines with some humanlike physical capabilities (robotics).

- **Human Resource Management.** Human resource information systems support human resource management in organizations. They include information systems for staffing, training and development, compensation administration, and performance appraisal.

- **Accounting and Finance.** Accounting information systems record and report business transactions and events for business firms and other organizations. Operational accounting systems emphasize legal and historical record-keeping and the production of accurate financial statements. Management accounting systems focus on the planning and control of business operations. Common operational accounting information systems include order processing, inventory control, accounts receivable, accounts payable, payroll, and general ledger systems. Information systems in finance support financial managers in decisions regarding the financing of a business and the allocation of financial resources within a business. Financial information systems include cash and securities management, capital budgeting, financial forecasting, and financial planning.

- **Transaction Processing.** Transaction processing systems play a vital role in processing data resulting from business transactions. They involve the basic activities of (1) data entry, (2) transaction processing, (3) database maintenance, (4) document and report generation, and (5) inquiry processing. However, transaction processing systems can also play a strategic role in gaining competitive advantages for a business.

- **Data Entry.** Traditional data entry methods in transaction processing systems requiring too many activities, people, and forms of data media are being replaced by more direct, automated methods known as source data automation. The high cost and potential for errors characteristic of traditional data entry methods can be minimized with source data automation that captures data as early and as close as possible to the source generating the data. Data is captured by using machine-readable media, prerecording data, or capturing data directly without the use of data media. Electronic data interchange methods allow the direct electronic transmission of source documents between companies.

- **Batch and Realtime Processing.** Two basic categories of transaction processing systems are batch processing, in which data is accumulated and processed periodically, and realtime (or online) processing, which processes data immediately. Realtime processing can be subdivided into several levels: inquiry, data entry, file processing, full capability, and process control.

Key Terms and Concepts

These are the key terms and concepts of this chapter. The page number of their first explanation is in parentheses.

1. Accounting information systems (325)
2. Accounts payable (327)
3. Accounts receivable (327)
4. Batch processing (338)
5. Business information systems (312)
6. Computer-aided design (321)
7. Computer-aided engineering (321)
8. Computer-aided manufacturing (317)
9. Computer graphics (321)
10. Computer-integrated manufacturing (317)
11. Control listing (343)
12. Cross-functional information systems (312)
13. Edit report (343)
14. Electronic data interchange (336)
15. Electronic funds transfer (337)
16. Fault tolerant system (340)
17. Financial information systems (328)

18. Financial planning models (328)
19. General ledger (328)
20. Human resource information systems (322)
21. Inquiry processing (344)
22. Inventory control (326)
23. Machine control (320)
24. Manufacturing information systems (317)
25. Marketing information systems (312)

26. Material requirements planning (317)
27. Online transaction processing (340)
28. Order processing (326)
29. Payroll (328)
30. Process control (319)
31. Realtime processing (340)
32. Robotics (320)
33. Sales force automation (314)
34. Source data automation (335)

35. Source document (334)
36. Strategic transaction processing systems (332)
37. Traditional data entry (334)
38. Transaction (332)
39. Transaction document (342)
40. Transaction processing cycle (332)
41. Transaction processing system (332)
42. Turnaround document (343)

Review Quiz

Match one of the key terms and concepts listed above with one of the brief examples or definitions listed below. Try to find the best fit for answers that seem to fit more than one term or concept. Defend your choices.

____ 1. An example is making a sale or a payment.

____ 2. Process data resulting from business transactions.

____ 3. Data entry, transaction processing, database maintenance, document and report generation, and inquiry processing.

____ 4. Has too many activities, people, media, costs, and errors.

____ 5. The automatic capture of data at the time and place of transactions.

____ 6. The electronic transmission of source documents between companies.

____ 7. Collecting and periodically processing transaction data.

____ 8. Processing transaction data immediately after it is captured.

____ 9. A sales order form is an example.

____ 10. Examples are paychecks, customer statements, and sales receipts.

____ 11. Part of a customer's invoice is returned for automated data entry.

____ 12. A payroll register is an example.

____ 13. Reports that identify errors occurring during transaction processing.

____ 14. Allows end users to check on the status of an order or the balance in an account and receive an immediate response.

____ 15. A nonstop transaction processing capability.

____ 16. A popular name for realtime transaction processing.

____ 17. Transaction processing systems can build strong relationships with customers and suppliers.

____ 18. Support marketing, production, accounting, finance, and human resource management with computer-based information systems.

____ 19. Information systems must integrate the activities and resources of the functional areas of a business.

____ 20. Information systems for sales management, product management, and promotion management.

____ 21. Uses computers to automate sales recording and reporting by salespeople.

____ 22. Information systems that support manufacturing operations and management.

____ 23. Using computers in a variety of ways to help manufacture products.

____ 24. Helps the design process using advanced graphics, workstations, and software.

____ 25. Helps engineers evaluate products and processes.

____ 26. A conceptual framework for all aspects of factory automation.

____ 27. Using computers to operate a petroleum refinery.

____ 28. Using computers to help operate machine tools.

____ 29. Computerized devices can take over some production activities from human workers.

____ 30. Translates the production schedule into a detailed plan for all materials required.

____ 31. Information systems to support staffing, training and development, and compensation administration.

____ 32. Accomplish legal and historical record-keeping and gather information for the planning and control of business operations.

____ 33. Handles sales orders from customers.

____ 34. Keeps track of items in stock.

____ 35. Keeps track of amounts owed by customers.

___ 36. Keeps track of purchases from suppliers.

___ 37. Produces employee paychecks.

___ 38. Produces the financial statements of a firm.

___ 39. Information systems for cash and securities manage-

___ 40. Provides a DSS capability for financial planning.

ment, capital budgeting, and financial forecasting.

___ 41. Systems for the capture and processing of money and credit transactions.

Discussion Questions

1. How can transaction processing systems play a strategic role in gaining competitive advantages for a business?

2. Why would electronic data interchange be "the ultimate in source data automation"?

3. Refer to the Real World Case on Continental Insurance and Northrup Grumman in the chapter. Why has "flattening the organization" made it harder to find people with the right skills?

4. What are several reasons for the continued growth of online transaction processing? When would an OLTP system need a fault tolerant capability?

5. What is sales force automation? How does it affect salesperson productivity, marketing management, and competitive advantage?

6. Refer to the Real World Case on PC Gifts and Flowers in the chapter. What do you think are the barriers to business on the Internet?

7. What is computer-integrated manufacturing? What is the role of computer-aided manufacturing, computer-aided engineering, and robotics in CIM?

8. How can computer-based information systems support human resource management in a business? Give a few examples.

9. What are the most common applications of computers in accounting? Why do most businesses computerize these accounting systems?

10. What are cross-functional information systems? Why is there a trend toward such systems?

Real World Problems

1. Holiday Inn Worldwide: Online Transaction Processing Systems

Holiday Inn, the world's largest hotel chain, utilizes a worldwide online transaction processing system to provide customer service and drive revenues. "We're constantly monitoring demand for rooms in real time," says Don Lynch, Holiday Inn's director for worldwide hotel systems development. Based on that demand, discount programs are used as required to maximize occupancy, so no room ever has to be sold for less than its real market value. Reservations taken at the front desk are constantly monitored. Holiday Inn's system can quickly respond to changing conditions regardless of the pace of reservation traffic.

Holiday Inn Worldwide (HIW) achieves this continually tuned balance through a carefully crafted IS architecture. The applications architecture forms a triangle connecting three points: the PC-based front desk applications running at each site, the IBM mainframe Transaction Processing Facility running in Atlanta headquarters, and the Informix-based HIRO (Holiday Inn Reservations Optimizer) system that runs on a Sun SPARCenter 2000 server, also located in Atlanta. A sophisticated satellite-based network provides instantaneous data communications between the hundreds of hotels dispersed across the globe and Holiday Inn's headquarters.

HIW is now implementing a data warehouse approach that will allow Holiday Inn to flexibly use all the information resources it maintains through its hotel operations as a powerful competitive weapon. "Within 72 hours of each day's closing, we have all the information on all our customers 'scrubbed' and in place," says Lynch. Being able to access this information instantly is essential for Holiday Inn to achieve strategic goals and execute critical operations.

a. What steps of the transaction processing cycle do you recognize in the HIRO system? Explain.

b. Why is the HIRO system being integrated with a data warehouse system?

Source: Adapted from "Holiday Inn and IT Double Up For Profits," Special Advertising Supplement, *Computerworld*, February 20, 1995, p. 30. Copyright 1995 by Computerworld, Inc., Framingham, MA 01701—Reprinted from *Computerworld*.

2. Pizza Hut Inc.: Market Research for Quality Management

Faced with falling profits in recent years, Pizza Hut Inc. has decided to quickly roll out systems that can contribute to quality and, ultimately, build the top line as well. One significant early example is Pizza Hut's customer satisfaction measurement system. Taking a page out of the playbook of Lexus and other masters of customer retention, Pizza Hut has begun calling thousands of customers each week to get feedback on their dining experiences. The system is built on Pizza Hut's impressive customer database, which the company has used for years to track the buying patterns of more than 25 million delivery customers. Each week, the new system downloads a representative set of 50,000 customer names and phone numbers to the Gallup Organization. Gallup polls those customers on speed of service, quality of food, and repurchase willingness. The results are represented in a "loyalty index," which is used to calculate management bonuses from the chief executive officer to store managers.

Whether Pizza Hut can translate customer survey data into improved quality and profits remains to be seen. But VP of MIS Dan Cooke says his group will use the feedback to refine restaurant control systems and processes. If customers report their pizzas weren't delivered hot enough, for example, IS can rewrite the code that controls baking and delivery routing. The system's hefty price tag—approximately $5 million per year, according to Chief Operating Officer Pat Williamson—may raise some eyebrows in the cost-sensitive industry. But the company's research shows that a customer is worth $7,200 over his or her lifetime, making the new system "worth more than any marketing program we could ever come up with," says Williamson.

a. What resources does Pizza Hut rely upon to do market research?

b. Do you think their customer satisfaction measurement system is a good idea, given its cost? Why or why not?

Source: Adapted from Brian McWilliams, "Coming Back For More," *Computerworld*, February 13, 1995, pp. 101–6. Copyright 1995 by Computerworld, Inc., Framingham, MA 01701—Reprinted from *Computerworld*.

3. HS Resources: Employee Performance Evaluations

When Lisa Norris began working for HS Resources, an oil and gas drilling and production company headquartered in San Francisco, the employee performance review was handwritten. But in hiring Norris as director of human resources and administration, the company—which last year doubled in size to nearly 200 employees—was looking for change. So she began searching for software that could familiarize new managers with the concept of performance evaluations as well as make the task easier. She decided that the *Performance Now!* program from KnowledgePoint would do both.

Norris finds Performance Now! particularly strong in supplying fresh ideas for motivating employees. Bosses running out of tactful or encouraging phrases can click on the program's help menus to bring up suggestions. "It's especially useful when you're dealing with employees that really need some support or need more training. It's very helpful in generating ideas and formulating them in ways that are very positive for the employee," adds Norris. The result is a nice-looking document that's customized for the employee being reviewed. It discussed how well the employee has done in the past year and what you as manager would like him or her to accomplish in the next. "It looks very good,"

Norris says. "It looks like a lot of work has gone into it—which it has!"

Performance Now! makes writing reviews much faster than scribbling them by hand, but Norris is quick to point out that it's still a time-consuming enterprise. She estimates that managers at her company spend about four hours writing an evaluation. "The bottom line isn't any product that you purchase," she says. "You have to train people on how to conduct performance evaluations, and that's generic, across any product. And there's no way to avoid the work that goes into an appraisal because it has to be tailored to the individual, and no computer product is going to do that for you."

a. How does Performance Now! help managers at HS Resources do performance evaluations?

b. Should it take a manager four hours to write up a performance evaluation for an employee, even with the help of software like Performance Now!? Why or why not?

Source: Adapted from Marti Remington, "Setting Standards High," *PC Today*, March 1995, p. 48.

4. Benner-Nawman Inc.: Multisegment Accounting

The state of accounting at Benner-Nawman Inc. would have raised the eyebrows of many savvy entrepreneurs when John Humphrey became CFO of the company about five years ago. Benner-Nawman, which grosses $13 million a year making telephone booths with plants in the United States and Canada, shared an outdated mainframe with several other companies. The mainframe would only keep two weeks worth of information and would not compile separate financial data for each plant. It wouldn't even convert the Canadian plant's figures, which were in Canadian dollars, into U.S. money. And, what wasn't stored or computed on the mainframe was done by hand. "I was kind of shocked when I came to work here in 1990 to find all of these manual records and penciled-in green sheets of what was going on in the business," Humphrey says. "They were 10 years behind the times at least."

Any accounting system would have improved the company's record-keeping, but Humphrey says the company chose *SunSystems Accounting Software,* a modular client/server accounting program from Systems Union Inc., because of its ability to do segment accounting and convert foreign currency. Benner-Nawman, headquartered in Benencia, California, keeps separate financial information for its plants in Illinois, Arizona, and Calgary, Alberta. "Prior to having SunSystems, we didn't have any way of measuring the different divisions and the entities of our business," Humphrey says.

The segments go well beyond each plant. Humphrey says the company can track costs and revenue at each of its sales divisions: international, domestic, and non–telephone booth items. SunSystems also tracks the performance of individual sales representatives. That's helped Benner-Nawman quickly spot poor-performing sales reps. The company used to let some unproductive reps work for two or three years after they started sliding. "Those are the kinds of calculations we have now that we weren't even close to having in the past," Humphrey says. "Before, we just had a consolidated financial statement of the whole business. We didn't have any details."

a. How does the SunSystems accounting package help managers at Benner-Nawman?

b. What are some other capabilities provided by accounting packages that are valuable for managers? Give several examples.

Source: Adapted from Ryan Steeves, "The Winning Call," *PC Today*, February 1995, p. 32.

5. Eastman Kodak: Sales Force Automation

Hoping to improve a so-so customer service record and boost lagging sales force productivity, Eastman Kodak's second largest division is untethering its salespeople from their desktops. So, Kodak's Professional & Printing Imaging Division is rolling out Apple PowerBook notebook computers to about 230 salespeople. They now access customer information from corporate databases using home-based PCs. In the past, Kodak salespeople have been handicapped by a lack of information about the individual customers who use their products. This is because the division sells primarily to distributors' processing labs and print and graphics shops, explained Jim Neitsche, information systems director for the division.

Under the mobile scheme, reps will have on-the-road access to a single data warehouse containing continuously refreshed information—including data about customer preferences. Users can replicate the warehouse on their portables via a newly developed Lotus Notes applications. Salespeople will have access to a broad base of information, ranging from sales reports to individual customers' film, camera, and processing preferences. This data will be available under a system called Pro Passport. Under the new system, the Pro Passport data—collected directly from the customers via questionnaires and various coupon and rebate programs—will be available to reps from a Lotus Notes server. "Access to this kind of data will allow us to clearly identify where significant customers are that we haven't been astute about contacting in the past," Altberg said.

a. How will notebook computers help sales reps at Kodak?

b. Why would a notebook PC be significantly more helpful to a sales rep than a home-based desktop PC?

Source: Adapted from Julia King, "Kodak Snaps Up Portables," *Computerworld*, February 6, 1995, pp. 1, 127. Copyright 1995 by Computerworld, Inc., Framingham, MA 01701—Reprinted from *Computerworld*.

6. Credit Agricole-Lazard: Developing Financial Products

At Credit Agricole-Lazard Financial Products Ltd. (CALfp), the IS staff has created their investment systems with an object-oriented development platform that allows the company to respond quickly to financial customers' needs. "In finance, you have to move fast. Being quick at implementing and deploying a software system has a direct correspondence to your revenue stream," said Philippe J. Stephan, a systems architect at CALfp in Paris. To date, the company has invested $10 million in hardware, software, and staff to develop and implement the system, according to Ravi Ziswanathan, general manager of CALfp in London. "It was a very large project in terms of scope, but we're pleased with its progress thus far," said Ziswanathan, who estimated that the company would invest an additional $10 million in the project during the next two years.

CALfp was formed in February 1994 when Credit Agricole and Lazard Freres established a 50-employee company with offices in London, Paris, and New York, specializing in structured finance. Back then, the concern was that new investment systems would be robust enough to process, monitor, and track transactions worth several hundred million dollars each. Plus, the systems would have to be flexible enough to incorporate new investment instruments on the fly. The systems would also require components to monitor complex financial derivatives to insulate CALfp and its investors from volatile market conditions and rogue trading. To avert these problems and position itself effectively against rivals such as Goldman Sachs & Co. and J. P. Morgan & Co., CALfp decided to develop an integrated set of applications. They chose Tower Technology's version of the Eiffel object-oriented language for their initiative, called the Rainbow project. Since Rainbow was launched last year, CALfp programmers have used Eiffel to develop several financial derivatives products, price them for customers, develop applications for risk analysis, and create accounting programs to maintain their customer accounts.

a. What computer-based financial systems is CALfp developing?

b. Why is CALfp using object-oriented development tools to develop financial products and systems?

Source: Adapted from Thomas Hoffman, "Object-Oriented Financial Package Tames Transactions," *Computerworld*, May 8, 1995, p. 75. Copyright 1995 by Computerworld, Inc., Framingham, MA 01701—Reprinted from *Computerworld*.

▲ *Application Exercises*

1. ABC Department Stores

ABC Department Stores uses POS terminals connected to a minicomputer in each store to capture sales data immediately and store them on a magnetic disk unit. Each night, the central computer in Phoenix polls each store's minicomputer to access and process the day's sales data, update the corporate database, and produce management reports. The next

morning, managers use their terminals to interrogate the updated corporate databases.

Identify how each of the following types of computer processing is occurring in the example above:

a. Batch

b. Realtime

c. Online

FIGURE 9.33
Sample rental transactions for one customer for one month.

Customer Name	Acct. #	Item Description	Rental Date	Daily Rental Rate	Rental Days	Total Charge
Builtrite	117	Backhoe	10/02/95	$150	2.5	$375
Builtrite	117	Cement Mixer	10/03/95	100	1.0	100
Builtrite	117	Port. Blower	10/03/95	50	2.0	100
Builtrite	117	Ditch Devil	10/06/95	175	1.0	175
Builtrite	117	Cement Mixer	10/07/95	100	0.5	50
Builtrite	117	Compressor	10/10/95	90	3.0	270
Builtrite	117	Nail Gun	10/10/95	30	3.0	90
Builtrite	117	Backhoe	10/15/95	150	1.0	150
Builtrite	117	Ditch Devil	10/16/95	175	2.0	350
Builtrite	117	Cement Mixer	10/21/95	100	1.5	150
Builtrite	117	Port. Blower	10/22/95	50	0.5	25
Builtrite	117	Backhoe	10/27/95	150	1.5	225
Builtrite	117	Compressor	10/28/95	90	2.0	180

d. Transaction
e. Data entry
f. Database maintenance
g. Inquiry processing

2. **Business Information Systems**
Which business information systems should be improved if the following complaints were brought to your attention? Identify the business function (accounting, finance, marketing, production/operations, or human resource management) and the specific information system in that functional area that is involved. (Refer to Figure 9.1.)
a. "Nobody is sure which of our sales reps is our top producer."
b. "Why was this part left out of the bill of materials?"
c. "I don't know why I didn't get a raise this year."
d. "Why were we overinvested in short-term securities?"
e. "Why are the balance sheet and income statement late this month?"
f. "Our sales reps are spending too much time on paperwork."
g. "The ROI and payback on this deal are all wrong."
h. "Which of our managers have overseas experience?"
i. "We need a workstation to design this product."
j. "Why are we being stuck with home office overhead expenses?"

3. **Accounting Information Systems**
Which common accounting information systems should be improved if the following complaints were brought to your attention? (Refer to Figure 9.16.)
a. "Month-end closings are always late."
b. "We are never sure how much of a certain product we have on the shelves."

c. "Many of us didn't get an earnings and deductions statement this week."
d. "We're tired of manually writing up a receipt every time a customer orders something."
e. "Our suppliers are complaining that they are not being paid on time."
f. "Our customers resent being sent notices demanding payment when they have already paid what they owe."

4. **Designing Information Products**
a. In your day-to-day living, you are a user of many transaction processing systems, including those used by banks, department stores, supermarkets, utility companies, and universities to process data generated by various end user transactions. Design a mockup of a report, document, or display that could be produced by a transaction processing system of your choice. Use a report generator from a database management or other software package to develop the report mockup if possible.
b. Evaluate how well the transaction processing system you chose performs its basic transaction processing activities. Write up a brief evaluation based on the activities illustrated in Figure 9.22.

5. **Ron's Rentals Customer Billing Report**
Ron's Rentals rents construction equipment to contractors. Approved customers are allowed to charge their rentals and are sent billings on a monthly basis. Ron would like to use database software to record information about each rental as it occurs and print up monthly billings to be sent to each customer. A set of rentals by one customer over a sample month is shown in Figure 9.33. You are to use this sample data to design a billing report that Ron's can send to its customers.

The report should be as informative as possible. You will certainly want to report the total amount billed, but your report should also give subtotals spent on different items.

a. Based on the sample data below, build a database file to store rental transaction records, and enter the sample data shown.

b. Using the report generation feature of your database package, create a monthly billing report for a customer.

This report should be laid out as nicely as possible and be as informative as possible. Print a copy of your report based on the sample data.

c. Critique your report. Are there elements of the report that you would like to have laid out differently, or features that you would like to have added? Did the datbase package you used limit your options in formatting this report?

Review Quiz Answers

1. 38	12. 11	23. 8	34. 22
2. 41	13. 13	24. 6	35. 3
3. 40	14. 21	25. 7	36. 2
4. 37	15. 16	26. 10	37. 29
5. 34	16. 27	27. 30	38. 19
6. 14	17. 36	28. 2	39. 17
7. 4	18. 5	29. 32	40. 18
8. 31	19. 12	30. 26	41. 15
9. 35	20. 25	31. 20	
10. 39	21. 33	32. 1	
11. 42	22. 24	33. 28	

Selected References

1. Andersen Consulting. *Foundations of Business Systems.* 2nd ed. Fort Worth, TX: Dryden Press, 1992.

2. Bakos, J. Yannis. "A Strategic Analysis of Electronic Marketplaces." *MIS Quarterly,* September 1991.

3. Battberg, Robert, Rashi Glazer; and John Little, eds., *The Marketing Information Revolution.* Boston: The Harvard Business School Press, 1994.

4. Cushing, Barry, and Marshal Romney. *Accounting Information Systems.* 6th ed. Reading, MA: Addison-Wesley Publishing, 1994.

5. Dams, Leila. "On the Fast Track to HR Integration." *Datamation,* September 15, 1991.

6. Douglass, David. "Computer Integrated Manufacturing." *SIM Executive,* First Quarter 1991.

7. Eliason, Alan. *Online Business Computer Applications.* 3rd ed. New York: Macmillan, 1991.

8. Fitzgerald, Michael. "Users Trying Again with Sales Force Automation." *Computerworld,* November 28, 1994.

9. Hess, Christopher, and Chris Kemerer. "Computerized Loan Origination Systems: An Industry Case Study of The Electronic Markets Hypothesis." *MIS Quarterly,* September 1994.

10. "Integration Strategies: Manufacturing." *Computerworld,* October 28, 1991.

11. Jiang, James. "Using Scanner Data." *Information Systems Management,* Winter 1995.

12. Lindholm, Elizabeth. "Transactions on the Desktop." *Datamation,* August 1, 1991.

13. McWilliams, Bryan. "Delighting the Marketer?" *Computerworld,* November 14, 1994.

14. Moad, Jeff. "Relational Takes on OLTP." *Datamation,* May 15, 1991.

15. Senn, James. "Electronic Data Interchange." *Information Systems Management,* Winter 1992.

16. Sloan, Robert, and Hal Green. "Manufacturing Decision Support Architecture: Achieving Effective Information Delivery." *Information Systems Management,* Winter 1995.

17. Snell, Ned. "Software to Tame the Sales Force." *Datamation,* June 1, 1991.

18. Trippi, Robert, and Efraim Turban. *Investment Management: Decision Support and Expert Systems.* Boston: Boyd & Fraser Publishing Co., 1990.

19. Wilder, Clinton. "Codex Goes Paperless with EDI." *Computerworld,* January 13, 1992.

REAL WORLD CASE

 ## Bernard Hodes and Others: Head Hunting on the Internet

Companies big and small are erecting "Help Wanted" bill-boards on the information superhighway hoping to capture the attention of passing cyber-motorists. And according to the Software Publishing Association, 27 percent of the Internet hosts are institutions of higher learning. This means that a lot of college students will be online, giving many companies the chance to have a presence at colleges that might not otherwise be economically feasible.

Usenet

The traditional way of posting job offerings and resumes is on Usenet newsgroups. Right now there are more than 150 jobs-related newsgroups organized by industry or locale. The reach is global and jobs offered range from file clerks to biologists.

To take advantage of this resource, start by making a quick trip to the newsgroup called Misc.jobs.misc. Once there, search for the two FAQs (collections of frequently asked questions) that provide posting guidelines and job-hunting resources. The methods for going to a newsgroup and searching it vary widely depending on which software you're using and how you're accessing the Internet.

The Resource FAQ lists current newsgroups and their focus. It doesn't make sense to post your job offer in every jobs newsgroup, just as you wouldn't want to advertise in every periodical. The guidelines will tell you, in detail, everything you always wanted to know about posting.

World Wide Web

If navigating through all those newsgroups seems more like a job for Christopher Columbus, there are a couple of money-makes-it-easy solutions that let you turn the grunge work over to a professional. Both these options can be found on the World Wide Web, which is actually the coolest corner of the Internet. In addition to other things, this is where hypermedia technology has been layered over the Internet to offer graphics, sound, and point-and-click usability—if you have the right kind of Internet access. Two places to check out on the WWW are the Online Career Center and the CareerMosiac (TM).

The Online Career Center accessible via http://www.iquest.net, attempts to bring together all the newsgroups and jobs gophers. It costs money to place ads directly with IQuest the sponsor of the Online Career Center. Reading resumes, however, is free.

The CareerMosiac is brought to you by Bernard Hodes Advertising Inc., a $250 million-plus recruitment advertising agency with offices around the world. One of CareerMosiac's functions is to sort and index the newsgroup listings into one convenient list. Visit the CareerMosiac via http://www.careermosiac.cp. Of course, Bernard Hodes Advertising will, for a fee, handle your Internet recruitment advertising needs. You never have to boot a computer, just send a check. Their Internet E-mail is: tglbbon@hodes.com.

Hints and Tips

Professional recruiter Michael Muller, of Scott Marlow Accounting and Financial Search Consultants in Ojai, California, uses the Internet to find accountants. He's had success locating qualified accounting applicants for jobs paying up to $125,000 a year.

For employers planning to post on the newsgroups, Muller offers a hint. "When asking for an E-mail response, specify sending a resume in ASCII format, otherwise you'll get files created by every word processing program out there. It's simpler to ask them to fax their resumes."

Professional recruiter Nick Cobb has been using the Internet for six months. "At the executive level, the Internet is not the best avenue. It is good, however, for entry-level and mid-level talent with computer skills," he says.

CASE STUDY QUESTIONS

1. Why are many companies using the Internet to attract, find, and recruit prospective employees?

2. Why is the Internet a good job-hunting ground for college students with computer skills or other specialties?

3. Have you begun job hunting or prospecting on the Internet? Why don't you give it a try, based on the information in this case? Then write up a short description of your experience.

Source: Adapted from Beth Slick, "Technology and the Human Factor" and "Head Hunting on the Internet," *PC Today*, March 1995, pp. 10–13.

Information Systems for Managerial Decision Making and Support

CHAPTER OUTLINE

LEARNING OBJECTIVES

The purpose of this chapter is to give you an understanding of the decision-making needs of the managers of organizations, and how management information, decision support, and executive information systems support managerial decision making.

Section I of this chapter emphasizes the major concepts involved in providing information to support decision making and the functions and roles of management.

Section II discusses basic concepts and components of management information, decision support, and executive information systems and provides examples of DSS and EIS applications.

After reading and studying this chapter, you should be able to:

1. Give examples of how information can support the four functions of management, the 10 roles of management, and the three levels of management activities.

2. Give examples of how information can support each of the four stages of the decision-making process.

3. Analyze the quality of a variety of information products using the three dimensions of information quality.

4. Identify the role and reporting alternatives of management information systems.

5. Describe how online analytical processing can meet key information needs of managers.

6. Explain the decision support system concept and how it differs from traditional information reporting systems.

7. Explain how executive information systems can support the information needs of top and middle managers.

8. Describe how group decision support systems can support group decision making.

SECTION I
Information and Managerial Decision Making

Information systems can significantly support managerial decision making. That is the goal which the information systems industry has been working toward since the concepts of management information systems (MIS), decision support systems (DSS), and executive information systems (EIS) were developed. Developing effective decision support systems requires understanding how information systems can contribute to the decision-making process, as well as to the many functions and roles performed by managers. This understanding is what we will pursue in this section.

Information and Management

In order to understand what information a manager needs, we need to review what management means. Figure 10.1 summarizes three fundamental conceptual frameworks that answer the question, "What does a manager do?" Let's take a closer look at each of these concepts to see how information systems can help meet the information needs of managers.

Information and the Functions of Management

Management is traditionally described as a process of leadership involving the **management functions** of planning, organizing, directing, and controlling. These functions of management are based on those expounded in the early 1900s by Henri Fayol, of France, a pioneer of management theory [17]. They give us a valuable way to think about what managers do. A manager should plan the activities of his or her organization, organize its personnel and their activities, direct its operations, and control its direction by evaluating feedback and making necessary adjustments.

- **Planning** involves the development of long- and short-range plans requiring the formulation of goals, objectives, strategies, policies, procedures, and standards. Planning also involves the perception and analysis of opportunities, problems, and alternative courses of action and the design of programs to achieve selected objectives.
- **Organizing** involves making assignments for the accomplishment of tasks to individuals and groups by delegating authority, assigning responsibility, and requiring accountability.
- **Directing** is the leadership of an organization through communication, inspiration, and motivation of organizational personnel.
- **Controlling** involves observing and measuring organizational performance and environmental activities and modifying the plans and activities of the organization when necessary.

Information systems can assist managers by providing information needed to accomplish each of these managerial functions. For example, information systems can help managers plan by providing both planning data and planning models. A typical example is the use of capital budgeting models to develop long-range plans for the major expenditures needed to build new factories or retail stores or to make other major additions to plant and equipment. Information systems could provide data on internal resource needs and external factors such as interest rates, as well as financial modeling software.

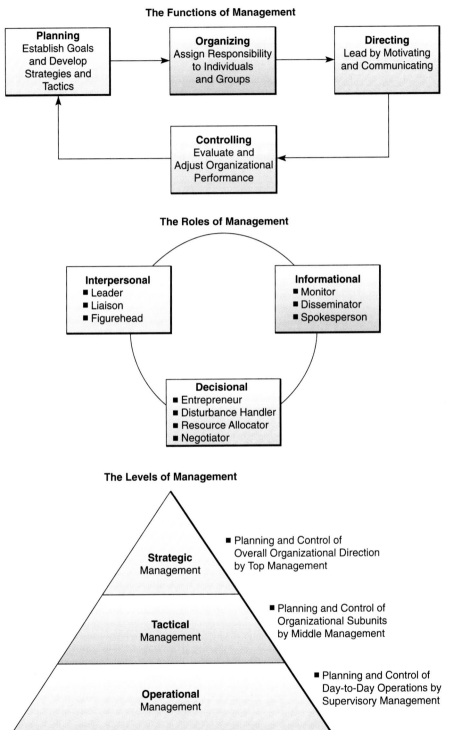

The Functions of Management

Planning
Establish Goals
and Develop
Strategies and
Tactics

Organizing
Assign Responsibility
to Individuals
and Groups

Directing
Lead by Motivating
and Communicating

Controlling
Evaluate and
Adjust Organizational
Performance

The Roles of Management

Interpersonal
■ Leader
■ Liaison
■ Figurehead

Informational
■ Monitor
■ Disseminator
■ Spokesperson

Decisional
■ Entrepreneur
■ Disturbance Handler
■ Resource Allocator
■ Negotiator

The Levels of Management

Strategic Management

Tactical Management

Operational Management

■ Planning and Control of
Overall Organizational Direction
by Top Management

■ Planning and Control of
Organizational Subunits
by Middle Management

■ Planning and Control of
Day-to-Day Operations by
Supervisory Management

FIGURE 10.1
What a manager does. This figure summarizes (1) the four functions of management, (2) the 10 major roles played by managers, and (3) the three levels of management activity.

Information systems can help managers organize and staff their organizations with human resources. For example, information from a personnel database and software for personnel requirements forecasting and an employee skills inventory can help managers organize present and proposed work groups and project teams. This helps ensure that employees with the necessary skills will be available when needed. Information systems can also help managers direct their organizations. For example, the electronic mail capabilities of office automation systems make it easier for managers to communicate with people in their organizations. Finally, information systems play a major role in the control function of management. Through such information products as exception reports, they help managers recognize deviations in performance from standards, forecasts, and budgets. This kind of feedback helps managers adjust a firm's operations to meet organizational objectives.

Information and the Roles of Management

Another useful management model was developed by management scholar Henry Mintzberg in the early 1970s [17]. This model views management as the performance of a variety of **managerial roles.** A manager has the authority and status to play the following roles:

- **Interpersonal roles.** A manager should be (1) a leader of subordinates, (2) a liaison with the external environment, and (3) a figurehead when ceremonial duties arise.
- **Information roles.** A manager should be (4) a monitor of information on organizational performance, (5) a disseminator of information within the organization, and (6) a spokesperson to the external environment.
- **Decision roles.** A manager should be (7) an entrepreneur in making innovative changes that affect the organization, (8) a disturbance handler when unanticipated events occur, (9) a resource allocator in determining the distribution of financial and other resources within the organization, and (10) a negotiator who resolves both internal and external disputes.

What information do managers need to perform these roles? How can information systems help? Mintzburg's studies of top-level executives showed that they did not get much help from computer-based information systems. Instead, they relied primarily on verbal information gathered from telephone calls, personal contacts, and meetings. However, improvements in office automation systems and executive information systems have been aimed at making information systems more attractive, easy to use, and helpful to top executives and other managers. For example, electronic mail systems allow electronic messages to be sent, stored, and forwarded among managerial and staff workstations. Executive information systems can make it easy for executives to gather critical information about organizational performance.

Another point to remember is that many of the 10 roles of management can be related to the four managerial functions. For example, the interpersonal role of a leader is directly related to the management functions of organizing, staffing, and directing. The information roles of a monitor and disseminator are directly related to the functions of directing and controlling. The decisional roles of an entrepreneur and resource allocator are directly related to the planning function. So, since information systems can supply information to support these managerial functions, they can also supply the information needed to perform the diverse roles of management.

FIGURE 10.2
Information requirements by management level. The type of information required by managers is directly related to their level of management and the structure of decision situations they face.

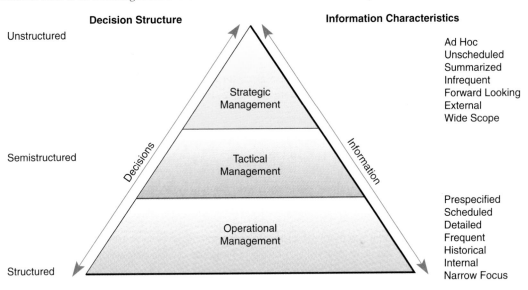

The information requirements of management depend heavily on the **management level** involved. Figure 10.1 emphasized that the activities of management can be subdivided into three major levels: (1) strategic management, (2) tactical management, and (3) operational management. These levels are related to the traditional management levels of top management, middle management, and operating or supervisory management. This "managerial pyramid" model of management was introduced in Chapter 2. It was popularized in the 1960s by Robert N. Anthony, another pioneer of management theory. It answers the question "What does a manager do?" by emphasizing that management consists of planning and control activities determined by the manager's specific level in an organization [1, 12].

Information and the Levels of Management

- **Strategic planning and control.** Top executives develop overall organizational goals, strategies, policies, and objectives through long-range strategic planning. They also monitor the strategic performance of the organization and its overall direction.

- **Tactical planning and control.** Middle managers develop short- and medium-range plans and budgets and specify the policies, procedures, and objectives for subunits of the organization. They also acquire and allocate resources and monitor the performance of organizational subunits, such as departments, divisions, and other work groups.

- **Operational planning and control.** Supervisory managers develop short-range planning devices such as production schedules. They direct the use of resources and the performance of tasks according to established procedures and within budgets and schedules established for the work groups of the organization.

Figure 10.2 emphasizes that the type of information required by managers is directly related to the level of management and the amount of structure in the decision situations they face. For example, the strategic management level requires more summarized, ad hoc, unscheduled reports, forecasts, and external intelligence to support its more unstructured planning and policy-making responsibilities. The operational management level, on the other hand, may require more regular internal reports emphasizing detailed current and historical data comparisons that support its more structured control of day-to-day operations. Thus, we can generalize that higher levels of management require more ad hoc, unscheduled, infrequent summaries, with a wide, external, forward-looking scope. On the other hand, lower levels of management require more prespecified, frequently scheduled, and detailed information, with a more narrow, internal, and historical focus.

Information and Decision Making

In Chapter 3, we discussed the conceptual framework that underlies the *systems approach* to problem solving. These same concepts have long been used to study and illustrate the process of decision making. The most widely used example of this is a model of the **decision-making process** by Herbert A. Simon, a Nobel prize-winning economist and scholar of management decision making. His model is a conceptual framework that divides the decision-making process into *intelligence, design,* and *choice* activities [2, 3]. Other researchers have emphasized that since managerial decision making is typically a problem-solving process, the *implementation* of a decision is as important to its success as the steps that lead up to making it [12]. Therefore, we can use a model of decision making that consists of four stages:

- **Intelligence activities.** Search the environment and identify events and conditions requiring decisions.
- **Design activities.** Develop and evaluate possible courses of action.
- **Choice activities.** Select a particular course of action.
- **Implementation activities.** Implement the decision and monitor its success.

As Figure 10.3 shows, this four-stage decision-making process includes the ability to cycle back to a previous stage if the decision maker is dissatisfied with the intelligence gathered, the alternatives developed, or the success of implementation activities. Also note that each of these stages of decision making has unique information requirements, which we will now explore.

Information for the Intelligence Stage

Information systems can help in the intelligence stage by providing information about internal and external conditions that might require decision making by appropriate managers. Thus, information systems can be used to scan the operations of an organization or the activities taking place in the business environment. Information systems can also scan the external environment to identify potential decision situations.

> **EXAMPLE**
> Sales analysis reports can be furnished to managers periodically, when exceptional sales situations occur, or on demand. These help managers identify the status of sales performance, sales trends, and exceptional sales conditions for the firm. Information from market research studies and external databases could also help managers identify changes in consumer preferences or competitive products.

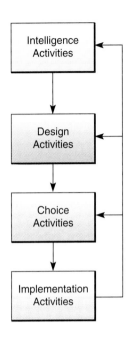

- Search for and identify conditions requiring a decision.
- Information systems should scan the internal organization and the external environment and help identify problems and opportunities.

- Develop and evaluate alternative courses of action.
- Information systems should help generate and evaluate decision alternatives.

- Select a course of action.
- Information systems should help emphasize and prioritize decision alternatives.

- Implement and monitor the success of the decision.
- Information systems should provide feedback on the implemented decision.

FIGURE 10.3
A model of the decision-making process. Note that the decision-making process is a four-stage process of intelligence, design, choice, and implementation activities that may cycle back to previous stages. Also note how information systems can support each stage of this process.

An important information system capability is needed in this stage. Managers should have the ability to make **ad hoc inquiries,** that is, unique, unscheduled, situation-specific information requests. The *prespecified reports* typically provided by management information systems periodically, on an exception basis, or even on demand may not be satisfactory. Such information products may not give a manager enough information to recognize whether a problem or opportunity exists.

EXAMPLE
A disturbing sales trend can be brought to a manager's attention by a weekly sales report that spotlights unusual or exceptional sales activity. However, the manager may need to make further inquiries to isolate the sales problem. Therefore, information systems frequently provide a query language capability to allow a manager to make ad hoc inquiries of a sales database to get the exact sales information he or she needs.

Information for the Design Stage

The design stage of decision making involves developing and evaluating alternative courses of action. A major consideration introduced by Simon for this stage (as well as for the other stages) is whether the decision situation is programmable or nonprogrammable or, more popularly, structured or unstructured.

Figure 10.4 shows the amount of structure in typical decisions faced by each level of management, based on the work of G. Anthony Gorry and Michael Scott Morton [12]. Their work emphasized that many of the changes in managers' information needs can be attributed to the degree of decision structure at each level of management. Decisions at the operational level tend to be more structured, those at the tactical level more semistructured, and those at the strategic level more unstructured. Therefore, information systems must be designed to produce a variety of information products to meet the changing decision needs of managers at different levels of an organization.

FIGURE 10.4
Examples of decisions by the type of decision structure and by level of management.

Decision Structure	Operational Management	Tactical Management	Strategic Management
Unstructured		Work group reorganization	New business planning
	Cash management	Work group performance analysis	Company reorganization
Semistructured	Credit management	Employee performance appraisal	Product planning
	Production scheduling	Capital budgeting	Mergers and acquisitions
	Daily work assignment	Program budgeting	Site location
Structured	Inventory control	Program control	

Structured Decisions

Structured decisions (also called programmable decisions) involve situations where the procedures to follow when a decision is needed can be specified in advance, Therefore, such decisions are structured or programmed by the decision procedures, or *decision rules,* developed for them. A structured decision may involve what is known as a deterministic or algorithmic decision. In this case, a decision's outcome can be determined with certainty if a specified sequence of activities (an algorithm) is performed. Or a structured decision may involve a *probabilistic* decision situation. In this case, enough probabilities about possible outcomes are known that a decision can be statistically determined with an acceptable probability of success.

> **EXAMPLE**
> The inventory reorder decisions faced by most businesses are frequently quantified and automated. Inventory control software includes decision algorithms that outline the computations to perform and the steps to take when quantities in inventory are running low. Computing *economic order points* and quantities is a typical example. Thus, one way that information systems can support structured decisions is by quantifying and automating a decision-making process. In other cases, prespecified information products such as periodic reports can provide most of the information needed by a decision maker faced with a structured decision situation.

Unstructured Decisions

Unstructured decisions (also called nonprogrammable decisions) involve decision situations where it is not possible or desirable to specify in advance most of the decision procedures to follow. Many decision situations in the real world are unstructured because they are subject to too many random or changeable events or involve too many unknown factors or relationships. At most, many decision situations are **semistructured.** That is, some decision procedures can be pre-specified, but not enough to lead to a definite recommended decision.

> **EXAMPLE**
> Decisions involved in starting a new line of products or making major changes to employee benefits would probably range from unstructured to semistructured. The many unknown or changeable factors involved would require a less-structured approach leading to subjective judgments by managers.

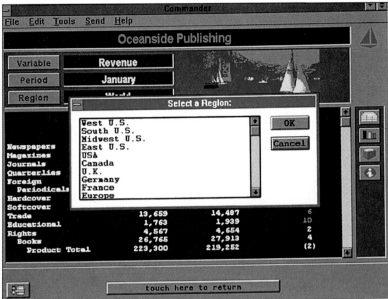

FIGURE 10.5
Using EXPRESS/EIS—a decision support/executive information system package. This analysis of revenue by product and region can help a marketing manager evaluate decision alternatives.

Information systems can support such decisions by providing (1) the ability to make ad hoc inquiries for information in company databases and (2) the ability to reach a decision in an interactive process using a decision support system.

As we mentioned in Chapter 2, decision support systems and expert systems can give managers such assistance. Models of business operations can be developed with decision support software, including advanced statistical, management science, and modeling packages, or less-complex spreadsheet programs. These *packages* and models can then be used to manipulate information collected in the intelligence stage to develop and evaluate a variety of alternatives. Figure 10.5 is a sales analysis display generated by a popular executive information system with DSS capabilities.

EXAMPLE
An electronic spreadsheet package can be used to build product performance models that incorporate some of the factors and relationships a product manager thinks are important. The product manager can then load the models with appropriate data and ask a series of what-if questions to see the effects on the spreadsheet display of a variety of alternatives. For example, "What would happen to the break-even point if we cut advertising expense by 10, 20, and 25 percent?" Or *goal* seeking questions could be used. For example, "How much would we have to cut fixed costs to get a 10 percent decrease in the break-even point?" As a product manager repeats this process, information is generated that helps develop and evaluate possible decision alternatives pertaining to product performance.

Information for the Choice Stage

Information systems should help managers select a proper course of action from the alternatives developed during the design stage. Of course, this assumes that enough information was gathered during the intelligence phase and a sufficient number of alternatives were developed and evaluated during the design stage. If not, the manager may choose to return to those stages for more data or alternatives.

However, given the time and resource constraints of the real world, most decision makers will choose to sacrifice rather than optimize when faced with a decision situation. That is, they will rarely act as rational economic beings who insist that all relevant information be gathered, that all rational alternatives be considered, and that only the optimum alternative be chosen. Instead, they will act with what Simon calls *bounded rationality*. That is, they will be satisfied to make a decision based on incomplete information and a limited number of alternatives, if it meets some of their subjective preferences and produces an acceptable level of results. We will discuss this topic further in the next chapter, when we discuss how humans process information.

In any case, information systems can help managers in the choice stage in several ways. Managers can be provided with summarized and organized information emphasizing the main points (such as major assumptions, resource requirements, and expected results) of each decision alternative. Various financial and marketing ratios and other methods can also be used to prioritize alternatives and thus help managers select the best course of action.

> **EXAMPLE**
> An information system can provide calculations of the net present value, internal rate of return, and payback period to rank several competing proposals from a financial point of view. Other criteria, such as expected market share, number of new personnel required, and training requirements, could also be used to rank alternatives.

Information for the Implementation Stage

The implementation stage involves accomplishing activities that implement the decision alternative selected during the choice stage. It also involves monitoring the success of the decision after it is implemented. Information systems can help managers monitor the successful implementation of a decision. They can provide feedback about business operations affected by the decision that was made. This helps a manager assess a decision's success or failure and determine whether follow-up decisions are needed.

> **EXAMPLE**
> If a decision to cut promotion costs is made, a sales manager can monitor the decision's effects on sales activity. If a larger drop in sales occurs than was expected, the manager must then decide what actions to take to correct the problem. The decision-making process then begins all over again.

Information Quality

What characteristics make information meaningful and useful to managers? What qualities give it value for end users? One way to answer these important questions is to examine the characteristics or attributes of **information quality**. Information that is outdated, inaccurate, or hard to understand would not be very meaningful, use-

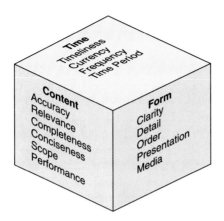

FIGURE 10.6
A summary of the attributes of
information quality. This outlines the attributes that should
be present in high-quality information products.

Time Dimension	
Timeliness	Information should be provided when it is needed
Currency	Information should be up-to-date when it is provided
Frequency	Information should be provided as often as needed
Time Period	Information can be provided about past, present, and future time periods

Content Dimension	
Accuracy	Information should be free from errors
Relevance	Information should be related to the information needs of a specific recipient for a specific situation
Completeness	All the information that is needed should be provided
Conciseness	Only the information that is needed should be provided
Scope	Information can have a broad or narrow scope, or an internal or external focus
Performance	Information can reveal performance by measuring activities accomplished, progress made, or resources accumulated

Form Dimension	
Clarity	Information should be provided in a form that is easy to understand
Detail	Information can be provided in detail or summary form
Order	Information can be arranged in a predetermined sequence
Presentation	Information can be presented in narrative, numeric, graphic, or other forms
Media	Information can be provided in the form of printed paper documents, video displays, or other media

ful, or valuable to managers. They want information of high quality, that is, information products whose characteristics, attributes, or qualities help make it valuable
to them. It is useful to think of information as having the three dimensions of time,
content, and form. Figure 10.6 summarizes the important attributes of information
and groups them into these three dimensions. Let's take a closer took at each of
them.

Information is frequently time sensitive. Making good decisions in day-to-day living,
working, and managing requires information when we need it (timeliness) as often
as we need it (frequency), and that is up-to-date when we receive it (currency).
That's why the **time dimension** of information is so important. Thus, information
systems can be designed to provide information whenever we want it (demand

The Time Dimension

reporting), whenever specified conditions occur (*exception* reporting), or at regular time intervals (*periodic* reporting). For example, a department store could have a sales transaction processing system that captures data on POS terminals and immediately updates sales files. Sales analysis information could then be provided to managers at executive workstations whenever they want it, whenever sales are above or below certain levels, or at the start of each business day. We will discuss information systems with these capabilities further in the next section.

Another time dimension attribute that is very important is the time *period* that the information describes. Information is frequently needed about past, present, and future time periods. For example, managers must be provided with information that helps them recognize and evaluate the impact of future trends. It is not enough to provide managers with historical (backward-looking) information and analysis. Future (forward-looking) information and analysis concerning trends developing inside the organization or in the business environment must also be provided. For example, an analysis of *past sales* performance may not provide management with adequate information. Sales management reports should also provide forecasts of *expected* trends in sales and in factors that might affect sales performance. Thus, future information is also known as planning information, since it results in forecasts, schedules, budgets, and plans for an organization.

The Content Dimension

The **content dimension** of information is usually considered its most important attribute. For example, what good is information that is attractive and timely if it is also wrong? Thus, accuracy is a vital attribute. However, if information is correct but not really related to one's information needs, then it is not relevant, and not very valuable. Also, even if information is accurate and relevant, it may be inadequate because it is incomplete. Thus, *completeness* is important, as is *conciseness*. The tendency of computer-based information systems to flood managers with unnecessary information must be restrained.

Information must frequently reveal the performance attained by individuals or organizations. Therefore, information can be provided about the *activities accomplished* during a specific period, such as last week's sales results. Or information could be provided about the *progress made* toward specified objectives or standards. For example, information could show the progress made in meeting sales forecasts or project schedules. This is related to the concept of *status* information, since information can reveal the status of a construction project or of a department's efforts to stay within its operating budget. It is also related to the concept of *exception* reporting, which reports information only if performance falls above or below specified levels. Finally, information about performance frequently reveals the *resources accumulated* by individuals or organizations at a point in time. For example, businesses need information on the quality and quantity of their financial assets, plant and equipment, product inventories, personnel, and other resources.

The Form Dimension

The **form dimension** of information emphasizes that information must be attractive and easy to understand and use. This dimension has been slighted by information systems in the past. There was greater emphasis on producing accurate and complete information (the content dimension) in a timely manner (the time dimension). However, there is now a greater appreciation that information that is unattractive or difficult to understand may not be used properly. So there is a new emphasis on improving the user interface and the *packaging* of information products to make them more attractive and usable for end users.

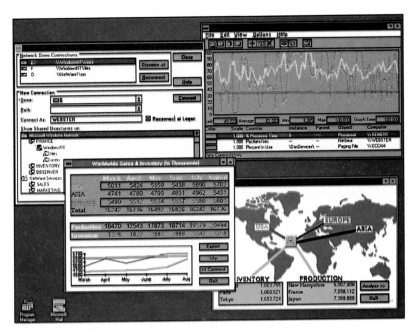

Courtesy of Microsoft Inc.

FIGURE 10.7
This sales management display uses a variety of forms to present information to sales managers.

For example, an information system can produce (1) *detailed* listings of all sales transactions, (2) sales product summary reports, which show only sales totals for each product, or (3) more condensed executive summary reports, which show sales totals by each department in a retail store. The *level of detail* needed depends on the information needs of a particular end user. Thus, salespersons might want a detailed listing of the sales they made, while department managers might be satisfied with product summaries of sales activity for their departments.

The way information is presented is also vital to its comprehension and use. High-quality information must therefore be properly presented using narrative, numeric, or graphics forms of presentation. For example, a good sales report to management should probably be a mix of narrative background information, numeric totals of sales results, and graphics displays of sales trends. See Figure 10.7.

Recent developments in graphics software, desktop publishing, and multimedia systems like interactive video have made it a lot easier for microcomputer users to present information properly. High-quality information can now be presented in a medium that is easy for people to access, understand, and use in their work activities. That is why video displays have become so popular, voice response systems are commonplace, multimedia presentations are growing, and printed reports and documents have been made more attractive for end users.

GTE Corporation: Data Warehousing for Decision Making

"I need a complete report on Hispanic households with a median income of less than $40,000 that generated more than $50 per month in telephone toll revenue during the third quarter of 1994."

That's exactly the kind of information a product manager needs to determine the viability of a new service or product offering. It's also the kind of query that might have taken GTE's Telephone Operations unit weeks to execute. Data from a variety of different sources would have to be accessed, integrated, and reconciled. And, in the end, all that work would have been done to satisfy a single request.

But no more. GTE's business managers can now get information requests answered fast because their enterprise data warehouse allows them to draw from a variety of disparate data sources. That's not only convenient, it's essential in the intensely competitive world of telecommunications services.

"If we can get data delivered to decision makers more quickly, we can beat the competition," says Perry Kosieniak, a senior application consultant.

The distinction between operational and decision-making needs was a key factor in GTE's move to data warehousing. While existing applications and infrastructure may be adequate to support day-to-day functions such as order taking and billing, they are often insufficient for strategic decision making.

"Decision making usually requires integration of data across multiple subject areas, such as customers, network usage and billing," says Kosieniak. "It may also require the use of sources outside the existing application environment, such as zip code tables or demographic data."

There are performance issues which also distinguish the two types of data management. Operations systems such as online transaction processing tend to place a fairly consistent burden on computing resources. Online query processing, on the other hand, tends to be unpredictable, with periods of tense activity alternating with periods of minimal use.

"You don't want to suddenly submit a large query to an operational server," says Kosieniak. "Not only could you get a slow response, but you may also adversely affect the performance of your operational system." By providing two distinct infrastructures for legacy systems and decision making, GTE can tailor each environment to meet specific needs.

Down the road, however, GTE plans to use a data warehouse to supplement some of its operational applications, such as customer profiling.

Speedier decision making isn't the only benefit that GTE expects to realize from its data warehouse solution. They also expect to increase the efficiency of both IT and the business units. On the IT side, the need for numerous staffers to service the constant stream of data requests is being significantly diminished. "With the data warehouse, you make available resources [that were] previously committed to extraction, replication and reporting," says Susan Guess, another GTE application consultant.

By improving these processes, GTE can reduce its costs and thereby lessen the need for outside contractors. The cost reductions enable the company to offer its own services at lower rates, which is essential to maintaining its competitive position.

On the business side, staff resources can be used more efficiently. "People in the business functions utilize querying tools as well," says Guess, "and they can spend a lot of time trying to obtain the data they need." Now they can focus on their real jobs, she says, to analyze and respond to decision data, rather than struggle to access it.

CASE STUDY QUESTIONS

1. What stages of decision making and management functions and roles are supported by GTE's data warehouse systems?

2. What other decision-making considerations are offered in this case?

3. What are the business benefits of GTE's data warehouse systems?

Source: "GTE Empowers Decision Makers" in "Shedding Light on Data Warehousing," Special Advertising Supplement, *Computerworld*, February 13, 1995, p. DW18. Copyright 1995 by Computerworld, Inc., Framingham, MA 01701—Reprinted from *Computerworld.*

SECTION II
Management Information and Support Systems

Previous chapters of this text have emphasized that information systems can support the diverse information and decision-making needs of managers. Figure 10.8 emphasizes the differing conceptual focuses of major types of information systems. In this section, we will explore in more detail how this is accomplished by management information, decision support, and executive information systems. We will concentrate our attention on how these information technologies have significantly strengthened the role information systems play in supporting the decision-making activities of managerial end users. See Figure 10.9.

Type of Information System	Focus
Expert systems	Knowledge—from experts
Decision support systems	Decisions—interactive support
Executive information systems	Information—for executives
Management information systems	Information—for managerial end users
Transaction processing systems	Data—from business operations

FIGURE 10.8
The differing focuses of major types of information systems.

Steve Niedorf/The Image Bank.

FIGURE 10.9
Every manager relies on information systems for information and decision support.

FIGURE 10.10
The management information
system concept. Note especially
that periodic, exception, and
demand reports and responses
are the information products
produced for managers by this
type of information system.

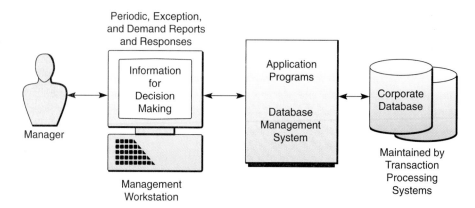

Management Information Systems

Management information systems, also called *information reporting systems,* were the original type of management support systems, and they are still a major category of information systems. MIS produce information products that support many of the day-to-day decision-making needs of management. Reports, displays, and responses produced by such systems provide information that managers have specified in advance as adequately meeting their information needs. Such predefined information products satisfy the information needs of managers at the operational and tactical levels of the organization who are faced with more structured types of decision situations. For example, sales managers rely heavily on sales analysis reports to evaluate differences in performance among salespeople who sell the same types of products to the same types of customers. They have a pretty good idea of the kinds of information about sales results they need to manage sales performance effectively.

Figure 10.10 illustrates the components of a management information system. Managers can receive information at their workstations that supports their decision-making activities. This information takes the form of periodic, exception, and demand reports and immediate responses to inquiries. Application programs and database management software provide access to information in the corporate databases of the organization. Remember, these databases are maintained by transaction processing systems. Data about the business environment is obtained from external databases when necessary.

Management Reporting Alternatives

Management information systems provide a variety of information products to managers. The three major reporting alternatives provided by such systems are summarized below. See Figure 10.11.

- **Periodic scheduled reports.** This traditional form of providing information to managers uses a prespecified format designed to provide managers with information on a regular basis. Typical examples of such periodic scheduled reports are weekly sales analysis reports and monthly financial statements.
- **Exception reports.** In some cases, reports are produced only when exceptional conditions occur. In other cases, reports are produced periodically but contain information only about these exceptional conditions. For example, a credit manager can be provided with a report that contains information only on customers who exceed their credit limits. Such exception reporting promotes management *by exception,* instead of overwhelming management with periodic detailed reports of business activity.

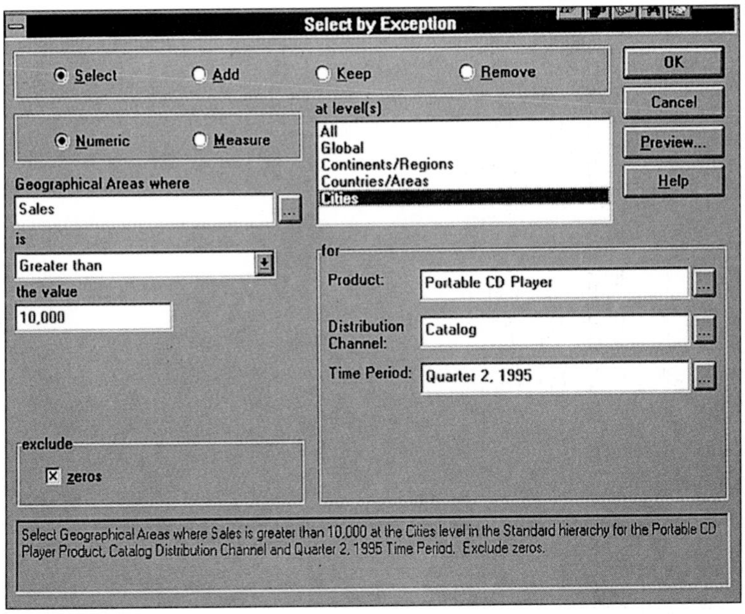

Courtesy of Information Resouces, Inc.

FIGURE 10.11
An example of how the ExpressView function of the Express/EIS package helps managers do exception analysis and reporting.

- **Demand reports and responses.** Information is provided whenever a manager demands it. For example, DBMS query languages and report generators allow managers at online workstations to get immediate responses or reports as a result of their requests for information. Thus, managers do not have to wait for periodic reports to arrive as scheduled.

Online Analytical Processing

The competitive and dynamic nature of today's global business environment is driving demands by business managers and analysts for information systems that can provide fast answers to complex business queries. The IS industry has responded to these demands with developments like the analytical databases, data warehouses, and multidimensional database structures introduced in Chapter 7, and with specialized servers and software products that support **online analytical processing** (OLAP). Online analytical processing is a capability of management, decision support, and executive information systems that enables managers and analysts to interactively examine and manipulate large amounts of detailed and consolidated data from many perspectives. OLAP involves analyzing complex relationships among thousands or even millions of data items stored in multidimensional databases to discover patterns, trends, and exception conditions. An OLAP session takes place online in realtime, with rapid responses to a manager's or analyst's queries, so that their analytical or decision making process is undisturbed [9]. See Figure 10.12.

Online analytical processing involves several basic analytical operations, including consolidation, "drill-down," and "slicing and dicing" [9]. See Figure 10.13.

- **Consolidation.** Consolidation involves the aggregation of data. This can involve simple roll-ups or complex groupings involving interrelated data. For example, sales offices can be rolled up to districts and districts rolled up to regions.

FIGURE 10.12
Online analytical processing may involve the use of specialized servers and multidimensional databases. OLAP provides fast answers to complex queries posed by managers and analysts using management, decision support, and executive information systems.

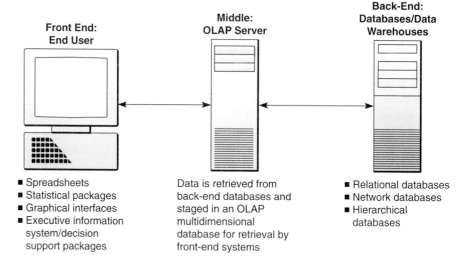

Front End:
End User

- Spreadsheets
- Statistical packages
- Graphical interfaces
- Executive information system/decision support packages

Middle:
OLAP Server

Data is retrieved from back-end databases and staged in an OLAP multidimensional database for retrieval by front-end systems

Back-End:
Databases/Data Warehouses

- Relational databases
- Network databases
- Hierarchical databases

FIGURE 10.13
An example of a display produced by an online analytical processing package.

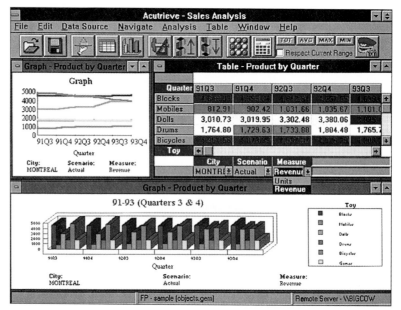

Courtesy of Kenan Systems, Inc.

- **Drill-Down.** OLAP can go in the reverse direction and automatically display detail data that comprises consolidated data. This is called drill-downs. For example, the sales by individual products or sales reps that make up a region's sales totals could be easily accessed.

- **Slicing and Dicing.** Slicing and dicing refers to the ability to look at the database from different viewpoints. One slice of the sales database might show all sales of product type within regions. Another slice might show all sales by sales channel within each product type. Slicing and dicing is often performed along a time axis in order to analyze trends and find patterns.

┌─── **EXAMPLE**
│ A marketing manager or analyst might use online analytical processing to
│ access a multidimensional database consisting of sales data that has been
│ aggregated by region, product type, and sales channel. In a typical OLAP
│ query, a manager might access a multigigabyte/multiyear sales database in
│ order to find all product sales in each region for each product type. After
│ reviewing the results, the manager might refine his or her query to find the
│ sales volume for each marketing channel within each sales region and product
│ classification. Finally, the marketing manager might perform quarter-to-quar-
│ ter or year-to-year comparisons for each marketing channel.

In summary, online analytical processing can provide rapid responses to complex queries for managers and analysts using management, decision support, or
executive information systems. OLAP applications:

- Access very large amounts of data—for example, several years of sales data in
  a data warehouse.
- Analyze the relationships between many types of business elements—such as
  sales, products, regions, and channels.
- Involve aggregated data—examples are sales volumes, budgeted dollars, and
  dollars spent in a region.
- Compare aggregated data over hierarchical time periods—monthly, quarterly,
  yearly, and the like.
- Present data in different perspectives—such as sales by region versus sales by
  channels and by product within each region.
- Involve complex calculations between data elements. For example, expected
  profits can be calculated as a function of sales revenue for each type of sales
  channel in a particular region.
- Are able to respond quickly to user requests so that managers or analysts can
  pursue an analytical or decision thought process without being hindered by
  the system [9].

Decision Support Systems

Decision support systems are a major category of management support systems.
They are computer-based information systems that provide interactive information
support to managers during the decision-making process. Decision support systems
use (1) analytical models, (2) specialized databases, (3) a decision maker's own
insights and judgments, and (4) an interactive, computer-based modeling process to
support the making of semistructured and unstructured decisions by individual
managers. Therefore, they are designed to be ad hoc, quick-response systems that
are initiated and controlled by managerial end users. Decision support systems are
thus able to directly support the specific types of decisions and the personal decision-making styles and needs of individual managers [24].

Management Reporting versus Decision-Making Support

Management information systems focus on providing managers with prespecified
information products that report on the performance of the organization. Decision
support systems, however, focus on providing information interactively to support
specific types of decisions by individual managers. Managers at the tactical and

	Management Information Systems	Decision Support Systems
Information Provided		
Information form and frequency	Periodic, exception, and demand reports and responses	Interactive inquiries and responses
Information format	Prespecified, fixed format	Ad hoc, flexible, and adaptable format
Information processing methodology	Information produced by extraction and manipulation of operational data	Information produced by analytical modeling of operational and external data
Decision Support Provided		
Type of support	Provide information about the performance of the organization	Provide information, and decision support techniques to confront specific problems or opportunities
Stages of decision-making supported	Support the intelligence and implementation stages of decision making	Support the intelligence, design, choice, and implementation stages of decision making
Types of decisions supported	Structured decisions for operational and tactical planning and control	Semistructured and unstructured decisions for tactical and strategic planning and control
Type of decision maker supported	Indirect support designed for many managers	Direct support tailored to the decision-making styles of individual managers

strategic levels of an organization need ad hoc types of information products to support their planning and control responsibilities. Decision support systems help such managers solve the typical semistructured and unstructured problems they face in the real world. In contrast, management information systems are designed to indirectly support the more structured types of decisions involved in operational and tactical planning and control.

Figure 10.14 summarizes and contrasts the differences between decision support and management information systems. Note that the objective of decision support systems is to provide information and decision support techniques needed to solve specific problems or pursue specific opportunities. In contrast, the objective of management information systems is to provide information about the performance of basic organizational functions and processes, such as marketing, manufacturing, and finance. Thus, decision support systems have a much more specific role in the decision-making process. Note also that a DSS is designed to support all four stages (intelligence, design, choice, and implementation) of decision making. Management information systems, on the other hand, are designed to provide information for the intelligence phase, which starts the decision-making process, and the implementation stage, which monitors its success.

> **EXAMPLE**
> An example might help at this point. Sales managers, typically, rely on management information systems to produce sales analysis reports. These reports contain sales performance figures by product line, salesperson, sales region, and so on. A decision support system, on the other hand, would also interactively show a sales manager the effects on sales performance of changes in a variety of factors (such as promotion expense and salesperson compensation). The DSS could then use several criteria (such as expected gross margin and market share) to evaluate and rank several alternative combinations of sales performance factors.

Examples of DSS Applications

Decision support systems are used for a variety of applications in both business and government. When a DSS is developed to solve large or complex problems that continually face an organization, it is called an *institutional* DSS. Decision support systems used for strategic corporate planning are an example of this type of DSS. Other DSS applications are developed quickly to solve smaller or less-complex problems that may be one-time situations facing a manager. These are called *ad hoc* DSS. Also, many decision support systems are developed to support the types of decisions faced by a specific industry (such as the airline, banking, or automotive industry) or by a specific functional area (such as marketing, finance, or manufacturing). Let's take a brief look at three examples to demonstrate the variety of DSS applications.

Airline DSS

The American Analytical Information Management System (AAIMS) is a decision support system used in the airline industry. It was developed by American Airlines but is used by other airlines, aircraft manufacturers, airline financial analysts, consultants, and associations. AAIMS supports a variety of airline decisions by analyzing data collected on airline aircraft utilization, seating capacity and utilization, and traffic statistics. For example, it produces forecasts of airline market share, revenue, and profitability. Thus, AAIMS helps airline management make decisions on aircraft assignments, route requests, ticket classifications, pricing, and so on [24].

Another successful decision support system for American Airlines is its *yield management* system. This DSS helps managers and analysts decide how much to overbook and how to set prices for each seat so that a plane is filled up and profits are maximized. American's yield management system deals with more than 250 decision variables. The system is estimated to generate up to 5 percent of American Airlines' revenue [3].

Real Estate DSS

RealPlan is a DSS used in the real estate industry to do complex analyses of investments in commercial real estate. For example, investing in commercial real estate properties, typically, involves highly detailed income, expense, and cash flow projections. RealPlan easily performs such analyses, even for properties with multiple units, lease terms, rents, and cost-of-living adjustments. Since RealPlan can also make forecasts of property values up to 40 years into the future, it helps decision makers not only with acquisition decisions but with real estate improvement and divestment decisions as well [25].

Geographic DSS

Geographic information systems (GIS) are a special category of DSS that integrate computer graphics and geographic databases with other DSS features. A geographic information system is a DSS that constructs and displays maps and other graphics

FIGURE 10.15
Using a geographic information system package for decision support.

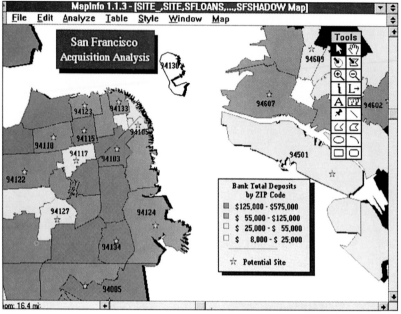

Courtesy of MapInfo, Inc.

displays that support decisions affecting the geographic distribution of people and other resources. Many companies are using GIS technology to choose new retail store locations, optimize distribution routes, or analyze the demographics of their target audiences. For example, companies like Levi Strauss, Arby's, Consolidated Rail, and Federal Express use GIS packages to integrate maps, graphics, and other geographic data with business data from spreadsheets and statistical packages. GIS software for microcomputers such as MapInfo and Atlas GIS are used for most business GIS applications. The use of the GIS for decision support should accelerate now that mapping capabilities have been integrated in the latest versions of spreadsheet packages such as Lotus 1-2-3 and Microsoft Excel [4, 15]. See Figure 10.15.

Components of a Decision Support System

Figure 10.16 illustrates the **components of a DSS** present in any decision support system. Note the hardware, software, data, model, and people resources needed to provide interactive decision support for managers. Let's first outline the functions of these components and then discuss DSS model and software requirements in more detail.

- **Hardware resources.** Personal computer workstations provide the primary hardware resource for a DSS. They can be used on a stand-alone basis, but are typically connected by wide area or local area networks to other computer systems for access to other DSS software, model, and data resources.
- **Software resources.** DSS software packages (DSS generators) contain software modules to manage DSS databases, decision models, and end user/system dialogue.
- **Data resources.** A DSS database contains data and information extracted from the databases of the organization, external databases, and a manager's

FIGURE 10.16
The decision support system concept. Note that hardware, software, data, model, and people resources provide interactive decision support for managers.

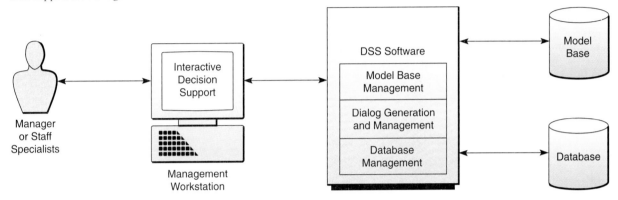

personal databases. It includes summarized data and information most needed by managers for specific types of decisions.

- **Model resources.** The model *base* includes a library of mathematical models and analytical techniques stored as programs, subroutines, spreadsheets, and command files.
- **People resources.** A DSS can be used by managers or their staff specialists to explore decision alternatives. Decision support systems can also be developed by such end users. However, the development of large or complex decision support systems and DSS generator software packages, typically, is left to information systems specialists.

Models for Decision Support

Unlike management information systems, decision support systems rely on model bases as well as databases as vital system resources. A DSS **model base** is an organized collection of mathematical models. It includes models developed to support specific decisions as well as general-purpose models. The model base can include models representing simple computational and analytical routines, or models that mathematically express complex relationships among many variables.

For example, models might express simple accounting relationships among variables, such as Revenue − Expenses = Profit. Or the DSS model base could include models and analytical techniques used to express much more complex relationships among variables. For example, it might contain linear programming models, multiple regression forecasting models, and capital budgeting present value models. Such models may be stored in the form of spreadsheet models or templates, programs and program modules, and command files. Model base management software packages can combine models and model components to create integrated models that support specific types of decisions.

Software for Decision Support

The software resources needed by decision support systems must integrate the management and use of the model bases, databases, and dialogue generation capabilities of a decision support system. **DSS software** ranges from special-purpose and full-featured **DSS generators** to more modest electronic spreadsheet and integrated packages.

FIGURE 10.17
The Commander DSS/EIS package provides data and model management and ad hoc querying capabilities to help managers make better business decisions.

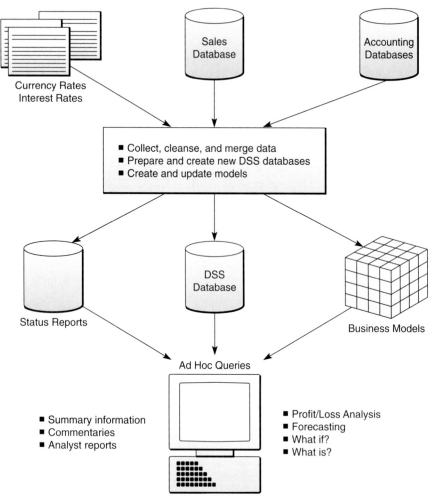

Source: Adapted from *Commander EIS: Delivering the Complete Solution* (Ann Arbor, MI: Comshare, 1993), p. 8.

Figure 10.17 illustrates the DSS capabilities of Commander EIS, a popular DSS/EIS generator. Notice how it extracts data from a variety of sources to create a DSS database, creates and updates business models, and provides a variety of ad hoc query and reporting capabilities. DSS software packages (such as IFPS/PLUS, ENCORE, STRATEGEM, and System W) or DSS/EIS packages (such as Express/EIS and Commander EIS) are available from independent consulting firms and computer manufacturers. Many are now available in microcomputer versions (e.g., PC/FOCUS, IFPS Personal, and ENCORE). In addition, statistical software packages (such as the SAS System and SPSS-X) are used as DSS generators for decision support that requires extensive statistical analysis.

DSS and Electronic Spreadsheets

Don't forget that electronic **spreadsheet packages** (such as Lotus 1-2-3, Excel, and Quattro Pro) are limited DSS generators. They provide some of the model building (spreadsheet models), analytical modeling (what-if and *goal* seeking analysis), database management, and dialogue management (menus, icons, and prompts)

FIGURE 10.18
An example of a simple spreadsheet.

	1994	1995	1996	Total	Average
ABC Company: Financial Performance					
Revenue	$1,000.00	$1,100.00	$1,200.00	$3,300.00	$1,100.00
Expenses	$600.00	$660.00	$720.00	$1,980.00	$660.00
Profit	$400.00	$440.00	$480.00	$1,320.00	$440.00
Taxes	$160.00	$176.00	$192.00	$528.00	$176.00
Profit after taxes	$240.00	$264.00	$288.00	$792.00	$264.00

FIGURE 10.19
These formulas and functions constitute the spreadsheet model for the spreadsheet in Figure 10.18.

	1994	1995	1996	Total	Average
ABC Company: Financial Performance					
Revenue	(C5)	(C5*(1.1)	(C5*(1.2)	@SUM(C5..E	@AVG(C5..E
Expenses	(C5*0.6)	(D5*0.6)	(E5*0.6)	(F5*0.6)	@AVG(C6..E
Profit	(C5–C6)	(D5–D6)	(E5–E6)	(F5–F6)	@TB1CD:
Taxes	(C8*0.4)	(D8*0.4)	(E8*0.4)	(F8*0.4)	@AVG(C9..E
Profit after taxes	(C8–C9)	(D8–D9)	(E8–E9)	(F8–F9)	@AVG(C11..E

offered by more powerful DSS generators. For example, we have discussed several times how a product manager could use a spreadsheet package to support his or her decision making.

An electronic spreadsheet package allows you to build models by entering the data and relationships (formulas) of a problem into the columns and rows of a worksheet format. Then you can do what-if analysis by making a variety of changes to data and formulas and visually evaluating the results of such changes either in worksheet or graphics displays. Spreadsheet programs provide many commands to manipulate the worksheet and also include built-in functions that perform common arithmetic, statistical, and financial computations needed for decision support. Figures 10.18, 10.19 and 10.20 provide examples of a simple spreadsheet, the formulas and functions that constitute the spreadsheet model, and graphics generated by the spreadsheet package.

An electronic spreadsheet package is a valuable tool for both business analysis and decision support. It can be used to solve problems that require the comparison, projection, or evaluation of alternatives. Therefore, spreadsheets are used for many

FIGURE 10.20
Examples of a bar graph and a pie chart of the data in the spreadsheet shown in Figure 10.18.

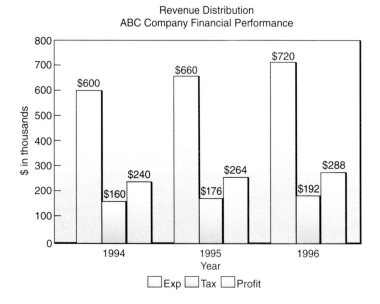

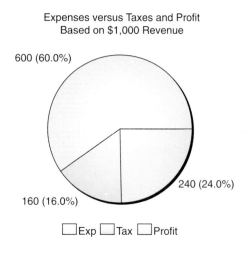

applications. Typical business uses include sales forecasting, profit and loss analysis, product pricing, investment analysis, budget development, cash flow analysis, financial statement preparation, construction bidding, real estate investment, and bank loan analysis.

Using Decision Support Systems

Using a decision support system involves an interactive **analytical modeling** process. Typically, a manager or staff specialist uses a DSS software package at his or her workstation. This allows managers to make inquiries and responses and issue commands using a keyboard, an electronic mouse, a touch screen, or possibly voice input. Output is typically in the form of text and graphics visual displays, but printed reports may be produced.

For example, using a DSS software package for decision support may result in a series of displays in response to alternative what-if changes keyed in by a manager. This differs from the demand responses of information reporting systems, since managers are not demanding prespecified information. Rather, they are exploring possible alternatives. Thus, they do not have to specify their information needs in advance. Instead, the DSS interactively helps them find the information they need to make a decision. That is the essence of the decision support system concept.

Analytical Modeling Alternatives

Using a decision support system involves four basic types of analytical modeling activities: (1) what-if analysis, (2) sensitivity analysis, (3) goal seeking analysis, and (4) optimization analysis [19]. Let's briefly look at each type of analytical modeling that can be used for decision support. See Figure 10.21.

What-if Analysis

In **what-if analysis,** an end user makes changes to variables, or relationships among variables, and observes the resulting changes in the values of other variables. As we mentioned earlier, a spreadsheet user might change a revenue amount (a variable) or

Type of Analytical Modeling	Activities and Examples
What-if analysis	Observing how changes to selected variables affect other variables. *Example:* What if we cut advertising by 10 percent? What whould happen to sales?
Sensitivity analysis	Observing how repeated changes to a single variable affect other variables. *Example:* Let's cut advertising by $100 repeatedly so we can see its relationship to sales.
Goal seeking analysis	Making repeated changes to selected variables until a chosen variable reaches a target value. *Example:* Let's try increases in advertising until sales reach $1 million.
Optimization analysis	Finding an optimum value for selected variables, given certain constraints. *Example:* What's the best amount of advertising to have, given our budget and choice of media?

FIGURE 10.21
Activities and examples of the major types of analytical modeling.

a tax rate formula (a relationship among variables) in a simple financial spreadsheet model. Then he or she could command the spreadsheet program to instantly recalculate all affected variables in the spreadsheet. A managerial user would be very interested in observing and evaluating any changes that occurred to the values in the spreadsheet, especially to a variable such as net profit after taxes. To many managers, net profit after taxes is an example of the bottom line, that is, a key factor in making many types of decisions. This type of analysis would be repeated until the manager was satisfied with what the results revealed about the effects of various possible decisions. Figure 10.22 is an example of what-if analysis.

Sensitivity analysis

Sensitivity analysis is a special case of what-if analysis. Typically, the value of only one variable is changed repeatedly, and the resulting changes on other variables are observed. So sensitivity analysis is really a case of what-if analysis involving repeated changes to only one variable at a time. Some DSS packages automatically make repeated small changes to a variable when asked to perform sensitivity analysis. Typically, sensitivity analysis is used when decision makers are uncertain about the assumptions made in estimating the value of certain key variables. In our previous spreadsheet example, the value of revenue could be changed repeatedly in small increments, and the effects on other spreadsheet variables observed and evaluated. This would help a manager understand the impact of various revenue levels on other factors involved in decisions being considered.

Goal Seeking Analysis

Goal seeking analysis reverses the direction of the analysis done in what-if and sensitivity analysis. Instead of observing how changes in a variable affect other variables, goal seeking analysis (also called *how* can analysis) sets a target value (a goal) for a variable and then repeatedly changes other variables until the target value is achieved. For example, a manager could specify a target value (goal) of $2 million for net profit after taxes for a business venture. Then he or she could repeatedly change the value of revenue or expenses in a spreadsheet model until a result of $2 million is achieved. The manager would discover what amount of revenue or level of expenses the business venture needs to achieve in order to reach the goal of $2

FIGURE 10.22
This example shows how what-if analysis done using Microsoft Excel is imported into a Microsoft Word document to prepare reports for management.

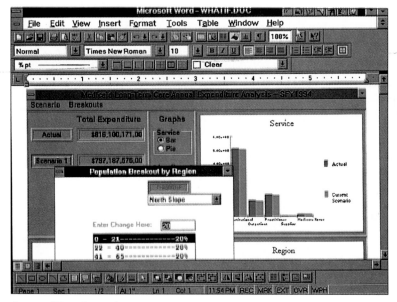

Courtesy of Kenan Systems, Inc.

million in after-tax profits. Therefore, this form of analytical modeling would help answer the question, "How can we achieve $2 million in net profit after taxes?" instead of the question, "What happens if we change revenue or expenses?" Thus, goal seeking analysis is another important method of decision support.

Optimization Analysis

Optimization analysis is a more complex extension of goal seeking analysis. Instead of setting a specific target value for a variable, the goal is to find the optimum value for one or more target variables, given certain constraints. Then one or more other variables are changed repeatedly, subject to the specified constraints, until the best values for the target variables are discovered. For example, a manager could try to determine the highest possible level of profits that could be achieved by varying the values for selected revenue sources and expense categories. Changes to such variables could be subject to constraints such as the limited capacity of a production process or limits to available financing. Optimization, typically, is accomplished by special-purpose software packages for optimization techniques such as linear programming, or by advanced DSS generators. The RealPlan DSS, mentioned earlier, is an example of a DSS that uses optimization and sensitivity analysis to support commercial real estate investment decisions.

Executive Information Systems

Executive information systems (EIS) are information systems that combine many of the features of management information systems and decision support systems. However, when they were first developed, their focus was on meeting the strategic information needs of top management. Thus, the first goal of executive information systems was to provide top executives with immediate and easy access to information about a firm's *critical success factors* (CSFs), that is, key factors that are critical to accomplishing an organization's strategic objectives. For example, the executives of a department store chain would probably consider factors such as its sales promotion efforts and its product line mix to be critical to its survival and success.

Studies have shown that top executives get the information they need from many sources. These include letters, memos, periodicals, and reports produced manually or by computer systems. Other major sources of executive information are meetings, telephone calls, and social activities. Thus, much of a top executive's information comes from noncomputer sources. Computer-generated information has not played a major role in meeting many top executives' information needs [17, 26].

Therefore, computer-based executive information systems were developed to meet the information needs of top management that were not being met by other forms of MIS. Executives and IS specialists have capitalized on advances in computer technology to develop attractive, easy-to-use ways to provide executives with the information they need. Software packages are now available that support EIS on mainframe, midsize, and networked microcomputer systems.

Executive information systems are still faced with resistance by some executives, plagued by high costs, and have had many publicized failures. However, the use of executive information systems is growing rapidly. They have spread into the ranks of middle management as more executives come to recognize their feasibility and benefits, and as less-expensive microcomputer-based systems for client/server networks become available.

For example, according to one recent study, 25 percent of the world's corporate executives are likely to be using an EIS [11]. One popular EIS software package reports that only 3 percent of its users are top executives [11]. Another example is the EIS of Conoco, one of the world's largest oil companies. Conoco's EIS is used by most senior managers, and by over 4,000 employees located at corporate headquarters in Houston and throughout the world [2].

Thus, executive information systems are becoming so widely used by managers, analysts, and other knowledge workers that they are sometimes humorously called "everyone's information systems." More popular alternative names are **executive support systems** (ESS), *enterprise information systems* (EIS), or *management support systems* (MSS). These names also reflect the fact that more features, such as DSS and expert system capabilities, electronic mail, and personal productivity aids such as electronic calendars, are being added to many systems to make them more attractive to executives [26, 28]. See Figure 10.23.

Rationale for EIS

As Figure 10.24 illustrates, executive workstations in an EIS are typically networked to mainframe or midsize systems or LAN servers for access to EIS software. The EIS package works with database management and telecommunications software to provide easy access to internal, external, and special management databases (such as multidimensional *analytical databases*) with almost instantaneous response times. Executive information systems provide information about the current status and projected trends in a company's critical success factors, as determined by its executive users. An analytical modeling capability to evaluate alternatives for decision support is also provided by newer EIS packages, as are some expert system features, such as an *explain* capability.

Of course, in an EIS, information is presented in forms tailored to the preferences of the executives using the system. For example, most executive information systems stress the use of a graphical user interface and graphics displays that can be customized to the information preferences of executives using the EIS. Other

Components of an EIS

FIGURE 10.23
Capabilities of executive information and support systems.

Executive Information Systems (EIS)
- Are tailored to individual executive users.
- Extract, filter, compress, and track critical data.
- Provide online status access, trend analysis, exception reporting, and "drill-down" capabilities.
- Access and integrate a broad range of internal and external data.
- Are user-friendly and require minimal or no training to use.
- Are used directly by executives without intermediaries.
- Present graphical, tabular, and/or textual information.

Executive Support Systems (ESS)
- Are EIS with additional capabilities.
- Support electronic communications (e.g., E-mail, computer conferencing, and word processing).
- Provide data analysis capabilities (e.g., spreadsheets, query languages, and decision support systems).
- Include personal productivity tools (e.g., electronic calendars, rolodex, and tickler files).

FIGURE 10.24
The executive information system concept. Note the hardware, software, and data resources involved.

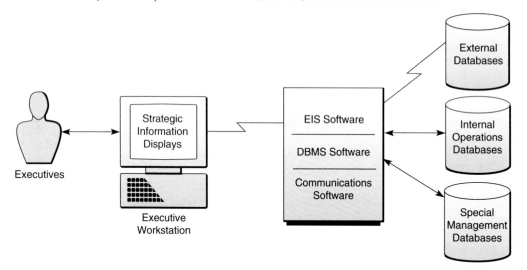

information presentation methods used by an EIS include exception reporting and trend analysis. The ability to drill down, which allows executives to quickly retrieve displays of related information at lower levels of detail, is another important capability of an EIS [2, 26, 28].

Examples of EIS

Figure 10.25 shows actual displays provided by the Commander executive information system. Notice how simple and brief these displays are. Also note how they provide executives with the ability to drill down quickly to lower levels of detail in areas of particular interest to them. This drill-down capability is related to the hypertext technology (discussed in Chapter 8), which allows end users to interactively retrieve

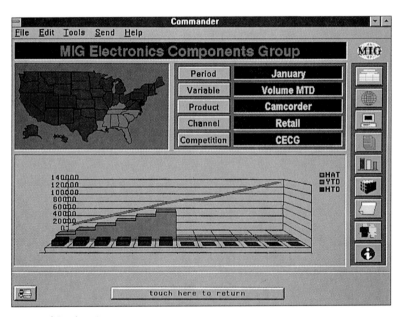

FIGURE 10.25
Displays provided by the Commander executive information system. Note the simplicity and clarity in which key information is provided, and the ability to drill down to lower levels of detail.

related pieces of information from text databases. That is why many EIS packages for microcomputers rely heavily on hypertext technology. Besides the drill-down capability, the Commander also stresses trend analysis and exception reporting. Thus, an executive can quickly discover the direction key factors are heading and the extent to which critical factors are deviating from expected results [7, 26].

FIGURE 10.26
Examples of EIS applications at Conoco.

Crude Oil Hot Key	Earnings Assumptions
U.S. Products Hot Key	DOE Statistics
U.S. Light Oil Spread Hot Key	Daily Market Update
European Light Oil Spread Hot Key	Volumes History
Natural Gas Futures Hot Key	RMS&T Vision Statement
Stocks/Price Relation	RMS&T Additions
RMS&T Industry Comparisons	Product Price Analysis
Market Status	Cash & Earnings Forecast Notes
COS&T Crude Postings	RMS&T Financial Perspectives
API Detail	Profit Objective
API Summary	Safety
RMNA Integrated Margin	Exploratory Wells
Industry Statistical Data	Product Demand
Marketing Update	Current Rack Prices
What's Hot on EIS?	Historical Rack Prices
Snapshot	Refining Indicators
Days Supply	Downstream Maps
API Refinery Capacity	Short-Term Economic Prices
Europe/Singapore Prices	Downstream Key Indicators
WTI vs. Postings	External Earnings Reporting
Organizational Bulletin	Net Cash Flow
EP Earnings	Crude Prices
RMS&T Earnings	Goldbook

Source: Adapted from Lloyd Belcher and Hugh Watson, "Assessing the Value of Conoco's EIS, *MIS Quarterly,* September 1993, p. 245.

As we mentioned earlier, Conoco, Inc., has a widely used EIS. Conoco's EIS is a large system with 75 different applications and hundreds of screen displays. Senior executives and over 4,000 managers and analysts worldwide use EIS applications ranging from analyzing internal operations and financial results to viewing external events that affect the petroleum industry. See Figure 10.26. Conoco's EIS is popular with its users and has resulted in improved employee productivity and decision making, and significant cost savings compared to alternative methods of generating information for managers and analysts [2]. See Figure 10.27.

Another successful EIS, developed by The Promus Companies, is described in detail in one of the Real World Case Studies in Appendix A [11]. Promus calls their EIS a *Management Support System* (MSS) since it combines office automation, decision support, and executive information services needed by managers in the hotel industry. Key factors recommended by Promus and others that should be considered in developing a successful EIS are shown in Figure 10.28.

Group Decision Support Systems

Decision making by groups of people is an important dimension of managerial decision making. In the real world, many decisions are not made by solitary decision makers. Instead, decisions are frequently made by groups of people coming to an agreement on a particular issue. Between these two extremes is a consultative type of decision making, combining both individual and group characteristics. For example, a manager may ask advice from other people individually before making a par-

FIGURE 10.27
Examples of EIS user feedback
at Conoco.

"We used the EIS graphics software to display our prices because no other product on the market can do it as well."—*Manager, Operations Group*

"I don't see the kinds of things you are doing occurring anywhere else in the company."—*Manager, Operations Group*

"I had EIS made accessible to my group so they would have the chance to feel a part of the operations. This has been a big boost to the morale of the group—an unquantifiable value."—*Manager, Service Group*

"EIS has helped break down some of the traditional barriers to interdepartmental information sharing."—*Analyst, Information Systems*

"EIS gives us instant access to information that we need on a daily basis. Previously, getting what we needed was a long and painful process."—*Operations Group*

"Our department is committed to putting necessary work online as much as possible. I'm requiring all my new analysts to learn the EIS software tools."—*Operating Group*

"If we didn't have graphics provided by the EIS, we'd hire someone to do them. I value this tool at $100,000 annually. It has significantly increased our confidence in our trading decisions."—*Manager, Trading Group*

"Based on my use of the statistics in the database, and the decisions affected, I would put a value on the database of $500,000 per year."—*Senior Manager, Planning*

"EIS is a necessary information source that eliminates the need for widespread paper distribution of financial and operational information."—*Manager, Planning & Finance*

"EIS is Conoco expatriates' one consistent and timely link to what is going on in the world of Conoco."—*Manager, Foreign Operating Subsidiary*

Source: Lloyd Belcher and Hugh Watson, "Assessing the Value of Conoco's EIS, *MIS Quarterly,* September 1993, p. 249.

ticular decision. Or the manager may bring a group of people together to discuss an issue but still makes the final decision.

Group Decision Making

Thus, managers are frequently faced with decision-making situations that require interaction with groups of people. Figure 10.29 outlines some of the major factors that affect group decision making. The success of **group decision making** depends on such factors as (1) the characteristics of the group itself, (2) the characteristics of the task on which the group is working, (3) the organizational context in which the group decision-making process takes place, (4) the use of information technology such as electronic meeting systems and group decision support systems, and (5) the communication and decision-making processes the group utilizes [6, 18].

A variety of methodologies and computer-based tools can be used to increase the effectiveness of group decision making. Examples are the brainstorming and nominal group methodologies. *Brainstorming* is the spontaneous contribution of ideas as they occur to members of a group. However, the nominal group technique

FIGURE 10.28
Key factors needed for a successful EIS.

Top Management Involvement and Commitment
Identify a dedicated executive sponsor with a strategic vision for information systems and a commitment to the strategic use of information technology.

Understanding Data Sources
A successful EIS implementation depends on the availability of accurate and complete data. For many organizations, this could mean that a significant investment in existing business systems is needed prior to implementing EIS.

Focusing on What Is Important
Organization CSFs, exception reporting, accessing information with drill-down capability are a key to success of an EIS.

Response Time
A successful EIS will increase in use, functionality, and scope over time. Ongoing system performance monitoring is key.

Understanding of Computer Literacy Level of Executives
Dictates presentation format, degree of use of graphics, text, mouse, touch screen, etc. The EIS must be easy to use.

Learning Curve for Development Team
Tools to be used are key, especially if developing a system. Familiar tools are best. Vendor support for an EIS package is essential.

Flexibility
Executives' needs will continue to evolve and change with time. As much flexibility as possible should be included.

Ongoing Support
EIS cannot be implemented and forgotten. Continuing support is critical to satisfy changing needs.

Source: John Southcott and Bruch Hooey, "EIS Big League Decision Support," *Edge*, November/December 1989, p. 29, and Chris Gibbons, Corrine Chaves, Ronald Wilkes, and Mark Frolick, "Management Support System at Promos," *Information Systems Management*, Summer 1994, p. 55.

FIGURE 10.29
Important factors affecting success of group decision making.

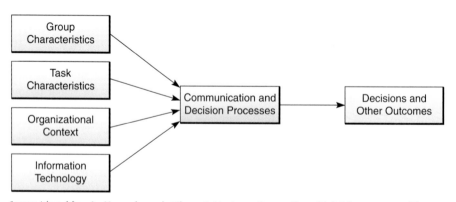

Source: Adapted from Jay Nunamaker et al., "Electronic Meetings to Support Group Work," *Communications of the ACM*, July 1991, p. 44. Copyright © 1991, Association of Computing Machinery, Inc. By permission.

(NGT) has proved to be significantly more effective than traditional or nonstructured methods. It uses four basic steps to reach a group decision [5].

1. The individuals in a group independently generate ideas about a problem or opportunity.
2. Each member of the group presents these ideas without decision and the ideas are listed before the group. This and the previous step are related to Simon's intelligence stage of decision making.
3. The members of the group discuss each idea to clarify and evaluate them. These are activities that correspond to the design stage of decision making.
4. Each individual independently ranks the ideas contributed, and these rankings are pooled to arrive at a group ranking and decision. This is part of the choice stage of the decision-making process.

Information technology can provide a variety of computer-based tools to increase the effectiveness of group decision making. Known generically as *group support systems* (GSS), these technologies include **group decision support systems** (GDSS), electronic meeting systems (EMS), and *computer mediated communications systems* (CMCS) such as electronic media. We discussed these systems in Chapter 8 in the context of work group computing and office automation. Research studies indicate that group support systems produce several important benefits. For example, computer support makes group communications easier, protects the anonymity of participants, and provides a public recording of group communications (*group memory*). This significantly improves the efficiency, creativity, and quality of group decision making in business meetings [6, 14, 18].

GDSS Packages

The unique needs of decision making by groups of people have spawned a variety of software packages for group decision support systems. For example, extensive electronic meeting systems packages are available that support the group decision-making activities that may take place in a computer-based *decision room* setting. Other GDSS software may be designed to support a specific application or task, such as a package for labor/management negotiations or a package that merely supports anonymous voting by members of a group. Figure 10.30 illustrates the group decision-making activities supported by the software tools in the GroupSystems EMS software package developed at the University of Arizona [18]. Figure 10.31 shows a typical EMS/GDSS decision room in action.

Groupware packages that support work group computing activities for members of a work group whose workstations are interconnected by local or wide area networks may also support group decision making. As we mentioned in Chapter 8, these packages are designed to support work group collaboration and communications by providing *computer-based systems for collaborative* work (CSCW) or *distributed group support systems* (DGSS). For example, they can support new product design and decision making, sales proposal preparation, financial planning, and other activities of work groups whose members may be located anywhere in the world [14, 25].

FIGURE 10.30
An example of the use of the software tools in the GroupSystems software package for conducting electronic meetings. Note the various group activities supported by the modules of this GDSS package.

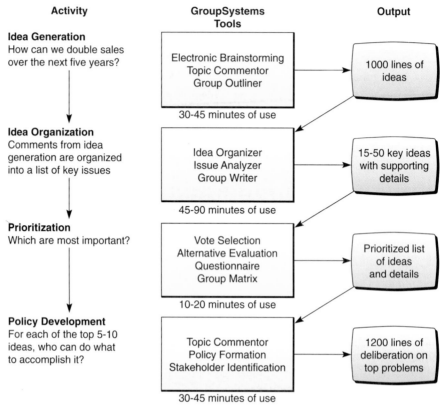

Activity	GroupSystems Tools	Output
Idea Generation How can we double sales over the next five years?	Electronic Brainstorming Topic Commentor Group Outliner *30–45 minutes of use*	1000 lines of ideas
Idea Organization Comments from idea generation are organized into a list of key issues	Idea Organizer Issue Analyzer Group Writer *45–90 minutes of use*	15–50 key ideas with supporting details
Prioritization Which are most important?	Vote Selection Alternative Evaluation Questionnaire Group Matrix *10–20 minutes of use*	Prioritized list of ideas and details
Policy Development For each of the top 5–10 ideas, who can do what to accomplish it?	Topic Commentor Policy Formation Stakeholder Identification *30–45 minutes of use*	1200 lines of deliberation on top problems

Source: Adapted from Jay Nunamaker et al., "Electronic Meetings to Support Group Work," *Communications of the ACM*, July 1991, p. 44. Copyright © 1991, Association for Computing Machinery, Inc. By permission, and H. Chen, P. Hsu, R. Orwig, L. Hoopes, and J.F. Nunamaker, "Automatic Classification from Electronic Meetings," *Communications of the ACM*, October 1994, p. 57.

FIGURE 10.31
Using a group decision support system in a decision room setting.

Courtesy of Ventana Corporation.

R E A L   W O R L D   C A S E

 SABRE Decision Technologies: Airline Decision Support

Like any industry with stiff competition, airline companies must seek innovative ways to create operational efficiency and thus entice and keep customers by ensuring their satisfaction. One of those ways is to employ scheduling software systems that better match supply with demand. These decision support systems (DSS) must take complex data, consumer preferences, and many different scenarios and come up with the most efficient flight schedules. Scheduling systems must consider historical data, all origin and destination market sizes, the airline's hubs, connections, passenger demand, estimated traffic, associated cost data, and each flight's finite number of seats. Complicating matters further is taking into account choices consumers can make.

Two years ago, SABRE Decision Technologies, a unit of AMR's SABRE Group, teamed up the Ansett Australia to develop a DSS called the Airline Profitability Model. SABRE Decision Technologies provides decision support system software packages, systems development, consulting, and automation services for the travel and transportation industry.

How does the Airline Profitability Model work? Steve Clampett, senior vice president at SABRE Decision Technologies, explains: "The system relies on its 'spill and recapture' process, which uses a probabilistic approach to finding preferred alternative routes for passengers." Because airplanes have a finite capacity, not all passengers get their first choice. Says Clampett, "The Airline Profitability Model takes into account that airlines 'protect' seats for higher-revenue passengers and the lower-fare passengers are more likely to have to seek alternative routes because of capacity constraints."

Using sophisticated forecasting algorithms, SABRE Decision Technologies first develops an estimate of the market size for each origin and destination city-pair being considered. This forecast is based on industry data, economic forecasts, and city demographics. The Airline Profitability Model then determines what the market share will be. According to Clampett, the system infers passenger preference (time of day, connections, airport preferences,

type of aircraft desired, etc.) via empirical data extracted from company databases. Other scheduling systems are available, but what makes the Airline Profitability Model unique is its ability to look at entire flight sequences, not just single flight segments, according to Clampett. In addition, its multitasking capabilities let schedulers process many profitability scenarios simultaneously.

The Airline Profitability Model takes six to nine months for calibration for a specific airline and its own data and market characteristics. It runs on a UNIX workstation and has a menu-driven graphical user interface.

Clients of the Airline Profitability Model include Lufthansa German Airlines, Ansett Australia, and Continental Airlines. According to Peter Froehlich, manager of Decision Support Systems Network Planning for Lufthansa German Airlines, "The Profitability Model, along with organizational and process flow changes at Lufthansa, is estimated to have increased Lufthansa's revenues by 300 million deutch marks per year." Says Glen Hauenstein, senior director of schedule planning at Continental, "The Airline Profitability Model provides Continental with a consistent platform that allows analysts to be more thorough in their analysis. The number crunching is done by the system, so the analysts can do what they are paid for—think."

So, if you've ever wondered how airlines determine flight schedules' frequency to specific cities, times of flight departures, or city preferences for connections, now you know that scheduling decision support systems are the brains behind the decisions. And instead of taking many people days, the model performs the analysis in a few hours.

CASE STUDY QUESTIONS

1. What characteristics and capabilities of the Airline Profitability Model make it a decision support system?

2. The Airline Profitability Model is an example of what type of analytical modeling? Explain.

3. Could other industries benefit from similar technology? Explain.

Source: Adapted from Patty Enrado, "Right on Schedule," *AI Expert*, December 1994, p. 48.

Summary

- **Information and Management.** Information systems can support a variety of management activities. These include the four functions of management (plan, organize, direct, and control), the 10 roles of management (leader, liaison, figurehead, monitor, disseminator, spokesperson, entrepreneur, disturbance handler, resource allocator, and negotiator), and the three levels of management activity (strategic, tactical, and operational planning and control).

- **Information and Decision Making.** Information systems can support the intelligence, design, choice, and implementation activities of the decision-making process. To do this, information systems should (1) scan the internal organization and the external environment to produce information that helps identify problems and opportunities, (2) help generate and evaluate decision alternatives, (3) provide information products that emphasize and prioritize decision alternatives, and (4) provide feedback on implemented decisions.

- **Decision Structure.** Decisions can be classified as structured, semistructured, or unstructured. Structured decisions involve situations where decision procedures can be specified in advance. Unstructured decisions are subject to too many random, changeable, or unknown factors for decision procedures to be specified in advance. Information systems can provide a wide range of information products to support many types of decisions.

- **Information Quality.** Managers have to be provided with information products that possess many attributes of information quality in each of the three dimensions of time (timeliness, currency, frequency, and time period), content (accuracy, relevance, completeness, conciseness, scope, and performance), and form (clarity, detail, order, presentation, and media).

- **Online Analytical Processing.** Management, decision support, and executive information systems can be enhanced with an online analytical processing capability. OLAP typically relies on specialized servers and software to interactively analyze complex relationships among large amounts of data stored in multidimensional databases. Managers and analysts can then discover patterns, trends, and exception conditions in an online, realtime process that supports their business analysis and decision making.

- **Decision Support Systems.** Decision support systems are interactive, computer-based information systems that use a model base and a database to provide information tailored to support semistructured and unstructured decisions faced by individual managers. They are designed to use a decision maker's own insights and judgments in an ad hoc, interactive, analytical modeling process leading to a specific decision.

- **DSS Components.** A decision support system consists of hardware, software, data, model, and people resources. Hardware resources include management workstations, departmental minicomputers, and corporate mainframes. Software resources include software packages such as DSS generators and spreadsheet packages that perform database management, model base management, and dialogue generation and management. Data and model resources include a database extracted from internal, external, and personal databases, and a model base that is a collection of mathematical models and analytical techniques. People resources include managers and staff specialists who explore decision alternatives with the support of a DSS.

- **Analytical Modeling.** Using a decision support system is an interactive, analytical modeling process, consisting of what-if analysis, sensitivity analysis, goal seeking analysis, and optimization analysis activities. Decision support system applications may be institutional or ad hoc but are typically developed to support the types of decisions faced by specific industries, functional areas, and decision makers.

- **Executive Information Systems.** Executive information systems are management information systems designed to support the strategic information needs of top management. However, their use is spreading to lower levels of management. EIS are easy to use and enable executives to retrieve information tailored to their needs and preferences. Thus, EIS can provide information about a company's critical success factors to executives to support their planning and control responsibilities.

- **Group Decision Support.** Managers are frequently faced with decision-making situations that require interactions with groups of people. Also, many decisions are made by groups of people coming to an agreement on a particular issue. The success of group decision making depends on many factors that can be enhanced by group decision-making methodologies and facilitated by using the computer-based facilities and software tools of electronic meeting systems and group decision support systems.

Key Terms and Concepts

These are the key terms and concepts of this chapter. The page number of their first explanation is in parentheses.

1. Analytical modeling (380)
   a. Goal seeking analysis (381)
   b. Optimization analysis (382)
   c. Sensitivity analysis (381)
   d. What-if analysis (380)
2. Components of a DSS (376)
3. Decision-making process (360)
   a. Intelligence activities (360)
   b. Design activities (361)
   c. Choice activities (364)
   d. Implementation activities (364)
4. Decision support versus manage-

ment reporting (373)
5. Decision support system (373)
6. DSS model base (377)
7. DSS software (377)
8. Executive information system (382)
9. Executive support system (383)
10. Functions of management (356)
11. Group decision making (387)
12. Group decision support system (386)
13. Information Quality (364)
    a. Content dimension (366)

   b. Form dimension (366)
   c. Time dimension (365)
14. Levels of management (359)
15. Management information system (370)
16. Online analytical processing (371)
17. Reporting alternatives (370)
18. Roles of management (358)
19. Semistructured decisions (362)
20. Spreadsheet DSS (378)
21. Structured decisions (362)
22. Unstructured decisions (362)

Review Quiz

Match one of the key terms and concepts listed above with one of the brief examples or definitions listed below. Try to find the best fit for answers that seem to fit more than one term or concept. Defend your choices.

____ 1. Information systems should help identify problems and opportunities.
____ 2. Information systems should help generate and evaluate decision alternatives.
____ 3. Information systems should help emphasize and prioritize decision alternatives.
____ 4. Inventory reorder decisions can frequently be quantified and automated.
____ 5. Decisions involved in starting a new line of products might involve a *lot* of unknown factors.
____ 6. Managers should plan, organize, staff, direct, and control an organization.
____ 7. A manager is a leader, liaison, monitor, spokesperson, entrepreneur, and negotiator, among other things.
____ 8. Top managers concentrate on strategic planning for the organization, whereas operational managers control day-to-day operations.
____ 9. Provide an interactive modeling capability tailored to the specific information needs of managers.
____ 10. Interactive responses to ad hoc inquiries versus pre-specified information.
____ 11. A management workstation, DSS software, database, model base, and manager or staff specialist.
____ 12. A collection of mathematical models and analytical techniques.

____ 13. Produce predefined reports for management.
____ 14. Managers can receive reports periodically, on an exception basis, or on demand.
____ 15. A software package that uses a worksheet format to help end users do analytical modeling.
____ 16. Analyzing the effect of changing variables and relationships and manipulating a mathematical model.
____ 17. Changing revenues and tax rates to see the effect on net profit after taxes.
____ 18. Changing revenues in many small increments to see revenue's effect on net profit after taxes.
____ 19. Changing revenues and expenses to find how best to achieve a specified amount of net profit after taxes.
____ 20. Changing revenues and expenses subject to certain constraints in order to achieve the highest net profit after taxes.
____ 21. People coming to an agreement on an issue.
____ 22. Computer-based tools can enhance the effectiveness of group decision making.
____ 23. Information systems for the strategic information needs of top and middle managers.
____ 24. Executive information systems that may have DSS, expert system, and office automation features.
____ 25. Whether information is valuable and useful to you.

___ 26. Information should be provided whenever it is needed and should be up-to-date.

___ 27. Information should be accurate, relevant, complete, and concise.

___ 28. Information should be presented clearly and attractively.

___ 29. Realtime analysis of complex business data.

Discussion Questions

1. How could a decision support system be used to support the planning, organizing, directing, and controlling functions of a department manager?

2. How could an executive information system be used to support the interpersonal, informational, and decisional roles of the CEO of a company?

3. Refer to the Real World Case on GTE Corporation in the chapter. What is the difference in the information technology requirements of operational versus decision-making business systems?

4. Can a DSS support all four of the stages of decision making? How about an EIS? Explain.

5. What is the difference between the ability of a manager to retrieve information instantly on demand using a networked workstation, and the capabilities provided by a DSS?

6. Refer to the Real World Case on SABRE Decision Technologies in the chapter. Why do you think it takes six to nine months to calibrate a DSS like the airline profitability model? Are the benefits worth it? Explain.

7. In what ways does using an electronic spreadsheet package provide you with the components and capabilities of a decision support system?

8. How do electronic meeting systems support group decision making? What benefits and limitations do you see to using an EMS for group decision support?

9. Why is the use of executive information systems expanding into the ranks of middle management?

10. Refer to the Real World Case on Blue Cross/Blue Shield of Rhode Island in the chapter. What additional types or capabilities of end user data access tools do you think their analysts and managers should have? Explain.

Real World Problems

1. Fidelity Investment Institutional Services: Strategic Decision Support

The financial analysts and strategic marketers at Fidelity Investment Institutional Services (FIIS) crawled into a black hole every time they queried their dinosaur mainframe system. "With our mainframe-based DB2 database, those power users could forget about creating accurate sales forecasts," said Mark Parsons, systems manager at the investment giant's Boston headquarters. "It was taking at least 24 hours to respond to those queries. Eventually, they just stopped making those requests." So they did the next month's and next year's sales projections the old-fashioned way: manually.

The analysts blew their chances because the DB2 database couldn't cope with decision support systems (DSS) and online transaction processing (OLTP) simultaneously. The new system is faster and smarter because Parsons and his team wisely decided to divide the DSS and OLTP functions. OLTP is now handled in the Dallas data center by a four-CPU Sun Microsystems SPARC1000 server. That configuration does the really heavy lifting, nightly crunching about 300M to 400M bytes, or about 40,000 daily transactions. Production data is then sent to Boston via wide area network into another four-CPU SPARC1000, where a Red Brick

Systems database system organizes the files for decision support analysis.

Now, in the client/server environment, the 50 analysts and marketers can compare sales of specific financial instruments and be sure they will receive a precise projection—in only four hours. "We had to put on users' desktops the ability to go after information in ways they hadn't been doing," Parsons said. "And we probably missed some business opportunities because we couldn't get the right information at the right time." "I can't quantify our competitive edge yet, but I guarantee this system will give us one," Parsons said. "We'll have a much greater ability to target the businesses that are most profitable for us. And we'll be able to create goals that are truly intelligent."

a. What managerial functions and decision making stages can you recognize in this case? Explain your reasoning.

b. What business decision support problems and solutions occurred at Fidelity Investment?

Source: Adapted from Willie Schatz, "When Data Is Not Enough," *Computerworld Client/Server Journal*, April 1995, p. 28. Copyright 1995 by Computerworld, Inc., Framingham, MA 01701—Reprinted from *Computerworld*.

2. Elizabeth Arden Inc.: Data Analysis and Presentation

Financial analysts can pore over the starkest of numbers and find valuable information. However, most managers are just interested in the bottom line. Paul West, chief financial officer at Elizabeth Arden Inc., knows this. So he began searching for a way to present numbers to his board of directors that would be an accurate, but visually attractive, picture of the company's finances. "We have a broad report that is very numbers oriented, and when you looked at it, it wasn't very appealing," West says. "It was my sense that people on our board weren't paying a lot of attention to it. We decided—given that we have a lot of creative and marketing types on the board—to do something in a graphic format."

West's research led him to Empower, a specialized presentation program from Metapraxis. He, as well as other financial managers at Elizabeth Arden, found Empower's analysis-oriented charts very attractive. "Initially that's why we looked at it," says West, "but it also allowed the financial people to drill down into detailed accounting data rather easily. So it was a combination of the two." West uses Empower to devise all his corporate reports. He immediately can view the Elizabeth Arden global financial system, including the United States and Europe, in raw detail. "We close our books in three days and on day four I've got it," he says.

With a source of fresh, virtually unlimited data, analysts at Elizabeth Arden can also forecast sales more accurately. Relying on Empower's "Windsock," or "window of credibility," analysis, for example, West can compare internal forecasts with statistical forecasts as the year progresses. "If there are deviations, they give us the ability to go back and question the logic [of the internal forecasts]," says West. Variances could be due to a new product introduction or to a promotion that changes the trajectories of historical patterns.

a. What attributes of information quality do you recognize in this case? Explain.

b. What are the business benefits of Elizabeth Arden's new Empower software?

Source: Adapted from Marti Remington, "Finding Beauty in Numbers," *PC Today,* January 1995, p. 42.

3. H.E. Butt Grocery Co.: Retail Decision Support

H. E. Butt Grocery Co., a 160-store chain based in San Antonio, has replaced its mainframe-enforced guessing game about which products will move fastest from which shelves with the client/server comfort of knowing its managers have made the right choice. Butt's 40,000 workers generated more than $4 billion in revenue in the fiscal year ended October 1994. Yet regardless of whether that ratio is good for the industry, top executives mandated a move to a client/server business intelligence system. "We'd been capturing scanning data for a long time," Danvers explained. "But the competition was getting so fierce that the delays in responding to queries were no longer acceptable. We had to manage our inventory in a timely fashion. Otherwise, we couldn't stay competitive with Wal-Mart, Kmart, and the other superstores."

Butt's client/server move began with the installation of a dual-processor, 200G-byte Hewlett-Packard HP9000 server. POS data flows into the IBM mainframe over the firm's widearea network, where it's processed. The data is then downloaded to the HP server, where a Red Brick Systems 80G-byte decision support DBMS resides. Butt's category managers then analyze that data from networked PCs using customized software with graphical user interfaces designed by Butt and built by A. C. Nielsen Co.

"Point-of-sale queries that took three to four weeks to answer with our mainframe system now take minutes, if not seconds," raved Claude Danvers, Butt's director of database administration. That information is absolutely vital to the 40 category managers, each of whom administers approximately 10 industry categories such as beverages or housewares. The managers receive the relevant field reports, massage them, and then fire the sanitized versions back to members of the sales force.

a. What category of information system is demonstrated by H.E. Butt's new business intelligence system? Explain your selection.

b. What business and IT problems and solutions are demonstrated in this case?

Source: Adapted from Willie Schatz, "When Data Is Not Enough," *Computerworld Client/Server Journal,* April 1995, pp. 27–28. Copyright 1995 by Computerworld, Inc., Framingham, MA 01701—Reprinted from *Computerworld.*

4. Aetna Life & Casualty: Executive Information Systems

Ron Compton, Aetna's president, says he can't imagine why any enterprise executive wouldn't use a computer religiously. Compton is hooked into an executive information system that features expert systems, E-mail, object-oriented databases, graphics programs, spreadsheets, word processors, and computer-based conferencing. He says that IT serves as an extension of his thought processes, helping him create strategies and retain information. Prior to taking the helm of Aetna, a firm with $94.5 billion in assets and more than 43,000 employees, Compton headed an Aetna subsidiary, American Reinsurance, that has since been sold. There he was instrumental in developing an executive information system build around critical information that he and other senior managers needed to achieve strategic and operational goals.

When Compton moved to Aetna, he participated in the customization of a similar EIS that collects data from multiple platforms across the enterprise. The EIS helps executives act on that information and then tracks the results of those actions. "I never design systems," he says. "I design output. I know how I want things to look." Compton also likes to preview the results of proposed decisions. For example, when he and his executive vice president at American Reinsurance had to structure compensation for the top 50 people in the company, the two of them holed up in a hotel room with their personal computers, "trying out all kinds of what-if budget scenarios until we got it right."

a. Can Aetna's executive information system also be called an executive support system? Why or why not?

b. Does Ron Compton also use his EIS as a decision support system? Explain.

Source: Adapted from David Morrison, "CEOs and PCs: Do They Compute?" *Beyond Computing,* January/February 1994, pp. 30–33. Reprinted with permission from *Beyond Computing* magazine, Jan/Feb. 1994 issue © Copyright 1994 IBM Corporation. All rights reserved.

5. Rhone-Poulenc Rorer and Blue Cross/Blue Shield of Maryland: Multidimensional Decision Analysis

"We're experiencing a real change in the type of questions managers pursue. We've entered the era of micromarketing where the devil is in the details," says Howard Mark, director of systems and programming at Rhone-Poulenc Rorer, Inc., a pharmaceutical company in Collegeville, Pennsylvania. Product managers at the company start at a high level, but when they spot something specific, such as a drop in market share in a certain area, they want to drill down fast to very low levels of detail.

"The business problems our users deal with are inherently multidimensional. They are looking at different slices of data, trending by time and by types of transactions, " notes Mark Max, director of financial systems at Baltimore-based Blue Cross/Blue Shield of Maryland. For example, a Blue Cross/Blue Shield manager might want to look at contract enrollment by product and by market over a period of time, a question with four dimensions. "People would throw numbers into spreadsheets and work it until they thought they had it right, but there was no inherent integrity to the results," Max explains.

Now managers at both Rhone-Poulenc Rorer and Blue Cross/Blue Shield use Information Resources, Inc.'s Express, which does online analytical processing against a multidimensional database. Managers can now perform such analyses quickly and simply with all the required calculations and aggregations already executed and validated. "We like the built-in analytical capabilities in Express," Max says.

a. What changes in the attributes of information that managers want is discussed in this case? Why do managers want such information now?

b. Does using Express provide the capabilities of and MIS, DSS, or EIS? Explain.

Source: Adapted from Alan Radding, "Is OLAP the Answer?" *Computerworld,* December 19, 1994, pp. 72–73. Copyright 1994 by Computerworld, Inc., Framingham, MA 01701—Reprinted from *Computerworld.*

6. Fellows Office Products: Client/Server Decision Support

"For many business intelligence applications, client/server is an essential architectural component," said Howard Dresner, an analyst at Gartner Group, Inc., in Stamford, Connecticut. "Those applications are very complex, and PCs aren't good at dealing with complex data relationships. You can't do things like predictive forecasting on the desktop." Well, you can, but not with any rigorous applications requiring a lot of data. According to Dresner, you need powerful servers to handle greater data complexity. Sophisticated business intelligence analysts want to digest the complex data and create a model around it that explains the reality of the company's business, he said.

For example, Fellows Office Products, Inc., sales reps needed help stacking the deck in their favor. Sales managers heard rumblings that the reps weren't spending enough fact time with their accounts, many of which were being courted by larger rivals. Using Ottawa-based Cognos, Inc.'s 4GL Powerhouse, the $200 million Chicago company developed a client/server program that instantly generates sales reports of 50 North American territories from static host data. Immediate access to this type of data is helping Fellows sales managers promote better service—and retain customers. "If the customer sees faster availability and more accurate information from us, the better position they'll be in to make a decision to buy our stuff," said Jeff Teitz, information systems manager.

a. What kind of information system does the new Fellows system appear to be? Explain your reasoning.

b. What role do servers play in client/server decision support systems?

Source: Adapted from Willie Schatz, "When Data Is Not Enough," *Computerworld Client/Server Journal,* April 1995, pp. 26–27. Copyright 1995 by Computerworld, Inc., Framingham, MA 01701—Reprinted from *Computerworld.*

Application Exercises

1. ABC Company: Spreadsheets for Decision Support

Use an electronic spreadsheet or integrated package available on the microcomputer or mainframe systems at your university to create the ABC Company Financial Performance spreadsheet as shown in Figure 10.18, using the formulas shown in Figure 10.19. Start by entering formulas for 1994 entries, which assume that expenses are 60 percent of revenue, profit is revenue minus expenses, taxes are 40 percent of profit, and profit after taxes equals profit minus taxes. Complete the 1995 and 1996 columns of the spreadsheet, which assume that 1995 revenue is 110 percent of 1994, and 1996 revenue is 120 percent of 1994. Assume that all other

formula relationships for 1994 entries also apply to 1995 and 1996. Then use SUM and AVERAGE functions to complete the final two columns of the spreadsheet.

a. Enter $1,000 for 1994 sales. Notice how the spreadsheet shown in Figure 10.18 is instantly generated and displayed. Store and print this spreadsheet as shown in Figure 10.18.

b. Then print out a version of the spreadsheet with all formulas displayed to document the formulas you used. See Figure 10.19.

c. Use the spreadsheet you created to perform what-if analyses. For example, change revenue, expense, or tax values or formulas in the ABC Company Financial Performance spreadsheet. (For example, increase revenue for 1994 by $1,000, increase expenses to 65 percent of revenue, and decrease taxes to 25 percent of profit.) What happens to the company's profit in each year? Print a copy of the spreadsheet with the results of these changes.

d. Create graphics displays of parts of the spreadsheet you developed. For example, develop a pie chart of profit after taxes, or a bar graph of expenses. See Figure 10.20. Make changes to entries in the spreadsheet and use graphics displays to help you perform what-if analyses.

e. Write a short explanation of what happened when you did what-if analysis and its implications for a managerial end user. What features need to be added or improved to make this package easier to use and a more effective DSS generator? Explain how and why you think this should be done.

2. **Designing Information Products**

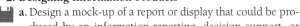

a. Design a mock-up of a report or display that could be produced by an information reporting, decision support, or executive information system for managers in a business or other organization.

b. Use a report generator from a database management or other software package to develop the report mock-up.

c. Evaluate the information quality of the information product you design. Write up a brief evaluation based on the attributes outlined in Figure 10.6.

Review Quiz Answers

1.	*3a*	9.	*5*	17.	*1d*	25.	*13*
2.	*3b*	10.	*4*	18.	*1c*	26.	*13c*
3.	*3c*	11.	*2*	19.	*1a*	27.	*13a*
4.	*21*	12.	*6*	20.	*1b*	28.	*13b*
5.	*22*	13.	*15*	21.	*11*	29.	*16*
6.	*10*	14.	*17*	22.	*12*		
7.	*18*	15.	*20*	23.	*8*		
8.	*14*	16.	*1*	24.	*9*		

Selected References

1. Anthony, Robert. *Planning and Control Systems: A Framework for Analysis.* Cambridge: Harvard University Graduate School of Business Administration, 1965.
2. Belcher, Lloyd, and Hugh Watson. "Assessing the Value of Conoco's EIS." *MIS Quarterly,* September 1993.
3. Betts, Mitch. "Efficiency Einsteins." *Computerworld,* March 22, 1993.
4. Betts, Mitch. "MapInfo/Microsoft Deal Puts Office Applications on the Map." *Computerworld,* November 28, 1994.
5. Burden, Kevin. "The CW Guide to Business Intelligence Software." *Computerworld,* December 19, 1994.
6. Chen, H.; P. Hsu; R. Orwig; L. Hoopes; and J. F. Nunamaker. "Automatic Concept Classification of Text from Electronic Meetings." *Communications of the ACM,* October, 1994.
7. *Commander EIS: Delivering the Complete EIS Solution.* Ann Arbor, MI: Comshare, 1993.
8. Dickson, Gary; Joo-Eng Lee Partridge; and Lora Robinson. "Exploring Modes of Facilitative Support for GDSS Technology." *MIS Quarterly,* June 1993.
9. Finkelstein, Richard. *Understanding the Need for Online Analytical Servers.* Ann Arbor, MI: Comshare, 1994.
10. Finlelstein, Richard. "When OLAP Does Not Relate." *Computerworld,* December 12, 1994.
11. Gibbons, Chris; Corrine Chaves; Ronald Wilkes; and Mark Frolick. "Management Support System at Promus." *Information Systems Management,* Summer 1994.
12. Gorry, G. Anthony, and Michael Scott Manon. "A Framework for Management Information Systems." *Sloan Management Review,* Fall 1971; republished Spring 1989.
13. Guimaraes, Tor; Magid Igbaria; and Ming-Te Lu. "The Determinants of DSS Success: An Analytical Model." *Decision Sciences Journal,* March/April 1992.
14. Jessup, Leonard, and David Tansuk. "Decision Making in an Automated Environment: The Effects on Anonymity and Proximity with a Group Decision Support System." *Decision Sciences Journal,* Spring, 1991.
15. Johnson, Mary Fran. "GIS Popularity Growing." *Computerworld,* March 22, 1993.
16. Draemer, Kenneth; James Danzinger; Deborah Dunkle; and John King. "The Usefulness of Computer-Based Information to Public Managers." *MIS Quarterly,* June 1993.
17. Mitzberg, Henry. *The Nature of Managerial Work.* New York: Harper & Row, 1983.
18. Nunamaker, Jay; Alan Dennis; Joseph Valacich; Douglas Vogel; and Joey F. George. "Electronic Meetings to Support Group Work." *Communications of the ACM,* July 1991.

19. Panko, Raymond. *End User Computing: Management Applications, and Technology.* New York: John Wiley & Sons, 1988.
20. Radding, Alan. "Is OLAP the Answer?" *Computerworld,* December 19, 1994.
21. Rochester, Jack, ed. "The New Role for Executive Information Systems." *I/S Analyzer,* January 1992.
22. Sengupta, Kishore, and Dov Te'eni. "Cognitive Feedback in GDSS: Improving Control and Convergence." *MIS Quarterly,* March 1993.
23. Simon, Herbert A. *The New Science of Management Decision.* Rev. ed. Englewood Cliffs, NJ: Prentice Hall, 1977.
24. Turban, Efraim. *Decision Support and Expert Systems: Management Support Systems.* 2nd Ed. New York: Macmillan, 1990.
25. Turoff, Murray; Starr Roxanne Hiltz; Ahmed Bahgat; and Ajaz Rava. "Distributed Group Support Systems." *MIS Quarterly,* December 1993.
26. Watson, Hugh; R. Kelly Ranier; and Chang Koh. "Executive Information Systems: A Framework for Development and a Survey of Current Practices." *MIS Quarterly,* March 1991.
27. Watson, Hugh, and Mark Frolick. "Determining Information Requirements for an EIS." *MIS Quarterly,* September 1993.
28. Watson, Hugh, and John Satzinger. "Guidelines for Designing EIS Interfaces." *Information Systems Management,* Fall 1994.

Blue Cross/Blue Shield of Rhode Island: Multidimensional Data Analysis

When Paul Mangili joined Blue Cross/Blue Shield of Rhode Island three years ago as a cost accountant, he spent many an hour pouring over documents, rekeying numbers into a Lotus 1-2-3 spreadsheet, and then creating reports. "It was caveman time," Mangili said. But his department was about to launch one of the first end user data access projects at the insurance company.

Today, the cost accounting department is far more evolved, to use Mangili's analogy. It now uses a multidimensional database system from Arbor Software, called Essbase Analysis Server, to analyze, slice, dice, chew up, and spit out data in a variety of reports.

Arbor is one of several companies that markets multidimensional database systems which have also become known as online analytical processing (OLAP) systems. Multidimensional databases specialize in very quick data access for complex queries.

"The overall objective was management needed cost information for faster decision making," said Norbert Charette, manager of cost accounting. "We felt that we had a level of detail that was just too much. We needed a process that would give us the ability to extract summary data in more digestible amounts."

To help sell management on the multidimensional database system, Charette said he tried to first "beat them up visually." He stacked up dozens of mainframe-generated reports, measuring 4 feet high by 10 feet long, in a conference room. That, he told his bosses, is what the cost accountants must work with every day, and what the new system would replace. It worked.

The cost accountants no longer feel like slaves to mainframe-generated reports, Mangili said. "It used to take three or four accountants to turn [a report] around in a week," he said. "Now, it'll take one person a day, maybe two," to produce a report.

At Blue Cross, the cost accounting system receives regular downloads of data from production mainframe applications. The data is then stored in the Arbor back-end multidimensional database. Essbase uses a front-end component that is a spreadsheetlike program and graphical user interface.

Cost accountants work with this front-end piece to view data and then create reports that track and explain spending for different groups in the insurance company.

The system has highlighted the need for more end-user technology and end-user data access tools, said George Trudell, a business and technology consultant at Blue Cross who worked with the cost accounting department on the project.

Trudell is working on a steering committee that is setting up guidelines for end-user data access tools and that will also address other end-user issues such as data warehousing. The committee's mission is to push information out to end users, Trudell said.

Among other lessons, the cost accounting experiment showed Blue Cross that it can address what can be an overwhelming issue—corporatewide end user data access—in manageable chunks. For starters, the cost accounting department was turned around at a small cost—just $30,000 for the Arbor system, according to Charette. Plus, with 18 people in the department, implementing the technology was not disruptive.

Trudell said the steering committee's work will focus on getting these kinds of results for other departments. The team is looking at warehousing guidelines and will incorporate information from other projects, such as a Lotus Notes pilot now under way. "That is seen as a means to reduce a lot of the bureaucracy and paperwork that's been there in the past," Trudell said.

CASE STUDY QUESTIONS

1. What is online analytical processing (OLAP), and what is its business purpose?

2. Is the use of the Essbase Analysis Server an example of a MIS? DSS? EIS? Explain.

3. How is Blue Cross/Blue Shield benefiting from the use of the Essbase tool?

Source: Adapted from Rosemary Cafasso, "Data Access Turns Around," *Computerworld*, April 3, 1995, p. 69. Copyright 1995 by Computerworld, Inc., Framingham, MA 01701—Reprinted from *Computerworld*.

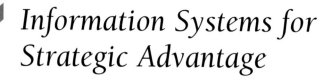

Information Systems for Strategic Advantage

CHAPTER OUTLINE

LEARNING OBJECTIVES

The purpose of this chapter is to give you an understanding of the role of information systems and technologies in helping an organization achieve a strategic advantage over its competitors.

Section I emphasizes competitive strategy concepts and the strategic roles information systems can play in gaining competitive advantages for an organization.

Section II provides many examples of the strategic business use of information technology and discusses the major managerial challenges posed by strategic information systems.

After reading and studying this chapter, you should be able to:

1. Identify several basic competitive strategies and explain how they can be used to confront the competitive forces faced by a business.

2. Identify several strategic roles of information systems and give examples of how information technology can implement these roles and give competitive advantages to a business.

3. Give examples of how information technology can break time, geographic, cost, and structural barriers in business.

4. Give examples of how business process reengineering involves the strategic use of information technology.

5. Identify how total quality management differs from business process reengineering in its use of information technology.

6. Identify how information technology can be used strategically to help a company be an agile competitor.

7. Explain how information technology can be used to form a virtual company to meet strategic business opportunities.

8. Identify several strategic business uses of the Internet and give examples of each.

┌ **SECTION I**
◢ *Fundamentals of Strategic Advantage*

Introduction

What are the new skills demanded of effective managers in the 1990s? Competence and comfort in handling information technology (IT) will be high on the list. IT—computers plus telecommunications plus workstations plus information stores—is one of the major forces reshaping competition [23].

As a prospective manager, it is important that you view information systems as more than a set of technologies that support end user computing and collaboration, efficient business operations, or effective managerial decision making. Information systems can change the way businesses compete. So you should also view information systems strategically, that is, as competitive networks, as a means of organizational renewal, and as a vital investment in technologies that help an enterprise achieve its strategic objectives. See Figure 11.1.

Thus, the strategic role of information systems involves using information technology to develop products, services, and capabilities that give a company strategic advantages over the competitive forces it faces in the global marketplace. This creates **strategic information systems,** information systems that support or shape the competitive position and strategies of an enterprise. So a strategic information system can be any kind of information system (TPS, MIS, DSS, etc.) that helps an organization gain a competitive advantage, reduce a competitive disadvantage, or meet other strategic enterprise objectives [30]. Let's look at several basic concepts that define the role of such strategic information systems.

Competitive Strategy Concepts

How should a managerial end user think about competitive strategies? How can competitive strategies be applied to the use of information systems by an organization? Several important conceptual frameworks for understanding and applying competitive strategies (which we briefly introduced in Chapter 1), have been developed by Michael Porter [32, 33], Charles Wiseman [39], and others. Figure 11.2 illustrates several important concepts. A firm can survive and succeed in the long run if it successfully develops strategies to confront five **competitive forces** that shape the structure of competition in its industry. These are: (1) rivalry of competitors within its industry, (2) threats of new entrants, (3) threats of substitutes, (4) the bargaining power of customers, and (5) the bargaining power of suppliers.

A variety of **competitive strategies** can be developed to help a firm confront these competitive forces. For example, businesses may try to counter the bargaining power of their customers and suppliers by developing unique business relationships with them. This effectively locks in customers or suppliers by creating "switching costs" that make it expensive or inconvenient for them to switch to another firm. Thus, competitors are also locked out by such strategies. Companies may use other strategies to protect themselves from the threat of new businesses entering their industry, or the development of substitutes for their products or services. For example, businesses may try to develop legal, financial, or technological requirements that create "barriers to entry" that discourage firms from entering an industry, or make substitution unattractive or uneconomical.

Another way that businesses can counter the threats of competitive forces that confront them is to implement five basic competitive strategies [31, 38]. As Figure 11.3 illustrates, they include the following:

Jon Feingersch/The Stock Market.

FIGURE 11.1
Information systems can involve the strategic use of information technology to gain competitive advantages.

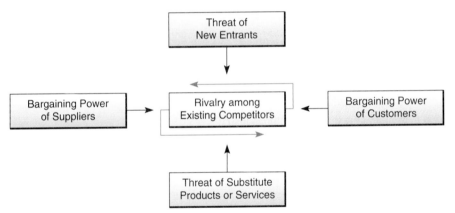

FIGURE 11.2
The competitive environment of an industry. Note the five competitive forces that determine the profitability and survival of the firms within an industry.

Source: Reprinted with the permission of The Free Press, an imprint of Simon & Schuster from *Competitive Advantage: Creating and Sustaining Superior Performance,* by Michael E. Porter. Copyright © 1985 by Michael E. Porter.

- **Cost leadership strategy.** Becoming a low-cost producer of products and services in the industry. Also, a firm can find ways to help its suppliers or customers reduce their costs or to increase the costs of their competitors.

- **Differentiation strategy.** Developing ways to differentiate a firm's products and services from its competitors' or reduce the differentiation advantages of competitors. This may allow a firm to focus its products or services to give it an advantage in particular segments or niches of a market.

- **Innovation strategy.** Finding new ways of doing business. This may involve the development of unique products and services, or entry into unique markets or market niches. It may also involve making radical changes to the business processes for producing or distributing products and services that

FIGURE 11.3
Businesses can develop competitive strategies to counter the actions of the competitive forces they confront in the marketplace.

Competitive Forces

	Supplier	Customer	Competitor	New Entrant	Substitute
Differentiation					
Cost					
Innovation					
Growth					
Alliance					
Other Strategies					

(Competitive Strategies — vertical axis label)

are so different from the way business has been conducted that they alter the fundamental structure of an industry.

- **Growth strategies.** Significantly expanding a company's capacity to produce goods and services, expanding into global markets, diversifying into new products and services, or integrating into related products and services.
- **Alliance strategies.** Establishing new business linkages and alliances with customers, suppliers, competitors, consultants, and other companies. These linkages may include mergers, acquisitions, joint ventures, forming "virtual companies," or other marketing, manufacturing, or distribution agreements.

Strategic Roles for Information Systems

How can the preceding competitive strategy concepts be applied to the **strategic role of information systems** in an organization? Put another way, how can managers use investments in information technology to directly support a firm's competitive strategies? These questions can be answered in terms of the key strategic roles that information systems can perform in a firm.

Figure 11.4 summarizes how information technology can be used to implement a variety of competitive strategies. These include not only the five basic competitive strategies, but also other ways that companies can use information systems strategically to gain a competitive edge. Figure 11.5 provides examples of how many corporations have used strategic information systems to implement each of the five basic strategies for competitive advantage [24, 25, 30, 39]. In the rest of this chap-

Lower Costs
- Use IT to substantially reduce the cost of business processes.
- Use IT to lower the costs of customers or suppliers.

Differentiate
- Develop new IT features to differentiate products and services.
- Use IT features to reduce the differentiation advantages of competitors.
- Use IT features to focus products and services at selected market niches.

Innovate
- Create new products and services that include IT components.
- Make radical changes to business processes with IT.
- Develop unique new markets or market niches with the help of IT.

Promote Growth
- Use IT to manage regional and global business expansion.
- Use IT to diversify and integrate into other products and services.

Develop Alliances
- Use IT to create virtual organizations of business partners.
- Develop interorganizational information systems that create strategic business relationships with customers, suppliers, subcontractors, and others.

Improve Quality and Efficiency
- Use IT to dramatically improve the quality of products and services.
- Use IT to make continuous improvements to the efficiency of business processes.
- Use IT to substantially shorten the time needed to develop, produce, and deliver products and services.

Build an IT Platform
- Leverage investment in IS people, hardware, software, and networks from operational uses into strategic applications.
- Build a strategic information base of internal and external data collected and analyzed by IT.

Other Strategies
- Use interorganizational information systems to create switching costs that lock in customers and suppliers.
- Use investment in IT to build barriers to entry against industry outsiders.
- Use IT components to make substitution of competing products unattractive.

FIGURE 11.4
A summary of how information technology can be used to implement competitive strategies.

ter, we will discuss and provide other examples of such strategic uses of information technology.

Using information technology to improve a company's operations can have many strategic effects. Investments in information technology can help make a firm's operations substantially more efficient. Improvements to its business processes could enable a company to cut costs dramatically and improve the quality and delivery of its products and services. For example, manufacturing operations for everything from automobiles to watches have been automated and significantly improved by computer-aided manufacturing (CAM) technologies. In the automobile industry, the distribution of cars and parts, and the exchange of vital business data have been substantially improved by telecommunications networks that electronically connect an automobile manufacturer's distribution facilities with car dealers. In the next section, we will discuss some of the major ways that using information technology for

Improving Business Operations

FIGURE 11.5

Examples of how companies used information technology to implement five competitive strategies for strategic advantage.

Strategy	Company	Strategic Information System	Business Benefit
Cost leadership	Levitz Furniture	Centralized buying	Cut purchasing costs
	Metropolitan Life	Medical care monitoring	Cut medical costs
	Deere & Company	Machine tool control	Cut manufacturing costs
Differentiation	Navistar	Portable computer-based customer needs analysis	Increase in market share
	Setco Industries	Computer-aided job estimation	Increase in market share
	Consolidated Freightways	Customer online shipment tracking	Increase in market share
Innovation	Merril Lynch	Customer cash management accounts	Market leadership
	Federal Express	Online package tracking and flight management	Market leadership
	McKesson Corp.	Customer order entry and merchandising	Market leadership
Growth	Citicorp	Global telecommunications network	Increase in global market
	Walmart	Merchandise ordering by Satellite network	Market leadership
	Toys 'R' Us Inc.	POS inventory tracking	Market leadership
Alliance	Walmart/Procter and Gamble	Automatic inventory replenishment by supplier	Reduced inventory Costs/Increased sales
	Levi Strauss/Designs Inc.	Electronic data interchange	Just-in-time merchandise replenishment
	Airborne Express/ Rentrak Corp.	Online inventory management/shipment tracking	Increase in market share

business process reengineering can improve the operational efficiency of business processes.

Operational efficiency may allow a firm to adopt a low-cost leadership strategy. However, a firm could decide instead to use its operational efficiency to increase quality and service by choosing a product differentiation strategy. This strategy would stress the unique quality of a firm's products and services. In either case, a firm would be better able to deter competitive threats. Its industry rivals and firms seeking to enter the industry using similar or substitute products would have a harder time beating an efficient competitor.

Promoting Business Innovation

Investments in information systems technology can result in the development of unique products and services or processes. This can create new business opportunities, and enable a firm to expand into new markets or into new segments of existing markets. The use of automated teller machines (ATMs) in banking is a classic example of an innovative investment in information systems technology.

By employing ATMs, Citibank and several other large banks were able to gain a strategic advantage over their competitors that lasted for several years [23, 25]. ATMs lured customers away from other financial institutions by cutting the cost of delivering bank services and increasing the convenience of such services. The more costly and less convenient alternative would have been to establish new bank branch offices. ATMs are also an example of product differentiation, since bank services are now provided in a new way. ATMs raised the cost of competition, which forced some smaller banks that could not afford the investment in new technology to merge with larger banks. ATMs represented an attractive and convenient new banking service produced and distributed to customers by making innovative changes in the delivery of bank services. Thus, information systems technology was used to develop a strategic new distribution process for bank services.

Investments in information technology can also allow a business to **lock in customers and suppliers** (and lock out competitors) by building valuable new relationships with them. This can deter both customers and suppliers from abandoning a firm for its competitors or intimidating a firm into accepting less profitable relationships. Early attempts to use information systems technology in these relationships focused on significantly improving the quality of service to customers and suppliers in a firm's distribution, marketing, sales, and service activities. Then businesses moved to more innovative uses of information technology.

Locking in Customers and Suppliers

For example, many telecommunications networks were designed to provide salespeople and customer service staff with up-to-date sales, shipping, inventory, and account status information for relay to their customers. Firms began to use the operational efficiency of such information systems to offer better-quality service and thereby differentiate themselves from their competitors. Some firms then began to extend these networks to their customers and suppliers in order to build innovative relationships that would lock in their business. This creates **interorganizational information systems** in which telecommunications networks electronically link the terminals and computers of businesses with their customers and suppliers, resulting in new business alliances and partnerships. Electronic data interchange (EDI) links between a business and its suppliers such as those between Motorola Codex and Texas Instruments are one example. (See Figure 9.25 in Chapter 9.) An even stronger link is the automatic inventory replenishment system that Proctor and Gamble has with Wal-Mart [9, 23].

A major emphasis in strategic information systems is to build **switching costs** into the relationships between a firm and its customers or suppliers. That is, investments in information systems technology can make customers or suppliers dependent on the continued use of innovative, mutually beneficial interorganizational information systems. Then, they become reluctant to pay the costs in time, money, effort, and inconvenience that it would take to change to a company's competitors.

Creating Switching Costs

A classic example is the computerized airline reservation systems used by most travel agents such as the SABRE system of AMR Corporation (American Airlines) and the APOLLO system of COVIA (United Airlines). Once a travel agency has invested a substantial sum in installing such an interorganizational system, and travel agents have been trained in its use, the agency is reluctant to switch to another reservation system. Thus, what seemed to be just a more convenient and efficient way of processing airline reservations has become a strategic weapon that gives these providers a major competitive advantage. Not only does an airline reservation system raise competitive barriers and increase switching costs, it also gives their providers an advantage in gaining reservations for themselves and provides them with a major new line of information products. Thus, computer-based reservation services are a major source of revenue for their providers, which charge a variety of fees to travel agencies and airlines who use their systems.

Raising Barriers to Entry

By making investments in information technology to improve its operations or promote innovation, a firm could also erect **barriers to entry** that would discourage or delay other companies from entering a market. Typically, this happens by increasing the amount of investment or the complexity of the technology required to compete in an industry or a market segment. Such actions would tend to discourage firms already in the industry and deter external firms from entering the industry. Merrill Lynch's cash management account is a classic example. By making major investments in information technology, they became the first securities brokers to offer a credit line, checking account (through BankOne), Visa credit card, and automatic investment in a money market fund, all in one account [30, 39]. Thus, large investments in computer-based information systems can make the stakes too high for some present or prospective players in an industry.

Building a Strategic IT Platform

Investing in information technology enables a firm to build a **strategic IT platform** that allows it to take advantage of strategic opportunities. In many cases, this results from a firm investing in advanced computer-based information systems to improve the efficiency of its own internal operations. Typically, this means acquiring hardware and software, developing telecommunications networks, hiring information system specialists, and training end users. Then, armed with this technology platform, the firm can **leverage investment in information technology** by developing new products and services. For example, the development by banks of remote banking services using automated teller machines was an extension of their expertise in teller terminal networks, which interconnect their branches.

Developing a Strategic Information Base

Information systems also allow a firm to **develop a strategic information base** that can provide information to support the firm's competitive strategies. Information in a firm's corporate databases has always been a valuable asset in promoting efficient operations and effective management of a firm. However, information about a firm's operations, customers, suppliers, and competitors, as well as other economic and demographic data, is now viewed as a strategic resource; that is, it is used to support strategic planning, marketing, and other strategic initiatives.

For example, many businesses are now using computer-based information about their customers to help design marketing campaigns to sell customers new products and services. This is especially true of firms that include several subsidiaries offering a variety of products and services. For example, once you become a customer of a subsidiary of Sears Roebuck and Co., you quickly become a target for marketing campaigns by their other subsidiaries, based on information provided by the Sears strategic information resource base. This is one way a firm can leverage its investment in transaction processing and customer accounting systems—by linking its databases to its strategic planning and marketing systems. This strategy helps a firm create better marketing campaigns for new products and services, build better barriers to entry for competitors, and find better ways to lock in customers and suppliers.

Information Systems and the Value Chain

Let's look at one final important concept that can help a manager identify opportunities for strategic information systems. The **value chain** concept was developed by Michael Porter [31] and is illustrated in Figure 11.6. It views a firm as a series, or "chain," of basic activities that add value to its products and services and thus add a margin of value to the firm. In the value chain concept, some business activities are primary activities, others are support activities. This framework can highlight where

FIGURE 11.6
The value chain of a firm. Note the examples of the variety of strategic information systems that can be applied to a firm's basic activities for competitive advantage.

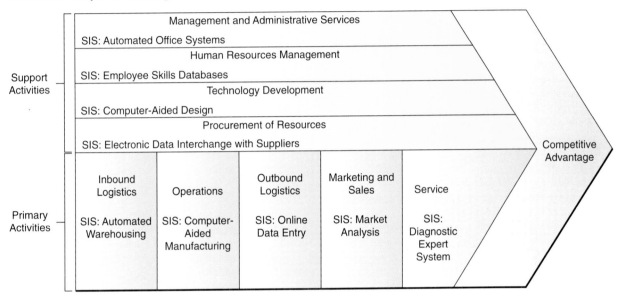

competitive strategies can best be applied in a business. That is, managerial end users should try to develop a variety of strategic information systems for those basic activities that add the most value to a company's products or services, and thus to the overall business value of the firm. Figure 11.6 provides examples of how and where information systems technology can be applied to basic business activities using the value chain framework.

For example, Figure 11.6 shows that office automation systems can increase the productivity of office communications and support activities in management and administrative services. Employee skills database systems can help the human resource management function locate and assign employees to important positions and projects. Computer-aided design (CAD) systems can automate the design of products and processes as part of technology development. Finally, electronic data interchange (EDI) systems can help improve procurement of resources by providing online telecommunications links to a firm's suppliers.

Other examples of strategic applications of information systems technology to primary business activities are identified in Figure 11.6. These include automated warehousing systems to support inbound logistic activities involving storage of inventory, computer-aided manufacturing (CAM) systems for manufacturing operations, and online order entry systems to improve *outbound logistics* activities that process customer orders. Information systems can also support marketing and sales activities by providing analyses of present and potential markets for goods and services, and can improve customer service by offering expert system diagnostic services to customers.

Thus, the value chain concept can help managers decide where and how to apply the strategic capabilities of information technology. It shows how various types of strategic information systems can be applied to the specific business activities that help a firm gain competitive advantages in the marketplace.

Capital One Financial: Strategic Data Mining

Some say the devil is in the details, but for Capital One Financial Corp. there is nothing but gold in its hugely detailed database of customer information. The once-sluggish company has taken off like a rocket, thanks to a savvy use of information technology that enables Capital One to extract rich insights from the data about the behavior of customers and prospects. "We know a lot about our customers," said James Donehey, Capital One's chief information officer. "We get a lot of empirical evidence from the thousands and thousands of tests we run every year."

The oldest credit-card provider in the United States, 41-year-old Capital One has risen from 18th to 11th place among credit-card companies in the past seven years. Last year alone, its credit-card loans grew by 60 percent. The company credits information technology for allowing it to develop marketing techniques that are now widely used in the industry and for giving it one of the lowest bad-debt write-off rates in the business.

"Our proprietary information–based strategy is the cornerstone of our success," the company wrote on the first page of its annual report. One of Capital One's most valuable assets does not show up on the balance sheet: millions of customer records built up from years of credit-card transactions. The company leverages those records—with mathematical models it developed—to test-market credit-card offerings in a risk-free environment.

"The credit-card business is not banking—it is really the information business," said Richard D. Fairbank, chairman and chief executive officer of Capital One.

At the foundation of its strategy are the records of customers, which are "mined" using computer models that employ actuarial and behavioral principles to predict individual risk and credit-card use patterns. The market success and risk associated with a product launch can be predicted, in part, from past usage patterns.

Many ideas crash and burn, but those that survive the tests have much of the risk wrung out of them, said John Pastore, an IT manager, "We base our marketing decisions more on risk than on profitability. If you manage the risk, profitability will happen," he said.

"Credit cards are credit cards are credit cards," Pastore said. "It's our computer models that make us unique. We start with brainstorming sessions," he added. "What factors should we test? What [is] the meaning of the factors, and how do you measure them? In any mailing there are hundreds of tests—from font sizes and colors on the envelope to fees and interest rates. We are good at predicting that if we use this color, we will get that response."

"We look at service and operations as opportunities for revenue, not as expenses," said Marge Connelly, a vice president and manager of customer service, back office operations, and quality assurance.

Connelly said many credit-card companies view functions such as customer statement preparations and mailing as commodities and outsource them. "But we have found tons of ways to manipulate those processes to bring us additional value," she said. For example, Connelly said the sort sequence of the customer file can be set to minimize postage costs or to allow a variety of inserts, each carefully calculated to appeal to certain customer segments.

Capital One's methods have led to industrywide innovations such as "balance transfer" offers in which the company offers a temporarily low interest rate to induce people to move balances on a competing card to a Capital One card. They have also enabled Capital One to reduce its annual charge-off rate from 5.6 percent in 1991 to 1.5 percent last year. Each percentage point is worth more than $70 million before taxes.

And in an industry where companies often have just four products—Visa and MasterCard in regular and "gold" versions—Capital One has thousands of offerings. The firm offers secured and unsecured cards, student cards, joint account cards, and affinity cards, each with various combinations of interest rates, fees, terms, and conditions.

"They were among the first to use very targeted solicitations and pricing strategies to attract the most profitable customers—low-risk customers who maintain a monthly balance," said Michael Freudenstein, a financial services analyst at J. P. Morgan Securities, Inc., in New York. "They were out-front with the 'balance transfer' product, for example." Now that other companies are going after the same balance transfer prospects, Capital One is mining the data for new opportunities, Freudenstein said. "They are searching for the next great product, and they want to be there first again," he said.

CASE STUDY QUESTIONS

1. Is data mining of customer records by Capital One Financial an example of the strategic use of information technology? Why or why not?

2. What competitive IT strategies are being implemented by Capital One in this case? Refer to Figure 11.4 to help you explain your choices.

3. What does Marge Connelly mean when she says that "we look at service and operations as opportunities for revenue, not as expenses"?

Source: Adapted from Gary Anthes, "Customer 'Data Mining' Pays Off," *Computerworld*, May 15, 1995, pp. 1,28. Copyright 1995 by Computerworld, Inc., Framingham, MA 01701—Reprinted from *Computerworld*.

┌─ **SECTION II**
│ *Strategic Applications and Issues in Information*
│ *Technology*
└─

How do most companies use information technology? Figure 11.7 illustrates various ways that organizations may view and use information technology. Companies may use information systems strategically, or may use them in defensive or controlled ways. For example, if a company emphasized strategic business uses of information technology, its management would view IT as a major competitive differentiator. It would then devote significant amounts of technology to support decision making, and to improve business processes. More and more businesses are beginning to use

Introduction

FIGURE 11.7
How a business may view and employ information technology.

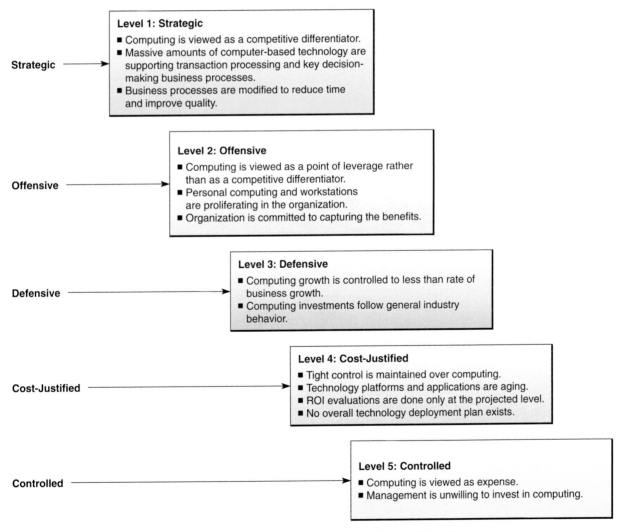

Source: Richard Murray, "The Quest for World Class IT Capability." *Information Systems Management,* Summer 1991, p. 13.

FIGURE 11.8
Information technology can break time, geographic, cost, and structural barriers.

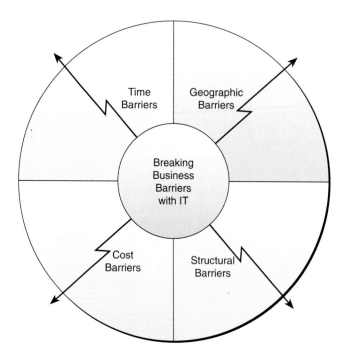

information systems strategically for competitive advantage. In this section, we will provide many examples of such strategic business applications of information technology.

Breaking Business Barriers

Figure 11.8 illustrates a useful framework for focusing on several vital capabilities of information technology that break traditional barriers to strategic business success. Two key capabilities of information technology seem obvious. First, computers and telecommunications networks break time barriers. Telecommunications is a lot faster than most other forms of communications. Second, computers and telecommunications break geographic barriers. Telecommunications networks enable you to communicate with people almost anywhere in the world as if you were there with them.

Two other business capabilities of information technology are not so obvious, or as easy to establish. First, information technology can break cost barriers. That is, computers and telecommunications networks can often significantly reduce the costs of business operations when compared with other means of information processing and communications. Second, telecommunications can break structural barriers. That is, computers and telecommunications networks can help a business develop strategic relationships by establishing new electronic linkages with customers, suppliers, and other business entities.

Figure 11.9 outlines examples of the four major strategic capabilities of information technology. This figure emphasizes how several strategic applications of information technology can help a firm capture and provide information quickly to

FIGURE 11.9
Examples of the strategic benefits of information technology.

Capabilities	Examples	Benefits
Break geographic barriers: Capture information about business transactions from remote locations	Transmission of customer orders from traveling salespeople to a corporate data center for order processing and inventory control	Provides better customer service by reducing delay in filling orders and improves cash flow by speeding up the billing of customers
Break time barriers: Provide information to remote locations immediately after it is requested	Credit authorization at the point of sale	Credit inquiries can be made and answered in seconds
Break cost barriers: Reduce the cost of more traditional means of communication	Video teleconferencing	Reduces expensive business trips; allows more people to participate in a meeting, thus improving the quality of decisions reached
Break structural barriers: Support linkages for competitive advantage	Electronic data interchange (EDI) of transaction data to and from suppliers and customers	Fast, convenient service locks in customers and suppliers

end users at remote geographic locations at reduced costs, as well as supporting its strategic organizational objectives. For example, telecommunications links between the computers of traveling salespeople and those at regional sales offices can be used to transmit customer orders, thus breaking geographic barriers. Point-of-sales terminals and an online sales transaction processing network can break time barriers by supporting immediate credit authorization and sales processing. Teleconferencing can be used to cut costs by reducing the need for expensive business trips since it allows more people from remote locations to participate in meetings and collaborate on group projects. Finally, electronic data interchange systems are used by the business to establish strategic relationships with their customers and suppliers by making the exchange of electronic business documents fast, convenient, and tailored to the needs of the business partners involved. Let's now look at examples of such applications in more detail.

How can information technology shorten the intervals between the various critical steps in a business process? That's the focus of *interval reduction* and *just-in-time* operations. Their goal is to shorten the response time to customer demands and reduce inventory investment to a minimum, thus helping to make a company an *agile competitor.*

Breaking Time Barriers

- Producers who deliver their products and services in *real time* relative to their competitors will have a strategic advantage. Operating in real time means no *lag time* between identification and fulfillment of a need [12].
- Every major on-line use of IT in core operations moves firms toward just-in-time something—inventory, sales, distribution, publishing, scheduling, or reporting. Reducing time and inventory is one of the new business imperatives [23].

FIGURE 11.10
Regional and global computing
networks support distributed
business operations.

John Feingersch/The Stock Market.

Toyota is a classic example of the use of computers and telecommunications networks for interval reductions and just-in-time operations that resulted in a significant strategic advantage [12]. In the early 1980s, Toyota found to its dismay that while it took them about 2 days to manufacture a car, it took about 25 to 30 days to process a customer's order for a car. From a total cost standpoint, Toyota then concluded that it was costing more to process the order on a car than to manufacture the car!

Toyota responded by developing a global telecommunications network that links the computers of its dealers and distribution centers to the computers at its headquarters in Toyota City, and the production and scheduling computers at its manufacturing centers. Its goal is to enable a customer in Japan to order a car that is not in inventory and have it delivered within 48 hours. As a result, Toyota gained a major competitive advantage measured by increases in customer satisfaction at the faster response times, and reductions in the costs involved in delivering a car from the factory to a customer.

Breaking Geographic Barriers

How can information technology break the geographic barriers that hinder the managerial control of operations, raise the cost of doing business, and limit the quality of services and the coverage of potential markets? Many businesses today operate from several locations and have customers or suppliers at distant locations. If a business is regional, national, or global in scope, then telecommunications networks become a vital component of its business operations. See Figure 11.10.

Telecommunications and computing technologies make it possible to distribute key business activities to where they are most needed, where they are best performed, or where they best support the competitive advantage of a business. Telecommunications networks link remote locations with company headquarters, other remote locations, and external entities such as suppliers, customers, and consultants. All of these entities can participate in business activities as if geographic barriers did not exist. Let's take a look at a few examples.

Citibank of New York moved its entire credit card operation to South Dakota during the 1980s because of high labor costs in New York City and restrictions by the State of New York on the interest rates it could charge for credit cards. Citibank uses leased satellite channels for data and voice communications, facsimile, and teleconferencing between its New York headquarters and its credit card operations center in South Dakota. Thus, Citibank's experience demonstrates that telecommunications networks enable a business to move part of its operations to distant locations with lower costs, a better workforce, or less restrictive government regulations [9].

Mobil Oil Corporation is another example of how information technology can break geographic barriers. Mobil has a worldwide computing network for oil exploration consisting of several HP9000 minicomputers and over 1,000 personal computers and technical workstations. Mobil can pool the expertise of its scientists and engineers at 11 locations around the globe. For example, it may use E-mail and data communications to call on its engineers in Canada, Australia, Dallas, and Singapore to help analyze the feasibility of drilling for oil in sandstone off the coast of Nigeria. Or a Mobil scientist performing graphics-based analysis in Indonesia can send drawings in real time to a colleague in Norway working a similar problem [17]. Thus, geographic barriers can effectively be ignored through the proper use of telecommunications for business operations.

Breaking Cost Barriers

How can information technology enable a business to gain strategic reductions in operating costs? Computers interconnected by telecommunications networks in key business areas can substantially reduce the costs of production, inventory, distribution, or communications for many business firms. Thus, information technology has helped companies cut labor costs, minimize inventory levels, reduce the number of distribution centers, and lower communications costs. Let's look at a specific example.

A few years ago, Hewlett-Packard (H-P) realized that it was spending $50 million to $100 million more each year than necessary on raw material purchases. That's because H-P is highly decentralized. It grants its operating divisions almost complete autonomy in purchasing and other operational decisions, "because they know their own needs best." However, because of this decentralization of purchasing, the company could not take advantage of high-volume discounts available from its suppliers.

Instead of centralizing purchasing, H-P used telecommunications networks to link the computers of divisional purchasing departments to a corporate procurement center's database. Each division at H-P still makes its own purchasing decisions. However, the corporate procurement office is able to integrate divisional purchasing information in the database to help it negotiate volume discounts for H-P's purchases, thus saving the company millions of dollars each year [23].

Breaking Structural Barriers

How can information technology enable a firm to break structural barriers that inhibit its operations or limit its drive for competitive advantage? Telecommunications networks can support innovations in the delivery of services, increase the scope and penetration of markets, and create strategic alliances with customers, suppliers, and even a firm's competitors. For example, automated teller machines shared by several banks and credit card companies placed in supermarkets and shopping malls break structural barriers between competing firms and expand the market for innovative financial services. Electronic data interchange (EDI)

FIGURE 11.11
How business process reengineering differs from business
improvement.

| | Spectrum of Reengineering | |
	Business Improvement	Business Reengineering
Definition	Incrementally improving existing processes	Radically redesigning business systems
Target	Any process	Strategic business processes
Potential Payback	10%–50% improvements	10-fold improvements
Risk and Level of Disruption	Low	High
What Changes?	Same jobs, Just more efficient	Big job cuts; new jobs Major job; redesign
Primary Enablers	IT and work simplification	IT and organizational redesign

Source: Adapted from Colleen Frye, "Imaging Proves Catalyst for Reengineering," *Computerworld/Client Server Journal,*
November 1994, p. 54. Copyright 1994 by Computerworld, Inc. Framingham, MA 01701—Reprinted from
Computerworld.

networks can create strategic links between a business and its customers and suppliers. They become "business partners," linked together by the convenience, efficiency, and the cost savings of their EDI network, and prospective customers for new
types of services.

For example, Miller Brewing Company is a customer of Reynolds Metals company and one of Reynolds' EDI business partners. Miller is helping Reynolds reduce
the inventory of aluminum coils used at tin can manufacturing plants, and track the
quality of aluminum that is received from Reynolds and other suppliers. Reynolds
developed software that enables Miller to use its EDI network links to Reynolds to
track in-transit inventories, as well as do materials forecasting and ordering and
quality control monitoring. Thus, Reynolds' EDI network is helping it develop a new
business alliance with one of its biggest customers [29].

Reengineering Business Processes

One of the most popular competitive strategies today is **business process reengineering** (BPR), most often simply called *reengineering*. In Chapter 1, we stressed that
reengineering is more than automating business processes to make modest improvements in the efficiency of business operations. We defined reengineering as a fundamental rethinking and radical redesign of business processes to achieve dramatic
improvements in cost, quality, speed, and service [19]. So BPR combines a strategy
of promoting business innovation with a strategy of making major improvements to
business operations so that a company can become a much stronger and more successful competitor in the marketplace. See Figure 11.11.

As Figure 11.11 points out, the potential payback of reengineering is high, but
so is its level of risk and disruption to the organizational environment. Making radical changes to business processes to dramatically improve efficiency and effectiveness is not an easy task. While many companies have reported impressive gains,
many others have failed to achieve the major improvements they sought through
reengineering projects [23, 25]. That's why organizational redesign approaches are
an important enabler of reengineering, along with the use of information technology.
For example, one common approach is the use of self-directed teams, where man-

FIGURE 11.12
The order management process.

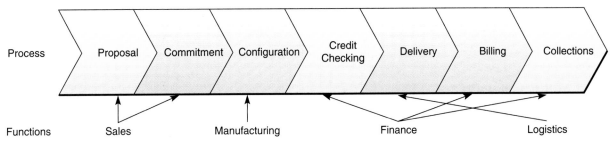

Source: Thomas Davenport, *Process Innovation: Reengineering Work through Information Technology* (Boston: Harvard Business School Press, 1993), p. 248.

- Prospect tracking and management systems.
- Portable sales force automation systems.
- Portable networking for field and customer site communications.
- Customer site workstations for order entry and status checking.
- Expert systems that match products and services to customer needs.
- Electronic data interchange and electronic funds transfer between firms.
- Expert systems for configuration, shipping, and pricing.
- Predictive modeling for continuous product replenishment.
- Composite systems that bring cross-functional information to employee workstations.
- Customer, product, and production databases.

FIGURE 11.13
Examples of information technologies that support reengineering the sales and order management processes.

Source: Adapted from Thomas Davenport, *Process Innovation: Reengineering Work through Information Technology* (Boston: Harvard Business School Press, 1993), p. 247.

agers become coaches and advisors to employees instead of supervisors. Another is the use of *case managers,* who handle almost all tasks in a business process, instead of splitting tasks among many different specialists [18, 19].

Of course, information technology plays a major role in reengineering business processes. The speed, information processing power, and ease-of-use of modern computer hardware, software, and networks can be used to dramatically increase the efficiency of business processes, and communications and collaboration among the people responsible for their operation and management. For example the order management process illustrated in Figure 11.12 is vital to the success of most companies. Many of them are reengineering this process with the help of the information technologies listed in Figure 11.13 [10].

The Role of Information Technology

The IBM Credit Corporation is one of the classic examples of how many companies are employing information technologies to reengineer business processes. IBM Credit reengineered a five step credit application process that formerly took four specialists an average of more than seven days to complete. Now 55 percent of the credit requests are processed almost instantaneously by computers. The other 45

IBM Credit Corporation

percent of credit applications are completely handled in one step and no more than four hours by case managers, called deal structurers, assisted by an easy-to-use computer-based credit processing system. In a few really tough cases, deal structurers consult and work as a team with a small group of credit experts. Now IBM Credit can process 100 times more credit requests than they formerly did with the same number of people [18, 19].

Ford Motor Company

Figure 11.14 shows how Ford Motor Company reengineered its procurement process. Procurement involves the purchasing, receiving, and accounts payable activities. Notice that the old process required the transmittal of five paper documents: (1) purchase order from purchasing to the vendor, (2) copy to accounts payable, (3) receiving document to accounts payable, (4) invoice from the vendor to accounts payable, and (5) check in payment from accounts payable to the vendor. Over 500 people were employed in accounts payable to process these documents. Much of this processing involved resolving discrepancies among the documents, especially when .he items in the receiving document did not match the items in the purchase order or the vendor's invoice.

Ford reengineered this procurement process with the help of information technology. Instead of waiting to begin the payment process until a vendor sends an invoice, Ford's new system triggers payment when the goods are received. Notice that a check in payment is now the only paper document involved. Now, an electronic purchase order is transmitted by the purchasing department to the vendor using electronic data interchange (EDI). The purchasing department also enters the data into a procurement database. When goods from a vendor arrive at Ford, the receiving department uses their computers to see whether they match the purchase order information in the database. If they do, the database is updated to show that the goods have been accepted. Payment is then sent to the vendor by accounts payable, which now needs only 125 people for the procurement process [18, 19].

CIGNA Corporation

CIGNA Corporation, a leading worldwide insurance and financial services company, is our final reengineering example. CIGNA employs 50,000 people in almost 70 countries. Between 1989 and 1993, CIGNA completed over 20 reengineering projects, saving over $100 million. At CIGNA,

> reengineering was refocused from excellence in operational business processes to enabling new business growth. Along the way, reengineering has begun to become part of the way that CIGNA employees and managers think. To CIGNA, business reengineering means "break-through innovation focused on customer needs." It is a vehicle to realign strategy, operations, and systems to deliver significantly increased financial results [6].

Thus, reengineering at CIGNA is a strategic business initiative. Figure 11.15 summarizes the objectives and accomplishments of reengineering programs of four major business areas at CIGNA. Major changes in business information systems and the use of information technology were involved in all of the projects. For example, the corporate medical presale process was reengineered with major revisions made to work activities and manual and computer-based procedures. The time to deliver a quote to a customer for corporate medical insurance was reduced from 17 days to 3. Fourteen manual "hand-offs" of work from one person to another were reduced to three all-electronic transfers. See Figure 11.16.

Before Reengineering: pay when invoice received.

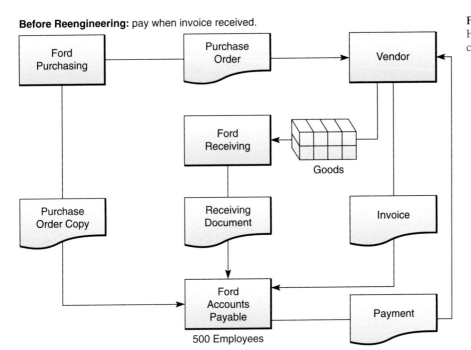

FIGURE 11.14
How Ford reengineered its procurement processes.

After Reengineering: pay when goods received.

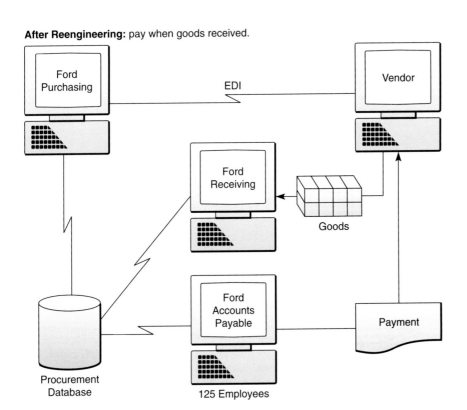

FIGURE 11.15
Objectives and accomplishments of reengineering projects at CIGNA.

Project	Initial Objectives	Accomplishments
CIGNA Re	▪ To dramatically reduce cost and enhance technology infrastructure.	▪ Staff reduced by 50%. ▪ Operating expenses reduced by 42%. ▪ 1,200% transaction time improvement. ▪ Team-based organization. ▪ Systems reduced from 17 mainframe-based systems to 5 PC-based systems.
CIGNA International Life and Employee Benefits-UK	▪ 30% improvement in cost. ▪ 50% improvement in quality. ▪ 50% improvement in cycle time. ▪ 30% improvement in customer satisfaction. ▪ 14% growth in business.	▪ 30% improvement in cost. ▪ 75% improvement in quality. ▪ 100% improvement in cycle time. ▪ 50% improvement in customer satisfaction.
Global Risk Management	▪ More effective estimate on costs and better pricing of products sold to foreign subsidiaries of U.S. corporations. ▪ Leveraging information and expertise residing at CIGNA's foreign offices.	▪ New products offered to customers. ▪ 25% staff reduction. ▪ $25 million reduction in operating expenses. ▪ Client server-based system that prices products considering local conditions and local losses.
Property and Casualty Claims Systems	▪ Improved working relationships between claims and systems, especially better communication. ▪ Faster response on systems changes. ▪ Better assessment of the business value of systems changes and new systems projects.	▪ Three organizational layers were flattened. ▪ Team-based organization. ▪ 32% reduction in systems staff. ▪ 63% reduction in reported systems problems. ▪ 100% accuracy on systems fixes. ▪ 43% reduction in systems requests.

Source: J. Raymond Caron, Sicrka Jarvenpaa, and Donna Stoddard, "Business Reengineering at CIGNA Corporation: Experiences and Lessons from the First Five Years," *MIS Quarterly*, September 1994, p. 235.

FIGURE 11.16
The results of reengineering the process to deliver an insurance quote to a corporate customer at CIGNA International—United Kingdom.

Corporate Medical Presale Process	
Before Reengineering	**After Reengineering**
▪ Seventeen-day cycle time.	▪ Three-day cycle time.
▪ Fourteen hand-offs—manual	▪ Three hand-offs—all electronic.
▪ Seven authorization steps.	▪ Zero authorization steps.
▪ Six hours of total work.	▪ Three hours of total work.
▪ Four hours of value-added work.	▪ Three hours of value-added work.
▪ Two hours of rework.	▪ Zero hours of rework.

Source: J. Rayond Caron, Sicrka Jarvenpaa, and Donna Stoddard, "Business Reengineering at CIGNA Corporation: Experiences and Lessons from the First Five Years," *MIS Quarterly*, September 1994, p. 240.

Improving Business Quality

No single approach to organizational change, including reengineering, is appropriate for all circumstances. Many companies have a portfolio of approaches to operational change including reengineering, continuous [quality] improvement, incremental approaches, and restructuring techniques. Some combine multiple approaches in one initiative—for example, using reengineering for a long-run solution and short-term process improvements in the current process to deliver quick benefit [11].

Thus, information technology can be used strategically to improve business performance in many ways other than in supporting reengineering initiatives. One

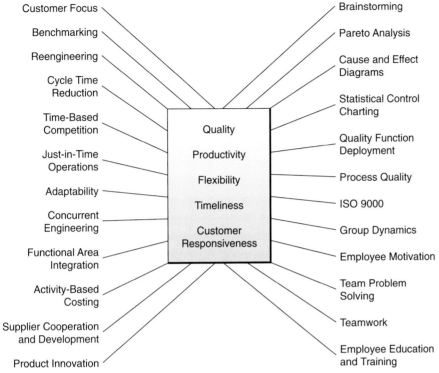

FIGURE 11.17
The objectives and methodologies of total quality management.

Source: Adapted from C. Carl Pegels, *Total Quality Management: A Survey of Its Important Aspects* (Danvers, MA: Boyd & Fraser Publishing Co., 1995), p. 6.

important strategic thrust is continuous quality improvement, popularly called *total quality management* (TQM). Previous to TQM, quality was defined as meeting established standards or specifications for a product or service. *Statistical quality control* programs were used to measure and correct any deviations from standards [10].

However, **total quality management** is a much more strategic approach to business improvement. Quality is emphasized from the customer's viewpoint, rather than the producer's. Thus, quality is defined as meeting or exceeding the requirements and expectations of customers for a product or service. This may involve many features and attributes, such as performance, reliability, durability, responsiveness, aesthetics, and reputation, to name a few [31, 40].

Total quality management is also a much broader management approach than quality control. As Figure 11.17 illustrates, TQM may use a variety of tools and methods to seek continuous improvement of quality, productivity, flexibility, timeliness, and customer responsiveness. According to quality guru Richard Schonberger, companies who use TQM are committed to:

1. Even better, more appealing, less variable quality of the product or service.
2. Even quicker, less-variable response—from design and development through supplier and sales channels, offices, and plants all the way to the final user.
3. Even greater flexibility in adjusting to customers' shifting volume and mix requirement.

Total Quality Management

FIGURE 11.18
Examples of improvements gained through total quality management.

- **AMP.** On-time shipments improved from 65% to 95%, and AMP products have nationwide availability within three days or less on 50% of AMP sales.
- **Asia, Brown, Boveri.** Every improvement goal customers asked for—better delivery, quality responsiveness, and so on—was met.
- **Chrysler.** New vehicles are now being developed in 33 months versus as long as 60 months 10 years ago.
- **Eaton.** Increased sales per employee from $65,000 in 1983 to about $100,000 in 1992.
- **Fidelity.** Handles 200,000 information calls in four telephone centers; 1,200 representatives handle 75,000 calls, and the balance is automated.
- **Ford.** Use of 7.25 man-hours of labor per vehicle versus 15 man-hours in 1980; Ford Taurus bumper uses 10 parts compared to 100 parts on similar GM cars.
- **General Motors.** New vehicles are now being developed in 34 months versus 48 months in the 1980s.
- **IBM Rochester.** Defect rates per million are 32 times lower than four years ago and on some products exceed six sigma (3.4 defects per million).
- **Pratt & Whitney.** Defect rate per million was cut in half; a tooling process was shortened from two months to two days; part lead times were reduced by 43%.
- **VF Corp.** Market response system enables 97% in-stock rate for retail stores compared to 70% industry average.
- **NCR.** Checkout terminal was designed in 22 months versus 44 months and contained 85% fewer parts than its predecessor.
- **AT&T.** Redesign of telephone switch computer completed in 18 months versus 36 months, manufacturing defects reduced by 87%.
- **Deere & Co.** Reduced cycle time of some of its products by 60%, saving 30% of usual development costs.

Source: Carl C. Pegels, *Total Quality Management: A Survey of Its Important Aspects* (Danvers, MA: Boyd & Fraser Publishing Co., 1995), p. 27.

4. Even lower cost through quality improvement, rework reduction, and non-value-adding waste elimination [31].

Figure 11.18 summarizes examples of many improvements to business performance attributed by companies to their total quality management programs [31]. Information technology was significantly involved in most of these improvements, along with a variety of organizational, management, and work redesign initiatives. Let's look at a few examples involving information technology in more detail.

AMP Corporation

AMP Corporation is a leading manufacturer of electrical/electronic connectors and interconnection systems. It has 28,000 employees and operates 180 facilities in 36 countries, with sales approaching $4 billion in 1994. AMP promotes total quality management in many ways, including several global online systems. One system, called Quality Scoreboard, enables over 2,500 managers at all levels to access key performance indicators for internal operations, customers, distributors, suppliers, and competitors. Managers can also view daily quality information about products manufactured or purchased by AMP. Quality Scoreboard can even be used to initiate corrective action by managers. Another system, called Delivery Scoreboard, provides managers with daily shipping and scheduling performance results for the company [5].

Ford is committed to designing quality into their cars, instead of relying on inspection during and after the production process. One key use of information technology that supports this quality strategy is an easy-to-use database of customer and quality information. The database is continuously updated with customer expectations and concerns, and lessons learned from customer feedback. This database is then accessed for information by quality professionals who are involved in the design and development, testing, and manufacturing-planning processes. Ford feels that the customer/quality database is a key element in increasing customer satisfaction. And that is important, since Ford estimates that each one-point gain in owner loyalty is worth $100 million in profit [5].

Ford Motor Company

We are changing from a competitive environment in which mass-market products and services were standardized, long-lived, information-poor, and exchanged in one-time transactions, to an environment in which companies compete globally with niche market products and services that are individualized, short-lived, information-rich, and exchanged on an ongoing basis with customers [15].

Becoming an Agile Competitor

Agility in competitive performance is the ability of a business to prosper in rapidly changing, continually fragmenting global markets for high-quality, high-performance, customer-configured products and services. An agile company can make a profit in markets with broad product ranges and short model lifetimes, can process orders in arbitrary lot sizes, and can offer individualized products while maintaining high volumes of production. Agile companies depend heavily on information technology to support and manage business processes, while providing the information processing capability to treat masses of customers as individuals [15].

Figure 11.19 illustrates that to be an agile competitor, a business must implement four basic strategies of agile competition. First, customers of an agile company feel enriched by products or services that they perceive as solutions to their individual problems. Thus, products can be priced based on their value as solutions, not on their cost to produce. Second, an agile company cooperates internally and with other companies, even competitors. This allows a business to bring products to market as rapidly and cost-effectively as possible, no matter where resources are located and who owns them. Third, an agile company organizes so that it thrives on change and uncertainty. It uses flexible, multiple organizational structures keyed to the requirements of different and constantly changing customer opportunities. Finally, an agile company leverages the impact of its people and the information and knowledge that they possess. By nurturing an entrepreneurial spirit, an agile company provides powerful incentives for employee responsibility, adaptability, and innovation [15].

The bottleneck to higher levels of performance in an agile company is not equipment but information flow, internally and among cooperating companies. Information is already an increasingly important and increasingly valuable component of consumer and commercial products. Packaging information, providing access to information, and information "tools"—for example, design software and database search software—will become increasingly valuable products in their own right, as well as increasingly valuable elements of hardware products, such as automobiles [15].

The Role of Information Technology

So information technology is a strategic requirement for agile product development and delivery. Information systems provide the information that people need to support agile operations, as well as the information built into products and services. Let's take a look at several examples.

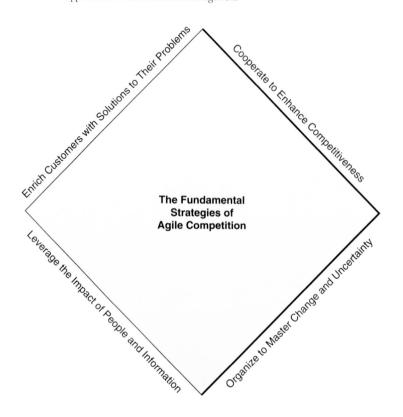

Ross Operating Valves

Ross Operating Valves manufactures hydraulic valves in Madison Heights, Michigan, in Lavonia, Georgia, and in Frankfurt and Tokyo. Ross uses a manufacturing system called Ross/Flex at the Lavonia plant. Ross/Flex consists of proprietary computer-aided design (CAD) software and a database of digitized valve designs. Ross/Flex enables valves to be custom-designed jointly by customers and by Ross "integrators"—engineers and skilled machinists. Designs are downloaded to computer-controlled machine tools. Prototypes are completed in one day at a typical cost of $3,000, one-tenth of the previous cost and time.

After the prototype is tested, customers can request changes to produce improved prototypes. When they are satisfied, customers can then approve production of the valves. Since introducing Ross/Flex in 1992 as a "free" service, business has increased dramatically and Ross has enjoyed extraordinary market success. In 1995, Ross began offering customers the option of remotely accessing its design software and database for a fee. Customers can then design their own valves and download them to Ross computer-controlled machinery for production [1, 15].

Ross/Flex demonstrates the strategic use of information technology to support agile competition. Ross (1) enriches customers with custom-designed solutions, (2) cooperates with them to enhance their own competitiveness, (3) organizes innovatively with teams of integrators who can easily handle changing customer needs, and (4) leverages their people and information resources to produce innovative and profitable business opportunities in a dynamic global market.

Motorola and Toshiba

Motorola manufactures customer-configured cellular pagers to order at its Boynton Beach, Florida plant. Pagers are assembled, tested, packaged, and shipped using

- **Adaptability.** Able to adapt to a diverse, fast-changing business environment.
- **Opportunism.** Created, operated, and dissolved to exploit business opportunities when they appear.
- **Excellence.** Possess all-star, world-class excellence in the core competencies that are needed.
- **Technology.** Provide world-class information technology and other required technologies in all customer solutions.
- **Borderless.** Easily and transparently synthesize the competencies and resources of business partners into integrated customer solutions.
- **Trust-Based.** Members are trustworthy and display mutual trust in their business relationships.

FIGURE 11.20
Six basic characteristics of successful virtual companies.

computer-controlled machinery, only hours after receiving the remotely entered customer orders. Motorola also has a built-to-order facility for two-way radios in Plantation, Florida. This plant produces 500 different models. The radios are made to individual customer order in two hours, compared to 10 days as recently as 1990 [15].

Toshiba manufactures more than 20 models of portable computers, each with many different customer-selected options. It assembles them on a single production line in batches of 20 per model, and can still make money on batches as small as 10 computers. At each work point on the production line, a notebook computer provides instructions for assembling the next model, the mix of options for each unit, and the number to be assembled [15].

Motorola and Toshiba both demonstrate the use of information technology to support agile competition. Many different models of products are quickly produced to order for their customers, using computer-controlled or -supported production lines. Thus, both companies are able to enrich their customers with products that they want, when they want them. And both are able to do so profitably even when producing small amounts of constantly changing made-to-order products.

Creating a Virtual Company

These days, thousands of companies, large and small, are setting up virtual corporations that enable executives, engineers, scientists, writers, researchers, and other professionals from around the world to collaborate on new products and services without ever meeting face to face. Once the exclusive domain of Fortune 500 companies with banks of powerful computers and dedicated wide-area networks, remote networking is now available to any company with a phone, a fax, and E-mail access to the Internet or an online service [34].

In today's dynamic global business environment, forming a **virtual company** can be one of the most important strategic uses of information technology. A virtual company (also called a *virtual corporation* or *virtual organization*) is an organization that uses information technology to link people, assets, and ideas. Figure 11.20 outlines six basic characteristics of successful virtual companies. It emphasizes that to be successful, a virtual company must be an adaptable and opportunity-exploiting organization, providing world-class excellence in its competencies and technologies, which transparently create integrated customer solutions in business relationships based on mutual trust [15].

FIGURE 11.21
A network structure facilitates the creation of virtual companies.

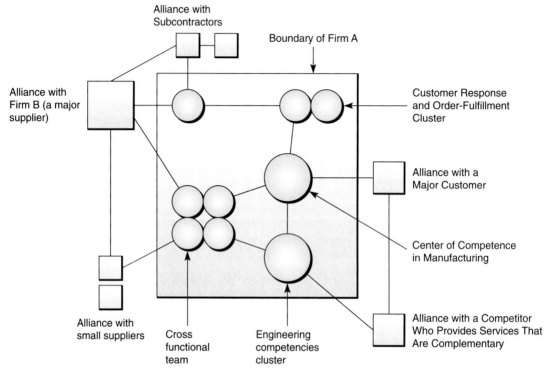

Source: James Cash, Jr., Robert Eccles, Nitin Nohria, and Richard Nolan, *Building the Information Age Organization: Structures, Control, and Information Technologies* (Burr Ridge, IL: Richard D. Irwin, 1994), p. 34.

Figure 11.21 illustrates that a business that forms virtual companies typically uses an organizational structure called a **network structure.** Notice that this company (Firm A) has developed alliances with suppliers, customers, subcontractors, and competitors. Thus the network structure makes it easy to create flexible and adaptable virtual companies keyed to exploit fast changing business opportunities [8].

Virtual Company Strategies

Why are people forming virtual companies? Several major reasons stand out, which are summarized in Figure 11.22. People and corporations are forming virtual companies as the best way to implement key business strategies that promise to ensure success in today's turbulent business climate.

For example, in order to exploit a diverse and fast-changing market opportunity, a business may not have the time or resources to develop the manufacturing and distribution infrastructure, people competencies, and information technologies needed. Only by quickly forming a virtual company of all-star partners can it assemble the components it needs to provide a world-class solution for customers that will capture the market opportunity. And, of course, computers, telecommunications networks, and other information technologies will be a vital component in creating a successful solution. Let's look at several examples.

- Share infrastructure and risk.
- Link complementary core competencies.
- Reduce concept-to-cash time through sharing.
- Increase facilities and market coverage.
- Gain access to new markets and share market or customer loyalty
- Migrate from selling products to selling solutions

FIGURE 11.22
Business strategies of virtual companies.

Steelcase, Inc.

Steelcase, Inc., is a major U.S. maker of office furniture. It has formed a virtual company called Turnstone as a subsidiary. Turnstone sells office furniture and office products through catalogs designed and printed by a third-party company. Customers of Turnstone phone in credit card orders to a telemarketing company based in Denver, which transmits the order data to computers at warehouses operated by Excel Logistics, Inc., in Westerville, Ohio. From there the products are shipped to customers by Excel, or by another carrier it has hired as a subcontractor. Excel's computer systems handle all order processing, shipment tracking, and inventory control applications. So marketing and financial management and coordinating the virtual company's business partners are the only major functions left to Turnstone's managers [26].

IBM Ambra

IBM's Ambra is a classic example of a virtual company formed to take advantage of a limited market opportunity. Ambra was a virtual company subsidiary of the IBM Corporation, formed by IBM to produce and market a PC clone. Ambra's headquarters were in Raleigh, North Carolina. There 80 employees used global telecommunications networks to coordinate the activities of five companies that were the other business partners that made up the virtual company.

This included Wearnes Technology, of Singapore, which did engineering design and subsystem development services, and manufactured or contracted for the Ambra PC components. SCI Systems manufactured the Ambra microcomputers in its assembly plants on a build-to-order basis from order data received by its computers from AI incorporated. AI, a subsidiary of Insight Direct, a national telemarketing company based in Tempe, Arizona, received orders for Ambra computers from customers over its 800-number telephone lines. Merisel Enterprises provided the product and delivery database used by AI, and handled Ambra order fulfillment and customer delivery. Finally, another IBM subsidiary provided field service and customer support [15].

Using the Internet

Companies will continue to use the Internet as a marketing channel—a place to publish information about themselves and their products—as well as to communicate with customers and business partners. But the Internet is capable of far more. Viewing the 'net merely as a gigantic bulletin board or electronic-mail system badly misses the point. With its extraordinary scope and growth, this global network of networks' true future will be to support distributed applications across companies and geographic boundaries [3].

FIGURE 11.23
Using the Internet for business.

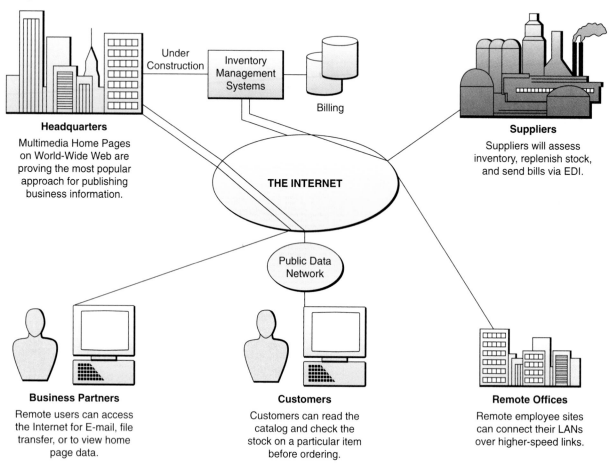

Source: Adapted from Ellis Booker, "A Tangled Web: Businesses Struggle to Leaverage the Internet," *Computerworld/Client Server Journal,* April 1995, p. 19. Copyright 1995 by Computerworld, Inc., Framingham, MA 01701—Reprinted from *Computerworld.*

Connecting to the Internet is one of the fastest growing and most popular ways that companies are trying to create strategic business applications of information technology. Figure 11.23 illustrates some of the present and potential business uses of the Internet. Notice that customers, suppliers, business partners, as well as the company headquarters and remote employee sites can be interconnected by the Internet.

Strategic Business Uses

Many businesses, both large and small, are viewing the Internet as a way to create strategic collaboration, operations, marketing, and alliances. These major **strategic business uses of the Internet** are summarized in Figure 11.24. Companies are using the global E-mail, bulletin board, file transfer, and remote computing capabilities of the Internet to support concurrent realtime collaboration among employees and business partners. This enables strategic gains to be made in the efficiency of business processes for developing, producing, marketing, or maintaining products and services. These same capabilities are fostering the growth of strategic alliances, including virtual companies, among business partners.

Many companies are dedicating servers to handle the hypermedia databases

- ▪ **Strategic Collaboration.** Realtime global communications and collaboration among employees and business partners to develop, produce, market, and maintain products and services.
- ▪ **Strategic Operations.** Global links to customers and suppliers using online ordering systems and electronic data interchange.
- ▪ **Strategic Marketing.** Promoting a company and its products and services by developing a variety of hyperlinked multimedia databases and information products for access by businesses and consumers.
- ▪ **Strategic Alliances.** Online global links to business partners. Electronic networking among the members of virtual companies.

FIGURE 11.24
Strategic business uses of the Internet.

and information products they are developing as *home pages* on the Internet's World Wide Web. This, typically, includes hyperlinked multimedia catalogs and promotional materials about a company's products and services that can be browsed using point-and-click browsing software like Mosaic or Netscape. Finally, some companies have begun to do online transaction processing on the Internet. This may involve electronic data interchange (EDI) between businesses and their suppliers, or electronic funds transfer (EFT) between businesses and their customers. However, the Internet lacks sufficient security, such as widespread use of secure servers and browsers, standard authorization techniques, and encryption of all monetary transactions. Once security is assured, the use of the Internet for online transaction processing should grow dramatically [3, 38]. See Figure 11.25.

General Electric Co. has established Home Pages on the Internet for its GE Plastics and GE Capital Services subsidiaries. GE Plastics Home Page contains more than 1,500 page of data and photos, between 35 and 50 megabytes of data. One of the main benefits of GE's Home Pages is to reduce the need for customers to call the GE help desk's 800-number, which receives over 80,000 calls yearly. GE hopes its Home Pages will strengthen its relationships with customers, while significantly cutting its phone bills and helping desk costs [3].

GE and Sun Microsystems

Sun Microsystems External Home Page is one of the most popular World Wide Web sites on the Internet. It has received over 50,000 accesses ("hits") from Internet users per month. Sun's External Home Page has 15 "buttons" hyperlinking customers, employees, and other users to everything from organizational maps to daily electronic news feeds. Because the External Home Page was so popular with its own employees, Sun has developed a Home Page for internal use by its staff. Called SunWeb, this Internet site is expected to improve communications and collaboration among Sun's employees worldwide [4].

Like other major corporations, Digital Equipment Corporation (DEC) and IBM, both leading computer manufacturers, make heavy use of the Internet. This includes sending and receiving thousands of E-mail messages daily, and providing standard and multimedia company or product information on servers. They also provide press releases, E-mail directories, and financial data. In addition, Digital has successfully used the remote computing capability of the Internet (Telenet) as a new way to market some of its computers. For example Digital connected two models of its latest high-performance Alpha computers to the Internet. It then invited Internet users to "test drive" the systems remotely using their own software to operate the machines. Several thousand potential customers logged on to the machines in six

Digital Equipment Corporation and IBM

FIGURE 11.25
The NEC Home Page on the
Internet's World Wide Web.

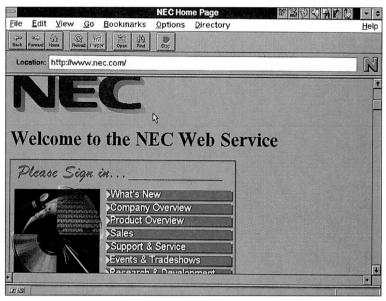

Sarah Evertson/Courtesy of NEC.

months. This resulted in sales of Alpha computers worth over $5 million to customers who had tried them on the Internet [38].

IBM includes an Internet Access Kit with its OS/2 Warp operating system. It also nurtures its relationship with OS/2 Warp users by providing easy access and 10 free hours of use to the IBM Global Network, also known as Advantis, and a World Wide Web point-and-click browser called WebExplorer. IBM also has developed an extensive Home Page Web Site called the IBM Internet Connection. Employees of IBM exchange over 30,000 Internet E-mail messages a day with outsiders. IBM engineers also use the Internet to collaborate with other companies in joint product development. For example, software engineers in Hawthorne, New York, use the Internet to collaborate with developers at Bellcore in New Jersey. They use Telenet to work on high performance workstations at Bellcore that they share with the Bellcore researchers [28, 38].

The Challenges of Strategic IS

As we have seen in this chapter, the strategic use of information technology enables managers to look at information systems in a new light. No longer is the information systems function merely an operations necessity; that is, a set of technologies for processing business transactions, supporting business processes, and keeping the books of a firm. It is also more than a helpful supplier of information and tools for managerial decision making. Now the IS function can help managers develop competitive weapons that use information technology to implement a variety of competitive strategies to meet the challenges of the competitive forces that confront any organization. However, this is easier said than done.

> We have learned over the past decade that it is not *the technology* that creates a competitive edge, *but the management process that exploits technology;* that there are not instant solutions, only difficult, lengthy, expensive implementations that involve organizational, technical, and market-related risk; and that competitive advantage comes from doing something others cannot match. If technology magically created competitive advantage for everyone, then there would effectively be no competitive edge for

FIGURE 11.26
Examples of the success and failure of strategic information systems.

	Strategic Success: Automated Teller Machines	Strategic Failure: Home Banking
Stimulus	Cost structures of branches; pressure on margins	Successes of ATMs and corporate cash management systems; perceived large market of personal computer users
First Major Mover(s)	Citibank (1976)	Chemical Bank (Pronto system) (1980)
Customer Acceptance	Rapid and consistent; convenience the draw	Minimal; no player in United States or Europe ever established a critical mass of customers. Many entrants to the market dropped out, as did Chemical, in 1989.
Catch-up Moves	"Shared access" networks (Cirrus, Monec); bank-specific networks, regional bank joint ventures	Mainly small-scale pilots and market tests; 19 American banks entered and abandoned the market, 1984–1989
First-Mover Expansion	Expanded locations in New York and other states; kept other banks from adding their ATM cards to the Citibank electronic franchise	Pronto abandoned in 1989
Commoditization	Strategic necessity by 1982. Almost every bank in the United States began offering ATM services.	Already complete, even before the market is established. No unique delivery base. Fifteen banks in 1990 were offering services through the Prodigy personal computer-based system. Still no evidence of a real market.
Comments	Highlights dilemma of cooperate versus compete. Consumer pressures for shared access plus operating costs of own networks forced expensive retrofit of systems. Cooperation earlier would have been cheaper for many.	The classic instance of the unmet potential: no technology blockages, but no self-justifying benefits seen by target customers

Source: Peter Keen, *Shaping the Future: Business Design through Information Technology* (Cambridge, MA: Harvard Business School Press, 1991), p. 48.

anyone. If innovation were easy, everyone would be an innovator. It is not easy, as evidenced by the many barriers to transforming IT from a problem to an opportunity. Among these barriers are the troubled history of IT in large organizations, particularly the limitations of the business management process; the culture gap between business and IS people; the rapid pace of technological change; and the immense and persistent difficulties associated with trying to integrate the many incompatible components of IT into a corporate platform [23].

So successful strategic information systems are not easy to develop and implement, as Figure 11.26 illustrates. They may require major changes in the way a

FIGURE 11.27

Key factors for sustaining strategic success in the use of information technology.

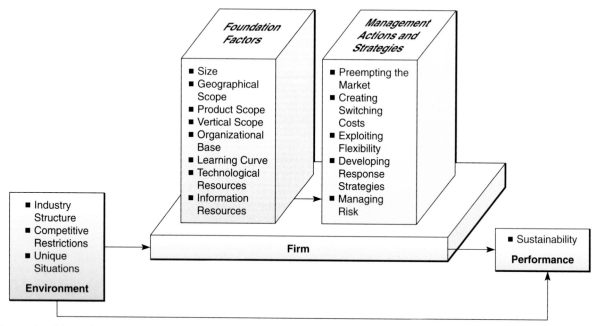

Source: Adapted from William Kettinger, Varun Grover, Subashish Guha, and Albert Segars, "Strategic Information Systems Revisited: A Study in Sustainability and Performance," *MIS Quarterly*, March 1994, p. 34.

business operates, and in their relationships with customers, suppliers, competitors, and others. The competitive advantages that information technology produces can quickly fade away if competitors can easily duplicate them, and the failure of strategic systems can seriously damage a firm's performance. Many of the examples and cases in this chapter and text demonstrate the challenges and problems as well as the benefits of the strategic uses of information technology. Thus, the effective use of strategic information systems presents managers with a major managerial challenge.

Sustaining Strategic Success

Figure 11.27 illustrates some of the factors that contribute to the success and sustainability of strategic information systems. Sustained success in using information technology strategically seems to depend on three sets of factors [24, 25].

- **The Environment.** A major environmental factor is the structure of an industry. For example, is it *oligopolistic*, that is, a closed structure with a few major players; or is it a wide open and level competitive playing field? Competitive restrictions and unique situations are environmental factors that involve political and regulatory restrictions to wide-open competition. For example, antitrust laws, patents, and government intervention can derail a company's plans for a preemptive business use of IT.

- **Foundation factors.** Unique industry position, alliance, assets, technological resources, and expertise are foundation factors that can give a company a competitive edge in a market. If such a company develops a strategic business use of IT, they have a winning combination for strategic success.

- **Management actions and strategies.** None of the other factors mentioned will ensure success if a company's management does not develop and initiate

FIGURE 11.28

Winners and losers in sustaining strategic advantage with IT. Sustained winners increased profits and market share for at least 5 to 10 years by strategic uses of information technology.

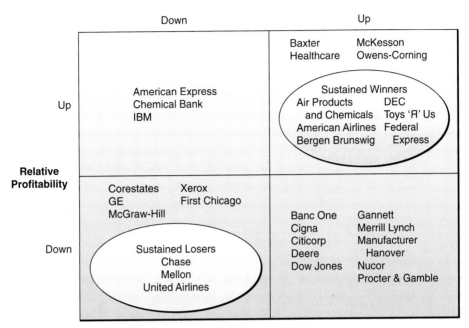

Relative Market Share

	Down	Up
Up	American Express Chemical Bank IBM	Baxter McKesson Healthcare Owens-Corning *Sustained Winners* Air Products DEC and Chemicals Toys 'Я' Us American Airlines Federal Bergen Brunswig Express
Down	Corestates Xerox GE First Chicago McGraw-Hill *Sustained Losers* Chase Mellon United Airlines	Banc One Gannett Cigna Merrill Lynch Citicorp Manufacturer Deere Hanover Dow Jones Nucor Procter & Gamble

Relative Profitability (left axis)

Source: William Kettinger, Varon Grover, and Albert Segars, "Do Strategic Systems Really Pay Off? An Analysis of Classic Strategic IT Cases," *Information Systems Management,* Winter 1995, p. 39

successful actions and strategies that shape how information technology is actually applied in the marketplace. Examples include (1) preempting the market by being first and way ahead of competitors in a strategic business use of IT, (2) creating switching costs and barriers to entry, (3) developing strategies to respond to the catch-up moves of competitors, and (4) managing the business risks inherent in any strategic IT initiatives.

Figure 11.28 provides an overview of recent research findings on companies who are winners and losers in terms of their strategic use of information technology [24]. Sustained winners include Air Products and Chemicals, American Airlines, Bergen Brunswig, DEC, Toys `R' Us, and Federal Express. These companies' investment in a specific strategic use of information technology continued to improve both their profitability and market share from 5 to 10 years after launching their strategic information systems. Sustained losers like Chase Manhattan, Mellon Bank, and United Airlines continued to suffer losses in profitability and market share for 5 to 10 years after making specific attempts to use IT strategically. As you can see, other companies had mixed success since they could not sustain profitability and market share for up to five years after introducing their strategic information systems.

So the lesson is clear. Sustained success in the strategic use of information technology is not a sure thing. Success depends on many environmental and foundation factors, but also on the actions and strategies of a company's management team. As a future manager, developing strategic business uses of information technology may be one of your biggest managerial challenges.

AMP, Inc.: Leveraging IT for a Quality Advantage

Ten years ago, electronic components manufacturer AMP, Inc., in Harrisburg, Pennsylvania, received 90 percent of all customer orders via telephone. By 1991, the number had dropped to 62 percent. More customers preferred to fax their orders, so AMP installed more fax machines for a total of five. But in 1994, statistics showed that only 61 percent of customers' faxes were getting through to the manufacturer on the first try. AMP again responded by increasing the number of inbound fax machines to 30. Three months later, another set of measurements revealed that the fax availability rate had jumped to 91.6 percent.

If you have not figured it out by now, AMP is a company driven—make that obsessed—by measurements, which in turn drive much of the systems development at its corporate logistics division.

"If it moves, we measure it," said Larry Brandt, associate director of customer service. To provide the best possible customer service, "we need to know what's coming at us, how it's coming and how much is coming," he explained.

AMP centralizes customer service, physical distribution, transportation, and several other functions into a single corporate logistics division. The unit's 50-person information systems group has created, among other things, an award-winning automated product information service and a system that lets customers track orders online.

Customers give both systems and the service they provide high marks for quality. "I'd rate AMP very high in customer service," said Andy Pisarski, an inventory management specialist at Anixter, Inc. "The tool we use most often is their dial-up system," Pisarski added. "I can go into the system and actually see on hand inventories, lead times and pricing. It takes me two seconds to look up an order instead of me asking them to look it up by a purchase order number."

At AMP, a call management system from AT&T does much of the measuring and number crunching. In addition to routing calls between the company's two main customer service centers in Harrisburg and California, the system measures the number of incoming calls, the number of calls completed before customers hang up, the time it takes to

answer a call and complete it, and the number of customer requests that are satisfied on the initial call.

On the systems side, these numbers help pinpoint where new kinds of services might improve overall customer satisfaction, according to Bryon Houtz, manager of systems planning and support.

For example, AMP's LAN-based outbound fax service was developed after statistics gleaned from the call management system identified customers' need for a fast way to access component specifications on demand.

AMP responded with AMPFAX, a 24-hour toll-free number that customers can use to download product drawings, instruction sheets, and component specifications to their fax machines from LAN-based PCs in the corporate logistics division.

In addition to generating statistics internally, AMP solicits performance feedback directly from customers via its Scorecard System. Under this program, customer keep their own AMP performance records, which are regularly compared with AMP's internal performance records.

Without fail, customers consistently rank on-time delivery as their number 1 priority, Brandt said. In response, AMP developed a forecast demand system, which gives customers such as Pisarski online access to the company's IBM mainframe-based inventory system. Using the dial-up system, customers can view inventory levels to plan forecasts and orders.

"We deploy technology that we can leverage best to our business," said John Stout, director of logistics systems.

CASE STUDY QUESTIONS

1. How is AMP using IT for quality management of customer service?

2. What competitive strategies are being implemented by AMP in this case? Refer to Figure 11.4 to help you explain your choices.

3. What could other companies learn from AMP's approach to customer service?

Source: Adapted from Julia King, "Electronics Firm Heeds Customers," *Computerworld*, May 1, 1995, p. 83. Copyright 1995 by Computerworld, Inc., Framingham, MA 01701—Reprinted from *Computerworld*.

Summary

- **The Role of Strategic Information Systems.** Information systems can play several strategic roles in businesses. They can help a business improve its operations, promote innovation, lock in customers and suppliers, create switching costs, raise barriers to entry, build a strategic IT platform, and develop a strategic information base. Thus, information technology can help a business gain a competitive advantage in its relationships with customers, suppliers, competitors, new entrants, and producers of substitute products. Refer to Figure 11.4 for a summary of the uses of information technology for strategic advantage.

- **Breaking Business Barriers.** Information technology can break traditional barriers to strategic business success. This includes time and geographic barriers broken by the speed and reach of global telecommunications networks. Information technology can also break cost barriers by significantly increasing the efficiency of business operations, and structural barriers by electronically linking a business to its customers, suppliers, and business partners.

- **Reengineering Business Processes.** Information technology is a key ingredient in reengineering business operations by enabling radical changes to business processes that dramatically improve their efficiency and effectiveness. IT can play a major role in supporting innovative changes in the design of work flows, job requirements, and organizational structures in a company.

- **Improving Business Quality.** Information technology can be used to strategically improve the quality of business performance. In a total quality management approach, IT can support programs of continual improvement in meeting or exceeding customer requirements and expectations in quality, services, cost, responsiveness, and other features that have a significant impact on a firm's competitive position.

- **Becoming an Agile Competitor.** A business can use information technology to help it become an agile company. Then it can prosper in rapidly changing markets with broad product ranges and short model lifetimes in which it must process orders in arbitrary lot sizes, and can offer individualized products while maintaining high volumes of production. An agile company depends heavily on IT to help it: (1) enrich its customers with customized solutions to their needs, (2) cooperate with other businesses to bring products to market as rapidly and cost-effectively as possible, (3) coordinate the flexible, multiple organizational structures it uses, and (4) leverage the competitive impact of its people and information resources.

- **Creating a Virtual Company.** Forming virtual companies has become an important competitive strategy in today's dynamic global markets. Information technology plays an important role in providing computing and telecommunications resources to support the communications, coordination, and information flows needed. Managers of a virtual company depend on IT to help them manage a network of people, knowledge, financial, and physical resources provided by many business partners to quickly take advantage of rapidly changing market opportunities.

- **Using the Internet.** Connecting to the Internet has become a key strategy for businesses seeking quick access to new markets. The Internet promises to be an attractive and cost-effective way for many companies to develop the strategic collaboration, operations, marketing, and alliances needed to solve and succeed in today's fast-changing global markets. Computing, telecommunications, and other information technologies are a necessary foundation for companies planning to implement such competitive strategies.

- **The Challenges of Strategic IS.** Successful strategic information systems are not easy to develop and implement. They may require major changes in how a business operates internally and with external stakeholders. Sustained success depends on many environmental and fundamental business factors, and especially on the actions and strategies of a company's management team. So developing strategic uses of information technology is a major managerial challenge.

Key Terms and Concepts

These are the key terms and concepts of this chapter. The page number of their first explanation is in parentheses.

1. Agile competitor (423)
2. Breaking business barriers (411)
   a. Cost barriers (415)
   b. Geographic barriers (414)
   c. Structural barriers (415)
   d. Time barriers (412)
3. Building a strategic IT platform (408)
4. Business process reengineering (416)
5. Competitive forces (402)
6. Competitive strategies (402)
7. Creating switching costs (407)
8. Developing a strategic information base (408)
9. Improving business operations (405)
10. Interorganizational information systems (407)
11. Leveraging investment in IT (408)

12. Locking in customers and suppliers (407)
13. Promoting business innovation (406)
14. Raising barriers to entry (408)
15. Strategic business use of the Internet (428)
16. Strategic information systems (402)
17. Strategic roles of information systems (404)
18. Total quality management (421)
19. Value chain (408)
20. Virtual company (425)

Review Quiz

Match one of the key terms and concepts listed above with one of the brief examples or definitions listed below. Try to find the best fit for answers that seem to fit more than one term or concept. Defend your choices.

_____ 1. A business must deal with customers, suppliers, competitors, new entrants, and substitutes.

_____ 2. Cost leadership, differentiation of products, and development of new products are examples.

_____ 3. Using investment in technology to keep firms out of an industry.

_____ 4. Making it unattractive for a firm's customers or suppliers to switch to its competitors.

_____ 5. Time, money, and effort needed for customers or suppliers to change to a firm's competitors.

_____ 6. Information systems that improve operational efficiency or promote business innovation are examples.

_____ 7. Information systems can help a business develop new products, services, and processes.

_____ 8. Information systems can help a business significantly reduce costs and improve productivity.

_____ 9. Information systems can help a business develop a strategic base of information.

_____ 10. A business can develop strategic capabilities in IT skills and resources.

_____ 11. Information systems can help a business develop electronic links to its customers and suppliers.

_____ 12. Highlights how strategic information systems can be applied to a firm's basic activities for competitive advantage.

_____ 13. A business can find strategic uses for the computing and telecommunications capabilities it has acquired to run its operations.

_____ 14. A business can use information systems to build barriers to entry, promote innovation, create switching costs, and so on.

_____ 15. A business can use information technology to develop low-cost ways to build close, convenient business relationships with global customers.

_____ 16. Information technology can help a business make radical improvements in business processes.

_____ 17. Programs of continual improvement in meeting or exceeding customer requirements or expectations.

_____ 18. A business can prosper in rapidly changing markets while offering its customers individualized solutions to their needs.

_____ 19. A network of business partners formed to take advantage of rapidly changing market opportunities.

_____ 20. Companies hope to use the Internet to gain a competitive advantage in their industry or in new markets.

Discussion Questions

1. Suppose you are a manager being pushed to use information technology to gain a competitive advantage in an important market for your company. What reservations might you have about doing so? Why?

2. How could a business use information technology to increase switching costs and lock in its customers and suppliers? Use business examples to support your answers.

3. How could a business leverage its investment in information technology to build a strategic IT platform that serves as a barrier to entry by new entrants into its markets?

4. Refer to the Real World Case of Capital One Financial in the chapter. What does John Pastore mean when he says that

"we base our marketing decisions more on risk than on profitability"? How is IT involved?

5. What strategic role can information technology play in business process reengineering and total quality management?

6. Refer to the Real World Case of AMP, Inc. in the chapter. Why is AMP "a company that is driven . . . by measurements"? How is IT involved?

7. How could a business use the Internet strategically? Be sure to include the concepts of breaking business barriers, forming a virtual company, and becoming an agile competitor in your answer.

8. Refer to the Real World Case of D. L. Boone & Co. and the KnowledgeNet in the chapter. What are the top business reasons for the growth of virtual corporations? What role does IT play in virtual companies?

9. "Information Technology can't really give a company a strategic advantage, because most competitive advantages don't last more than a few years and soon become strategic necessities which just raise the stakes of the game." Discuss.

10. MIS author and consultant Peter Keen says: "We have learned over the past decade that it is not *technology* that creates a competitive edge, but *the management process that exploits technology*." What does he mean? Do you agree or disagree. Why?

Real World Problems

1. Security APL, Inc.: Strategic Success on the Internet

Every day, an IBM RS/6000 server at Security APL, Inc., in Chicago processes a half million inquiries from across the worldwide Internet, spitting out free stock quotes that are 15 minutes old. This is the Quote Server, one of the most popular landing sites on the World Wide Web (www.secap1.con/cgt-bin/qs). But the Quote Server is just the tip of the iceberg at Security APL, which appears to have done more than any other financial services company to leverage the power of the Internet. The company also has a fee-based service called Portfolio Accounting World-Wide or PAWWS. For $8.95 per month, PAWWS customers get an Internet-accessible service that offers a comprehensive and growing portfolio management and accounting system. The portfolio service includes automated links to Securities and Exchange Commission archives, corporate home pages, news and online stock trading services such as Howe Barnes Investment, Inc.'s The Net Investor.

"Our mission has always been to be the premier provider of portfolio accounting and measurement to independent investment and money managers," said Jay N. Whipple III, who founded the company in 1978. The company's clients include money management firms, bank trust departments, insurance companies, and brokerage houses. "We're taking utilities that were once price prohibitive and giving them to money managers, financial advisers, and retail customers," said Valerie Kahn, president of PAWWS. Although she would not specify the number of PAWWS customers, she said the firm has fewer than 100,000 clients.

Security APL is "way ahead of the curve," said Richard Crone, a senior manager in the Center for Electronic Banking at KPMG Peat Marwick in Los Angeles. Few of the 400 financial services company domains on the Internet have any kind of interactive presentation, he noted. Each of Security's 90 employees, who work in offices in Chicago, Jersey City, New Jersey, Boston, and San Diego, maintain their own Web home pages. Those home pages can be accessed by other employees or external clients. "Customizing the information that customers see is the key to success" in this environment, Crone added.

a. Is Security APL using the Internet for strategic advantage? Explain.

b. How could companies in other industries learn from Security's success on the Internet? Use an example to illustrate your answer.

Source: Adapted from Ellis Booker, "Financial Services Spread across the Web," *Computerworld*, May 15, 1995, p.12. Copyright 1995 by Computerworld, Inc., Framingham, MA 01701—Reprinted from *Computerworld*.

2. Safeco and Toro: Debating the Strategic Value of IT

Today, after a decade of often disappointing (and costly) computing adventures, more top executives are grasping what sophisticated chief information officers have known for years: information technology is best used as an enabler, not a savior. "There's more realism now," says Gerald T. Knight, CEO at the Toro Co., in Bloomington, Minnesota. "Anybody can get state-of-the-art quickly across all systems. Technology moves too quickly to provide any kind of advantage."

However, Richard J. Anderson, senior vice president of administration at $3.9 billion Seattle-based insurer Safeco, disagrees. "Capitalizing on the technology available out there can be a very high level proprietary advantage," he says. "I regard it to be one of our three or four primary points of advantage." To illustrate, he points to a PC-based automobile underwriting expert system installed a few years ago. Now, 50 percent of policies are authorized, laser-printed, and mailed the day of application. "That's a very effective competitive use," Anderson notes.

But Toro's Knight says: "Businesses used to lock up a channel for 10, 15, or 20 years. Today, channels of distribution and customer bases are changing a lot more rapidly." To keep up, Toro's 75-person IS department has just begun a three-year effort to install an enterprisewide client/server system that will eventually link dozens of existing databases. "We're not doing this to get savings out," explains Knight. "We need the added flexibility of going to market and of faster product innovation. Our ability to respond to the customer will be faster and more reliable. We need the ability to support a fast-changing business mode."

a. Do you agree with Gerard Knight's critique of using IT for competitive advantage? Why or why not?

b. Do you agree with Richard Anderson's view of the strategic business impact of information technology? Why or why not?

Source: Adapted from Joseph Maglitta, "Anxious Allies," Special Report: 1995 CEO/CFO Survey, *Computerworld*, June 12, 1995, pp. 5–9. Copyright 1995 by Computerworld, Inc., Framingham, MA 01701—Reprinted from *Computerworld*.

3. Citgo Corporation: Reengineering Corporate Culture and Technology

Experts and executives say reengineering has opened many eyes about technology's potential.

"The transformation necessary to take advantage of technology is more complex than executives give it credit for," says David Shpilberg, national director of information technology consulting for Ernst & Young in New York. "It is a transformation of people and process and technology. But they wrongly think technology transformation can be dictated."

Take Steven Berlin, Citgo's senior vice president and CFO. "We thought that if you put in faster processing, we'd get a lot of different abilities to roll up and analyze data," he explains. "But we weren't getting the benefits we thought we should be getting. Then the light went on: We had a 1950s way of working and 1990s technology."

So Citgo's CEO brought in consultants to help gain a fresh look. Over an eight-month period, every executive and employee got continuous improvement training. Berlin credits the move with getting the ball rolling to recreate the whole 4,600-person company, including the 180-member IT department. The Tulsa-based firm is now beginning to replace aging systems handling such functions as general ledger maintenance tracking and personnel. "We finally realized the problem is on the people side," Berlin explains. "The new approach starts with company culture and every employee and what they do and how they do it. Everybody is thinking about the big process and how they fit it."

a. What is a common mistake some executives make about business process reengineering? What would be a more correct view of BPR? Explain.

b. What lessons did CITGO learn about success in implementing business process engineering?

Source: Adapted from Joseph Maglitta, "Anxious Allies," Special Report: 1995 CEO/CFO Survey, *Computerworld*, June 12, 1995, pp. 5–9. Copyright 1995 by Computerworld, Inc., Framingham, MA 01701—Reprinted from *Computerworld*.

4. MCA/Universal: A Strategic Choice of the Internet

MCA/Universal has an Internet Web server (www.mca.com). But the movie industry giant takes the Web so seriously that it also installed an internal Internet server as a central resource for the entire company. And, after only two months online, the central server has been packed with video and music clips, promotional material, and general information by the company's motion pictures and music entertainment groups. The result? "We're being accessed more than 1,000 times a day," says CIO George Brenner.

MCA/Universal's foray into the Internet World Wide Web began after a diligent search for the best way to deliver its content in an online, electronic format. "We're in the entertainment business, and we have a vision to use public networks as a way to deliver digital content," Brenner says. About two years ago, an executive committee of senior management and division heads considered a number of alternatives, including CompuServe and America Online, but concluded that "it's not easy to get content to the public through a commercial service," Brenner says. Also, "you don't necessarily have control of the content after giving it to a commercial service." So MCA/Universal chose the Internet. Yet for MCA/Universal, this is only the beginning. Brenner intends to install Netscape Communications' Netsite Commerce Server to allow credit-card transactions and the sale of MC/Universal products. Brenner says he also plans to develop other "original content" for the Web.

a. Is MCA/Universal's use of the Internet an example of the strategic use of IT? Why or why not?

b. Why did MCA/Universal pick the Internet over CompuServe and America OnLine? Do you agree with their choice? Why or why not?

Source: Adapted from Garrett Ray, "Internet Tough Guys," *Computerworld*, January 23, 1995, pp. 100–102. Copyright 1995 by Computerworld, Inc., Framingham, MA 01701—Reprinted from *Computerworld*.

5. Kmart and Johnson & Johnson: Strategic Supply Chain Systems

Three years ago, Kmart Corp. stunned its top suppliers with a chilling change in strategy. The discounter, under pressure from rivals such as Wal-Mart, wanted to shrink its warehouse and distribution center structure dramatically. No more buildings overflowing with inventory—Kmart wanted each of its 300 largest suppliers to adopt a just-in-time retailing approach. If they didn't, they would face a crushing loss of revenue from one of their biggest customers. Kmart hoped that automatic replenishment of empty store shelves would reduce its costs dramatically.

For Jeffrey Gora, senior replenishment planner at Johnson & Johnson's consumer products unit, Kmart's ultimatum was a spur to action. J&J bought into the commercial technology of the 1990s: supply- or value-chain management systems.

To improve their top and bottom lines, J&J and many companies are building a new business model based on the internetworking of the computer systems of trading partners. They are using realtime, database-driven software and WAN links to replace fax messages, mag tapes, phone calls, and all the other inefficient, multilayered, and manual processes usually employed by trading partners to enhance commerce. Supply chain management links trading partners from beginning to end of their business process: product design, marketing, ordering, delivery, payment, and reordering. The trickle of companies going beyond EDI to adopt this new paradigm is about to swell to a flood. The growth of commercial domains on the Internet is laying the foundation for a surge of electronic, value chain commerce. Once security and payment issues are resolved, supply chain systems will become a strategic necessity.

a. How and why did Kmart stun 300 of its top suppliers?

b. How do supply or value chain systems meet the strategic challenge posed by companies like Kmart?

Source: Adapted from Larry Marion, "New Links in the Value Chain," White Paper: Enterprise Software Directions, *Computerworld*, June 12, 1995, pp. S8–S12. Copyright 1995 by Computerworld, Inc., Framingham, MA 01701— Reprinted from *Computerworld*.

6. Johnson Controls and Levi Strauss: Strategic Value Chain Management

Some pioneers in implementing value chain management systems are aware of not only the risks but also the effort required to reduce their vulnerability. For example, the automotive systems group of Johnson Controls uses the Internet, an industry-specific private network, and direct computer network linkages to exchange data on car seat design, production, and delivery with key customers. "The top priority is the security of data," says Andrew Drummond, LAN systems manager. "We want to make sure that each customer's information, such as product drawings, will be confidential and secure, so Ford doesn't see what Chrysler is doing." According to Drummond, securing data is a long, tedious process involving a series of what-if challenges. "We invest weeks of security-related work for each customer that we add to the network. And we have to repeat the process for the next customer."

Another serious challenge for managers in the midst of a value chain implementation is the flip-side of security: insuring interoperability of systems among partners. "Tools to enable the seamless virtual enterprise aren't there yet," contends Gevenie Delsol, director of global network services, Levi Strauss & Co. "Even if everyone is using a standard protocol like TCP/IP, the implementations are not always completely interoperable." Levi Strauss has found that each supplier or customer link requires systems and network managers to knit together a labor-intensive custom solution. "You have to understand the client's environment," notes Delsol. "It seems like it consumes all of our time, trying to get the same vocabulary and baseline of understanding with our trading partners."

a. What are the security and interoperability challenges of value chain systems?

b. How do Johnson Controls and Levi Strauss meet these challenges when implementing strategic value chain systems?

Source: Adapted from Larry Marion, "New Links in the Value Chain," White Paper: Enterprise Software Directions, *Computerworld*, June 12, 1995, pp.S8–S12. Copyright 1995 by Computerworld, Inc., Framingham, MA 01701—Reprinted from *Computerworld*.

Application Exercises

1. The Glamoral Corporation

The Glamoral Corporation is considering the development of a marketing information system that will allow them to do a better job of targeting promotional mailings to the customers most likely to purchase particular product lines. The proposed system is considered to be a strategic information system in marketing. Its impact is expected to come in the form of increased sales due to improved marketing penetration. Because of the speculative nature of the benefits of the system, only the first three years of operation of the system are to be considered in evaluating its profitability.

The information systems department estimates that the system would cost $350,000 for initial development. Development should be completed in one year. Once the system becomes operational, its maintenance is expected to require $30,000 per year.

The best estimate of the impact of the system on sales is that it would increase sales from their current projected levels by 5 percent in the first year of operation and by 10 percent for the second and third years of operation. The level of sales for the products affected by this system is currently $10,500,000 and this sales level is expected to remain constant through the projection period unless the new system is developed. The marginal contribution of a dollar of sales to profits is 25 cents.

a. Based upon these figures construct a spreadsheet which clearly displays all of the important elements of the costs and benefits of the proposed system. Your spreadsheet should include a row or column showing the net contribution of the system to corporate profits for the development year and for each of the first three years of operation.

b. Assume that Glamoral requires a return on investment of at least 20 percent for this type of investment. Add a net present value calculation to your spreadsheet and determine whether this project would be justified.

c. Modify your spreadsheet to include the internal rate of return for this investment. Based upon the figures presented, do you think that Glamoral should invest in this system?

d. If you have a spreadsheet with a goal seeking function, find the level of initial development cost for the system that would produce a net present value of zero in part b, assuming all other parameters remain unchanged.

2. ABC Shipping Human Resources Information System

ABC Shipping Company's current Human Resources Information System is badly out of date. Inadequacies in the system require Personnel workers to make numerous manual calculations to accommodate standard information requests. Three alternatives to rectify this problem have been proposed: (1) *Modification* of the current system, (2) *Development* of an entirely new system by ABC's information systems department, and (3) *Purchase* of a third party human resources software package and modification of it to meet ABC's needs. A spreadsheet will be used to compare the costs and benefits of these alternatives over the next 10 years.

Modification of the existing system is the least costly alternative; it is projected that the modified system would cost $135,000 to develop and could be operational within a year. Purchase of a third party package is expected to cost $195,000 plus an additional $115,000 to adapt it to meet ABC's needs. A purchased system could also be operational within a year. Development of a new system internally would require two years and would cost $475,000. With the cost being spread evenly over the two years of development.

Benefits from the new system would come predominantly in the form of reduced time required by clerical staff in the Personnel Department to answer information requests. These benefits have been measured in terms of staff hours saved compared to the current system. The greatest time saving can be achieved if a new system tailored exactly to ABC's needs is developed. Modification of the existing system will produce substantially less time savings, since not all of the desired features could be built into the system. The expected work hours per year saved for each proposed system are shown below. Including fringe benefits, the average cost of an hour of clerical work is $12. Assume that both the cost of a clerical hour and the number of hours saved will not change over the 10-year period.

System	Clerical Hrs. Saved
Modification	2,000
Development	10,000
Purchase	5,000

a. Based on these figures develop a spreadsheet showing the costs and benefits of each alternative system over the next 10 years.
b. Modify your spreadsheet so that it includes calculations of the net present value (assumes a required return on investment of 10 percent per year) and internal rate of return for each alternative.
c. Which alternative would you choose? Why?
d. The clerical time saved under each system was assumed to be constant over the entire 10-year period. Do you think that this is a realistic assumption? If not, what pattern of savings would you expect for each alternative?

Review Quiz Answers

1.	5	6.	16	11.	10	16.	4
2.	6	7.	13	12.	19	17.	18
3.	14	8.	9	13.	11	18.	1
4.	12	9.	8	14.	17	19.	20
5.	7	10.	3	15.	2	20.	15

Selected References

1. Alter, Allan, "Jack be Agile, Jack be Quick." *Computerworld,* November 7, 1994.
2. Bakos, J. Yannis. "A Strategic Analysis of Electronic Marketplaces." *MIS Quarterly,* September 1991.
3. Booker, Ellis. "A Tangled Web: Businesses Struggle to Leaverage the Internet." *Computerworld/Client Server Journal,* April 1995.
4. Booker, Ellis. "GE Places Services on the Internet." *Computerworld,* October 31, 1994.
5. Bowles, Jerry. "Quality 2000: The Next Decade of Progress." *Special Advertising Supplement, Fortune,* October 3, 1994.
6. Caron, J. Raymond, Sicrka Jarvenpaa, and Donna Stoddard. "Business Reengineering at CIGNA Corporation: Experiences and Lessons from the First Five Years." *MIS Quarterly,* September 1994.
7. Cash, James, Jr.; F. Warren McFarlan, James McKenney; and Lynda Applegate. *Corporate Information Systems Management.* 3rd ed. Homewood, IL: Richard D. Irwin, 1992.
8. Cash, James, Jr.; Robert Eccles; Nitin Nohria; and Richard Nolan. *Building the Information Age Organization: Structures, Control, and Information Technologies.* Burr Ridge, IL: Richard D. Irwin, 1994.
9. Clemons, Eric, and Michael Row. "Sustaining IT Advantage: The Role of Structural Differences." *MIS Quarterly,* September, 1991.
10. Davenport, Thomas. *Process Innovation: Reengineering Work through Information Technology.* Boston: Harvard Business School Press, 1993.
11. Davenport, Thomas, and Donna Stoddard. "Reengineering: Business Change of Mythic Proportions." *MIS Quarterly,* June 1994.
12. Davis, Stanley. *Future Perfect.* Reading, MA: Addison-Wesley, 1989.
13. Feeney, David, and Blake Ives. "In Search of Sustainability: Reaping Long-Term Advantages from Investments in Information Technology." *Journal of Management Information Systems,* Summer 1990.
14. Frye, Colleen. "Imaging Proves Catalyst for Reengineering." *Computerworld/Client Server Journal,* November 1994.
15. Goldman, Steven; Roger Nagel; and Kenneth Preis. *Agile Competitors and Virtual Organizations: Strategies for Enriching the Customer.* New York: Van Nostrand Reinhold, 1995.
16. Guha, Subashish; William Kettinger; and James Teng. "Business Process Reengineering: Building a Comprehensive Methodology." *Information Systems Management,* Summer 1993.

17. Halper, Mark. "Mobil Nets Unite Staff." *Computerworld,* January 11, 1993.

18. Hammer, Michael. "Reengineering Work: Don't Automate, Obliterate." *Harvard Business Review,* July/August 1990.

19. Hammer, Michael, and James Champy. *Reengineering the Corporation: A Manifesto for Business Revolution.* New York: Harper Collins, 1993.

20. Hooper, Max. "Rattling SABRE—New Ways to Compete in Information." *Harvard Business Review,* May–June 1990.

21. Jacobson, Ivar; Maria Ericsson; and Agneta Jacobson. *The Object Advantage: Business Process Reengineering with Object Technology.* New York: The ACM Press, 1995.

22. Keen, Peter. *Computing in Time: Using Telecommunications for Competitive Advantage.* New York: Ballinger Publishing Co., 1988.

23. Keen, Peter. *Shaping the Future: Business Design through Information Technology.* Cambridge, MA: Harvard Business School Press, 1991.

24. Kettinger, William; Varon Grover; and Albert Segars. "Do Strategic Systems Really Pay Off? An Analysis of Classic Strategic IT Cases." *Information Systems Management,* Winter 1995.

25. Kettinger, William; Varun Grover; Subashish Guha; and Albert Segars. "Strategic Information Systems Revisited: A Study in Sustainability and Performance." *MIS Quarterly,* March 1994.

26. King, Julia. "Logistics Providers Enable 'Virtual' Firms." *Computerworld,* July 18, 1994.

27. Konsynski, Ben, and F. Warren McFarlan. "Information Partnerships—Shared Data, Shared Scale." *Harvard Business Review,* January–February 1991.

28. Lieberman, Philip. "A Guide to OS/2 Warp's Internet Access Kit." *Personal Systems,* March/April 1995.

29. Lindquist, Christopher. "Miller Finds Pardox Brew Tasty." *Computerworld,* February 8, 1993.

30. Neumann Seev. *Strategic Information Systems: Competition through Information Technologies.* New York: MacMillan College Publishing Co., 1994.

31. Pegels, C. Carl. *Total Quality Management: A Survey of Its Important Aspects.* Danvers, MA: Boyd & Fraser Publishing Co., 1995.

32. Porter, Michael. *Competitive Advantage.* New York: Free Press, 1985

33. Porter, Michael, and Victor Milar. "How Information Gives You Competitive Advantage." *Harvard Business Review,* July–August, 1985.

34. Resnick, Rosalind. "The Virtual Corporation." *PC Today,* February 1995.

35. Roche, Edward M. *Telecommunications and Business Strategy.* Chicago: Dryden Press, 1991.

36. Schonberger, Richard. "Is Strategy Strategic? Impact of Total Quality Management on Strategy." *Academy of Management Executive,* August 1992.

37. Sprague, Ralph, Jr., and Barbara McNurlin. *Information Systems Management in Practice,* 3rd ed. Englewood Cliffs, NJ: Prentice Hall, 1993.

38. Tetzelli, Rick. "The Internet and Your Business." *Fortune,* March 7, 1994.

39. Wiseman, Charles. *Strategic Information Systems,* Homewood, IL: Richard D. Irwin, 1988.

40. Zahedi, Fatemeh. *Quality Information Systems,* Danvers, MA: Boyd & Frazer Publishing Co., 1995.

D. L. Boone & Co. and KnowledgeNet: Debating the Virtual Corporation

An organization that's using the Internet and other online networks to create a virtual network of small businesses is KnowledgeNet, a worldwide consulting firm with more than 100 member practices in 16 countries. The group's members all fall under the umbrella of professional services, engaging in activities as diverse as systems analysis, accounting, technical writing, sales and marketing, project management, and software development.

KnowledgeNet is the brainchild of entrepreneur David Boone, who heads D. L. Boone & Co., an international systems and management consulting firm in Vienna, Virginia, that coordinates the activities of the worldwide network. Boone's goal is to put together a world-class consulting firm composed of small firms and individuals being driven from the corporate world by the current economic climate, and to market the firm's services under a single internationally known trademark. Because D. L. Boone & Co. is a "virtual corporation," it doesn't have any fixed facilities and maintains only those permanent employees essential for corporate operations.

Each of KnowledgeNet's affiliate offices—called Associates—contributes to the financing of the company's operations and shares in its profits. Boone also uses online networks to distribute copies of his business plan to consultants interested in joining. Associates who link up with KnowledgeNet use the Internet and other networks to communicate via E-mail. Boone says half the Associates have Internet accounts; the other half use commercial online services. Boone himself has accounts on Compu-Serve, America Online, Prodigy, and the Internet.

While virtual corporations are clearly a big hit with entrepreneurs, virtual workers can have mixed feelings. Freelance professionals like virtual corporations because they can provide the marketing clout and the administrative infrastructure the workers could not afford on their own, such as accountants and lawyers on the membership team who provide advice and assistance to all members. By linking up in virtual corporations, professionals can also price their work more competitively. Ordinarily, a company would have to hire an expensive consulting firm to locate many of the people that a company like KnowledgeNet already has in place. Instead of finding, hiring, and relocat-

ing a person for a position, a company can simply use KnowledgeNet's services to provide the expertise required for the work more economically.

Isolation, however, can be a problem for virtual workers. Some of Boone's Associates, for example, are lukewarm about the concept. Associate David Habercom says that the virtual corporation concept "actually does not appeal to me very much at all. I much prefer to work with people I can see and touch and go to lunch with. The noise of people walking by, laughter down the hall, a meeting with sleeves rolled up and intense, face-to-face debate, in my mind at least, [are] half of what makes work satisfying."

However, Habercom says he likes the idea of joining forces with colleagues who have complementary skills and of reaching more clients than he could hope to reach alone.

"Whether KnowledgeNet or D. L. Boone & Co.—or any virtual corporation, for that matter—will actually deliver on the promise remains to be seen," Habercom says. "David Boone is clearly doing the right things: working hard, thinking smart, and pulling in the right people. But the other side of the equation is that corporation customers have to become comfortable with a company they can hardly see. Most executives are like me and prefer doing business face-to-face. When something goes wrong, I want to be able to get my hands around the other guy's throat—that, and knowing he can do the same to me helps keep us honest. So, there is a trust curve here, and it may be steeper on the customer's side than ours.

"In short, we're committed and ready to blaze new trails, but the terrain is the human mind, not electronic pathways. Techies don't change the world, they just hand out the tools. For virtual corporations, the real struggle has hardly begun."

Ankur Lal, an Associate from New Delhi, takes a more optimistic view. Lal, who has helped American and Canadian firms develop software applications in India for the past five years, works with a group of 10 experienced software engineers at an Indian facility linked via E-mail to overseas clients. By going online, Lal and his group can send and receive specification, code, and messages through their computers.

"I am sure the virtual corporation idea will pick up more

and more with people able to work wherever they are and give it their best," Lal says. "With the information super-highway, distance will be [only] a psychological barrier since the quality of work would be the same in one's own office or 10,000 miles away. So good business sense will mean using the best services at the most economical cost anywhere in the world. The virtual corporation is very much here to stay and will take the world by storm."

Source: Adapted from Rosalind Resnick, "The Virtual Corporation," *PC Today*, February 1995, pp. 65–66.

CASE STUDY QUESTIONS

1. Is KnowledgeNet an example of a virtual company? Explain.

2. Do you agree with David Habercom's critique of virtual corporations? Why or why not?

3. Do you agree with Ankur Lal's endorsement of virtual corporations? Why or why not?

Information Systems and Artificial Intelligence Technologies

CHAPTER OUTLINE

LEARNING OBJECTIVES

The purpose of this chapter is to give you an understanding of developments in artificial intelligence and human information processing and the use of AI developments such as expert systems for business applications.

Section I of this chapter gives an overview of artificial intelligence application areas, including neural networks, fuzzy logic, and virtual reality, and introduces basic concepts in human information processing and information theory.

Section II explores the fundamentals of expert systems, including their relationship to other knowledge-based systems, and provides examples of the business use of expert systems and other AI technologies.

After reading this chapter, you should be able to:

1. Identify the present and future impacts of artificial intelligence on business operations, managerial decision making, and strategic advantage.

2. Give examples of the use of concepts about human information processing and cognitive styles in designing information products for managers.

3. Identify how neural networks, fuzzy logic, virtual reality, and intelligent agents can be used in business.

4. Identify the major components of an expert system and explain how its knowledge and software components contribute to its conclusions.

5. Explain how expert systems are developed, emphasizing the roles of knowledge engineers and expert system shells.

6. Give examples of several ways expert systems or hybrid AI systems can be used in business decision-making situations.

SECTION I

Artificial Intelligence and Human Information Processing

An Overview of Artificial Intelligence

The field of information systems and its applications in business and society are being increasingly affected by developments in the field of artificial intelligence. Developments such as natural languages and multisensory user interfaces, industrial robots, expert systems, and "intelligent" software are some examples of this impact. As a potential managerial end user, you should be aware of the importance of such developments. Businesses and other organizations are significantly increasing their attempts to assist the human intelligence and productivity of their knowledge workers with artificial intelligence tools and techniques.

But what is artificial intelligence? **Artificial intelligence** (AI) is a science and technology based on disciplines such as computer science, biology, psychology, linguistics, mathematics, and engineering. The goal of AI is to develop computers that can think, as well as see, hear, walk, talk, and feel. A major thrust of artificial intelligence is the development of computer functions normally associated with human intelligence, such as reasoning, learning, and problem solving, as summarized in Figure 12.1. That's why the term artificial intelligence was coined by John McCarthy at MIT in 1956. Besides McCarthy, AI pioneers included Herbert Simon and Allen Newell at Carnegie-Mellon, Norbert Wiener and Marvin Minsky at MIT, Warren McCulloch and Walter Pitts at Illinois, Frank Rosenblatt at Cornell, Alan Turing at Manchester, Edward Feigenbaum at Stanford, Roger Shank at Yale, and many others [18].

Debate has raged around artificial intelligence since serious work in the field began in the 1950s. Not only technological, but moral and philosophical questions abound about the possibility of intelligent, "thinking" machines. For example, British AI pioneer Alan Turing in 1950 proposed a test for determining if machines could think. According to the Turing test, a computer could demonstrate intelligence if a human interviewer, conversing with an unseen human and an unseen computer, could not tell which was which [18].

Though much work has been done in many of the subgroups that fall under the AI umbrella, critics believe that no computer can truly pass the Turing test. They claim that developing intelligence to impart true humanlike capabilities to comput-

FIGURE 12.1
Attributes of intelligent behavior. AI is attempting to duplicate these capabilities in computer-based systems.

- Think and reason.
- Use reason to solve problems.
- Learn or understand from experience.
- Acquire and apply knowledge.
- Exhibit creativity and imagination.
- Deal with complex or perplexing situations.
- Respond quickly and successfully to new situations.
- Recognize the relative importance of elements in a situation.
- Handle ambiguous, incomplete, or erroneous information.

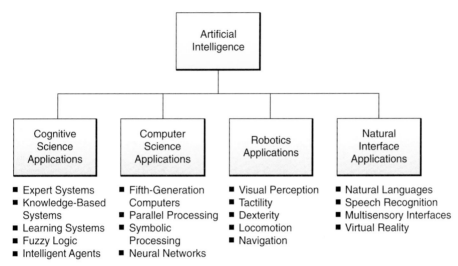

ers is simply not possible. But progress continues, and only time will tell if the ambitious goals of artificial intelligence will be achieved and equal the popular images found in science fiction.

Figure 12.2 illustrates the major domains of AI research and development. Note that AI **applications** can be grouped under the four major areas of cognitive science, computer science, robotics, and natural interfaces, though these classifications do overlap each other, and other classifications can be used. Also note that expert systems are just one of many important AI applications. Let's briefly review each of these major areas of AI and some of their current applications. We will discuss several of these applications in greater detail in Section II.

The Domains of Artificial Intelligence

Cognitive Science

This area of artificial intelligence is based on research in biology, neurology, psychology, mathematics, and many allied disciplines. It focuses on researching how the human brain works and how humans think and learn. The results of such research in **human information processing** are the basis for the development of a variety of computer-based applications in artificial intelligence. We will discuss some of these important concepts in human information processing in this section.

Applications in the cognitive science area of AI include the development of expert systems and other *knowledge-based* systems that add a knowledge base and some reasoning capability to information systems. Also included are *adaptive learning* systems that can modify their behaviors based on information they acquire as they operate. Chess-playing systems are primitive examples of such applications, though many more applications are being implemented. *Fuzzy logic systems* can process data that are incomplete or ambiguous, that is, *fuzzy data*. Thus, they can solve unstructured problems with incomplete knowledge by developing approximate inferences and answers, as humans do [10].

Computer Science

This area of AI applications focuses on the computer hardware and system software needed to produce the powerful supercomputers required for many AI applications. At the forefront of this area are efforts to create a *fifth generation* of "intelligent" computers, which use the *parallel processing* architecture discussed in Chapter 4. Such computers will be designed for optimum *logical* inference processing, which depends on symbolic processing instead of the numeric processing of traditional computing. Other attempts are being made to develop *neural networks,* including massively parallel, neurocomputer systems whose architecture is based on the human brain's meshlike neuron structure. Neural network computers can process many different pieces of information simultaneously. Neural network software for traditional computers can "learn" by being shown sample problems and their solutions. As they start to recognize patterns, they can begin to program themselves to solve such problems on their own [32].

Robotics

AI, engineering, and physiology are the basic disciplines of **robotics.** This technology produces robot machines with computer intelligence and computer-controlled, humanlike physical capabilities. This area thus includes applications designed to give robots the powers of sight or visual *perception,* touch or tactile capabilities, *dexterity* or skill in handling and manipulation, *locomotion* or the physical ability to move over any terrain, and *navigation* or the intelligence to properly find one's way to a destination [26]. The use of robotics in computer-aided manufacturing is discussed in Chapter 9.

Natural Interfaces

The development of natural *interfaces* is considered a major area of AI applications and is essential to the natural use of computers by humans. The development of natural languages is a major thrust of this area of AI. Being able to talk to computers and robots in conversational human languages and have them "understand" us as easily as we understand each other is the goal of many AI researchers. Thus, this application area involves research and development in linguistics, psychology, computer science, and other disciplines. Applications include human language understanding, speech recognition, and the development of multisensory devices that use a variety of body movements to operate computers. Thus, this area of AI drives developments in the voice recognition and response technology discussed in Chapter 4, and the natural programming languages discussed in Chapter 5. Finally, an emerging application area in AI is *virtual reality.* This field is developing multisensory human/computer interfaces that enable human users to experience computer-simulated objects, spaces, activities, and "worlds" as if they actually exist.

Neural Networks

Neural networks are computing systems modeled after the brain's meshlike network of interconnected processing elements, called *neurons.* Of course, neural networks are a lot simpler in architecture (the human brain is estimated to have over 100 billion neuron brain cells!). However, like the brain, the interconnected processors in a neural network operate in parallel and interact dynamically with each other. This enables the network to "learn" from data it processes. That is, it learns to recognize patterns and relationships in the data it processes. The more data examples it receives as input, the better it can learn to duplicate the results of the examples it processes. Thus, the neural network will change the strengths of the interconnections between the processing elements in response to changing patterns in the data it receives and the results that occur [29, 34].

Note in Figure 12.3 that before training, the neural net gave equal weight to all six neurons that represent possible criteria for credit risk determination and their "synapses," or connections, to the *profitable customer* and *default customer* neurons, which are the next level of the net. Then the net was given several rounds of train-

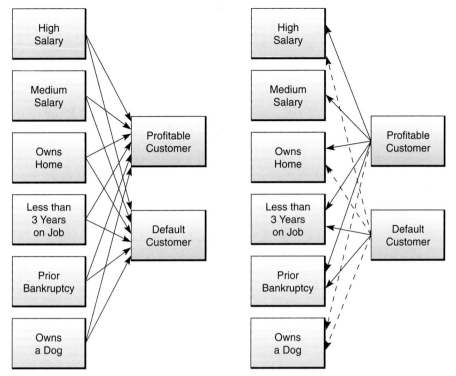

FIGURE 12.3
Training a neural network for a credit application evaluation system. Note how training has changed the strength of the connections between the credit criteria and customer neurons. The untrained neural net is on the left, the net after one round of training is on the right.

Source: Adapted from Ralph Sprague and Barbara McNurlin, *Information Systems Management in Practice*, 3rd ed. (New York: Prentice-Hall, 1993), p. 443.

ing, which consists of processing data about actual credit applications and whether the resulting loans were paid back properly or not [32].

After the first round of training, the neural net has kept its strong connections to the profitable customer neuron by sending "strengthen your signal" messages back to credit criteria like "high salary" and "own home." But it has weakened several connections to the default customer neuron by sending "send a weaker signal" messages back to some of the other criteria. It has also weakened the connection between the irrelevant "own a dog" criterion and the customer neurons.

Thus, the neutral network begins to learn which credit characteristics result in good or bad loans. The developers of the neural network would provide it with many more examples of credit applications and loan results to process, and opportunities to adjust the signal strengths between its neurons. The neural network would continue to be trained until it demonstrated a high degree of accuracy in correctly duplicating the results of recent cases. At that point it would be trained enough to begin making credit evaluations on its own.

Neural networks can be implemented on microcomputers and other traditional computer systems by using software packages that simulate the activity of a neural network. Specialized neural network coprocessor circuit boards for PCs are also available that provide significantly greater processing power. In addition, special-purpose neural net microprocessor chips are being used in specific application areas such as military weapons systems, image processing, and voice recognition. However, most business applications depend primarily on neural net software packages to accomplish applications ranging from credit risk assessment to check signature verification, investment forecasting, and manufacturing quality control [16, 32].

FIGURE 12.4
A display of a neural net software
development package. Notice the
variety of options for building
and using the neural network.

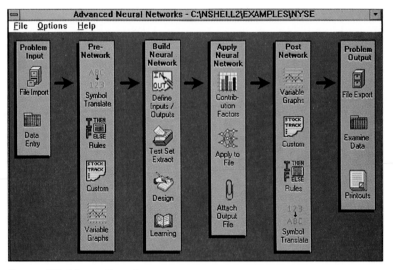

Courtesy of Ward Systems Group, Inc.

See Figure 12.4. Let's take a closer look at a business example to get a better feel for a neural network application.

Consumer Lending

Security Pacific Bank of California has developed a neural net system for helping it make consumer lending decisions. Most banks rely on a *credit scoring* service provided by outside companies who collect and analyze statistics on the credit patterns of consumers who wish to qualify for a bank loan. Security Pacific replaced these "score card vendors" with a loan-underwriting neural net system it developed with the help of an AI consulting firm. They designed the net and then "trained" it by having it review 6,000 previous loan-underwriting cases in the bank's files.

The loan-underwriting system analyzes 27 credit factors about a potential borrower and makes one of two possible recommendations: (1) strongly applicable to an accept or (2) strongly indicative of a decline. If a decline recommendation is made by the system, the loan application is referred to a human loan officer for review. But all other loan requests are approved by the bank, which rates its neural net system as "very successful" [16].

Fuzzy Logic Systems

In spite of the funny name, **fuzzy logic** systems represent a small, but serious and growing, application of AI in business. Fuzzy logic is a method of reasoning that resembles human reasoning since it allows for approximate values and inferences (fuzzy logic) and incomplete or ambiguous data (fuzzy data) instead of relying only on *crisp data,* such as binary (yes/no) choices. For example, Figure 12.5 illustrates a partial set of rules (fuzzy rules) and a fuzzy SQL query for analyzing and extracting credit risk information on businesses that are being evaluated for selection as investments. Notice how fuzzy logic uses terminology that is deliberately imprecise, such as *very high, increasing, somewhat decreased, reasonable,* and *very low.* This enables

FIGURE 12.5
An example of fuzzy logic rules and a fuzzy logic SQL query in a credit risk analysis application.

Fuzzy Logic Rules

Risk should be acceptable
If debt-equity is very high
   then risk is positively increased
If income is increasing
   then risk is somewhat decreased
If cash reserves are low to very low
   then risk is very increased
If PE ratio is good
   then risk is generally decreased

Fuzzy Logic SQL Query

Select companies
   from financials
      where revenues are very large
      and pe_ratio is acceptable
      and profits are high to very high
      and (income/employee_tot) is reasonable

Source: Adapted from Earl Cox, "Solving Problems with Fuzzy Logic," *AI Expert,* March 1992, p. 30, and "Applications of Fuzzy System Models," *AI Expert,* October 1992, p. 37.

FIGURE 12.6
The components of a fuzzy logic credit analysis, screening, and selection system.

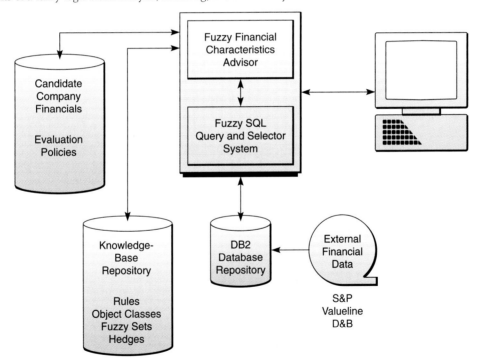

fuzzy systems to process incomplete data and quickly provide approximate, but acceptable, solutions to problems that are difficult for other methods to solve [7, 9].

    Fuzzy logic queries of a database, such as the SQL query shown in Figure 12.5, promise to improve the extraction of data from business databases. Queries can be stated more naturally in words that are closer to the way business specialists think about the topic for which they want information. Figure 12.6 illustrates the

FIGURE 12.7
The components of a fuzzy process controller.

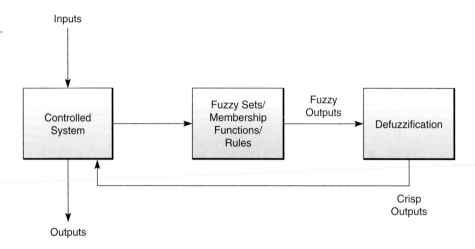

components of a fuzzy credit analysis, screening, and selection system that uses fuzzy SQL queries to interrogate company and external financial databases [8].

Examples of applications of fuzzy logic are numerous in Japan, but rare in the United States. The United States has tended to prefer using AI solutions like expert systems or neural networks. But Japan is a hotbed of fuzzy logic applications, especially the use of special-purpose fuzzy logic microprocessor chips, called *fuzzy process controllers*. Thus, the Japanese ride on subway trains, use elevators, and drive cars that are guided or supported by fuzzy process controllers made by Hitachi and Toshiba. They can even trade shares on the Tokyo Stock Exchange using a stock-trading program based on fuzzy logic rules. Many new models of Japanese-made products also feature fuzzy logic microprocessors. The list is growing, but includes auto-focus cameras, auto-stabilizing camcorders, energy-efficient air conditioners, self-adjusting washing machines, and automatic transmissions [21, 22]. Figure 12.7 illustrates the components of a fuzzy process controller.

Virtual Reality

Virtual reality (VR) is computer-simulated reality. Also known as artificial reality and *cyberspace,* it is an area of artificial intelligence that had its origins in efforts to build more natural, realistic, multisensory human/computer interfaces. So virtual reality relies on multisensory input/output devices such as a headset with video goggles and stereo earphones or a *data glove* or jumpsuit with fiber-optic sensors that track your body movements. Then you can experience computer-simulated "virtual worlds" three dimensionally through sight, sound, and touch. Thus, virtual reality is also called *telepresence.* For example, you can enter a computer-generated virtual world, look around and observe its contents, pick up and move objects, and move around in it at will. Thus virtual reality allows you to interact with computer-simulated objects, entities, and environments as if they actually exist [19, 28]. See Figure 12.8.

Current applications of virtual reality are wide ranging and include computer-aided design (CAD), medical diagnostics and treatment, scientific experimentation in many physical and biological sciences, flight simulation for training pilots and astronauts, and entertainment, especially 3-D video arcade games. CAD is the most widely used industrial VR application. It enables architects and other designers to

Courtesy of Ford Motor Company.

FIGURE 12.8
Using virtual reality in product design. This Ford Motor Company engineer is using a virtual reality headset and data glove to help design improved car interiors at Ford's Advanced Engineering Center in Dearborn, Michigan.

design and test electronic 3-D models of products and structures by entering the models themselves and examining, touching, and manipulating sections and parts from all angles. This *scientific-visualization* capability is also used by pharmaceutical and biotechnology firms to develop and observe the behavior of computerized models of new drugs and materials, and by medical researchers to develop ways for physicians to enter and examine a virtual model of a patient's body.

VR designers are creating everything from virtual weather patterns and virtual wind tunnels to virtual cities and virtual securities markets. For example, by converting stock market and other financial data into three-dimensional graphic form, securities analysts can use VR systems to more rapidly observe and identify trends and exceptions in financial performance. Also promising are applications in information technology itself. This includes the development of 3-D models of telecommunications networks and databases. These virtual graphical representations of networks and databases make it easier for IS specialists to visualize the structure and relationships of an organization's telecommunications networks and corporate databases, thus improving their design and maintenance.

VR becomes *telepresence* when users that can be anywhere in the world use VR systems to work alone or together at a remote site. Typically, this involves using a VR system to enhance the sight and touch of a human who is remotely manipulating equipment to accomplish a task. Examples range from *virtual surgery* where surgeon and patient may be on either side of the globe, to the remote use of equipment in hazardous environments such as chemical plants or nuclear reactors.

The use of virtual reality seems limited only by the newness and cost of its technology. For example, a VR system consisting of a headset with goggles and headphones, a fiber-optic data glove, a motion-sensing device, and a microcomputer workstation with 3-D modeling software may cost up to $50,000. If you want less-cumbersome devices, more realistic displays, and a more natural sense of motion in your VR world, costs can escalate into several hundred thousand dollars. Organizations such as NASA, the Department of Defense, IBM, Digital Equipment Corporation, Lockheed, Matsushita Electric, and several universities are investing millions of dollars in virtual reality R&D projects involving the use of supercomputers, complex modeling software, and custom-made sensing devices. However, the cost of highly realistic multisensory VR systems is expected to drop substantially in the future, making virtual reality available for a wide array of business and end user applications [3, 19, 28].

Human Information Processing

Before we can build artificial intelligence into computers and robots, we must understand human intelligence better. How do humans recognize and accept sensory data, process and store information, and use this information to select and make a variety of responses? This is the question researchers of our cognitive **process** have been studying for many years. Researchers realize that humans do not process information as computers do. For example, humans naturally create and use *concepts* as frameworks for thinking about the real world. They use *analogies* and metaphors as techniques to develop associations among real-world phenomena and learn about their environment. Humans also reason, that is, they make inferences based on knowledge and rules of behavior. However, such reasoning is, typically, not a blind following of rules but an intuitive, instinctive, subjective thinking process capable of solving unstructured and incomplete problems.

The research findings of cognitive psychology and other disciplines form the basis for **cognitive theory,** which is a foundation discipline of artificial intelligence and the source of many AI applications, including expert systems, natural languages, and learning systems. Cognitive theory also provides conceptual frameworks that help us understand how information systems can more effectively serve their human users.

The Human Information Processing System

Figure 12.9 illustrates the components and flows of a human information processing system, based primarily on the work of Allen Newell and Herbert Simon [14]. In this model, visual, audio, tactile, and other stimuli from our environment are captured by our sensing subsystem (eyes, ears, skin, etc.) and transferred to the brain. The brain uses several specialized processing centers and memory units to handle different types of processing and memory functions. This results in a variety of response outputs, such as decisions made and tasks performed. The brain also transmits the results of its processing to our bodies, which provide the *physical effectors* that result in speech, movement, and other responses.

Short-Term Memory

The brain seems to have a short-term memory (STM), which stores only a few units or chunks of information for a few seconds. A chunk can be a symbol or group of symbols such as a word, a group of digits, or an image. Research shows that the STM has a storage capacity of between five and nine chunks, that is, seven plus or minus two units of information. Some researchers believe the STM is part of the processor unit and is used to support input/output processing. That is, the STM may work with a specialized subunit of the processor on chores such as the temporary capture and filtering of sensory input. It also contributes to our ability to work on more than one task at a time, even though research shows that humans process information serially, that is, one unit at a time.

Long-Term Memory

The brain's long-term memory (LTM) seems to have an almost unlimited capacity to store information. It takes only a fraction of a second to recall a unit of information from long-term memory. However, it takes much longer to store (memorize) information. A unit of information may have to move from a receptor to temporary storage in the STM, to the processor, and to the LTM several times in a learning or rehearsal process before it is finally stored. Much of this is due to the complex pro-

FIGURE 12.9
A human information processing system. This model is derived from research and theories about the cognitive process and illustrates its components and flows using an information processing context.

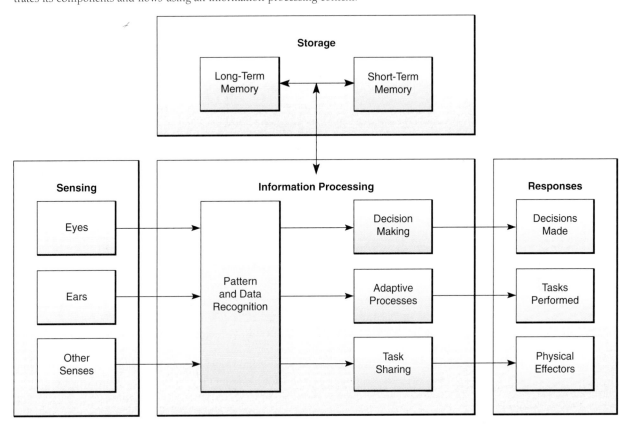

cessing, storage, and access methods we use, including various filtering, categorizing, searching, and retrieval methods. For example, we may process and store information about an event, a concept, a name, a sound, or an image differently, using a variety of processing centers, filtering methods, and memory search networks [18].

Our environment provides us with more stimuli than we can process as information. Therefore, we prevent information *overload* by an **information filtering** process that screens out some stimuli while selecting others for processing. We do this in many ways, depending on a variety of factors, some which we are born with and others arising from our knowledge, experience, and cultural backgrounds [20, 23]. See Figure 12.10.

Information Filtering

Humans seem to use a variety of conceptual frameworks to selectively process information. For example, research shows that humans develop frames of *reference,* or intuitive patterns of information acquisition and processing. As we develop expertise in any area of life, we develop and use frames of reference more skillfully to handle stimuli that confront us. For example, think of the many frames of reference we would use when trying to catch something thrown at us unexpectedly while in a

Selective Frameworks

FIGURE 12.10
The role of information filtering in human decision making. Note how we filter information from the environment before it enters our cognitive process.

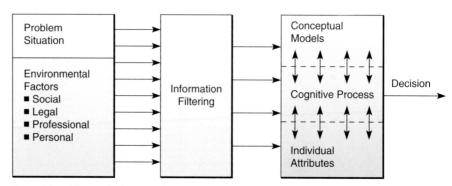

Source: Adapted from Michael Bonner, Clarence Gratto, Jerry Gravander, and Mark Tuttle. "A Behavioral Model of Ethical and Unethical Decision Making," *Journal of Business Ethics,* June 1987, p. 275.

crowd. We would use a variety of frames of reference to capture and process information selectively about the object, the person throwing it, the people and area around us, and so on, all of this in a matter of seconds.

Humans also tend to develop a problem space when confronted with a task. That is, we build a conceptual "workspace" to structure and limit our input and recall of information and processing methods. Thus, we might use a variety of rules of thumb, or heuristics, to help us reduce the number of alternatives we have to consider. Similarly, we exhibit a trait called *bounded rationality,* which was introduced in Chapter 10. That is, we usually develop a simplified conceptual model of a task that limits the alternatives we have to consider.

For example, we will intuitively (1) ignore some places or sources of information when beginning to search for an article, (2) use rules of thumb when conducting the search, and (3) limit possible search alternatives. More specifically, if you were a salesperson and could not find a weekly sales analysis report, you probably would intuitively (1) not look for it in the employee cafeteria, (2) look first on your desk, then in the conference room where today's sales meeting was held, and (3) discount the probability it was taken by a friend of yours.

Cognitive Limitations

There seem to be other major sources of our filtering of information, such as limitations or biases in our cognitive process. For example, some information is filtered out just because of the limitations on the number of units of information (seven plus or minus two) that can be effectively stored in short-term memory. We also tend to be biased as intuitive statisticians. That is, we tend to assign higher probabilities to outcomes we subjectively prefer, even though there is no objective basis for this in the information received. We also tend to overlook small changes in a value, even though they may be statistically significant. For example, many of us inflate our chances of winning a lottery and ignore small percentage changes in important statistics, such as interest rates.

Humans also do things such as anchoring, that is, using previously stored information to judge stimuli of the same type. Or we will favor information with concreteness, that is, information that does not require further processing before storage. For example, we intuitively tend to compare the amount of this week's paycheck with last week's. We also tend to pay more attention to the net amount of our paycheck than to the information about hours worked, pay rates, and deductions that determined that amount.

Another characteristic that affects the information we select is our tendency to store information we do not really need or use. We seem to need information systems to provide us with some information for psychological reassurance, rather than as the basis for decision making. For the same reason, humans need some form of feedback information about the results of their information processing activities. We seem to need reassurances that we have produced correct responses. For example, we prefer systems that give us some type of confirmation that a message we sent was properly received.

What implications do filtering methods in human information processing have for the design of information products and systems? Obviously, we must develop systems that can penetrate such filters with information products that reinforce the most important or relevant information while filtering out irrelevant data. Let's look at a few examples.

Highlighting, reverse video, color, and graphics are often used in computer-generated displays to emphasize important information that might be overlooked. Computer software packages are designed, typically, to prompt users to consider a variety of alternatives, thus expanding the boundaries of their conceptual workspaces. Also widely used is the redundant display of information and user prompts by computer-based systems. This reinforces the normal human rehearsal or learning process, as well as helps penetrate the filtering methods of the human users of an information system. Information systems can also perform statistical analyses of data when appropriate, instead of leaving such analyses to their human users. Finally, software packages are, typically, designed to provide feedback messages to users during data entry and processing activities to reinforce and confirm the accomplishment of correct procedures.

Filtering and Information Systems

We all know that people differ in how they handle the same information and confront the same problems. Researchers would say that their **cognitive styles** are different [20]. When people with a *receptive* style gather information, they tend to focus on the *details* in order to derive knowledge. People with a more *perceptive* style, on the other hand, get an overall knowledge that focuses on the *relationships* between units of the same information. For example, people with a receptive style would focus more on the details of a sales analysis report. Perceptive people, on the other hand, would focus more on sales performance summaries such as the totals for various product categories.

Another dimension of cognitive style is the way we evaluate information once we gather it. People who have more of an *analytic* style use a structured or deductive approach in their cognitive process as they move toward a conclusion. The intuitive style, on the other hand, is more of an unstructured, heuristic approach using trial-and-error strategies to reach a conclusion. For example, the systems approach outlined in Chapter 3 stresses a structured problem-solving methodology that would be attractive to people who prefer an analytic, rather than an intuitive, cognitive style.

Cognitive Style and Information Systems

Another popular explanation of differences in **cognitive** style has to do with research on the functions of various parts of the human brain [35]. As Figure 12.11 illustrates, some research studies have shown that various parts of the brain may contribute to either a *rational* or intuitive style of cognitive processes, which the whole brain integrates in its information processing activities. Due to factors including

Cognitive Style and the Brain

FIGURE 12.11
A whole-brain model of cognitive functions. Note how major
areas of the brain may support
different elements of cognitive
styles in human information
processing.

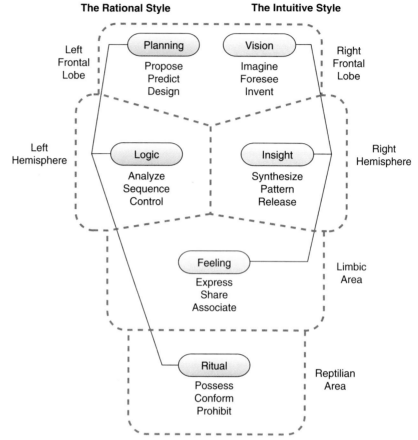

Source: Adapted from William Taggart, "A Human Information Processing Model for the Managerial Mind: Some MIS
Implications," in *Human Factors in Management Information Systems,* ed. Jane Carey (Norwood, NJ: ABLEX Publishing
Corp., 1988).

genetics, education, experience, and cultural background, we tend to favor more of
one type of processing than the other when we gather and evaluate information.
Thus, people with an intuitive style tend to "act on a hunch" without having to know
all of the facts. People with more of a rational style, however, have to review the facts
about a situation and "see the bottom line" before making a decision. Therefore,
information systems should be designed to appeal to both types of cognitive styles.
For example, if reports and displays offer information in narrative, numeric, and
graphic forms, they should communicate more effectively to end users with a variety of cognitive styles.

Information Theory and Information Systems

Information theory, which is also called the mathematical theory of communication, was developed by Norbert Weiner, a pioneer in the field of artificial intelligence
who developed the concept of *cybernetics;* that is, the concept of automated systems
that monitor their own feedback and control their own actions [30]. Information
theory contains several important concepts used in artificial intelligence and that are
useful in designing effective information systems. In this theory, the term *communication* is used to describe any procedure by which a person may affect the mind of

another person. This includes not only oral and written communications, but also other types of behavior, such as *body language* and other *nonverbal cues*. Communication of the many types of data resources and information products present in information systems is also included in this concept.

Information theory helps us evaluate the communication of information in three major dimensions. It emphasizes that we should find answers to three basic questions when we evaluate information systems:

- **The technical dimension.** How accurately can information be transmitted?
- **The semantic dimension.** How precisely does information convey the desired meaning?
- **The effectiveness dimension.** How effectively does information affect the behavior of its recipient?

Redundancy

The technical dimension of information theory stresses the use of **redundancy,** which is the repetition of part or all of a message. Thus, a message may contain extra information, or it may be repeated different times in different ways. This increases an information system's effectiveness—that is, the chance that the correct information will be understood by the recipient. Of course, this makes an information system less efficient, since more information than the simple message itself is transmitted. Also, redundancy can reduce the effectiveness of an information system if so much redundant information is transmitted that it overwhelms the recipient. So redundancy can be overdone.

Let's look at examples of redundancy found in many reports produced by information systems. Information about sales results, for example, is presented in detail, in subtotals by various categories, and by grand totals for a period. Graphics displays of the same results may also be used. Actual sales results for a period may be compared with previous periods and with forecasted sales. The differences, or variances, between these results may also be reported as additional items of information. These types of redundancy are used to "get the message through" about sales performance to the managers receiving such reports.

Other Factors

As important as the technical accuracy dimension of information are its semantic and effectiveness dimensions. Even an accurate message can be misinterpreted or misused. For example, suppose you want to communicate the current trend in sales performance. A correct but detailed listing of sales results will be more subject to misinterpretation (a semantic problem) than a trend line or bar graph display of the same information. If you want sales managers and salespeople to get excited about the trend in sales results (the effectiveness dimension), a graphics display will also probably be more effective than a listing of sales figures.

However, that doesn't mean that graphics displays of information are always superior. As we mentioned in Chapter 8, poorly designed or labeled graphs are easily subject to misinterpretation and misuse. In many instances, managers and others still need to "see some numbers" before they can make a decision. Estimating results by interpreting graphics displays is not a satisfactory way to present information in these cases. So the effectiveness dimension may require us to produce narrative and numeric summaries, as well as graphics, for managers.

REAL   WORLD   CASE

Earl Cox of Metus Systems: Fuzzy Logic Database Queries

A few months ago, while attending a conference on advanced technologies, I heard a speaker from the National Science Foundation discuss fuzzy database operations. Unfortunately, her perspective on how fuzzy logic and relational database operations should be combined had little relevance to the real world. Her talk centered on the mechanisms that could be employed to store fuzzy information in a database. As it happened, I was sitting next to the CIO of a very large insurance company.

"Would you actually store fuzzy information in your customer database?" I asked as neutrally as possible.

"Well, no, the information would be meaningless for our analytical programs. Second, any really useful information is either very volatile or very perishable. Thus, the contents of, say, the age or disposable income column, would change on a regular basis. And third, our databases are shared by many departments. What is middle aged to our actuarial department, might be young or old to our marketing or sales departments. No," he continued seriously, "we already have the facts. What we would like to do is treat the facts in a fuzzy manner."

"Bingo!" I said. "Let me tell you a story of one company that's doing just that."

A few years ago, actually, it was after the October 1987 stock market crash, when the specter of insider trading haunted every trader, I met with the head of a very large New York investment house. Michael T stood with his back to me, his sleeves rolled up, looking out over the East River. "Our analysts are scared to death. If they work through the night to find a company we can recommend—bang! We got inquiries from the SEC. Everyone, suspects an insider deal."

"What do you want from me?" I asked. Just outside the door, behind a thick curved glass barrier, a double rack of beige computer consoles flowed with amber ticker symbols or fluctuated with yellow and blue graphs. A trio of tired little men in crumpled white shirts and baggy trousers sat among cigarette butts talking without blinking into dirty telephones.

Michael waved at tapes labeled Valueline, S&P, Dunn and Bradstreet. "I want a way to look through all these databases and find those perfect recommendations. I'd like to try that weird stuff you've been proposing for the past three months."

"Fuzzy logic," I muttered.

"Yeah, fuzzy what ever it is."

I've never been a proud man. I mean, I'll do anything to advance the cause of fuzzy logic, so I didn't even mind that Michael was desperate, that I was his last resort. After all, I did have a solution to his problem. That solution used the same tools his analysts knew and loved (or despised)—the interactive database query. Except instead of looking into the database with crisp, sharp cut-off points and rigid limits, they would now employ a vocabulary that mapped a lot closer to the way they actually thought about their problem. Refer to Figures 12.5 and 12.6.

The application of fuzzy logic in this database retrieval, screening, and analysis application provides an order-of-magnitude improvement to the solution of the problem. In the case of the investment house looking for acquisition opportunities, a query is cast in the form of linguistic statements like:

```
select companies

  from value line
    where revenues are large
    and pe__ratio is acceptable
    and profits are high to quite high
```

In practice, this query not only selects a broad set of company records that meet these requirements, but also returns the truth value associated with each record (i.e., how well or to what degree each record matched the fuzzy query.) Also, since the analysts communicate through a vocabulary that matches their way of thinking about the problem, changes in the selection criteria can be made with a much higher degree of confidence than in the nonfuzzy form the analysts were previously using.

CASE STUDY QUESTIONS

1. Why does Earl Cox recommend using fuzzy logic for database queries but not for storing data?

2. Why is the investment company's selection problem a good application for fuzzy database queries?

3. What are some other business applications of fuzzy logic? Give an example of one application.

Source: Adapted from Earl Cox, "Applications of Fuzzy System Models," *AI Expert*, October 1992, pp. 34–39, and "Relational Database Queries Using Fuzzy Logic," *AI Expert*, January 1995, pp. 23–25.

┌ **SECTION II**
Expert Systems and Other Knowledge-Based Systems

One of the most practical and widely implemented applications of artificial intelligence in business is the development of expert systems and other knowledge-based information systems. A **knowledge-based information system** (KBIS) adds a knowledge base to the major components found in other types of computer-based information systems. An **expert system** (ES) is a knowledge-based information system that uses its knowledge about a specific, complex application area to act as an expert consultant to end users. As we said in Chapter 2, expert systems can be used for either operational or management applications. Thus, they can be classified conceptually as either operations or management support systems, depending on whether they are giving expert advice to control operational processes or to help managerial end users make decisions. See Figure 12.12

Expert systems are related to knowledge-based decision support systems, which add a knowledge base to the database and model base of traditional decision support systems. However, unlike decision support systems, expert systems provide answers to questions in a very specific problem area by making humanlike inferences about knowledge contained in a specialized knowledge base. They must also be able to explain their reasoning process and conclusions to a user. So expert systems can provide decision support to managers in the form of advice from an expert consultant in a specific problem area [27].

The integration of expert systems into decision support systems and other types of information systems is expected to become a major characteristic of a trend toward expert-assisted information systems. This integration adds expertise as well as a knowledge base to information systems. An important example is the integration of

Knowledge-Based Information Systems

Expert-Assisted IS

Roger Tully/Tony Stone Images.

FIGURE 12.12
Large banks have been heavy users of expert systems and other AI technologies for applications such as screening loan applications and detecting credit card fraud.

FIGURE 12.13
An example of a knowledge-based information system. This executive support system integrates decision support and expert system components with an executive information system.

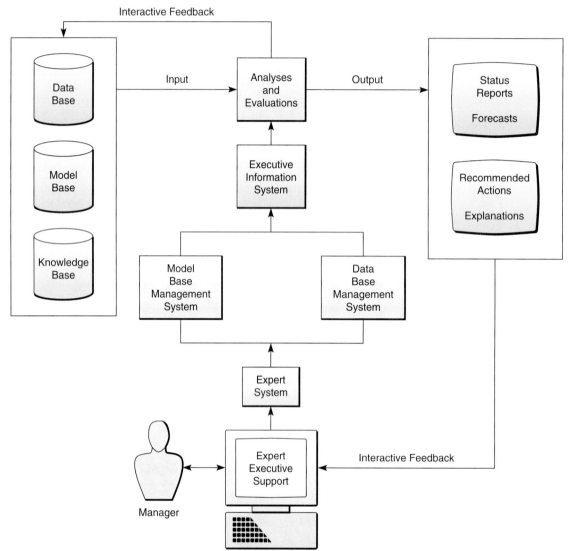

Source: Adapted from Guisseppi Forgionne," Decision Technology Systems," *Information Systems Management*, fall 1991, p. 38.

expert systems and decision support systems with executive information systems. For example, Figure 12.13 illustrates how an expert system and a decision support system have been built into an EIS. This executive support information system or *management support system* provides executives with expert-assisted information retrieval and decision support [13].

Components of an Expert System

The **components** of an expert system include a knowledge base and software modules that perform inferences on the knowledge and communicate answers to a user's questions. Figure 12.14 illustrates the interrelated components of an expert system. Note the following components:

FIGURE 12.14

Components of an expert system. The software modules perform inferences on a knowledge base built by an expert and/or knowledge engineer. This provides expert answers to an end user's questions in an interactive process.

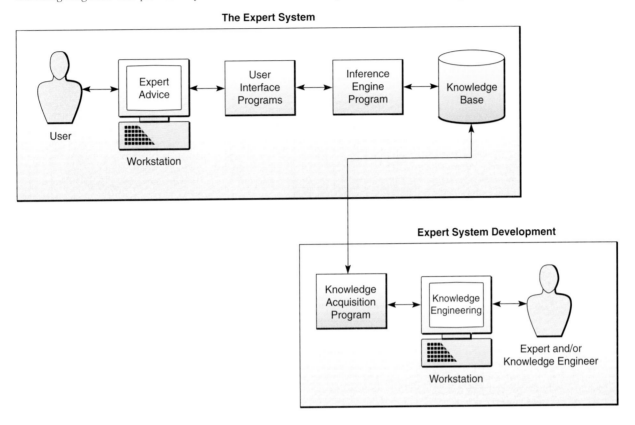

- **Knowledge base.** The knowledge base of an expert system contains (1) facts about a specific subject area (for example, John is an *analyst*) and (2) heuristics (rules of thumb) that express the reasoning procedures of an expert on the subject (for example: IF John is an analyst, THEN he needs a workstation). We will discuss the contents of the knowledge base in more detail shortly.
- **Software resources.** An expert system software package contains an **inference engine** and other programs for refining knowledge and communicating with users. The inference engine program processes the knowledge (such as rules and facts) related to a specific problem. It then makes associations and inferences resulting in recommended courses of action for a user. User interface programs for communicating with end users are also needed, including an explanation program to explain the reasoning process to a user if requested.

    Knowledge acquisition programs are not part of an expert system but are software tools for knowledge base development. Other software packages, such as expert system shells, are important software resources for developing expert systems.

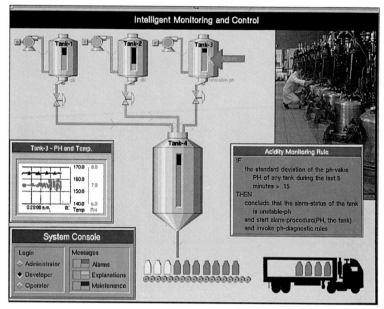

Courtesy of Gensym Corporation.

- **Hardware resources.** These include stand-alone microcomputer systems, as well as microcomputer workstations and terminals connected to servers and midsize computers or mainframes in telecommunications networks.
- **People resources.** An expert system provides expert advice to end users. This expertise is captured in a knowledge base by a knowledge engineer from facts and rules provided by one or more experts. Or experts and end users can be their own knowledge engineers and use expert system shells as development tools to build their own knowledge bases and expert systems.

Examples of Expert Systems

Using an expert system involves an interactive computer-based session, in which the solution to a problem is explored, with the expert system acting as a consultant to an end user. The expert system asks questions of the user, searches its knowledge base for facts and rules or other knowledge, explains its reasoning process when asked, and gives expert advice to the user in the subject area being explored. For example, Figure 12.15 illustrates one of the displays of an expert system.

Expert System Applications

Expert systems are being used for many different types of applications, and the variety of applications is expected to continue to increase. However, you should realize that expert systems, typically, accomplish one or more generic uses. Figure 12.16 outlines six generic categories of expert system activities, with specific examples of actual expert system applications. As you can see, expert systems are being used in many different fields, including medicine, engineering, the physical sciences, and business. Expert systems now help diagnose illnesses, search for minerals, analyze compounds, recommend repairs, and do financial planning. So from a strategic busi-

---

Application Categories and Typical Uses

Decision management—Systems that appraise situations or consider alternatives and make recommendations based on criteria supplied during the discovery process:
> Loan portfolio analysis
> Employee performance evaluation
> Insurance underwriting
> Demographic forecasts

Diagnostic/troubleshooting—Systems that infer underlying causes from reported symptoms and history:
> Equipment calibration
> Help desk operations
> Software debugging
> Medical diagnosis

Maintenance/scheduling—Systems that prioritize and schedule limited or time-critical resources:
> Maintenance scheduling
> Production scheduling
> Education scheduling
> Project management

Design/configuration—Systems that help configure equipment components, given existing constraints:
> Computer option installation
> Manufacturability studies
> Communications networks
> Optimum assembly plan

Selection/classification—Systems that help users choose products or processes, often from among large or complex sets of alternatives:
> Material selection
> Delinquent account identification
> Information classification
> Suspect identification

Process monitoring/control—Systems that monitor and control procedures or processes.
> Machine control (including robotics)
> Inventory control
> Production monitoring
> Chemical testing

FIGURE 12.16
Major application categories and examples of typical expert systems. Note the variety of applications that can be supported by such systems.

ness standpoint, expert systems can and are being used to improve every step of the product cycle of a business, from finding customers to shipping products to them. Let's look at three actual examples more closely.

ADCAD (ADvertising Communications Approach Designer) is an expert system that assists advertising agencies in setting marketing and communications objectives, selecting creative strategies, and identifying effective communications approaches. In particular, it is designed to help advertisers of consumer products with the development of advertising objectives and ad copy strategy, and the selection of communications techniques. Figure 12.17 illustrates the stages in the advertising design process and some of the factors affecting advertising design decisions on which ADCAD is based. ADCAD's knowledge base consists of rules derived from various

Advertising Strategy

FIGURE 12.17
Some of the stages and factors in the advertising design process on which the ADCAD expert system is based.

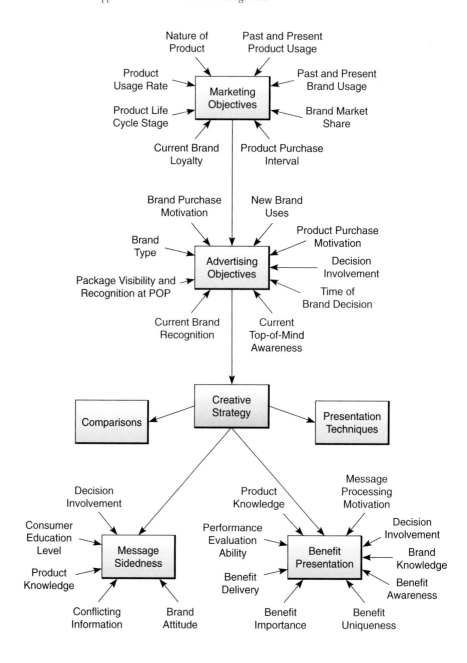

sources, including consultations with the creative staff of the Young & Rubicam advertising agency. For example, here are two of the hundreds of rules in ADCAD's knowledge base:

- **IF** ad objective = convey brand image or reinforce brand image
  AND brand purchase motivation = sensory stimulation, **AND** message processing motivation = high
  THEN emotional tone = elation

- **IF** ad objective = change brand beliefs
  AND message processing motivation = low, **AND** purchase anxiety = low,
  AND brand use avoids fearful consequences = yes
  THEN emotional tone = high fear.

ADCAD uses a question and answer format, asking the user a series of questions about the advertising problem. It then searches through its knowledge base, matching user answers against its rules to draw inferences. Then ADCAD presents its recommendations, along with a rationale for each recommendation if asked. For example, here's how ADCAD responded, when asked to explain its recommendation to use a celebrity to present an ad on television for a shampoo product:

- Just a moment please . . .
  The advertising objective is to communicate or reinforce your brand's image, mood, or an associated lifestyle to consumers who are not highly motivated to process your ad message. A celebrity presenter can attract the consumer's attention, enhance your brand's image, and become a memorable cue for brand evaluation.

ADCAD has been popular with advertising and brand managers since it provides them with a rationale for their current advertising, as well as ideas for new communications approaches. Another benefit of ADCAD is its support of what-if analysis of advertising options. ADCAD allows users to easily change their responses to questions and investigate the impact of alternative product or market assumptions. This feature has also made ADCAD a valuable training tool for students and novice advertising managers [5].

Insurance Evaluation

The Kaiser Foundation Health Plan uses an expert system known as SIMR (System for Individual Marketing and Review) to evaluate applications for health insurance coverage. SIMR helps evaluate applicants to determine whether they medically qualify for membership with Kaiser. Processing such applications used to take four to six weeks since every application had to be reviewed by doctors or other medical staffers. Kaiser used the Aion DS expert system development tool to develop a knowledge base of rules extracted from the rules that medical staffers use when they review applications.

The SIMR expert system now automatically handles 40 percent of all insurance applications without requiring a review by medical personnel. For example, SIMR has been recommending 28 percent immediate acceptances and 12 percent immediate rejections of applications it reviews. SIMR also has cut in half the time a doctor or other medical staffer needs to review the remaining applications. By simplifying and automating what was formerly a manual process, SIMR has significantly improved some of Kaiser's business processes, cut operating expenses, and provided better service to customers [4].

Bank Auditing

Banks have been at the forefront of using expert systems, neural nets, and other AI technologies to audit key financial operations [36]. For example, Royal Bank of Canada has implemented an expert system for credit card fraud detection that has cut millions of dollars of losses each year, while reducing the operating costs of their fraud analysis operations by $200,000 a year. Royal Bank's system helps their fraud analysts quickly identify and analyze suspected fraudulent activity, so that they can shut down bad accounts within hours of the first transactions.

FIGURE 12.18
Criteria for applications that are
suitable for expert systems
development.

Suitability Criteria

Domain: The domain, or subject area, of the problem is relatively small and limited to a well-defined problem area.

Expertise: Solutions to the problem require the efforts of an expert. That is, a body of knowledge, techniques, and intuition is needed that only a few people possess.

Complexity: Solution of the problem is a complex task that requires logical inference processing, which would not be handled as well by conventional information processing.

Structure: The solution process must be able to cope with ill-structured, uncertain, missing, and conflicting data, and a problem situation that changes with the passage of time.

Availability: An expert exists who is articulate and cooperative, and who has the support of the management and end users involved in the development of the proposed system.

Banque Populaire De Lorraine, of France, has developed an expert system for the analysis and control of customer loans and other liabilities. Called SESAME, this expert system reviews the status of over 25,000 large and complex business customer accounts each month. It analyzes a client's business activity, identifies any irregularities, and makes recommendations on actions to be taken.

Chemical Bank of New York uses an expert system, called Inspector, and a communications network spanning 23 countries to review over a billion dollars in worldwide foreign exchange transactions each day. Because of the large dollar amounts involved in such transactions, Inspector paid for itself many times over, the first time it identified a fraudulent trade.

Developing Expert Systems

As the previous examples show, many organizations are developing expert system solutions to business problems. However, before developing an expert system, the following questions need to be answered:

- What applications are suitable for expert systems?
- What benefits and limitations of expert systems should be considered?
- Should the expert system be (1) purchased as a completely developed system, (2) developed with an expert system shell, or (3) developed from scratch as a custom system?

Expert System Suitability

Obviously, expert systems are not the answer to every problem facing an organization. People using other types of information systems do quite well in many problem situations. So what types of problems are most suitable to expert system solutions? One way to answer this is to look at examples of the applications of current expert systems, including the generic tasks being accomplished, as were summarized in Figure 12.16. Another way is to identify criteria that make a problem situation suitable for an expert system. Figure 12.18 outlines some important criteria [6, 13].

Figure 12.18 should emphasize that many real-world situations do not fit the suitability criteria for expert system solutions. Therefore, expert systems should be developed cautiously, especially if sensitive or strategic applications are involved. Hundreds of rules may be required to capture the assumptions, facts, and reasoning that are involved in even simple problem situations. For example, a task that might

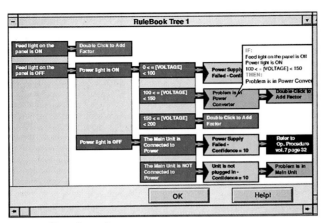

Courtesy of Exsys Expert Systems.

FIGURE 12.19
Using the Exsys Professional expert system shell to develop an expert system for a chemical refining process.

take an expert a few minutes to accomplish might require an expert system with hundreds of rules and take several months to develop. A task that may take a human expert several hours to do may require an expert system with thousands of rules and take several years to build [7, 13].

Expert Systems: Make or Buy?

Once the suitability and feasibility of a proposed expert system application have been evaluated, it's time to confront the make-or-buy decision. As you saw in a previous example, complete expert system packages like the ADCAD can be purchased by advertising companies and other businesses. Many other packages are available in a variety of application areas, and the number is increasing each year. As in other make-or-buy decisions, the suitability of the expert system package for an end user's needs must be balanced against the cost in time and money of developing a custom system.

Expert System Shells

The easiest way to develop your own expert system is to use an **expert system shell** as a developmental tool. An expert system shell is a software package consisting of an expert system without its kernel, that is, its knowledge base of facts and rules. This leaves a *shell* of software (the inference engine and user interface programs) with generic inferencing and user interface capabilities. Other development tools (such as rule editors and user interface generators) are added in making the shell a powerful expert system development tool.

Expert systems shells are now available as relatively low cost software packages that help users develop their own expert systems on microcomputers. They allow trained users to develop the knowledge base for a specific expert system application. For example, one shell uses a spreadsheet format to help end users develop IF-THEN rules, automatically generating rules based on examples furnished by a user. Once a knowledge base is constructed, it is used with the shell's inference engine and user interface modules as a complete expert system on a specific subject area. Expert system shells have accelerated the widespread development and use of expert systems. See Figure 12.19.

Custom Expert System Development

Instead of using an expert system shell, an expert system can be developed from scratch. This requires using one or more programming languages to develop the inference engine and user interface programs and to build a knowledge base. For example, two programming languages, LISP and PROLOG, have long been used for expert systems development. LISP is a procedural, list processing language specifically designed to handle many types of logical text processing (symbolic processing). PROLOG is a nonprocedural language that uses statements defining values and relationships between objects to produce logical inferences. It thus is more efficient than LISP in constructing rule-based knowledge bases. Obviously, this is a much more difficult, time-consuming, and costly undertaking. However, early expert systems were developed this way, as are many large expert system projects. Their developers want the design flexibility that is not supported by the generic nature and basic capabilities of many shells. Thus, they prefer to develop an expert system that is more tailored to their specific needs.

Knowledge Engineering

Expert systems are developed using a prototyping process, as explained in Chapter 3. However, developing expert systems is different because it results in the development of a knowledge base, and it frequently requires the services of a knowledge engineer.

A **knowledge engineer** is a professional who works with experts to capture the knowledge (facts and rules of thumb) they possess. The knowledge engineer then builds the knowledge base (and the rest of the expert system if necessary), using an iterative, prototyping process until the expert system is acceptable. Thus, knowledge engineers perform a role similar to that of systems analysts in conventional information systems development. Obviously, knowledge engineers must be able to understand and work with experts in many subject areas. Therefore, this new information systems specialty requires good "people skills," as well as a background in artificial intelligence and information systems.

Once the decision is made to develop an expert system, a team of one or more domain experts and a knowledge engineer may be formed. Or experts skilled in the use of expert system shells could develop their own expert systems. If a shell is used, facts and rules of thumb about a specific domain can be defined and entered into a knowledge base with the help of a rule editor or other knowledge acquisition tool. A limited working prototype of the knowledge base is then constructed, tested, and evaluated using the inference engine and user interface programs of the shell. The knowledge engineer and domain experts can modify the knowledge base, then retest the system and evaluate the results. This process is repeated until the knowledge base and the shell result in an acceptable expert system.

The Value of Expert Systems

Before deciding to acquire or develop an expert system, it is important that managerial end users evaluate its **benefits and limitations.** In particular, they must decide whether the benefits of a proposed expert system will exceed its costs.

Benefits of Expert Systems

An expert system captures the expertise of an expert or group of experts in a computer-based information system. Thus, it can outperform a single human expert in many problem situations. That's because an expert system is faster and more consistent, can have the knowledge of several experts, and does not get tired or distracted by overwork or stress.

Expert systems also help preserve and reproduce the knowledge of experts. They allow a company to preserve the expertise of an expert before he or she leaves the organization. This expertise can then be shared by reproducing the software and knowledge base of the expert system. This allows novices to be trained and supported by copies of an expert system distributed throughout an organization. Finally, expert systems can have the same competitive advantages as other types of information technology. That is, the effective use of expert systems can allow a firm to (1) improve the efficiency of its operations, (2) produce new products and services, (3) lock in customers and suppliers with new business relationships, and (4) build knowledge-based strategic information resources.

The major limitations of expert systems arise from their limited focus, inability to learn, maintenance problems, and developmental cost. Expert systems excel only in solving specific types of problems in a limited domain of knowledge. They fail miserably in solving problems requiring a broad knowledge base and subjective problem solving. They do well with specific types of operational or analytical tasks, but falter at subjective managerial decision making. For example, an expert system might help a financial consultant develop alternative investment recommendations for a client. But it could not adequately evaluate the nuances or current political, economic, and societal developments, or the personal dynamics of a session with a client. These important factors would still have to be handled by the human consultant before a final investment decision could be reached.

Expert systems may also be difficult and costly to develop and maintain properly. The costs of knowledge engineers, lost expert time, and hardware and software resources may be too high to offset the benefits expected from some applications. Also, expert systems can't maintain themselves. That is, they can't learn from experience but must be taught new knowledge and modified as new expertise is needed to match developments in their subject areas. However, some of these limitations can be overcome by the use of expert system shells and other developmental tools that make the job of development and maintenance easier.

Limitations of Expert Systems

In the case of the intelligent agent, we are seeing such AI-ish routines embedded in our latest spreadsheet and word processing packages and made available for use on networks such as the Internet. Indeed, almost any software package in the late 1990s will have to have an intelligent agent capability if it hopes to compete in the competitive software marketplace [11].

Intelligent agents are growing in popularity as a way to use artificial intelligence routines in software to help users accomplish many kinds of tasks. An intelligent agent is a *software surrogate* for an end user or a process that fulfills a stated need or activity. An intelligent agent uses its built-in and learned knowledge base about a person or process to make decisions and accomplish tasks in a way that fulfills the intentions of a user. Many times, an intelligent agent is given a graphic representation or persona, such as Einstein for a science advisor, Sherlock Holmes for an information search agent, and so on. Thus, intelligent agents (also called intelligent assistants and *wizards*) are special-purpose knowledge-based information systems that accomplish specific tasks for users. Figure 12.20 illustrates the components of an intelligent agent for commodity buying [17, 26].

As we mentioned in Chapter 5, intelligent agents are evidence of a trend toward *expert-assisted* software packages. One of the most well-known uses of intelligent agents are the *Wizards* found in Microsoft Word, Excel, Access, and Powerpoint. These Wizards are built-in capabilities that can analyze how an end user is using a software package and offer suggestions on how to complete various tasks. Thus, Wizards might help you change document margins, format spreadsheet cells,

Intelligent Agents

FIGURE 12.20
Components of an intelligent agent for commodity buying.

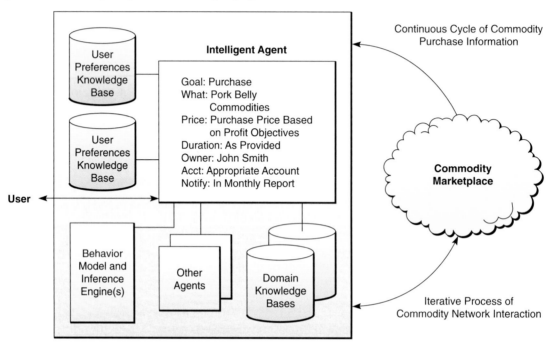

query a database, or construct a graph. Wizards and other software agents are also designed to adjust to your way of using a software package so that they can anticipate when you will need their assistance. See Figure 12.21.

The use of intelligent agents is expected to grow rapidly as a way to simplify software use, access to network resources, and information screening and retrieval for users. Intelligent agents are becoming necessary as software packages become more sophisticated and powerful, as networks like the Internet became more vast and complex, and as information sources and media proliferate exponentially. In fact, some commentators forecast that much of the future of computing will consist of intelligent agents performing their work for users. So instead of using agents to help us accomplish computing tasks, we will be managing the performance of intelligent agents as they perform computing tasks for us. Figure 12.22 summarizes a few of the many types of intelligent agents that are in use or currently being developed [17].

Hybrid AI Systems

To be competitive in today's global environment, businesses are turning to high-technology solutions that employ increasingly sophisticated systems. Today, businesses are looking for systems beyond management information systems and decision support systems to help them solve problems that have capabilities displayed by human experts. The answers to their problems are being met by two applications of artificial intelligence (AI)—expert systems and neural networks. The strengths of these two technologies can be integrated into systems that provide best features of both technologies [27].

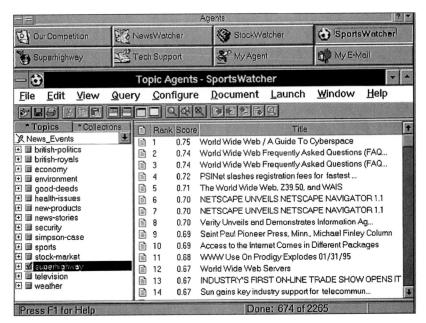

FIGURE 12.21
Intelligent agents like those in Verity's Topic Information Server help you find information in a variety of categories from many online sources.

FIGURE 12.22
Examples of intelligent agents.

User Interface Agents

- **Interface Tutors.** Observe user computer operations, correct user mistakes, and provide hints and advice on efficient software use.

- **Presentation Agents.** Show information in a variety of reporting and presentation forms and media based on user preferences.

- **Network Navigation Agents.** Discover paths to information and provide ways to view information that are preferred by a user.

- **Role-Playing Agents.** Play what-if games and other roles to help users understand information and make better decisions.

Information Management Agents

- **Search Agents.** Help users find files and databases, search for desired information, and suggest and find new types of information products, media, and resources.

- **Information Brokers.** Provide commercial services to discover and develop information resources that fit the business or personal needs of a user.

- **Information Filters.** Receive, find, filter, discard, save, forward, and notify users about products received or desired, including E-mail, voice mail, and all other information media.

Increasingly, AI developers are constructing products which integrate several AI technologies into a single **hybrid AI system.** As the opening quotation of this section emphasizes, this frequently includes two popular AI technologies: expert systems and neural nets. For example, an integrated ES/NN system might detect trends or find hidden relationships (as neural nets do), then make inferences and decisions about them in a specific problem area (as expert systems do). See Figure 12.23.

FIGURE 12.23
Examples of integrated expert systems and neural nets.

Example	Expert System (ES) and Neural Network (NN) Functions
Underwater welding robot temperature controller	NN classifies using digital signal processor; ES suggests corrective action
Market timing	NN preprocesses Computrac data; ES generates rules from NN
Jet engine diagnostic	NN diagnoses problem; ES suggests corrective action
Construction decision support	NN finds an initial choice; ES performs economic analysis
Commercial loan advisor	ES preprocesses data; NN assigns a rating value
DNA amplification	ES creates a file of inputs; NN clusters similar characteristics
Architecture scoring model	ES finds a preliminary score; NN tunes the score
Stock selection	ES uses expert rules; NN provides value to rate stock performance and provides learning
Human resource requirements	ES estimates requirements; NN provides projections based on historical data
Realtime vision	ES searches for objects; NN models objects

Most integrated AI systems are designed to provide the best features of expert systems, neural nets, or fuzzy logic technologies, and to offset each other's strengths and weaknesses. For example, the difficulties in acquiring and representing knowledge for expert systems can be offset by how neural networks can learn from sample data. Conversely, a neural network's weakness in explaining the rationale for its recommendations can be improved with the strong explanation capabilities of an expert system [27]. On the other hand, an expert system's limited ability to handle incomplete or ambiguous data can be offset by a fuzzy logic system's ability to process imprecise data values to better describe a real world problem situation.

Figure 12.23 includes many examples of hybrid AI systems using expert system and neural net technologies. Figure 12.24 illustrates a hybrid system that combines fuzzy logic and neural net technologies for an insurance policy risk analysis application. Hybrid systems such as these are expected to grow in business use as companies look for more complete AI solutions to the tough problems they face in today's competitive markets.

Technical Note: How Expert Systems Work

The Knowledge Base

Read the next few pages if you want to know in more detail how expert systems work. Remember that the two unique components of an expert system are its knowledge base and inference engine. Let's examine these components in more detail.

Expert systems have a knowledge base consisting of knowledge extracted from experts, sometimes with the help of a specialist called a knowledge engineer. As we said earlier, the knowledge in a knowledge base can be subdivided conceptually into two categories:

- Facts about a specific subject area (called a domain). Facts could include definitions, relationships, measurements, probabilities, observations, constraints, and hypotheses.
- Rules of thumb (called heuristics) describing the reasoning procedures by which an expert uses facts to arrive at conclusions.

FIGURE 12.24
A hybrid fuzzy logic and neural network system for insurance policy risk determination.

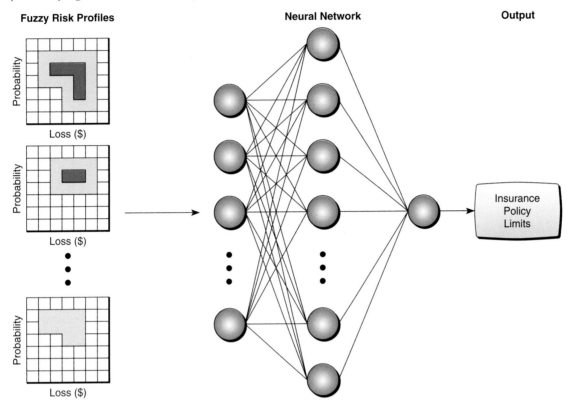

There are many ways that such knowledge is represented in expert systems. Four of the most popular are rule-based, frame-based, object-based, and case-based methods of knowledge representation.

Rule-based expert systems represent knowledge in the form of rules and statements of fact. They are the most common type of expert system because they relate facts and reasoning procedures in an intuitively familiar way and are thus easier for end users to learn. Figure 12.25 illustrates that rule-based expert systems have two major components: a knowledge base and an inference engine. The knowledge base is a collection of facts about a subject area stored in the form of statements such as "IBM is a corporation," "Compaq makes microcomputers," and "John needs a workstation."

The **rules** in an expert system are called *production rules,* decision rules, or IF-THEN rules. Collections of rules are stored in the knowledge base. Rules typically take the form of a premise and a conclusion, such as IF (condition), THEN (conclusion), or IF (situation), THEN (action).

For example:
IF John is an analyst, THEN he needs a workstation.

However, a rule can have several conditions and conclusions, and the IF (condition), THEN (conclusion), ELSE (conclusion) form is used in many systems.

Rule-Based Knowledge

FIGURE 12.25
A rule-based expert system.
Note that such systems have an
inference engine program that
manipulates a knowledge base
consisting of facts and rules in
order to reach conclusions.

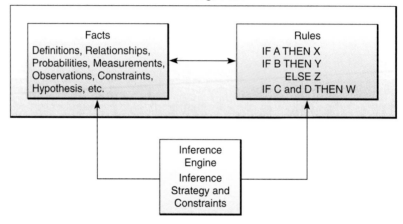

For example:
IF Compaq makes microcomputer workstations,
and
Compaq's workstations have the best price/performance ratio,
and
IBM's workstations are equivalent to Compaq's,
THEN John should select a Compaq workstation,
ELSE John should select an IBM workstation.

Frame-Based Knowledge

Frame-based expert systems represent knowledge in the form of a hierarchy or net-work of frames. A **frame** is a collection of knowledge about an entity or other con-cept. Each frame is a complex package of *slots*, that is, data values describing the many characteristics or attributes of an entity, including its relationships to other entities. Thus, each slot contains the name of an attribute and either:

- The current value of the attribute.
- Procedures for transferring to another frame to compute or develop the value of the attribute.
- "Inheritance" procedures for obtaining the value of the attribute (called a default value) by finding it in a related frame.

Figure 12.26 illustrates a frame-based knowledge base representing a few of the frames, slots, and interactions needed to answer the question, "Does John need a workstation?" Notice the relationships between frames based on the attribute val-ues they have in common. Also note that the value for John's resources is obtained from the analyst frame, while his current salary will be computed by a salary com-putation procedure.

Object-Based Knowledge

In Chapter 5 we introduced the concepts of *objects* and object-oriented program-ming (OOP) languages, while in Chapter 7 we briefly discussed object-oriented databases. Expert system shells that use object-oriented programming tools to develop object-based expert systems are available. These expert systems are related to frame-based systems, but represent knowledge as a network of objects rather than

FIGURE 12.26
A frame-based knowledge base. Notice how knowledge is represented in the form of slots and interrelated frames.

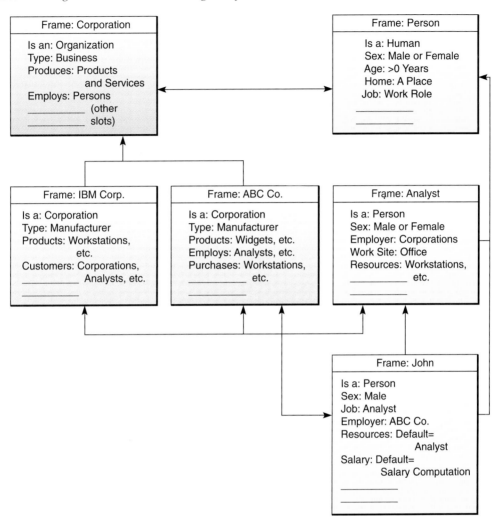

frames. An object consists of data values describing the attributes of an entity, plus the operations (methods, procedures, or actions) that can be performed upon the data.

For example, if Figure 12.26 represented objects instead of frames, the program code for computing John's salary could be contained within the object for John. Alternately, John's salary could be performed by a program code for computing analysts' salaries that was stored in the analyst object, which is one of John's parent objects. This method of inheritance capability allows an object to inherit program code from its parent objects in an object-based expert system.

Case-based reasoning (CBR) is a fairly new but increasingly popular alternative to rule-based expert systems. CBR expert systems store knowledge in the form of cases, that is, examples of past performance, occurrences, and experiences. See Figure 12.27. Hundreds or thousands of those cases may be stored in a case library or *case*

Case-Based Reasoning

Identification:
- Company name
- Ticker symbol
- S&P bond rating
- Industry
- Base year of data

**Balance Sheet
Information:**
- Total assets
- Current assets
- Cash
- Market/Book
- Total liabilities
- Current liabilities

Income Statement:
- Sales
- Net income
- Interest expense

Other Data:
- Dividends paid
- Stock price
- Shares outstanding
- Earnings growth (one year)
- Cash flow

Key Financial Ratios:
- Current ratio
- Quick ratio
- Debt ratio
- Debt/equity ratio
- Payout ratio
- Sales/total assets
- Return on assets
- Interest coverage
- Cash flow liabilities

FIGURE 12.28
The case-based reasoning expert
system process.

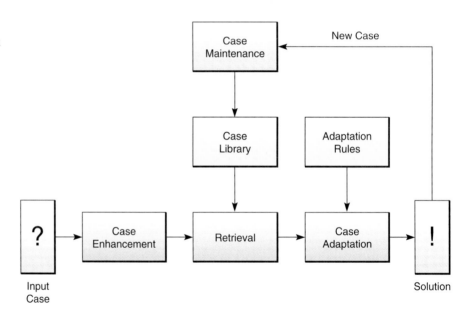

knowledge base. Figure 12.28 illustrates that when a user encounters a problem (a new case), the expert system may first enhance the case by editing it to fit its case format. Then it searches the case knowledge base for similar cases, retrieves the case with the closest fit, and adapts the old cases to solve the problem presented in the new case. The new case and its solutions may then be added to the case library to keep it up to date with new and unique examples and a record of successful and unsuccessful solutions. Thus, the case knowledge base can be continually expanded and improved the more it is used [2,6].

The Inference Engine

The inference engine is the most important software component of an expert system. This program evaluates and manipulates the facts and rules (or the frames or objects) in a knowledge base. Then it makes associations and inferences resulting in a recommended course of action for a user. This process produces an inference chain, that is, a linking of the various facts and rules needed to reach the conclusion. That's what is displayed by an expert system when it is asked to explain its reasoning process to an end user. An inference engine uses two basic strategies or processes to create inference chains and reach conclusions—*forward chaining* and *backward chaining*. Let's look at rule-based systems to see how this is done.

A **forward-chaining** inference strategy reaches a conclusion by applying rules to facts. The inference engine examines the premise (the "IF condition" part) of one rule at a time and scans the knowledge base to see if it contains any facts that satisfy that rule's conditions. If it does, that rule is said to "fire," and the conclusion of that rule (the "THEN conclusions" part) is added to a temporary or working memory of the knowledge base as a new fact. The inference engine continues until it searches the entire knowledge base for any more matches to the premise of the rule being examined. Then it selects the next rule in the knowledge base, and the entire process is repeated until all rules have been examined this way and all inferences made. This iterative process results in one or more conclusions, which are then communicated to the expert system user.

Forward Chaining

For example, an inference engine could search a knowledge base of rules and facts about our employees and suppliers to help us decide on the purchase of workstations for our employees. Assume we asked the expert system to help us answer the question, "Should John have a workstation?" The inference engine could select a rule we used in our earlier example:

IF John is an analyst, THEN he needs a workstation.

This rule would fire if a search of the fact base revealed that John is indeed an analyst. The other rule we used earlier as an example (concerning John's choice of workstations) would fire if the knowledge base also indicated that both COMPAQ and IBM make high-quality workstations. The expert system could then reach the conclusion that John should be authorized to purchase either a COMPAQ or IBM workstation.

A **backward-chaining** inference process justifies a proposed conclusion by determining if it will result when rules are applied to the facts. Thus, the process starts with a hypothesis or goal and is said to be goal-driven. The goal is compared to the conclusion of each rule in the rule base. Each time there is a match between the goal and the conclusion of a rule, the premise of the rule is examined by the inference engine and compared to the facts in the knowledge base. If, after repeated trials, facts are found that satisfy all of a rule's conditions, that rule fires and the goal is achieved—that is, the hypothesis is justified. If some conditions cannot be satisfied, the expert system reports this to the user.

Backward Chaining

For example, we could state the goal as "John should have a workstation." The inference engine could select the rule "IF John is an analyst, THEN he needs a workstation," since its conclusion matches the hypothesis. The inference engine could then search the knowledge base to find out if John is an analyst. Once it found this fact, the rule would fire and the goal would be justified and recommended to the user of the expert system.

Canada Trust: Banking on Expert Systems

While most top-tier U.S. banks have been applying neural network technologies to stop credit-card fraud, Canada Trust has a somewhat different approach: an expert system. The $163 billion savings and loan used Trinzic Corp.'s Aion Development System to develop an expert system with more than 250 rules that calculate and analyze credit-card transaction patterns.

The system has worked. Since the expert system went into production in July 1993, Canada Trust has eliminated its use of reports from MasterCard International. More important, the bank has avoided more than $1.2 million in MasterCard losses since the software was installed.

Credit-card fraud is rampant, and the losses continue to spiral. MasterCard issuers reported more than $450 billion in worldwide losses in 1993—the last full year statistics were available—and the number continues to climb.

"It's still a very serious problem, and the numbers aren't going down," said David Medeiros, an analyst at the Tower Group, a banking and technology consultancy. Consumer credit-card fraud is very difficult to detect with any certainty, even when using the most advanced techniques on card transaction data. At best, the most effective neural network models cannot provide more than a 25 percent to 33 percent certainty of actual fraud, according to Medeiros. To combat this, Canada Trust uses SAS Institute software to extract data from its IBM ES/9000 mainframe-based credit-card authorization records. Data is extracted every two hours during the business day and once nightly.

The expert system then automates the search for deviations from a customer's profile, such as big-ticket purchases outside the customer's normal purchasing patterns and transactions such as cash advances or jewelry or electronic purchases, which are frequent targets of fraud.

The expert system then assigns an overall score to a transaction incident based on the likelihood of fraud and routes the data to the bank's fraud department for analysis.

For example, the system identified a Canada Trust MasterCard customer who had not used his credit card for three months but whose account suddenly showed a large jewelry purchase. The purchase turned out to be fraudulent.

Prior to the development of the expert system, Canada Trust relied on "velocity reports," or credit-card usage reports, from MasterCard to analyze suspected fraudulent activity. But the data was two to three days old before Canada Trust fraud experts could begin analyzing, it, and the bank wanted to be able to detect fraudulent activity before customer statements were produced, according to Paul Martinello, audit information analyst at the bank's London, Ontario, office.

Canada Trust spent $9,000 for IBM OS/2-based versions of AionDS and approximately $45,000 for the IBM MVS component. The bank received the return on its investment after half a month of using the software, Martinello said.

According to MasterCard figures, credit-card fraud in Canada rose 46.4 percent in 1993. Although there are no fail-safe credit-card fraud detection technologies on the market, Canada Trust's expert system has helped the bank reduce its credit-card fraud to an annual rate of less than 25 percent, Martinello said. "We can't cover everything, but we're running well below the industry average," he said.

CASE STUDY QUESTIONS

1. How does an expert system work to help Canada Trust and credit card losses?

2. What expert system components and resources (refer to Figure 12.14) do you recognize in this case?

3. Why do you think credit card systems have such huge losses? How could IT help reduce such losses even more?

Source: Adapted from Thomas Hoffman, "Bank Turns to Third-Party Expert System to Combat Skyrocketing Credit-Card Fraud," *Computerworld*, April 24, 1995, p. 82. Copyright 1995 by Computerworld, Inc., Framingham, MA 01701—Reprinted from *Computerworld*.

Summary

- **Artificial Intelligence.** The major application domains of artificial intelligence (AI) include a variety of applications in cognitive science, computer science, robotics, and natural interfaces. The goal of AI is the development of computer functions normally associated with human physical and mental capabilities, such as robots that see, hear, talk, feel, and move, and software capable of reasoning, learning, and problem solving. Thus AI is being applied to many applications in business operations and management, as well as in many other fields.

- **Human Information Processing.** Models of the human information processing system provide us with important concepts about the human cognitive process in an information processing context. These models emphasize that humans selectively process information, which should be considered in the design of information products and systems. Also important are several concepts about cognitive styles, such as the rational and intuitive tendencies of human thought processes. Information theory also helps us evaluate the communication of information in terms of technical, semantic, and effectiveness dimensions. Such concepts help us understand how information products can accommodate the different cognitive styles of end users.

- **Expert Systems.** Expert systems are knowledge-based information systems that use a knowledge base about a specific, complex application area and an inference engine program to act as an expert consultant to users. An expert system consists of hardware, software, knowledge, and people resources. Hardware includes workstations and other computers. Software includes an inference engine program that makes inferences based on the facts and rules stored in a knowledge base. Other software includes user interface programs and expert system shells for expert system development. A knowledge base consists of facts about a specific subject area and heuristics (rules of thumb) that express the reasoning procedures of an expert. Users, domain experts, and knowledge engineers are the people resources of an expert system.

- **Types of Expert Systems.** There are four basic forms of expert systems: rule-based, frame-based, case-based reasoning, and object-based systems. Rule-based systems express knowledge in the form of statements of facts and production rules. Frame-based and object-based systems express knowledge in the form of a hierarchy or network of frames or objects. Case-based reasoning stores knowledge in the form of examples of past performances. Inference engine programs process such knowledge by using either a forward- or backward-chaining strategy to produce inferences and reach conclusions.

- **Expert System Development.** Expert systems can be purchased or developed if a problem situation exists that is suitable for solution by expert systems rather than by conventional experts and information processing. The benefits of expert systems (such as preservation and replication of expertise) must be balanced with their limited applicability in many problem situations. If the decision is made to develop an expert system, the use of an expert system shell should be considered. It allows end users to develop their own expert systems in an interactive prototyping process.

- **Other AI Technologies.** The many application areas of AI are summarized in Figure 12.2, including neural networks, fuzzy logic, virtual reality, intelligent agents, and hybrid AI systems. Neural nets are hardware or software systems based on simple models of the brain's neuron structure that can learn to recognize patterns in data. Fuzzy logic systems use rules of approximate reasoning to solve problems where data is incomplete or ambiguous. Virtual reality systems are multisensory systems that enable human users to experience computer-simulated environments as if they actually existed. Intelligent agents are knowledge-base software surrogates for a user or process in the accomplishment of selected tasks. Hybrid AI systems are knowledge-based systems that integrate several AI technologies, such as expert systems, neural networks, and fuzzy logic systems.

Key Terms and Concepts

These are the key terms and concepts of this chapter. The page number of their first explanation is in parentheses.

1. Artificial intelligence (446)
   a. Application areas (447)
   b. Objectives (446)
2. Backward chaining (479)
3. Case-based reasoning (477)
4. Cognitive functions of the human brain (457)
5. Cognitive styles (457)
6. Expert system (461)
   a. Benefits and limitations (470)
   b. Components (462)
   c. Generic applications (464)
   d. Suitable applications (468)
7. Expert system development (468)
8. Expert system shell (469)
9. Forward chaining (479)
10. Frame-based knowledge (476)
11. Fuzzy logic (450)
12. Human information processing (454)
13. Hybrid AI systems (472)
14. Inference engine (478)
15. Information filtering (455)
16. Information theory (458)

17. Intelligent agent (471)

18. Knowledge base (474)

19. Knowledge-based systems (461)

20. Knowledge engineer (470)

21. Neural network (448)

22. Object-based knowledge (476)

23. Redundancy (459)

24. Robotics (448)

25. Rule (475)

26. Rule-based knowledge (475)

27. Virtual reality (452)

Review Quiz

Match one of the key terms and concepts listed above with one of the brief examples or definitions listed below. Try to find the best fit for answers that seem to fit more than one term or concept. Defend your choices.

____ 1. Sensory stimuli are processed and stored and result in a variety of behavioral responses.

____ 2. Humans develop frames of reference and other methods to screen and select stimuli for processing.

____ 3. This month's financial results are reported in detail and summary form, using text and graphics displays.

____ 4. Some people seem to focus on the details, others on the relationships among units of information they receive.

____ 5. Some people display more logical, verbal, and analytic reasoning versus more intuitive, symbolic, and creative thought processes.

____ 6. Information technology that focuses on the development of computer functions normally associated with human physical and mental capabilities.

____ 7. Applications in cognitive science, computer science, robotics, and natural interfaces.

____ 8. Development of computer-based machines that possess capabilities such as sight, hearing, dexterity, and movement.

____ 9. Computers can provide you with computer-simulated experiences.

____ 10. An information system that has a knowledge base as a major system component.

____ 11. A knowledge-based information system that acts as an expert consultant to users in a specific application area.

____ 12. A workstation, user interface programs, inference engine, knowledge base, and an end user.

____ 13. Applications such as diagnosis, design, prediction, interpretation, and repair.

____ 14. Small, well-defined problem areas that require experts and logical inference processing for solutions.

____ 15. They can preserve and reproduce the knowledge of experts but have a limited application focus.

____ 16. A collection of facts and reasoning procedures in a specific subject area.

____ 17. A software package that manipulates a knowledge base and makes associations and inferences leading to a recommended course of action.

____ 18. A software package consisting of an inference engine and user interface programs used as an expert system development tool.

____ 19. One can either buy a completely developed expert system package, develop one with an expert system shell, or develop one from scratch by custom programming.

____ 20. An analyst who interviews experts to develop a knowledge base about a specific application area.

____ 21. Knowledge-based software surrogates who do things for you.

____ 22. Knowledge-based combinations of several AI technologies.

____ 23. Express knowledge in the form of rules and statements of fact.

____ 24. If John is an analyst, then he needs a workstation.

____ 25. Express knowledge in the form of a hierarchical network of packages of knowledge about concepts in a subject area.

____ 26. Express knowledge in the form of a hierarchical network of packages of knowledge that include both data values and the program code for operations to be performed upon the data.

____ 27. Store knowledge in the form of examples of past performance.

____ 28. Reaches a conclusion by applying rules to facts.

____ 29. Justifies a proposed conclusion by determining if it will result when rules are applied to facts.

____ 30. AI systems that use neuron structures to recognize patterns in data.

____ 31. AI systems that use approximate reasoning to process ambiguous data.

Discussion Questions

1. Can computers think? Will they ever be able to? Explain why or why not.

2. What are some of the most important applications of AI in business? Defend your choices.

3. Refer to the Real World Case on of Earl Cox and Metus Systems in the chapter. Why is fuzzy logic a better approach than non-fuzzy methods for querying some business databases?

4. How can information systems take a manager's cognitive style into consideration? Give several examples to illustrate your answer.

5. Why would neural nets or fuzzy logic be better for some applications than expert systems? How do hybrid AI systems integrate such technologies?

6. Refer to the Real World Case on Canada Trust in the chapter. Are expert systems or neural nets a better technology for detecting credit card fraud? Explain.

7. What are several good applications of expert systems in business? Defend your choices based on the content of Figures 12.16 and 12.18.

8. How are expert systems developed? What is the role of a knowledge engineer and an expert system shell?

9. Refer to the Real World Case on Harvey P. Newquist III in the chapter. What does he mean when he says that the "information superhighway needs onramps, and passing lanes and rest stops and roadside information kiosks?"

10. What are some of the limitations or dangers you see in the use of AI technologies such as expert systems, virtual reality, and intelligent agents? What could be done to minimize such effects?

Real World Problems

1. Lockheed Corporation and Others: Expert Systems for Business Process Reengineering

If you look at most of the recent AI applications to go online, most fit under the large umbrella of BPR—business process reengineering. A glance at some of the American Association for Artificial Intelligence's 1994 Innovative Applications of Artificial Intelligence (IAAI) awards is a case in point. Lockheed's Palo Alto Research Laboratory, for example, was an IAAI winner for a purchasing advisory expert system that automated the procurement process. Changing from the manual practice to automation reduced the average processing time per procurement from 30 days to 4. The AI component of the application is saving Lockheed $600,000 to $800,000 annually.

IAAI winner Countrywide Funding Corporation built an underwriting expert system that automates the processing of 50 percent of the loans and reduces underwriting time from 50 to 15 minutes. E. I. duPont de Nemours & Co. received an IAAI award for an overtime scheduling expert system that automates the process, saving $30,000 each week in overtime costs through more effective scheduling. In addition, worker's grievances filed with the union for overtime reasons have dropped by 90 percent since the system was installed, because workers feel that the distribution of opportunities to work overtime is more fair and even. Singapore Press Holdings won for an expert system that automates advertising layout, reducing daily layout time from 12 hours to 30 minutes at an estimated savings of $800,000 annually.

These are but a few of the most recent IAAI winners that illustrate how AI is being used for BPR. The final winner to mention here is AT&T Global Business Communications Systems, which built a customer-service help desk using case-based reasoning, designed to improve agents' responses. AT&T reports that it has significantly reduced replacement part costs, field service costs, and training requirements for help-desk staff.

a. Why might business process reengineering be a good applications area for expert systems?

b. Analyze one of the business examples in this case in terms of their suitability for expert systems as outlined in Figure 12.18.

Source: Adapted from Sara Hedberg, "Where's *AI Hiding*?" *AI Expert*, April 1995, pp. 17–19.

2. Spartan Stores Inc.: Neural Nets for Buying Decisions

Spartan Stores Inc. (Grand Rapids, Michigan) is a $2 billion retail food chain that has used California Scientific's BrainMaker neural net development program to assist buyers in forecasting product purchases. Buyers formerly evaluated nearly 1,000 recommended purchase orders per day. These orders were generated by Spartan's computer forecasting system. After scanning these potential orders, buyers normally discarded three-quarters of them as inapplicable, based on a variety of criteria (ranging from product popularity to seasonal value).

To alleviate some of this mind-numbing analysis, Spartan chose to develop a neural net that could make simple applicability decisions, thereby letting buyers concentrate on more complex tasks. The company created an application built on 27 variables that were applied to purchases such as inventory on hand, rate of sale, number on order, items planned as part of a promotional or advertising campaign, and so on.

After lengthy testing of the neural net system (using Kellogg's products as a test bed), Spartan found that there was an agreement rate of better than 90 percent between the software and the human buyers. So, like all good intelligent systems, the application has now been put into practical use and is being modified for other areas of the company.

a. How did Spartan develop their neural net purchasing system?

b. Why did Spartan's buying process have good potential for a neural net solution?

Source: Adapted from H. P. Newquist "Spring Ahead, Fall Back," *AI Expert*, February 1995, pp. 42–43.

3. Veratex Corporation: Hybrid Telemarketing Systems

Sometimes it takes two AI technologies to create a successful application, and Veratex Corp. (Troy, Michigan), a $58 million per year dental and medical supply company, has proven it within its sales department. Veratex was experiencing large turnover in the telemarketing sales force. Says Mary Lamphier, vice president of information systems and CIO at Veratex, "We needed quicker, better, and more thorough training and sales support, and I felt we could use AI as a remedy." Veratex needed a system that had integrated, comprehensive telemarketing and sales support that included customer credit histories and buying patterns. The sales agents needed to access the information quickly, letting them customize customer needs such as suggesting products and raising credit limits.

Veratex teamed up with IBM and a business partner, Churchill Systems, which specializes in commercial applications of AI technologies, to develop a hybrid expert/neural net system. The resulting system gives Veratex a one-two punch in five teleservicing sales areas: complementary products, substitute products, specialization in medical and dental products, credit management, and sales analysis. Lamphier and Veratex were quite pleased with the results. For example, sales staff training takes only three to six weeks, and sales increased 14 percent on one product line within the first month of the system's installation.

Now, when a customer calls in a request, the expert system generates a list and description of suggestions for a variety of products. This helps sales agents offer other related products to the customer. For customers who have back orders, sales agents can retrieve a list, price, and description of substitute products. According to Harve Light, president of Churchill Systems, "By comparing profiles of low-volume customers to neural network-generated profiles of high-volume Veratex customers, the neural network application helps sales agents predict which low-volume customers have greatest potential to become a future high-volume customer."

a. How do an expert system and neural net work together to help the sales department of Veratex?

b. How might another industry or business function use a hybrid AI system like Veratex?

Source: Adapted from Patty Enrado, "Two Is Better Than One," *AI Expert*, March 1995, p. 48.

4. IBM Corporation: Using Case-Based Reasoning

IBM is not only hoping to bring artificial intelligence back to the fore of its computing products, it is using AI internally as well. In an attempt to get third-party software development of OS/2 applications up and running, IBM developed AskPSP, a help desk application built with Inference's CBR Express/CasePoint software. AskPSP (which stands for Ask Personal Software Products) assists developers with technical problems during the creation of OS/2 software by finding solutions from a library of cases relating to OS/2. When developers run into difficulties, they can tell AskPSP—in conversational English—what their problems are. AskPSP then seeks to identify similar cases that will explain the trouble.

The cases were created and stored by IBM's tech-support people—those brave souls who staff the front lines and phone lines between developers and IBM itself and know, via customers, where the pitfalls lie. In the rare instances when there is no case to resolve a particular application development problem, users can send their problem cases back to IBM, where they are resolved and become new cases in the library. By stockpiling these cases, IBM potentially can cover most of its "bug" bases with each new release of its OS/2 operating system.

a. Why do you think case-based reasoning has become a popular approach for building a knowledge base for expert systems?

b. How does a case-based reasoning approach help IBM's OS/2 application development effort?

Source: Adapted from H. P. Newquist, "Spring Ahead, Fall Back," *AI Expert*, February 1995, pp. 42–43.

5. Tom Hall: Using an E-Mail Agent

Interoffice E-mail is popular these days—all too popular for Dallas-based Unix programmer Tom Hall, who says he could spend an hour a day filing, deleting, and responding to E-mail. Don't get him wrong—Hall thinks E-mail is great. "On my current project," he says, "we have to coordinate efforts of programmers between here and Phoenix. Paper mail just wouldn't have the response time we need." His group relies heavily on Microsoft Mail (MS-Mail) and a wide-area network of hundreds of PCs. Nevertheless, E-mail has its down side. For example, it's typical for enthusiastic E-mailers to broadcast low-priority messages across wide swathes of the company. Another headache is composing multiple replies to similar E-mail queries. In Hall's case, he found himself repeatedly being asked to send the same project status reports. To cope with his mail deluge, Hall enlisted MailBot, a software agent for MS-Mail developed by Daxtron Laboratories Inc.

Hall programmed Mailbot by giving it rules for a variety of E-mail jobs, including screening out unwanted E-mail and sending multiple E-mail replies to repeated E-mail queries. Hall figures his Mailbot saves him between 30 and 60 minutes a day. "Even if you take into account all of the time I spent learning and programming, Mailbot gave that time back to me within the first month." Hall trusts his agent, but out of healthy paranoia he still deletes messages himself. "Mailbot rakes the Wastebasket folder every night and nukes anything over two weeks old."

Having spent about 30 hours learning, programming, and playing with Mailbot, Hall has an agent that does things just the way he likes them. He thinks agents are essential for weeding out junk E-mail, but believes they'd be even more helpful if people would adopt keyword conventions to help the agents sort the mail. "I think that will evolve naturally," Hall says, "as more and more people use agents to deal with their mail."

  a. What is an intelligent agent? How does an agent help Tom Hall with his E-mail?

  b. How could intelligent agents help businesspeople in other ways? Use an example to illustrate your answer.

Source: Adapted from Marti Remington, "Booking A Software Agent," *PC Today*, March 1995, p. 52.

6. MacMillan Bloedel Corp.: Developing an Expert System

MacMillan Bloedel Corp. is a forest products conglomerate in British Columbia that produces particle board used in building items such as bookshelves, furniture, and kitchen cupboards. Due to high staff turnover and a reorganization of divisional personnel at the particle board plant, only two senior employees nearing retirement had the comprehensive, operational know-how and training capability necessary to operate the facility.

When the only people who knew the idiosyncracies of each machine were no longer with the firm, the only alternative was to call them back as consultants—very expensive

consultants. "They had a former manager named Herb who was making a fortune," says Beverly Smith, vice president of AcQuired Intelligence, Inc., which makes the ACQUIRE expert system development package. "He was making more than he did as an employee because they kept having to bring him back from the golf course to tell them that when the board bubbled here, you made an adjustment there. And he didn't really appreciate it, he was retired."

So the company decided to implement an expert system solution. The task was two-pronged: to document the procedures inherent in the routine operation of the facility and to provide a vehicle for training and upgrading personnel. "The machinery had been tinkered with over the years," says Smith, "so the manuals were of no use. Every piece of machinery in the plant was beyond the manufacturer's setting."

The ACQUIRE knowledge-based acquisition system was used to pick Herb's brain for his knowledge of how to start up, clean up, and set up the particle board coating line. The line consisted of machines whose operations parameters changed according to the coating to be applied. Herb was able to provide expert information that was captured in the expert system's knowledge base, so it could consistently provide quality maintenance and operations advice to the mill operators.

  a. Why did MacMillan Bloedel need an expert system? How did they develop the expert system?

  b. Is this a suitable application for an expert system? Use Figure 12.18 to help you explain your answer.

Source: Adapted from Richard Egan, "The Expert Within," *PC Today*, January 1995, p. 39.

Application Exercises

1. The ADCAD System

Evaluate the ADCAD expert system on page 465 in the chapter. Write up your evaluation based on the following points:

  a. The components of an expert system that you recognize. (See Figure 12.14.)

  b. How well it fits the suitability criteria and application categories for expert systems. (See Figures 12.16 and 12.18.)

  c. The benefits and limitations of this expert system.

2. The Kaiser Foundation

Evaluate the SIMR expert system of the Kaiser Foundation on page 467 in the chapter. Write up your evaluation based on the following points:

  a. The components of an expert system that you recognize. (See Figure 12.14.)

  b. How well it fits the suitability criteria and application categories for expert systems. (See Figures 12.16 and 12.18.)

  c. The benefits and limitations of this expert system.

3. ABC Department Stores: End User Development

The Marketing Department at ABC Department Stores main-

tains a small library of periodicals and reference works for their staff. This library has been run on an honor system. The employee checking out an item is to write his or her name, the date, and the title and issue of the publication checked out on a cardboard form and put it in a box beside the library shelves. Employees are asked to keep a publication no longer than one week. When they return the publication, they so indicate on the cardboard form and put it in a different box.

This system has not always worked well; most employees do remember to fill out the form, but many forget to return the items they have borrowed. Also, whenever someone needs to get information from a publication that is checked out, they have to search through all of the cards to find out which employee has the publication they want.

Suppose you were asked to develop a simple computer-based application to manage checkouts from this library. You can assume that it is not necessary to keep an inventory of the books in the library; only a listing for checked-out books is to be maintained. A sample set of data is listed in Figure

FIGURE 12.29
Sample employee checkout data.

Employee Name	Checkout Date	Periodical Name	Returned
Smith S.	9/19/95	Marketers Guide	No
Wick J.	9/20/95	Lotus Users Guide	No
Adams A.	9/17/95	Media Week, 25-2	Yes
Smith S.	9/21/95	A Guide to BEA Data	No
Smith S.	9/24/95	Media Week, 24-7	No
Bates N.	9/19/95	Ad Era, 39-14	No
Davis R.	9/20/95	Statistics Made Simple	No
Law V.	9/25/95	Ad Era, 40-2	Yes
Davis R.	9/27/95	Ratings Rater, 34-7	No
Morris M.	9/26/95	Media Week, 25-4	No
Adams M.	9/27/95	Sampling Methods	No
Wick J.	9/27/95	Retail Trends 32-17	No
Law V.	9/28/95	Marketer's Guide	No
Bates N.	9/28/95	A DBASE Primer	No

12.29. Use a database management package or an integrated package to do the following:

a. Create a database file to store the appropriate data for this application, and enter the sample data shown in Figure 12.29.

b. Retrieve information needed to satisfy the following end user requests. Get printed listings of your results.

(1) An employee wants to know who has checked out *Statistics Made Simple*.

(2) Sue Smith (Smith, S.) wants to know which books she has checked out.

(3) You want to know how many books are currently checked out.

(4) You want a list of each publication that has been checked out longer than one week and the name of the employee who checked it out. (Assume the current date is 9/28/95).

4. Anderson Products Software Training

Anderson Products Company encourages its workers to seek training in the use of common software packages. Anderson does not provide the training internally but pays the fees for training provided by a local university. The company will pay the full cost for up to 15 days of software training for each employee. For any additional training beyond 15 days, the employee must pay half of the fee.

You have been assigned the responsibility for managing the software training in your department. You decide to create a database file to keep track of training. You want to keep information identifying the employee's name, the length of the training, the type of software that the training addresses, and an indication of whether or not the training has been completed. When an employee informs you that they plan to enroll for a training session, you will add a new record to the database filling in all information and placing an "N" in the Completed field. Once an employee completes the training session, they submit a request for reimbursement. At that time, the value for the Completed field is changed to a "Y." A set of historical data for this database file is shown below.

Anderson Product Employee Software Training History

Employee Name	Software Type	Number of Training Days	Training Completed?
Evans, D.	Database	2	Y
Andrews, A.	Word Processing	3	Y
Barnes, W.	DOS	2	Y
Evans, D.	Spreadsheet	3	Y
Barnes, W.	Word Processing	3	Y
Norris, B.	DOS	2	N
Andrews, A.	Spreadsheet	3	Y
Evans, D.	DOS	2	N
Dale, E.	Database	2	N
Barnes, W.	Spreadsheet	3	Y
Barnes, W.	DOS	2	N
Norris, B.	Spreadsheet	3	Y

a. Create a database file to store the data needed for this application and enter the set of historical data shown.

b. Create a report listing all of your training data sorted by employee name. Your report should have subtotals showing the total days of training for each employee and a grand total for training days.

c. Using the retrieval capabilities of your database software package, perform the following retrievals:

(1) Get a list of the names of employees who have completed spreadsheet training sessions.

(2) Retrieve the total number of days of training that Barnes, W. has completed.

(3) Retrieve the total number of days of DOS training that is pending (Completed = "N").

Review Quiz Answers

1. *12*	9. *27*	17. *14*	25. *10*
2. *15*	10. *19*	18. *8*	26. *22*
3. *23*	11. *6*	19. *7*	27. *3*
4. *5*	12. *6b*	20. *20*	28. *9*
5. *4*	13. *6c*	21. *17*	29. *2*
6. *1*	14. *6d*	22. *13*	30. *21*
7. *1a*	15. *6a*	23. *26*	31. *11*
8. *24*	16. *18*	24. *25*	

Selected References

1. Anthes, Gary. "Smart Models Float." *Computerworld,* October 31, 1994.
2. Allen, Bradley. "Case-Based Reasoning: Business Applications". *Communications of the ACM,* March 1994.
3. Ashline, Peter, and Vincent Lai. "Virtual Reality: An Emerging User-Interface Technology." *Information Systems Management,* Winter 1995.
4. Ballou, Melinda-Carrol. "Expert System Modernizes Kaiser." *Computerworld,* November 14, 1994.
5. Blattberg, Robert; Rashi Glazer; and John Little. *The Marketing Information Revolution.* Boston: The Harvard Business School Press, 1994.
6. Buta, Paul. "Mining for Financial Knowledge with CBR." *AI Expert,* February 1994.
7. Cox, Earl. "Application of Fuzzy System Models." *AI Expert,* October 1992.
8. Cox, Earl. "Relational Database Queries Using Fuzzy Logic." *AI Expert,* January 1995.
9. Cox, Earl. "Solving Problems with Fuzzy Logic." *AI Expert,* March 1992.
10. Cox, Earl. "The Great Myths of Fuzzy Logic." *AI Expert,* January 1992.
11. Eliot, Lance. "Intelligent Agents Are Watching You." *AI Expert,* August 1994.
12. Enrado, Patty. "Giving Credit Where It Is Due." *AI Expert,* September 1991.
13. Forgionne, Guisseppi. "Decision Technology Systems." *Information Systems Management,* Fall, 1991.
14. Jablonowski, Mark. "Fuzzy Risk Analysis: Using AI Systems." *AI Expert,* December 1994.
15. Jiang, James. "Using Scanner Data." *Information Systems Management,* Winter 1995.
16. Keyes, Jessica. "Getting Caught in a Neural Network." *AI Expert,* July 1991.
17. King, James. "Intelligent Agents: Bringing Good Things to Life." *AI Expert,* February 1995.
18. Kurszweil, Raymond. *The Age of Intelligent Machines.* Cambridge, Ma., The MIT Press, 1992.
19. Larijani, L. Casey. The Virtual Reality Primer. New York: McGraw-Hill, 1994.
20. McKenney, James, and Peter Keen. "How Managers' Minds Work." *Harvard Business Review,* May–June 1974.
21. McNeill, F. Martin, and Ellen Thro. *Fuzzy Logic: A Practical Approach.* Boston: AP Professional, 1994.
22. Munakata, Toshinori, Guest Ed. "Artificial Intelligence." Special Section, *Communications of the ACM,* March 1994.
23. Newell, Allen, and Herbert Simon. *Human Problem Solving.* Englewood Cliffs, NJ: Prentice Hall, 1972.
24. Newquist, H. P. "The Dark Side of Hybrid Systems." *AI Expert,* March 1995.
25. Newquist, Harvey. "Virtual Reality's Commercial Reality." *Computerworld,* March 30, 1992.
26. *On the Cutting Edge of Technology.* Carmel, IN: SAMS Publishing, 1993.
27. Osyk, Barbara, and Bindieanavale Viayaraman. "Integrating Expert Systems and Neural Nets." *Information Systems Management,* Spring 1995.
28. Pimentel, Ken, and Kevin Teixeira. *Virtual Reality: Through the New Looking Glass.* 2nd ed. New York: Intel/McGraw-Hill, 1995.
29. Pracht, William. "Neural Networks for Business Applications." *Interface: The Computer Education Quarterly,* Summer 1991.
30. Raisbeck, Gordon. *Information Theory.* Cambridge, MA: MIT Press, 1964.
31. Rhingoid, Howard. "How Real Is Virtual Reality?" *Beyond Computing,* March/April 1992.
32. Sprague, Ralph, and Barbara McNurlin. *Information Systems Management in Practice.* 3rd ed. New York: Prentice Hall, 1993.
33. Stottler, Richard. "CBR for Cost and Sales Prediction." *AI Expert,* August, 1994.
34. Tafti, Mohammed. "Neural Networks: A New Dimension in Expert System Applications." *Data Base,* Winter 1992.
35. Taggart, William, and E. Valenzi. "Assessing Rational and Intuitive Styles: A Human Information Processing Metaphor." *Journal of Management Studies,* March 1990.
36. Trinzic Corporation. *An Introduction to Business Process Automation.* Palo Alto, CA: Author, 1993.
37. Turban, Efraim. *Decision Support and Expert Systems: Managerial Support Systems.* 2nd ed. New York: Macmillan Publishing Co., 1990.
38. Zadeh, Lotfi. "Fuzzy Logic, Neural Networks, and Soft Computing." *Communications of the ACM,* March 1994.

Harvey P. Newquist III: Surfing the Information Superhighway with AI

I'm whipping down the information superhighway. I can't find off-ramp 357, which supposedly is the location for horror movies from the 1960s, as well as related scholarly texts on how these films affected our national psyche. I can't find the off-ramp because it's not very well marked among all the other off-ramps that are jammed together on this highway. I accidentally get off at exit 358, which to my dismay is the celebrity interviewers channel. Suddenly I am besieged by options that let me sit in with Oprah, Phil, Geraldo, Montel, Sally Jesse, and a host of other talking heads.

This is not where I want to be, so I try another route and find that I am listening to Barbara Walters interviewing Connie Chung. I am trapped and can find no way out. I am in hell, and I deserve it for taking my chances on the information superhighway without an intelligent assistant.

A bizarre scenario, to be sure, but navigating the information superhighway will be no day at the beach. Though the above nightmare sounds unnatural from the perspective of TV channel surfing, think of it more along the lines of navigating your way through a bulletin board service.

You begin with a simple mission, follow the appropriate pathways, and expect to work your way from directory to directory until you work down to your intended destination. But for those of you who have ever gotten lost in the bulletin board systems or CompuServe, you know that once you work far enough into the maze, extricating yourself and returning to the appropriate menu or information path can be almost impossible. Oftentimes, you feel tempted to log off and then start the whole thing over again.

Use this metaphor for the information superhighway and you see how you might get lost in a world of utter despair, frustration, and mindlessness. How do you exit this mess and arrive at your final destination? Unfortunately, no one

has an answer for this yet. Everyone is too ga-ga over the "potential" of all this video data and text-based information screaming down some form of national network that they haven't considered how difficult it really will be to make this entire concept useful to the average couch potato.

Advanced technologies such as AI will have to be critical components of superhighway information technology. One of the problems of the information superhighway will be the need for a new interface that adequately addresses the inability of most people to navigate their way across town, let along through an invisible world of digital information. While this is a major concern, a bigger concern will be finding exactly the information you want and discarding what you don't want.

You will, alas, need something extremely powerful to help you out. You shouldn't expect to surf the information superhighway without some sort of computer device to perform context interpretation. And context interpretation is based on understanding, which leads us back to some form of artificial intelligence.

Intelligent agents now are available for traditional document retrieval systems aiding the search for data by context. Filtering systems have been built into E-mail programs that discard the unwanted junk that flows into mailboxes. But the emphasis on video and interactivity on the superhighway opens a new can of worms. Video may well become the primary source of data in a globalized nonstop business environment, but no one has quite prepared for that fact of life. And if big companies aren't ready, you can bet you won't be any better off in the comfort of your living room.

The information superhighway needs on-ramps and passing lanes and rest stops and roadside information kiosks, but nobody has addressed these issues. In practice, we will need a lot of machine intelligence to aid us biologically limited humans.

Will it be neural nets recognizing the patterns of our first tentative highway searches? Will it be case-based reasoning, which compares our interests and needs to cases that are programmed into the highway interface? Will it be simple rule-based structures that make if-then decisions for us? Will it be fuzzy logic that provides us with a traffic guide that incorporates not only our specific interests but also gray areas of interest? Will it be an intelligent TV Guide agent that gives us an hourly update of all the things that we claim to be interested in? I don't have the answers yet, but at least I'm thinking about it.

NOTE: Harvey P. Newquist III is an AI consultant and the author of *The Brainmakers: A History of the AI Industry*, published by SAMS Publishing.

CASE STUDY QUESTIONS

1. What problem does Harvey Newquist see in surfing the information superhighway? Do you agree? Why or why not?

2. Why does he think that AI techniques will be needed to solve this problem? What technologies does he recommend?

3. What AI technologies would you like to see developed to help you navigate the information superhighway? Explain your choices.

Source: Adapted from Harvey P. Newquist III, "In Practice: More Notes from Route 666," *AI Expert*, March 1994, pp. 41–43.

Managing Information Technology

What managerial challenges do information systems pose for the managers of modern organizations? The three chapters of this module are designed to emphasize how managers and end users can plan, implement, and control the use of information technology in a global information society.

Chapter 13, "Managing IT: Enterprise and Global Management," emphasizes the impact of information technology on management and organizations, the importance of information resource management, and the managerial implications of global information technology.

Chapter 14, "Managing IT: Planning and Implementing Change," covers the role of managers in planning for the strategic and operational use of information systems, and managerial issues in the implementation of new information technologies.

Chapter 15, Managing IT: Security and Ethical Challenges," discusses the controls needed for information system performance and security, as well as the ethical implications and societal impacts of information technology.

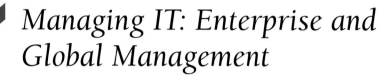

Managing IT: Enterprise and Global Management

CHAPTER OUTLINE

LEARNING OBJECTIVES

The purpose of this chapter is to give you an understanding of the managerial challenges that information technology presents to managerial end users by analyzing (1) the managerial implications of information technology and (2) how IT can support global business operations.

Section I of this chapter discusses the impact of information technology on managers and organizations and the use of an information resource management approach in managing the performance of the information systems function.

Section II discusses how cultural, political, and geoeconomic considerations affect global business and IT strategies, applications, technology platforms, data issues, and systems development.

After reading and studying this chapter, you should be able to:

1. Identify the major ways information technology has affected managers.

2. Explain how problems of information system performance can be solved by management involvement in IS planning and control.

3. Explain how information technology is affecting the structure and activities of organizations.

4. Identify the five major dimensions of the information resource management concept and explain their impact on the management of the information systems function.

5. Identify several cultural, political, and geoeconomic challenges that confront managers in the management of global information technology.

6. Explain the effect on global IT strategy of the trend toward a transnational business strategy by international business organizations.

7. Identify several considerations that affect the choice of IT applications, IT platforms, data definitions, and systems development methods made by a global business.

Introduction

The strategic and operational importance of information technology in business is no longer questioned.

> What is less clear is how business executives can ensure that their firms benefit from new opportunities afforded by IT and avoid its well-known, oft-repeated pitfalls: botched development projects; escalating costs with no apparent economic benefit; organizational disruption; and technical glitches. Competence and confidence in handling IT will clearly be key to effective management in the coming decade. Senior executives can no longer delegate IT policy and strategic decision making to technical professionals [16].

Thus, there is a real need for business end users to understand how to manage this vital organizational function. In this section, we will explore how IT has affected managers and organizations, and stress the concept of *information resource management* as a key framework for managing information technology by both end user managers and IS managers. So whether you plan to be an entrepreneur and run your own business, a manager in a corporation, or a managerial-level professional, managing information system resources and technologies will be one of your major responsibilities. See Figure 13.1.

Managers and Information Technology

When computers were first introduced into business, predictions were made that there would be significant changes in management and organizations. The information processing power and programmed decision-making capability of computer-based information systems were supposedly going to cause drastic reductions in employees, including middle management and supervisory personnel. Centralized computer systems would process all of the data for an organization, control all of its operations, and make most of its decisions [19].

This did not prove to be the case. Changes in organizational structure and

FIGURE 13.1
Information technology is having a major impact on the management, structure, and work activities of organizations.

Courtesy of IBM Corporation.

FIGURE 13.2

Information technology must be managed to meet the challenges of the business and technology environment of the 1990s.

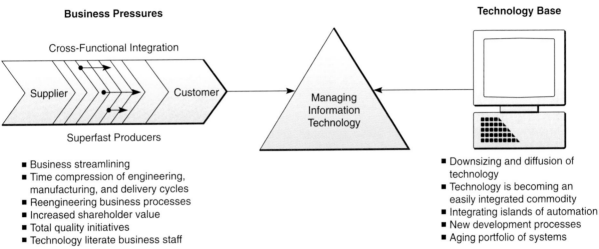

Source: Adapted and reprinted from Richard Murray and Richard Hardin, "The IT Organization of the Future," *Information Systems Management* (New York: Auerbach Publications), Fall 1991. © 1991 Warren, Gorham & Lamont. Used with permission.

types of personnel did occur, but they were not as dramatic as predicted. Naturally, highly automated systems do not require as many people as manual methods. Therefore, there have been significant reductions in the number of people required to perform manual tasks in many organizations. For example, computerized accounting systems have drastically reduced the need for clerical accounting personnel, and factory automation has greatly reduced the demand for many types of factory workers. However, these reductions were countered by dramatic increases in sales and service personnel, knowledge workers, and managers as businesses increased the depth and scope of their operations. It was also countered to some extent by the need for more technicians and professionals to develop and run the computer-based information systems of organizations [23].

Now, however, a variety of forces seem to be causing a significant change in the structure and distribution of managers in organizations in which information technology plays a major role. For example, Peter Drucker, the visionary management scholar and author, predicts that by the end of the 1990s, the typical large business will have fewer than half the levels of management and no more than one-third of the managers it had in the 1980s. He also predicts that information technology will allow the structure of information-based organizations to be more like those of hospitals, universities, and symphony orchestras. They will be *knowledge-based,* "composed largely of specialists who direct and discipline their own performance through organized feedback from colleagues, customers, and headquarters" [13].

As Figure 13.2 illustrates, the competitive pressures of the business and technology environment of the 1990s are forcing major firms to rethink their use and management of information technology. Many business executives now see information technology as an *enabling technology* for managing the *cooperative advantage* that business units must have to successfully confront the competitive measures they face. For example, telecommunications networks and more cost-effective hardware and software are enabling individuals, business units, and organizations to be "wired

FIGURE 13.3
Information technologies are
enablers of innovation in managerial processes.

- Executive information systems that provide realtime information.
- Electronic linkages to external partners in strategic processes.
- Computer-based simulations that support learning-oriented planning.
- Electronic conferencing and group decision support systems.
- Expert systems for planning and capital allocation.
- Information technology infrastructure for communications and group work.

together" in close business relationships that can provide the communication and coordination needed in today's competitive global marketplace [25].

Thus, **information technology,** that is, the technologies of modern computer-based information systems, is once again being portrayed as a major force for organizational and managerial change. Thanks to telecommunications networks and personal computers, computing power and information resources are now more readily available to more managers than ever before. In fact, these and other information technologies are already promoting innovative changes in managerial decision making, organizational structures, and managerial work activities in companies around the world [12]. See Figure 13.3.

For example, the decision support capability provided by information systems technology is changing the focus of managerial decision making. Managers freed from "number crunching" chores must now face tougher strategic policy questions in order to develop realistic alternatives for today's dynamic competitive environment. The use of telecommunications networks, electronic mail, and electronic meeting systems to coordinate work activity is another example of the **impact of** information technology on management. Middle managers no longer need to serve as conduits for the transmission of operations feedback or control directives between operational managers and top management. Thus, drastic reductions in the layers and numbers of middle management, and the dramatic growth of work groups consisting of task-focused teams of specialists are forecast [13, 23].

Finally, information technology presents managers with a major managerial challenge. Managing the information system resources of a business is no longer the sole province of information systems specialists. Instead, **information resource management** (IRM) has become a major responsibility of all managers. That is, data and information, computer hardware and software, telecommunications networks, and IS personnel should be viewed as valuable resources that must be managed by all levels of management to ensure the effective use of information technology for the operational and strategic benefit of a business.

Information Systems Performance

As Figure 13.4 illustrates, the information systems function has performance problems in many organizations. The promised benefits of information technology have not occurred in many documented cases. Studies by management consulting firms, computer user groups, and university researchers have shown that many businesses have not been successful in managing their computer resources and information services departments. Figure 13.4 dramatizes the results of research on the types of problems that arise when new information technologies, especially client/server networks, are implemented in many businesses [20]. Thus, it is evident that, in many organizations, information technology is not being used effectively, efficiently, or economically [12, 23]. For example:

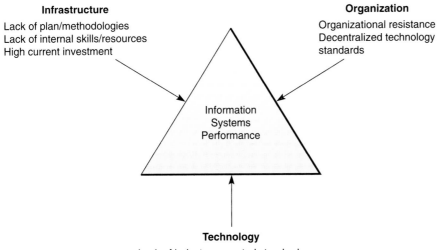

Infrastructure
Lack of plan/methodologies
Lack of internal skills/resources
High current investment

Organization
Organizational resistance
Decentralized technology
standards

Information
Systems
Performance

Technology
Lack of industry-accepted standards
Lack of client/server applications
Lack of maturity in client/server products

FIGURE 13.4
Performance problems in information systems. New information technologies can cause infrastructure, organization, and technology problems in an organization.

Source: Adapted and reprinted from John Levis and Peter Von Schilling, "Lessons from Three Implementations: Knocking Down Barriers to Client/Server," *Information Systems Management* (New York: Auerbach Publications), Summer 1994. © 1994 Warren, Gorham & Lamont. Used with permission.

- Information technology is not being used *effectively* by companies that use IT primarily to computerize traditional business processes instead of using it for decision support and innovative processes and products to gain competitive advantages.

- Information technology is not being used *efficiently* by information services groups that provide poor response times, frequent downtimes, incompatible systems, unintegrated data, and applications development backlogs.

- Information technology is not being used *economically* in many cases. Information technology costs have risen faster than other costs in many businesses, even though the cost of processing each unit of data is decreasing due to dramatic price reductions and improvements in hardware and software technology.

What is the solution to problems of poor performance in the information systems function? There are no quick and easy answers. However, the experiences of successful organizations reveal that the basic ingredient of high-quality information systems performance is extensive and meaningful *involvement* of managers and end users in the *governance* of the IS function [4, 25]. This should be the key ingredient in shaping the response of management to the challenge of improving the business value of information technology.

Proper involvement of managers in the management of IT requires the development of governance structures that encourage the active participation of managerial end users in planning and controlling the business uses of IT. Thus, many organizations have developed policies and procedures which require managers to be involved in IT decisions that affect their business units. This helps managers avoid IS performance problems in their business units' in the key areas outlined in Figure 13.4. Without this high degree of involvement, managers cannot hope to improve the strategic business value of information technology. Figure 13.5 illustrates several major levels of **management involvement** and governance of information technology.

Management Involvement and Governance

FIGURE 13.5
Levels of management involvement in IS governance. Successful information systems performance requires the involvement of managers in IS governance.

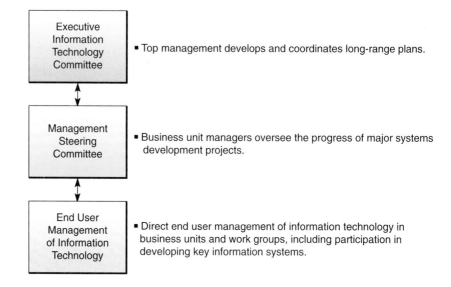

- Top management develops and coordinates long-range plans.

- Business unit managers oversee the progress of major systems development projects.

- Direct end user management of information technology in business units and work groups, including participation in developing key information systems.

- Many organizations use an *executive information technology committee* of top management to do strategic information system planning and to coordinate the development of major information systems projects. This committee includes senior management of the major divisions of the firm, as well as the **chief information officer** (CIO) of the organization, who is the senior executive responsible for governance of the IS function.

- A *steering committee* of business unit managers, operating managers, and management personnel from the information services department may be created to oversee the progress of critical systems development projects. The committee meets on a regular basis to review progress made, to settle disputes, and to change priorities, if necessary.

- Development of decision support and work group systems requires managerial involvement in the prototyping process for such projects. End user managers must also accept their responsibility for managing the resources and quality of information services provided to their business units and work groups.

Let's now look at two actual examples of management involvement and governance of information technology in business [2].

Hughes Space and Communications Co.

Hughes has established rules, institutions and a process to manage information, according to CIO Gary R. Osborn. To manage a specific item of information, the business unit divides responsibility between "process owners," such as a manufacturing vice president, and the IS department. Process owners are the sources of data, and they define its quality, accuracy, and accessibility. IS sets rules distinguishing different kinds of data and dictating how it is formatted on the system. A policy board meets every two to four weeks to decide changes in information policy. Broader information issues are discussed, along with corporate issues, in a quarterly meeting of senior Hughes executives. Osborn sits on both boards.

Chemical Banking Corporation

After Chemical Bank and Manufacturers Hanover Trust Co. merged, a business technology management council was established to set technology direction for the com-

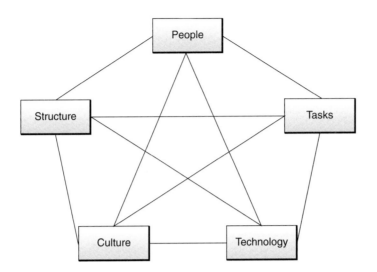

FIGURE 13.6
Organizations as sociotechnical
systems. Information systems
must accommodate the people,
tasks, technology, culture, and
structure components and relationships of an organization.

bined companies. The council is chaired by Denis J. O'Leary, Chemical's executive vice president and CIO. It includes the top IS executives from both central IS and Chemical's business units, senior non-IS executives from Chemical business units and the controller's office. The council sets policies, standards and guidelines that direct technology policies for both line managers and IS managers. The council then spun off subcommittees such as the two-year-old information management committee. The committee is cochaired by O'Leary, the CFO, and the head of credit policy. It establishes rules and principles for managing information across the company.

Organizations and Information Technology

One way to understand the organizational impact of information technology is to view an **organization as a sociotechnical system.** In this context, people, tasks, technology, culture, and structure are the basic components of an organization. Figure 13.6 illustrates this conceptual framework, which was first developed by Harold Leavitt [18]. This concept emphasizes that to improve an organization's performance, managers must (1) change one or more of these components and (2) take into account the relationships among these interdependent components. This is especially important for the proper use of information technology. In the past, information systems technology has been used to automate organizational tasks without sufficient consideration given to its strategic impact on the organization. Thus, a major managerial challenge of information technology is to develop information systems that promote strategic improvements in how an organization supports its people, tasks, technology, culture, and structure.

People

Managers are individuals with a variety of preferences for information and diverse capabilities for effectively using information provided to them. As we pointed out in Chapter 10, information systems must produce information products tailored to meet managers' individual needs, as management information, decision support, and executive information systems can do.

Tasks

The tasks of many organizations have become quite complex and inefficient over time. In many cases, information technology has been used "to do the same old thing, only faster." However, as we discussed in Chapter 11, IT can play a major role in fighting organizational complexity by supporting the **reengineering of business**

processes. For example, IT developments such as electronic data interchange dramatically reduce the need for several departments to be involved in preparing, authorizing, checking, and sending paper business documents. This can eliminate many manual tasks and required procedures, and significantly improve communication and strategic cooperation between organizations.

Technology

The technology of computer-based information systems continues to grow more sophisticated and complex. However, this technology should not dictate the information needs of end users in the performance of their organizational tasks. It should accommodate the management culture and structure of each organization. For example, executive information systems have shown they can overcome many of the objections of top executives to the lack of individual and task flexibility of previous types of management information systems.

Culture

Organizations and their subunits have a culture which is shared by managers and other employees. That is, they have a unique set of organizational values and styles. For example, managers at some organizations share an informal, collegial, entrepreneurial spirit that stresses initiative, collaboration, and risk taking. Managers at other organizations may stress a more formal "do it by the book," "go through the chain of command," or "don't risk the stockholders' money" approach. Naturally, the designs of information systems and information products must accommodate such differences. For example, managers in a corporate culture that encourages entrepreneurial risk taking and collaboration will probably favor executive information systems that give them quick access to forecasts about competitors and customers, and E-mail and groupware systems that make it easy to communicate with colleagues anywhere.

Structure

Organizations structure their management, employees, and job tasks into a variety of organizational subunits. However, we have just mentioned how Drucker and others are emphasizing that information technology must support a process of *organizational redesign*. So the IS function must no longer assume a hierarchical, centralized, organizational structure which it supports by centralizing processing power, databases, and systems development at the corporate headquarters level. This type of structure emphasizes gathering data into centralized databases and producing reports to meet the information needs of functional executives.

Instead, IT must be able to support a more decentralized, collaborative type of organizational structure, which needs more interconnected client/server networks, distributed databases, "downsized" computers, and systems development resources distributed to business unit and work group levels. Thus, information technology must emphasize quick and easy communication and collaboration among individuals, business units and other organization work groups, using electronics instead of paper. For example, information technologies such as E-mail, groupware, and desktop videoconferencing enable the development of interorganizational information systems and network organizational structures that are vital to the formation of the virtual companies discussed in Chapter 11.

Information Resource Management

Information resource management (IRM) has become a popular way to emphasize a major change in the management and mission of the information systems function in many organizations. IRM can be viewed as having five major dimensions. Figure 13.7 illustrates this conceptual framework [27].

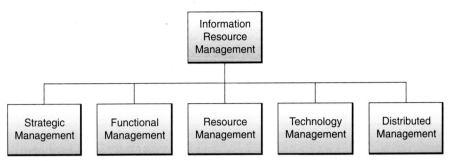

Source: Adapted from James A. O'Brien and James N. Morgan, "A Multidimensional Model of Information Resource Management," *Information Resources Management Journal,* Spring 1991, p. 4. Copyright 1991. *Information Resources Management Journal,* Idea Group Publishing, Harrisburg, PA. Reprint by permission.

FIGURE 13.7
The information resource management (IRM) concept. Note that there are five major dimensions to the job of managing information systems resources.

- **Strategic management.** Information technology must be managed to contribute to a firm's strategic objectives and competitive advantages, not just for operational efficiency or decision support.
- **Functional management.** Information technology and information systems can be managed by functional organizational structures and managerial techniques commonly used throughout other business units.
- **Resource management.** Data and information, hardware and software, telecommunications networks, and IS personnel are vital organizational resources that must be managed like other business assets.
- **Technology management.** All technologies that process, store, and communicate data and information throughout the enterprise should be managed as integrated systems of organizational resources.
- **Distributed management.** Managing the use of information technology and information system resources in business units or work groups is a key responsibility of their managers, no matter what their function or level in the organization.

Strategic Management

The IRM concept emphasizes a strategic management view that we emphasized in Chapter 11 and have stressed throughout this text. That is, the IS function must manage information technology so that it makes major contributions to the profitability and strategic objectives of the firm. Thus, the information systems' function must change from an *information services utility* focused only on serving a firm's transaction processing or decision support needs. Instead, it must become a producer or packager of information products or an *enabler* of organizational structures and business processes that can give a firm a comparative advantage over its competitors. As we saw in Chapter 11, companies can develop strategic information systems to gain a competitive edge. Thus, information resource management focuses on developing and managing information systems that significantly improve operational efficiency, promote innovative products and services, and build strategic business alliances and information resources that can enhance the competitiveness of an organization.

The Chief Information Officer

Many companies have created a senior management position, the **chief information officer** (CIO), to oversee all use of information technology in their organizations. Thus, all traditional computer services, telecommunications services, office

FIGURE 13.8
How CIOs spend their time.

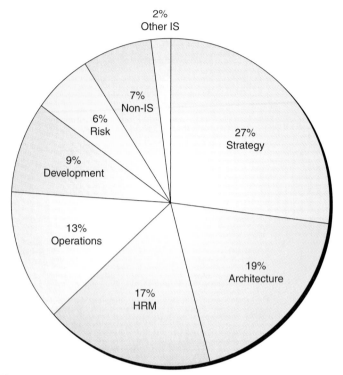

Source: Adapted from Lynda Applegate and Joyce Elam, "New Information Systems Leaders: A Changing Role in a Changing World," *MIS Quarterly*, Dec. 1992, p. 481. Reprinted with permission from the *MIS Quarterly*.

automation systems, and other IS technology support services are the responsibility of this executive. Also, the CIO does not direct day-to-day information service activities. Instead, CIOs concentrate on long-term planning and strategy. They also work with other top executives to develop strategic information systems that help make the firm more competitive in the marketplace. Several firms have filled the CIO position with executives from outside the IS field to emphasize the strategic business role of information technology. Figure 13.8 illustrates how new CIOs (most of whom had previous management experience outside of the IS function) spend their time [3].

Functional Management

The IRM concept stresses that managerial functions and techniques common to most businesses and organizational structures must be used to manage information technology. IS managers must use managerial techniques (such as planning models, financial budgets, project management, and functional organization) just as they do with other major resources and activities of the business.

In many large organizations, the information systems function is organized into a departmental or divisional unit. We will use the name *information services department* for this group, though such names as information systems, computer services, data processing, EDP, MIS, and IRM department are also used. Information services departments perform several basic functions and activities. These can be grouped into three basic functional categories: (1) systems development, (2) operations, and (3) technical services. Figure 13.9 illustrates this grouping of information services functions and activities in a functional IS organizational structure.

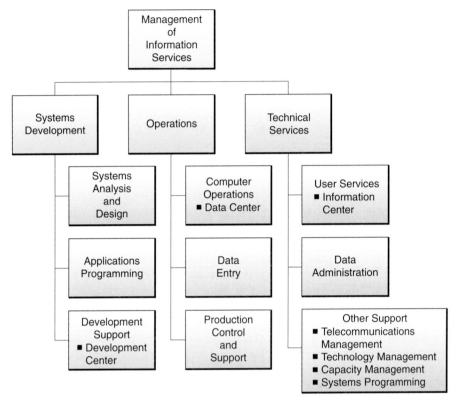

FIGURE 13.9
A functional organizational structure for an information services department. Note the activities that take place under each of the major functions of information services.

Centralization versus Decentralization

Experience has shown that modern computer-based information systems can support either the **centralization or decentralization** of information systems, operations, and decision making within computer-using organizations. For example, centralized computer facilities connected to all parts of an organization by telecommunications networks allow top management to centralize decision making formerly done by lower levels of management. It can also promote centralization of operations, which reduces the number of branch offices, manufacturing plants, warehouses, and other work sites needed by the firm.

On the other hand, there is an increasing trend toward downsized and distributed networks (of micro and server computers at multiple work sites) that allow top management to delegate more decision making to middle managers. Management can also decentralize operations by increasing the number of branch offices (or other company units) while still having access to the information and communications capabilities they need to control the overall direction of the organization.

Therefore, computer-based information systems can encourage either the centralization or decentralization of information systems, business operations, and management. The philosophy of top management, the culture of the organization, the need to reengineer its operations, and its use of aggressive or conservative competitive strategies all play major roles with information technology in shaping the firm's organizational structure and information systems architecture [24, 3].

Changing Trends

Thus, companies continue to use a variety of organizational arrangements for the delivery of information services. In the early years of computing, when computers could barely handle a single department's workload, decentralization was the only option. Subsequently, the development of large mainframe computers and telecommunications networks and terminals caused a centralization of computer hardware and software, databases, and information specialists at the corporate level of organizations. Next, the development of minicomputers and microcomputers accelerated a **downsizing** trend, which prompted a move back toward decentralization by many business firms. Distributed processing networks of micro- and minicomputers at the corporate, department, work group, and end user levels came into being. This promoted a shift of databases and information specialists to some departments, and the creation of information centers to support end user computing.

Lately, the trend has been to establish tighter control over the information resources of an organization, while still serving the strategic needs of its business units. This has resulted in a centralizing trend at some organizations and the development of hybrid structures with both centralized and decentralized components at others. Some companies have even spun off their information systems function into *IS subsidiaries* that offer information processing services to external organizations as well as to their parent company.

Other corporations have **outsourced**, that is, turned over all or part of their information systems operation to outside contractors known as *systems integrators* or facilities management companies. Such changes in the organizational alignment of the information systems function are expected to continue into the future. Organizations will continue to experiment with ways to both control and encourage the use of information system resources to promote end user productivity and the achievement of their strategic objectives. Figure 13.10 is a *business-focused* organizational structure for an IS department. Figure 13.11 illustrates how IS personnel can be organized into *delivery teams* and assigned to business units [31].

Let's take a quick look at the recent experiences of two major corporations to dramatize how radically businesses are restructuring their IS function.

Du Pont Corporation

Du Pont slashed annual spending on its total IS function from $1.2 billion in 1989 to $770 million in 1994, a 40 percent cut. Du Pont, which generated $38 billion in sales in fiscal 1994, also cut the number of people working in IS services by over 30 percent in the same period, from 7,000 to 4,800 employees. Nearly 200 data centers (computer centers) spread throughout the global company were merged into 40, according to Cinda Hallman, vice president of IS at Du Pont. She says that IS can now move away from cost cutting and work on integrating their customers and suppliers [21].

Del Monte Foods

Del Monte outsourced all of its data centers to Electronic Data Systems Corporation several years ago, so it no longer runs its own IS computer operations. Del Monte has been aggressively implementing a "Top 20" plan to develop strategic applications of information technology for its top 20 customers and suppliers. Del Monte is also pursuing strategic alliances outside of its company walls, says David A. McPherson, CIO and vice president. He says that the cost savings from business reengineering projects at Del Monte are used to finance such new IS programs [21].

Managing Systems Development

Systems development management means managing activities such as systems analysis and design, prototyping, applications programming, project management, quality assurance, and system maintenance for all major systems development pro-

FIGURE 13.10
A business-focused organizational structure assigns delivery teams of IS specialists to business units and functions.

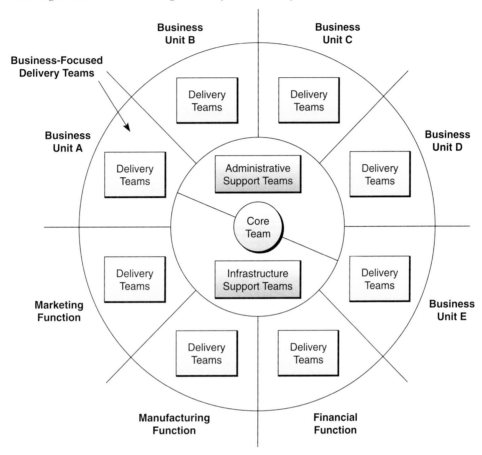

jects. Planning, organizing, and controlling the systems development function of an information services department is a major managerial responsibility. It requires managing the activities of systems analysts, programmers, and end users working on a variety of information systems development projects. In addition, many systems development groups have established **development centers,** staffed with consultants to the professional programmers and systems analysts in their organizations. Their role is to evaluate new applications development tools and help information systems specialists use them to improve their application development efforts.

IS operations management is concerned with the use of hardware, software, and personnel resources in the corporate or business unit **data centers** (computer centers) of an organization. Operational activities that must be managed include data entry, equipment operations, production control, and production support.

Most operations management activities are being automated by the use of software packages for computer system performance management. These **system performance monitors** monitor the processing of computer jobs, help develop a planned schedule of computer operations that can optimize computer system performance, and produce detailed statistics that are invaluable for effective planning and control of computing capacity. Such information is used to evaluate computer system utilization, costs, and performance. This evaluation provides information for capacity planning, production planning and control, and hardware/software

Managing IS Operations

FIGURE 13.11
How an IS delivery team could be organized.

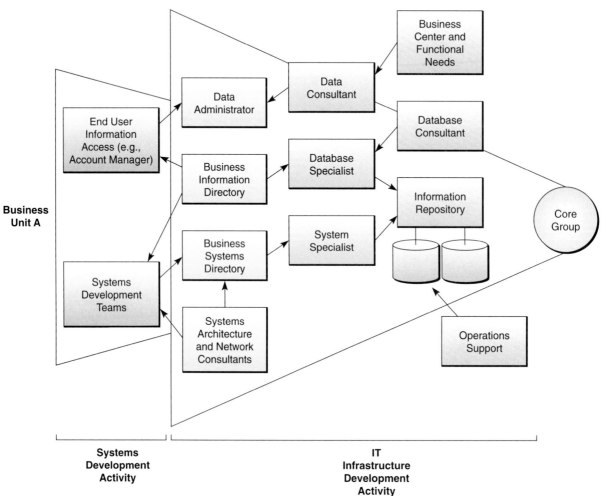

acquisition planning. It is also used in *quality assurance* programs, which stress quality control of services to end users. See Figure 13.12.

System performance monitors also supply information needed by **chargeback systems,** which allocate costs to users based on the information services rendered. All costs incurred are recorded, reported, allocated, and charged back to specific end user departments, depending on their use of system resources. Under this arrangement, the information services department becomes a "service center" whose costs are charged directly to computer users, rather than being lumped with other administrative service costs and treated as an overhead cost.

Many performance monitors also feature *process control* capabilities. Such packages not only monitor but automatically control computer operations at large data centers. Some use built-in expert system modules based on knowledge gleaned from experts in the operations of specific computer systems and operating systems. These performance monitors provide more efficient computer operations than human-operated systems. They also are leading toward the goal of "lights out" data centers, where computer systems can be operated unattended, especially after normal business hours.

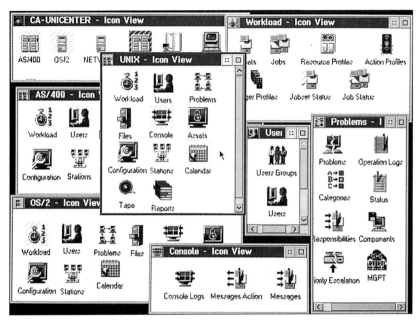

FIGURE 13.12
A computer system performance monitor in action. The CA-UNI-CENTER package can monitor and manage a variety of computer systems and operating systems.

Courtesy of Computer Associates, Inc.

Resource Management

From an information resource management point of view, data and information, hardware and software, telecommunications networks, and IS personnel are valuable resources that should be managed for the benefit of the entire organization. If plant and equipment, money, and people are considered vital organizational resources, so should its data, information, and other information system resources. This is especially true if the organization is committed to building a strategic information resource base to be used for strategic IT applications, and if it wants to develop innovative products and services that incorporate information systems technology. We discussed managing data as an organizationwide resource through programs of data administration and data resource management in Chapter 7. In this chapter, let's now look at several human resource management issues.

Human Resource Management of IT

The success or failure of an information services organization rests primarily on the quality of its people. Many computer-using firms consider recruiting, training, and retaining qualified IS personnel as one of their greatest challenges. Millions of persons are employed in the information services organizations of computer users. National employment surveys continually forecast shortages of qualified information services personnel. Employment opportunities in the computer field are excellent, as businesses continue to expand their use of computers. For these reasons, it is important to analyze the types of jobs and the managerial problems associated with information services personnel.

Figure 13.13 gives valuable insight into the variety of job types and salaries commanded by many information services personnel. Actual salaries range higher and lower than the averages shown, depending on such factors as the size and geographic location of the information services organization.

Managing information services functions involves the management of managerial, technical, and clerical personnel. One of the most important jobs of information service managers is to recruit qualified personnel and to develop, organize,

FIGURE 13.13
Examples of important job categories and annual salaries in information services.

Top IS Management			
CIO/VP IS/ MIS/DP: $144,800	Director, systems development: $88,800	Director, networks: $85,600	Director, IS operations: $90,900
Networks			
Telecommunications manager: $65,550	Telecommunications specialist: $50,700	Network administrator: $51,200	LAN manager: $51,900
Systems Development			
Project manager, systems and programming: $65,900	Senior systems analyst: $56,500	Database manager: $63,300	Database analyst: $52,600
PC End User Support			
Microcomputer manager/End user computing manager: $66,800	Technical support manager/Help desk manager: $53,200	Business services analyst: $47,900	PC technical support specialist: $36,800

Source: Adapted from "Computerworld's Eighth Annual Salary Survey" by Stephen Earls, Computerworld, Sept. 5, 1994, p. 84. Copyright 1994 by Computerworld, Inc., Framingham, MA 01701—Reprinted from *Computerworld*.

and direct the capabilities of existing personnel. Employees must be continually trained to keep up with the latest developments in a fast-moving and highly technical field. Employee job performance must be continually evaluated and outstanding performances rewarded with salary increases or promotions. Salary and wage levels must be set, and career paths must be designed so individuals can move to new jobs through promotion and transfer as they gain in seniority and expertise.

For example, many firms provide information services personnel with individual career paths, opportunities for merit salary increase, project leadership opportunities, and attendance at professional meetings and educational seminars. These opportunities help provide the flexible job environment needed to remain competent personnel. Challenging technological and intellectual assignments and a congenial atmosphere of fellow professionals are other major factors frequently cited in helping to retain information services personnel [1]. Figure 13.14 illustrates some of the career paths available to information systems professionals.

Technology Management

An information resource management philosophy emphasizes that all technologies that process, store, and deliver data and information must be managed as integrated systems of organizational resources. Such technologies include telecommunications and office automation systems, as well as traditional computer-based information processing. These "islands of technology" are bridged by IRM and become a primary responsibility of the CIO, since he or she is in charge of all information technology services. Thus, the information systems function can become "a business within a business," whose chief executive is charged with strategic planning, research and development, and coordination of all information technologies for the strategic benefit of the organization [8, 9].

Telecommunications Management

The rapid growth of telecommunications networks in computer-using firms has made **telecommunications management** a major technology management function. This function manages the wide area networks for applications such as online

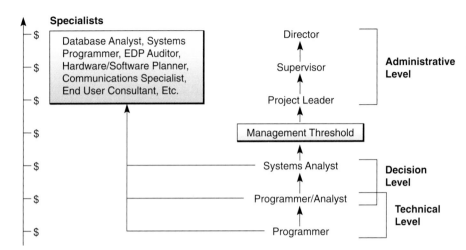

FIGURE 13.14
Career paths for systems development personnel can lead into management, or branch into a variety of specialist positions.

transaction processing, electronic data interchange, and electronic mail, and the local area networks for work group and end user computing. These networks require a major commitment of hardware and software resources, as outlined in Chapter 6. They also require the creation of managerial and staff positions to manage their use. Thus, telecommunications management is responsible for overseeing all telecommunications services provided to end users and the information services function.

Telecommunications managers are usually responsible for evaluating and recommending the acquisition of communications media, communications carriers, and communications hardware and software for end user, departmental, and corporate telecommunications networks. They work with end user managers to improve the design, operational quality, and security of an organization's telecommunications networks and services. Network managers, typically, manage the operation of specific wide area and local area telecommunications networks. They monitor and evaluate telecommunications processors (such as network and file servers), network control software (such as network operating systems), and other common network hardware and software resources to ensure a proper level of service to the users of a network.

Telecommunications networks need a lot of managing to operate efficiently and effectively. That's why the quality of an organization's telecommunications managers and staff is a vital concern. Acquiring, training, and retaining good *network managers* or *administrators* should be a top priority. For example, even a small LAN needs a network manager who is responsible for its management and maintenance. New workstations and software must be installed, data and program files must be maintained, operations problems must be diagnosed and solved, and network security must be maintained. So manageability is a *key* managerial concern in any decision involving an organization's telecommunications activities.

The management of rapidly changing technology is important to any organization. Changes in information technology have come swiftly and dramatically and are expected to continue into the future. Developments in information systems technology have had, and will continue to have, a major impact on the operations, costs, management work environment, and competitive position of many organizations. Therefore, many firms have established separate groups to identify, introduce, and

Advanced Technology Management

monitor the assimilation of new information systems technologies into their organizations, especially those with a high payoff potential [8]. These organizational units are called *technology management, emerging technologies,* or *advanced technology* groups.

Such advanced technology groups (ATGs), typically, report to the chief information systems officer and are staffed with former senior systems analysts and other specialists in information systems technology. Their job is to monitor emerging technological developments and identify innovative developments that have high potential payoffs to the firm. Then they work with end user managers and information services management to introduce new technologies into the firm. They also audit a firm's current applications of technology so they can recommend improvements. We will discuss planning and implementation issues in the introduction of new information technologies in Chapter 14.

Distributed Management

Responsibility for managing information technology is increasingly being distributed to the managers of an organization at all levels and in all functions. Information resource management is not just the responsibility of an organization's chief information officer. If you're a manager, IRM is one of your responsibilities, whether you are a manager of a company, a department, a work group, or a functional area. This is especially true as telecommunications networks and developments such as cooperative processing, end user computing, work group computing, and interorganizational information systems drive the responsibility for managing information systems out to all of an organization's functional and work group managers [24, 25].

Managing End User Computing

As we saw in Chapter 8, the number of people in organizations who use or want to use computers to help them do their jobs has outstripped the capacity of many information services departments. As a result, a revolutionary change to end user computing has developed. End users now use personal computer workstations, software packages, and local area networks to develop and apply computer-based information systems to their own business activities. Organizations have responded by creating an **end user services,** or *client services,* function to support and manage this explosion in end user computing.

End user computing provides both opportunities and problems for end user management. Establishing an **information center** in an organization or end user department is one solution. However, other organizations have dismantled their information centers and distributed end user support specialists to departments and other work groups. For example, some firms create user liaison positions, or "help desks," with end user "hot lines." IS specialists with titles such as *user consultant, account executive,* or *business analyst* may be assigned to end user work groups. These specialists perform a vital role by troubleshooting problems, gathering and communicating information, coordinating educational efforts, and helping end users with application development. Their activities improve communication and coordination between end user work groups and the corporate information services department and avoid the runaround that can frustrate end users.

In addition to these measures, most organizations must still establish and enforce policies concerning the acquisition of hardware and software by end users.

FIGURE 13.15
Three strategies for managing
end user computing.

User Autonomy
Equipment (primarily microcomputers) is purchased without corporate standards. End users are fully responsible for design and support of systems. End users totally control the budget.

User Partnership
Equipment and software are purchased by end users using a corporate standard. Applications are developed by end users. Systems training and support are given by the IS function. Budget responsibility is shared.

Central Control
Equipment and software are purchased by the IS function. Applications are developed by both end users and IS staff. The IS staff provides support and training. The budget is controlled by the IS function.

Source: Adapted from Thomas Clark, "Corporate Systems Management: An Overview and Research Perspective," *Communications of the ACM*, February 1992, p. 65. Copyright 1992. Association for Computing Machinery, Inc. By permission.

This ensures their compatibility with existing hardware and software systems. Even more important is the development of applications with proper controls to promote correct performance and safeguard the integrity of corporate and departmental databases. We will discuss such IS controls in Chapter 15. Figure 13.15 summarizes three basic strategies organizations use to manage end user computing [9].

Levi Strauss & Co.: Managing IT in a Global Company

The blue jeans that Levi Strauss & Co. makes are ubiquitous; some day its network will be too. One of the company's corporate goals is to have a constant brand image around the world. As a result of that mission, "all of our key strategic issues are global," says Gevenie Delsol, director of global network services for the company.

Levi Strauss, which last year enjoyed sales of more than $6 billion, needs a global network to support a worldwide virtual enterprise consisting of subcontractors, distributors, and retailers. To achieve that, the company had to shift from a mainframe-centered IS structure to one in which the network was the core processing resource. "That puts more reliance on management tools, to not just manage change and solve problems but to predict what will happen," Delsol says.

Levi Strauss has already deployed 182 servers worldwide with another 180 servers in rollout. Currently the servers provide only bare-bones file and print services, but the company plans to add global E-mail, video conferencing, and other applications, which it will either move from the mainframe or build from scratch.

Overall, the project is part of a three-year $850 million revamping of its technology strategy. This year's budget is $200 million. "We're investing heavily in upgrading our worldwide operations to deliver superior customer service," notes George James, senior vice president and chief financial officer. The massive conversion of the company's IS infrastructure will not be completed until 1996.

Eventually, the company's 10,000 employee PC workstations plus its major trading partners will be linked to a computing web managed by data centers in Dallas, Brussels and Singapore. This IS strategy was formulated by CIO Bob Eaton and the Global Network Forum, a group of 35 managers from the decentralized business units.

To minimize the headaches that are sure to accompany a strategy this ambitious, the forum decided to adopt systems and networking standards such as Microsoft Windows and Microsoft Office, Novell NetWare running Ethernet for the LANs, and the TCP/IP protocol for the WAN.

In addition, the Global Network Forum selected Hewlett-Packard's OpenView as the global systems and network management platform. "OpenView is better suited than other products for a global environment," explains Delsol. Another reason for the selection of OpenView, Delsol notes, is that "we see HP's commitment to being open and adhering to standards." OpenView will also help the company integrate its different computing platforms around the world, so that the network "appears seamless to the user," she says.

Last year, Levi Strauss united their computing systems management and telecommunications network management systems. Delsol gives three reasons for that decision: the convergence of the tools themselves, economies of scale, and the need for crosstraining within the company.

Automated systems and network management tools are crucial if Levi Strauss is to realize its global IS vision. Backup-and-restore activities and other heretofore manual systems tasks are scheduled to be automated. "We believe in automating any process that we can, from trouble tickets and alerts to help desks," says Delsol.

"We can't build a support staff large enough to do it manually," she adds. "Levi Strauss's business is making and selling jeans, not technology. We need to make the technology work for us."

CASE STUDY QUESTIONS

1. What global computing and network strategies are being implemented by Levi Strauss? What do you think of them? Explain.

2. How are Levi's managers involved in global IT management? Is this a good approach? Explain.

3. Should other global companies use Levi's approach? Give examples to illustrate you answer.

Source: Adapted from Larry Marion, "The Globalist: Systems and Network Management in Networked Environments," Special Advertising Supplement, *Computerworld*, June 12, 1995, pp. S18–S19. Copyright 1995 by Computerworld, Inc., Framingham, MA 01701—Reprinted from *Computerworld*.

SECTION II
Global Information Technology Management

It's no secret that international dimensions are becoming more and more important in managing a business in the global economies and markets of the 1990s. Whether you become a manager in a large corporation or the owner of a small business, you will be affected by international business developments, and deal in some way with people, products, or services whose origin is not from your home country. For example:

> The global corporation may have a product that was designed in a European country, with components manufactured in Taiwan and Korea. It may be assembled in Canada and sold as a standard model in Brazil, and in the United States as a model fully loaded with options. Transfer pricing of the components and assembled product may be determined with an eye to minimizing tax liability. Freight and insurance may be contracted for relet through a Swiss subsidiary, which earns a profit subject only to cantonal taxes. The principal financing may be provided from the Eurodollar market based in London. Add the complexities of having the transactions in different countries, with foreign exchange hedge contract gains and losses that sometimes offset trading losses and gains, and one has a marvelously complex management control problem [17].

So international issues in business management are vitally important today. This means that international issues in accounting, marketing, finance, production/operations, human resource management, and, of course, information systems and information technology are also very important to business success. Properly designed and managed information systems using appropriate information technologies are a key ingredient in international business. They provide vital information resources needed to support business activity in global markets. See Figure 13.16.

The International Dimension

Jon Feingersh/The Stock Market.

FIGURE 13.16
Business managers must now deal with international and global issues.

FIGURE 13.17
The major dimensions of global
IT management.

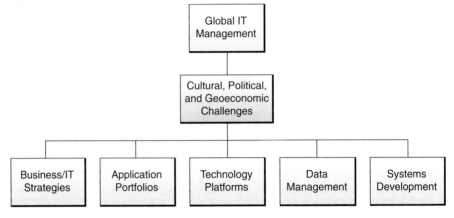

Global IT Management

Figure 13.17 illustrates the major dimensions of the job of managing global information technology that we will cover in this section. Notice that all global IT activities must be adjusted to take into account the cultural, political, and geoeconomic challenges that exist in the international business community. Developing appropriate business and IT strategies for the global marketplace should be the first step in **global IT management.** Once that is done, end user and IS managers can move on to developing the *portfolio of applications* needed to support *business/IT strategies;* the hardware, software, and telecommunications technology *platforms* to support those applications; the *data management* methods to provide necessary databases; and finally the *systems development* projects that will produce the global information systems required.

Cultural, Political, and Geoeconomic Challenges

"Business as usual" is not good enough in global business operations. The same holds true for global IT management. There are too many cultural, political, and geoeconomic (geographic and economic) realities that must be confronted in order for a business to succeed in global markets. As we have just said, global IT management must focus on developing global business IT strategies and managing global application portfolios, technologies, platforms, databases, and systems development projects. But managers must also accomplish that from a perspective and through methods that take into account the cultural, political, and geographic differences that exist when doing business internationally.

For example, a major *political challenge* is that many countries have rules regulating or prohibiting transfer of data across their national boundaries (*transborder data flows*), especially personal information such as personnel records. Others severely restrict, tax, or prohibit imports of hardware and software. Still others have *local content* laws that specify the portion of the value of a product that must be added in that country if it is to be sold there. Other countries have *reciprocal trade agreements* that require a business to spend part of the revenue they earn in a country in that nation's economy [28].

Geoeconomic challenges in global business and IT refer to the effects of geography on the economic realities of international business activities. The sheer physical distances involved are still a major problem, even in this day of electronic telecommunications and jet travel. For example, it may still take too long to fly in specialists when IT problems occur in a remote site. It is still difficult to communicate conveniently across the world's 24 time zones. It is still difficult to get good-quality telephone and telecommunications service in many countries. There are still problems finding the job skills required in some countries, or enticing specialists from other countries to live and work there. Finally, there are still problems (and opportunities) in the great differences in the cost of living and labor costs in various countries [23]. All of these geoeconomic challenges must be addressed when developing a company's global business and IT strategies.

Cultural challenges facing global business and IT managers include differences in languages, cultural interests, religions, customs, social attitudes, and political philosophies. Obviously, global IT managers must be trained and sensitized to such cultural differences before they are sent abroad or brought into a corporation's home country. Other cultural challenges include differences in work styles and business relationships. For example, should one take one's time to avoid mistakes, or hurry to get something done early? Should one go it alone or work cooperatively? Should the most experienced person lead, or should leadership be shared? The answers to such questions would depend on the culture you are in, and would spotlight cultural differences that might exist in the global workplace. Let's take a look at a recent example.

Located on the tip of the Malaysian peninsula, the city-state nation of Singapore is one of the economic powerhouses of Asia. Singapore is also a preeminent user of information technology for strategic advantage in business and government. A recent study demonstrated the role of cultural differences between the United States and Singapore in the use of electronic meeting systems as group support systems (GSS) [32]. For example:

The Republic of Singapore

1. Singaporean groups had higher premeeting consensus than U.S. groups.
2. All groups in both cultures had the same level of postmeeting consensus.
3. Change in consensus was greater in United States groups than in Singaporean groups.
4. After controlling for premeeting consensus, influence among participants was more equal in Singaporean groups than in U.S. groups.
5. In Singaporean groups, a GSS led to unequal influence among participants in groups with a high level of agreement before their meeting.

Thus, the use of group support systems is a good example of how culture can affect the impact of information technology. Singaporean culture places a high priority on group harmony and the maintenance of social structure. When there is a high premeeting agreement within a group, cultural pressure promotes an acquiescence of group members' opinions to that of a dominant member of the group. Therefore, group members are sufficiently satisfied with a group solution to suppress their personal opinions in favor of supporting cultural norms. Thus, GSS voting tools enable a team with an initially high level of consensus to discover rapidly their accord and quickly reach agreement on an issue [32].

What does it mean to be a **global company**? How does one know if a business is truly a global company? Here's one definition:

The Global Company

> A global company is a business that is driven by a global strategy, which enables it to plan and treat all of its activities in the context of a whole-world system, and therefore serve its local and global customers with excellence [6].

Figure 13.18 illustrates this view of a global company. It emphasizes that a global company balances its strategies and activities to ensure serving customers in

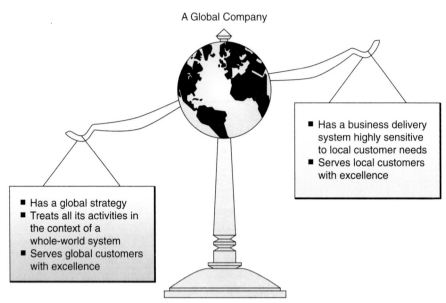

A Global Company

■ Has a business delivery
system highly sensitive
to local customer needs
■ Serves local customers
with excellence

■ Has a global strategy
■ Treats all its activities in
the context of a
whole-world system
■ Serves global customers
with excellence

Source: Adapted and reprinted by permission of Harvard Business School Press from *Globalization, Technology, and Competition: The Fusion of Computers and Telecommunications in the 1990s* by Stephen P. Bradley, Jerry A. Hausman, and Richard L. Nolan. Boston: 1993, p. 245. Copyright © 1993 by the President and Fellows of Harvard College.

each locality with sensitivity and excellence, while still implementing a whole-world strategy that serves its global customers with excellence. Becoming a global company is a major undertaking, a process requiring fundamental business transformation. According to MIS professor and international consultant Richard Nolan, becoming a global company is a multiyear process, driven by the vision of achieving a fundamentally different state than the current one, and involving simultaneous changes in just about every aspect of the business [6]. Figure 13.19 emphasizes the scope of the changes required to become a global company.

IBM Corporation

IBM is a global company, deriving more than 60 percent of its revenue from outside the United States. IBM continues to study how to improve its structure, operations, and management, in response to the challenges of "being global." IBMs 500 largest international customers represent more than 20 percent of the company's revenue, more than $13 billion, and this customer base is growing approximately twice as fast as IBM's domestic base. The demands of these international customers are a powerful business incentive. Also, IBM's strategy is to cooperate with its business partners, of which the company has thousands around the world. Working with its global business partners, many of which are intent on making use of IBM's international dimensions, has raised new and difficult issues for IBM management. However, IBM believes the business opportunity inherent in being global opens the field for new applications and services, which the company is eager to exploit [6].

Rosenbluth Travel

Rosenbluth Travel is one of the five largest travel industries in the United States, with annual sales over $1.3 billion. Its success is characterized by:

- Rapid and creative innovation driven by closeness to its market and a clear vision of its corporate customers' changing needs.
- Aggressive use of information technology (IT) to build infrastructure for the delivery of services and to form a platform for continued innovation [6].

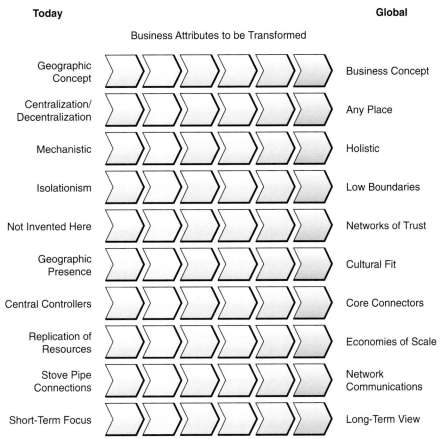

Today   **Global**

Business Attributes to be Transformed

Today		Global
Geographic Concept		Business Concept
Centralization/ Decentralization		Any Place
Mechanistic		Holistic
Isolationism		Low Boundaries
Not Invented Here		Networks of Trust
Geographic Presence		Cultural Fit
Central Controllers		Core Connectors
Replication of Resources		Economies of Scale
Stove Pipe Connections		Network Communications
Short-Term Focus		Long-Term View

FIGURE 13.19
What it takes to become a global company.

Source: Adapted and reprinted by permission of Harvard Business School Press from *Globalization, Technology, and Competition: The Fusion of Computers and Telecommunications in the 1990s* by Stephen P. Bradley, Jerry A. Hausman, and Richard L. Nolan. Boston: 1993, p. 58. Copyright © 1993 by the President and Fellows of Harvard College.

Rosenbluth offers global travel services in an effort to keep pace with its customers, which have globalized their operations in response to market pressure, competitor actions, and changing supplier relations. Rosenbluth chose a unique structure for globalization, the Rosenbluth International Alliance (RIA). Rather than relying on expansion through development of its own offices abroad and attempting to develop local travel management expertise and to capture the necessary shares of foreign markets, the company chose to work with the best foreign partners it could find. RIA, a cooperative alliance of independent agencies, comprises 32 partners spanning 37 countries. The benefits of this approach are as follows:

- Even for multinational corporate clients, the bulk of travel is regional or local, requiring local expertise. RIA's structure reflects this.
- When necessary, local markets can be linked. Providing service for traveling executives and resolving unanticipated problems requires more than presence; it requires local expertise coupled with global access to information. RIA's structure reflects this as well.
- The need for global coordination is expected to increase as clients demand consolidated reporting of travel patterns and global travel management services. RIA's structure, being flexible, can evolve as global travel support needs change [6].

FIGURE 13.20
Companies operating internationally are moving toward a transnational business strategy. Note some of the chief differences between international, global, and transnational business and IT strategies.

International	Global	Transnational
▪ Autonomous operations.	▪ Global sourcing.	▪ Virtual operations.
▪ Region specific.	▪ Multiregional.	▪ World markets.
▪ Vertical integration.	▪ Horizontal integration.	▪ Transparent order fulfillment
▪ Specific customers.	▪ Some transparency of cus-	and customers.
▪ Captive manufacturing.	tomers and production.	▪ Transparent manufacturing.
▪ Customer segmentation and	▪ Some cross regionalization.	▪ Global sourcing.
dedication by region and plant.		▪ Dynamic resource management.

Information Technology Characteristics

International	Global	Transnational
▪ Standalone systems.	▪ Regional decentralization.	▪ Logically consolidated, physi-
▪ Decentralized/no standards.	▪ Interface dependent.	cally distributed.
▪ Heavy reliance on interfaces.	▪ Some consolidation of applica-	▪ Common data.
▪ Multiple systems, high redun-	tions and use of common sys-	▪ Integrated systems.
dancy and duplication of ser-	tems.	▪ Specialized workstation-based
vices and operations.	▪ Reduced duplication of opera-	applications.
▪ Lack of common systems and	tions.	▪ Transnational IT policies and
data.	▪ Some worldwide IT standards.	standards.

Source: Adapted and reprinted from Michael Mische, "Transnational Architecture: A Reengineering Approach," *Information Systems Management* (New York: Auerbach Publications), Winter 1995, © 1995 Warren, Gorharn & Lamont. Used with permission.

Global Business and IT Strategies

How much of a business need is there for **global information technology?** That is, do we need to use IT to support our company's international business operations? Figure 13.20 helps answer these questions by showing that many firms are moving toward **transnational strategies** in which they integrate their global business activities through close cooperation and interdependence among their international subsidiaries and their corporate headquarters. Businesses are moving away from (1) *multinational* strategies where foreign subsidiaries operate autonomously; (2) *international* strategies in which foreign subsidiaries are autonomous but are dependent on headquarters for new processes, products, and ideas; or (3) *global* strategies, where a company's worldwide operations are closely managed by corporate headquarters [17, 24].

In the transnational approach, a business depends heavily on its information systems and appropriate information technologies to help it integrate its global business activities. Instead of having independent IS units at its subsidiaries, or even a centralized IS operation directed from its headquarters, a transnational firm moves to integrate its IS operations. Thus, a transnational business tries to develop an integrated and cooperative worldwide hardware, software, and telecommunications architecture for its IT *platform*. Figure 13.21 illustrates how a transnational business and IT strategy for a global company can be implemented with an integrated network organizational structure [6].

Global Business and IT Applications

The applications of information technology developed by global companies depend on their business and IT strategies and their expertise and experience in IT. However, their IT applications also depend on a variety of **global business drivers,** that is, business requirements caused by the nature of the industry and its competitive or environmental forces. One example would be companies like airlines or hotel

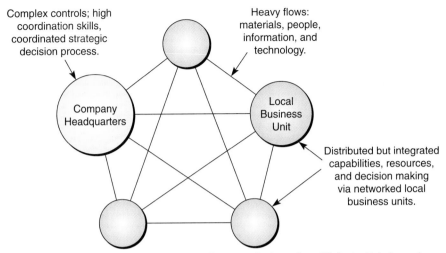

Source: Adapted and reprinted by permission of Harvard Business School Press from *Globalization, Technology, and Competition: The Fusion of Computers and Telecommunications in the 1990s* by Stephen P. Bradley, Jerry A. Hausman, and Richard L. Nolan. Boston: 1993, p. 86. Copyright © 1993 by the President and Fellows of Harvard College.

FIGURE 13.21
An example of how a transnational business and IT strategy can be implemented with an integrated network organizational structure.

chains that have *global customers,* that is, customers who travel widely or have global operations. Such companies will need global IT capabilities for online transaction processing so they can provide fast, convenient customer service to their customers or face losing them to their competitors. The economies of scale provided by global business operations are another business driver that requires the support of global IT applications [15].

Companies whose products are available worldwide would be another example of how business needs can shape global IT. For example, Coca Cola or Pepsi might use teleconferencing to make worldwide product announcements, and use computer-based marketing systems to coordinate global marketing campaigns. Other companies with global operations have used IT to move parts of their operations to lower-cost sites. For example, Citibank moved its credit card processing operations to Sioux Falls, South Dakota, American Airlines moved much of its data entry work to Barbados, while other firms have looked to Ireland and India as sources of low-cost software development [15, 21]. Figure 13.22 summarizes some of the business requirements that make global IT a competitive necessity.

Of course, many global IT applications, particularly finance, accounting, and office applications, have been in operation for many years. For example, most multinational companies had global financial budgeting and cash management systems, and more recently office automation applications such as fax and E-mail systems. However, as global operations expand and global competition heats up, there is increasing pressure for companies to install global transaction processing applications for their customers and suppliers. Examples include global point-of-sale (POS) and customer service systems for customers and global electronic data interchange (EDI) systems for suppliers. Figure 13.23 illustrates the distribution of global IT applications based on whether they are single-purpose or collaborative systems owned by a single global company, or a cooperative venture involving several companies [29].

Chase Manhattan Bank is an example of a global company with global information systems for customer service. At Chase's Global Securities Services (GSS), more than 200 managers around the world use the Account Service Planning and Analysis

Chase Manhattan Bank

FIGURE 13.22
Business drivers for global IT.
These are some of the business
reasons behind global IT applications.

Global customers. Customers are people who may travel anywhere or companies with global operations. Global IT can help provide fast, convenient service.

Global products. Products are the same throughout the world or are assembled by subsidiaries throughout the world. Global IT can help manage worldwide marketing and quality control.

Global operations. Parts of a production or assembly process are assigned to subsidiaries based on changing economic or other conditions. Only global IT can support such geographic flexibility.

Global resources. The use and cost of common equipment, facilities, and people are shared by subsidiaries of a global company. Global IT can keep track of such shared resources.

Global collaboration. The knowledge and expertise of colleagues in a global company can be quickly accessed, shared, and organized to support individual or group efforts. Only global IT can support such electronic collaboration.

Source: Adapted from Blake Ives and Sirkka Jarvenpaa, "Applications of Global Information Technology: Key Issues for Management," *MIS Quarterly*, Volume 15, Number 1, March 1991, p. 40 Reprinted with permission from the *MIS Quarterly.*

FIGURE 13.23
Families of global IT applications and information systems.

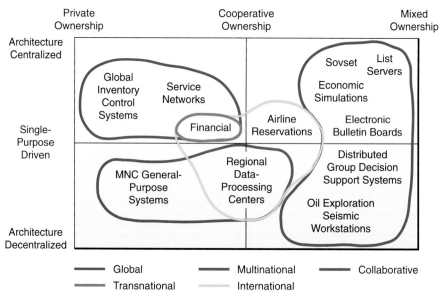

Source: Adapted with the permission of Simon & Schuster from the Macmillan College text *Managing Information Technology in Multinational Corporations,* by Edward Roche. Copyright © 1992 by Macmillan College Publishing Company, Inc.

(ASPA) system. ASPA, along with two related systems, helps GSS develop service and production plans, as well as monitor success against these plans according to customer service expectations and revenue targets. By analyzing specific customer service data by various dimensions quickly, Chase is able to identify key service problems in its global transaction processing systems and drill down through countries and customer accounts anywhere in the world, zero in on the problem, and take corrective action to prevent recurrence.

A customer service manager in any of Chase's service centers around the world can check for problems in performance with a few mouse clicks on his or her PC. A typical problem could be something like dividend or settlement payments taking

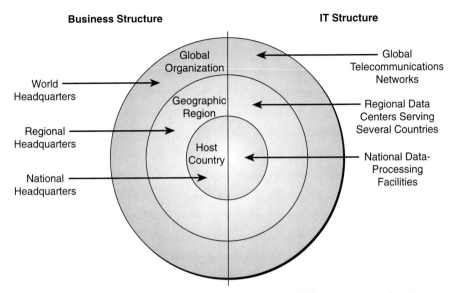

Business Structure

IT Structure

Global Organization

Geographic Region

Host Country

World Headquarters

Regional Headquarters

National Headquarters

Global Telecommunications Networks

Regional Data Centers Serving Several Countries

National Data-Processing Facilities

Source: Adapted with the permission of Simon & Schuster from the Macmillan College text *Managing Information Technology in Multinational Corporations,* by Edward Roche. Copyright © 1992 by Macmillan College Publishing Company, Inc.

FIGURE 13.24
Global business and technology structures. Note how a global IT structure reflects a company's global business structure.

longer than normal. Once a service problem is identified, the GSS customer service manager can use the system to analyze the situation and, working with the customer—who may be unaware of the problem—put together a program that will correct the problem within a specific time limit [4].

The choice of *technology platforms* (also called the *technology infrastructure*) is another major dimension of global IT management. That is, what hardware, software, telecommunications networks, and computing facilities will be needed to support our global business operations? Answering this question is a major challenge of global IT management. The choice of a global IT platform is not only technically complex, but also has major political and cultural implications.

For example, hardware choices are difficult in some countries because of high prices, high tariffs, import restrictions, long lead times for government approvals, lack of local service or spare parts, and lack of documentation tailored to local conditions. Software choices can also present unique problems. Software packages developed in Europe may be incompatible with American or Asian versions, even when purchased from the same hardware vendor. Well-known U.S. software packages may be unavailable because there is no local distributor, or because the software publisher refuses to supply markets that disregard software licensing and copyright agreements [14].

Telecommunications network and computing facilities decisions also present major challenges in global IT management. In Chapter 6, we discussed some of the managerial challenges posed by telecommunications network technologies. Obviously, global telecommunications networks that cross many international boundaries make such issues even more complex.

Figure 13.24 shows that companies with global business operations usually establish or contract with systems integrators for additional data centers in their subsidiaries in other countries. These data centers meet local and regional computing needs, and even help balance global computing workloads through communications

Global IT Platforms

FIGURE 13.25
The global telecommunication command center of Electronic Data Systems.

Courtesy of EDS Corporation.

satellite links. However, off-shore data centers can pose major problems in headquarter's support, hardware and software acquisition, maintenance, and security.

> Establishing locations for international data centers presents several challenges: overlapping working hours; local computing and labor regulations; potential theft; sabotage and terrorism; unreliable power sources; availability of completely redundant network backup capability; and the like [15].

That's why many global companies turn to systems integrators like EDS or IBM to manage their overseas operations. See Figure 13.25.

Global Data Issues

Global data issues have been a subject of political controversy and technology barriers in global business operations for many years. A major example is the issue of **transborder data flows** (TDF), in which business data flows across international borders over the telecommunications networks of global information systems. Many countries view transborder data flows as violating their national sovereignty because TDF avoids customs duties and regulations for the import or export of goods and services. Other countries may view TDF as a violation of their privacy legislation since, in many cases, data about individuals is being moved out of the country without stringent privacy safeguards. Still others view transborder data flows as violating their laws to protect the local IT industry from competition, or their labor regulations for protecting local jobs [7].

Figure 13.26 outlines some of the fears and responses of several countries to global data issues. Notice that this includes not only transborder data flows, but also regulation of files and databases stored in a host country. Recent research seems to indicate that data issues have not been as much of a problem for global business as had been feared. This is due primarily to difficulties in enforcing such laws, and to efforts by host countries to encourage foreign investment. However, the data issues that still seem politically sensitive are those that affect the movement of personal data in payroll and personnel applications [7, 15].

Country	Presumed Fear	Actual Response
Brazil	Information colonialism and a lack of development of a domestic information industry.	All companies must maintain copies of all databases physically within the country; offshore processing is prohibited.
Canada	Exportation of corporate information to headquarters in other countries (especially the United States). Abuses of the personal privacy of its citizens. Loss of cultural and national sovereignty.	1980 Banking Act prohibits processing data transactions outside of the country unless approved by the government. Limitations on the number of direct access links for international data transmission and limitations on satellite usage.
France	Basically the same as Canada.	Imposition of taxes on and duties on information and information transfers. Requires every database maintained in France to be registered with the government.
Germany	A lack of development of a domestic information industry. Abuses of personal privacy.	Regulations which favor the domestic information industry and control of private leased telecommunication lines which connect to public communications networks. Data records on German nationals must be kept in Germany.
Sweden	Abuses of privacy. Domestic economic data may not be accessible if stored abroad.	Has a data protection law and a commission to license and approve all data systems. Prohibits offshore processing and storage of data.
Taiwan	National and economic security	Government monitoring of data transmissions.

FIGURE 13.26
Global data issues. Note the fears and responses by some countries to the issues of transborder data flows and control of global databases.

Source: Copyright © 1992. *The Global Issues of Information Technology Management*, Idea Group Publishing, Harrisburg, PA. Reprint by permission.

Other important global data issues are concerned with global data management and standardization of data. Common data definitions are necessary for sharing data among the parts of an international business. Differences in language, culture, and technology platforms can make global data standardization quite difficult. For example, a sale may be called "an 'order booked' in the United Kingdom, an 'order scheduled' in Germany, and an 'order produced' in France" [29]. However, businesses are moving ahead to standardize data definitions and structures. By involving their subsidiaries in data modeling and database design, they hope to develop a global data architecture that supports their global business objectives [14].

Global Systems Development

Just imagine the challenges of developing efficient, effective, and responsive applications for business end users domestically. Then multiply that by the number of countries and cultures that may use a global IT system. That's the challenge of managing global systems development. Naturally, there are conflicts over local versus

FIGURE 13.27
The global use of information technology depends on international systems development efforts.

L. D. Gordon/The Image Bank.

global system requirements, and difficulties in agreeing on common system features such as multilingual user interfaces and flexible design standards. And all of this effort must take place in an environment that promotes involvement and "ownership" of a system by local end users. Thus, one IT manager estimates that

> it takes 5 to 10 times more time to reach an understanding and agreement on system requirements and deliverables when the users and developers are in different countries. This is partially explained by travel requirements and language and cultural differences, but technical limitations also contribute to the problem [15].

Other systems development issues arise from disturbances caused by systems implementation and maintenance activities. For example: "An interruption during a third shift in New York City will present midday service interruptions in Tokyo." Another major development issue relates to the trade-offs between developing one system that can run on multiple computer and operating system platforms, or letting each local site customize the software for its own platform [15]. See Figure 13.27.

Several strategies can be used to solve some of the systems development problems that arise in global IT [15, 29]. First is transforming an application used by the home office into a global application. However, often the system used by a subsidiary that has the best version of an application will be chosen for global use. Another approach is setting up a *multinational development team* with key people from several subsidiaries to ensure that the system design meets the needs of local sites as well as corporate headquarters.

A third approach is called *parallel development*. That's because parts of the system are assigned to different subsidiaries and the home office to develop at the same time, based on the expertise and experience at each site. Another approach is the concept of *centers of excellence*. In this approach, an entire system may be assigned for development to a particular subsidiary based on their expertise in the business or technical dimensions needed for successful development. Obviously, all of these approaches require managerial oversight and coordination to meet the global needs of a business.

You and Global IT Management

Most companies fail to have in place a coherent information-*technology* strategy. Their IT infrastructure does not match or facilitate their emerging global *business* strategy. Few multinationals have discovered the potential of computer and communications

FIGURE 13.28

Basic steps toward becoming a global company.

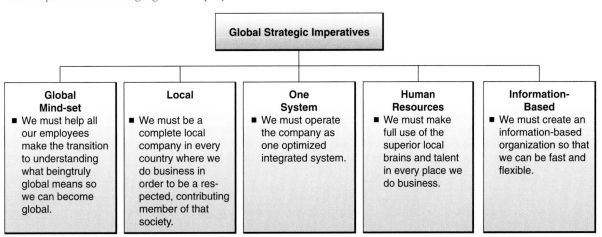

Source: Adapted and reprinted by permission of Harvard Business School Press from *Globalization, Technology, and Competition: The Fusion of Computers and Telecommunications in the 1990s* by Stephen P. Bradley, Jerry A. Hausman, and Richard L. Nolan. Boston: 1993, p. 248. Copyright © 1993 by the President and Fellows of Harvard College.

technology to transform their operations on a global basis. A company may have a single product sold globally, but no globally rationalized product database. It may be fighting a battle for centralized control when the business strategy needs to be different for each national market. It most likely has many different national data centers when it could better serve strategy with regionalized data processing of selected applications and resources [29].

Now that we have covered the basic dimensions of global IT management, it is time to acknowledge that much work remains to be done to implement global IT strategies. As a future managerial end user or IS manager, the global business success of the company you work for will be in your hands. But now at least you know the dimensions of the problems and opportunities that arise from the use of information technology to support global business operations.

First, you must discover if your company has a global business strategy and a strategy for how information technology can support global business operations. If not, you can begin to play a role, however small, in developing such strategies. Then you must discover or help develop the IT applications to support your global business activities. This includes providing your ideas for the hardware, software, and telecommunications platform and databases you need to do business globally. This process can be a gradual one. For example, as a managerial end user, you can follow the lead of a global corporation that laid out the five basic actions it had to accomplish to become a truly successful global company, as shown in Figure 13.28.

As a managerial end user, global IT management will be one of your many managerial responsibilities. Like other areas of global business management, it requires an added dimension of sensitivity to the cultural, political, and geoeconomic realities of doing business with people in other countries. But it also offers an exciting challenge of competing successfully in a dynamic global arena to bring your products or services to customers throughout the world.

R E A L   W O R L D   C A S E

ABB Asea Brown Boveri: Managing IT in a Global Multidomestic Company

The world's largest electrical engineering firm, ABB Asea Brown Boveri Ltd., began life by tackling global computing complexity. ABB hasn't stopped since.

Formed in 1987 by the merger of engineering giants Asea AB in Sweden and BBC Brown Boveri Ltd. in Switzerland, ABB gave its information systems personnel a daunting task: to create, within months, a single financial reporting application for 1,300 companies employing more than 200,000 people in 140 countries. Some other statistics:

Annual IS spending	$700 million
IS spending per employee	$3,390
Annual IS spending as percentage of revenue	2.5%
Number of IS employees	5,000

"You know how that goes: The IS people may say it's going to take two years to develop, and we say, 'No, guys, it should be ready the first quarter of 1988,'" says Begt Skantze, a corporate development manager who now manages ABB Group Information Systems. "And it was ready the first quarter of 1988."

Today, the unified reporting system remains one of Zurich-based ABB's few standard applications. The $28 billion giant continues to balance the paradoxes facing an "international, multidomestic organization." The company considers itself global but with deep local roots; large overall but individually small, with 5,000 profit centers; decentralized but with centralized reporting.

Indeed, Skantze says his current challenge is balancing a diverse, decentralized structure while leveraging centralized efficiencies in purchasing and other operations. It's a big job. Even more remarkable is the fact that he directs ABB technology on a part-time basis with only two staffers. "We're lean and mean," Skantze chuckles.

How do they do it? IS operations mirror a two-dimensional company matrix. Each ABB company around the world has its own board of directors, president, and CIO. All these executives enjoy a good deal of autonomy from the home office in Switzerland. Despite this, many ABB companies have found it useful to share data with formerly separate subsidiaries. An IS steering committee serves major geographic and business entities. Each group meets several times a year to approve budgets and ensure that

technology plans fit overall company direction. Committees comprise the top IS manager, financial officers, board members, and chief executive officers. IS managers serve each of the three geographic regions, five business segments, and 45 business areas.

Each business chooses its own applications, but ABB has standardized its office automation infrastructure. The company began rolling out Lotus Notes 18 months ago. "We have one chance in a lifetime to standardize because it's something new," Skantze explains.

For example, several ABB companies have developed Notes applications that have been replicated around the world. One such application: a manufacturing defect Notes database. If an ABB employee in the United States finds a foreign-made part that doesn't conform to specifications, simply logging that fact in a Notes database will result in immediate notification of all interested ABB employees worldwide. This allows the affected ABB overseas manufacturing plant to embark on an immediate explanation or correction.

ABB now boasts 13,000 Notes users worldwide. "ABB is an interesting example of how companies can move, in this case to Notes, to build a global information infrastructure cutting through the national hierarchies," says Sean Phelan, an analyst at The Yankee Group in Watford, England.

Beyond that, some 1,000 staffers populate major IS centers in Sweden, Germany, Switzerland, and the United States. These centers house mainframes that handle host-based applications. For a chargeback fee, IS staffers also help install client/server systems for ABB companies.

CASE STUDY QUESTIONS

1. Is ABB a global, transnational company? Do you think their organizational structure is a good way to organize their company? Explain.

2. How is the IS function organized and managed at ABB? Do you think this is a good idea? Why or why not?

3. What is the role of Lotus Notes in ABB's business operations and management?

Summary

- **Managers and IT.** Information technology is changing the distribution, relationships, resources, and responsibilities of managers. That is, IT is eliminating layers of management, enabling more collaborative forms of management, providing managers with significant information and computing resources, and confronting managers with a major information resource management challenge.

- **IS Performance.** Information systems are not being used effectively, efficiently, or economically by many organizations. The experiences of successful organizations reveal that the basic ingredient of high-quality information system performance is extensive and meaningful management and user involvement in the governance of information technology. Thus, managers may serve on executive steering committees and create an IS management function within their business units.

- **Organizations and IT.** The people, tasks, technology, culture, and structure of an organization affect how it will organize and use information technology. Thus, many variations exist, which reflect the attempts of organizations to tailor their organizational structures and applications to their particular business activities and management philosophy, as well as to the capabilities of centralized or distributed information systems. Lately, the trend has been to a combination of centralized and distributed arrangements for the management of information technology.

- **Information Resource Management.** Managing the use of information technology in an organization has become a major managerial responsibility. End user managers should use an information resource management approach to manage the data and information, hardware and software, telecommunications networks, and people resources of their business units and work groups for the overall benefit of their organi-

zations. The information systems function in an organization may be headed by a chief information officer who oversees the organization's strategic use of information technology (strategic management). IRM also involves managing data and IS personnel (resource management), telecommunications and advances in information technologies (technology management), and end user computing (distributed management). The activities of information services can be grouped into basic functional categories such as systems development, operations, and technical services (functional management).

- **Managing Global IT.** The international dimensions of managing global information technology include dealing with cultural, political, and geoeconomic challenges posed by various countries, developing appropriate business and IT strategies for the global marketplace, and developing a portfolio of global IT applications and a technology platform to support them. In addition, database management methods have to be developed and systems development projects managed to produce the global information systems that are required to compete successfully in the global marketplace.

- **Global Business and IT Strategies and Issues.** Many businesses are becoming global companies and moving toward transnational business strategies in which they integrate the global business activities of their subsidiaries and headquarters. This requires that they develop a global IT platform, that is, an integrated worldwide hardware, software, and telecommunications architecture. Global companies use this IT platform to develop and deliver global IT applications that meet their unique global business requirements. Global IT and end user managers must deal with restrictions on the availability of hardware and software, restrictions on transborder data flows and movement of personal data, and difficulties with developing common data definitions and system requirements.

Key Terms and Concepts

These are the key terms and concepts of this chapter. The page number of their first explanation is in parentheses.

1. Centralization or decentralization (503)
   a. Information systems (504)
   b. Operations and management (503)
2. Chargeback systems (506)
3. Chief information officer (501)
4. Cultural, political, and geoeconomic challenges (514)
5. Data center (505)
6. Development center (505)
7. Downsizing (504)
8. End user services (510)
9. Global business drivers (518)
10. Global company (515)
11. Global information technology (518)
12. Global IT management (514)
    a. Applications (518)
    b. Business/IT strategies (518)
    c. Data issues (522)
    d. IT platforms (521)
    e. Systems development (523)
13. Human resource management of IT (507)

14. Impact of information technology (494)
    a. On management (494)
    b. On organizations (499)
15. Information center (510)
16. Information resource management (500)
    a. Five dimensions of IRM (501)

17. Information services functions (502)
18. Information systems performance (496)
19. Management involvement (497)
20. Operations management (505)
21. Organizations as sociotechnical systems (499)
22. System performance monitor (505)

23. Systems development management (504)
24. Technical services (502)
25. Technology management (508)
26. Telecommunications management (508)
27. Transborder data flows (522)
28. Transnational strategy (518)

Review Quiz

Match one of the key terms and concepts listed above with one of the brief examples or definitions listed below. Try to find the best fit for answers that seem to fit more than one term or concept. Defend your choices.

___ 1. Managers now have a lot of information, information processing power, and responsibility for information systems.

___ 2. Information technology affects the people, tasks, technology, culture, and structure of organizations.

___ 3. Information system resources can be distributed throughout an organization or consolidated in corporate data centers.

___ 4. Information systems can help management increase the number of regional and branch offices or consolidate operations.

___ 5. The management of data, information, hardware, software, and IS personnel as organizational resources.

___ 6. Managing information technology is a distributed, functional responsibility focusing on the strategic management of IS resources and technologies.

___ 7. Computers have not been used efficiently, effectively, and economically.

___ 8. A management steering committee is an example.

___ 9. End users need information centers or other forms of liaison, consulting, and training support.

___10. Includes the basic functions of systems development, operations, and technical services.

___11. An executive that oversees all information systems technology for an organization.

___12. Managing systems analysis and design, computer programming, and systems maintenance activities.

___13. Planning and controlling data center operations.

___14. Corporate locations for computer system operations.

___15. A support group for an organization's professional programmers and systems analysts.

___16. A support group for an organization's end users.

___17. Rapidly changing technological developments must be anticipated, identified, and implemented.

___18. An IS function that includes user services, telecommunications management, and technology management.

___19. Telecommunications networks and their hardware and software must be developed, administered, and maintained.

___20. Software that helps monitor and control computer systems in a data center.

___21. The cost of IS services may be allocated back to end users.

___22. Recruiting and developing information services employees.

___23. Many business firms are replacing their mainframe systems with networked microcomputers.

___24. A business that is driven by a global strategy.

___25. Using IT to support a company's international business operations.

___26. Integrating global business activities through cooperation among international subsidiaries and corporate headquarters.

___27. Differences in customs, governmental regulations, and the cost of living are examples.

___28. Global customers, products, operations, resources, and collaboration.

___29. Applying IT to global transaction processing systems is an example.

___30. The goal of some organizations is to develop an integrated worldwide hardware, software, and telecommunications platform.

___31. Transborder data flows and security of personnel databases are top concerns.

___32. Standardizing computer systems, software packages, telecommunications networks, and computing facilities.

___33. Agreement is needed on common user interfaces and other design features in global IT.

___34. Global telecommunications networks move data across national boundaries.

Discussion Questions

1. What has been the impact of information technology on the work relationships, activities, and resources of managers?

2. What can end user managers do about performance problems in the use of information technology and the development and operation of information systems in a business?

3. Refer to the Real World Case on Levi Strauss & Co. in the chapter. What are the automated systems and network management tools mentioned in the case? What strategic and operational roles do they play at Levi Strauss?

4. How is information technology affecting the structure and work roles of modern organizations? For example, will middle management wither away? Will companies consist primarily of self-directed project teams of knowledge workers? Explain your answer.

5. Should the IS function in a business be centralized or decentralized? What recent developments support your answer?

6. Refer to the Real World Case on Barclays Bank, Nestlé, and Elf Altochem in the chapter. Will video conferencing ever replace most physical, face-to-face meetings in Global business management? Why or why not?

7. What do you think are the most important cultural, political, or geoeconomic challenges facing managers of global companies? Why?

8. What are several major dimensions of global IT management? How would cultural, political, or geoeconomic challenges affect each of them?

9. Why do you think firms with global business operations are moving away from multinational, global, and international strategies toward a transnational business strategy? How does this affect global IT management?

10. What important business "drivers" or requirements do you think are most responsible for a company's use of global IT? Give several examples to illustrate your answer.

Real World Problems

1. Harris Methodist Health System: The CIO as Change Agent

Meet Larry Blevins, change agent. He doesn't just talk the talk. In once recent undertaking, Blevins, chief information officer of privately held Harris Methodist Health System, in Fort Worth, Texas, led an effort to get San Diego-based systems integrator Science Applications International Corp. (SAIC) care to co-develop a knowledge base to be accessed by doctors and clinicians. The knowledge base (which includes a database of patient, diagnostic, treatment, and billing information; communications; and personal-productivity tools) would replace Harris's paper-based system, which is more difficult for doctors and others to access, and carries support costs in staffing, copying, and storage. Blevins personally pitched the concept to SAIC's board. He has also participated in the co-development effort, ensuring that Harris gets a system that will meet its needs well into the future. The system, which will be implemented within the next 12 months, is expected, conservatively, to save Harris "hundreds of thousands of dollars," Blevins says. "It eliminates administrative costs and improves quality."

Blevins, who wouldn't reveal the details of his compensation package, says his role as CIO often takes him into territory normally reserved for executives who specialize in strategic partnerships. In another instance, he went out and convinced several companies, including Microsoft, VTEL Corp, Image PSL, and Southwestern Bell to co-develop a diagnostic image-management system that Harris wanted. The radiology system, implemented in February, took about two years to create. It was worth the wait. Harris' old system cost $10 per film to store and maintain its library of hun-

dreds of thousands of films. The new system costs five cents per film and takes users four seconds or less to access it, Blevins boasts. The system, named the Electronic Diagnostic Image Management System, is a combination of technologies, including high-quality direct video capture, communications, compressed video, low-cost optical-disk storage, PCs, and advanced software-development tools, Blevins says.

a. How does Larry Blevins use his position as the CIO to act as a change agent at Harris Methodist Health System?

b. Do you think other CIOs should act as change agents in their companies? Why or why not?

Source: Adapted from Lawrence Aragon, "Change Agents," *PCWeek/Executive*, March 27, 1995, p. E1, E14.

2. Allied Signal and Pfizer, Inc.: Shared versus Decentralized IS Services

To centralize or not to centralize is no longer the burning issue for information systems organizations under pressure to achieve greater economies of scale from multimillion-dollar technology investments. These days, the question is what to consolidate and where, according to IS executives at the growing number of companies involved in the cost-cutting process of converting some or all IS operations to so-called *shared services*. Under shared services—a familiar management model in areas such as finance and human resources—scattered IS operations are pulled together into megaservice centers, which then serve all of the company's business units around the globe.

"IS is a natural candidate for shared services because technology touches all facets of business," said Albert Ritardi, former vice president of administrative services at Allied Signal, Inc., and current president of Ritardi & Associates, Inc., a shared services consultancy in Basking Ridge, New Jersey. During 1993 and 1994, Allied's shared services initiatives—which included the consolidation of 17 data centers into a single data processing megacenter in Tempe, Arizona—cut costs by about $42 million, he said. "And these are cost savings that occur year after year after year. They're not onetime events," Ritardi said.

Pfizer, Inc., in New York, is converting data processing, telecommunications, and PC LAN management to shared services. In doing so, Cathy O'Connor, vice president of corporate information technology, estimates the pharmaceutical giant will save millions of dollars on telecommunications costs alone. "We now spend $15 million annually on telecommunications. By going to vendors and negotiating with a full set of requirements, we're hoping to get savings or cost avoidance in the $3 million to $4 million area," O'Connor said.

a. What is the difference between shared and decentralized IS services? Shared and the centralized IS approach?

b. What are the benefits and limitations of the shared services approach?

Source: Adapted from Julia King, "Cost Cutters Turning to Shared Services," *Computerworld*, March 13, 1995, p. 28. Copyright 1995 by Computerworld, Inc., Framingham, MA 01701—Reprinted from *Computerworld*.

3. Empire Blue Cross/Blue Shield: Outsourcing IS for Poor Performance

Two weeks after firing about 20 percent of its systems staff, New York's largest health care insurer—calamity-ridden Empire Blue Cross/Blue Shield—is looking to outsource a large chunk of its information systems operations. Last week, J. Rock Tonkel, senior vice president of IS and administrative services, disclosed in an interview that Empire has solicited bids from Electronic Data Systems, Computer Sciences Corp., IBM's Integrated Systems Solutions Corp., and Andersen Consulting. Empire now employs 900 IS workers, and its 1994 IS expenditures totaled $135 million. Analysts characterized Empire's decision to outsource IS as highly unusual in an industry where data processing—particularly claims processing—is considered a critical core competency by virtually all other companies.

The company has been migrating to a new claims processing system known as CS/90 since 1992. Currently, about 50 percent of the 26 million claims the company handles annually are processed on that system. Two mainframe-based legacy systems, both more than 25 years old, process the other half of claims filed by the company's 5.4 million individual subscribers. The insurer also has completed two other systems under an estimated $160 million revamp that began in the late 1980s. An imaging system from Sigma Imaging Systems has been fully operational for more than a year, scanning about 100,000 claims daily. The other system, named Excel, is a customer service application that enables customer service agents at OS/2-based PCs to access data from the new and old claims processing systems.

But according to several accounts, including those by company insiders, customer service remains dismal. Last year, for example, the average time it took to process an institutional claim in the downstate region was 14.7 days, up from 9.4 days in 1993. Also, of the 26,000 customers who called in for help on a daily basis, 5 percent, or 1,300, received a busy signal, up from 4.2 percent the years before. Some other stats:

- Empire's 1994 enrollments totaled 2.7 million, down 48 percent, from 5.2 million contracts in 1988.
- Last year, 10.2 percent of subscribers trying to contact an Empire customer service representative hung up before getting through
- Empire's former CEO, Donald Morchower, publicly acknowledged that the insurer's erratic billing systems were unable to detect false claims, resulting in losses exceeding $40 million.

a. Why do you think that Empire has such poor performance in their computer-based customer service systems?

b. Do you think outsourcing the IS function is a good solution? Why or why not?

Source: Adapted from Julia King and Thomas Hoffman, "Troubled Insurer to Get IS," *Computerworld*, May 29, 1995, pp. 1, 127. Copyright 1995 by Computerworld, Inc., Framingham, MA 01701—Reprinted from *Computerworld*.

4. Ford Motor Company: Linking Global Business Operations

Few have looked harder or wider at linking global resources than Ford. On Jan 1, 1995, the $108 billion Dearborn, Michigan, automaker completed a massive global reorganization, called Ford 2000. Once major goal is a $6 billion international program to build "world cars" on three continents. To that end, five vehicle program centers were established in Germany, England, and the United States. Moreover, Ford created six new international design centers in Europe, Asia, and North America. These studios are linked to the company's new $84 million advanced engineering center in Dearborn via land-based and satellite-linked WANs and LANs. Engineers and designers will be able to do collaborative crash test and air flow analysis, simulations, and other electronic work from networked workstations. Company officials say better use of global resources will boost design efficiency by 25 to 35 percent.

How do you provide information technology support for such far-flung operations in 30 countries? What gets globalized and what doesn't? Bill Powers, Ford's new executive director of IS and research, follows a rough guideline: "Anything that is basically purely technical should be global. As you run toward business, you hit a gray zone. Anything close to actual customers—sales and marketing—or employee relations should be more local. Data resides locally, but it's linked to a global system."

In other words, globalize only as needed. To support worldwide design, Powers' teams have deployed 500 Silicon Graphics workstations, 90 Onyx Graphics computers, and two Convex C4 supercomputers. Ford says the approach will trim product development time from 36 months to 24 months and save $3 billion to $4 billion starting with the

1999 model year. Ford also now boasts worldwide purchasing and parts systems, which significantly contribute to the efficient linking of its global operations.

  a. How and why is Ford linking its global business operations?

  b. Do you agree with Bill Powers on what business operations should be globalized with IT? Why or why not?

Source: Adapted from Joseph Maglitta, "Global Titans," in "The Global 100," Supplement to *Computerworld,* May 1, 1995, pp. 14–18. Copyright 1995 by Computerworld, Inc., Framingham, MA 01701—Reprinted from *Computerworld.*

5. Nissan Motor Corp: Cultural Challenges of Global IT

"The American decision-making process tends to be very direct—maybe to the point of being aggressive or confrontational," says Evan Wride, director of information services at Nissan Motor Corp., a U.S. subsidiary of Japanese automotive manufacturer Nissan Motor Ltd. European and Asian corporate cultures will probably require a different approach, he says.

"In Japan, for example, they tend to want to build relationships and consensus over time, so things can take a little longer or feel as though they are moving more slowly," Wride says. While this may be frustrating for a U.S.-based CIO, Wride says, "it may also result in better long-term results since things are thought through more carefully."

At Nissan, Wride had to learn quickly that when a Japanese counterpart said yes or nodded, he wasn't "necessarily agreeing with me," he says. "In Japan, a yes means, 'I heard you.' Nothing more."

For this reason, Wride makes sure he gets everything in writing when working with an overseas superior or colleague. Currently developing a new warranty claims system for his U.S.-based operation, Wride is in frequent contact with Japan to ensure his system will coexist peacefully with the warranty system at the home office.

"We always make sure we are absolutely clear on what actions are being taken or not being taken," he says. Generally, this means firing off an electronic-mail message or, better yet, a fax or a formal memo containing a signature. "For some reason, receiving a personally signed document makes a big difference in Japan," he says.

  a. What cultural challenges in global IT management does Evan Wride experience at Nissan?

  b. What are some other cultural challenges you might experience as a manager in a global company? Give several examples.

Source: Adapted from Alice La Plante, "Life in the Foreign Lane," *Computerworld,* February 20, 1995, p. 117–21. Copyright 1995 by Computerworld, Inc., Framingham, MA 01701—Reprinted from *Computerworld.*

6. Chemical Banking Corp.: Outsourcing Global PC Support

In a cost-cutting move that industry analysts expect other large banks to quickly follow, $185 billion Chemical Banking Corp. in New York last week turned over support and service of its worldwide PC base to an outside company. Under the terms of a three-year, multimillion-dollar deal, Unisys Corp. will maintain some 30,000 multivendor PCs, servers, printers, and terminals previously supported under separate contracts Chemical Bank had with manufacturers and other providers. The bank has 30 strategic business units at more than 100 locations worldwide. The contract is significant because it is one of the few desktop outsourcing agreements that encompasses a company's global PC resources.

"Even more than cost savings, a constant level of service is among the specific benefits we expect to get from this," said John Irvine, a vice president in Chemical Bank's information technology and operations unit. PC life cycle costs, which include service and support costs, add up to about $40,000 per desktop over five years, according to the Gartner Group, Inc.

Chemical Bank's 30 individual business units will design their own support plans, choosing from Unisys Desktop Services that include the following:

- PC and LAN asset management.
- On-site and/or depot repairs.
- PC procurement, installation, and integration.
- Help desk support.
- End user training.

  a. Do you think Chemical's outsourcing of global PC support is a good business decision? Why or why not?

  b. Should global companies outsource other parts of the IS function as a global business/IT strategy? Explain.

Source: Adapted from Julia King, "Chemical Bank Outsources PC Support, Services to Unisys," *Computerworld,* May 15, 1995, p. 6. Copyright 1995 by Computerworld, Inc., Framingham, MA 01701—Reprinted from *Computerworld.*

Application Exercises

1. Acme Trucking Company

The Acme Trucking Company is planning to distribute a year-end bonus to their drivers. They want the bonuses they distribute to give an extra reward to drivers who have been with the firm for several years, since turnover has been a problem for Acme and drivers whose efficiency rating is particularly high. Thus a two-part bonus is planned, with a portion determined by years of service and a second component paid only to those drivers with a high efficiency rating.

The President of Acme has proposed the following criteria for bonuses:

Employees with less than five years of service	$500
Employees with more than five years of service	$900
Additional bonus for employees whose efficiency rating is 90 or above	$750

However, he wants to be able to see the effects of changes in any of the bonus parameters (years of service to earn the higher bonus, efficiency rating needed to earn the additional bonus, and the bonus dollar amounts) on the amount of bonus money paid. Then he will meet with the vice presidents of operations, finance, and human resource management to finalize plans for distributing the bonuses.

a. Prepare a spreadsheet based on the data shown in Figure 13.29, which will give the amount of bonus paid to each driver and the total cost of the bonus plan using the president's initial estimates, and produce a printout of your results.

b. Change the parameters of your spreadsheet as follows:
Years of service required for the higher
bonus: seven years
Efficiency rating required for added bonus: 95
Bonus levels:
Less than seven years $ 500
Seven years or more $1,100
Efficiency bonus $1,000
Get a printout showing the results of these changes.

c. Write a short memo recommending a bonus plan for Acme, with an explanation of why you are recommending it.

d. Write a short critique of the bonus planning process at Acme, with recommendations on how it could be improved.

2. ABC Shipping Company

ABC Shipping Company has decided to implement a new inventory control system by purchasing a software package from a vendor and adapting it. A three-member committee was selected to evaluate the packages supplied by competing vendors and select the best package. This committee has identified four vendors whose software seems to meet their minimum requirements. It has developed a set of criteria, shown below, to be used in evaluating the alternative packages. The committee has also agreed on a set of weights to be used based on the relative importance of these criteria. For instance, flexibility is considered three times as important as

efficiency for this system and thus is assigned 30 percent of the total evaluation, while efficiency counts for only 10 percent.

Criteria	Weight
Efficiency	10%
Flexibility	30%
Security	10%
Language	15%
Documentation	20%
Hardware	15%

After demonstrations by vendors, each of the three committee members evaluated the performance of each of the alternative software packages in each of the evaluation categories, giving a score from 1 to 10. The ratings compiled by the committee members for each vendor (A, B, C, etc.) in each category are shown below:

Category	John Jones				Jean Ellis				Sandra Flowers			
	A	B	C	D	A	B	C	D	A	B	C	D
Efficiency	7	8	5	9	6	9	7	8	5	7	6	9
Flexibility	8	6	8	7	9	7	8	8	7	7	9	8
Security	5	7	9	6	6	8	10	7	6	7	9	5
Language	8	9	7	8	8	10	7	10	7	8	7	9
Documentation	9	5	8	7	10	4	9	7	9	6	9	7
Hardware	9	7	9	5	9	6	9	6	10	6	8	5

An overall rating for each package is to be computed by averaging the three ratings for each category, multiplying that average by the weighing factor for that category, and finally adding these weighted scores for all categories to produce an overall score. For example, the overall rating for vendor A would be calculated as follows:

FIGURE 13.29
Drivers' years of service and efficiency ratings.

Driver's Name	Years of Service	Efficiency Rating
Barnes, Joseph	3	92
Coles, Joyce	6	97
Varney, Alex	9	82
Norris, Bill	5	90
Ferris, John	2	94
Lewis, Ann	4	88
Adams, Ansel	12	98
Yates, Billie	1	93
Mason, Berry	5	76
Davis, Jack	1	91
Evans, Alan	6	86
Macy, Doyle	16	89
Towns, Dawn	3	95
Smith, Dan	5	77

Category	Ratings			Average Rating	Weight	Weighted Score
	Jones	Ellis	Flowers			
Efficiency	7	6	5	6	.10	.60
Flexibility	8	9	7	8	.30	2.40
Security	5	6	6	5.67	.10	.57
Language	8	8	7	7.67	.15	1.15
Documentation	9	10	9	9.67	.20	1.93
Hardware	9	9	10	9.33	.15	1.40
Total weighted score						8.05

a. Create a spreadsheet to record these ratings and calculate the weighted score for each package. Your spreadsheet should have an output area that allows just the weighted scores, by category and total, to be printed. Get a printout of the entire spreadsheet and a separate printout showing just this output area.

b. Create a graph of your spreadsheet that will allow the weighted average scores for the packages on each evaluation category to be compared.

c. Briefly explain how the committee could use their weighted scores to select the best software package.

Review Quiz Answers

1. *14a*
2. *14b*
3. *1a*
4. *1b*
5. *16*
6. *16a*
7. *18*
8. *19*
9. *8*
10. *17*
11. *3*
12. *23*
13. *20*
14. *5*
15. *6*
16. *15*
17. *25*
18. *24*
19. *26*
20. *22*
21. *2*
22. *13*
23. *7*
24. *10*
25. *11*
26. *28*
27. *4*
28. *9*
29. *12a*
30. *12b*
31. *12c*
32. *12d*
33. *12e*
34. *27*

Selected References

1. Alavi, Maryam, and Greggry Young. "Information Technology in an International Enterprise: An Organizing Framework." In Palvia et al., *The Global Issues of Information Technology Management.* Harrisburg, PA: Idea Group Publishing, 1992.
2. Alter, Allan. "Profiles in Governance" in "A More Perfect Union," *Computerworld,* November 28, 1994.
3. Applegate, Lynda, and Joyce Elam. "New Information Systems Leaders: A Changing Role in a Changing World." *MIS Quarterly,* December 1992.
4. Bowles, Jerry. "Quality 2000: The Next Decade of Progress," *Fortune,* Special Advertising Supplement, October 3, 1994.
5. Boynton, Andrew; Robert Zmud; and Gerry Jacobs. "The Influence of IT Management Practice on IT Use in Large Organizations." *MIS Quarterly,* September 1994.
6. Bradley, Stephen; Jerry Hausman; and Richard L. Nolan. *Globalization, Technology, and Competition: The Fusion of Computers and Telecommunications in the 1900s.* Boston: Harvard Business School Press, 1993.
7. Carper, William. "Societal Impacts and Consequences of Transborder Data Flows." In Palvia et al., *The Global Issues of Information Technology Management.* Harrisburg, PA: Idea Group Publishing, 1992.
8. Cash, James, Jr.; Robert Ecrles; Nitin Nohria; and Richard Nolan. *Building the Information Age Organization.* Homewood, IL: Richard D. Irwin, 1994.
9. Clark, Thomas. "Corporate Systems Management: An Overview and Research Perspective." *Communications of the ACM,* February 1992.
10. Corett, Michael. "Outsourcing and the New IT Executive." *Information Systems Management,* Fall, 1994.
11. Couger, J. Daniel. "New Challenges in Motivating MIS Personnel." *Handbook of IS Management.* 3rd ed. Boston: Auerbach, 1991.
12. Davenport, Thomas. *Process Innovation: Reengineering Work through Information Technology.* Boston: Harvard Business School Press, 1993.
13. Drucker, Peter. "The Coming of the New Organization." *Harvard Business Review,* January–February 1988.
14. Frenzel, Carroll. *Management of Information Technology.* Boston: Boyd & Fraser, 1992.
15. Ives, Blake, and Sirkka Jarvenpaa. "Applications of Global Information Technology: Key Issues for Management." *MIS Quarterly,* March 1991.
16. Keen, Peter. *Shaping the Future: Business Design through Information Technology.* Boston: Harvard Business School, 1991.
17. King, William, and Vikram Sethi. "A Framework for Transnational Systems." In Palvia et al., *The Global Issues of Information Technology Management.* Harrisburg, PA: Idea Group Publishing, 1992.
18. King, William, and Vikram Sethi. "An Analysis of International Information Regimes." *International Information Systems,* January 1992.

19. Leavitt, H. J., and T. L. Whisler. "Management in the 1980s." *Harvard Business Review,* November–December 1985.

20. Levis, John, and Peter Von Schilling. "Lessons from Three Implementations: Knocking Down Barriers to Client/Server." *Information Systems Management,* Summer 1994.

21. Magletta, Joseph. "CIOs Warned to Get Their Shops in Shape." *Computerworld,* November 7, 1994.

22. Manheim, Marvin. "Global Information Technology: Issues and Strategic Opportunities." *International Information Systems,* January 1992.

23. McFarlan, F. Warren. "The Expert's Opinion." *Information Resources Management Journal,* Fall 1991.

24. Mische, Michael. "Transnational Architecture: A Reengineering Approach." *Information Systems Management,* Winter 1995.

25. Murray, Richard, and Richard Hardin, "The IT Organization of the Future." *Information Systems Management,* Fall 1991.

26. Niederman, Fred; James Brancheau; and James Weatherbe. "Information Systems Management Issues for the 1990s." *MIS Quarterly,* December 1991.

27. O'Brien, James, and James Morgan. "A Multidimensional Model of Information Resource Management." *Information Resources Management Journal,* Spring 1991.

28. Palvia, Shailendra; Prashant Palvia; and Ronald Zigli, eds. *The Global Issues of Information Technology Management.* Harrisburg, PA: Idea Group Publishing, 1992.

29. Roche, Edward. *Managing Information Technology in Multinational Corporations.* New York: Macmillan, 1992.

30. Rochester, Jack, and David Douglass. "Building a Global IT Infrastructure." *I/S Analyzer,* June 1991.

31. Sloan, Robert, and Hal Green. "Manufacturing Decision Support Architecture." *Information Systems Management,* Winter 1995.

32. Watson, Richard; Teck Hua Ho; and K.S. Raman. "Culture: A Fourth Dimension of Group Support Systems." *Communications of the ACM,* October 1994.

R E A L   W O R L D   C A S E

 Barclays Bank, Nestlé, and Elf Atochem: Global IT Challenges

Barclays Bank

It's time again for Ken Hamilton's monthly sit-down with his information systems peers at Barclays Bank PLC. Off he goes, briefcase in hand, down the hall and into the elevator. Once out the door, he fights through tangled New York traffic to Kennedy International Airport, where he boards a plane for the more than six-hour flight to London's Heathrow Airport. After getting through red tape in customs, he hails a cab that threads its way through crowded London streets to Barclays' headquarters. Voila—he's arrived.

Finally, a jet-lagged Hamilton—who is, in effect, the chief information officer of Barclays' North American operations—joins other senior Barclays IS managers from 75 countries around the globe for their monthly meeting of the minds. "We've found that physically being in the same room on a regular basis is absolutely essential for keeping out worldwide IS groups running smoothly," Hamilton says.

Hamilton makes sure he stays in close personal touch by his monthly visits to London. These trips are especially important because the monthly consortium of Barclays CIOs has no authority to set worldwide standards. That responsibility falls to a dedicated London-based architectural standards team that issues guidelines for Hamilton and his peers to follow. The monthly trek is thus a preemptive strike by Hamilton and the other scattered Barclays CIOs to make sure their in-the-trenches needs will not be put out of mind simply because they are out of sight.

"Being CIO of an American entity, even a multinational one, is completely different," says Hamilton, who formerly worked for a U.S. bank. It can be a bit of a jolt moving from a leadership to an "advisory" role, he says.

Nestlé

"Nestlé is . . . more of a federated association of 200 operating companies than a monolithic Procter & Gamble," said Jean Claude Dispaux, senior vice president of group information technology and logistics at Nestec, the technical assistance company of Nestlé, in Vevey, Switzerland. But three and a half years ago "there was a concern that we were not taking advantage of our strength, size, and value of our

Source: Adapted from Alice La Plante, "Life in the Foreign Lane," *Computerworld,* February 20, 1995, pp. 117–21, and Larry Marion, "Cross-Border Confections," *Computerworld Client/Server Journal,* June 1995, pp. 44–45.

products," Dispaux said. With 20,000 products made in 494 factories around the world, "some of these could profit from sharing inventory and manufacturing operations." The solution consisted of the following:

- Create strategic business units with global views of the enterprise.
- Standardize business processes.
- Populate the countries with similar client/server financial, commercial, supply chain, and even manufacturing systems to enable more sharing among the subsidiaries.

Nestlé is just about halfway into this six- to seven-year project. But the going has been rough. For one, the Nestle subsidiaries were accustomed to buying "whatever systems they wanted," said Jeri Bender, assistant vice president of management services/technology and standards at Nestec. But for transborder systems to work, standards had to be set in systems development methodology, operating systems, database management, and client applications.

A second problem is language support, particularly for double-byte character sets used for Japanese, Chinese, Thai, and Korean. Although the issue is thorny, Nestlé is on the right path. It is down to 50 general ledger systems, from more than 120 systems eight years ago. "By the turn of the century, we'll be down to three or four," Dispaux said.

Nestlé is also custom-developing strategic transborder applications. A current project is to enable one manufacturing site's system (say, Nestlé France) to automatically fulfill another Nestlé site's inventory needs based on inventory data, sales figures, and forecasts sent by the recipient's system.

Developing standards, determining business requirements, and testing versions of software means bringing together cross-cultural and crossfunctional teams, sometimes for months at a time. Nestlé has, however, given up on cross-cultural programming teams. "We found it was a Tower of Babel," Dispaux said. "We provide project management from here and subcontract most of the code-writing."

Elf Altochem

At Elf Atochem ETO is the Philadelphia-based subsidiary of the Paris-based pharmaceuticals giant, Bob Rubin, vice president of information services for Elf's North American operations, is not a fan of international E-mail, primarily because of language and cultural barriers.

"We find that 'delayed' communications such as E-mail don't work terribly well," he says. The dangers of hastily fired off E-mail messages are well-know within domestic organizations. There is always the danger of forgetting or

ignoring social niceties because of the impersonal nature of the medium. E-mail can also unintentionally offend the receiver because of the lack of accompanying visual clues indicating the sender's tone or attempts to humor. Language and cultural differences can dramatically exaggerate these problems.

If it's impossible to arrange a face-to-face or telephone meeting, Rubin says, "we prefer to use faxes. They tend to be more thought-out [and] more formally written and [to] contain less imprecise language."

Yet despite rosy predictions that technologies such as E-mail, groupware, and interactive videoconferencing will replace traditional face-to-face communication—a major expense and hassle when working for a foreign boss—U.S.-based CIOs flatly say this simply isn't the case. "Because of the cultural differences, you absolutely cannot replace the traveling, no matter how sophisticated your E-mail or videoconferencing network happens to be," says Bruce Hawthorne, president of Hawthorne Associates, Inc., a Peapack, New Jersey-based international IS consulting firm.

A case in point: Elf Atochem installed videoconferencing systems at its offices around the world with the idea of cutting down on worldwide travel. However, travel has remained fairly constant. But now it is supplemented with ever-greater frequency by "virtual" meetings, Rubin says. This enables Elf employees to work together much more closely.

The realtime aspect of videoconferencing means you can ask questions and get immediate answers when a language or cultural miscommunication arises, he says. Also, you get the visual clues missing from a telephone conversation or faxed memos.

Of course, this would also be the case if trying to collaborate with a domestic colleague who happens to be located in another state, he says. "But the fact that you are part of an international company increases the complexity because of the range of possible differences—cultural, linguistic, political," Rubin says.

CASE STUDY QUESTIONS

1. Do you agree that Ken Hamilton needs to travel and meet with his Barclays' CIO counterparts each month in London? Why or why not?

2. What business/IT strategies, application portfolio and technology platform choices, and systems development and cultural challenges do you recognize at Nestlé?

3. Why doesn't global E-mail work at ELF Altochem? What is the role of videoconferencing at ELF? Explain.

Managing IT: Planning and Implementing Change

CHAPTER OUTLINE

LEARNING OBJECTIVES

The purpose of this chapter is to give you an understanding of some of the key issues facing managers in the planning and implementation of business changes supported by information technology.

Section I of this chapter explores how companies can plan the strategic and operational use of information technology to support their business vision and the strategies and goals they establish for business success.

Section II explores the activities and management considerations in the implementation process for major changes in business processes, information technology and information systems.

After reading and studying this chapter, you should be able to:

1. Discuss the role of planning in organizations and the purpose of strategic, tactical, and operational planning for information systems.

2. Give examples of how planning methodologies and tools support the information systems planning process.

3. Identify the activities involved in the implementation process for organizational and technological change, and give examples of some of the major management techniques involved.

4. Discuss how end user resistance to changes in business processes or information technology can be minimized by end user involvement in systems development and implementation.

5. Describe several evaluation factors that should be considered in evaluating the acquisition of hardware, software, and IS services.

6. Identify the activities involved in the implementation of new information systems.

SECTION I
Planning for Business Change with IT

Introduction

Is planning important for the successful management of information technology? Listen to what this international consultant has to say:

> Betting on new IT innovations can mean betting the future of the company. Leading-edge firms are sometimes said to be on the "bleeding edge." Almost any business executive is aware of disastrous projects that had to be written off, often after large cost overruns, because the promised new system simply did not work [12].

So effective planning of investments in information technology is a key ingredient in avoiding disaster and achieving strategic business success with IT. Now let's look at an example of what happens when a large organization fails to properly plan its use of information technology.

The U.S. Department of State

The U.S. Department of State has been struggling with deficiencies in its financial systems for more than a decade. Yet, it is not on a course likely to solve those problems anytime soon. This is because efforts to correct the problems are hampered by inadequate planning and management. That is the central conclusion of a recent report by the U.S. General Accounting Office (GAO), the audit and investigative arm of the U.S. Congress. Planning problems cited include the following:

- The lack of an agencywide information strategy, no single person to oversee financial systems, and no documentation describing an anticipated new financial management structure.
- An inability to produce auditable financial statements of its $5 billion annual expenditures.
- Multiple, nonintegrated financial systems, with estimates ranging from 10 to 76 such systems.
- Five major systems plans, none of which addresses agencywide needs or attempts to tie together ongoing systems development efforts [2].

What the Department of State needs is strategic business and information systems planning. Without it, this agency will continue to fumble along with unauditable accounting statements, unintegrated financial systems, an uncoordinated planning effort, and no coherent information technology strategy. That's why success in the business use of information technology requires information systems planning. See Figure 14.1.

Organizational Planning

Planning is deciding what to do before you do it. Most of us would agree planning is an important ingredient of success. If you spend time and effort thinking about the best way to reach a goal before you begin to reach for it, you are planning, and your chances of accomplishing your goal should be enhanced. That's why organizations and their managers plan. They go through an **organizational planning** process of (1) evaluating what they have accomplished and the resources have acquired, (2) analyzing their environment, (3) anticipating future developments, (4) deciding on what goals they want to achieve, and (5) deciding what actions to take to achieve their goals.

The result of this planning process is called a **plan**, which formally articulates

Seth Resnick/Liaison International.

FIGURE 14.1
Strategic business planning is a vital ingredient for the successful use of information technology.

FIGURE 14.2
The organizational planning process. Note how implementation and control methods provide feedback for the planning process.

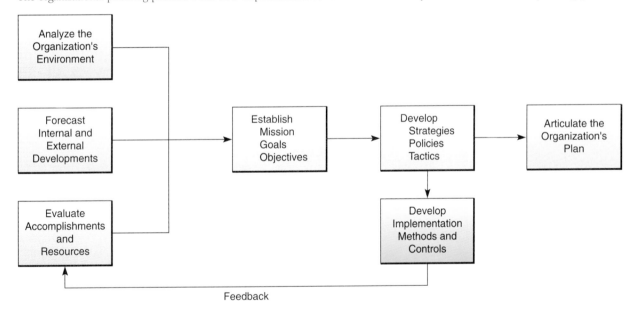

the actions we feel are necessary to achieve our goals. Thus, a plan is an action state-ment. Plans lead to actions, actions produce results, and part of planning is learning from results. That's why we said in Chapter 10 that planning is one of the functions of management. In this context, the planning process should be followed by imple-mentation, which should be followed by control measures, which feedback for plan-ning. That's why implementation and control of IT are the subjects of the next section and chapter. Figure 14.2 illustrates the organizational planning process.

Planning Terminology

Let's review briefly some of the terms used in the organizational planning process. A **mission** is an organization's "reason for being." It is a statement of the basic purpose or purposes for which the organization exists. For example, the mission of a utility company could be: "To supply energy to consumers." **Goals** are broad statements of the ends the organization intends to accomplish in order to fulfill its mission. **Objectives** are more specific, measurable elements of a goal. For example, the utility company might have increased profitability and energy utilization as goals, measured by objectives such as specific increases in earnings per share and kilowatt hours used.

Strategies are general approaches that show how goals should be achieved, and **tactics** are more specific guides to actions that would implement strategies. For example, a company strategy of "becoming the low-cost producer in its industry" would probably require a tactic such as increasing investments in automation. Policies are general guidelines that direct and constrain decision making within an organization. For example, many organizations have a policy of "promoting from within" that guides managers in filling job openings that occur. Policies are implemented by **rules** and **procedures,** which are more specific statements that direct decision making. For example, procedures to follow in hiring employees, and rules protecting employee job rights, would help implement a policy of promoting from within an organization.

Types of Planning

Planning is discussed, typically, in terms of the **level** of planning (strategic, tactical, and operational) and the planning time frame. **Strategic planning** deals with the development of an organization's mission, goals, strategies, and policies. Corporations may call this *strategic* business planning, and begin the process by developing a **business vision.** Organizations may use a variety of techniques, including *mental mapping,* as shown in Figure 14.3, and by asking and answering questions such as those shown in Figure 14.4 [24]. **Tactical planning** involves the design of tactics, the setting of objectives, and the development of procedures, rules, schedules, and budgets. **Operational planning** is planning done on a short-term basis to implement and control day-to-day operations. Typical examples are project planning and production scheduling.

Long-range planning usually involves looking three to five years (or more) into the future. However, many organizations have a planning process that reviews and modifies their long-range plans on a regular basis, such as six months to a year. **Short-range planning** can range from daily, weekly, or monthly planning to a one-year or two-year time frame. Typical examples are the development of financial and operating budgets, production scheduling, and planning for the development and implementation of projects. All operational planning and much tactical planning are done on a short-range basis. Most strategic planning and some tactical planning are done using a medium- to long-range planning horizon. However, if unforeseen developments with major strategic implications occur, an organization would use strategic planning methods within a short time frame in order to confront a crisis.

The Role of Information Systems Planning

Information systems planning is an important component of organizational planning. This text has emphasized how information technology can play a vital role in the efficiency of a company's operations, the effectiveness of managerial decision making, and the success of an organization's strategic initiatives. Therefore, managing IT requires a planning process that is part of the strategic, tactical, and operational planning of the organization. Figure 14.5 illustrates how information systems

FIGURE 14.3

Creating a business/IT vision can be helped by creativity techniques such as this mental mapping of vision relationships.

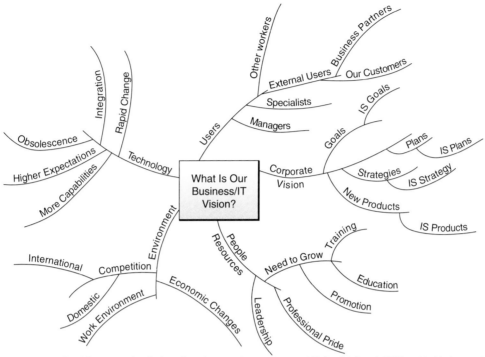

What is happening in our industry and around its edges?
- Where are the new sources of innovation and competitive advantage?
- Where does "service" give an edge?
- What are the leaders doing and why?
- What does all this mean for the basic direction and priorities of our business?

What makes us special? What must we do to remain so?
- What is the core of our business?
- How do we maintain differentiation?
- Why will customers give us their loyalty or give it to others?

Who is our competition?
- Who is our competition now?
- Who will our competition be five years from now?
- What caused the change?
- What pressures does this create for us?
- What opportunities does it open up for us?

What style of organization do we want to be?
- What is our culture and how do we keep it vital and effective?
- How do we want our customers and competitors to *see* us?
- What makes it easy to work here and what makes it hard?
- What do we mean by *productivity* and how would we recognize it if we saw it?

How can we run our business better?
- Should we improve coordination and responsiveness and combine decentralization with centralization?
- Should we eliminate delays in getting needed information?
- Should we speed up decision making?
- Should we eliminate such problems as service delays, reaching customers, or answering queries?

FIGURE 14.4

How to gain a business vision. These are questions that organizations must ask and answer about themselves.

FIGURE 14.5

Strategic planning uses a business vision and business drivers to create an IT architecture and tactical IS plans for the business use of information technology.

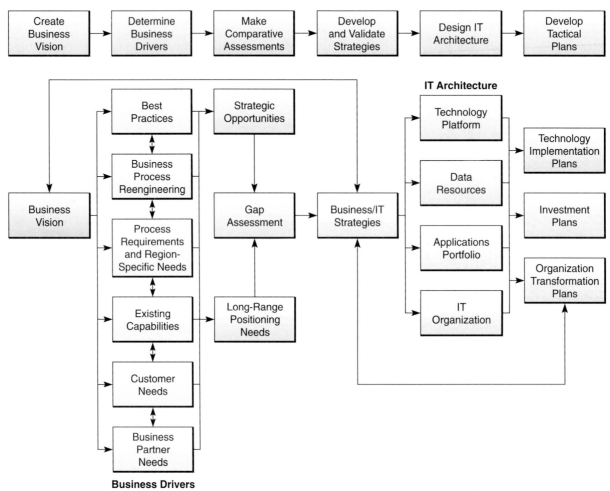

Source: Adapted and reprinted from Michael Mische, "Transnational Architecture: A Reengineering Approach," *Information Systems Management* (New York: Auerbach Publications), Winter 1995, © 1995 Warren, Gorham & Lamont. Used with permission.

planning fits into an organization's planning process. It emphasizes the activities and outputs of strategic planning and the role of the business vision, business drivers, and the IT architecture in the IT planning processes.

Strategic Information Systems Planning

Companies do strategic information systems planning, as illustrated in Figure 14.5, with four main objectives in mind:

- **Business alignment.** Aligning investment in information technology with a company's business vision and strategic business goals.
- **Competitive advantage.** Exploiting information technology to create innovative and strategic business information systems for competitive advantage.

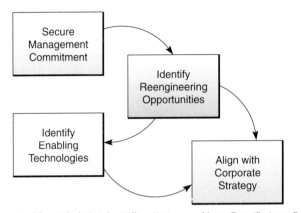

Source: Adapted and reprinted from Subashish Guha, William Kettinger, and James Teng, "Businesss Process Reengineering: Building a Comprehensive Methodology," *Information Systems Management* (New York: Auerbach Publications), Summer 1993. © 1993 Warren, Gorham & Lamont. Used with permission.

FIGURE 14.6
Reengineering opportunities must be aligned with a company's business strategies and earn a commitment from top management before BPR can begin.

- **Resource management.** Developing plans for the efficient and effective management of a company's information system resources, including IS personnel, hardware, software, data, and network resources.
- **Technology architecture.** Developing technology policies and designing an information technology architecture for the organization [7].

The strategic IS planning process illustrated in Figure 14.5 is *business driven*, not *technology driven*. Notice that a business vision and business drivers, such as business process reengineering to achieve the best industry practices and the needs of customers and business partners, are what drive the planning process. Business/IT strategies can then be developed based on the strategic opportunities that are revealed. Only then can the IT architecture for the company be designed. For example, Figure 14.6 shows that reengineering opportunities must first be aligned with a company's business strategies and earn a commitment from top management before business process reengineering can begin.

Figure 14.5 also shows that the **IT architecture** that is created by the strategic-planning process is a conceptual design, or *blueprint*, that includes the following major components:

The Information Technology Architecture

- **Technology platform.** Computer systems, system and application software, and telecommunications networks provide a computing and communications infrastructure, or *platform*, that supports the use of information technology in the business.
- **Data resources.** Many types of operational and specialized databases, including data warehouses, analytical databases, and external data banks (as discussed in Chapter 7) store and provide data and information for business processes and managerial decision support.
- **Applications portfolio.** Business applications of information technology are designed as a diversified *portfolio* of information systems that support key business functions as well as crossfunctional business processes. In addition, an applications portfolio should include support for interorganizational

business linkages, managerial decision making, end user computing and collaboration, and strategic initiatives for competitive advantage.

- **IT organization.** The organizational structure of the IS function within a company, and the distribution of IS specialists among corporate headquarters and business units can be designed or redesigned to meet the changing strategies of a business. The form of the IT organization depends on the managerial philosophy, business vision, and business/IT strategies formulated during the strategic planning process.

Tactical and Operational Planning

Tactical information systems planning builds on the business/IT strategies developed in the strategic IS planning stages. Tactical planning is the last stage of the planning process shown in Figure 14.5. Tactical IS planning produces project proposals for the development of new or improved information systems that implement the IT architecture created during strategic IS planning. These projects are then evaluated, ranked, and fitted into a multiyear development plan. Finally, a resource allocation plan is developed to specify the IS resources, financial commitments, and organizational changes needed to implement the strategic IT development plan of the company.

Operational information systems planning involves detailed planning for the accomplishment of new information systems development projects, including the preparation of operating budgets. Annual operating budgets specify the allocation of financial and other resources needed to support the organization's information services operations and systems development and maintenance activities. This also holds true for end user departments and other work groups that do a lot of their own information processing and application development.

Project planning is an important operational planning function. It involves the development of plans, procedures, and schedules for an information systems development project. Such planning is an important part of a **project management** effort that plans and controls the implementation of systems development projects. This is necessary if a project is to be completed on time and within its proposed budget and if it is to meet its design objectives.

Several techniques of project management produce charts to help plan and control projects. One is the Gantt chart, which specifies the times allowed for the various activities required in information systems development. Another is produced by network methodologies such as CPM (critical path method) and the PERT system (Program Evaluation and Review Technique), which develops a network diagram of required activities. Network methodologies view a project as a network of distinct tasks and milestones and specify the amount of time budgeted for the completion of each task. Figure 14.7 is an example of a Gantt chart prepared by a project management software package.

S.C. Johnson & Son, Inc.

S.C. Johnson & Son, more commonly known as Johnson Wax, emphasizes a *portfolio management* approach in its use of IS planning [15]. Johnson divides all IT applications into six portfolios according to the business function they support. These include sales, marketing, distribution, finance, manufacturing, and logistics. Each portfolio consists of a mix of computer-based applications that keep a particular business function operating successfully. An IS specialist serves as the manager of each application portfolio. Portfolio managers are given annual goals for the portfolio, which usually require them to lower the portfolio's fixed costs and come up with innovative IT solutions.

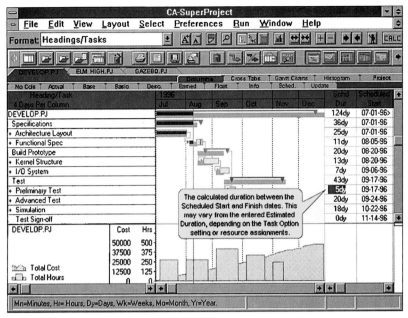

Courtesy of Computer Associates, Inc.

FIGURE 14.7
A Gantt chart for a business project produced by a project management package.

The general managers of each Johnson business unit meet regularly with the IS staff to define major goals for improvements in business processes in their units. For example, they might want a 15 percent reduction in the cost of closing a sale, or a 5 percent reduction in inventory levels. Then an information technology team headed by a portfolio manager develops an IT strategy to meet these business goals. Finally, the IT team proposes system development projects to create new systems or enhance present systems to meet the business unit's goals.

Information Systems Planning Methodologies

Business organizations may use a formal information systems **planning methodology** to ensure that all important planning activities and products are accomplished and produced. This methodology helps an organization translate its strategic goals into a detailed information systems development plan to achieve those goals. Many formal planning methodologies exist. For example, two popular methodologies are Business Systems Planning (BSP) and critical success factors (CSF). We will briefly discuss these and other methods in order to give you an idea of how they help managers do strategic and tactical information systems planning.

Business Systems Planning

Business Systems Planning (BSP) was first developed by IBM. It is a structured approach that assists an organization in developing information systems plans to satisfy its short- and long-term information requirements. One of the basic premises of BSP methodology is that an organization's information systems should be planned from the top down and implemented piece-by-piece from the bottom up. Figure 14.8 illustrates this view of the BSP approach.

Top-down planning requires that a group of top executives lay out the strategic mission and objectives of the organization. Then managers throughout the organization propose how these objectives should be implemented in the basic functions

FIGURE 14.8
A Business Systems Planning approach. Note how BSP accomplishes top-down planning and bottom-up implementation.

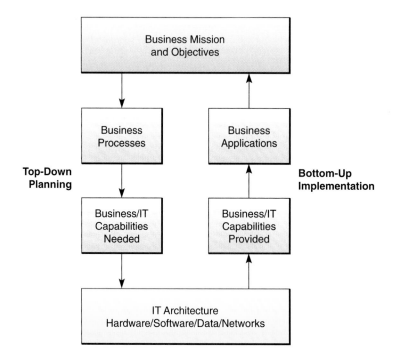

(marketing, manufacturing, etc.) and processes (order entry, shipping, receiving, etc.) of the business. Next, managers and IS specialists suggest the IT capabilities that might be needed to support these basic processes. Finally, an **IT architecture** is developed that designs the technology platform (computer systems, software, and networks) and the organizational databases that can provide the capabilities needed by the business.

Bottom-up implementation involves application development activities that are performed by end users and information systems professionals. Their goal is to develop specific business applications (such as electronic data interchange) that rely on a technology platform whose design was determined by the hardware, software, databases, and networks of the IT architecture. Each application should therefore serve a business function that supports the mission and objectives of the organization.

Critical Success Factors

The **critical success factors** (CSF) approach is another important methodology for information systems planning. It can be used by itself or incorporated into other planning methodologies as a key component of their planning process. This approach was developed by John Rockart and others who were dissatisfied with the lack of emphasis on the key information needs of managers in other information systems planning methodologies [15]. Its major premise is that the information requirements of an organization should be determined by its **critical success factors**, a small number of key factors that executives consider critical to the success of the enterprise. These are key areas where successful performance will ensure the success of the organization and the attainment of its goals. Thus, information systems are designed to continually measure performance in each CSF and report this informa-

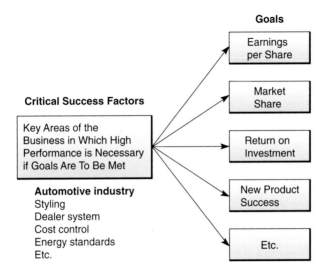

Goals

FIGURE 14.9
Examples of goals versus critical success factors. Success in a firm's CSFs should ensure the attainment of its organizational goals.

tion to management. Examples of goals and critical success factors are shown in Figure 14.9.

In the CSF approach to information systems planning, interviews are held with groups of managers to determine their individual critical success factors and their view of the CSFs for the organization. Managers are asked to identify their goals and the critical success factors that would ensure the attainment of those goals. This includes consideration of the competitive strategies of the firm, its position in the industry, and its economic and political environment. Managers are asked to identify a limited number of key areas (about 5 to 10) where "things have to go right," "failure would hurt most," or they would most want information about if they had been gone for a while. These are their critical success factors.

For example, managers in the supermarket industry may consider pricing, product mix, inventory turnover, and sales promotions as critical success factors. Performance in these areas could be measured by gross margin and net margin percentages, product shelf space comparisons, inventory turnover ratios, and tracking sales results with the timing and amount of sale promotions. Finally, critical success factors can be used to help develop an IT architecture and IS application portfolio. This results in the development of project priorities and design criteria for the information systems needed by the organization.

Planning for competitive advantage is especially important in today's competitive arena. So strategic IS planning includes an analysis of the potential the firm has for using information technology for competitive advantage. In Chapter 11, we introduced a model of *competitive forces* (competitors, customers, suppliers, new entrants, and substitutes) and *competitive strategies* (cost leadership, differentiation, growth, innovation, and alliances), as well as a *value chain* model of basic business activities. These models can be used in the strategic planning process to help generate ideas for the strategic use of IT. Also popular in strategic IS planning is the use of a **strategic opportunities matrix,** as illustrated in Figure 14.10. SWOT analysis (strengths, weaknesses, opportunities, and threats) is used to evaluate the impact that each

Planning for Competitive Advantage

FIGURE 14.10
A strategic opportunities matrix.
This matrix helps planners iden-
tify strategic uses of IT.

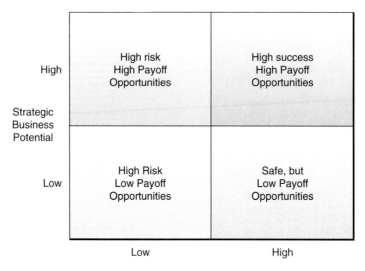

Source: Adapted and reprinted by permission of Harvard Business School Press from *Shaping the Future: Business Design through Information Technology* by Peter G. W. Keen. Boston: 1993, p. 44. Copyright © 1993 by Peter G. W. Keen.

possible strategic opportunity can have on the business and its use of information technology [8, 28].

Managers must ask and answer many key questions to uncover and evaluate potential business/IT opportunities for competitive advantage [12]. Examples include:

- How might a business or technological development or trend represent a competitive opportunity?
- Does it change the core business drivers of our company? Our industry?
- What are the main risks associated with this opportunity: market risk, or technical, implementation, financial, regulatory, or organizational risk?
- Are there any indicators that this combination of business and technology will become a competitive necessity within a few years?
- Is the necessary IT platform in place? Do any competitors have an equivalent platform? Will the innovation require major changes to our IT platform? What is the required lead time to make such changes?
- Can this opportunity be pursued alone, or should we look for business part-ners? Should they be industry partners or partners from other industries (e.g., suppliers, customers).

Reach and Range Analysis

Figure 14.11 illustrates a useful planning framework for determining how to posi-tion the information technology capabilities of an organization [12]. **Reach** refers to the types of business stakeholders and locations that can be connected by telecom-munications network links to a firm's hardware, software, network, and database resources—that is, its IT *platform or base.* **Range** refers to the types of information and information processing that can be shared through computers and telecommu-nications networks.

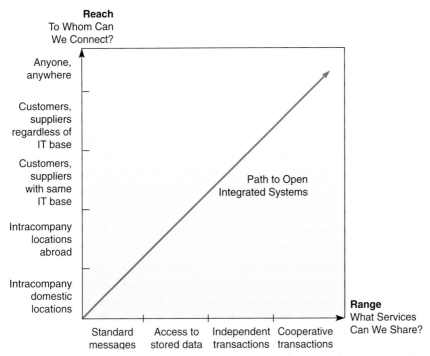

Source: Adapted and reprinted by permission of Harvard Business School Press from *Shaping the Future: Business Design through Information Technology* by Peter G. W. Keen. Boston: 1993, p. 40. Copyright © 1993 by Peter G. W. Keen.

FIGURE 14.11
A reach and range planning framework. Information technology can help a business develop open integrated systems to build strategic relationships among its internal locations and external stakeholders.

Many companies are determined to reach anyone, anywhere, with a wide range of products and services. For example, companies as diverse as McDonald's and Coca-Cola or Microsoft and Citibank are determined to use information technology to pursue customers anytime, anywhere they are. They are counting on global IT networks to enable them to manage the production and delivery of a variety of products and services to the consumers of the world.

Figure 14.10 also emphasizes that one of the most important information technology strategies of many organizations is to use telecommunications and other information technologies to develop *open integrated* information systems. That is, these organizations are committed to developing an open IT architecture whose networks and resources can be easily accessed by a variety of internal and external computer systems, software packages, and networks. This allows them to provide an integrated selection of business applications to service their internal needs and those of their present and future stakeholders. Planning and implementing open, integrated business systems through information technology has thus become a strategic business goal for many companies.

> Planning and budgeting processes are notorious for their rigidity and irrelevance to management action. Rigid adherence to a process of rapid or efficient completion may only make the process less relevant to the true management agenda [6].

The Scenario Approach

Managers and planners continually try different approaches to make planning easier, more accurate, and more relevant to the dynamic, real world of business. Thus, the scenario approach to IS planning is gaining in popularity, as are computer-assisted planning techniques we will discuss shortly.

In the **scenario approach**, managers and planners create scenarios of what a business will be like three to five years or more into the future, and the role that information technology can or will play in those future scenarios. Alternative scenarios are created based on combining a variety of developments, trends, and environmental factors, including political, social, business, and technological changes that might happen [21].

Royal Dutch Shell

For example, Royal Dutch Shell shifted their planning process over 20 years ago from the idea that planning involves "producing a documented view of the future" to a scenario approach where planning involves "designing scenarios so managers would question their own model of reality and change it when necessary." Royal Dutch Shell believes this change to scenario-based planning was rewarded by their successful actions during the oil market upheavals of the 1970s and 1980s [6].

Denny's, Inc.

Denny's uses scenario-based planning to develop five-year plans for the business use of information technology. Department managers gather off-site for several days to create business and IS scenarios. They assess the success of scenarios from the past, to help them anticipate what the company might be like five years into the future. The managers create several most-likely business scenarios, and develop a high-level IS plan for the information technology needed to support each one. Then the IS director analyzes these IS plans to identify the common IT resources required by each one. The managers then reconvene to discuss these findings, and decide on one IS plan for Denny's [21].

Computer-Aided Planning Tools

The planning process can be quite difficult and time-consuming. That's what gives organizations the "we don't have time to plan" excuse for not using a formal planning process. So vendors have developed **computer-aided planning** (CAP) tools to help ease the burden of planning. For example, PC Prism is a CAP package from Intersolv Corporation, the makers of the Excelerator CASE tool. PC Prism is a menu-driven software package that helps managerial end users develop strategic, tactical, and operational information systems plans. It provides generic planning features that can support other planning methodologies such as the BSP and CSF methodologies. PC Prism is used to define a planning environment (strategic, tactical, etc.) and planning structures such as critical success factors, organizational units, business processes, data structures, and so on. Then it is used to identify and analyze relationships between planning structures.

This results in an *enterprise model* of the business, as shown in Figure 14.12. An enterprise model defines the structures and relationships of business processes (process models) and data elements (data models), as well as other planning structures. Once the enterprise model is developed, managers and planners can analyze the relationships between planning structures. For example, the relationships between a specific business process, such as "update inventory on hand," and a specific data element, such as "quantity of item on hand," can be explored. Also, a manager can create what-if scenarios to analyze the effects of changes to selected structures and relationships. This type of analysis helps planners recognize what changes need to be made to develop information systems plans and systems development projects that support the organization's critical success factors.

Enterprise Model

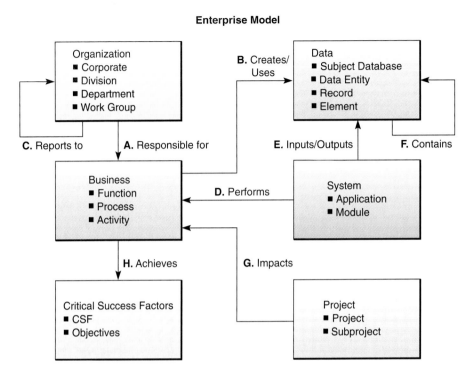

FIGURE 14.12
An enterprise model diagram developed using a computer-aided planning package.

R E A L   W O R L D   C A S E

Dunlop Tire Corp.: Strategic IS Planning

Fragmented, outdated information systems were once the bane of Dunlop Tire's existence. The company was rapidly losing ground to competitors which could process orders faster and run their operations at lower cost. To respond more quickly and efficiently to the demands of a competitive marketplace, Dunlop developed an ambitious IS plan based on open systems and a clear strategic direction. "Having the right architecture design strategy is essential for us to meet our goals," says Dennis Courtney, Dunlop's director of information systems. In Dunlop's case, that approach features GUI application software, Oracle database management systems, and Sun servers as the primary technology platform.

Central to Dunlop's strategy is separating data and applications from each other. "That's key to our goal of getting information to whoever needs it," says Courtney. The strategy calls for each of Dunlop's three main locations to have two Sun SPARCserver 1000s—one for running their Oracle database, the other for running core business applications. Not only is data access improved, system performance is maximized.

Other applications are run on the dozen or so SPARCserver 10s and 20s that Courtney reserves for that purpose. "A modular approach to CPU deployment is more flexible and easier to manage," says Courtney. "And the Sun servers have yet to go down."

Dunlop has made a strategic decision to wherever possible become a software package-oriented shop, buying applications from outside vendors that conform to open standards and fit into Dunlop's strategic framework. "Instead of coders and legacy systems specialists, we're becoming process analysts and integrators," says Courtney.

This decision has a two-fold benefit. First, it allows Dunlop to satisfy application requirements without the burdensome expense of developing them from the ground up. Second, it allows the IS staff to get closer to their customers on the business side, instead of burying themselves in extended programming projects.

Thus, IS staffers build strategic core competencies, rather than focusing on commodity skills easily purchased elsewhere. This strategy makes vendor selection critical. Dunlop has chosen Oracle Corp. as a strategic software partner. They not only provide their own financial, manufacturing, and analytical application packages but also have strong third-party vendor support. "With Oracle, we can add best-of-breed products from other vendors and integrate them with what we already have in place," says Courtney. Sun Microsystems is also a key technology partner in Dunlop's new approach. "Sun not only makes great hardware, they are an invaluable source of expertise for infrastructure planning and design," says Courtney.

With a centralized database architecture and a distributed network infrastructure, Dunlop is well positioned to support the type of crossfunctional operation that makes for a responsive, fast-moving business. At the same time, Dunlop has had to change its IS subculture. Courtney has built crossfunctional teams responsible for project design, rollout, and maintenance. "We put Unix people, network people, and support people together," says Courtney. "They're in self-directed teams that take full responsibility for results—no finger-pointing allowed."

The approach extends beyond the IS department to include Dunlop's strategic suppliers. "We have the Sun and Oracle people sit down with our own staff so we can work together on current and long-range issues," says Courtney. "As business partners, we share expertise and make strategic architectural decisions together."

CASE STUDY QUESTIONS

1. What strategic and tactical business/IS planning activities do you recognize at Dunlop Tire? Refer to Figure 14.5 to help you.

2. What components of an IT architecture are being implemented at Dunlop?

3. What role do Oracle Corp. and Sun Microsystems play in Dunlop's planning? Do you think this is a good idea? Why or why not?

Source: Adapted from "Dunlop Tire Races to an Open Future," in "The Client/Server Advantage," Special Advertising Supplement, *Computerworld*, February 20, 1995, p. 28. Copyright 1995 by Computerworld, Inc., Framingham, MA 01701—Reprinted from *Computerworld*.

SECTION II
Implementing Business Change with IT

Implementation is an important managerial responsibility. Implementation is doing what you planned to do. You can view implementation as a process that carries out the plans for changes in the business use of information technology developed in the planning process described in Section I.

Introduction

The implementation process can also be viewed as a major stage that follows the investigation, analysis, and design stages of the systems development process introduced in Chapter 3. Therefore, implementation is an important activity in the deployment of information technology to support the business changes planned by an organization and its end users.

> IT increasingly changes jobs, skill needs, work, and relationships. Technical change has become synonymous with organizational change. Such change can be complex, painful, and disruptive. The people side of IT is often more difficult to anticipate and manage smoothly than is the technological side [12].

Managing Organizational Change

So implementing changes in information technology, typically, is only part of a larger process of managing major changes in business processes, organizational structures, job assignments, and work relationships. Figure 14.13 illustrates some of the major managerial activities that organizations use to help manage business change. Notice that **change management** requires the involvement and commit-

FIGURE 14.13
Some of the major activities involved in organizational change management.

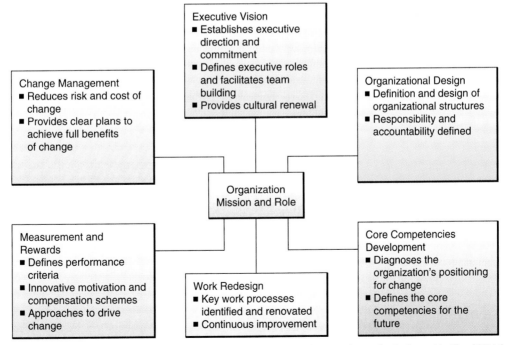

Source: Adapted and reprinted from Louis Fried and Richard Johnson, "Gaining the Technology Advantage: Planning for the Competitive Use of IT," *Information Systems Management* (New York: Auerbach Publications), Fall 1991. © 1991 Warren, Gorham & Lamont. Used with permission.

FIGURE 14.14
Reasons for user resistance to reengineering business processes.

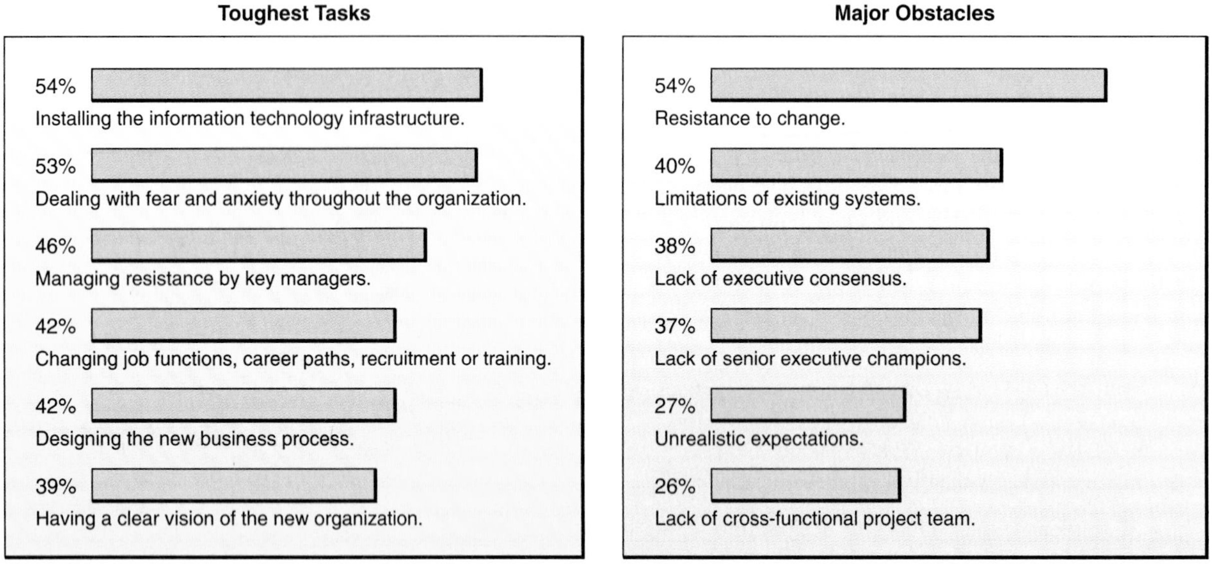

Source: Adapted from "Rocks in the Gears: Reengineering the Workplace," by Joseph Maglitta, Computerworld, 10/3/94, p. 96. Copyright 1994 by Computerworld, Inc., Framingham, MA 01701—Reprinted from *Computerworld.*

ment of top management and a formal process or organizational design. This supports changes in business and technology generated by the reengineering of business processes or other work redesign activities [20].

Human resource management is a major focus of other organizational change management activities shown in Figure 14.13. This includes activities such as developing innovative ways to measure, motivate, and reward performance. So is designing programs to recruit and train employees in the core competencies required in a changing workplace. Finally, change management involves analyzing and defining all changes facing the organization, and developing programs to reduce the risks and costs, and to maximize the benefits of change. For example, implementing a reengineered business process might involve developing a change *action plan,* assigning selected managers as *change sponsors,* developing employee *change teams,* and encouraging open communications and feedback about organizational changes. To summarize, change experts recommend:

- Involve as many people as possible in reengineering and other change programs.
- Make constant change part of the culture.
- Tell everyone as much as humanly possible about everything as often as possible, preferably in person.
- Make liberal use of financial incentives and recognition.
- Work within the company culture, not around it [16].

Implementing Information Technology

Any "new way of doing things" generates some resistance by the people affected. Thus, the reengineering of business processes, including the implementation of new computer-based work support technologies, can generate a significant amount of end user fear and reluctance to change. Figure 14.14 outlines many reasons for such

FIGURE 14.15

A technology implementation cycle. Technology implementation activities can minimize end user resistance to the changes brought on by new information technologies.

	Activity	Goal
1. **Preimplementation**	Gather data on workplace, personnel work, tasks, etc.	Determine planning alternatives, needed resources, and possible roadblocks
2. **Human design**	Study automated workplace and establish criteria for its human design	Eliminate deterrents and establish incentives for productivity, human physiology, and psychology
3. **Marketing**	Develop and implement a strategy for "selling" technical systems and the changes they cause	Introduce technology so that worker "buys" the system and "owns" the system
4. **Education**	Educate workers about the demands new technology will make on them and the benefits it will provide	Reduce worker stress concerning technology and increase confidence in the ability to use it productively
5. **Training**	Develop and implement a sequential, natural program of skill growth	Develop workers who are minimally computer competent and primed for additional computer skills evolution
6. **Documentation**	Compose and distribute documents that explain how the system works	Provide easy access to and effective assistance from reference materials so that workers can complete automated tasks
7. **Human communications**	Establish and maintain continuing means of communication with workers	Create opportunities for dialogue between workers and information technology, technicians, and management
8. **Postimplementation**	Compile evaluation of each phase into one document and review entire implementation process	Feed forward evaluation results to improve the next technology implementation

Source: Adapted from Computerizing the *Corporation: The Intimate Link Between People and Machines* by Vicki McConnell and Karl Koch (New York: Van Nostrand Reinhold, 1990), p. 100.

end user resistance, some of which we explore in a discussion concerning societal impacts of IT in Chapter 15. However, end user resistance can be minimized by formal **technology implementation** programs, which end user managers and IS consultants can develop to encourage user acceptance and productive use of reengineered business processes and new information technologies. So, one of the keys to solving problems of end user resistance is proper end user education and training, improved communications with IS professionals, and end user involvement in the development and implementation of new systems. See Figure 14.15.

Direct end user participation in systems development projects *before* a system is implemented is especially important in reducing the potential for end user resistance. This involvement helps ensure that end users "assume ownership" of a system, and that its design meets their needs. Systems that tend to inconvenience or frustrate their users cannot be effective systems, no matter how technically elegant they are and how efficiently they process data. Let's look at two examples.

FIGURE 14.16
Why systems development
projects succeed or fail.

Top five reasons for success:	Top five reasons for failure:
▪ User involvement.	▪ Lack of user input.
▪ Executive management support.	▪ Incomplete requirements and specifications.
▪ Clear statement of requirements.	▪ Changing requirements and specifications.
▪ Proper planning.	▪ Lack of executive support.
▪ Realistic expectations.	▪ Technological incompetence.

Source: Adapted from "Few IS Projects Come in on Time, on Budget," by Rosemary Cafasso, Computerworld, 12/12/94, p. 20. Copyright 1994 by Computerworld, Inc., Framingham, MA 01701—Reprinted from *Computerworld*.

Federal Express Corporation

Federal Express emphasizes the change management value of on-the-job training. Fed Ex has installed more than 1,000 interactive video workstations for training of their couriers and customer service personnel. The workstations enable rapid learning of new products and services as they are rolled out. When Fed Ex, for example, initiates international package delivery service to a new country, it uses the training systems to acquaint employees with customs requirements for the country. Fed Ex views the systems as a strategic advantage and has integrated them into many of its human resource policies. For example, under its policy of learning-based compensation, when a Federal Express employee completes a training module, the workstation automatically triggers an increase in the employee's compensation level in the payroll database [6].

TRW Information Services

TRW Information Services encourages employee "buy-in" for its reengineering projects by making reengineering efforts part of everyone's job. Over 200 employees are part of a reengineering team, which includes the executive vice president and general manager. Employee motivation is kept high through financial and travel bonuses. TRW publishes a special biweekly newsletter and provides a telephone hot line to provide information on reengineering projects. These information sources help reduce anxiety by employees over rumors they might hear about possible job cuts [16].

Implementing Information Systems

The **implementation process** for newly designed information systems, involves a variety of acquisition, testing, documentation, installation, and conversion activities. It also involves the training of end users in the operation and use of the new information system. Thus, implementation is a vital step in ensuring the success of new systems. Even a well-designed system can fail if it is not properly implemented. See Figure 14.16. Figure 14.17 illustrates the major activities of the implementation process for new systems. In this section, we will concentrate on the acquisition and installation of IS resources and other managerial implementation issues.

Acquiring Hardware, Software, and Services

Acquiring hardware, software, and external IS services is a major implementation activity. These resources can be acquired from many sources in the **computer industry**. For example, Figure 14.18 lists the top 10 mainframe, midrange, microcomputer, software, services, and data communications companies in 1995. Of course, there are many other firms in the computer industry that supply hardware, software, and services. For example, you can buy microcomputer hardware and software from

FIGURE 14.17

An overview of the implementation process. Implementation activities are needed to transform a newly developed information system into an operational system for end users.

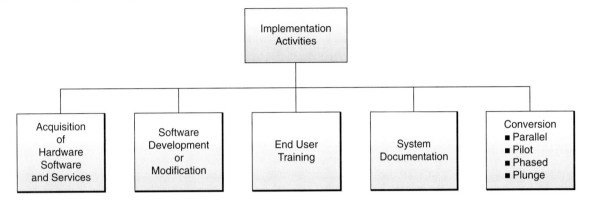

FIGURE 14.18

Major companies in the computer industry that provide mainframes, midrange computers, microcomputers, software, services, and data communications products.

Microcomputer Systems			Midrange Systems			Mainframe Systems		
Rank	Company	Revenues ($ millions)	Rank	Company	Revenues ($ millions)	Rank	Company	Revenues ($ millions)
1	Compaq	9,018.8	1	IBM	5,764.7	1	IBM	5,956.8
2	IBM	8,775.1	2	AT&T GIS	5,042.0	2	Unisys	1,243.2
3	Apple	7,161.8	3	Hewlett-Packard	2,688.0	3	Amdahl	819.3
4	Dell	2,870.0	4	Tandem	1,538.9	4	Cray	571.4
5	Gateway 2000	2,700.0	5	Digital	1,174.5	5	Intel	460.8
6	Packard Bell	2,600.0	6	Motorola	616.8	6	Silicon Graphics	163.1
7	AST Research	2,311.0	7	Data General	536.5	7	Convex	76.4
8	AT&T GIS	1,718.9	8	Sun Microsystems	534.8	8	Digital	40.5
9	Digital	1,350.0	9	Unisys	497.3	9	Control Data	5.2
10	Hewlett-Packard	1,152.0	10	Apple	477.5			

Computer Software			IS Services			Data Communications		
Rank	Company	Revenues ($ millions)	Rank	Company	Revenues ($millions)	Rank	Company	Revenues ($millions)
1	IBM	11,529.4	1	IBM	16,653.5	1	IBM	3,586.9
2	Microsoft	4,464.0	2	EDS	10,052.4	2	AT&T	2,979.3
3	Computer Associates	2,454.7	3	Digital	6,345.0	3	Cisco	1,500.0
4	Novell	1,918.1	4	Hewlett-Packard	4,608.0	4	Motorola	1,162.4
5	Oracle	1,901.6	5	Unisys	3,108.0	5	Bay Networks	1,080.0
6	Lockheed Martin	1,242.0	6	Computer Sciences	3,085.0	6	Hewlett-Packard	960.0
7	Digital	1,215.0	7	KPMG Peat Marwick	2,300.0	7	3Com	912.3
8	AT&T	916.7	8	Andersen Consulting	2,206.8	8	Cabletron	729.6
9	Lotus	873.6	9	Entrex	1,300.0	9	Newbridge	672.0
10	Unisys	683.8	10	Deloitte & Touche	1,041.0	10	Memorex Telex	457.5

Source: Adapted from "The Datamation 100," Datamation, June 1, 1995, pp. 47–65.

mail-order firms like Dell and Gateway, or from retail chains like Computerland and MicroAge, while thousands of small consulting firms provide a broad range of IS services.

Hardware and Software Suppliers

The major computer manufacturers shown in Figure 14.18 produce many types of computer systems, as well as peripheral equipment and software. Of course, you can buy software packages directly from large software developers such as Microsoft and Lotus Development, or through computer retailers and mail-order companies. Many larger business and professional organizations, educational institutions, and government agencies have employee purchase plans that let you buy computer hardware and software at substantial discounts. These *corporate buying* plans are arranged through negotiations with hardware manufacturers and software companies.

Original equipment manufacturers (OEMs) produce and sell computers by assembling components produced by other hardware suppliers. Plug-compatible manufacturers (PCMs) manufacture computer mainframes and peripheral devices that are specifically designed to be compatible (by just "plugging in") with the computers made by IBM, Digital Equipment Corporation, and others. Value-added resellers (VARs) specialize in providing industry-specific hardware and software from selected manufacturers.

Computer retailers and mail-order firms sell microcomputers and peripherals to individuals and small businesses, and even many large corporate accounts. They are an important source of hardware, software, and services for microcomputer systems. Retail computer stores include thousands of independent retailers, as well as national chains such as Computerland, MicroAge, and JWP Businessland, and "superstore" chains like CompuAdd, CompUSA, and Computer City SuperCenters. Mail-order firms include Dell, Gateway, and Zeos, to name a few.

Suppliers of IS Services

The major sources of **external information systems services** are computer manufacturers, computer retailers, computer service centers, time-sharing companies, systems integrators, and independent consultants. These and other types of firms in the computer industry offer a variety of services. For example, computer service centers (or service bureaus) provide off-premises computer processing of customer jobs, and time-sharing companies provide realtime mainframe computing via wide area networks to subscribers. Systems integrators take over complete responsibility for an organization's computer facilities when an organization outsources its computer operations. They may also assume responsibility for developing and implementing large systems development projects that involve many vendors and subcontractors. Many other services are available to end users, including computer rentals, systems design services, contract programming, consulting, education, and hardware maintenance.

Evaluating Hardware, Software, and Services

How do computer-using organizations evaluate and select hardware and software? Typically, they require suppliers to present bids and proposals based on system specifications developed during the design stage of systems development. Minimum acceptable physical and performance characteristics for all hardware and software requirements are established. Most large business firms and all government agencies formalize these requirements by listing them in a document called an RFP (request for proposal) or RFQ (request for quotation). The RFP or RFQ is then sent to appropriate vendors, who use it as the basis for preparing a proposed purchase agreement. See Figure 14.19.

ABC DEPARTMENT STORES INC.

PHONE (602)323-4557 BOX 5124 PHOENIX, ARIZONA 86581-0058

REQUEST FOR PROPOSAL

REQUEST NO	PAGE	OF
0001	1	1

1 ACME COMPUTER SUPPLY CO.
2704 E. MCDOWELL ROAD
PHOENIX, ARIZONA 85283

2

3

TERMS: (1) YOU ARE INVITED TO BID ON GOODS AND/OR SERVICES ITEMIZED BELOW.
(2) THIS REQUEST FOR PROPOSAL IS NOT INTENDED TO BE RESTRICTIVE. BRAND NAME OR MANUFACTURER'S NAME MAY BE USED FOR PURPOSE OF DESCRIPTION AND/OR TO ESTABLISH THE QUALITY DESIRED. BIDS ARE NOT RESTRICTED TO SUCH BRAND OR MANUFACTURER.
(3) THE ATTENTION OF THE BIDDER IS DIRECTED TO THE TERMS AND CONDITIONS ON THE REVERSE SIDE WHICH ARE INCORPORATED HEREIN.

WE RESERVE THE RIGHT TO REJECT ANY AND ALL BIDS.

RETURN THIS QUOTATION TO PURCHASING DEPT. AT ABOVE ADDRESS

DATE	BUYER	REQUISITION NO.	QUOTATION DUE DATE
6/24/9X	G. WILLIAMS	0001	7/24/9X

LINE	OBJECT CODE	QUANTITY	UNIT	PART NUMBER AND DESCRIPTION	UNIT PRICE	AMOUNT
1	08561	10	1	IMPACT DOT MATRIX PRINTER		
				MINIMUM SPECIFICATIONS:		
				FULLY COMPATIBLE WITH ALL IBM PERSONAL SYSTEM/2 MODELS		
				PRINTING SPEED: 200 CHARACTERS PER SECOND		
				PRINTING DIRECTION: BIDIRECTIONAL, LOGIC SEEKING		
				COLUMN WIDTH: 80 COLUMNS PICA		
				PAPER FEED: ADJUSTABLE SPROCKET FEED		
				PRINT HEAD: DISPOSABLE 24 PIN IMPACT DOT MATRIX		
				RIBBON TYPE: CARTRIDGE RIBBON		
				GRAPHICS CAPABILITY: HIGH-RESOLUTION GRAPHICS. SIX DENSITIES AND A GRAPHICS CHARACTER SET.		

IMPORTANT → SHOW ARIZONA AND LOCAL SALES TAX WHEN APPLICABLE. IF NOT SHOWN AS SEPARATE ITEM, IT WILL BE ASSUMED TO BE INCLUDED IN UNIT AND TOTAL PRICES. | SALES TAX |

THIS IS NOT AN ORDER | **TOTAL** |

SHIPMENT WILL BE MADE	TERMS	F.O.B. POINT
_______ Days after Receipt of Order		ABC DEPARTMENT STORES PHOENIX, ARIZONA

We quote as shown, except as otherwise noted. The undersigned agrees that this proposal is a firm offer which shall be irrevocable and open for acceptance for _______ calendar days (60 calendar days unless otherwise specified) from the date set for submission of quotes.

SIGNATURE _______ DATE _______

FIGURE 14.19
Example of a request for proposal (RFP). Note how it specifies the capabilities that must be met in the supplier's bid.

Computer users may use a scoring system of evaluation when there are several competing proposals for a hardware or software acquisition. Each **evaluation factor** is given a certain number of maximum possible points. Then each competing proposal is assigned points for each factor, depending on how well it meets the specifications of the computer user. Scoring each evaluation factor for several proposals helps organize and document the evaluation process. It also spotlights the strengths and weaknesses of each proposal. See Figure 14.20.

A formal evaluation process reduces the possibility of buying inadequate or unnecessary computer hardware or software. Badly organized computer operations, inadequate systems development, and poor purchasing practices may cause inadequate or unnecessary acquisitions. Therefore, it is necessary to use various methods of evaluation to measure key factors for computer hardware, software, and services. See Figures 14.21, 14.22, and 14.23.

Whatever the claims of hardware manufacturers and software suppliers, the performance of hardware and software must be demonstrated and evaluated. Independent hardware and software information services (such as the Datapro and Auerbach reporting services) should be used to gain detailed specification information and evaluations. Hardware and software should be demonstrated and evaluated.

FIGURE 14.20
Evaluating microcomputer operating systems. Note the use of a scoring system to evaluate operating systems based on eight key criteria.

	IBM OS/2 Warp	Microsoft Windows NT Workstation 3.5	Microsoft Windows 95 (Beta version)
Reliability	7.1	7.4	6.2
Recovery from failure	6.5	6.6	5.8
Multitasking	8.0	7.4	6.5
Speed	7.3	7.2	7.0
Technical support	7.0	6.2	5.8
Ease of use	7.7	7.0	7.3
Applications breadth	5.0	6.0	6.5
Memory management	7.4	6.8	6.6
Average rating	**7.0**	**6.8**	**6.5**

Source: Michael Sullivan-Trainor, "IBM OS/2 Wins Tech Points." *Comuterworld*, April 24, 1995, p. 118. Copyright 1995 by Computerworld, Inc., Framingham, MA 01701—Reprinted from *Computerworld*.

This can be done on the premises of the computer user or by visiting the operations of other computer users who have similar types of hardware or software. Other users are frequently the best source of information needed to evaluate the claims of manufacturers and suppliers. Vendors should be willing to provide the names of such users.

Large computer users frequently evaluate proposed hardware and software by requiring the processing of special benchmark test programs and test data. Users can then evaluate test results to determine which hardware device or software package displayed the best performance characteristics. Special software simulators may also be available that simulate the processing of typical jobs on several computers and evaluate their performances.

Hardware Evaluation Factors

When you evaluate computer hardware, you should investigate specific physical and performance characteristics for each hardware component to be acquired. This is true whether you are evaluating mainframes, microcomputers, or peripheral devices. Specific questions must be answered concerning many important factors. These **hardware evaluation factors** and questions are summarized in Figure 14.21.

Notice that there is much more to evaluating hardware than determining the fastest and cheapest computing device. For example, the question of possible obsolescence must be addressed by making a *technology* evaluation. The factor of ergonomics is also very important. Ergonomic factors ensure that computer hardware and software are user-friendly, that is, safe, comfortable, and easy to use. *Connectivity* is another important evaluation factor, since so many computer systems are now interconnected within wide area or local area telecommunications networks.

Software Evaluation Factors

You should evaluate software according to many factors that are similar to those used for hardware evaluation. Thus, the factors of performance, cost, reliability, availability, compatibility, modularity, technology, ergonomics, and support should be used to evaluate proposed software acquisitions. In addition, however, the software evaluation factors summarized in Figure 14.22 must also be considered. You should answer the questions they generate in order to properly evaluate software

Hardware Evaluation Factors	Rating
Performance What is its speed, capacity, and throughput?	
Cost What is its lease or purchase price? What will be its cost of operations and maintenance?	
Reliability What is the risk of malfunction and its maintenance requirements? What are its error control and diagnostic features?	
Availability When is the firm delivery date?	
Compatibility Is it compatible with existing hardware and software? Is it compatible with hardware and software provided by competing suppliers?	
Modularity Can it be expanded and upgraded by acquiring modular "add on" units?	
Technology In what year of its product life cycle is it? Does it use a new untested technology or does it run the risk of obsolescence?	
Ergonomics Has it been "human factors engineered" with the user in mind? Is it user-friendly, designed to be safe, comfortable, and easy to use?	
Connectivity Can it be easily connected to wide area and local area networks of different types of computers and peripherals?	
Environmental Requirements What are its electrical power, air-conditioning, and other environmental requirements?	
Software Is system and application software available that can best use this hardware?	
Support Are the services required to support and maintain it available?	
Overall Rating	

FIGURE 14.21
A summary of major hardware evaluation factors. Notice how you can use this to evaluate a computer system or a peripheral device.

purchases. For example, some software packages are notoriously slow, hard to use, or poorly documented. They are not a good choice, even if offered at attractive prices.

Most suppliers of hardware and software products and many other firms offer a variety of IS services to end users and organizations. Examples include assistance during installation or conversion of hardware and software, employee training, customer hot lines, and hardware maintenance. Some of these services are provided without cost by hardware manufacturers and software suppliers. Other types of services can be contracted for at a negotiated price. Evaluation factors and questions for IS services are summarized in Figure 14.23.

Evaluating IS Services

FIGURE 14.22
A summary of selected software evaluation factors. Note that most of the hardware evaluation factors in Figure 14.21 can also be used to evaluate software packages.

Software Evaluation Factors	Rating
Efficiency Is the software a well-written system of computer instructions that does not use much memory capacity or CPU time?	
Flexibility Can it handle its processing assignments easily without major modification?	
Security Does it provide control procedures for errors, malfunctions, and improper use?	
Language Is it written in a programming language that is used by our computer programmers and users?	
Documentation Is the software well documented? Does it include helpful user instructions?	
Hardware Does existing hardware have the features required to best use this software?	
Other Factors What are its performance, cost reliability, availability, compatibility, modularity, technology, ergonomics, and support characteristics? (Use the hardware evaluation factor questions in Figure 14.21.)	
Overall Rating	

Other Implementation Activities
Testing

Testing, documentation, and training are keys to successful implementation of a new system. See Figure 14.24. The testing of a newly developed system is an important implementation activity. **System testing** involves testing hardware devices, testing and debugging computer programs, and testing information processing procedures. Programs are tested using test data, which attempts to simulate all conditions that may arise during processing. In good programming practice (structured programming), programs are subdivided into levels of modules to assist their development, testing, and maintenance. Program testing usually proceeds from higher to lower levels of program modules until the entire program is tested as a unit. The program is then tested along with other related programs in a final systems *test*. If computer-aided software engineering (CASE) methodologies are used, such program testing is minimized, since any automatically generated program code is more likely to be error-free.

An important part of testing is the production of tentative copies of displays, reports, and other output. These should be reviewed by end users of the proposed systems for possible errors. Of course, testing should not occur only during the system's implementation stage, but throughout the system's development process. For example, input documents, screen displays, and processing procedures are examined and critiqued by end users when a prototyping methodology is used during the systems design stage. Immediate end user testing is one of the benefits of a prototyping process.

Evaluation Factors for IS Services	Rating
Performance What has been their past performance in view of their past promises?	
Systems Development Are systems analysis and programming consultants available? What are their quality and cost?	
Maintenance Is equipment maintenance provided? What is its quality and cost?	
Conversion What systems development, programming, and hardware installation services will they provide during the conversion period?	
Training Is the necessary training of personnel provided? What is its quality and cost?	
Backup Are several similar computer facilities available for emergency backup purposes?	
Accessibility Does the vendor have a local or regional office that offers sales, systems development, and hardware maintenance services? Is a customer hot line provided?	
Business Position Is the vendor financially strong, with good industry market prospects?	
Hardware Do they have a wide selection of compatible hardware devices and accessories?	
Software Do they offer a variety of useful system software and application packages?	
Overall Rating	

FIGURE 14.23
Evaluation factors for IS services. These factors focus on the quality of support services computer users may need.

Howard Grey/Tony Stone Images.

FIGURE 14.24
Testing, documentation, and training are keys to successful implementation.

FIGURE 14.25
The contents of system documentation organized and stored using a CASE software package.

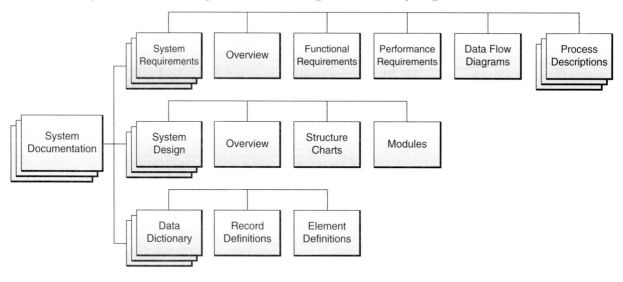

Documentation

Developing good user **documentation** is an important part of the implementation process. Examples include manuals of operating procedures and sample data entry display screens, forms, and reports. During the implementation stage, system documentation manuals may be prepared to finalize the documentation of a large system. When computer-aided systems engineering methods are used, documentation can be created and changed easily. Figure 14.25 illustrates the contents of system documentation stored in the repository of a CASE package.

Documentation serves as a method of communication among the people responsible for developing, implementing, and maintaining a computer-based system. Installing and operating a newly designed system or modifying an established application requires a detailed record of that system's design. Documentation is extremely important in diagnosing errors and making changes, especially if the end users or systems analysts who developed a system are no longer with the organization.

Training

Training is a vital implementation activity. IS personnel, such as user consultants, must be sure that end users are trained to operate a new system or its implementation will fail. Training may involve only activities like data entry, or it may also involve all aspects of the proper use of a new system. In addition, managers and end users must be educated in the fundamentals of information systems technology and its application to business operations and management. This basic knowledge should be supplemented by training programs for specific hardware devices, software packages, and end user applications. As we mentioned in Chapter 8, this educational role is a typical service of an organization's information center.

Conversion Methods

The initial operation of a new computer-based system can be a difficult task. Such an operation is usually a **conversion** process in which the personnel, procedures, equipment, input/output media, and databases of an old information system must

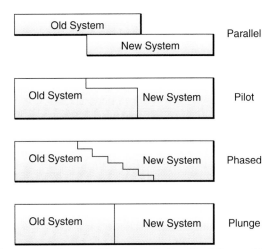

Source: Adapted with the permission of Simon & Schuster from the Macmillan College text *Managing Information Technology: What Managers Need to Know* by E. Wainwright Martin, Daniel DeHayes, Jeffrey Hoffer, and William Perkins. Copyright © 1991 by Macmillan College Publishing Company.

FIGURE 14.26
The four major forms of conversion to a new system.

be converted to the requirements of a new system. Four major forms of system conversion are illustrated in Figure 14.26. They include:

- Parallel conversion.
- Phased conversion.
- Pilot conversion.
- Plunge or direct cutover.

   Conversions can be done on a parallel basis, whereby both the old and the new system are operated until the project development team and end user management agree to switch completely over to the new system. It is during this time that the operations and results of both systems are compared and evaluated. Errors can be identified and corrected, and the operating problems can be solved before the old system is abandoned. Installation can also be accomplished by a direct cutover or *plunge* to the newly developed system. It can also be done on a phased basis, where only parts of a new application or only a few departments, branch offices, or plant locations at a time are converted. A phased conversion allows a gradual implementation process to take place within an organization. Similar benefits accrue from using a pilot conversion, where one department or other work site serves as a test site. A new system can be tried out at this site until developers feel it can be implemented throughout the organization.

Maintenance

Once a system is fully implemented and being operated by end users, the maintenance function begins. **System maintenance** is the monitoring, evaluating, and modifying of operational information systems to make desirable or necessary improvements. For example, the implementation of a new system usually results in the phenomenon known as the *learning curve*. Personnel who operate and use the system will make mistakes simply because they are not familiar with it. Though such errors usually diminish as experience is gained with a new system, they do point out areas where a system may be improved. Maintenance is also necessary for other failures and problems that arise during the operation of a system. End users and information systems personnel then perform a troubleshooting function to determine the causes of and solutions to such problems.

The maintenance activity includes a postimplementation review process to ensure that newly implemented systems meet the systems development objectives established for them. Errors in the development or use of a system must be corrected by the maintenance process. This includes a periodic review or audit of a system to ensure that it is operating properly and meeting its objectives. This audit is in addition to continually monitoring a new system for potential problems or necessary changes. Maintenance includes making modifications to a system due to changes in the business organization or the business environment. For example, new tax legislation, company reorganizations, and new business ventures usually require making a variety of changes to current business information systems.

The World Bank: User Resistance to Change with IT

Before the business benefits of information technology such as groupware can emerge within a company, employees must be willing to actually use the technology. And that can be the biggest stumbling block of all.

At the World Bank, in Washington, for example, a large-scale plan to move 10,000 users of Digital Equipment's All-In-1 electronic mail package to its Teamlinks desktop groupware package ran into snags when many users balked at the change. One pilot group "nearly revolted," said Lesley Shneier, an information officer at the bank.

"We're not paying enough attention to where the real costs are—to people," Shneier said. "The typical attitude has been, 'Put new technology on their desks and go away.'"

World Bank made its move to a groupware network to support an effort to decentralize the global development organization and broaden the organization's focus beyond its Washington headquarters. The information systems department introduced the new technology to four divisions participating in pilot tests, but, Shneier said, despite extensive training and on-site support, "the majority of staff remain reluctant to change to a new system."

One concern centered on changing job functions. The bank's professional staff will use the new desktop software to draft their own reports rather than dictating them or writing longhand drafts. But some object to performing work now done by secretaries, she said.

Introducing groupware enterprisewide is bound to be difficult, said Scott McCready, an analyst at IDC/Avante Technology, a Framingham, Massachusetts–based research company. "I'm not convinced you can or should institutionalize groupware," he said. "Unless new technology makes a difference in people's daily lives, they don't want to be bothered with it."

Another reason users may not be receptive to groupware is that they have not been given a legitimate business rationale for using it, said Karen Moser, a senior analyst at Aberdeen Group, in Boston.

World Bank's use of Teamlinks was intended to improve collaboration globally and streamline the process of producing reports that go through as many as 100 rewrites before they are finalized. But the organization's employees

were "saturated with new technology and didn't see its relevance to their work," Shneier said.

World Bank IS officer Lesley Schneier suggests that organizations can combat or defuse user resistance to adopting groupware in the following ways:

- *Communicate* the business reasons for moving to a new system or users may see new technology as an obstacle to getting their jobs done.
- *Provide training* in small bites, then retrain periodically to ensure that users understand how to take advantage of new features.
- *Provide proactive, not just reactive, support.* This could mean dropping by a user's office and offering to show the individual how to use a more advanced feature.
- *Involve line managers* in evangelizing and supporting the change.

Other end users say problems with user acceptance of new technologies can be overcome by establishing mechanisms for user feedback. During a work flow implementation project at the Pentagon, for instance, the IS staff recognized the importance of user feedback and set up a special E-mail box and voice-mail box to encourage responses, said a Defense Department official who asked to remain anonymous.

"We haven't created a culture that says to users that their feedback is important," said Dan Polito, vice president of NationsBank Corp., in Charlotte, North Carolina. "We need to make people feel that it's OK to say they don't like something."

CASE STUDY QUESTIONS

1. What caused employee resistance to new groupware technology at the World Bank?
2. Why didn't the World Bank's attempts to manage organizational change succeed?
3. What should the World Bank do differently to manage future introductions of new technology?

Source: Adapted from Elizabeth Heichler, "Move to Groupware Sparks User Resistance," *Computerworld*, March 13, 1995, p. 12. Copyright 1995 by Computerworld, Inc., Framingham, MA 01701—Reprinted from *Computerworld*.

Summary

- **Planning for Business Change.** Managing information technology requires planning for changes in business goals, processes, structures, and technologies. Planning is a vital organizational process that analyzes and evaluates an organization's internal and external environments; forecasts new developments; establishes an organization's mission, goals, and objectives; develops strategies, tactics, and policies to implement its goals; and articulates plans for the organization to follow. A good planning process helps organizations examine themselves, uses resources efficiently and effectively, promotes change, and builds a business vision.

- **IS Planning.** Information systems planning includes strategic, tactical, and operational planning activities. Strategic IS planning involves aligning investment in information technology with a company's business vision and strategic organizational goals such as reengineering business processes or gaining competitive advantages. It results in a strategic plan that outlines a business vision, business/IT strategies, and a technology architecture for the IS function. The technology architecture is a conceptual blueprint that specifies a company's technology platform, data resources, applications portfolio and IT organization. Tactical information systems planning evaluates current and projected information needs of the organization; defines, prioritizes, and schedules information systems development projects; and develops allocation plans for hardware, software, personnel, telecommunications,

facilities, and financial resources. Operational IS planning develops operational plans such as annual operating budgets and individual system development project plans.

- **IS Planning Methodologies.** Business organizations may use a variety of formal IS planning methodologies, including business systems planning, critical success factors, a strategic opportunities matrix, reach and range analysis, and a scenario approach. Computer-aided planning software tools are also available to help planners develop strategic, tactical, and operations IS plans for a company.

- **Implementing Business/IT Change.** Implementation activities carry out the plans for the business use of information technology developed during the planning process. This includes managing the introduction and implementation of changes in business processes, organizational structures, job assignments, and work relationships resulting from reengineering projects, strategic business alliances, and the introduction of new technologies. Companies use change management programs to reduce the risks and costs and maximize the benefits of such major changes in business and information technology.

- **Implementation.** The implementation process for information systems consists of activities that carry out the operational plans developed during the information systems planning process. As summarized in Figure 14.27, it involves acquisition, testing, documentation, training, installation, and con-

FIGURE 14.27
A summary of IS implementation activities.

Acquisition
Evaluate and acquire necessary hardware and software resources and information system services. Screen vendor proposals.

Software Development
Develop any computer programs that will not be acquired externally as software packages. Make any necessary modifications to software packages that are acquired.

Training
Educate and train management, end users, and operating personnel. Use consultants or training programs to develop user competencies.

Testing
Test and make necessary corrections to the programs, procedures, and hardware used by a new system.

Documentation
Record and communicate detailed system specifications, including procedures for end users and IS personnel and examples of input/output displays and reports.

Conversion
Convert from the use of a present system to the operation of a new or improved system. This may involve operating both new and old systems in *parallel* for a trial period, operation of a *pilot* system on a trial basis at one location, *phasing in* the new system one location at a time, or an immediate *cutover* to the new system.

version activities that transform a newly designed information system into an operational system for end users.

- **Evaluating Hardware, Software, and Services.** Business end users should know how to evaluate the acquisition of information system resources. Manufacturers and suppliers can be required to present bids and proposals based on sys-

tem specifications developed during the design stage of systems development. A formal evaluation process reduces the possibility of incorrect or unnecessary purchases of computer hardware or software. Several major evaluation factors, summarized in Figures 14.21, 14.22, and 14.23, can be used to evaluate hardware, software, and IS services.

Key Terms and Concepts

These are the key terms and concepts of this chapter. The page number of their first explanation is in parentheses.

1. Applications portfolio (543)
2. Business vision (540)
3. Change management (553)
4. Computer industry (556)
5. Computer-aided planning (551)
6. Conversion methods (564)
7. Documentation (564)
8. End user resistance (555)
9. Evaluation factors (559)
   a. Hardware (560)
   b. Software (560)
   c. IS services (561)
10. External IS services (558)
11. Information systems planning (540)
    a. Strategic (542)
    b. Tactical (544)
    c. Operational (544)
12. Information technology architecture (543)
13. IS implementation process (556)
14. Organizational planning concepts (538)
15. Planning for competitive advantage (547)
16. Planning methodologies (545)
    a. Business Systems Planning (545)
    b. Critical success factors (546)
    c. Strategic opportunities matrix (547)
    d. Reach and range analysis (548)
    e. Scenario approach (549)
17. Project management (544)
18. Systems maintenance (565)
19. System testing (562)
20. Technology implementation (555)

Review Quiz

Match one of the key terms and concepts listed above with one of the brief examples or definitions listed below. Try to find the best fit for answers that seem to fit more than one term or concept. Defend your choices.

____ 1. An organization should decide on its business vision and plan how it will achieve its strategic goals and objectives.

____ 2. A company should decide what kind of organization it wants to be, and what kind of business it wants to be in.

____ 3. Outlines a business vision, business/IT strategies, and technical architecture for the information systems function.

____ 4. Defines, prioritizes, and schedules the development and implementation of major information systems projects for an organization.

____ 5. Develops operating budgets for the information systems function.

____ 6. Management of the development work for new information systems.

____ 7. A comprehensive, business goal- and business process-driven methodology for information systems planning.

____ 8. Planning that concentrates on determining a few key areas where a manager feels performance information is vital to the success of the organization.

____ 9. The mix of investments in IS applications developed to support basic business functions.

____10. Strategic IS planning should develop a blueprint for information technology in a company that specifies a technology platform, applications portfolio, data resources, and IT organization structure.

____11. IS planning should focus on developing strategies for using information technology to gain competitive advantages.

____12. Evaluating strategic opportunities based on their business impact and a company's ability to use IT.

____13. Planning to reach all of your potential stakeholders with an integrated range of IT-enabled applications.

____14. Planning how you would use information technology in various hypothetical business situations.

___15. Companies should try to minimize the risks and costs, and maximize the benefits of major changes in business and technology.

___16. Acquiring hardware and software, testing and converting to a new system, and training people to use it.

___17. The source of hardware, software, and services for users.

___18. Contracting with outside firms for computer processing, education, maintenance, and so on.

___19. Performance, cost, reliability, technology, and ergonomics are examples.

___20. Performance, cost, efficiency, language, and documentation are examples.

___21. Maintenance, conversion, training, and business position are examples.

___22. End users frequently resist the introduction of new technology.

___23. User resistance to the introduction of IT can be overcome by their involvement and training.

___24. Operate in parallel with the old system, use a test site, switch in stages, or cut over immediately to a new system.

___25. Checking whether hardware and software work properly for end users.

___26. A user manual communicates the design and operating procedures of a system.

___27. New business ventures or legislation will probably require changes to some of our information systems.

Discussion Questions

1. How should strategic IS planning support reengineering business processes and gaining competitive advantages? Give several examples.

2. Which planning technique is better: Business Systems Planning or critical success factors, reach and range analysis, or the scenario approach? Explain your reasoning.

3. Refer to the Real World Case on Dunlop Tire Corp. in the chapter. How do Dunlop's changes to the IS organization improve their role in implementing organizational changes through IT?

4. How can a company use change management to minimize the risks and costs and maximize the benefits of changes in business and technology? Give several examples.

5. What are the three most important factors you would use in evaluating computer hardware? Explain why.

6. Refer to the Real World Case on The World Bank in the chapter. Does introducing new groupware technology have more potential for provoking end user resistance than other types of IT implementations? Why or why not?

7. What are the three most important factors you would use in evaluating computer software? Explain why.

8. Assume that in your first week on a new job you are asked to use a type of software package that you have never used before. What kind of user training should your company provide to you before you start?

9. Refer to the Real World Case on GMAC and General Chemical in the chapter. What non-technical business reasons helped them make their selection decisions? Do you agree with the weight they gave to such factors? Why or why not?

10. What is the difference between the parallel, plunge, phased, and pilot forms of IS conversion? Which conversion strategy is best? Explain why.

Real World Problems

1. Owens-Corning Fiberglass: Planning Radical IT Change

Some might call Owens-Corning Fiberglass Corp.'s information systems plans insane. But to Chief Information Officer Mike Radcliff, they are merely aggressive. A good five years after the paperless revolution failed to materialize, observers are agog over the corporation's bid to forcibly eradicate paper in just a little more than a year. Last week, Owens-Corning broke ground for a $100 million world headquarters building in Toledo, Ohio, which is scheduled to open in May 1996. Hidden in that seemingly mundane announcement is the fact that file cabinets were intentionally excluded from the design. This gives employees at the $3.3 billion materials manufacturer exactly 13 months to figure out how to live without paper. They also must figure out how and where to deploy videoconferencing facilities, multimedia kiosks, electronic whiteboards, docking stations, and wireless LANs. And that is just for starters.

Along with the company's 250-person IS department, workers will evaluate palmtops, laptops, satellite and cable service, CD-ROM publication systems, Internet services, and handwriting recognition systems. And in their spare time, IS staffers will rip out virtually every one of the company's current information systems and implement SAP America's client/server R/3 enterprise software. But that schedule is a tad more leisurely. IS has 24 months to bring up manufacturing, sales, and research facilities in more than 30 countries.

The activities are all part of the company's migration to a

new customer-focused work culture, which is based on employee teaming, worker mobility, ongoing learning, and a paperless work environment. As for the total cost of all the new technologies, that has yet to be determined, said Jerry McColough, leader of the technology transition team. "It's not like we have a budget set up. We're working instead with a range," McColough said. "The idea is, if the businesses feel they can use a technology to work differently and it is a business advantage, it will be available to them."

So is this company insane or what? "I think we do have one of the most aggressive schedules you'll find," Radcliff said last week. But are they crazy? Not at all, he insisted. "It's simply that we're looking to make a very rapid transition," he explained. "The fact that we were building a new headquarters was such a wonderful icon for workplace transformation. We figured it is where we can really bring it all together."

To do it all on schedule, Owens-Corning has asked users to evaluate the technologies they will be expected to use. Employees also are charged with defining precisely how new high-tech gear should be used, said John Lee, who works in medical services and is on the 11-member employee design integration team. Known as the EDIT, the team functions as a liaison between IS and the company's 1,000-person headquarters staff.

a. Do you think that Owens-Corning has done a good job of organizational and IS planning? Why or why not?

b. Do you think that Owens-Corning is doing a good job of implementing IT and organizational change? Why or why not?

Source: Adapted from Julia King, "Owens-Corning to Go Paperless in New Building," *Computerworld,* March 27, 1995, p. 2. Copyright 1995 by Computerworld, Inc., Framingham, MA 01701—Reprinted from *Computerworld.*

2. US West Inc.: Failure in Reengineering Planning

Frustration over a slow-moving, multimillion-dollar customer service reengineering project has prompted the departure of several top information systems executives and a complete overhaul of US West's 5,000-person IS organization. Last week, a company spokesman confirmed that the telecommunications carrier spent $290 million on the project last year, but reengineering "was not proceeding as fast or as well as we had anticipated." He also confirmed the departure of Will Smith, former president of Denver-based US West Technologies, the $11 billion telecommunications company's now-defunct IS subsidiary. Also gone from the company are Lloyd Linnell, vice president of billing and corporate systems; Ed Fontenot, vice president of network systems engineering; and Bob Factor, vice president of enterprise architecture and corporate systems. US West would not say whether the departures were voluntary. However, under the restructuring, the former information technology services group and an information application development group will be absorbed by US West

Communications, the company's main telecommunications services business.

Announced in 1995, US West's reengineering initiative calls for consolidating 530 customer service offices in 14 states into 26 customer service, repair, and maintenance "megacenters" in 10 cities. So far, nine centers have been opened, with the remainder scheduled for completion by the end of 1996. Overly ambitious project completion estimates on the part of IS account for many of the project shortfalls, according to Dennis Dempsey, vice president of information application development. What has proved especially problematic is a system of intelligent workstations and servers, he said. "That is one of the systems that got out to centers before we fully understood what it would take to support it. We had significant stability issues in that environment, which has aggravated some of the service problems," Dempsey said. Runaway costs are another thorn, he added. "Our run rates for the budget in 1994 and 1995 are too high," he said. As a result, US West plans to lay off 450 IS employees and 400 of 1,000 contractors, he said.

a. What planning failures led to US West's firing of top IS executives?

b. What changes should US West make to improve the planning and implementation of its reengineering project?

Source: Adapted from Julia King, "US West's Failed Restructuring Spells IS Overhaul," *Computerworld,* February 27, 1995, p. 6. Copyright 1995 by Computerworld, Inc., Framingham, MA 01701—Reprinted from *Computerworld.*

3. CSX and Washington National Insurance: Criticizing Client/Server

Want to win the hearts of CIOs? Better do better. Listen to Wade Brown, CIO of Washington National Insurance Co. "It's a big lie," says Brown of client/server technology. "It was supposed to make us more productive and cost less—and so far, neither has happened." And he's a *fan.*

Some early customers are so furious about C/S's unrealized promise that they're ripping the stuff out. Take George Sekely, who retires at the end of the month after three years as senior vice president for technology at CSX. His predecessor installed first-generation client/server systems from DEC and Banyan to control CSX's office and train operations. But they couldn't handle the round-the-clock demands of a $9 billion railroad company. A massive central computer was needed to synchronize the movement of thousands of locomotives and freight cars. CSX is sticking with the mainframe. "It's a complete mirage," says Sekely of client/server today. "A complete waste of money."

Other CIOs aren't so apocalyptic. But many are very sharp—and specific—in their criticisms. Washington National's Brown began installing a client/server system a year ago. His main gripe: He couldn't find a vendor to deliver an integrated suite of system management software. So he had to cobble together best-of-breed software components to provide data integrity, backup, and security. It didn't work. The technologies clashed. Fortunately for Brown, Legent

Corporation now offers just the package he requires to do the job—Paradign/XP. Now Legent has a loyal customer, and Brown finally has the performance he was promised.

a. What planning and implementation challenges do client/server systems present to IS managers and their business organizations?

b. What planning and implementation activities might have avoided CSX's failed client/server installation? Washington National's client/server problems?

Source: Adapted from Steve Hamm, "Hell Hath No Fury Like a CIO Burned," *PCWeek*, March 27, 1995, pp. A1, A10.

4. Arizona Daily Star: Implementing Internet Services

You can't tell Robert S. Cauthorn that the Internet has insurmountable security, technical, and cost issues that prevent it from being a serious medium for commercial ventures. "A lot of this jazz is overblown," says Cauthorn, director of new technology at the *Arizona Daily Star,* in Tucson. "There's a mystique surrounding the complexity and security. There isn't that much to it." To prove his point, Cauthorn is leading a project to establish the *Arizona Daily Star* as both a subscription-based World Wide Web site and an Internet connection service provider. The newspaper's venture, called StarNet, just became available to residents and businesses within the *Star's* circulation area. Cauthorn found implementation a lot easier than the hype suggests. "I'm a journalist and a computer person, so the combination of content and technology came easy to me," he said. On the other hand, "it was hard to find a systems administrator to help me out. There weren't that many knowledgeable applicants," Cauthorn said.

Despite the optimism of Internet pioneers such as Cauthorn, about half of the 5,000 companies that have established a commercial site on the Web use outsourcers—either Internet service providers or systems integrators—to manage the server and maintain the connection. "We're in the service bureau phase of the Internet," says Peter Raulerson, principal at ParaTechnology, a consultancy in Bellevue, Washington. "In many companies, the marketing group wants to begin a pilot project on the Internet, and the IS group doesn't have the expertise so they decide to outsource." However, eventually the IS people will do it themselves because the Internet will allow companies to streamline business processes, and internal connections will be necessary to do that," says Tom Missato, project leader at CommerceNet, an Internet consortium of users and vendors in California's Silicon Valley.

a. Why do you think that Robert Cauthorn has not found it difficult to plan and implement business services on the Internet?

b. Why are many other companies outsourcing the job of establishing and managing their business site on the Internet? Do you think this is a good idea? Why or why not?

Source: Adapted from Michael Sullivan-Trainor, "Serving Up the

Web," *Computerworld,* May 15, 1995, p. 62. Copyright 1995 by Computerworld, Inc., Framingham, MA 01701—Reprinted from *Computerworld.*

5. Alamo Rent A Car and PMI Food Equipment: IT Selection Criteria

Alamo Chooses Iceberg

Availability, performance, and price compelled Alamo Rent A Car, Inc., in Fort Lauderdale, Florida, to select StorageTek's Iceberg RAID (redundant array of independent disks) system. But the race was close, says Tom Loane, vice president of computer and communications services at Alamo. IBM's Ramac and the Iceberg magnetic disk drive systems are similar in many aspects, Loane says. "It just happened that StorageTek had the best deal the week we went shopping." Loane also looked at EMC's Symmetrix. "EMC also has a good product, but it does not perform in our environment. Our use is write-intensive, and we felt it was not right for us," he says.

Alamo considered traditional DASD (direct access storage devices) magnetic disk units before it selected the RAID system. But the economies were 100 percent on the RAID side; its a lot cheaper than conventional DASD, Loane says. "Once you invest in the software to made RAID work, the disks are cheap. It's also nice to have a box that is an order of magnitude smaller than what it's replacing, thus saving floor space and requiring less air conditioning," he says. The Iceberg storage system at Alamo is configured for 200G bytes of storage with 512M bytes of RAM memory.

PMI Chooses Ramac

Compatibility was PMI Food Equipment Group's no. 1 concern in its search for a RAID product last year. "Whatever we purchased had to use our existing files without modification, handle our database tasks, provide the response times we required, have high availability, and equal the present total capacity, plus give us some room to grow. IBM's Ramac fit the bill," says Ray Florence, director of PMI's Corporate Data Center in Troy, Ohio. PMI, a manufacturer of restaurant food processing equipment, replaced several IBM 3390 model DASDs. The firm wanted something that could use the existing controllers and the IBM 3390 data structures as is, and was compatible with its IBM ES/9000 mainframe system. Cost was important, but compatibility was the main issue.

These requirements led PMI to choose IBM's RAID product, Ramac, last October. The installation went smoothly and without any problems, Florence says. "It's great to have just one little box sitting there humming, replacing a string of big heavy ones," he says. "We looked at StorageTek's and EMC's offerings but were concerned about the controller issue and selected IBM. They gave us the best deal with compatibility and cost." The installed Ramac configuration can be expanded to 90.8G bytes of storage.

a. What criteria did Alamo use to choose a RAID product from StorageTek? Do you agree with their decision? Explain.

b. What criteria did PMI use to choose a RAID drive from IBM? Do you agree with their decision? Explain.

Source: Adapted from Robert Callery, "Buying Issues Turned Upside Down," *Computerworld,* January 30, 1995, pp. 78–79. Copyright 1995 by Computerworld, Inc., Framingham, MA 01701—Reprinted from *Computerworld.*

6. Ameritech Corp.: The Challenge of Reengineering IS

Eighteen months ago, the chairman of Chicago-based telecommunications holding company Ameritech Corp. called together his senior information systems executives. "He said, 'What are you doing for me? Explain why I need you at all,'" recalls Eric Christensen, director of consulting services at the $11.7 billion telecommunications giant. That question prompted Christensen to explore ways to measure the contribution of IS to Ameritech's rapidly expanding businesses. It also led to a major restructuring of Ameritech's IS function.

Christensen didn't start out to reengineer information systems at Ameritech's 2,500-person technology unit. "It was more a 52-card pickup of the whole business," says Christensen. One IS change just led to another, driven by a 15-member process innovation team. Now Ameritech's IS group is organized around key business processes instead of traditional IS functions.

"IS groups are the shoemaker's kids," Christensen says. "It's a matter of being so focused on solving other people's problems that you don't have time to look at your own." So Christensen says getting IS professionals and managers on board can be tough. "It's a never-ending battle," he says. And because it's difficult and lengthy, internal IS reengineering requires prolonged top-level support, says John Wyatt, CEO of James Martin and Co., a reengineering consultancy. Interest can be tough to maintain, he says. "The logical end to the horror story is outsourcing the IS function."

Lack of vision is often a problem, too. University of Colorado professor Daniel J. Couger says reengineering in IS is often doomed by a lack of creativity. Technologists, he says, "have lots of tools that talk about how you analyze a process. But they only advocate one tool for redesigning a process—brainstorming, the least effective of all the creative tools." Couger, author of *Creative Problem Solving and Opportunity Finding,* published by Boyd and Fraser, says in the long run, money spent on expensive consultants would be better spent on teaching IS staffers creative tools and techniques.

a. Why was reengineering Ameritech's IS function an important but difficult assignment?

b. What can be done to improve this change process?

Source: Adapted from Alice La Plante, "It's Got What It Takes," *Computerworld,* October 3, 1994, pp. 87–88, and Joseph Maglitta, "Weak Links," *Computerworld,* February 6, 1995, pp. 94–96. Copyright 1995 by Computerworld, Inc., Framingham, MA 01701—Reprinted from *Computerworld.*

Application Exercises

1. Daylight Distributing Implements a Distributed System

Daylight Distributing Company is implementing a system whereby their salespersons will be issued portable computers. Salespersons will record sales and inventory information for each store as the call on that store is completed. Summary information about the day's sales will be transmitted every evening from the salespersons' PCs to Daylight's central database at corporate headquarters using a modem and standard phone lines. Information about recent stockage and sales for stores that will be visited the following day will be downloaded to the salesperson's PC each evening, as well.

You have been asked to develop a simple database application to track this program. For each call, the following information is to be recorded: the date, the salesperson's name, and the length of the call in minutes. Sample data are shown below.

Based upon the description above and the sample data:

a. Design and implement a database file and enter the sample data into it.

b. Prepare a summary report showing the number of times each salesperson called in.

c. Assuming that all calls are billed at the rate of 12 cents per minute, prepare a report showing the total cost of the program, and the cost of each salesperson's calls.

Salesperson Name	Date	Length of Call
Al Johnson	04/03	12
Ann Flowers	04/03	9
Dan Warren	04/03	16
Al Johnson	04/04	11
Ann Flowers	04/04	13
Sue Jones	04/05	18
Al Johnson	04/05	14
Ann Flowers	04/05	10
Dan Warren	04/05	19
Ann Flowers	04/06	8
Al Johnson	04/07	17
Ann Flowers	04/07	11
Sue Jones	04/07	19

2. Electronic Data Interchange at Daylight Distributing

Daylight Distributing Company is investigating the costs and benefits of developing an electronic data interchange (EDI) system to connect it with its customers. Many of the larger department stores Daylight serves are already involved in EDI relationships with Daylight's competitors and some have threatened to quit stocking Daylight's products if they do not implement EDI. You have been asked to prepare a rough estimate of the costs and benefits of implementing an EDI system.

You find that the cost of hardware and software to support an EDI system would be approximately $180,000 the first year, with maintenance costs of $15,000 per year thereafter. Additional training and personnel costs in the IS department are estimated to be $50,000 the first year and $30,000 in each succeeding year.

Benefits of the system will come from reduction in the clerical time required to process orders and from improved market share. The impact on market share is difficult to quantify, so you decide to base the quantitative analysis only on the savings in clerical time.

Daylight processes 45,000 orders per year. It is estimated that the use of EDI could save 30 minutes of processing time on each order. The average cost of clerical labor (including benefits) is $9.50 per hour. If Daylight implements EDI, they expect to process 25 percent of their orders using the EDI system during the first year. They expect the percentage of total orders processed by EDI to increase to 50 percent for the second year and then to increase by 5 percentage points in each succeeding year.

Use this information to develop a spreadsheet comparing the costs and benefits of EDI over the first five years of operation. Based upon your results, would you recommend that Daylight Distributing proceed with the EDI project?

Review Quiz Answers

1.	14	8.	16b	15.	3	22.	8
2.	2	9.	1	16.	13	23.	20
3.	11a	10.	12	17.	4	24.	6
4.	11b	11.	15	18.	10	25.	19
5.	11c	12.	16c	19.	9a	26.	7
6.	17	13.	16d	20.	9b	27.	18
7.	16a	14.	16e	21.	9c		

Selected References

1. Allen, Brandt, and Andrew Boynton. "Information Architecture—In Search of Efficient Flexibility." *MIS Quarterly,* December 1991.
2. Anthes, Gary. "Management Problems Plague State Department IS." *Computerworld,* October 17, 1994.
3. Belmonte, Richard, and Richard Murray. "Getting Ready for Strategic Change." *Information Systems Management,* Summer 1993.
4. Cafasso, Rosemary. "Few IS Projects Come in on Time, on Budget." *Computerworld,* December 12, 1994.
5. Das, Sidhartha; Shaker Zahra; and Merrill Warkentin. "Integrating the Content and Process of Strategic MIS Planning with Competitive Strategy." *Decision Sciences Journal,* November/ December 1991.
6. Davenport, Thomas. *Process Innovation: Reengineering Work through Information Technology.* Boston: Harvard Business School Press, 1993.
7. Earl, Michael. "Experiences in Strategic Information Systems Planning." *MIS Quarterly,* March 1993.
8. Frenzel, Carroll. Management *of Information Technology.* Boston: Boyd & Fraser, 1992.
9. Fried, Louis, and Richard Johnson. "Gaining the Technology Advantage: Planning for the Competitive Use of IT." *Information Systems Management,* Fall 1991.
10. Guha, Subashish; William Kettinger; and James Teng. "Business Process Reengineering: Building a Comprehensive Methodology." *Information Systems Management,* Summer 1993.
11. Hershey, Gerald, and Donna L. Kizzier. *Planning and Implementing End-User Information Systems.* Cincinnati: South-Western Publishing, 1992.
12. Keen, Peter. *Shaping the Future: Business Design through Information Technology.* Boston: Harvard Business School, 1991.
13. Kumar, Kaldeep. "Post-Implementation Evaluation of Computer-Based Information Systems: Current Practices." *Communications of the ACM,* February 1990.
14. Lederer, Albert, and Vijay Sethi. "Critical Dimensions of Information Systems Planning." *Decision Sciences Journal,* Winter 1991.

15. LaPlante, Alice. "No Doubt About IT." *Computerworld,* August 15, 1994.
16. Maglitta, Joseph. "Rocks in the Gears: Reengineering the Workplace." *Computerworld,* October 3, 1994.
17. McConnell, Vicki, and Karl Koch. *Computerizing the Corporation: The Intimate Link between People and Machines.* New York: Van Nostrand Reinhold, 1990.
18. Mische, Michael. "Transnational Architecture: A Reengineering Approach." *Information Systems Management,* Winter 1995.
19. Murray, Richard, and Dorothy Trefts. "Building the Business of the Future: The IT Imperative." *Information Systems Management,* Fall 1992.
20. Murray, Richard, and Richard Hardin. "The IT Organization of the Future." *Information Systems Management,* Fall 1991.
21. Sprague, Ralph, and Barbara McNurlin. *Information Systems Management in Practice.* 3ed. Englewood Cliffs, NJ: Prentice Hall, 1993.
22. Swanson, Burton. *Information Systems Implementation.* Homewood, IL: Richard D. Irwin, 1988.
23. Walton, Richard. *Up and Running: Integrating Information Technology and the Organization.* Boston: Harvard Business School, 1991.
24. Zahedi, Fatemeh. *Quality Information Systems.* Danvers, MA. Boyd & Fraser, 1995.

GMAC and General Chemical: Evaluating Novell NetWare versus Windows NT

GMAC Chooses Netware

Technical and cost issues factored into Niraj Patel's decision to upgrade his NetWare 3.12 network operating system to NetWare 4.1 rather than Windows NT 3.5. But a nontechnical issue was the most telling, according to Patel, network and telecommunications manager at General Motors Acceptance Corp. (GMAC) Mortgage Co.

When he tried to set up a comparison of NetWare 4.1 and Windows NT 3.5 nine months ago, Novell sent a service engineer to his office for a full day to set up a NetWare 4.1 server and teach the staff how to use it. Microsoft, on the other hand, sent an evaluation copy of Windows NT and gave Patel a telephone number he could call for technical support.

Despite a minor prejudice in favor of NetWare, Patel was willing to move to Windows NT as a primary server platform if necessary. And the two net operating systems were comparable in almost every respect under the low-load testing Patel did. They supported the same range of hardware and compared closely in security, stability, single-server administration, and file and print throughput. But technical factors, as well as some intangibles, clinched the deal.

"People have a lot more confidence in NetWare because it's been around a long time," Patel said. "We've been doing a lot of consolidation onto larger servers, and I was just a lot more comfortable doing that with NetWare than NT."

Patel's group supports 100 branch offices that dial in to centralized Unix servers to access mortgage applications, and a 2,000-user, 15-server, six-site NetWare network that runs corporate support, accounting, electronic mail, and other applications for corporate administration.

On the technical front, Patel's group opted for NetWare 4.1 on the strength of its enterprisewide administration features, which translated into bigger cost savings than those possible with Windows NT.

Key to NetWare 4.1's ease of administration is its Network Data Services (NDS), which lets users log on to any server with just one authentication. By the same token, it lets network managers administer the network from one location, which saves manpower and money. Windows NT's server-based directory, by contrast, requires server-by-

server management.

"In a lot of my remote branches I have third parties maintaining the servers for me," Patel said. "I'm looking to cut down their role and save money that way." We will also save money by cutting staff in the company's second-largest site, in Waterloo, Iowa. "I have two LAN administrators right now. I could probably get away with one," he said.

Patel is consolidating NetWare servers at the headquarters as well and will reduce the number of LAN administrators there by two. The cost savings from staff cuts will be a least $100,000, which is equal to the total amount GMAC Mortgage spends on new Novell products in a year, he said.

It will also make the firm's fluid organizational chart easier to maintain, Patel said. The company moves people around left and right. They may cross departments, things like that. The time the company's saving doing drag and drop changes automatically in NDS rather than making server-by-server changes is astronomical, he said.

General Chemical Chooses Windows NT

For General Chemical Corp., the sum of the parts in Microsoft's product collection may be greater than the whole. The chemical company in recent years has been deploying Microsoft products—from Windows for Workgroups to SQL Server—throughout its network. It now appears that Windows NT will help tie those components together and in so doing, push Novell NetWare out the door.

"As Microsoft began to discuss its directions for Windows NT Server, we became more interested," said Michael Smith, MIS manager and supervisor of General Chemical's Materials Microsoft SQL Server-Base Maintenance/Decision Support System. "Microsoft Office is our desktop standard. Why not keep the number of vendors that we deal with to a minimum, especially since Microsoft's pricing is so great."

Novell, meanwhile, has done little to advance beyond its traditional strengths in file and print sharing since General Chemical first installed NetWare 2.X in the 1980s, according to Smith.

Smith cited a host of other reasons for migrating from NetWare to Windows NT as a strategic enterprise network

Source: Adapted from Peggy Watt and Kevin Fogarty, "NetWare versus NT: Two Users, Two Different Paths," *Network World,* March 13, 1995, pp. 1, 88. Copyright 1995 by Network World, Inc., Framingham, MA 01701—Reprinted from *Network World.*

platform. These include Windows NT's stronger TCP/IP product support, General Chemical's positive experience with SQL Server since installing it two years ago, an existing relationship in place with Hewlett-Packard under which General Chemical gets Microsoft support, and Microsoft's tightly integrated BackOffice suite of Windows NT-based server products.

General Chemical already runs Windows for Workgroups on over 600 HP Vetra personal computers, which are located primarily in seven sites, most of which are linked to form the company's enterprise network. Most of those PCs are tied to NetWare LANs for file and print services.

Moving from NetWare to Windows NT has enabled General Chemical to swap the less than satisfactory performance on Novell's wide area IPX protocol for TCP/IP, Smith said. "IPX is a very fast protocol locally, but it does not route well," Smith said. On top of that, NetWare broadcasts messages that add traffic overhead and clog netlinks, he said. TCP/IP is also the protocol used by General Chemical's new HP 3000, Model 987, which hosts the company's decision support system.

Windows NT also had some other things going for it, Smith said. For example, he liked Microsoft's directory services technology more than Novell's. "NetWare 4.1's directory services seem very robust but complicated and hierarchial," Smith said. Windows NT's "registry and domains were easier to deal with." However, Smith wishes Windows NT had NetWare Directory Services' ability to limit the amount of disk space that work groups can have on a server.

But given the overall attractiveness of Microsoft's BackOffice suite, Smith can deal with some of Windows NT's shortcomings. His staff is already evaluating the Systems Management Server piece of BackOffice and is eagerly anticipating Exchange Server, Microsoft's promised messaging technology.

BackOffice's licensing structure is also inviting in that it features a set server price and options of per client charges or fees based on the number of desktops in concurrent use, Smith said. "I think Novell is starting to come around on pricing but it used to be that every time you added another server you had to buy another multiuser license. That was a pain," he added.

CASE STUDY QUESTIONS

1. Why did GMAC choose the Novell NetWare network operating system over Windows NT?

2. Why did General Chemical replace Novell NetWare with Windows NT?

3. Based on this case, what choice would you recommend to a business considering these two network operating system products? Why?

Managing IT: Security and Ethical Challenges

CHAPTER OUTLINE

LEARNING OBJECTIVES

The purpose of this chapter is to give you an understanding of how managers should manage and control the use of information systems in an organization by analyzing (1) control methods for information system performance and security, and (2) ethical and societal challenges of information technology.

Section I discusses how the quality and security of information systems can be promoted by a variety of information system, procedural, and facility controls.

Section II discusses fundamental ethical concepts in business and information technology and how society is affected by IT in employment, individuality, working conditions, privacy, crime, health, and solutions to societal problems.

After reading and studying this chapter, you should be able to:

1. Outline several types of information system controls, procedural controls, and facility controls that can be used to ensure the quality and security of information systems.

2. Discuss ways to control the performance and security of end user computing systems.

3. Identify several ethical principles that affect the use and management of information technology.

4. Identify several ethical issues in how information technology affects employment, individuality, working conditions, privacy, crime, health, and solutions to societal problems.

5. Identify what end users and IS managers can do to lessen the harmful effects and increase the beneficial effects of information technology.

Why Controls Are Needed

As a manager, you will be responsible for the control of the quality and performance of information systems in your business unit. See Figure 15.1. Like any other vital business asset, the resources of information systems hardware, software, and data need to be protected by built-in controls to ensure their quality and security. That's why controls are needed. Computers have proven that they can process huge volumes of data and perform complex calculations more accurately than manual or mechanical information systems. However, we know that (1) errors do occur in computer-based systems, (2) computers have been used for fraudulent purposes, and (3) computer systems and their software and data resources have been accidentally or maliciously destroyed.

There is no question that computers have had some detrimental effect on the detection of errors and fraud. Manual and mechanical information processing systems use paper documents and other media that can be visually checked by information processing personnel. Several persons are usually involved in such systems and, therefore, cross-checking procedures are easily performed. These characteristics of manual and mechanical information processing systems facilitate the detection of errors and fraud.

Computer-based information systems, on the other hand, use machine-sensible media such as magnetic disks and tape. They accomplish processing manipulations within the electronic circuitry of a computer system. The ability to check visually the progress of information processing activities and the contents of databases is significantly reduced. In addition, a relatively small number of personnel may effectively control processing activities that are critical to the survival of the organization. Therefore, the ability to detect errors and fraud can be reduced by computerization. This makes the development of various control methods a vital consideration in the design of new or improved information systems.

Effective controls are needed to ensure **information system security,** that is, the accuracy, integrity, and safety of information system activities and resources. Controls can minimize errors, fraud, and destruction in an information services organization. Effective controls provide **quality assurance** for information systems. That is, they can make a computer-based information system more free of errors and fraud and able to provide information products of higher quality than manual types of information processing. This can help reduce the potential negative impact (and increase the positive impact) that information technology can have on business survival and success and the quality of life in society.

What Controls Are Needed

Three major types of controls must be developed to ensure the quality and security of information systems. These control categories, illustrated in Figure 15.2 are:

- Information system controls.
- Procedural controls.
- Physical facility controls.

Information System Controls

Information system controls are methods and devices that attempt to ensure the accuracy, validity, and propriety of information system activities. Controls must be developed to ensure proper data entry, processing techniques, storage methods, and

Bob Krist/Tony Stone Images.

FIGURE 15.1
Managers are responsible for the control of the quality and performance of information systems in their business units.

FIGURE 15.2
The controls needed for information system security. Specific types of controls can be grouped into three major categories: information system, procedural, and physical facility controls.

Physical Facility Controls

Procedural Controls

Information System Controls

Managing
Information
System
Performance
and Security

Input, Processing, Output,
and Storage Controls

Separation of Duties • Standard Procedures
Documentation• Authorization Requirements • Auditing

Physical Protection • Computer Failure Controls
Telecommunications Controls • Insurance

information output. Thus, information system controls are designed to monitor and maintain the quality and security of the input, processing, output, and storage activities of any information system. See Figure 15.3.

Have you heard the phrase "garbage in, garbage out" (GIGO)? Figure 15.4 shows why controls are needed for the proper entry of data into an information system. Examples include passwords and other security codes, formatted data entry screens, audible error signals, templates over the keys of key-driven input devices, and prerecorded and prenumbered forms. Input of source documents can also be controlled by registering them in a logbook when they are received by data entry personnel. Realtime systems that use direct access files frequently record all entries into the system on magnetic tape *control logs* that preserve evidence of all system inputs. Computer software can include instructions to identify incorrect, invalid, or

Input Controls

FIGURE 15.3
Examples of information system controls. Note that they are designed to monitor and maintain the quality and security of the input, processing, output, and storage activities of an information system.

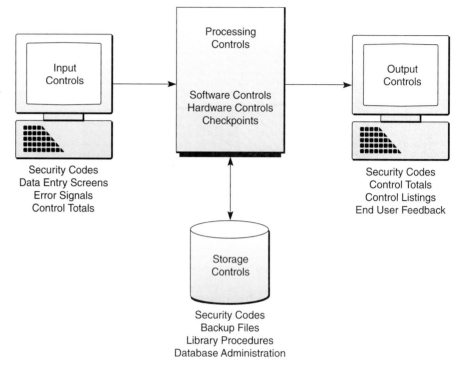

improper input data as it enters the computer system. For example, a data entry program can check for invalid codes, data fields, and transactions. Also, the computer can be programmed to conduct "reasonableness checks" to determine if input data exceeds certain specified limits or is out of sequence. This includes the calculation and monitoring of selected **control totals.**

Data entry and other systems activities are frequently monitored by the use of control totals. For example, a record count is a control total that consists of counting the total number of source documents or other input records and comparing this total to the number of records counted at other stages of input preparation. If the totals do not match, a mistake has been made. Batch totals and hash totals are other forms of control totals. A *batch total* is the sum of a specific item of data within a batch of transactions, such as the sales amounts in a batch of sales transactions. *Hash totals* are the sum of data fields that are added together for control comparisons only. For example, employee social security numbers could be added to produce a control total in the input preparation of payroll documents.

Processing Controls

Once data is entered correctly into a computer system, it must be processed properly. Processing controls are developed to identify errors in arithmetic calculations and logical operations. They are also used to ensure that data are not lost or do not go unprocessed. Processing controls can include hardware controls and software controls.

Hardware Controls

Hardware controls are special checks built into the hardware to verify the accuracy of computer processing. Examples of hardware checks include:

- **Malfunction detection circuitry** within a computer or telecommunications processor that can monitor their operations. For example, *parity checks* are

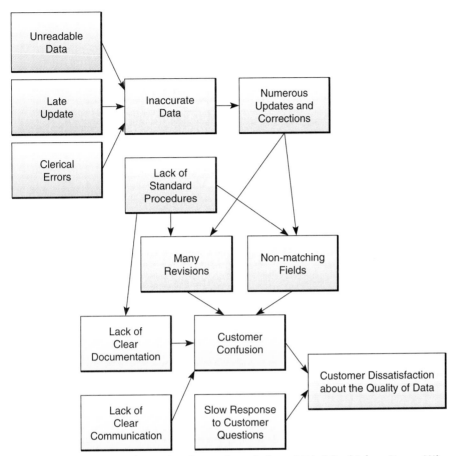

FIGURE 15.4
Garbage in, garbage out. Input controls are needed for the proper entry of data into a computer system.

made to check for the loss of the correct number of bits in every byte of data processed or transmitted on a network. Another example is *echo checks,* which require that a signal be returned from a device or circuit to verify that it was properly activated. Other examples are redundant circuitry checks, arithmetic sign checks, and CPU timing and voltage checks.

- **Redundant components.** For example, multiple read-write heads on magnetic tape and disk devices check and promote the accuracy of reading and recording activities.

- **Special-purpose microprocessors and associated circuitry** that may be used to support *remote diagnostics* and maintenance. These allow off-site technicians to diagnose and correct some problems via a telecommunications link to the computer.

Software Controls

Some software controls are designed to ensure that the right data is being processed. For example, the operating system or other software checks the internal file labels at the beginning and end of magnetic tape and disk files. These labels contain information identifying the file as well as provide control totals for the data in the file. These internal file labels allow the computer to ensure that the proper storage file is being used and that the proper data in the file have been processed.

FIGURE 15.5
Using CA-UnicenterStar, the
security monitor module of the
CA-UNICENTER performance
monitor system.

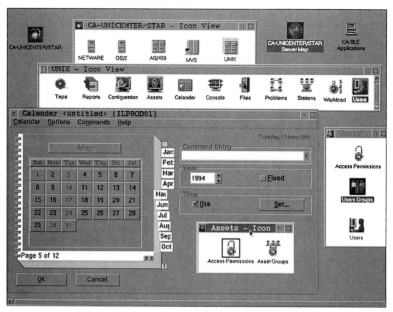

Courtesy of Computer Associates, Inc.

Another major software control is the establishment of checkpoints during the processing of a program. *Checkpoints* are intermediate points within a program being processed where intermediate totals, listings, or "dumps" of data are written on magnetic tape or disk or listed on a printer. Checkpoints minimize the effect of processing errors or failures, since processing can be restarted from the last checkpoint (called a *rollback*), rather than from the beginning of the program. They also help build an **audit trail,** which allows transactions being processed to be traced through all of the steps of their processing.

Many input, processing, output, and storage controls may be provided by specialized system software packages known as **system security monitors.** System security monitors are programs that monitor the use of a computer system and protect its resources from unauthorized use, fraud, and destruction. Such programs provide the computer security needed to allow only authorized users to access the system. For example, identification codes and passwords are frequently used for this purpose. Security monitors also control the use of the hardware, software, and data resources of a computer system. For example, even authorized users may be restricted to the use of certain devices, programs, and data files. Finally, such programs monitor the use of the computer and collect statistics on any attempts at improper use. They produce reports to assist in maintaining the security of the system. See Figure 15.5.

Output Controls

How can we control the quality of the information products produced by an information system? Output controls are developed to ensure that information products are correct and complete and are transmitted to authorized users in a timely manner. Several types of output controls are similar to input control methods. For example, output documents and reports are frequently logged, identified with route slips, and visually verified by input/output control personnel. Control totals on output are usually compared with control totals generated during the input and processing stages. Control listings can be produced that provide hard copy evidence of all output produced.

Prenumbered output forms can be used to control the loss of important output documents such as stock certificates or payroll check forms. Distribution lists help input-output control personnel ensure that only authorized users receive output. Access to the output of realtime processing systems is controlled, typically, by security codes that identify which users can receive output and the type of output they are authorized to receive. Finally, end users who receive output should be contacted for feedback on the quality of the output. This is an important function of systems maintenance and quality assurance activities.

Storage Controls

How can we protect our data resources? First, control responsibilities for files of computer programs and organizational databases may be assigned to a librarian or database administrator. These employees are responsible for maintaining and controlling access to the libraries and databases of the organization. Second, many databases and files are protected from unauthorized or accidental use by security programs that require proper identification before they can be used. Typically, the operating system or security monitor protects the databases of realtime processing systems from unauthorized use or processing accidents. Account codes, passwords, and other **security codes** are frequently used to allow access to authorized users only. A catalog of authorized users enables the computer system to identify eligible users and determine which types of information they are authorized to receive.

Typically, a three-level password system is used. First, an end user logs on to the computer system by entering his or her unique identification code or user ID. The end user is then asked to enter a *password* in order to gain access into the system. Finally, to access an individual file, a unique *file name* must be entered. In some systems, the password to read the contents of a file is different from that required to write to a file (change its contents). This feature adds another level of protection to stored data resources. However, for even stricter security, passwords can be scrambled, or *encrypted*, to avoid their theft or improper use.

Many firms also use *backup files,* which are duplicate files of data or programs. Such files may be stored off-premises, that is, in a location away from the computer center, sometimes in special storage vaults in remote locations. Many realtime processing systems use duplicate files that are updated by telecommunication links. Files are also protected by *file retention* measures, which involve storing copies of master files and transaction files from previous periods. If current files are destroyed, the files from previous periods are used to reconstruct new current files. Usually, several *generations* of files are kept for control purposes. Thus, master files from several recent periods of processing (known as *child, parent, grandparent* files, etc.) may be kept for backup purposes.

Facility Controls

Physical facility controls are methods that protect physical facilities and their contents from loss or destruction. Computer centers are subject to such hazards as accidents, natural disasters, sabotage, vandalism, unauthorized use, industrial espionage, destruction, and theft of resources. Therefore, physical safeguards and various control procedures are necessary to protect the hardware, software, and vital data resources of computer-using organizations.

FIGURE 15.6

The encryption process of the controversial Clipper chip proposed by the U.S. government. The Clipper microprocessor would allow law enforcement surveillance of encrypted data transmissions and files.

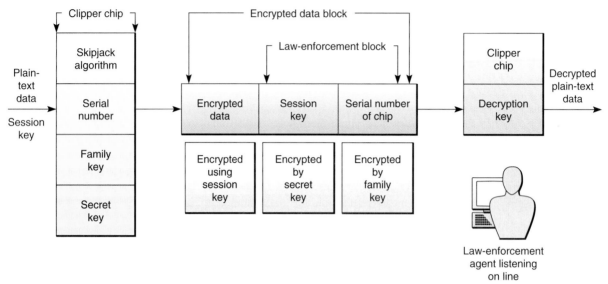

Source: Adapted from "Crypto Policy and Business Privacy," by Winn Schwartau, *PC Week*, June 28, 1993 p. 207. Reprinted from *PC Week*. Copyright © 1993, Ziff-Davis Publishing Company.

Encryption and Fire Walls

Encryption of data and the use of fire wall computers have become important ways to protect computer network resources. Passwords, messages, files, and other data can be transmitted in scrambled form and unscrambled by computer systems for authorized users only. This process is called **encryption.** Typically, it involves using a special mathematical algorithm, or key, to transform digital data into a scrambled code before it is transmitted, and to decode the data when it is received. Special microprocessors and software packages can be used for the encryption process. There are several competing encryption standards, including DES (Data Encryption Standard), RSA (by RSA Data Security), and the Skipjack algorithm of the U.S. government's proposed Clipper encryption microprocessor chip. See Figure 15.6.

Another important method for control and security of telecommunications networks are **fire wall** computers. A network fire wall is a computer that protects computer networks from intrusion by serving as a safe transfer point for access to and from other networks. It screens all network traffic, and only allows authorized transmissions in and out of the network. Fire walls have become an essential component of organizations connecting to the Internet, because of its vulnerability and lack of security. Figure 15.7 illustrates the Internet fire wall system of AT&T [35].

Fire walls can deter, but not completely prevent, unauthorized access (*hacking*) into computer networks. In some cases, a fire wall may allow access only from trusted locations on the Internet to particular computers inside the fire wall. Or it may allow only "safe" information to pass. For example, a fire wall may permit users to read E-mail from remote locations but not to run certain programs. In other cases, it is impossible to distinguish safe use of a particular network service from unsafe use and so all requests must be blocked. The fire wall may then provide substitutes for some network services (such as E-mail or file transfer) that perform most of the same functions but are not as vulnerable to penetration [35].

FIGURE 15.7
AT&T's Internet fire wall system.

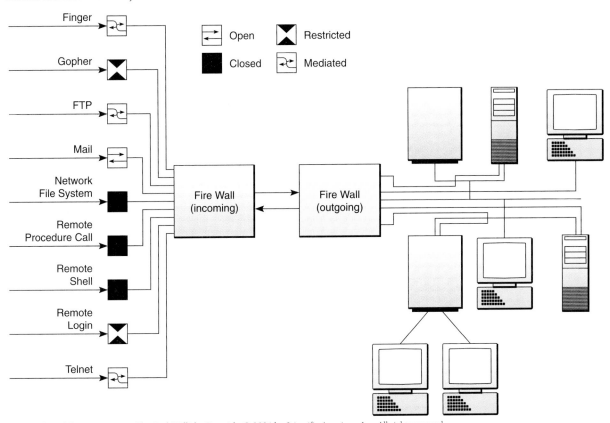

Providing maximum security and disaster protection for a computer installation requires many types of controls. Only authorized personnel are allowed access to the computer center through such techniques as identification badges for information services personnel, electronic door locks, burglar alarms, security police, closed-circuit TV, and other detection systems. The computer center should be protected from disaster by such safeguards as fire detection and extinguishing systems; fireproof storage vaults for the protection of files; emergency power systems; electromagnetic shielding; and temperature, humidity, and dust control.

Physical Protection Controls

Biometric controls are a fast-growing area of computer security. These are security measures provided by computer devices which measure physical traits that make each individual unique. This includes voice verification, fingerprints, hand geometry, signature dynamics, keystroke analysis, retina scanning, face recognition, and genetic pattern analysis. Biometric control devices use special-purpose sensors to measure and digitize a *biometric profile* of an individual's fingerprints, voice, or other physical trait. The digitized signal is processed and compared to a previously processed profile of the individual stored on magnetic disk. If the profiles match, the individual is allowed entry into a computer facility or given access to information system resources.

Biometric Controls

FIGURE 15.8
Methods of fault tolerance in computer-based information systems.

Layer	Threats	Fault-Tolerant Methods
Applications	Environment, hardware and software faults	Application-specific redundancy and rollback to previous checkpoint
Systems	Outages	System isolation, data security, system integrity
Databases	Data errors	Separation of transactions and safe updates, complete transaction histories, backup files
Networks	Transmission errors	Reliable controllers; safe asynchrony and handshaking; alternative routing; error-detecting and error-correcting codes
Processes	Hardware and software faults	Alternative computations, rollback to checkpoints
Files	Media errors	Replication of critical data on different media and sites; archiving, backup, retrieval
Processors	Hardware faults	Instruction retry; error-correcting codes in memory and processing; replication; multiple processors and memories

Source: Adapted from Peter Neumann *Computer-Related Risks* (New York: ACM Press), 1995, p. 231. Copyright 1995, Association for Computing Machinery, Inc. by permission.

Computer Failure Controls

"Sorry, the computer is down" is a well-known phrase to many end users. A variety of controls are needed to prevent such computer failure or minimize its effects. Computers fail for several reasons—power failure, electronic circuitry malfunctions, mechanical malfunctions of peripheral equipment, hidden programming errors, and computer operator errors. The information services department, typically, takes steps to prevent equipment failure and to minimize its detrimental effects. For example, computers with automatic and remote maintenance capabilities may be acquired. A program of preventive maintenance of hardware may be established. Adequate electrical supply, air conditioning, humidity control, and fire prevention standards must also be set. A backup computer system capability may be arranged with other computer-using organizations. Major hardware or software changes should be carefully scheduled and implemented to avoid problems. Finally, computer operators should have adequate training and supervision.

Many firms also use **fault tolerant** computer systems to ensure against computer failure. These systems have multiple central processors, peripherals, and system software. This may provide a *fail-safe* capability where the computer system continues to operate at the same level even if there is a major hardware or software failure. However, many fault tolerant computer systems offer a *fail-soft* capability where the computer system can continue to operate at a reduced but acceptable level in the event of a major system failure. Figure 15.8 outlines some of the fault tolerant capabilities used in many computer systems and networks.

Procedural Controls

Procedural controls are methods that specify how the information services organization should be operated for maximum security. They facilitate the accuracy and integrity of computer operations and systems development activities.

Separation of Duties

Separation of duties is a basic principle of procedural control. It requires that the duties of systems development, computer operations, and control of data and program files be assigned to separate groups. For example, systems analysts and computer programmers may not be allowed to operate corporate mainframes or make changes to data or programs being processed. In addition, the responsibility for maintaining a library of data files and program files is assigned to a librarian or database administrator. Finally, a production control section may monitor the progress of information processing jobs, data entry activities, and the quality of input/output data. This is an important *quality assurance* function.

Standard Procedures and Documentation

Manuals of standard procedures for the operation of information systems, typically, are developed and maintained. Following standard procedures promotes uniformity and minimizes the chances of errors and fraud. It helps employees know what is expected of them in operating procedures and output quality. It is important that procedures be developed for both normal and unusual operating conditions. For example, procedures should tell employees what to do differently when their computers are not working. Finally, system, program, and operations documentation must be developed and kept up-to-date to ensure the correct processing of each application. Documentation is also invaluable in the maintenance of a system as needed improvements are made.

Authorization Requirements

Requests for systems development, program changes, or computer processing are frequently subjected to a formal review before authorization is given. For example, program changes generated by maintenance programmers should be approved by the manager of programming after consultation with the manager of computer operations and the manager of the affected end user department. Conversion to new hardware and software, installation of newly developed information systems, and changes to existing programs should be subjected to a formal notification and scheduling procedure. This minimizes their detrimental effects on the accuracy and integrity of ongoing computer operations.

Disaster Recovery

Natural and man-made disasters do happen. Hurricanes, earthquakes, fires, floods, criminal and terrorist acts, and human error can all severely damage an organization's computing resources, and thus the health of the organization itself. Many organizations, like airlines and banks, for example, are crippled by losing even a few hours of computing power. Many firms could survive only a few days without computing facilities. That's why organizations develop **disaster recovery** procedures and formalize them in a *disaster recovery plan*. It specifies which employees will participate in disaster recovery and what their duties will be, what hardware, software, and facilities will be used, and the priority of applications that will be processed. Arrangements with other companies for use of alternative facilities as a disaster recovery site and offsite storage of an organization's databases are also part of an effective disaster recovery effort.

Controls for End User Computing

In Chapter 8, we outlined some of the risks of end user application development. We also discussed measures companies are taking to ensure the quality and security of end user applications. However, what many firms are beginning to realize is that, in many cases, end user-developed applications are performing extremely important business functions. Instead of merely being systems for personal productivity or decision support, these applications are supporting the accomplishment of important business activities that are critical to the success and survival of the firm. Thus, they can be called *company-critical* end user applications.

FIGURE 15.9
Criteria and controls for company-critical end user applications.

- Methods for testing user-developed systems for compliance with company policies and work procedures.
- Methods for notifying other users when changes in mission-critical user-developed systems are planned.
- Thorough documentation of user-developed systems.
- Training several people in the operation and maintenance of a system.
- A formal process for evaluating and acquiring new hardware and software.
- Formal backup and recovery procedures for all user systems.
- Security controls for access to user and company computer systems, networks, and databases.

Figure 15.9 outlines controls that can be observed or built in to all *company-critical end user applications*. Many companies are insisting on such end user controls to protect themselves from the havoc that errors, fraud, destruction, and other hazards could cause to these critical applications and thus to the company itself. The controls involved are those that are standard practice in applications developed by professional IS departments. However, such controls were ignored in the rush to end user computing.

Figure 15.9 emphasizes a major point for managerial end users. Who is ultimately responsible for ensuring that proper controls are built in to company-critical applications? End users managers are! This emphasizes once again that all managers must accept the responsibility for managing the information system resources of their work groups, departments, and other business units.

Auditing Information Systems

An information services department should be periodically examined, or *audited*, by internal auditing personnel from the business firm. In addition, periodic audits by external auditors from professional accounting firms are a good business practice. Such audits should review and evaluate whether proper and adequate information system controls, procedural controls, physical facility controls, and other managerial controls have been developed and implemented. There are two basic approaches for **auditing information systems**—that is, auditing the information processing activities of computer-based information systems. They are known as (1) auditing around the computer and (2) auditing through the computer.

Auditing around the computer involves verifying the accuracy and propriety of computer input and output without evaluating the computer programs used to process the data. This is a simpler and easier method that does not require auditors with programming experience. However, this auditing method does not trace a transaction through all of its stages of processing and does not test the accuracy and integrity of computer programs. Therefore, it is recommended only as a supplement to other auditing methods.

Auditing through the computer involves verifying the accuracy and integrity of the computer programs that process the data, as well as the input and output of the computer system. Auditing through the computer requires a knowledge of computer operations and programming. Some firms employ special EDP auditors for this assignment. Special test data may be used to test processing accuracy and the control procedures built into the computer program. The auditors may develop special test programs or use audit software packages. See Figure 15.10.

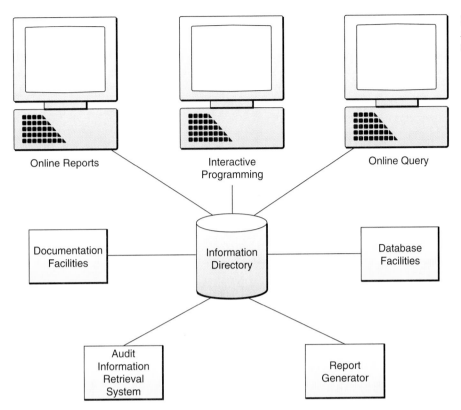

FIGURE 15.10
An example of the capabilities of an audit software package.

EDP auditors use such programs to process their test data. Then they compare the results produced by their audit programs with the results generated by the computer user's own programs. One of the objectives of such testing is to detect the presence of unauthorized changes or patches to computer programs. Unauthorized program patches may be the cause of "unexplainable" errors or may be used for fraudulent purposes.

Auditing through the computer may be too costly for some computer applications. Therefore, a combination of both auditing approaches is usually employed. However, both auditing approaches must effectively contend with the changes caused by computer-based information systems to the *audit trail*.

An **audit trail** can be defined as the presence of documentation that allows a transaction to be traced through all stages of its information processing. This journey begins with a transaction's appearance on a source document and ends with its transformation into information on a final output document. The audit trail of manual information systems was quite visible and easy to trace. However, computer-based information systems have changed the form of the audit trail. Information formerly available to the auditor in the form of visual records is no longer available or is recorded on media that can be interpreted only by machines. For example, real-time transaction processing systems have increased the invisibility of the traditional audit trail. Paper documents and historical files are frequently eliminated when remote terminals and direct access files are used.

Such developments make the auditing of such systems a complex but vital assignment. Therefore, auditing personnel should be included on the project team of all major systems development projects and consulted before smaller critical systems projects are implemented. In addition, auditing personnel should be notified of changes to major computer programs caused by program maintenance activities. Such procedures give the auditor the opportunity to suggest methods of preserving the audit trail. The auditor can also ensure that adequate controls are designed into systems being developed or modified.

Kevin Mitnick and Tsutomu Shimomura:
The Cyber Thief and the Security Expert

Every now and then a stunning breach propels Internet security into the limelight. One such security breach occurred Christmas day 1994 when hacker Kevin Mitnick scaled significant hurdles to break into the computer at the San Diego Supercomputer Center of security expert Tsutomu Shimomura, who was away on a cross-country skiing vacation near Lake Tahoe. The attacker slipped past a firewall computer by disguising his identity through a form of *spoofing* called sequence number attack. He made himself appear to the firewall as a trusted machine. Until this breach, firewalls were considered to be virtually fail-safe protection. But since 1985, Internet security experts have known of the particular weakness exploited by the attacker. Since the Christmas raid, the smug reassurance firewalls once provided has been shattered.

Mitnick, a 31-year-old fugitive hacker thought to have cracked open dozens of corporate and government computers since 1982, was arrested by agents of the U.S. Federal Bureau of Investigation in February 1995 at his home in Raleigh, North Carolina. The criminal charges against Mitnick are access device fraud and computer fraud, including the snatching of thousands of credit card numbers from the Internet. Kent Walker, assistant U.S. attorney in San Francisco, will prosecute the case.

According to an affidavit from FBI Special Agent Levord M. Burns, the cyber-manhunt went into high gear when Andrew Gross, a systems/network administrator at the San Diego Supercomputer Center, reported the Christmas Day intrusion into the files of computer security expert Shimomura. The intruder used known but apparently heretofore unused techniques called "IP spoofing and session hijacking" to get in, as outlined below.

- **Infiltration: IP spoofing.** This allows an intruder, essentially, to impersonate a local system's Internet protocol address. Other local systems can be tricked into believing incoming connections from the intruder actually originate from a local "trusted host" and will not require a password.

  Defense. Filter packets as they enter a firewall from the Internet, blocking any packet that claims to have originated inside a local domain.

- **Infiltration: Session hijacking.** Once the intruders gain top-level, system administrator *root access* on a system, they can use a hacker program to dynamically modify the Unix operating system, allowing them to hijack, or take over, an existing terminal and

log-in connections from any user on the system.

Defense. Prevent root compromise through careful system management. Installation of security patches and network controls such as firewalls.

Mitnick, who calls himself "the Condor," left an insulting digitized voice message for Shimomura, then added back-door access programs to Shimomura's computer. This allowed him to copy files, including advanced security software that other hackers could exploit. For example, one of the files was an unreleased copy of a program called SATAN (Security Administrators Tool for Analyzing Networks), which allows anyone to probe for security flaws in a network.

Some of Shimomura's files, as well as a compressed file of stolen credit-card numbers, wound up stored on the servers of the Well, an Internet access provider in San Francisco. The credit-card numbers were stolen from Netcom On-Line Communication Services, Inc., in San Jose, California, another Internet access provider that helped authorities with the electronic chase.

"The Well's files were not compromised or stolen, but some old and unused accounts became a storage bin for files that were stolen from other systems," a Well spokeswoman said. The huge illicit files tipped off Well technicians.

The Well then allowed Shimomura and the FBI to use a back room outfitted with three of Shimomura's powerful SPARC laptop workstations to monitor and track the hacker's continuing online activities, the spokeswoman said. The FBI affidavit alleged that Mitnick, to cover his tracks, used cellular modems to dial in to Internet access lines across the country. But the cellular numbers were eventually traced by Shimomura and FBI and Sprint security experts to Mitnick's new apartment in Raleigh, where he was arrested.

CASE STUDY QUESTIONS

1. How did Kevin Mitnick break into Tsutomu Shimomura's computer system? What security measures and controls would guard against such tactics?

2. What do you think was Mitnick's motive in breaking into Shimomura's computer system? What crimes did he commit? Explain.

3. How was Mitnick caught? How should he be punished? Defend your sentence.

Source: Adapted from Gary Anthes, "Hackers Try New Tacks," *Computerworld*, January 30, 1995, p. 12; Mitch Betts and Gary Anthes, "FBI Nabs Notorious Hacker," *Computerworld*, February 20, 1995, p. 4; Alan Radding, "Crash Course in 'Net Security," *Computerworld*, March 6, 1995, p. 90; and Jeff Goodell, "The Samurai and the Cyber Thief," *Rolling Stone*, May 4, 1995, pp. 40–45, 71.

SECTION II
Ethical and Societal Challenges of Information Technology

The Ethical Dimension

Ethical questions are involved in many strategic decisions, such as investment in human resources, modernization, product development and service, marketing, environmental decisions, and executive salaries. Often strategic issues are threats or opportunities that may significantly affect the firm's performance and are characterized by their novelty, complexity, and speed. Obviously, such threats or opportunities may involve a large ethical component. For example, Johnson & Johnson had to remove Tylenol from store shelves, and Manville Corporation quickly decided how to preserve the company's assets while meeting its obligations to victims during asbestos liability suits [17].

Whether we are in an ethical crisis or not is a subject of debate. But what is not debatable is that we are in the midst of an **information revolution,** in which information technology has dramatically magnified our ability to acquire, manipulate, store, and communicate information. Thanks to information technology, we have electronic tools which let us retrieve and communicate information in seconds to practically any person, in any place, at any time of the day. Thanks to IT, we can now communicate easily, work cooperatively, share resources, and make decisions, all electronically. But also thanks to information technology, it has now become possible to engage in ethical or unethical business practices electronically anywhere in the world.

That's why it is important for you to understand the ethical dimensions of working in business and using information technology. As a future managerial end user, it will be your responsibility to make decisions about business activities and the use of IT which will always have an ethical dimension that must be considered. See Figure 15.11.

For example, should you electronically monitor your employees' work activities and electronic mail? Should you let employees use their work computers for private business, or take home copies of software for their personal use? Should you electronically access your employees' personnel records or workstation files? Should you sell information about your customers, extracted from transaction processing systems, to other companies? These are a few examples of the types of decisions you will have to make which have a controversial ethical dimension. So let's take a closer look at ethical considerations in business and information technology.

Ethical Foundations

There are several **ethical philosophies** which you can use to help guide you in ethical decision making. Four basic ethical philosophies are: egoism, natural law, utilitarianism, and respect for persons [10]. Briefly, these alternative ethical philosophies are:

Egoism. What is best for a given individual is right.

Natural law. Humans should promote their own health and life, propagate, pursue knowledge of the world and God, pursue close relationships with other people, and submit to legitimate authority.

Utilitarianism. Those actions are right that produce the greatest good for the greatest number of people.

Tom Carroll/Phototake.

FIGURE 15.11
Managers must consider the ethical dimension of the business use of IT. Computer networks managed from this control room are designed to control refinery processes, ensure worker safety, and protect environmental quality.

Respect for persons. People should be treated as an end and not as a means to an end; and actions are right if everyone adopts the moral rule presupposed by the action.

There are many **ethical models** of how humans apply their chosen ethical philosophies to the decisions and choices they have to make daily in work and other areas of their lives. For example, one theory focuses on people's decision-making processes, and stresses how various factors of our perceptions of them affect our ethical decision-making process. Figure 15.12 illustrates this model. Notice how individual attributes; personal, professional, and work environments; and government/legal and social environments may affect our decision processes and lead to ethical or unethical behavior.

Another example is a *behavioral stage* theory which says that people go through several stages of *moral evolution* before they settle on one level of ethical reasoning. Figure 15.13 illustrates the stages in this model of ethical behavior. In this model, if you reach the final stage of moral evolution, your actions are guided by self-chosen ethical principles, not by fear, guilt, social pressure, and so on.

Business Ethics

Business ethics can be subdivided into two separate areas [18]. The first concerns the illegal, unethical, or questionable practices of managers or organizations, their causes, and their possible remedies. The second is concerned with the numerous ethical questions that managers must confront as part of their daily business decision making. For example, Figure 15.14 outlines some of the basic categories of ethical issues and specific business practices that have serious ethical consequences. Notice that the issues of employee privacy, security of company records, and workplace safety are highlighted because they have been major areas of ethical controversy in information technology.

How can managers make ethical decisions when confronted with business issues such as those listed in Figure 15.14? Several important alternatives based on theories of *corporate social responsibility* can be used [29,30].

FIGURE 15.12

A model of ethical decision making. Note the factors that may affect our ethical decision-making process.

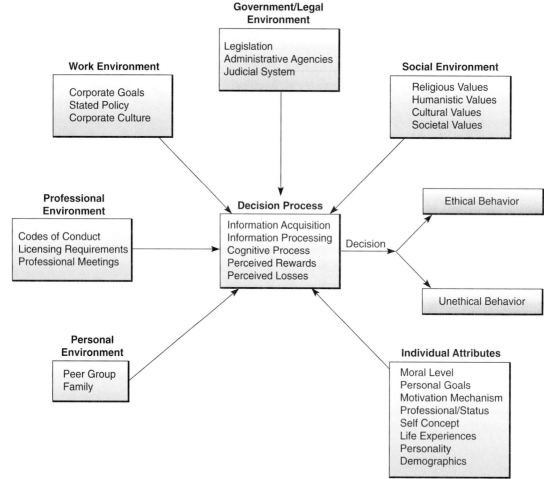

Source: Adapted from "A Behavioral Model of Ethical and Unethical Decision Making" by Michael Bonner, Clarence Gratto, Jerry Gravander, and Mark Tuttle, *Journal of Business Ethics*, June 1987, pp 265–280. Copyright © 1987 Kluwer Academic Publishers.

- **The stockholder theory** holds that managers are agents of the stockholders, and their only ethical responsibility is to increase the profits of the business without violating the law or engaging in fraudulent practices.
- **The social contract theory** states that companies have ethical responsibilities to all members of society, which allow corporations to exist based on a *social contract*. The first condition of the contract requires companies to enhance the economic satisfaction of consumers and employees. They must do that without polluting the environment or depleting natural resources, misusing political power, or subjecting their employees to dehumanizing working conditions. The second condition requires companies to avoid fraudulent practices, show respect for their employees as human beings, and avoid practices which systematically worsens the position of any group in society.

Stages of Morality		Illustrative Behavior
Level 1: Preconventional morality		
Stage 1	Punishment orientation	Obeys rules to avoid punishment
Stage 2	Reward orientation	Conforms to obtain rewards or to have favors returned
Level II: Conventional morality		
Stage 3	Good-boy/good-girl orientation	Conforms to avoid disapproval of others
Stage 4	Authority orientation	Upholds laws and social rules to avoid censure of authorities and guilt about not "doing one's duty"
Level III: Postconventional morality		
Stage 5	Social-contract orientation	Actions guided by principles commonly agreed on as essential to the public welfare—upheld to retain respect of peers and self-respect
Stage 6	Ethical principle orientation	Actions guided by self-chosen ethical principles (that usually value justice, dignity, and equality)—upheld to avoid self-condemnation

FIGURE 15.13
Stages of moral evolution. Note how people may evolve in their moral orientation through several levels of ethical reasoning.

Source: Adapted from "Education for the Moral Development of Managers: Kohlberg's Stages of Moral Development and Interactive Education" by Gerald D. Baxter and Charles A. Karick, *Journal of Business Ethics*, June 1987, pp. 243–248. Copyright © 1987 Kluwer Academic Publishers.

FIGURE 15.14
Basic categories of ethical business issues. Information technology has caused ethical controversy in the areas of employee privacy, security of company records, and workplace safety.

Equity	Rights	Honesty	Exercise of Corporate Power
Executive Salaries	Corporate Due Process	Employee Conflicts of Interest	Political Action Committees
Comparable Worth	Employee Health		*Workplace Safety*
Product Pricing	Screening	*Security of Company Records*	Product Safety
	Employee Privacy	Inappropriate Gifts	Environmental Issues
	Sexual Harassment	Advertising Content	Disinvestment
	Affirmative Action	Government Contract Issues	Corporate Contributions
	Equal Employment Opportunity	Financial and Cash Management Procedures	Social Issues Raised by Religious Organizations
	Shareholder Interests	Questionable Business Practices in Foreign Countries	Plant/Facility Closures and Downsizing
	Employment at Will		
	Whistle-blowing		

Source: Adapted from The Conference Board, "Defining Corporate Ethics," in Peter Madsen and Jay Shafritz, *Essentials of Business Ethics* (New York: Meridian, 1990), p. 18.

- **The stakeholder theory** maintains that managers have an ethical responsibility to manage a firm for the benefit of all of its *stakeholders,* which are all individuals and groups that have a stake in or claim on a company. This usually includes the corporation's stockholders, employees, customers, suppliers, and the local community. Sometimes the term is broadened to include all

FIGURE 15.15
Major aspects of the ethical and
societal dimensions of information technology. Remember that
IT can have both a positive and
a negative effect on society in
each of the areas shown.

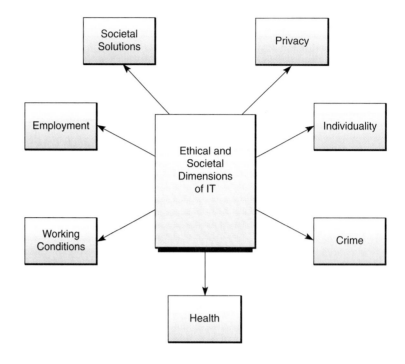

FIGURE 15.15
Major aspects of the ethical and
societal dimensions of information technology. Remember that
IT can have both a positive and
a negative effect on society in
each of the areas shown.

groups who can affect or be affected by the corporation, such as competitors,
government agencies, special interest groups, and the media. Balancing the
claims of conflicting stakeholders is obviously not an easy task for managers.

Ethical and Societal Dimensions of IT

Figure 15.15 illustrates several important aspects of the ethical and societal dimensions of information technology. It emphasizes that the use of information technology in business has major impacts on society, and thus raises serious ethical
considerations in areas such as privacy, crime, health, working conditions, individuality, employment, and the search for societal solutions through IT. However, you
should realize that information technology can have a beneficial effect as well as a
negative effect in each of these areas. For example, computerizing a production process may have the adverse effect of eliminating jobs, and the beneficial effect of
improving the working conditions and job satisfaction of employees that remain,
while producing products of higher quality at less cost. So your job as a managerial
end user should involve managing your work activities and those of others to try to
minimize the negative effects of IT and maximize its beneficial effects. That would
represent an ethically responsible use of information technology.

Ethics and Information Technology

To help you in making such ethical choices, it might be helpful to keep in mind four
ethical principles that can serve as guidelines in the implementation of any form of
technology [22]. Figure 15.16 illustrates some of the ethical risks that may arise in
the use of IT.

- **Proportionality.** The good achieved by the technology must outweigh the
  harm or risk. Moreover, there must be no alternative that achieves the same
  or comparable benefits with less harm or risk.

FIGURE 15.16
Ethical considerations of the potential harms or risks of the business use of IT.

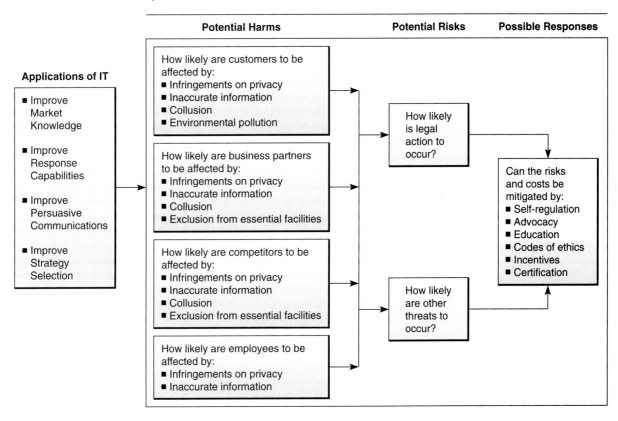

- **Informed consent.** Those affected by the technology should understand and accept the risks.
- **Justice.** The benefits and burdens of the technology should be distributed fairly. Those who benefit should bear their fair share of the risks, and those who do not benefit should not suffer a significant increase in risk.
- **Minimized risk.** Even if judged acceptable by the other three guidelines, the technology must be implemented so as to avoid all unnecessary risk.

Information Ethics

Another way to understand the ethical dimensions of IT is to consider the basic ethical issues that arise from its use to gather, process, store, and distribute information. Richard Mason [10] has posed four basic ethical issues, which deal with the vulnerability of people to this aspect of information technology. It is based on the concept that information forms the intellectual capital of individual human beings. However, information systems can rob people of their intellectual capital. For example, people can lose information without compensation and without their permission. People can also be denied access to information or be exposed to erroneous information. Mason summarizes these four ethical issues with the acronym PAPA—privacy, accuracy, property, and accessibility.

- **Privacy.** What information about one's self or one's associations must a person reveal to others, under what conditions, and with what safeguards? What things can people keep to themselves and not be forced to reveal to others?
- **Accuracy.** Who is responsible for the authenticity, fidelity, and accuracy of information? Similarly, who is to be held accountable for errors in information and how is the injured party to be made whole?
- **Property.** Who owns information? What are the just and fair prices for its exchange? Who owns the channels, especially the airways, through which information is transmitted? How should access to this scarce resource be allocated?
- **Accessibility.** What information does a person or an organization have a right or a privilege to obtain, under what conditions, and with what safeguards?

In answering these questions, Mason proposes the development of a new social contract, where information technology will help ensure everyone's right to fulfill his or her human potential. In this new social contract, information systems should be designed to ensure accuracy and not invade a person's privacy. Channels of information should be protected and information made accessible to avoid information illiteracy or deprivation. Finally, information systems should be designed to protect an individual's intellectual capital from unauthorized exposure, loss, or damage. Developing, protecting, and enforcing this social contract then becomes the responsibility of end users, managers, and IS professionals.

IT and Employment

The impact of information technology on **employment** is a major ethical concern and is directly related to the use of computers to achieve automation. There can be no doubt that the use of information technology has created new jobs and increased productivity, while also causing a significant reduction in some types of job opportunities. Computers used for office information processing or for the numerical control of machine tools are accomplishing tasks formerly performed by many clerks and machinists. Also, jobs created by information technology within a computer-using organization require different types of skills and education than do the jobs eliminated by computers. Therefore, individuals may become unemployed unless they can be retrained for new positions or new responsibilities.

However, there can be no doubt that information technology has created a host of new job opportunities for the manufacture, sale, and maintenance of computer hardware and software, and for other information system services. Many new jobs, such as systems analysts, computer programmers, and computer operators, have been created in computer-using organizations. New jobs have also been created in service industries that provide services to the computer industry and to computer-using firms. Additional jobs have been created because information technology makes possible the production of complex industrial and technical goods and services that would otherwise be impossible to produce. Thus, jobs have been created by activities that are heavily dependent on information technology, in such areas as space exploration, microelectronic technology, and scientific research.

IT and Individuality

A frequent criticism of information technology concerns its negative effect on the **individuality** of people. Computer-based systems are criticized as impersonal systems that dehumanize and depersonalize activities that have been computerized, since they eliminate the human relationships present in noncomputer systems. Although it is more efficient for an information system to deal with an individual as a number than as a name, many people feel a loss of identity when they seem to be "just another number."

Another aspect of the loss of individuality is the regimentation of the individual that seems to be required by some computer-based systems. These systems do not seem to possess any flexibility. They demand strict adherence to detailed procedures if the system is to work. The negative impact of IT on individuality is reinforced by horror stories that describe how inflexible and uncaring computer-based systems are when it comes to rectifying their own mistakes. Many of us are familiar with stories of how computerized customer billing and accounting systems continued to demand payment and send warning notices to a customer whose account has already been paid, despite repeated attempts by the customer to have the error corrected.

However, computer-based systems can be ergonomically engineered to accommodate **human factors** that minimize depersonalization and regimentation. People-oriented and user-friendly information systems can thus be developed. The computer hardware, software, graphical user interface, and other IT capabilities that make such systems possible are increasing rather than decreasing. For example, use of microcomputers has dramatically improved the development of people-oriented end user and work group information systems. Even everyday products and services have been improved through microprocessor-powered "smart" products.

IT and Working Conditions

Information technology has eliminated monotonous or obnoxious tasks in the office and the factory that formerly had to be performed by people. For example, word processing and desktop publishing make producing office documents a lot easier to do, while robots have taken over repetitive welding and spray painting jobs in the automotive industry. In many instances, this allows people to concentrate on more challenging and interesting assignments, upgrades the skill level of the work to be performed, and creates challenging jobs requiring highly developed skills in the computer industry and within computer-using organizations. Thus, information technology can be said to upgrade the *quality of work* because it can upgrade the quality of working conditions and the content of work activities.

Of course, it must be remembered that some jobs created by information technology, data entry, for example, are quite repetitive and routine. Also, to the extent that computers are utilized in some types of automation, IT must take some responsibility for the criticism of assembly-line operations that require the continual repetition of elementary tasks, thus forcing a worker to work like a machine instead of like a skilled craftsperson. Many automated operations are also criticized for relegating people to a "do-nothing" standby role, where workers spend most of their time waiting for infrequent opportunities to "push some buttons." Such effects do have a detrimental effect on the quality of work, but they must be compared to the less-burdensome and more creative jobs created by information technology.

Computer Monitoring

One of the most explosive ethical issues concerning the quality of work is **computer monitoring.** That is, computers are being used to monitor the productivity and behavior of millions of employees while they work. Supposedly, computer monitoring is done so employers can collect productivity data about their employees to increase the efficiency and quality of service. However, computer monitoring has been criticized as unethical because it monitors individuals, not just work, and is

FIGURE 15.17
Computer monitoring can be
used to record the productivity
and behavior of people while
they work.

Joan Feingersh/Uniphoto Picture Agency.

done continually, thus violating workers' privacy and personal freedom. For example, when you call to make a reservation, an airline reservation agent may be timed on the exact seconds he or she took per caller, the time between calls, and the number and length of breaks taken. In addition, your conversation may also be monitored [9, 11]. See Figure 15.17.

Computer monitoring has been criticized as an invasion of the privacy of employees because, in many cases, they do not know that they are being monitored or don't know how the information is being used. Critics also say that an employee's right of due process may be harmed by the improper use of collected data to make personnel decisions. Since computer monitoring increases the stress on employees who must work under constant electronic surveillance, it has also been blamed for causing health problems among monitored workers. Finally, computer monitoring has been blamed for robbing workers of the dignity of their work. In effect, computer monitoring creates an "electronic sweatshop," where workers are forced to work at a hectic pace under poor working conditions.

Political pressure is building to outlaw or regulate computer monitoring in the workplace. For example, a Privacy for Consumers and Workers Act has been introduced in both houses of the U.S. Congress. This proposed law would regulate computer monitoring, and protect the worker's right to know and right to privacy. Public advocacy groups, labor unions, and many legislators are pushing for action. In the meantime, lawsuits by monitored workers against employers are increasing rapidly. Jury awards to workers have been in the hundreds of thousands of dollars [10]. So computer monitoring of workers is one ethical issue that won't go away.

Privacy Issues

Information technology makes it technically and economically feasible to collect, store, integrate, interchange, and retrieve data and information quickly and easily. This characteristic has an important beneficial effect on the efficiency and effectiveness of computer-based information systems. However, the power of information technology to store and retrieve information can have a negative effect on the **right to privacy** of every individual. For example, confidential E-mail messages by employees are monitored by many companies. Confidential information on individuals contained in centralized computer databases by credit bureaus, government

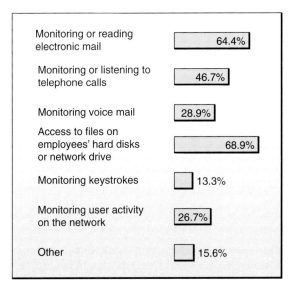

Source: Adapted from "Privacy Issue Comes of Age in a Networked World" by Laura Smith, *PC Week*. Copyright © 1993, Ziff-Davis Publishing Company.

FIGURE 15.18
Areas covered by a privacy policy in a survey of companies.

agencies, and private business firms has been stolen or misused, resulting in the invasion of privacy, fraud, and other injustices. The unauthorized use of such information has seriously damaged the privacy of individuals. Errors in such databases could seriously hurt the credit standing or reputation of an individual. See Figure 15.18.

Some of the important privacy issues being debated in business and government include the following [30]:

- Accessing individuals' private E-mail conversations and computer records (*violation of privacy*).
- Always "knowing" where a person is, especially as mobile and paging services become more closely associated with people rather than places (*computer monitoring*).
- Using customer information to market additional business services (*computer matching*).
- Collecting telephone numbers and other personal information to build individual customer profiles (*unauthorized personal files*).
- Using automated equipment either to originate calls or to collect caller information (*caller identification*).

Companies differ on their privacy policies, especially as they apply to electronic mail. For example, First Bancorporation of Ohio vows that it will never monitor the E-mail system used by its over 1,000 employees. It views E-mail correspondence as private. However, Eastman Kodak's policy states that it retains the right to monitor employee E-mail. But the company says that it will exercise that right only if there is reason to suspect that an employee is involved in illegal or unauthorized activity. The Bank of Boston, on the other hand, has a written policy banning all use of

E-Mail Privacy

FIGURE 15.19

Why companies do computer matching.

	Customer (Internal Information)	Customer (External Information)	Prospect
Acquire	1. Profile own customers based on existing transaction data.	2. Acquire new information about existing customers from a third party.	3. Acquire information about prospective customers from a third party.
Use	4. Target own customer for new or repeat business.	5. Market-research or cross-market own customers for new business.	6. Target prospective customers for new business.
Transfer	7. Transfer information about own customers within organization.	8. Transfer information about customers to a third party.	9. Transfer information about prospects to other third parties.

Source: Adapted from "How Did They Get My Name? An Exploratory Investigation of Consumer Attitudes toward Secondary Information Use" by Mary Culnane, *MIS Quarterly*, September 1993, p. 347. Reprinted with permission of the *MIS Quarterly*.

computers for personal business, and warns employees that it will actively monitor E-mail to enforce that policy. To underscore its reasons, the bank revealed that it had discovered an employee running a gambling operation and handicapping dog races over its E-mail system. [25, 31].

Computer Matching

Unauthorized use or mistakes in the **computer matching** of personal data is another controversial threat to privacy. Individuals have been mistakenly arrested and jailed, and people have been denied credit because their physical profiles or social security numbers have been used to match them incorrectly or improperly with the wrong individuals. A newer threat is the unauthorized matching of computerized information about you extracted from the databases of sales transaction processing systems, and sold to *information brokers* or other companies. You are then subjected to a barrage of unsolicited promotional material and sales contacts [11]. See Figure 15.19.

Such developments were possible before the advent of computers. However, the speed and power of large computer systems networked to direct access databases and remote terminals greatly increases the potential for such injustices. The trend toward nationwide telecommunication networks with integrated databases by business firms and government agencies substantially increases the potential for the misuse of computer-stored information.

Privacy Laws

In the United States, the Federal Privacy Act strictly regulates the collection and use of personal data by governmental agencies (except for law enforcement investigative files, classified files, and civil service files). The law specifies that individuals have the right to inspect their personal records, make copies, and correct or remove erroneous or misleading information. It also specifies that federal agencies (1) must annually disclose the types of personal data files they maintain, (2) cannot disclose personal information on an individual to any other individual or agency except under certain strict conditions, (3) must inform individuals of the reasons for requesting personal information from them, (4) must retain personal data records only if it is "relevant and necessary to accomplish" an agency's legal purpose, and (5) must "establish appropriate administrative, technical, and physical safeguards to ensure the security and confidentiality of records" [10, 11, 34].

In 1986, the Electronic Communications Privacy Act and the Computer Fraud and Abuse Act were enacted by the U.S. Congress. These federal **privacy laws** are a major attempt to enforce the privacy of computer-based files and communications. These laws prohibit intercepting data communications messages, stealing or destroying data, or trespassing in federal-related computer systems. In 1988, the Computer Matching and Privacy Act became law in the United States. It regulates the matching of data held in federal agency files to verify eligibility for federal programs. Such legislation should emphasize and accelerate the efforts of systems designers to use hardware, software, and procedural controls to maintain the accuracy and confidentiality of computerized databases.

The opposite side of the privacy debate is the right of people to know about matters others may want to keep private (freedom of information), the right of people to express their opinions about such matters (freedom of speech), and the right of people to publish those opinions (freedom of the press). One of the biggest battlegrounds in the debate are the bulletin boards, E-mail boxes, and online files of the Internet and public information networks such as Prodigy, CompuServe, and America Online. The weapons being used in this battle include *flame mail,* libel laws, and censorship.

Flaming is the practice of sending extremely critical, derogatory, and often vulgar E-mail messages (*flame mail*), or electronic bulletin board postings to other users on the Internet or online services. Flaming is especially prevalent on some of the bulletin board systems of special interest discussion groups such as the Internet's Usenet. There have been several incidents of racist or defamatory messages that have led to calls for censorship and lawsuits for libel. In addition, the presence of sexually explicit photographs and text at Internet locations has triggered lawsuits and censorship actions by the institutions involved [28]. See Figure 15.20.

Computer Libel and Censorship

Computer crime is a growing threat caused by the criminal or irresponsible actions of a small minority of computer professionals and end users who are taking advantage of the widespread use of computers and information technology in our society. It thus presents a major challenge to the ethical use of IT. Computer crime also poses serious threats to the security of computer-based information systems and makes the development of effective control methods a top priority. See Figure 15.21.

Computer Crime

One way to understand computer crime is to see how current **laws** define it. A good example of this is the U.S. Computer Fraud and Abuse Act of 1986. In a nutshell, this law says that computer crime involves access of "federal interest" computers (used by the federal government), or operating in interstate or foreign commerce (1) with intent to defraud, (2) resulting in more than a $1,000 loss, or (3) to gain access to certain medical computer systems. Trafficking in computer access passwords is also prohibited. Penalties for violations of this law are severe. They include 1 to 5 years in prison for a first offense, 10 years for a second offense, and 20 years for three or more offenses. Fines could range up to $250,000 or twice the value of the stolen data [9, 11].

Computer Crime Laws

FIGURE 15.20
Examples from the computer
libel and censorship debate, and
software piracy controversy.

Flaming liability

On-line service provider Prodigy Services Co. is under legal siege for defamatory remarks posted against a business.

Long Island-based securities firm Stratton Oakmont, Inc. filed a $200 million libel suit against the user who posted the defamatory comments and against Prodigy for failing to remove the offending message. Prodigy already screens E-mail for obscenities or racist comments; the "flame" in question accused Stratton Oakmont of fraudulent securities offerings.

Cyberspace censorship?

Against the objections of civil liberties activists, Pittsburgh-based Carnegie Mellon University has decided to cut sexually oriented newsgroups from its Internet servers because some of these on-line discussion forums are dedicated to posting explicit digitized photographs. Pennsylvania obscenity laws prohibit distribution of such images. These images have been downloaded or viewed more than 6 million times at the school, according to a study by one Carnegie Mellon research associate.

Copycat

David LaMacchia, a 20-year-old student at MIT, is in court for using the school's Internet servers to distribute copyrighted software.

LaMacchia faces charges of conspiracy to commit wire fraud. A conviction could bring him as many as five years in federal prison, plus fines well beyond the scope of ordinary school loans.

The twist for the defense is that LaMacchia collected no money for his efforts and neither uploaded nor downloaded any of the copyrighted programs. He only operated a bulletin board that made such activities possible.

Source: Adapted from "Cyberspace and The Law," by Derek Slater, *Computerworld*, December 5, 1994, p. 115. Copyright 1994 by Computerworld, Inc., Framingham MA 01701—Reprinted from *Computerworld*.

The Data Processing Management Association (DPMA) defines computer crime more specifically. In its Model Computer Crime Act, the DPMA defines computer crime as including (1) the unauthorized use, access, modification, and destruction of hardware, software, data, or network resources, (2) the unauthorized release of information, (3) the unauthorized copying of software, (4) denying an end user access to his or her own hardware, software, data, or network resources, and (5) using or conspiring to use computer resources to illegally obtain information or tangible property.

Examples of Computer Crime

Another way to understand computer crime is to examine examples of major types of criminal activity involving computers. Typically, this involves the theft of money, services, software and data; destruction of data and software, especially by *computer viruses;* and malicious access, or *hacking* of computer networks, and violations of privacy.

Money Theft

Many computer crimes involve the theft of money. They frequently involve fraudulent alteration of computer files to cover the tracks of the thieves, or to swindle money from others based on falsified records. For example, in the famous Volkswagen AG case of 1987, a group of company executives altered computerized foreign exchange accounting files to hide their theft of almost $253 million. In the most famous computer swindle, The Equity Funding Case of 1977, a group of con artists used a large insurance company's computers to generate thousands of falsified insurance policies with a face value of over $2 billion. The policies were then used as collateral to swindle investors out of more than $600 million for worthless stock in a fictitious company.

Mode	Misuse Type
External (EX):	
1. Visual spying	Observing of keystrokes or screens
2. Misrepresentation	Deceiving operators and users
3. Physical scavenging	Dumpster-diving for printout
Hardware misuse (HW):	
4. Logical scavenging	Examining discarded/stolen media
5. Eavesdropping	Intercepting electronic or other data
6. Interference	Jamming, electronic or otherwise
7. Physical attack	Damaging or modifying equipment, power
8. Physical removal	Removing equipment and storage media
Masquerading (MQ):	
9. Impersonation	Using false identities external to computer systems
10. Piggybacking attacks	Usurping communication lines, workstations
11. Spoofing attacks	Using playback, creating bogus nodes and systems
12. Network weaving	Masking physical whereabouts or routing
Pest programs (PP):	Setting up opportunities for further misuse
13. Trojan horse attacks	Implanting malicious code, sending letter bombs
14. Logic bombs	Setting time or event bombs (a form of Trojan horse)
15. Malevolent worms	Acquiring distributed resources
16. Virus attacks	Attaching to programs and replicating
Bypasses (BY):	Avoiding authentication and authority
17. Trapdoor attacks	Utilizing existing flaws
18. Authorization attacks	Password cracking, hacking tokens
Active misuse (AM):	Writing, using, with apparent authorization
19. Basic active misuse	Creating, modifying, using, denying service, entering false or misleading data
20. Incremental attacks	Using salami attacks
21. Denials of service	Perpetrating saturation attacks
Passive misuse (PM):	Reading, with apparent authorization
22. Browsing	Making random or selective searches
23. Inference, aggregation	Exploiting database inferences and traffic analysis
24. Covert channels	Exploiting covert channels or other data leakage
Inactive misuse (IM/25):	Willfully failing to perform expected duties, or committing errors of omission
Indirect misuse (IN/26):	Preparing for subsequent misuses, as in offline preencryptive matching, factoring large numbers to obtain private keys, autodialer scanning

FIGURE 15.21
Types of computer crime. Note the many ways that computer systems and networks have been misused for criminal purposes.

Source: Adapted from *Computer-Related Risks* by Peter Neumann (New York: ACM Press), 1995, p. 102. Copyright 1995, Association for Computing Machinery, Inc. By permission.

We do not know the extent of other major computer frauds, though losses from automated teller machines (ATMs) are smaller, but numerous. Financial institutions do not usually report them, because they fear a loss of consumer confidence and increases in insurance premiums. A lot of unsuccessful frauds have been reported, but many have been foiled more by accident than by vigilance. For example, in 1988, the Union Bank of Switzerland was automatically processing a money transfer of $54.1 million, when a computer failure caused a manual check of the transaction, which revealed it was fraudulent [23].

Service Theft

The unauthorized use of a computer system is called service theft. A common example is unauthorized use of company-owned microcomputers by employees. This may range from doing private consulting or personal finances to playing video games. So, if it's unauthorized use of someone else's computer, it's service theft. More serious cases are also more blatant. In one example, the manager of a university computer center in New York state and his assistant secretly used the school's computer to provide a variety of commercial computing services to their business clients.

Software Theft

Computer programs are valuable property and thus are the subject of theft from computer systems. However, unauthorized copying of software, or **software piracy,** is also a major form of software theft. Several major cases involving the unauthorized copying of software have been widely reported. These include lawsuits by the Software Publishers Association, an industry association of software developers, against major corporations that allowed unauthorized copying of their programs. Lotus Development Corporation and other software companies have also won lawsuits against competitors who marketed copies or clones that had the "look and feel" of their popular software packages.

Unauthorized copying is illegal because software is intellectual property that is protected by copyright law and user licensing agreements. For example, in the United States, commercial software packages are protected by the Computer Software Piracy and Counterfeiting Amendment to the Federal Copyright Act. In most cases, the purchase of a commercial software package is really a payment to license its "fair use" by an individual end user. Therefore, many companies sign *site licenses* that allow them to legally make a certain number of copies for use by their employees at a particular location. Other alternatives are *shareware,* which allows you to make copies of software for others, and *public domain* software, which is not copyrighted.

Data Alteration or Theft

Making illegal changes to data is another form of computer crime. For example, an employee of the University of Southern California was convicted of taking payments from students and changing their grades in return. Other reported schemes involved changes in credit information, and changes in Department of Motor Vehicles records that facilitated the theft of the cars to which the records referred. More recently, employees of the U.S. Social Security Administration were indicted for selling confidential personal information to *information brokers.* Also indicted were Virginia state police and other officers who sold criminal histories from the National Crime Information Center databases [4].

Computer Viruses: Destruction of Data and Software

One of the most destructive examples of computer crime involves the creation of **computer viruses** or *worms.* Virus is the more popular term but, technically, a virus is a program code that cannot work without being inserted into another program. A *worm* is a distinct program that can run unaided. In either case, these programs copy annoying or destructive routines into the networked computer systems of anyone who accesses computers "infected" with the virus or who uses copies of magnetic disks taken from infected computers. Thus, a computer virus or worm can spread destruction among many users. Though they sometimes display only humorous messages, they more often destroy the contents of memory, hard disks, and other storage devices. Copy routines in the virus or worm spread the virus and destroy the data and software of many computer users.

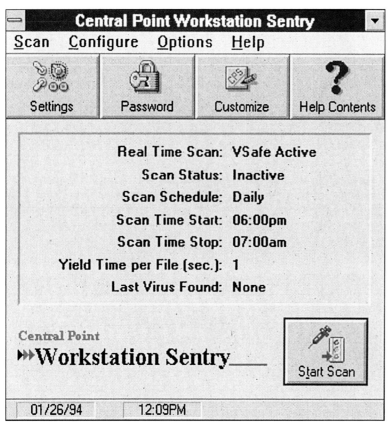

Courtesy of Central Point Software.

FIGURE 15.22
An example of the display of a computer vaccine program to eliminate computer viruses.

Computer viruses enter a computer system, typically, through illegal or borrowed copies of software, or through network links to other computer systems. Copies of software downloaded from electronic bulletin boards can be another source of viruses. A virus usually copies itself into the files of a computer's operating system. Then the virus spreads to main memory and copies itself onto the computer's hard disk and any inserted floppy disks. The virus spreads to other computers through telecommunications links or floppy disks from infected computers. Thus, as a good end user computing practice, you should avoid using software from questionable sources without checking for viruses. You should also regularly use vaccine programs which can help diagnose and remove computer viruses from infected files on your hard disk or in a network. See Figure 15.22.

Hacking, in computerese, is the obsessive use of computers, or the unauthorized access and use of networked computer systems. Illegal hackers (also called *crackers*) may steal or damage data and programs. One of the issues in hacking is what to do about a hacker who commits only "electronic breaking and entering," that is, gets access to a computer system, reads some files, but neither steals nor damages anything. This situation is common in computer crime cases that are prosecuted. In California, a court found that the typical computer crime statute language

Malicious Access

prohibiting "malicious" access to a computer system did apply to any users gaining unauthorized access to others' computer systems [10].

Crime on the Internet

Widely publicized attacks by hackers on the Internet have splashed the open electronic playground with a dose of cold reality and sent newcomers scrambling to beef up network security plans. In recent years, as the Internet has changed from the casual chat line of the academic and research communities to the playground of the computationally hip, attacks have increased. The influx has created a new breed of intruder who uses sophisticated software programs designed to automatically probe the Internet looking for system weaknesses [2].

Someone breaks into computer systems at Rice University and steals files of thousands of passwords, changes passwords, and destroys several files. Someone takes over a student's account on a computer at Northern Arizona University and sends a racist E-mail message to over 15,000 Internet users worldwide. Someone breaks into computers at IBM, Sprint, and an Internet service provider and sends an *electronic mail bomb* of thousands of angry E-mail messages to *Wired* magazine and a pair of *Newsday* reporters, jamming their Internet mailbox and knocking them off the Net. Someone breaks into the heavily protected computer networks of General Electric, causing them to disconnect from the Internet for three days. The Computer Emergency Response Team (CERT) of Carnegie Mellon University notices that someone is using network monitoring software (*sniffers*) to capture passwords over 110 times in 10 months on the Internet [1, 12].

These are just some of the computer crimes that hackers commit on the Internet each day, according to CERT. Figure 15.23 shows that computers connected to the Internet are vulnerable to hacking in many different ways. Services such as Gopher, FTP (file transfer protocol), electronic mail, or a network file system may be used to extract passwords or other vital files or to plant data that will cause a system to welcome intruders. A cracker may also use services that allow one computer on a network to execute programs on another computer—including remote procedure call (rpc), remote shell (rshell) and remote login (rlogin). This allows the intruder to gain *privileged access* directly. Telnet, a tool for interactive communication with remote computers, or Finger, a service that provides data about users, can help a cracker discover information to plan other attacks. A hacker may telnet to a computer's E-mail port, for example, to find out whether a particularly vulnerable mail program is running or to determine whether certain privileged user accounts may be easily accessible.

How can companies and end users protect themselves from such intruders? Password encryption and fire wall computers are tops on the list, followed by tight security management of a company's networks and encryption of sensitive files and databases. Frequent changing of user passwords helps, but a list of one-time passwords (only used once) carried by an end user is a lot better. In *challenge-response* password encryption systems, users carry a special calculator which encrypts a number provided by the system which they can use as a password into the system. Encryption of private E-mail messages and other data by popular E-mail and groupware packages is another good security measure for the Internet [35].

Health Issues

The use of information technology in the workplace raises a variety of **health issues**. Heavy use of computers is reportedly causing health problems like job stress, damaged arm and neck muscles, eye strain, radiation exposure, and even death by com-

FIGURE 15.23

Hackers can break into the Internet by using the vulnerability of its services to break into files, steal passwords, and take over an Internet server.

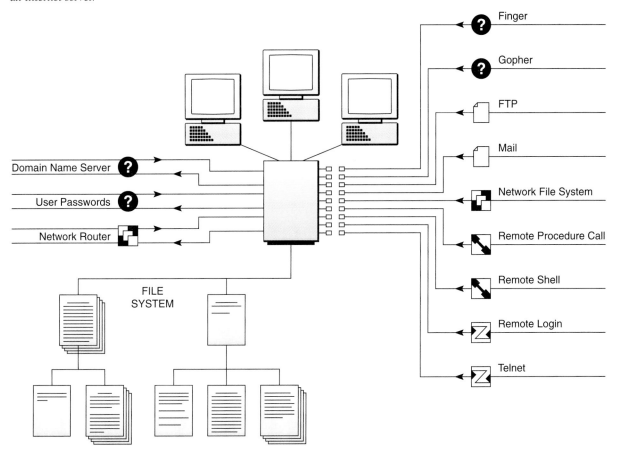

puter-caused accidents. For example, *computer monitoring* is blamed as a major cause of computer-related job stress. Workers, unions, and government officials criticize computer monitoring as putting so much stress on employees that it leads to health problems [10, 11].

People who sit at PC workstations or visual display terminals (VDTs) in fast-paced, repetitive keystroke jobs can suffer a variety of health problems known collectively as *cumulative trauma disorders* (CTDs). Their fingers, wrists, arms, necks, and backs may become so weak and painful that they cannot work. Many times strained muscles, back pain, and nerve damage may result. In particular, some computer workers may suffer from *carpal tunnel syndrome,* a painful, crippling ailment of the hand and wrist that, typically, requires surgery to cure [19].

Prolonged viewing of video displays causes eyestrain and other health problems in employees who must do this all day. Radiation caused by the *cathode ray tubes* (CRTs) that produce most video displays is another health concern. CRTs produce an electromagnetic field which may cause harmful radiation of employees who work too close for too long in front of video monitors. Some pregnant workers have

FIGURE 15.24
Ergonomic factors in the work-place. Note that good ergonomic design considers tools, tasks, the workstation, and environment.

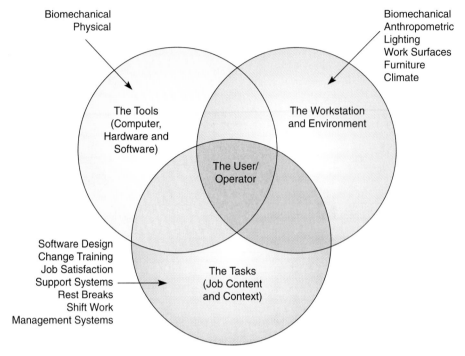

Solutions to some of these health problems are based on the science of **ergonomics,** sometimes called *human factors engineering.* The goal of ergonomics is to design healthy work environments that are safe, comfortable, and pleasant for people to work in, thus increasing employee morale and productivity. Ergonomics stresses the healthy design of the workplace, workstations, computers and other machines, and even software packages. Other health issues may require ergonomic solutions emphasizing *job design,* rather than workplace design. For example, this may require policies providing for work breaks every few hours from heavy VDT use, while limiting the CRT exposure of pregnant workers. Ergonomic job design can also provide more variety in job tasks for those workers who spend most of their workday at computer workstations. See Figure 15.24.

reported miscarriages and fetal deformities due to prolonged exposure to CRTs at work. However, several studies have failed to find conclusive evidence concerning this problem. Still, several organizations recommend that female workers minimize their use of CRTs during pregnancy. [10, 11].

Ergonomics

Societal Solutions

Before we conclude this section, it would be good to emphasize that information technology can have many beneficial effects on society. We can use information technology to solve human and social problems through **societal solutions** such as medical diagnosis, computer-assisted instruction, governmental program planning, environmental quality control, and law enforcement. For example, computers can be used to help diagnose an illness, prescribe necessary treatment, and monitor the progress of hospital patients. Computer-assisted instruction (CAI) allows a computer to serve as "tutor," since it uses conversational computing to tailor instruction to the needs of a particular student. This is a tremendous benefit to students, especially those with learning disabilities.

Information technology can be used for crime control through various law enforcement applications. For example, computerized alarm systems allow police to identify and respond quickly to evidences of criminal activity. Computers have been used to monitor the level of pollution in the air and in bodies of water, to detect the sources of pollution, and to issue early warnings when dangerous levels are reached. Computers are also used for the program planning of many government agencies in such areas as urban planning, population density and land use studies, highway planning, and urban transit studies. Computers are being used in job placement systems to help match unemployed persons with available jobs. These and other applications illustrate that information technology can be used to help solve the problems of society.

As a managerial end user, you have a responsibility to do something about some of the abuses of information technology in the workplace. Whether you are a manager, end user, or IS professional, you should accept the ethical responsibilities that come with your work activities. That includes properly performing your role as a vital human resource in the computer-based information systems you help develop and use in your organization. In this section, we have outlined several ethical principles that can serve as the basis for ethical conduct by managers, end users, and IS professionals. But what more specific guidelines might help your ethical use of information technology?

One way to answer this question is to examine statements of responsibilities contained in codes of professional conduct for IS professionals. A good example is the code of professional conduct of the Data Processing Management Association (DPMA), an organization of professionals in the computing field. Its code of conduct outlines the ethical considerations inherent in the major responsibilities of an IS professional. Figure 15.25 is a portion of the DPMA code of conduct.

The DPMA code provides guidelines for ethical conduct in the development and use of information technology. End users and IS professionals would live up to their ethical responsibilities by voluntarily following such guidelines. For example, you can be a **responsible end user** by (1) acting with integrity, (2) increasing your professional competence, (3) setting high standards of personal performance, (4) accepting responsibility for your work, and (5) advancing the health, privacy, and general welfare of the public. Then you would be demonstrating ethical conduct, avoiding computer crime, and increasing the security of any information system you develop or use.

As a managerial end user, you should insist that the ethical and societal dimensions of information technology be considered when computer-based information systems are being developed and used. For example, a major design objective should be to develop systems that can be easily and effectively used by people. The objectives of the system must also include protection of the privacy of the individuals and the defense of the system against computer crime. Control hardware, software, and procedures must be included in the systems design. The potential for misuse and malfunction of a proposed system must be analyzed and controlled with respect to all of an organization's present and potential stakeholders, individuals, and society as a whole.

You and Ethical Responsibility

FIGURE 15.25
Part of the DPMA standards of professional conduct. This code can serve as a model for ethical conduct by end users as well as IS professionals.

DPMA Standards of Professional Conduct

In recognition of my obligation to my employer I shall:

- Make every effort to ensure that I have the most current knowledge and that the proper expertise is available when needed.
- Avoid conflicts of interest and ensure that my employer is aware of any potential conflicts.
- Protect the privacy and confidentiality of all information entrusted to me.
- Not misrepresent or withhold information that is germane to the situation.
- Not attempt to use the resources of my employer for personal gain or for any purpose without proper approval.
- Not exploit the weakness of a computer system for personal gain or personal satisfaction.

In recognition of my obligation to society I shall:

- Use my skill and knowledge to inform the public in all areas of my expertise.
- To the best of my ability, ensure that the products of my work are used in a socially responsible way.
- Support, respect, and abide by the appropriate local, state, provincial, and Federal laws.
- Never misrepresent or withhold information that is germane to a problem or a situation of public concern, nor will I allow any such known information to remain unchallenged.
- Not use knowledge of a confidential or personal nature in any unauthorized manner to achieve personal gain.

Source: Adapted from Bruce E. Spiro, "Ethics in the Information Age," *Information Executive*, Fall 1989, p. 40.

It should be obvious to you that many of the detrimental effects of information technology are caused by individuals or organizations who are not accepting the ethical responsibility for their actions. Like other powerful technologies, information technology possesses the potential for great harm or great good for all humankind. If managers, end users, and IS professionals accept their ethical responsibilities, then information technology can help make this world a better place for all of us.

REAL WORLD CASE

 ## Jennifer Hart and Others: Flaming on the Internet

Dear Editor:

I am a marketing manager for a software vendor, so I use electronic mail frequently for communication, both internally and externally. I received my first flame mail letter when I accidentally sent a message to an entire Internet user group asking to be added to the subscriber list. Most users ignored this mistake, but one participant sent a flame message that made my hands shake.

The flame message was demeaning, insulting, and cruel. What was I, an idiot woman, doing on the Internet? Who was I to try to access this male-dominated domain? Didn't I know the basic rules of this world? What could I add to the user group when I couldn't even subscribe correctly? And on and on.

The whole experience so disgusted me that I never did get onto the user list (our company is a member of this organization), and when someone nicely responded with the correct information on how to subscribe, I was afraid to read the message. Later I learned that this was only a mild flame as flames go and that flaming is "part of the Internet experience." Sorry—it's not a part that I want to share.
Jennifer Hart
San Francisco

Dear Editor:

Responding to an honest question on the Internet with a flame letter is a form of cruelty. I have been on the receiving end of sarcasm, and I know how it made me feel. If flaming is done in person, the look on the flamee's face usually draws an immediate apology from the flamer. Unfortunately, the impersonal 'net keeps the flamer from seeing the effects of his or her message.
George W. Ball
Alfred, N.Y.

Dear Editor:

Many years ago, one of my friends wrote a paper for a sociology class on what is now in some circles called flaming or "keyboard lycanthropy."

He suggested that the root of this behavior lay in the poor bandwidth of the medium. E-mail lacks the stabilizing force of personal presence and the come-back-to-haunt-you character of the written letter. Consequently, people write things in newsgroups and E-mail that would result in

their being punched out, sued, or disowned by their parents if they had said it face-to-face.

These individuals are often charming enough in person; they exhibit sociopathic traits in computer-mediated communication simply because cultural forms lag behind technological trends. For many people, the mores and practices of culture are the only factors regulating their behavior. One need not be capable of independent ethical reasoning, or even common sense, to use a computer.

For that reason, I fear your call for ostracism of flamers is noble but unlikely to be heard.
Patty A. Hardy
Emeryville, California

Dear Editor:

I used to get offended by flame mail but I got some great advice from a buddy, a Houston police officer with about 12 years of experience dealing with obnoxious people: When one resorts to name-calling and personal attacks, it's because he's run out of intelligent arguments and knows it. The next time you get flamed, sit back and smile smugly; You won.
Ray LaFrance
Golden, Colorado

Dear Editor:

I guess cyberspace is just like the real world: A few bad apples—virus writers, hate groups, criminals of all sorts—make life miserable for all. The hardcore bullies won't change, but perhaps *Computerworld's* opinion pieces will help those on the fence not to get drawn into the negative and destructive. We can be part of the solution rather than part of the problem.
David K. Tao
West Chester, Pennsylvania

CASE STUDY QUESTIONS

1. What is flame mail?

2. Is sending flame mail over the Internet a crime? Is it ethical? Why or why not?

3. Have you been flamed? If so, what was your reaction? What should be done about flaming?

Summary

- **IS Security and Control.** One of the most important responsibilities of the management of computer-using business firms is to assure the security and quality of its information services activities. Controls are needed that ensure the accuracy, integrity, and safety of the information system activities and resources of the organization and its end users. Such controls attempt to minimize errors, fraud, and destruction, and can be grouped into three major categories: (1) information system controls, (2) procedural controls, and (3) physical facility controls, as summarized in Figures 15.2 and 15.3.

- **The Ethical Foundations of IT.** Business and IT activities involve many ethical considerations. Various ethical philosophies and models of ethical behavior may be used by people

in forming ethical judgments. These serve as a foundation for ethical principles and codes that can serve as guidelines for dealing with ethical business issues that may arise in the use of information technology.

- **Ethical and Societal Dimensions of IT.** Information technology raises serious ethical and societal issues in terms of the impact of IT on employment, individuality, working conditions, computer monitoring, privacy, computer matching, health, and computer crime. Managerial end users and IS professionals can help solve the problems of improper use of IT by assuming their ethical responsibilities for the ergonomic design, beneficial use, and enlightened management of information technology in our society.

Key Terms and Concepts

These are the key terms and concepts of this chapter. The page number of their first explanation is in parentheses.

1. Auditing information systems (590)
2. Audit trail (591)
3. Biometric controls (587)
4. Business ethics (595)
5. Computer crime (605)
   a. Examples (606)
   b. Laws (605)
6. Computer matching (604)
7. Computer monitoring (601)
8. Computer virus (608)
9. Control of end user computing (589)
10. Control totals (582)
11. Disaster recovery (589)
12. Encryption (586)
13. Ergonomics (612)
14. Ethical and societal dimensions of IT (598)
   a. Employment (600)
   b. Individuality (600)
   c. Health (610)
   d. Privacy (602)
   e. Societal solutions (612)
   f. Working conditions (601)
15. Ethical models (595)
16. Ethical philosophies (594)
17. Ethical principles (598)
18. Fault tolerant (588)
19. Fire wall (586)
20. Hacking (609)
21. Human factors (601)
22. Information system controls (580)
23. Information system security (580)
24. Physical facility controls (585)
25. Privacy laws (605)
26. Procedural controls (588)
27. Responsible end user (613)
28. Security codes (585)
29. Software piracy (608)
30. System security monitor (584)

Review Quiz

Match one of the key terms and concepts listed above with one of the brief examples or definitions listed below. Try to find the best fit for answers that seem to fit more than one term or concept. Defend your choices.

____ 1. Ensuring the accuracy, integrity, and safety of information system activities and resources.

____ 2. A computer system that acts as a safe transfer point for access to and from other networks by a company's networked computers.

____ 3. Control totals, error signals, and security codes are examples.

____ 4. The separation of the duties of computer programmers and computer operators is an example.

____ 5. Fire and access detection systems are examples.

____ 6. Software that can control access and use of a computer system.

____ 7. A computer system can continue to operate even after a major system failure if it has this capability.

____ 8. Periodically examine the accuracy and integrity of computer processing.

____ 9. The presence of documentation that allows a transaction to be traced through all stages of information processing.

___10. Managerial end users are responsible for information system controls in their business units.

___11. Using your voice or fingerprints to identify you electronically.

___12. A plan to continue IS Operations during an emergency.

___13. The sum of subtotals must equal a grand total.

___14. Scrambling data during its transmission.

___15. Passwords, user IDs, and account codes are examples.

___16. Examples are egoism, natural law, utilitarianism, and respect for persons.

___17. Ethical choices may result from decision-making processes or behavioral stages.

___18. Managers must confront numerous ethical questions in their businesses.

___19. Ethical guidelines in the use of information and information technology.

___20. Employees may have to retrain or transfer.

___21. Computer-based systems may depersonalize human activities.

___22. Constant long-term use of computers at work may cause health problems.

___23. Personal information is in computer-accessible files.

___24. Computer-based monitoring of environmental quality is an example.

___25. Tedious jobs are decreased and jobs are made more challenging.

___26. Using computers to identify individuals that fit a certain profile.

___27. Regulate the collection, access, and use of personal data.

___28. Using computers to monitor the activities of workers.

___29. People have a variety of needs when operating computers.

___30. Using computers to steal money, services, software, or data.

___31. It is illegal to access a computer with intent to defraud.

___32. Unauthorized copying of software.

___33. Electronic breaking and entering into a computer system.

___34. A program makes copies of itself and destroys data and programs.

___35. Designing computer hardware, software, and workstations that are safe, comfortable, and easy to use.

___36. End users should act with integrity and competence in their use of information technology.

Discussion Questions

1. How do IS controls, procedural controls, and facility controls improve IS performance and security? Give several examples to illustrate your answer.

2. Refer to the Real World Case on Kevin Mitnick and Tsutomu Shimomura in the chapter. What can be done to improve security on the Internet? Give several examples of controls and other security measures.

3. What artificial intelligence techniques can a business use to improve computer security and fight computer crime?

4. What controls are needed for end user computing? Give an example of three controls that could be used at your school or work.

5. What is disaster recovery? How could it be implemented at your school or work?

6. Refer to the Real World Case on Jennifer Hart and Others. What other Internet and online network customs or activities raise ethical issues in your mind? Give several examples, then evaluate the ethical issues involved and recommend an ethical position on that issue.

7. Is there an ethical crisis in business today? What role does information technology play in unethical business practices?

8. What business decisions will you have to make as a manager that have both an ethical and IT dimension? Give several examples to illustrate your answer.

9. Refer to the Real World Case on David LaMacchia of MIT in the chapter. Why did he do it? That is, what do you think LaMacchia's motive was in doing what he did? What ethical issues are involved?

10. What would be examples of one positive and one negative effect for each of the ethical and societal dimensions of IT illustrated in Figure 15.15? Give it a try.

Real World Problems

1. SABRE Computer Services and American Airlines: The Business Impact of IT Security

Once past the retina scanner, blast doors and half a dozen checkpoints, Terry Jones threads his way through myriad mainframes and 10 terabytes of stored data. Here, in the heart of American Airlines and the SABRE global travel reservations network, the president of SABRE Computer Services points to one of his group's latest accomplishments—floor space. That clearing in the 57,000-sq. ft. underground data center in Tulsa, Oklahoma, is the result of upgrades to higher-density processors and disk units. Drive arrays, robotic tape silos, and optical storage also contributed to better utilization of space.

"Since our big growth started in 1982, we have always

FIGURE 15.26
The financial impact on businesses when computers and networks go down.

Industry	Hourly Financial Impact	Average Hourly Financial Impact
Brokerage (retail)	$5.6 million–$7.3 million; range due to market conditions	$6.45 million
Credit card sales authorizations	$2.2 million–$3.2 million; range due to seasonal shopping	$2.6 million $89,500
Package shipping service requests	$24,500–$32,000; range due to peak shipping times	$23,250

been running into constraints, ranging from the number of digits we could handle in an entry field to the size of the data center," said Scott Nason, vice president of operations planning and performance at American Airlines. As the major user of the flight operations system and a significant user of the reservations system, Nason has high demands for reliability, quick fixes, and fast access that echo those of any information systems client. But he is more than a typical user. "We're unable to run the airline for more than a few minutes without SABRE Computer Services," Nason said.

But American Airlines is not alone. Biometric controls, high-security data centers, uninterruptable power sources, fire walls, backup databases, fault tolerant computers, and disaster recovery plans have become vital business requirements for companies who want to survive in today's networked marketplace. See Figure 15.26.

a. What categories and types of IS controls are mentioned in this case?

b. How important is IS security to businesses today? Explain with examples from this case.

Source: Adapted from Thomas Hoffman, "Risk Mounts for Mission Critical Data," *Computerworld*, March 27, 1995, pp. 1, 82, and Patrick Dryden, "American Airlines Copes by Consolidating," *Computerworld*, June 12, 1995, p. 75. Copyright 1995 by Computerworld, Inc., Framingham, MA 01701—Reprinted from *Computerworld*.

2. State of Virginia, U.S. Department of Labor, and Garber Travel: Computer Games at Work

The Virginia state government and the U.S. Department of Labor recently ordered employees to erase from their office PCs all games, including the Minesweeper and Solitaire applets included in Microsoft's Windows 3.1. Game playing by state employees during business hours is unproductive and "a clear-cut example of misuse of taxpayer funds," said Cliff Schroeder, a spokesman for Virginia's Secretary of Administration office in Richmond. "We wanted to nip it in the bud."

Government agencies are taking a hard line, perhaps to dispel taxpayer notions that civil servants are goofing off. A recent memo issued by John G. Dinneen, director of information resources management at the U.S. Labor Department in Washington, said office PCs "are to be used for official business purposes" with the possible exception of training

courses where games are useful for teaching mouse skills. "Otherwise, the playing of computer games is simply not in the interest of government, and games should be removed from all computers," Dinneen said.

Other organizations that reportedly have cracked down on PC games include Ford Motor Co., Sears Roebuck, the Boeing Co., and Garber Travel Services. Boston-based Garber has deleted Solitaire, Minesweeper, and Paintbrush from all 700 company PCs, said Rock Blanco, senior vice president of information technology. "Actually, from an information systems point of view, I'm far more concerned about unauthorized software and viruses than about users playing games," Blanco said. But the company feared it would lose clients if they discovered travel agents playing games, he said.

a. Why are the organizations in this case removing and prohibiting computer games at work?

b. Is playing computer games at work ethical? Why or why not?

Source: Adapted from Mitch Betts, "Drop That Mouse! The Boss Is Coming!" *Computerworld*, January 23, 1995, p. 12. Copyright 1995 by Computerworld, Inc., Framingham, MA 01701—Reprinted from *Computerworld*.

3. Southern Benefits Consultants and Utica Enterprises: Corporate Software Piracy

"We've run across situations where the IS department, including the IS manager, is personally installing or reproducing unlicensed software. Or they are allowing more users access off a server than they have licenses to support," says Robert Kruger, director of enforcement at the Business Software Alliance (BSA), in Washington. Software piracy in a corporate setting is "directly traceable to IS people," Kruger declares. "Either they're allowing it to happen or actively engaging in it." The problem is of more than academic interest because the BSA is famous for calling federal marshals to raid corporate sites. The cost of criminal or civil penalties, or even of an out-of-court settlement, is at least twice the cost of "getting legal" in the first place. If a piracy case actually goes to trial and the defendant loses, the penalties can be up to $100,000 per copyrighted work, which can add up to millions of dollars in liability, Kruger notes.

Last December, the BSA and federal marshals raided the offices of Southern Benefits Consultants, Inc., an insurance administrator in Dallas, after a tip from a former IS employee. By March, the company had agreed to pay a $110,000 settlement. "The problem was known by everybody in the company, but they had insufficient resolve to deal with it," Kruger says.

Similarly, Utica Enterprises, Inc., a leading auto parts maker in Shelby, Michigan, was turned in by a former IS employee who had helped the company do its own software audit; when the audit was complete, the managers of the company did nothing about the problems the audit had uncovered, Kruger says. In November, the company paid $260,000 to settle the lawsuit.

a. Why does Robert Kruger blame the IS function for much of the software piracy in business? Do you agree? Explain.

b. Is copying copyrighted software for more than backup purposes ethical behavior? Why or why not?

Source: Adapted from Mitch Betts, "Dirty Rotten Scoundrels?" *Computerworld,* May 22, 1995, pp. 1, 104. Copyright 1995 by Computerworld, Inc., Framingham, MA 01701—Reprinted from *Computerworld.*

4. Fitness Magazine: Computer Virus Attack

"Your data was delicious." That's the computer message that greeted Anthony Ferdaise and his business partner when they returned from a lunch break one day last October. To his horror, Ferdaise discovered that every file on their personal computer's hard drive had been erased, the casualties of a computer virus.

Ferdaise and his partner, who are developing San Diego–based Fitness Magazine, used data-recovery software in a vain attempt to recover some of the lost files. Unfortunately, they hadn't backed up their hard disk for more than two months. Ferdaise estimates that the time it took to reinstall the partners' software, re-create their data, and once again scan in photos set the magazine's launch back by six months.

Ferdaise says he has learned two valuable—if painful—lessons from his experience: check for viruses regularly, and back up religiously. He has purchased a tape backup system, which performs automatic, incremental backups in the middle of the night. Ferdaise says he also scans his system for viruses about once a week. To those who think viruses won't strike them, Ferdaise cautions, "I said the same thing—and it happened to me."

a. What is a computer virus? How do you think it might have invaded Fitness Magazine's computer system?

b. What can be done to prevent damage by computer viruses?

Source: Adapted from Martha Mangelsdorf, "Managing Technology," *Inc.,* March 1995, p. 121.

5. Canter and Siegel: Spamming on the Internet

Advertising on the Internet is still fairly new, and it's causing its share of controversy. The Internet is opening up to more commercial activities, but there are still some activities that are definitely taboo. A law firm in Phoenix, Canter and Siegel, posted ads for its immigration services to more than 5,000 Usenet newsgroups. The problem was that the vast majority of these newsgroups, or discussion areas, had nothing to do with the subject of immigration. According to

"netiquett," a widely followed set of Internet etiquette standards, this was a big no-no. One of the law firm's partners, Laurence Canter, was quoted as saying he knew his actions were offensive to many Usenet users, but he placed the ads anyway for purely business reasons.

In retaliation for this "shotgun advertising," also called *spamming,* hundreds of Usenet users flooded the law firm with junk faxes, obscene phone calls, and E-mail "mail bombs." The mail bombs clogged the system of Performance Systems International, the company providing Canter and Siegel with Internet access. The next morning, it pulled the plug on the law firm's Internet account. Canter and Siegel, in turn, threatened to sue.

Afterward, according to a statement released by Performance Systems, both parties reached an "interim agreement." The law firm agreed to "refrain from mass electronic postings of any unsolicited, non-contextual, non-topic advertisements." Performance Systems acknowledged that better education is needed to avoid similar situations in the future.

a. What is spamming? Why do Internet members frown on spamming?

b. Is spamming legal? Is it ethical? Defend your position.

Source: Adapted from Reid Goldsborough, "Advertising on the Internet," *PC Today,* February 1995, pp. 23–26. *PC Today,* 120 W. Harvest Drive, Lincoln, NE 68521.

6. Johnson Controls Inc.: Controlling Corporate Cyberspace

Fears that an employee's outburst in cyberspace will land the company in court are prompting many firms to set some rules. Employers are concerned about a variety of legal entanglements such as employees' downloading copyrighted software without authorization or sending flaming E-mail messages on the Internet or other online networks that could lead to charges of libel or harassment. A big fear is that outsiders will view an employee's posting as an official company statement. This could open the door for an injured party to file suit against both the individual and his or her employer.

For example, Johnson Controls, in Milwaukee, has developed a draft policy for internal and external electronic mail networks. The policy prohibits the following activities:

- Operating a business for personal gain, searching for jobs outside Johnson Controls, sending chain letters, or soliciting money for religious or political causes.
- Offensive or harassing statements, including "disparagement of others based on their race, national origin, sex, sexual orientation, age, disability, religious, or political beliefs."
- Sending or soliciting sexually oriented messages or images.
- Dissemination or printing of copyrighted materials (including articles and software) in violation of copyright laws.

Johnson Controls' policy was prompted by "the explosion of

user interest in the Internet," said Thomas McCullough, project leader for electronic messaging.

  a. Is Johnson Controls justified in developing a policy on employee use of the Internet and other online networks? Why or why not?

  b. Do you agree with the prohibitions in Johnson Controls'

policy? Would you add or delete any to protect the company or its employee's rights? Explain.

Source: Adapted from Mitch Betts and Ellis Booker, "Firms Draft Cyber-Safeguards," *Computerworld*, March 6, 1995, pp. 1, 12. Copyright 1995 by Computerworld, Inc., Framingham, MA 01701—Reprinted from *Computerworld*.

Application Exercises

1. Computer Ethics: A Quiz

What is ethical? Unethical? These were the questions behind a landmark study of computing ethics by SRI International in Menlo Park, California. Some 27 business and information systems professions, ethical philosophers, and lawyers were asked to respond to two dozen scenarios and decide if they were ethical. Their responses later formed the basis of a book entitled *Ethical Conflicts: In Information and Computer Science, Technology and Business* (published by QUED Information Sciences, Inc., 1990). Here are five typical scenarios:

Situation 1: The silent manager. A programming department manager discovers that one of his programmers and another from the inventory control department are involved in a corporate plan to defraud company stockholders by inflating company assets. The programs in question passed his quality assurance testing because they were identified as simulation and test files. Eventually, the fraud was discovered and the perpetrators were prosecuted. The programming manager—who is responsible for all application programming throughout the company but who had told no one of the scheme—was identified as an unindicted conspirator.

  Question: Was the manager unethical in not responding to evidence of wrongdoing?

Situation 2: The bare-bones system. A programming analyst at a large retailer is charged with project responsibility for building a customer billing and credit system. During the project, money runs out. The programming analyst had continually warned management about impending problems but was told to keep going and finish the development of a bare-bones system as quickly and cheaply as possible. To meet this directive, several key features—including safeguards, error detection, and correction—had to be left out until later versions. After a difficult and costly conversion to the new system, a great many unfixable problems arose, including wrong and unreadable billings and credit statements. Customers were outraged, fraud increased, company profits fell, and the project leader was blamed for it all.

  Question: Was it unethical for the project leader to order the system into production prematurely?

Situation 3: The nosy security manager. The information security manager at a large company also acted as administrator of a huge electronic mail network. During his regular

monitoring of mail, the manager discovered personal messages about football bets, sexual encounters, and other non-business matters. Printed listings of the messages were regularly given to the company's human resources director and corporate security director. In some cases, managers punished employees, using the messages as evidence. Employees became angry, charging their privacy rights on E-mail were the same as on the company's telephone or interoffice mail system.

  Question: Was it ethical for the information security manager to monitor E-mail and inform management of personal use?

Situation 4: All work, no play. The manager of research at a computer company explicitly told workers that anyone found playing games on company computers would be subject to dismissal. On a random inspection, a computer game was discovered in the files of a programmer, who was then punished?

  Question: Was it ethical for the manager to prohibit the use of computer games in employee files?

Situation 5: It's not our job. A software professional was charged with developing control software for part of a large system. The job looked straightforward and trouble-free. To work, the software required input from other units in the system. The developer then read an article by a noted software specialist and was convinced that input from the other units could be trusted. So he decided that neither the software he was designing nor the unit his company was providing would do the job they were supposed to. He showed his supervisor the article and explained his concerns, but was told only to worry about his group's part of the project.

  Question: Was it ethical for the developer to continue working on the project?

Responses of the SRI Panel:

Situation 1: *Unethical, 23; not unethical, 1; no ethics issue, 0.*

Situation 2: *Unethical, 24; not unethical, 0; no ethics issue, 0.*

Situation 3: *Unethical, 22; not unethical, 2; no ethics issue, 0.*

Situation 4: *Unethical, 7; not unethical, 5; no ethics issue, 13.*

Situation 5: *Unethical, 12; not unethical, 7; no ethics issue, 1.*

  Prepare an outline that evaluates the ethical dimensions of each of the preceding scenarios as follows:

a. Answer the ethical questions after each scenario.

b. Explain your ethical reasoning for each answer.

c. Explain why you think the SRI panel responded as it did to each question.

2. Computer Ethics: The Clipper Chip Controversy

In April 1993, the Clinton administration proposed a new standard for encryption technology, developed with the National Security Agency. The new standard is a plan called the Escrowed Encryption Standard. Under the standard, computer chips would use a secret algorithm called Skipjack to encrypt information.

The Clipper Chip

The Clipper Chip is a semiconductor device designed to be installed on all telephones, computer modems, and fax machines to encrypt voice communications. The Clipper Chip contains a powerful algorithm that uses an 80-bit encryption scheme that is considered impossible to crack with today's computers within a normal lifetime. Clipper uses a long key, which could have as many as 1,024 values. The only way to break Clipper's code would be to try every possible combination of key values. A single supercomputer would take a billion years to run through all of Clipper's possible keys.

The chip also has secret government master keys built in, which would be available only to government agencies. Proper authorization, in the form of a court order, would be necessary to intercept communications.

The difference between conventional data encryption chips and the Clipper Chip is that the Clipper contains a law enforcement access field (LEAF). The LEAF is transmitted along with the user's data and contains the identity of the user's individual chip and the user's key—encrypted under the government's master key. This would stop eavesdroppers from breaking the code by finding out the user's key. Once an empowered agency knew the identity of the individual chip, it could retrieve the correct master key, use that to decode the user's key, and so decode the original scrambled information. (Refer back to Figure 15.6 for an illustration of the Clipper Chip.)

The Government's Case

The Clinton administration's proposed new standards for encryption technology—the Clipper Chip—was supposed to be the answer to the individual's concern for data security and the government's concern for law enforcement. Law-abiding citizens would have access to the encryption they need and the criminal element would be unable to use encryption to hide their illicit activity.

Despite opposition from the computer industry and civil libertarians, government agencies are phasing in the Clipper technology for unclassified communications. Commercial use of Clipper is still entirely voluntary, and there is no guarantee it will be adopted by any organizations other than government ones. Yet several thousand Clipper-equipped telephones are currently on order for government use.

The Justice Department is evaluating proposals that would prevent the police and FBI from listening in on conversations without a warrant. A possible solution to the concerns about privacy invasion would be to split the decryption key into two or more parts and give single parts to trustees for separate government agencies. In theory, this would require the cooperation of several individuals and agencies before a message could be intercepted. This solution could compromise the secrecy needed to conduct a clandestine criminal investigation, but the Justice Department is investigating its feasibility.

The Opponents' Case

Computer industry and civil libertarian opponents of the plan have criticized its implementation on several counts:

- Terrorists and drug dealers would circumvent telephones if the telephones had the Clipper Chip. Furthermore, they might use their own chip.

- Foreign customers would not buy equipment from American manufacturers if they knew that their communications could be intercepted by United States government agents.

- The integrity of the "back door" system could be compromised by unscrupulous federal employees, thus violating the privacy of citizens.

- The remote possibility exists that an expert cryptologist could somehow break the code and sell the information to privacy violators.

The Ethical Dilemma

No method of data encryption will always protect individual privacy and society's desire to stop criminal activities. Electronic funds transfer systems and the information superhighway have made the need for private communications more important than ever before. Society's problems with drugs and terrorism complicate the issues, highlighting the sensitive balance among the individual's right to privacy, society's need to protect itself, and everyone's fear of Big Brother government tools.

a. Briefly summarize the ethical case for the Clipper Chip.
b. Briefly summarize the ethical case against the Clipper Chip.
c. What is your position? Explain your ethical reasoning, identifying any ethical principles you are using to support your position on this controversy.

Source: Adapted from Edward H. Freeman, "When Technology and Privacy Collide," *Information Systems Management*, Spring 1995, pp. 43–46, (New York: Auerbch Publications) © 1995 Warren, Gorham, & Lamont. Used with permission.

Review Quiz Answers

1. 23	10. 9	19. 17	28. 7
2. 19	11. 3	20. 14a	29. 21
3. 22	12. 11	21. 14b	30. 5a
4. 26	13. 10	22. 14c	31. 5b
5. 24	14. 12	23. 14d	32. 29
6. 30	15. 28	24. 14e	33. 20
7. 18	16. 16	25. 14f	34. 8
8. 1	17. 15	26. 6	35. 13
9. 2	18. 4	27. 25	36. 27

Selected References

1. Anthes, Gary. "Internet Hackers Hit GE, Others." *Computerworld,* December 5, 1994.
2. Anthes, Gary, and James Daly. "Internet Users Batten Down Hatches." *Computerworld,* February 7, 1994.
3. Austin, Nancy. "Personal vs. Professional Ethics: Handling the Job/Ethics Clash." *Working Women,* September 1992.
4. Betts, Mitch. "Personal Data More Public Than You Think." *Computerworld,* March 9, 1992.
5. Bloom, Paul; Robert Adler; and George Milne. "Identifying the Legal and Ethical Risks and Costs of Using New Information Technologies to Support Marketing Programs." In *The Marketing Information Revolution,* ed. Robert Blattbert, Rashi Glazer, and Hon Littel. Boston: Harvard Business School Press, 1994.
6. Carey, Jane, ed. *Human Factors in Information Systems: An Organizational Perspective.* Norwood, NJ: Ablex, 1991.
7. Cash, James, Jr.; Robert Eccles; Nitin Nohria; and Richard Nolan. *Building the Information Age: Structure, Control, and Information Technologies.* Homewood, IL: Richard D. Irwin, 1994.
8. Cheswick, William, and Steven Bellovin. "In Depth: Repelling the Wily Hacker." *Computerworld,* May 16, 1994.
9. Culnane, Mary. "How Did They Get My Name?: An Exploratory Investigation of Consumer Attitudes Toward Secondary Information Use." *MIS Quarterly,* September 1993.
10. Dejoie, Roy; George Fowler; and David Paradice, eds. *Ethical Issues in Information Systems.* Boston: boyd & fraser, 1991.
11. Dunlop, Charles, and Rob Kling, eds. *Computerization and Controversy: Value Conflicts and Social Choices.* San Diego: Academic Press, 1991.
12. Elmer-DeWitt, Phillip. "Terror on the Internet." *Time,* December 12, 1994.
13. Freeman, Edward, ed. *Business Ethics: The State of the Art.* New York: Oxford University Press, 1991.
14. Freeman, Edward. "When Technology and Privacy Collide: Encoded Encryption and the Clipper Chip." *Information Systems Management,* Spring 1995.
15. Fried, Louis. "Information Security and New Technology." *Information Systems Management,* Summer 1994.
16. Ganesan, Ravi, and Ravi Sandhu, guest editors. "Security Cyberspace." *Special Section: Communications of the ACM,* November 1994.
17. Harrington, Susan. "What Corporate America Is Teaching about Ethics." *Academy of Management Executive* 5, no. 1 (1991).
18. Kallman, Earnest, and John Grillo. *Ethical Decision Making and Information Technology: An Introduction with Cases.* New York: Mitchel McGraw-Hill, 1993.
19. Keppler, Kay. "A New Kind of Cutting Edge." *AI Expert,* February 1995.
20. Knouse, Stephen, and Robert Giacalone. "Ethical Decision Making in Business." *Journal of Business Ethics,* May 1992.
21. Madsen, Peter, and Jay Shafritz, eds. *Essentials of Business Ethics.* New York: Meridian, 1990.
22. McFarland, Michael. "Ethics and the Safety of Computer Systems." *Computer,* February 1991.
23. Neumann, Peter. *Computer-Related Risks.* New York: ACM Press, 1995.
24. Ranier, Rex, Jr.; Charles Snyder; and Houston Carr. "Risk Analysis for Information Technology." *Journal of Management Information Systems,* Summer 1991.
25. Rothfeder, Jeffrey. "Computers May Be Personal, but Are They Private?" *Beyond Computing,* January/February 1994.
26. Schuler, Doug, guest editor. "Social Computing." Special Section, *Communications of the ACM,* January 1994.
27. Schwartau, Winn. "Crypto Policy and Business Privacy." *PCWeek,* June 28, 1993.
28. Slater, Derek. "Cyberspace and the Law." *Computerworld,* December 5, 1994.
29. Smith, H. Jefferson, and John Hasnas. "Debating the Stakeholder Theory." *Beyond Computing,* March/April 1994.
30. Smith, H. Jefferson, and John Hasnas. "Establishing an Ethical Framework." *Beyond Computing,* January/February 1994.
31. Smith, Laura. "Privacy Issue Comes of Age in a Networked World." *PCWeek,* June 28, 1993.
32. Solomon, Robert. *Ethics and Excellence: Cooperation and Integrity in Business.* New York: Oxford University Press, 1992.
33. Stark, Andrew. "What's the Matter with Business Ethics?" *Harvard Business Review,* May–June 1993.
34. Straub, Detmar, and Rosann Collins. "Key Information Liability Issues Facing Managers: Software Piracy, Proprietary Databases, and Individual Rights to Privacy." *MIS Quarterly,* June 1990.
35. Wallich, Paul. "Wire Pirates." *Scientific American,* March 1994.
36. Wolinsky, Carol, and James Sylvester. "From Washington: Privacy in the Telecom Age." *Communications of the ACM,* February 1992.
37. Zahedi, Fatemeh. *Quality of Information Systems.* Danvers, MA. boyd & frazer, 1995.

REAL WORLD CASE

David LaMacchia of MIT: Software Piracy on the Internet

The Judge Rules

MIT student David LaMacchia escaped conviction on criminal charges that he ran an electronic bulletin board that others used to illegally upload and download more than $1 million in copyrighted software. U.S. District Court Judge Richard Stearns, in Massachusetts, ruled that the old federal wire fraud law under which LaMacchia was indicted was not applicable in his case.

Successful use of the wire fraud law against LaMacchia would have served to "criminalize...the myriad of home computer users who succumb to the temptation to copy even a single software program for private use," Stearns wrote in his decision.

While LaMacchia escaped a fine and a federal prison term, his alleged behavior won no support from the court. "If the indictment is to be believed, one might at best describe his actions as heedlessly irresponsible and at worst nihilistic, self-indulgent, and lacking in any fundamental sense of values," Stearns wrote.

He also said current copyright law could not be used against the MIT student because its criminal provisions require showing that copyright infringement was made "for purposes of commercial advantage or private financial gain," something LaMacchia was not alleged to have done. However, Stearns also wrote, "criminal as well as civil penalties should probably attach to willful, multiple infringements of copyrighted software, even absent a commercial motive on the part of the infringer."

The Editor's View

Let's suppose I advertise, through various means, a service for thieves. I will appear at the back door of, say, a sporting goods store at midnight. I'll bypass alarms and hold the door open, and anyone responding to my solicitation is free to walk in and take what he wants. I don't profit from this. I am motivated by the belief that some capitalist pig created the goods therein, and thus they should be free to the people.

Only the lunatic fringe would say I wouldn't be committing a crime. But this is pretty much what an MIT student is alleged to have done in allowing thieves to cart away more than $1 million worth of software, free of charge. Instead of standing at the door, David LaMacchia posted the software on a bulletin board and exhorted anyone to copy it. He knew it was wrong and tried to cover his tracks. He got caught.

Now mix in a silver-tongued lawyer, a Clinton-appointed prosecutor, a job-for-life federal judge and most of all, federal wiretap laws drafted before anyone reading this was born. Voila! LaMacchia walked.

With luck, this sorry episode will serve as one more reminder to the 104th U.S. Congress that business needs the protection of copyright laws revised to fit the times. Imagine the chilling effect on would-be software pirates of a $200,000 fine and a few years behind bars for Mr. LaMacchia. Hey, we're talking about the assisted theft of more than a million dollars' worth of goods!

Instead, the judge said, "he didn't do anything illegal." That ruling sets a precedent to exonerate the next person who holds open the back door. Make no mistake about it. There will be a next time and a time after that. And each will cost you money, as someone somewhere takes something without paying for it. Let your congressperson know the time is long past for the creation of laws to govern clearly illicit activity in cyberspace.

CASE STUDY QUESTIONS

1. Should David LaMacchia's actions be classified as a computer crime? Why or why not?

2. Is what LaMacchia did ethical behavior? Why or why not?

3. If LaMacchia had been convicted, of software piracy, how should he have been punished? Defend your sentence.

Source: Adapted from Gary Anthes, "Wire Fraud Law Falls Short," *Computerworld,* January 9, 1995, p. 16, and Bill Laberis, Editor-in-Chief, "Editorial: A Crime That Pays," *Computerworld,* January 9, 1995, p. 34. Copyright 1995 by Computerworld, Inc., Framingham, MA 01701—Reprinted from *Computerworld.*

Real World Case Studies

Introduction

This appendix contains the following 7 case studies:

- Unum Corporation: The Changing Role of the Chief Information Officer
- Merck Corporation: Global Systems Development
- Middleton Mutual: The Expert System Project
- The Union Bank of Switzerland: Using CASE for Development on a LAN
- Dominion-Swann Industries: The Ethics of Work Support Technology
- The Promus Companies: Management Support Systems
- The Condor and the Samurai: Crime and Ethics in Cyberspace

These real world cases describe the problems and opportunities faced by a variety of computer-using organizations. They are based on real situations faced by actual organizations, though the names of organizations and their employees have been changed in two of the cases to ensure confidentiality. Four cases are relatively short, two are of medium length, and one is a relatively long case study. However, they are all designed to give you an opportunity to integrate the knowledge of major information system concepts gained from reading and studying the text material, and to apply it to situations faced by real-world business firms and other organizations.

Solving Case Studies

Several approaches can be used in analyzing cases. The simplest approach is to read the case and then try to find the answers to the questions at the end of each case study. This should give you a good exposure to the business and information system situations contained in the case. A more formal methodology was discussed in Chapter 3 and is outlined in Figure A.1. Be sure to review the solution to the Auto Shack Stores case used as an example in Chapter 3. It will give you a good example of the use of this methodology to develop an information system solution to a business problem. Use this methodology to help you analyze a case study, develop an information system solution, and write up your results. Of course, you must first read the case, highlighting phrases or making notes that identify problems, opportunities, or other facts that may have a major bearing on your solution of the case.

Solution Constraints

The analysis you perform and the solutions you develop with the methodology outlined in Figure A.1 will be limited by several major constraints. Being aware of these constraints will help you use this methodology more effectively. These constraints are:

FIGURE A.1
A systems solutions methodology. Use this methodology to
help you analyze an actual or
case study situation, develop a
solution, and write up your
results.

1. **Identification of problems, opportunities, and symptoms.** Separate major problems or opportunities from their symptoms. Identify the major components of systems you feel are most involved in the problems or opportunities that you discover.

2. **Statement of the problem.** Briefly state the major problems or opportunities facing the organization.

3. **Summary of alternative solutions.** Briefly identify several alternative solutions to the problems you have identified.

4. **Evaluation of alternative solutions.** Evaluate the alternative solutions using evaluation criteria that reveal their advantages and disadvantages.

5. **Rationale for the selected solution.** Select the solution that best meets the evaluation criteria, and briefly explain the reasons for its selection.

6. **Information system design proposal.** Propose a design for any new or improved information systems required by the selected solution. Use one or more tools of analysis and design to illustrate your design proposal.

7. **Implementation plan.** Propose an implementation plan for the selected solution.

- **Information.** The amount of data and information you can gather in a situation or find in case study material. Remember that in the real-world, decisions usually have to be based on incomplete information.

- **Assumptions.** The number of assumptions you make or are allowed to make. Good, rational assumptions are a key ingredient in good solutions, since there is never enough information available in either real-world situations or case studies. You should identify and explain the reasons for any major assumptions you make.

- **Knowledge.** The amount of knowledge about business and information systems you possess. Hopefully, this will increase as you cover more of this textbook and as you progress in your business education and career. For now, do the best you can with the knowledge you have.

- **Time.** The amount of time you spend on the analysis of the problem. Obviously, the more time you have, the more information you can gather, and the more analysis you can perform. Of course, time constraints are typical in the real world, so make judicious use of the time you have.

Unum Corporation: The Role of the Chief Information Officer

Interested in the top information systems post at a consistently prosperous company that has a well-regarded track record in new product development, customer service, and innovative use of information technology? If so, pack your bags and head north along the Maine coast to Portland. Destination: Unum Corporation, a $3.4 billion disability insurance company in search of a corporate chief information officer. Qualifications for the job include extensive international business experience, a commitment to customer service, and a passion for keeping costs down.

And oh yes, you must have an ability to work well in the long shadows cast by the company's two previous high-profile CIOs. See Figure A.2.

IS professionals with an affinity for making grand plans involving bleeding-edge technology need not apply. Instead, Unum is seeking an implementer, someone who can steer an IS course initially charted by former CIO John Alexander, then recharted by his successor, Bob Best, who left Unum in June after less than a year on the job. Unum Corp. grew tired of life at the bleeding edge of technology and hired Bob Best as a business-minded CIO to replace John Alexander. Then the new CIO left.

Today, Best holds the top IS post at Provident Life and Accident Co. in Chattanooga, Tennessee. Alexander, who served as Unum's CIO for six years, now

Help Wanted

The Revolving Door

IMMEDIATE OPENING—WANTED: THE PERFECT CIO

A $3.4 billion disability insurance company with a proven track record in new product development, customer service, and innovative use of information technology seeks top information systems manager.

QUALIFICATIONS INCLUDE:

- Extensive international business experience.
- Commitment to customer service.
- Passion for keeping costs down.
- Ability to steer an already-chartered IS course.

Send resume to Unum Corporation, Portland, Maine.

FIGURE A.2
What Unum wants in a CIO.

Source: Julia King. "Help Wanted: The Perfect CIO." *Computerworld,* September 26, 1994, pp. 101–104. Copyright 1995 by Computerworld, Inc., Framingham, MA 01701—Reprinted from *Computerworld.*

runs his own consulting company, Business Technology Consulting, Inc., also in Portland. Both men have left their stamp on the IS strategy that Unum now wants a new CIO to oversee.

The Bleeding Edge

For instance, it was during Alexander's tenure that much of the distributed technology in use today was introduced. This includes more than 4,000 PCs running under DOS, Windows, and OS/2, as well as a sophisticated network infrastructure that links some 7,200 employees across the United States and Canada, the United Kingdom, and Japan. "Under John, we had a strong technical focus. Before he came, we had some not very successful implementations, and he was seen as a technical turnaround person," explains Dick Curry, vice president of enterprise technology services and acting CIO. "He was very successful at introducing new technologies and taking us pretty much from a mainframe to a more distributed mind-set."

Others who recall Alexander characterize him as a CIO who liked to push the technology envelope. They also say it was this aggressiveness that eventually caused him to fall out of favor with higher-ups. "John was driving Unum to the brink of the bleeding edge, so they got rid of the bleeding-edge guy and brought in someone to drive the technology for business' sake," says a company source who requested anonymity.

Looking back on his tenure, Alexander concedes a certain amount of high-tech pyrotechnics. Between 1990 and 1992, for example, he says Unum implemented client/server systems with IBM 3270 terminals and Windows- and OS/2-based PCs on the client side and Unix and OS/2 servers—without commercially available communications software to link the disparate platforms. "We got out on the leading edge of client/server technology and built some proprietary tools," Alexander says. "Maybe we were a hair ahead of our time."

A Business Focus for IT

Best's focus, on the other hand, was strictly business. He came to the company from Colonial Life & Accident Co. in Columbia, South Carolina, which Unum acquired in early 1993. What he brought with him, company insiders say, was a keen eye for value as well as a talent for devising IS solutions to meet real business needs. A prime example is Colonial's PC-and-mainframe-based client view system. This system lets Unum representatives view all of a customer's transactions and note customers' questions and concerns online. Using the system, the same customer service staffer can answer all of a customer's questions in a single phone call. Moreover, the marketing and product development teams use the information collected during these calls to design new offerings.

It was during Best's tenure that Unum reorganized. Under its current structure, 12 affiliate companies—and their IS departments—operate more or less independently within a strategic framework. That framework is set by a corporate team of six senior officers, including James F. Orr, chairman and chief executive officer. By allowing each affiliate "to find its own way," Orr says Unum can more easily meet its ambitious goals by 1998, its 150th anniversary. These include increasing revenue growth, reducing operating expenses, and significantly bolstering overall customer satisfaction.

One of Best's first actions was to state in a brochure how IS would help meet these goals. This document became the foundation for the company's overall IS strategy. Essentially, the brochure states that any and all information systems should be designed, managed, and maintained by the business units that use them, rather than by a centralized IS department. Best also imported a strong user-oriented approach to building information systems and soliciting ideas and feedback. This, too, remains intact.

During a recent printer acquisition process, for example, business users accompanied IS staffers to all vendor presentations. "They went to all of the meetings and understood all of the pieces and had an equal voice in the decision-making process," Curry says.

The Search for a CIO

In the coming months, he says, business users from Unum's 12 affiliates will also help decide whether the company should lease or buy additional mainframe computing capacity. But for now, Unum's main IS challenge is to recruit a CIO who can move forward with the information technology strategy the company has laid out for itself. IS is directly involved in the search, says Curry, who helped write the job specifications and is participating in the interview process.

"It's going to take a very special person. Of that, there's no doubt in my mind," says Ann Waecker, Unum's head of operating excellence within enterprise technology services. "Someone who looks at our strategy and says 'This is great but I want to do this to it' is not the person we're looking for," she says. "What we're looking for is more of a relationship builder, a collaborative person, and I think it will be very difficult to find that person."

Some say what Unum seems to want is for Best to return to finish what he started. "Bob was a very hands-on kind of CIO who built our [IS] strategy and then jumped ship. I just don't think he gave it enough time," one manager says. That a company would search for a new CIO with a similar philosophy to the one who left isn't very unusual, says Jerry Loev, a consultant at CSC Impact, an IS consulting firm in Cambridge, Massachusetts. "The only thing peculiar is that they'd admit it," Loev says.

For whatever reason, Best doesn't want to talk about Unum or why he left. Several calls to his office went unanswered. But Paul Bonaca, vice president of IS at Colonial and a close co-worker of Best's when he was at the company, thinks he has a pretty good idea. Best, Bonaca says, was operations-oriented, having worked his way to the management ranks through underwriting and policy claims functions. At Colonial "he had almost all of the company. He was running the company internally," Bonaca says. By contrast, Best's role at Unum was strictly IS. "He was in a staff position and didn't have people working for him," Bonaca says.

What Unum Wants

Ann Beadle, CIO at Unum America, the company's largest affiliate, says she will look to the new corporate CIO for assistance in acquiring different kinds of IS expertise. Four new systems initiatives, all of which call for the use of outside contractors, are currently under way or being planned at Unum America. "So one of the things I'll be looking for from the new CIO is help in executing an [outside] vendor strategy," she says.

Curry says the new corporate CIO can expect to work with business colleagues well-versed in information technology. Much of their knowledge, Curry says, stems from Unum's 15-year-old chargeback system under which individual affiliates are billed for things like seconds of CPU time and cylinders of data storage capacity. Whoever fills the CIO slot can expect to play a key role in Unum's ongoing program of leveraging IS to bolster external customer service. Last year, the corporation set a five-year goal of reducing by 40 percent the number of insurance customers who do not rate Unum's service as excellent or very good.

Last but not least, prospective candidates for the CIO post should have a lot of experience in international business because Unum's plans call for aggressive expansion in overseas markets. The company already has a presence in Europe, thanks to its acquisition last year of Duncanson & Holt, Inc., a $500 million London-based insurer. In Canada, Unum's business has continued to grow during the past several years, and now the company is targeting the Pacific Rim. In March, following its acquisition of a license to do business there, Unum opened its first office in Japan, Curry says.

For the time being, Curry says, "we're still several months off from confirming anyone." So far, Unum has interviewed several candidates for the CIO job, but has still not selected anyone.

CASE STUDY QUESTIONS

1. **The revolving door:**
   a. Why did Unum hire John Alexander as their CIO?
   b. Why did Unum replace Alexander with Bob Best?
   c. Do you approve of Unum's CIO decisions? Why or why not?

2. **Business versus technology focus:**
   a. What are the advantages and disadvantages of Alexander's "bleeding-edge" IT strategy?
   b. What are the benefits and limitations of Best's business focus for IT at Unum?

3. **Unum's search for a CIO:**
   a. Do you approve of what Unum wants in its new CIO? Why or why not?
   b. What type of CIO and what strategic IT focus do you think Unum needs? Why?
   c. What should be the top priority and first actions taken by Unum's new CIO? Explain your position.

Merck Corporation: Global Systems Development

Introduction

Merck Corporation is one of the largest and most successful pharmaceutical companies in the world. It has been selected as the "most admired" U.S. corporation several years in a row. Merck is a $5 billion dollar company, number one in the world. It has 10 products that each bring in more than $100 million in sales per year, and it has 2 or 3 products that bring in more than $1 billion per year.

Besides making hefty profits, Merck has provided incalculable service to developing countries free of charge. For example, it gives away a drug that stops river blindness, a particularly horrible disease that has plagued sub-Saharan Africa for generations. Before Merck's discovery, river blindness was so widespread that it had actually become part of the culture of many tribal groups in sub-Saharan Africa (around Niger). The population had become so used to becoming blind at the age of six or so that its entire structure was premised on this disease. Merck's drug gives sight to millions of people and awakens them to a new and richer life. There is no way to measure the beneficence of this act on the part of Merck.

Approximately 47 to 52 percent of Merck's sales are overseas, depending on the exchange rate. Approximately 70 percent of these overseas sales are made in Europe (France, England, Italy, Spain, Portugal, and other countries). Its drugs are sold at an approximate 70 percent markup, which is needed to recoup the very high costs of research and development.

As a drug company, Merck faces intense regulation in each market in which it conducts business. Each country has a different and highly restrictive regime for managing the legal drug trade. This regulation has a great impact on the prices that Merck is *allowed* to charge. In many national markets, the largest customer is the national health service, which purchases large amounts of drugs to dispense to patients of the plan. Negotiations with these national health services determine the prices that Merck will charge. The high degree of variability among countries and their markets forces Merck to tailor its business activities to each market. For example, in Europe, Merck has 13 subsidiaries.

The Role of Information Technology

This regulatory and business operations structure drives the information technology support system. In the 1990 Computerworld Premier list, Merck was ranked as "the most effective user of information systems" in the drug market. At the time it was reported, Merck had an information systems budget of $185 million and was employing approximately 1,000 MIS professionals. Merck is a heavy user of

Source: Edward M. Roche, *Managing Information Technology in Multinational Corporations* (New York: Macmillan Publishing Co., 1992), pp. 99–103. Reprinted with the permission of Simon & Schuster from the Macmillan College text *Managing Information Technology in Multinational Corporations* by Edward Roche. Copyright © 1992 by Macmillan College Publishing Company, Inc.

computers in the drug development phase, using them for molecular modeling and crystallography. In 1989–1990, Merck installed an IBM 3090 supercomputer. In the 1980s, Merck had been one of the first companies to equip its sales force with portable personal computers. Merck uses a great deal of automation in its manufacturing. It was reported in 1989 that Merck used an automated line to package 240 bottles per minute for a physician's sample pack of two new drugs in a "one-by-four" package designed by Merck.

According to Merck, it has a "United Nations" type of organization in its information systems function: it has separate IS departments in each country. The larger of these departments, or *satellites,* has approximately 40 to 50 MIS professionals. The United Nations model refers to a type of multinational organization that has specific replicable units in each country. It is very different from a business in which a single unit or function serves many different countries simultaneously. We see in the case of Merck that although a single organization, perhaps for Europe as a whole, might be more efficient, regulatory structures prevent this from happening. Some writers distinguish what they term a *multidomestic* firm and a *global* firm. They use the term *multidomestic* in the same way Merck uses *United Nations model* and point out that in multidomestic industries a company pursues separate strategies in each of its foreign markets while viewing the competitive challenge independently from market to market, whereas a global industry pits one multinational's entire worldwide system of product and market positions against another's.

The International Financial Consolidation System

The financial reporting structures of Merck are tightly controlled. It is one of the most profitable multinational corporations in the world, although it has not formed its own internal bank, as some other multinational corporations have. Each month, 89 financial reports arrive at Rahway, New Jersey, from the various overseas locations of the company. It takes Merck approximately three weeks to close its books for the preceding month. It is necessary for Merck to get this information before it can formulate financial strategy.

Prior to this, the consolidation process was manual. The various subsidiaries around the world would create their local reports and then use facsimile to transmit these to headquarters. After the summary reports arrived in Rahway, they would go through data entry and consolidation. The format of the incoming reports was not entirely standard, which produced the need for a great deal of manual accounting work at headquarters. A staff was set up to handle this job. This process was essentially manual in spite of the great investments that had been made in information technology in the past.

Designing a New System

To simplify this process, management decided to work toward building an information system that would link headquarters with the satellite locations. This would be done by uploading the reports from the field to headquarters. A high-level task force was appointed to solve this problem. After much study and more than one year, the team developed a system to achieve this. Unfortunately, it would require rewriting code at each location. Their solution called for an aggressive programming effort that was beyond the capability of the number of team members allocated for this project. In addition, the particular approach selected would require constant recoding, and the number of programs would proliferate.

The problem lay in the preference for building a "supersystem" at headquarters that was capable of dealing with the incoming format of each of the different subsidiaries reporting. It was estimated that creation of this system would have taken approximately $500,000 on the conservative side.

An additional complication was that the subsidiary satellite locations did not all have the same type of equipment. Some of the locations had IBM System 36 minicomputers, while others had the more advanced System 38.

As realization spread of the impending problems, a new management team was brought in to assess the situation. The new team quickly realized that the situation was impossible. In order to meet the schedule, the team would have had to use eight people to write more than 700 programs in eight weeks. This was highly unlikely considering the time it had taken just to write a simple program to handle only a portion of the requirements.

A New System Design

The new management of the project realized that the original team had invested a great amount of time and effort into the solution they had come up with. There would be a great deal of demoralization and frustration if the effort was quashed at the start, and this frustration could lead to outright rebellion.

The new management then divided the team into two parts. One-half was assigned to continue working on the old approach, and the other half was assigned to work on an alternative solution (which won out in the end). The alternative solution was based on a Lotus 1-2-3 type of program that would work with a database-type application. Only 40 programs were required, and they were written in RPG and were far less complex. This was a great simplification over the original plan, which required more than 700 programs of much greater complexity.

The second solution was based on the S/36 architecture, which was less advanced than the S/38 but was a common architecture. Programs and applications developed on the S/36 would run on the S/38, but not the other way around. The S/38 platform was more sophisticated and ran better software, but the S/36 was a "common denominator" among the platforms available. When the idea of using the common denominator came up, there were complaints that the solution would "not be using the full capabilities of the S/38." In addition, the software would also operate on a PC. From the point of view of the locations that were operating S/38s, the solution proposed would amount to "running inferior software on a superior machine." On the surface, this appeared to be a waste of computing capacity.

The counterargument to this was that using an application common to all of the machines would radically reduce the amount of coding required to get the operation up and running. Because of its simplicity, this solution quickly won out. Not only was it easier to manage, but the first "solution" was incapable of being implemented because of the tremendous coding and programming required.

Additional savings were realized when the time for installation came. The packets of the new program were simply mailed to each of the locations, with instructions for use. After a few hours on the phone during the initial setup phase of troubleshooting, the systems were up and running. This was a very different outcome than would have resulted if a programming team were required to go out to each remote location and practically customize a package. In addition, should changes to the system be required, much of this could be done centrally in Rahway.

Death of a System Proposal

The second team immediately realized that the Rahway operation could be very quickly simplified, eliminating the need for much of the manual accounting work that was required for consolidation. In effect, it would be possible to achieve one- or two-day consolidations using a modification of the linkages between the remote S/36s and the machines in Rahway. However, this could have taken away work from some of the persons on the accounting staff who had built a career on knowing how to reconcile the different types of statements from around the world. When it was realized that the information technology system could replace much of the administrative function of these people, then the issue became more *political* in nature. The project was killed.

CASE STUDY QUESTIONS

1. **The role of IT:**
   a. How effectively does Merck use IT in its business? Explain.
   b. Do you approve of how Merck organizes its IS function? Explain your reasoning.

2. **Designing a new system:**
   a. Does Merck need a new financial consolidation system? Explain.
   b. Which of the two proposed financial consolidation systems do you prefer? Why?

3. **Death of a system proposal:**
   a. Why was the new system proposal killed? Do you approve? Why or why not?
   b. What went wrong in the attempt to introduce new information technologies and a new financial system at Merck?
   c. What would you have done differently? Defend your proposal.

Middleton Mutual: The Expert System Project

Introduction

Middleton Mutual is a large insurance company headquartered in Philadelphia. Its chief information officer, Dennis Devereaux, and vice president of information systems planning, Max Vargo, are about to request $1 million to develop an expert system for Linda Peterson's property and casualty (P&C) underwriting department. They've discussed the expert system with President Bill Hayes, CFO Hal Atkins, and other members of the capital expense committee and until now have felt confident it would be approved. But according to the messages in the company's electronic mailbox, the project seems less certain.

The Expert System Proposal

Welcome to Middleton E-mail.
You have 1 new message.
To:　　DDevereaux, CIO
From:　MVargo, VP, IS planning
　　　Finished the paperwork for expert systems underwriting program. Expected benefits are soft—intangibles like more consistent underwriting and faster turnaround—but compelling. Absent any big changes, we can get it to Capital Expense Committee for next week's meeting. Are you checking with Bill Hayes? I'll check if you want.

Welcome to Middleton E-mail.
You have 1 new message.
To:　　WHayes, president
From:　DDevereaux, CIO
　　　Just wanted to confirm that we will be submitting our expert systems proposal to the CEC next week. We've pinned down the figures, and they're well within the $1 million we budgeted. We've selected a shell program from a first-rate vendor and lined up a top-notch knowledge engineering consultant who specializes in insurance applications. Two of our most experienced underwriters and eight programmers from my department will work closely with the consultant. We're excited about this program and are anxious to get started.

Justifying IT Investments

Welcome to Middleton E-mail.
You have 1 new message.
To: DDevereaux, CIO
From: WHayes, president
    Sorry I haven't had a chance to get to you sooner. Given last quarter's results, we're not in a position to approve any projects that don't pay for themselves almost immediately. Be sure your justification form shows concrete and immediate financial benefits. Promises of "better service" won't cut it.

Welcome to Middleton E-mail.
You have 1 new message.
To: WHayes, president
From: DDevereaux, CIO
    Bill, this isn't like replacing 50 people with a computer in the back office. How can you quantify staying in business? I thought we agreed this was the first step to getting Middleton on a level IS playing field. You remember the progression: first, the expert system for multiperil, then we take it to commercial auto and workers' comp. Next we'll upgrade the mainframes and connect our databases and other systems with the expert systems. When we're all connected, we'll be ready for our ultimate goal of letting agents analyze risk and quote policies on the spot. If we delay, we'll be left in the dust. I've seen it in other companies—you try to save a few dollars, and you wind up broke.

Welcome to Middleton E-mail.
You have 1 new message.
To: DDevereaux, CIO
From: WHayes, president
    I'd like to see you do the project, but we need to know what the payoff is. Everything should have a number attached. If expert systems are more efficient, the committee will want to know how much more efficient. I'm just cautioning you to be straightforward about the financial implications.

Welcome to Middleton E-mail.
You have 1 new message.
To: HAtkins, CFO
From: WHayes, president
    Any more thoughts on the expert systems project? Dennis may not be able to document concrete savings, but I keep looking over my shoulder at companies that are getting into this artificial intelligence business: Cigna, Travelers, USAA, Fireman's Fund. I heard about an expert system that analyzed an application and said to write it at substandard when the company's best underwriter had decided it was standard. They reexamined the case and found out the underwriter was wrong.

Welcome to Middleton E-mail.
You have 1 new message.
To: WHayes, president
From: HAtkins, CFO
    I think we should stand firm on this unless we see convincing numbers. It looks to me like another black hole we'll keep throwing money into. We can't afford any more runaway technology projects. Devereaux says he wants to get us into laptops, but he doesn't have any idea whether that's going to cut our administrative costs or underwriting losses or what. He's got a technology solution looking for a

problem. If he can prove there are direct productivity benefits, he'll have my support. But we're getting hit from all sides—taxes, interest rates, soft prices. I'm worried about next quarter. And the quarter after that.

Welcome to Middleton E-mail.
You have 1 new message.
To: LPeterson, VP, P&C
From: DDevereaux, CIO
    Some members of the CEC, including Bill Hayes, are leaning against the expert system project. I know I've got your support on this, but I'd appreciate it if you'd let Bill and Hal know that you're behind the project. They don't seem to realize that this application has very real benefits for your department.

Welcome to Middleton E-mail.
You have 1 new message.
To: DDevereaux, CIO
From: LPeterson, VP, P&C
    Sorry to hear the committee is going against your proposal, but I don't think I can say anything to change the outcome. Bill and Hal are running things by the numbers. Roger Lerch, my best underwriter, is retiring in six months, and Lucy Townsend and Henry Ballard are going next year. That kind of experience is hard to replace. But let's not worry too much about it. I can get something started under my budget which is how things usually work around here. If I didn't use the back door, I'd have an abacus on my desk. Besides, my people will accept it better if we take the lead. Right now, the underwriters say there's too much judgment involved for expert systems to do their job. They have to get used to the idea.

Welcome to Middleton E-mail.
You have 1 new message.
To: LPeterson, VP, P&C
From: DDevereaux, CIO
    I haven't given up on the project, and I've budgeted for it. It's just a matter of convincing Hal and Bill that it's worth the money. A word from you would certainly reinforce the idea that there's a real business need.

Welcome to Middleton E-mail.
You have 1 new message.
To: MVargo, VP, IS planning
From: DDevereaux, CIO
    This is going to be a harder sell than I thought. I'm sure Hal Atkins has talked Bill out of it. Atkins is dead set against technology investments of any kind unless they have immediate financial benefits. Why don't you put together some fancy slides of the data you got—show how expert systems make fewer mistakes than human experts and how much time it takes to process an application with and without the system. Use some of the material the vendors gave us. And reserve the conference room for Monday afternoon. Meanwhile, I'll decide how to play this—shelve the proposal for now or give Bill and Hal the numbers they want, even if they're half-baked.

Involving End User Management

Playing IT Politics

Welcome to Middleton E-mail.

You have 1 new message.

To: DDevereaux, CIO

From: MVargo, VP, IS planning

　　　Not surprised Atkins is giving this department a hard time. Maybe we should do development in-house. We can promise less trouble with integration and more functionality with a customized system. DP can do the project. We can hire a knowledge engineer to work with programmers who are interested in artificial intelligence rule sets and neural networks, things other companies are afraid of. Should I talk to the guys in DP?

Welcome to Middleton E-mail.

You have 1 new message.

To: MVargo, VP, IS planning

From: DDevereaux, CIO

　　　Let's not reopen the make-buy issue. I'm firm on using a shell. If we produce a functional stand-alone system in months instead of years, we won't get our water turned off. Then we can tackle the integration. Just get the data and sit on this for now. Don't discuss it with anyone in DP, and whatever you do, don't talk about neural networks or neural-computing with anyone outside the department. People might get the wrong idea about what we're trying to do.

The Ways Things Get Done

Welcome to Middleton E-mail.

You have 1 new message.

To: JParker, secretary

From: LPeterson, VP, P&C

　　　Joan, let me know how much is left in our budget for office supplies and furniture. Also, get me a list of our approved software vendors. And set up a meeting with Roger Lerch and Lucy Townsend. I have a special project for them.

 CASE STUDY QUESTIONS

1. **The expert system proposal:**

   a. What are the benefits and limitations of Middleton's proposed expert system?

   b. Should the expert system proposal be approved? Why or why not?

2. **The politics of IT investments:**

   a. Do you approve of how CIO Dennis Devereaux has promoted the expert system project with top and end user management? Explain.

   b. What is VP Linda Peterson's position? Do you agree with what she is proposing? Why or why not?

   c. What would you do at this point? Explain your reasoning.

The Union Bank of Switzerland: Using CASE for Development on a LAN

Christian Gabathuler is a tall, sensitive-looking man with a doctorate in physics. Swiss companies often are run by people with PhDs; there is an emphasis on academics in that country that enables young people to move leisurely through the educational process, taking a required break for mandatory military service, then to join a large corporation, and finally to work their way up through the ranks. The country's military heritage translates into an emphasis on the hierarchical organizational structure. There is also a tendency to manage by consensus. Although this allows for good long-term strategy, Gabathuler thinks it slows the decision-making process.

Dr. Gabathuler runs the information services organization at the Union Bank of Switzerland (UBS), North American region, with responsibility for operations, telecommunications, application development, and the information center. Gabathuler had received the mandate from Zurich to move forward with the implementation of LANs into the company's North American region, beginning with the New York office, then proceeding to offices in Toronto, Houston, Los Angeles, San Francisco, and other locales.

The implementation of LANs at UBS was initially driven by the need for a more effective communication platform. Bank personnel would often find themselves with a plethora of host computer terminals, PCs, printers, and online service terminals in order to access information. Implementing LANs at UBS would enable users to tap these multiple resources through a server; in other words, users could log onto a host session, then "hot key" and log onto another session for an online service, and hot key to another session for a local PC application—all from one workstation.

Introduction

It soon became apparent to Gabathuler that the usefulness of LANs was more than the technology they provided: "To use the full power of the LAN you need a cooperative environment," which requires strong teamwork and the ability to overcome a "turf" mentality. "It's more than technology," says Gabathuler. "It's a way of thinking."

The UBS telecommunications group was assigned the task of installing and configuring the LAN, and training the staff of the first targeted LAN for the private

The Inspiration for the Change to LANs

Source: Don Thompson, *Reorganizing MIS: The Evolution of Business Computing in the 90's* (Carmel, IN: SAMS Publishing, 1992), pp. 161–165.

banking group in the New York office. Private banking had a particularly pressing need for a LAN—that group had a business plan to expand business substantially over the next few years and needed the capability to effectively service those clients. The business manager of investment services who ran the private banking business for the bank understood well the implications of more computing power on his doorstep and his ability to become more competitive with that processing power. Business needs were driving his interest in LANs.

The telecommunications group successfully installed the initial pilot LAN. The Zurich office, again seeing the requirements of the LAN primarily within the realm of communications, had laid out very specifically the physical configuration of the LAN, without dictating the applications platform (including software tools) that were to be installed.

The information center was responsible for installing a suite of tools on the LAN for end users. These tools included application development tools, spreadsheets, document and word processors, and even computer-aided systems engineering (CASE) tools. Down the line, the information center was given the responsibility of implementing a pilot imaging application.

It became quickly apparent that the LAN tools would enable the business manager to move around the somewhat slow application development process that was the norm within the central or corporatewide, development staff and to get an application up and running quickly. The worries of central IS and of Dr. Gabathuler were that the proliferation of LAN application development would create a mess—poorly documented applications lacking anything resembling standardization.

Although the central development staff may have been slower, at least they developed solutions that worked within an overall architecture, effectively addressed security issues, and were maintainable by their IS professionals. At the business unit, a consultant or summer intern might be brought in to develop a system, then leave, having neither documented the system effectively nor "passed the baton" to another staff person with equal or better knowledge.

Standardizing User-Developed Systems

The CASE tool was envisioned as a method of offering standardization within this decentralized, departmental development effort if and where such standardization was needed. Standards would be enforced through the tool itself, with its data dictionary, diagrams, and self-documenting environment.

In evaluating several CASE tools, however, managers quickly found that not all were appropriate for the kind of development envisioned at the departmental level. Some tools were very expensive and obviously meant for a mainframe or large-scale development environment. The following characteristics were deemed necessary for a CASE tool purchased to perform departmental and rapid application development:

- Good network version.
- Support of multiple methodologies (meaning different types of diagramming standards).
- Ease of use and ability to be learned quickly.
- Support for the desired rapid development cycle.

The inherent fear among some computer-literate business users was that the introduction of the CASE tool into a LAN development environment would slow things down. Why? The programmer could not immediately jump into coding the system (the real work), but would have to spend inordinate amounts of time performing analysis that would not directly result in productive activity (coding). Documentation, in this sense, was not a primary concern to the business user; or if it was, it took a back seat to getting the application up and running quickly.

The platform for proving the value of a CASE tool wound up being the development of a pilot application on the pilot LAN in private banking. This pilot was, however, a highly visible, critical application that was deemed by upper management as essential to the business goals of private banking. Such an application underscored the importance it had, on the one hand, and the imperative, on the other, for the information center to successfully pilot this theoretical CASE tool environment into a real-world situation.

A pilot application in investment services (INVS) was chosen to demonstrate the usefulness of CASE tools on a LAN. The application was an analyst reporting system (ARS) that was used to track private banking account closings and acquisitions and give a consolidated view of private banking accounts for performance measurement. The application was developed by a CASE-experienced IS analyst working closely with the investment services LAN administrator and prospective system users. The application uses a combination of downloads. A monthly analyst's report, also maintained within the system, is reconciled with the download. See Figure A.3.

This pilot application will introduce an environment, tools, and techniques for LAN development. Once supported by a rigorous training program, the environment could become a platform through which consistent, quality LAN applications are developed throughout the firm.

Fortunately for the information center, the pilot application was up and running in three months, and was well-documented to boot. The CASE tool included diagrams on how the system was structured that could be maintained by other departments or offices for similar applications. Most importantly, the system actually

Pilot Application for CASE Tool Environment—Investment Services

---

The CASE tool was used to do the following:

- Develop a process diagram to document system processes.
- Develop a table description diagram that describes the tables in the system.
- Check the data dictionary for any interface standards that may apply to the application.

The document library/data dictionary and the application development tool were used to develop:

- Design specifications (logical design).
- Table specifications (physical implementation).
- Source code.

A rapid development tool was used to:

- Prototype the system and demonstrate it to users.
- Generate most of the code to support system functions.
- Create all reporting and input functions.

FIGURE A.3
How the LAN-based CASE tool was used at Union Bank.

worked. This success instantly sold the concept of LAN application development to other business managers, who knew that IS had projected a year and a half for development of the same system on the traditional platform.

Results of the LAN Strategy at UBS

As the LAN strategy evolved, it became evident that CASE would not work for every application. According to Joel Kizer, the bank's information center manager, the bank is now moving toward application generators in addition to CASE tools. Kizer believes that CASE is planned for only the more complex applications. Many smaller applications will be well served by tools and application generators that free the user from the constraints of code- or analysis-intensive projects.

The LAN application was particularly timely in that it followed right on the heels of implementation of a global accounting system in New York. The Zurich development group required no less than eight years and millions of dollars to build the system. Dr. Gabathuler felt that the accounting system never had adequate user involvement in its design; the result was user unhappiness with the application. If he had it to do over again? "Get visible results quickly," he stated, "within a year at most."

To say the least, quick results did not factor into the bank's eight-year, multi-million dollar integrated accounting application that wound up on the scrap heap. Quick results were, however, a large part of the bank's first (although simple) LAN application that met a critical business requirement of a highly profitable unit of the bank. Obviously, there is quite a bit of difference between a global accounting system geared to meet the needs of disparate corporate offices and a small application on a LAN geared to meet the needs of one department. Nonetheless, the business manager was quickly on a plane to Europe telling the story of his demands for this application that had gone unmet, and his final ability to develop on his LAN, with his people and his budget, an application that he desperately needed in relatively short order.

This business manager may have started a revolution at one of the world's leading banks by showing that applications could be so easily and quickly developed on the network. To say the least, the following year's budgets found business managers requesting large sums to create applications on their LANS, with networks likely becoming the primary future development platform.

As Dr. Gabathuler noted about technology in organizations in general, "Once you recognize the advantages of a certain structure, change goes very fast."

CASE STUDY QUESTIONS

1. **Moving to LANs:**
   a. Do you agree with the business and technology reasons that prompted Union Bank to move toward developing local area networks? Explain.
   b. Do you approve of how Union Bank began to implement the LAN strategy? Explain.

2. **CASE and end user development on a LAN:**
   a. What were the perceived benefits and limitations of end user development on a LAN at Union Bank? Do you agree? Why or why not?
   b. What steps of the systems development life cycle do you recognize in this case? Explain.

   c. What was the role of CASE tools in prototyping systems development on a LAN?

   d. Do you approve of how end users were involved in developing the analyst reporting system (ARS)? Why or why not?

3. The results of CASE on a LAN:

   a. Was Union Bank's first development project on a LAN successful? Explain.

   b. Do you agree with the conclusions of Dr. Gabathuler and the manager of private banking on the implications of the project for future systems development at Union Bank? Why or why not?

Dominion-Swann Industries: The Ethics of Work Support Technology

Introduction

The following is an excerpt from Dominion-Swann Industries' 1995 Employee Handbook. DS is a $1 billion diversified company, primarily in the manufacture of electrical components for automobiles. This section of the handbook was prepared by the corporate director of personnel, in consultation with the human resource management firm SciexPlan Inc.

Dominion-Swann's New Workplace: Hope for Industry through Technology

We are a technology-based company. We respect our employees, whose knowledge is the core of the technological enterprise. We care about the DS community. We value honesty, informed consent, and unfettered scientific inquiry. Our employees understand company strategy. They are free to suggest ways to improve our performance. We offer handsome rewards for high productivity and vigorous participation in the life of our company. Committed to science, we believe in careful experimentation and in learning from experience.

Since 1990, we have instituted changes in our work environment. The reasons for change were clear enough from the start. In 1990, DS faced an uncertain future. Our productivity and quality were not keeping pace with overseas competition. Employee turnover was up, especially in the most critical part of our business—automotive chips, switches, and modules. Health costs and work accidents were on the rise. Our employees were demoralized. There were unprecedented numbers of thefts from plants and offices and leaks to competitors about current research. There was also a sharp rise in drug use. Security personnel reported unseemly behavior by company employees not only in our parking lots and athletic fields but also in restaurants and bars near our major plants.

In the fall of 1990, the company turned to SciexPlan Inc., a specialist in employee-relations management in worldwide companies, to help develop a program for the radical restructuring of the work environment. We had much to learn from the corporate cultures of overseas competitors and were determined to benefit from the latest advances in work-support technology. The alternative was continued decline and, ultimately, the loss of jobs.

Frankly, there was instability while the program was being developed and implemented. Some valued employees quit and others took early retirement. But widespread publicity about our efforts drew to the program people who sincerely sought a well-ordered, positive environment. DS now boasts a clerical, professional, and factory staff that understands how the interests of a successful company corre-

1. **Make the company a home to employees.** Break down artificial and alienating barriers between work and home. Dissolve, through company initiative, feelings of isolation. Great companies are made by great people; all employee behavior and self-development counts.

2. **Hire people who will make a continuing contribution.** Bring in people who are likely to stay healthy and successful, people who will be on the job without frequent absences. Candor about prospective employees' pasts may be the key to the company's future.

3. **Technical, hardware-based solutions are preferable to supervision and persuasion.** Machines are cheaper, more reliable, and fairer than managers. Employees want to do the right thing; the company wants nothing but this and will give employees all the needed technical assistance. Employees accept performance evaluation from an impartial system more readily than from a superior and appreciate technical solutions that channel behavior in a constructive direction.

4. **Create accountability through visibility.** Loyal employees enjoy the loyalty of others. They welcome audits, reasonable monitoring, and documentary proof of their activities, whether of location, business conversations, or weekly output. Once identified, good behavior can be rewarded, inappropriate behavior can be improved.

FIGURE A.4
The four principles that underlie the work-support philosophy of Dominion-Swann Industries.

spond with the interests of individual employees. To paraphrase psychologist William James, "When the community dies, the individual withers." Such sentiments, we believe, are as embedded in Western traditions as in Eastern—they are the foundation of world community. They are also a fact of the new global marketplace.

The Fundamentals

Since 1990, productivity per worker is up 14 percent. Sales are up 23 percent, and the work force is down 19 percent. Employees' real income is up 18 percent, due in large part to our bonus and profit-sharing plans. Many of these efficiencies can be attributed to reform of our factories' production technologies. But we can be proud to have been ahead of our time in the way we build our corporate spirit and use social technologies. At DS four principles underlie work-support restructuring. See Figure A.4.

These principles have yielded an evolving program that continues to benefit from the participation and suggestions of our employees. The following summary is simply an introduction. The personnel office will be pleased to discuss any aspect of community performance or breaches of company policy in detail with employees. (You may call for an appointment during normal business hours at X-2089.)

Entry-Level Screening

As a matter of course and for mutual benefit, potential employees are screened and tested. We want to avoid hiring people whose predictive profile—medications, smoking, obesity, debt, high-risk sports, family crises—suggests that there will be serious losses to our community's productivity in the future.

Job applicants volunteer to undergo extensive medical and psychological examinations and to provide the company with detailed personal information and records, including background information about the health, lifestyle, and employment of parents, spouses, siblings, and close friends. Company associates seek permission to make discreet searches of various databases, including education, credit, bankruptcy and mortgage default, auto accident, driver's license suspension, insurance, health, worker's compensation, military, rental, arrest, and criminal activity.

The company opposes racial and sexual discrimination. DS will not check databases containing the names of union organizers or those active in controversial political causes (whether on the right or the left). Should the company's inquiry unwittingly turn up such information, it is ignored. We also use a resume verification service.

Since our community is made up of people, not machines, we have found it useful to compare physiological, psychological, social, and demographic factors against the profiles of our best employees. Much of this analysis has been standardized. It is run by SciexPlan's expert system, INDUCT.

Community Health

We want employees who are willing to spend their lives with the company, and we care about their long-term health. The company administers monthly pulmonary tests in behalf of the zero-tolerance smoking policy. Zero tolerance means lower health insurance premiums and improved quality of life for all employees.

In cooperation with Standar-Hardwick, one of the United States' most advanced makers of medical equipment and a valued customer, we've developed an automated health monitor. These new machines, used in a private stall and activated by employee thumbprint, permit biweekly urine analysis and a variety of other tests (blood pressure, pulse, temperature, weight) without the bother of having to go to a health facility. This program has received international attention: at times, it has been hailed; at times, severely criticized. People at DS often express surprise at the fuss. Regular monitoring of urine means early warning against diabetes and other potentially catastrophic diseases—and also reveals pregnancy. It also means that we can keep a drug-free, safe environment without subjecting people to the indignities of random testing or the presence of an observer.

The Quality Environment

Drawing on SciexPlan's research, our company believes that the physical environment is also important to wellness and productivity. Fragrant aromas such as evergreen may reduce stress; the smell of lemon and jasmine can have a rejuvenating effect. These scents are introduced to all work spaces through the air-conditioning and heating systems. Scents are changed seasonally.

Music is not only enjoyable to listen to but can also affect productivity. We continually experiment with the impact of different styles of music on an office's or plant's aggregate output. Since psychologists have taught us that the most serious threat to safety and productivity is stress, we use subliminal messages in music such as "safety pays," "work rapidly but carefully," and "this company cares." Personal computers deliver visual subliminals such as "my world is calm" or "we're all on the same team."

At the start of each month, employees are advised of message content. Those who don't want a message on their computers may request that none be transmitted—no questions asked. On the whole, employees who participate in the program feel noticeably more positive about their work. Employees may borrow from our library any one of hundreds of subliminal tapes, including those that help the listener improve memory, reduce stress, relax, lose weight, be guilt-free, improve self-confidence, defeat discouragement, and sleep more soundly.

On the advice of SciexPlan's dietitians, the company cafeteria and dining room serve only fresh, wholesome food prepared without salt, sugar, or cholesterol-producing substances. Sugar- and caffeine-based, high-energy snacks and beverages are available during breaks, at no cost to employees.

Work Monitoring

Monitoring system performance is our business. The same technologies that keep engines running at peak efficiency can keep the companies that make engine components running efficiently too. That is the double excitement of the information revolution.

At DS, we access more than 200 criteria to assess productivity of plant employees and data-entry personnel. These criteria include such things as the quantity of keystroke activity, the number of errors and corrections made, the pressure on the assembly tool, the speed of work, and time away from the job. Reasonable productivity standards have been established. We are proud to say that, with a younger workforce, these standards keep going up, and the incentive pay of employees who exceed standards is rising proportionately.

Our work units are divided into teams. The best motivator to work hard is the high standards of one's peers. Teams, not individuals, earn prizes and bonuses. Winning teams have the satisfaction of knowing they are doing more than their share. Computer screens abound with productivity updates, encouraging employees to note where their teams stand and how productive individuals have been for the hour, week, and month. Computers send congratulatory messages such as "you are working 10 percent faster than the norm" or messages of concern such as "you are lowering the team average."

Community Morale

There is no community without honesty. Any community must take reasonable precautions to protect itself from dishonesty. Just as we inspect the briefcases and purses of visitors exiting our R&D division, the company reserves the right to call up and inspect without notice all data files and observe work-in-progress currently displayed on employees' screens. One random search discovered an employee using the company computer to send out a curriculum vitae seeking employment elsewhere. In another, an employee was running a football pool.

Some companies try to prevent private phone calls on company time by invading their employees' privacy. At DS, encroachments on employees' privacy are obviated by telecommunications programs that block inappropriate numbers (dial-a-joke, dial-a-prayer) and unwanted incoming calls. In addition, an exact record of all dialing behavior is recorded, as is the number from which calls are received. We want our employees to feel protected against any invalid claims against them.

Video and audio surveillance too protects employees from intruders in hallways, parking lots, lounges, and work areas. Vigilance is invaluable in protecting our community from illegal behavior or actions that violate our safety and high commitment to excellence. All employees, including managers, check in and out of various workstations—including the parking lot, main entrance, elevator, floors, office, and even the bathroom—by means of an electronic entry card. In one case, this surveillance probably saved the life of an employee who had a heart attack in the parking lot: when he failed to check into the next workstation after five minutes, security personnel were sent to investigate.

Beyond Isolation

Our program takes advantage of the most advanced telecommunications equipment to bind employees to one another and to the company. DS vehicles are equipped with onboard computers using satellite transponders. This offers a tracking service and additional two-way communication. It helps our customers keep inventories down and helps prevent hijacking, car theft, and improper use of the vehicles. Drivers save time since engines are checked electronically. They also drive more safely, and vehicles are better maintained since speed, gear shifts, and idling time are measured.

In addition to locator and paging devices, all managers are given fax machines and personal computers for their homes. These are connected at all times. Cellular telephones are provided to selected employees who commute for more than half an hour or for use while traveling,

Instant communication is vital in today's international economy. The global market does not function only from 9 to 5. Modern technology can greatly increase productivity by ensuring instant access and communication. Periodic disruptions to vacations or sleep are a small price to pay for the tremendous gains to be won in worldwide competition. DS employees share in these gains.

Great companies have always unleashed the power of new technology for the social welfare, even in the face of criticism. During the first industrial revolution, such beloved novelists as Charles Dickens sincerely opposed the strictures of mass production. In time, however, most of the employees who benefited from the wealth created by new factories and machines came to take progress for granted and preferred the modern factory to traditional craft methods. Today we are living through a Second Industrial Revolution, driven by the computer.

Advanced work-support technology is democratic, effective, and anti-hierarchical. DS's balance sheet and the long waiting list of prospective employees indicate how the new program has helped everybody win. To recall the phrase of journalist Lincoln Steffens, "We have been over into the future, and it works." We are a company of the 21st century.

CASE STUDY QUESTIONS

1. **Work support technology:**

   a. What does Dominion-Swann mean by the phrase *work-support technology?*

   b. Why did Dominion-Swann implement work-support technology?

   c. Has the use of work-support technology been successful at Dominion-Swann?

2. **The ethics of work-support technology:**

   a. Do you approve of any of the ways Dominion-Swann is using work-support technology? Explain.

   b. Do you disagree with any of the ways Dominion-Swann is using work-support technology? Explain.

   c. Do you think that any of the ways that Dominion-Swann is using work-support technology is unethical? Explain your ethical reasoning, mentioning any ethical philosophies or principles you hold.

   d. Would you like to work at Dominion-Swann Industries? Why or why not?

The Promus Companies: Management Support Systems

Promus was created in February 1990, when Holiday Corp. transferred its Holiday Inn hotel business to British brewer Bass PLC and spun off its remaining brands—Harrah's casino/hotels and the Embassy Suites, Hampton Inn, and Homewood Suites hotels—into a new company: The Promus Companies, Inc. The organization has an unwavering commitment to customer satisfaction. If for any reason customers are unhappy with their stay at any of the Promus hotels, their stay is free. This approach has been successful. The company's net income more than doubled in its first two years of operation, and its stock has soared by 150 percent in the past year. The technology represented by the organization's management support systems (MSS) is a key to continuing this success.

Introduction

The management philosophy at Promus is that all personnel should be self-managed, from senior executives all the way down to the lowest level of the organization, to ensure customer satisfaction through true total quality management. Senior management saw the need for information technology mechanisms to empower all of the organization's personnel. This led to the development of the management support system at Promus to provide a common pool of information to support the decision making of all employees, from executives down to the hotel housekeepers. As a result, senior executives spread decision-making authority and responsibility for customer satisfaction and customer service throughout the organization.

Self-Management Philosophy

The number of properties in the hospitality industry has grown significantly during the past decade, with most increases coming in the number of syndicators in the market in relation to the number of individual hotel owners. There are over 60 new hotel chains more than there were 10 years ago. A consequence of this growth has been significant declines in industrywide profits.

To be successful, Promus needed to differentiate itself from others in the hospitality industry. The name Promus was chosen to denote the promise the company made to ensuring customer satisfaction. The total commitment to quality leadership led to a decision to empower employees throughout the organization so that those close to the customer could take the necessary and appropriate action to guarantee the satisfaction of customers. The use of technology has played an essential role in the formulation and implementation of this strategy.

The Business Challenge

Source: Chris Gibbons, Corrine Chaves, Ronald B. Wilkes, and Mark N. Frolick, "Management Support Systems At Promus: Using IT to Ensure Customer Satisfaction," *Information Systems Management*, Summer 1994, pp. 51–56, (New York: Auerbach Publications), © 1995 Warren, Gorham & Lamont. Used with permission.

The Information Systems Challenge

Management decided to develop and implement a computer-based system to facilitate the empowerment of employees throughout the organization and to assist in the overall management of Promus. The objective of the MSS was to provide the same tool set for all levels of the organization, with various components plugged in as people needed them. Promus identified several levels of computer users and made hardware and software recommendations for each of these levels. The IS staff would then support only these predetermined hardware and software standards. The reasoning was that by having corporate staff members migrate to individual pieces of software before the MSS interface was introduced, user resistance would be reduced. By the time the MSS was implemented, it would be seen as just one more piece of technology to support the business user.

Enterprise Data Modeling

A critical requirement of the MSS was that all employees at all levels be able to see the relevant information for managing their responsibilities and that the information provided to each of the users be consistent. Many EIS failures have been attributed to the problem of data inconsistencies—for example, when executives look at two sets of numbers that should be the same but are not.

To address the data inconsistency issue, IS developed an enterprise data model. The entity-relationship (E-R) model was used for modeling the enterprise. All the people in the organization who were responsible for data definitions were brought together in joint application development (JAD) sessions to develop the data model. The complete data model, along with narrative descriptions of all entities, was distributed to relevant parties in the organization, including selected members of the user community.

The following key principles guided development of the enterprise data model:

- *A clear understanding of the nature of this business comes first.* The business, rather than the data structures of existing application systems, guided the design of the end user–oriented database.
- *Concentrate on what is rather than what's needed now.* A focus on current needs may preclude the ability to handle future needs. Capturing the true nature of the business, rather than trying to solve specific existing problems, allows current needs to be addressed but also provides the flexibility to meet future needs.
- *Database design is relationship oriented.* The nature of the business is best represented through the things that make up the business and the relationships among them.
- *There are more similarities than differences.* Many apparent differences in the business are superficial and largely disappear when the underlying structure of the business is understood. For example, although franchise and company-owned hotels have been viewed as different in the past, all hotels have a franchise holder. In the case of company-owned hotels, the franchise holder is the company. A strong attempt was made to focus on the identification of similarities in development of the enterprise data model.
- *Design precedes implementation.* While it seems obvious that design should precede implementation, it is common to see implementation of systems before design is complete or, in the worst cases, without any design work at all.

The resulting enterprise data model facilitated standardized data aggregation and consequently eliminated data inconsistencies. The model covers virtually all aspects of Promus's activities, extending beyond the areas incorporated into the current MSS. The intention is to maintain the enterprise data model and use it as a guide for future expansion and enhancement of the MSS as well as other systems in the organization.

Lessons in Commercial Tool Use

Although Promus used a commercially available MSS software product to develop the initial version of its MSS, over time this product did not prove to be flexible enough for many of the required tasks. To achieve this flexibility, Promus used programming languages such as Visual Basic for subsequent versions of the MSS.

The use of a commercially available MSS product did, however, enforce a design discipline that was crucial to the quality of the resulting system; it also facilitated a fundamental understanding of MSS among developers. Consequently, for initial MSS development, the use of a commercial MSS product can have significant benefits, even if there is the possibility of eventually moving away from the commercial MSS product.

Management Support System Components

The MSS at Promus operates in a windows-based desktop environment. It offers online help that is both graphical and intuitive, allowing employees to obtain help without having to refer to a manual.

The MSS enables broader span of control by providing more immediate access to information. Specifically, the impact of competitive decisions, such as pricing changes, can be immediately visible, which means management is able to respond quickly to changing market conditions. This responsiveness permits decentralized decision making while allowing a review of the impact of the decisions.

Direct access to a wide range of information gives employees an extensive view of their organization, a fuller understanding of the impact and importance of their function, and a sense of partnership in the operation of the entire organization. They can validate their mental models of the business and hence contribute more broadly across the organization. Leaders in the organization, given the opportunity, can contribute more broadly when they have information by which to better judge the potential impact of their decisions or recommendations.

The MSS has three major components: an office automation component, a decision support component, and an executive information component (see Figure A.5). These subsystems address different information needs and serve all functions of the organization.

To realize the full potential of an MSS, the three components must be fully integrated. Individuals using the MSS should have a common user interface. That is, all the screens should function consistently across the MSS components.

Office Automation Component

Communication within the organization is improved by clearly defining and publishing, through the MSS, the company's goals. If goals change during the year, these changes can be immediately communicated. The annual cycle of goal setting and determining priorities can be modified to more closely reflect the time compression required by changes in the marketplace. A healthy competitiveness can also be encouraged if operating goals and statistics are made public.

Office automation tools support cross-functional team activities by enabling specialists from multiple disciplines or business units to work together for the life of a project, without team members having to relocate. If teams are physically dispersed, the MSS provides a communication medium for mail, status updates, to-do lists, priorities, and project management.

FIGURE A.5
Information functions of an
MSS.

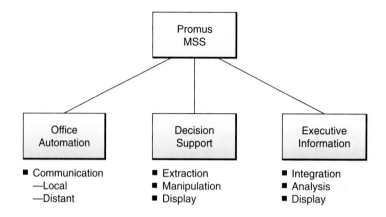

Decision Support Component

Newer generation decision support system (DSS) tools provide many easy-to-use features that allow information manipulation by a much broader spectrum of employees. A relatively low level of technical sophistication is required to effectively manipulate data using these new tools. To use the tools effectively, however, users need background knowledge about the company's data and how it is stored. The process of acquiring the required background knowledge can be time-consuming, given the large volume of data available.

The ease of use of newer-generation DSS tools empowers employees to access information directly. System experts no longer reside exclusively in the IS area but in other functional areas of the organization as well. The ease of use of the newer DSS tools also means that the user can view the company's information in different and innovative ways. Decision support tools make it easier to answer questions that require manipulating data, either in its raw form or in nonstandard ways.

Executive Information Component

While the definition of EIS has evolved, a typical EIS can be thought of as a computer-based information system that provides executives with easy access to high-level strategic information about a firm's current status. The information that is displayed is well structured and synthesizes information from multiple sources, both internal and external to the organization. The EIS allows users to drill down from a high-level summary to the source data.

The System's Impact

To be effective, the MSS had to satisfy both business and technical requirements. On the business side, the MSS had to solve or support a well-defined business problem, it must have management's support in the form of one or more sponsors, and it must add value to the information delivery process. On the technical side, the MSS had to be managed as an evolutionary system, it must be kept as simple as possible, and the technicians must avoid reinventing the wheel each time the technology platform changes.

The MSS at Promus provides transparent access to data from anywhere in the organization, at any time, to support speed and accuracy in decision making. This system is driven so far down into the organization that some service-level quality information is entered by housekeepers. Information is maintained for future review at this level, delivered in summary form to property managers, and rolled up in a more aggregated form for senior executive consumption in the EIS component and for data manipulation in the DSS component.

CASE STUDY QUESTIONS

1. **Management philosophy and strategy:**

   a. What is the Promus management philosophy and strategy?

   b. How does IT support this philosophy and strategy?

   c. Do you approve of Promus's management and IT strategy? Why or why not?

2. **IS strategy and tactics:**

   a. Do you agree with the strategy and tactics of the IS staff in implementing the MSS at Promus? Explain.

   b. What was the role of the enterprise data model in developing the MSS?

   c. What were the benefits and limitations of the commercial MSS package formerly used at Promus?

3. **The MSS at Promus:**

   a. How do the office automation, decision support, and executive information components of the MSS support Promus employees and managers?

   b. What are the benefits and limitations of the MSS at Promus?

   c. How would you improve the performance of the MSS?

   d. What business benefits would result from these improvements?

The Condor and the Samurai: Crime and Ethics in Cyberspace

The Busted Vacation

On the day after Christmas last year, Tsutomu Shimomura tossed some clean clothes, his sunglasses, and his 2.4-gigabyte, 85MHz SPARC laptop into a rental car and set off for his cabin in California near Lake Tahoe. This was the start of a long-awaited winter break for the world-renowned expert on computer crime, and he was looking forward to a few weeks of cross-country skiing and kicking back. He'd been on the road a couple of hours when his Oki cellular phone rang. It was Andrew Gross, a graduate student at the San Diego Supercomputer Center. Gross told him the startling news: Someone had hacked into one of Shimomura's computers at his beach house in San Diego—his home computer.

It was a humbling moment for Shimomura, 30, a computational physicist whose work in San Diego is funded by a consortium of government agencies and private industries. The Japanese-born researcher moves easily in a realm of pure science, constructing computer models of such abstruse phenomena as lattice gases and designing custom computer architectures and potentially lethal software that can penetrate network security.

But pride wasn't the only thing damaged in the break-in—the intruder screwed up Shimomura's vacation. Three or four years ago the scientist had discovered cross-country skiing as a great way to recharge his brain, and he'd focused on it with characteristic intensity ever since. He'd rented a cabin near Truckee, California, for the winter, a 70s-era A-frame with big windows, a wood stove, and enough room for all the equipment he needed for a long winter hibernation. That would include, of course, three powerful Sun SPARC workstations, a few Apple PowerBooks, call routers, and a fiber-distributed data-interface ring—more computing power in one spot than many Third World countries possess.

The Search Begins

When Shimomura returned to San Diego the next morning, he immediately went to work reconstructing the attack, seeking a telltale trace of the intruder's identity. This process, according to those who know, is incredibly demanding and tedious. "Imagine searching through the entire federal budget looking for a stray nickel," says John Gage, a friend of Shimomura's and the director of the science office at Sun Microsystems. "That's the kind of concentration and patience it took."

At the end of his efforts, Shimomura knew for certain what the intruder had copied: some personal files, E-mail, various security tools, and valuable cellular-phone software. He also took a program called Berkeley Packet Filter, a surveillance tool developed under a research grant from the National Security Agency that can be slipped into a computer while it's running and can then snatch valuable bits of information as they fly by on a network. What Shimomura didn't know was who stole it.

To Shimomura, this was serious business. In his ongoing quest to test the limits of network security, he has, according to colleagues, written some of the most potentially destructive software in the world—what he calls Class 10 tools. "Tsutomu has built software that can literally destroy an alien computer," says Brosl Hasslacher, a physicist at Los Alamos National Laboratory, in New Mexico, and a close friend of Shimomura's. "They can, for example, tell the computer to sit in one register until it literally melts the circuitry in the chip or command the hard drive to hit the same track 33,000 times—until it destroys the drive." Many security wizards doubt such tools could work on anything but old-fashioned PCs, and Shimomura, perhaps wary of giving away his secrets, wouldn't comment. Fortunately, these weapons—whatever their capabilities—were stored in a safe place.

But just breaking into a world-class security expert's computer wasn't enough for this cyberthief. As a final jab, he left voice mail messages intended to incite Shimomura to the chase. "Damn you," one message said in an unidentifiable foreign accent, perhaps mock British or mock Japanese, "my technique is best. . . . Don't you know who I am?"

Biography of a Hacker

Shimomura did not know, but he had a few ideas. There was for example, a hacker who had been running from the law for two years, a rude and much-mythologized grifter who had emerged as the federal government's most-wanted computer criminal. The authorities sneeringly referred to him as Mr. Cyberpunk. Shimomura knew him as Kevin Mitnick.

Mitnick grew up in Panorama City, California, a bleak, depressed chunk of the San Fernando Valley that is neither panoramic nor a city. A shy only child with lifelong stomach problems, he was raised by his mother, Shelly Jaffe, after his parents separated when Kevin was three. To pay the bills for their small condo at 8933 Willis St., Jaffe worked long hours as a waitress at a popular deli and restaurant in nearby Encino.

Mitnick discovered his aptitude quickly. While still an overweight teenager at Monroe High School, he broke into the computer system of the Los Angeles Unified School District; he worked his way up to adolescent pranks like disconnecting the phone lines of then celebrities like Kristy McNichol. Early on, Mitnick developed an appetite for more serious targets like the North American Air Defense Command, where he hacked his way in but apparently didn't mess with anything. Away from the computer, his boldness dissipated. He turned into a mad-mannered loner with a weight problem. "He didn't drink or smoke, he wasn't interested in girls, he was lousy at sports," says Troy Fromin a boyhood friend.

It seemed that Mitnick's only talent was for exploring the arcane webs of telephone and computer systems, but even as a hacker, he was not an extraordinary technician. What elevated Mitnick from the pack was his boldness and persistence. "Social engineering is what I excelled in," Mitnick told a computer-security conference in 1992, during one of his periodic attempts to go straight. Typically, he would pose as a maintenance worker or an executive and trick an employee at a computer or telephone company into revealing privileged information, In 1981 when Mitnick was 17, he talked his way past a security guard at Pacific Bell and, along with two accomplices, walked out with an armload of technical manuals. He was caught and eventually pleaded guilty to charges of computer fraud and burglary. His sentence was a year of probation.

After a first arrest most kids realize hacking is a dead end. Not Mitnick. Information was a trophy for him, a way of feeling superior to his friends. Entranced by the myth of the outsider, he began going by the code name Condor, after the Robert Redford character in *Three Days of the Condor,* an innocent on the run who trusts no one. At one point, Mitnick had the final digits of his unlisted home phone changed to 007 and reportedly billed the phone to the name James Bond.

It is almost poignant that at several times in his life, Mitnick tried to leave his hacking behind and make the leap into adulthood. In 1986, when he was 23, he met a petite woman named Bonnie Vitello at a Computer Learning Center in Los Angeles. Naturally, he communicated first by screen, but soon enough they were chatting. Before long they married.

Marriage didn't cure Mitnick's lust for cracking computers. In 1988 he was arrested for breaking and entering the system at Digital Equipment Corp., one of the largest computer manufacturers in the country. He copied the precious source code for Digital's operating system software, which would give him wide-open access to any Digital machine he wanted. This was clearly a serious matter, but it was trophy hunting, not industrial espionage. "I [never wanted] to use technology as a tool for crime," Mitnick said at the 1992 security conference. "I was just an electronic joy rider having fun in cyberspace."

Nevertheless, after he was indicted, Mitnick spent seven and a half months in solitary confinement, prevented from using a telephone, presumably out of fear that he would start World War III by whistling into the receiver. "They treated him worse than any drug dealer or violent criminal," says Alan Rubin, who was his attorney at the time. "To judges and prosecutors, most of whom didn't know the first thing about computers or technology, he was some kind of an evil wizard." In part because Digital was embarrassed that Mitnick had cracked their system and didn't want to go public with the news, the charges against him were reduced. He then served four and a half months at Lompoc Federal Penitentiary, near Santa Barbara, California, the same minimum-security prison that later held Ivan Boesky, Wall Street's fallen angel.

After he was released, Mitnick spent about six months at an AA-style residential treatment program in Los Angeles, during which he was not allowed to touch a computer. He seems to have genuinely tried to reform. He lost weight, worked at various jobs, including one with a private investigator and another as a network-security consultant. His progress was rocked by tragedy: His half brother Adam, to whom Mitnick had grown closer in recent years, was found dead in his car, a suspected suicide. Soon after, Mitnick disintegrated.

In 1992 investigators for the California Department of Motor Vehicles got wind of a phone scam someone was using to get information out of the DMV's database. They staked out a copy shop in Studio City, where the scam artist was having information faxed. They expected to find a rogue cop. Instead they found Mitnick, who dropped everything and ran. He failed to show up for meetings with his probation officer in the following week; a warrant was later issued for his arrest.

Now he was on the run, just like Redford in *Three Days of the Condor.*

The Samurai's Story

Compared with Mitnick's hardscrabble life, Shimomura's has been a privileged existence. Born in Japan and raised in Princeton, New Jersey, by parents who are biochemists, he left high school at 14 and started hanging around the department of astrophysics at Princeton University, where he helped write software to track satellites. After a stint at Caltech, he ended up as a staff physicist at Los Alamos National Laboratory. Eight years later he moved on to the Supercomputer Center in San Diego, where he is a kind of *wunderkind* in residence. In his office at the center and at his fully equipped beachfront home, he has the freedom to work on whatever interests him, which at the moment is computer architecture and security.

Unlike many scientists who tend to live in pristine, theoretical worlds, Shimomura is well known for his strong sense of civic duty and has testified before Congress on digital crime. His life is full of motion: flying back and forth between Silicon Valley and San Diego, speaking in his intense, rapid-fire style at various security conferences, rollerblading along the beach. He is at once humble and arrogant, a kind of intellectual warrior who has little patience for sloppy thinking but who is perfectly willing to spend hours discussing the merits of different formulas of kick and glide wax on cross-country skis.

As the details of the Christmas Day break-in became clearer, Shimomura began to have his doubts that Mitnick was possible. Although he knew that the tools on his machine might have interested Mitnick, the method of the cracker seemed too complex. "He is not that smart," says Shimomura. The intruder, he explains, had used a long-known but little-publicized strategy that exploits the friendly relationship between two computers on the Net. In essence, an alien floods one computer with messages, knocking it out of commission, then quickly assumes that computer's identity to gain access to the third computer. It's called spoofing. Once inside the foreign machine, the intruder is able to do more or less whatever he wants—including erase any trace of his presence.

Shimomura knew, however, that Mitnick had been on the prowl lately. A few weeks before the Christmas break-in, for example, Lae Elam, a friend of Shimomura's who runs a Web site called Art on the Net, was working late one night when she noticed something odd about an account logged into her Web site—a user dialed in from a remote on an artist's account that wasn't set up for tel-net access. Elam had enough experience in these matters to know it only meant one thing: Someone cracked the account and was roaming around in her machine. She followed his electronic trail back to Netcom, a large Internet provider in San Jose, California, and read the account file. As she searched through the directory on status, the file suddenly changed to OWNER READ/WRITE ONLY. Her palms went clammy on the keyboard. The cracker was onto her.

Next thing Elam knew, the intruder had initiated a realtime chat with her. "It was very scary at first," Elam says. She didn't know how much damage—if any—had been done to her system or whether the intruder had created any trapdoors that would allow him easy access later. "I bet you're really pissed because I broke into your system and you don't know who I am," the intruder wrote on her screen. Elam admits she was more frightened than angry. Had he singled out her machine for attack?

Why? Had he hatched some plan to take her computer down? They talked for more than an hour, and eventually he put Elam at ease. "I think he was just curious," says Elam. "He just wanted to come into my site and look around and see what was going on."

A few days later a message left on the answering machine of a friend of Elam's referred to the break-in at Art on the Net. A second friend, knowledgeable about the hacker underground, identified the voice: Kevin Mitnick. Apparently the Condor

Trail of the Intruder

was getting busy. In December someone broke into a computer at Stanford University and cracked the account of a young cryptographer named Paul Kocher. The intruder—"I'm 99 percent sure it was Mitnick," Kocher says—was after the source code for a cryptanalytic algorithm, an encryption program Kocher co-authored with a colleague in Israel. When the intruder didn't find it, he assumed the electronic identity of Kocher's colleague and sent Kocher forged E-mail hoping to trick Kocher into sending it to him (it didn't work). In another case a person later presumed to be Mitnick called one of Shimomura's friends and demanded cell-phone software. "You know I'm going to get it anyway," the cracker boasted. "Why don't you just give it to me now?"

Accepting the Challenge

When Shimomura heard about break-ins like these, he decided he had to do something. "Tsutomu has a samurai sense of honor," says Brosl Hasslacher of Los Alamos. "He believes deeply in a kind of unspoken code of ethical behavior."

In the first days of the new year, Shimomura put off the idea of hunting for Mitnick. He might have postponed it indefinitely had a call not come from John Perry Barlow, co-founder of the Electronic Frontier Foundation (EFF) and a leading voice for civil liberties in cyberspace. System administrators at the WELL, an established Bay Area bulletin-board service that is the electronic nexus of Silicon Valley, said their system had been cracked.

Barlow called Shimomura and asked him to look into it. Around the same time, Bruce Koball, a technical consultant in Berkeley, California, and one of the organizers of the annual Computers, Freedom and Privacy conference, got a call from the WELL telling him that one of the conference's files on the WELL was taking up an unusually large amount of space: 158 megabytes. Strange, Koball thought. He checked the file and discovered, among other things, more than two megabytes of compressed private E-mail, most of it to or from "tsutomu@sdsc.edu." He had no idea who that was. But by chance, Koball read a story in the next day's *New York Times* by John Markoff that detailed the Christmas Day break-in at Shimomura's home computer, and he quickly realized those were Shimomura's files stashed on the WELL.

Markoff had been a central figure in this drama from the very beginning. In 1992 he and his former wife, Katie Hafner, now a contributing editor for *Newsweek*, published *Cyberpunk: Outlaws and Hackers on the Computer Frontier,* one of the first and most detailed accounts of the computer underground. In a section titled "Kevin: The Dark-Side Hacker," the book chronicled Mitnick's early escapades, including the break-in at Digital. Mitnick later wrote a brief, poorly argued rebuttal to the book in a hacker magazine called *2600: The Hacker Quarterly,* charging that Markoff and Hafner trashed him because he had refused to cooperate with them (he had wanted to be paid for his time) and that the book was "20 percent fabricated."

"He thought Markoff was out to get him," says Mark Seiden, a computer network and security consultant involved in the chase who later watched as a person he believed to be Mitnick talked to friends on the Net about the *Times* reporter. "He thought Markoff was feeding information to the FBI."

Markoff, who is also a friend and ski buddy of Shimomura's, dismisses that idea. "I took great pains to be a chronicler of events, not a participant."

During the first week of February, Shimomura finally got down to work. Along with a few colleagues and his pal Andrew Gross, he began surveillance at the WELL in Sausalito, California, while Seiden watched from the offices of Internex, another

Internet provider in the Bay Area that had been broken into. Shimomura noticed that the intruder attacked the machines in a similar way every time and that the break-ins came at about the same hour every night. "If he would have been less consistent or if he would have taken a few days off," says Shimomura, "he would have been much tougher to catch."

Shimomura didn't know it at the time, but federal authorities had narrowly missed catching the Condor a few months earlier. In August 1994, Kevin Pazaski, a fraud analyst for McCaw Cellular Communications, in Washington, was alerted to strange calling patterns in the Seattle area. After checking it out for a few days, he determined that it must be a "cloned" phone, a standard-issue cellular phone that has been reprogrammed with a pilfered phone number and security code. Clones are often used in 'call sell' operations, 'in which a street entrepreneur rakes in thousands of dollars a day selling cheap overseas calls. For companies like McCaw, phone fraud is serious business. Last year it cost the industry an estimated $1 billion in lost revenues.

A Near Miss

Pazaski hadn't seen much of this kind of crime in Seattle, however. To help track down the perpetrator, he called in Todd Young, a security consultant who specialized in phone "phreaks" and other cellular criminals. He had, in fact, been hired by a company in California (he won't say which one) to hunt down Mitnick a year or so earlier—to no avail. This time he had no idea it was Mitnick. Says Young: "We just thought it was some kid with a cell phone. We had no idea it was Mr. Cyberpunk."

If you know the number on which a person is dialing out, locating someone who is using a cellular phone—cloned or otherwise—isn't difficult. By analyzing the direction and strength of a couple of cellular broadcasting towers, Pazaski was able to narrow down the perp's location to an area 15 blocks wide and 3 blocks deep. Then, using equipment called a CellScope, which is basically a radio tuner, and a "yagi"—a special directional-finder antenna—he and Young were able to drive through the area and tune into the cellular signal just as if they were tuning into a radio station. Within 20 minutes they were guided to a 16-unit apartment complex in the University District. At that point, Young got out and walked to an apartment on the first floor. He heard a voice through the door—the same one he had heard on the CellScope—talking about "file transfers" and "system access." Young had found his man.

Now, in order to document the crimes, they began surveillance. For more than two weeks they tracked a man who claimed to be Brian Merrill but who was in fact Kevin Mitnick. They eavesdropped on his calls, they followed him into the nearby Safeway, into Taco Bell. He was always alone; they never saw any friends go in or out of the apartment. "He seems to have had a fairly lonely life," says Young. According to David Drews, the manager of the apartment complex, Mitnick paid $500 a month for his furnished one-bedroom apartment. Exactly where he got the money to pay his bills has always been a question. In Seattle, at least, he'd had a 9-to-5 job at Virginia Mason Medical Center. The hospital won't comment on what position Mitnick held, but it was apparently low-level administration in the information-systems department. "He wasn't any different than anyone else who works here," says one hospital employee, who recalls Mitnick as "a friendly, low-key guy." The only odd note, Drews says, was that he always paid his rent in cash.

On October 27 a search warrant was issued for Mitnick's apartment. The

Seattle police joined up with the Secret Service, which shares jurisdiction on many phone- and computer-fraud cases, and staked out Mitnick's apartment that night, hoping to catch him in action. After two hours the cops got tired of hanging around and, in a move they'd later regret, decided to go in. They kicked down the door and entered, guns drawn. They found a rat's nest of technology—several modems, a Toshiba T4400SX laptop, cell phones, manuals. One investigator noticed an X-ray of what appeared to be Mitnick's colon on the kitchen table, along with medical bills.

At 11:30 that night, about an hour after the police left the scene, Drews heard a knock on his door. It was Mitnick. Drews would later conclude that Mitnick had been on his way home when he saw the police inside his apartment. He had waited until they were gone, then sneaked into the complex via the back alley.

"Sorry to bother you," Mitnick said politely. "Did you let somebody into my apartment?"

"No, they kicked in the door," Drews said.

"Who's they?"

"The Seattle police and the Secret Service."

"Oh, f——," Mitnick said and once again disappeared into the night.

The Hunt Continues

After several long hours of surveillance at the WELL, Shimomura and Gross determined that most of the intruder's activity was coming through Netcom. So they moved their operation down to San Jose, hoping to get a better vantage point. Netcom's headquarters are in the heart of Silicon Valley in a glassy building directly across the street from the Winchester Mystery House, an enduring landmark of the Old West that was built at the turn of the century with the fortune made on the Winchester repeating rifle.

The first night, Shimomura and Gross set up shop in the office of Robert Hood, network manager of Netcom. Shimomura spent most of his time watching his screen, matching tel-net logs from the WELL with outgoing logs from Netcom. By doing this they were able to determine an important clue: The intruder was gaining access to Netcom on an account named gkremen. When Shimomura and Gross looked up the name in the membership directory, they discovered it was a legitimate user's account that the intruder had hacked into and taken over. It was Shimomura's first major breakthrough. By tracking the phone call to that account, it would be possible to determine from which part of the country the intruder was calling.

Like most Internet providers, Netcom has points of presence (POPs), phone numbers in various regions of the country so customers don't need to make a long-distance call to dial into its system. Unlike with most customer traffic, which is consistently dialed into the nearest POP, the activity on the Netcom account was coming from all over the country: Denver; Minneapolis; Raleigh, North Carolina. To make it even more difficult to track, once the wily intruder was connected to Netcom, he would bounce through as many sites as he could. Thus, he would sometimes dial in through Netcom in Raleigh, then bounce over to Escape, a small Internet provider in New York where a lot of hackers and crackers hang out, then bounce again to Internex, then to the WELL, and finally, his trail covered, to his destination computer, be it Shimomura's or someone else's.

Knowing the account the intruder was using also allowed Shimomura to monitor his activity in real time, just as it was happening. They could watch him log onto the WELL, read someone's mail, transfer a file, then hopscotch to another Internet provider and begin prowling around. Using his own special home-brewed software,

Shimomura was able to capture all this activity keystroke for keystroke in a precisely timed log, almost as if he were making a video of a burglar in action.

"We could tell from the way he broke into various computers and from the kinds of files he was moving around that this was probably Mitnick," says Rick Francis, vice president of software engineering at Netcom. He would, for example, open Markoff's E-mail file at the WELL, then do a search by the letters *ick* to see if his name was mentioned Also, one of the passwords Mitnick used was fucknmc, which presumably referred to the initials of a researcher at Leeds University, in England, named Neill Clift, against whom Mitnick had long carried a grudge.

While all this was going on at Netcom, Seiden was conducting additional surveillance at Internex. It was Seiden who made the next critical discovery. After watching the intruder stash a 140-megabyte file on the WELL for safekeeping, Seiden decided to download it and have a look. He was startled to find, among other things, the encrypted password file for Apple's Internet gateway, various tools for breaking into Sun computers as well as a controversial—and at the time unreleased—program called SATAN (an acronym for Security Administrators Tool for Analyzing Networks), which had been developed by Dan Farmer, until recently the security guru at Silicon Graphics, and Wietse Venema, his Dutch colleague. SATAN allows anyone to probe the security flaws in a machine as easily as clicking open a file on a Macintosh. It's a double-edged sword: Great for quick security checks, but it also has the potential to transform every 13-year-old geek with a modem into an expert cracker.

But most significant of all from the law enforcement point of view was that in this 140-megabyte stash, Seiden found the complete Netcom customer database, including a file named Cards, which contained some 32,000 customer records—names, addresses, and phone numbers, as well as 21,600 credit-card numbers. Whether the intruder was the one who actually copied the credit-card numbers is an open question. "Every teenager in America knew that Netcom was an open book," says hacker extraordinaire Mark Abene, aka Phiber Optik. There is no evidence that these stolen credit-card numbers were ever used to make purchases or to acquire cash. Nevertheless, the discovery piqued the interest of law enforcement. Stealing source code is one thing; everyone understands credit-card theft.

In hindsight, what is remarkable about the intruder's activity was how he targeted the heart of the computer culture. He stashed his stolen goods in a file belonging to Computers, Freedom and Privacy; besides breaking into Shimomura's machine, he cracked the computer of John Gilmore, a leading cryptography advocate. It was as if Mitnick wanted to cement his reputation among the People Who Mattered.

Either that or he had a wicked sense of humor. "If you knew the joke, it was great stuff," says EFF's Barlow.

Flight of the Condor

On January 4, Mitnick checked into the Friendship Inn at Raleigh. Since leaving Seattle he had shaved off his mustache and appropriated a new alias: David Stanfill. The next day he rented a car at the nearby U-Save auto rental. Mitnick told the clerk that he had just moved to Raleigh from Las Vegas, where he had lived for the past four years and had suffered a painful divorce from his wife. He gave the clerk the business card of a fictitious company in Las Vegas called American Infotechnical, where he said he had worked until recently. The clerk was so charmed by Mitnick's hard-luck tale that he gave Mitnick a break on the rental rate of a Plymouth Horizon: a month for the price of three weeks. Again, Mitnick paid in cash. What attracted him to Raleigh? Mitnick told the clerk at U-Save that he had come to North Carolina because *Money* magazine had listed it as one of the best places in America to live. He also said he wanted to get a job in the computer industry, and Raleigh's Research Triangle Park was just the kind of high-tech Mecca he was looking for.

There may have been other motives. Donn Parker, a security expert at SRI International, a Bay Area think tank for government and industry, points out that one of the biggest phone-card fraud operations in history was busted not long ago in Raleigh. And it may not be dead yet. "I have a suspicion that there has been a loose, ongoing conspiracy in North Carolina," says Parker, who estimates that at its height, the scam was bringing in $18,000 a day.

If Mitnick was making anything like that kind of money, however, he sure didn't act like it. On February 4, a few days before Shimomura arrived at the WELL to begin surveillance, Mitnick signed a lease at the Players Club apartments under the name Glenn Case. Rent for a one-bedroom furnished apartment wasn't much more than he paid in Seattle, but the Players Club had a few luxuries—pool, gym, spa, tennis courts. He still didn't own a car, however, and his personal possessions didn't amount to much more than a laptop, modems, and cellular phones.

The Endgame

The endgame began on Shimomura's third night of monitoring the intruder's activity at Netcom. Gross was still there, as was Markoff, who had dropped by to check out the action. All attention was focused on trying to pinpoint the intruder's whereabouts with a phone trace. They had noticed that most of the calls were coming in via the Raleigh POP, and by then federal authorities got authorization for a "trap and trace." When a call came in to the Raleigh "dial up" that they suspected might be Mitnick, it was automatically traced to the point of origin.

In this case, however, the trap and trace led them to a blind alley. Mitnick had apparently broken into GTE's phone switch in Raleigh and monkeyed around with it so that it looked like the call was coming in over a regular land line when in fact it was coming in over a cellular phone. When Shimomura called the number, he could hear the *clunk, clunk, clunk* of the call being forwarded back and forth in an endless loop.

By then the FBI had put two and two together about Mitnick's near bust in Seattle, and the feds assumed his MO would be similar—he was probably operating off a cloned cell phone that was attached via modem to his laptop. So Kent Walker, then an assistant U.S. attorney who had been closely involved with the Mitnick case from the beginning, subpoenaed the records of cellular-phone companies in Raleigh. By matching the times of the calls that had been dialed into the various Netcom POPs with cellular calls in the area, the team hoped to figure out exactly which cellular phone Mitnick was using. Within three hours, Jim Murphy, an engineer for Sprint Cellular in Raleigh, had a match. From there it was fairly easy to identify which transmitter was handling Mitnick's calls, which in turn allowed them to pinpoint him in an area roughly one and a quarter square miles.

Less than 12 hours later, Shimomura was on a plane to North Carolina.

It was windy that night in Raleigh when Shimomura was met at the airport by Murphy and Joe Orsak, a senior maintenance engineer for Sprint Cellular. The group then teamed up with a local FBI agent, who briefed the engineers on what he knew about Mitnick, warning that he was a slippery character who might be easily spooked. The agent gave them a few pointers about tracking. "He warned us about keeping our equipment as hidden as possible as we drove around," recalls Orsak. "He also told us not to drive in circles, because that would draw attention to ourselves, and not to use a cellular phone to communicate, because Mitnick probably had a scanner that could pick up conversations in the area."

Then the FBI agent left, and Orsak and Shimomura drove to another location and picked up Markoff, who had flown in earlier that day. Perhaps understandably, given his proximity to such a hot story, Markoff wanted to keep his identity as a journalist quiet. He was introduced to Orsak as Mr. Markoff—Orsak assumed he was one of Shimomura's team. After a few minutes of discussion, the threesome piled into Orsak's Chevy Blazer and went out to find Mitnick, stopping only to fuel up with peanuts and bottled water from an all-night market.

Orsak's equipment was similar to what Young had used in Seattle: a CellScope and a yagi. Shimomura rode in the passenger seat, tracking the signal as it grew stronger, then weaker, then stronger again as they homed in on Mitnick like a dog circling a field for the scent of a rabbit. Mitnick, perhaps a little wiser after his near miss in Seattle, would sometimes switch phones and dial out on another line. But whenever he did, Murphy and Gary Whitman, an engineer at CellularOne, a phone carrier that Mitnick was using, would catch it and send the number via pager to Orsak in the Blazer. Then Shimomura would switch frequencies on the CellScope, and the search would continue.

It was only about 40 minutes before the signal pulled them to the Players Club apartments. But it was impossible to pinpoint Mitnick's whereabouts any more precisely than being sure he was in one of several apartments along the eastern edge of the complex. Still, that was enough for one day. It was nearly 3 A.M. by the time Shimomura and the rest of the team headed back to their hotel rooms.

The next day, Levord Burns, an FBI agent from the computer-crimes squad in Washington, D.C., arrived on the scene. Murphy, Shimomura, Orsak, Markoff, and Burns all met for dinner at Ragazzi's, an Italian restaurant nearby. It was something of an awkward situation for Markoff because Burns didn't know he was a reporter, and Markoff, wanting to stay close to the story, was in no rush to call attention to that fact. Nevertheless, after that dinner, Markoff decided to bow out of the action—"I realized I was just going to get in the way," he says.

Later that evening, Orsak and Burns drove over to the Players Club apartments together. They pulled quietly into the parking lot, and Burns stepped out with what looked like a small camera bag that he'd brought with him from Washington. Inside was a smaller, more sophisticated version of the radio direction finder Orsak and Shimomura had used the night before. Burns walked into the apartment complex and down the hallway, tracking the signal right up to the door of Apartment 202.

The next night, a warrant was issued for Mitnick's arrest. At 2 A.M. Wednesday, February 15, while Shimomura, exhausted, watched from a safe distance, FBI agents knocked on the door of Apartment 202.

Postgame Wrap-Up

"My goal in hunting down Kevin," Shimomura said one recent afternoon, watching a Sierra blizzard rage outside the window of a ski lodge, "was to try to encourage responsible behavior on the Net. It's up to the people who are a part of this community to make statements about what is acceptable to do and what is not. And what Kevin did was not very polite. He was a nuisance who caused a lot of trouble. At a certain point it is easier to just deal with the problem once and get it over with. Hopefully, some lessons will be learned."

One of the more obvious lessons is that networks are by definition insecure and that the only real answer to the problem of malicious hackers—short of rebuilding the Internet from the ground up—is the widespread use of encryption. Shimomura has fought hard for what's called public-key encryption, which would allow users to routinely code information in a way that does not leave any "back door" open for electronic surveillance. It is an idea the Justice Department has bitterly fought, arguing that it would limit law enforcement's ability to perform wiretaps on dangerous suspects. In effect, instead of using technology to solve the problem, law enforcement still prefers to rely on guns and subpoenas to keep people in line.

Since his arrest and arraignment, Mitnick has been in a North Carolina jail waiting for his trial. If convicted, he could easily face 35 years in prison for his crimes. The question remains, Does he deserve punishment this severe? Does it fit the crime? Even if he broke into all the computers with which he is accused of tampering, and even if he copied gigabytes of valuable software, there is still no evidence that he sold any of these files for profit or that he damaged the machines he had broken into. "Mitnick was a tumor," says Seiden, "but he was benign."

Mitnick's punishment surely won't be. Law enforcement can be a game of symbols, especially in a new and arcane form of activity, and Mitnick is the unfortunate poster boy. His indictment lists 23 counts of access fraud, each with a possible sentence of 20 years in prison. With prosecutors in at least three states (California, Washington, and North Carolina) clamoring for his hide, more indictments are likely. "Kevin's going to be the one that they hang outside the gates to show everyone what happens to hackers," says Barlow, who fears that overly severe punishment of outlaw hackers will ultimately do more harm than good. "Soon enough these kids are going to find out that you might as well get hung for a sheep as a lamb."

And it's unlikely that the EFF—or anyone else—is going to come rushing to Mitnick's defense. "Five years ago there might have been freelancers and consultants out there who would defend him," says Barlow. "Not anymore. A lot of those freelancers and consultants are now wearing suits, and if you work for a major corporation, you don't say nice things about Kevin Mitnick."

It would be a sad irony if Shimomura's good deed played into the hands of the oppressors: the cops, congressmen, and fat cats who would like to see the Net whipped into submission and lost boys like Mitnick burned at the stake. The specter clearly haunts Shimomura. His sense of morality may have sent him after Mitnick in the first place, but his physicist's desire to see a problem to an aesthetically pleasing conclusion has left him questioning his prey's potential punishment. "Prison is not a very elegant solution to the problem of Kevin Mitnick," Shimomura says.

Some have suggested that a hackers conservation corps be set up or that Mitnick's considerable skills be put to use, say, wiring libraries in the Bronx. None of these options appeals to Shimomura. "I don't know what should be done," he confesses. One can't help but feel that some of the discomfort in Shimomura's reaction can be traced to the fact that he and Markoff have signed a reported $600,000 book deal with a movie to follow.

For Kevin Mitnick there is only the satisfaction that he was taken down by the best. Perhaps he tried to acknowledge that as he was being led out of the courtroom in cuffs and shackles after his prearraignment hearing in Raleigh. He turned to Shimomura and whispered, "Hello, Tsutomu, I respect your skills." Or perhaps this was just another hack, one last attempt to tweak Shimomura's head.

Gentleman that he is, Shimomura held Mitnick's eye and said nothing.

CASE STUDY QUESTIONS

1. The break-in:

  a. How did Kevin Mitnick break into Tsutomu Shimomura's computer system?

  b. What computer crimes or unethical practices did he commit? Explain.

2. The motive:

  a. What do you think was Mitnick's motive in breaking into Shimomura's computer system? Explain.

  b. Why do you think that Mitnick chose a life of hacking and computer crime?

3. The security:

  a. How vulnerable is the Internet to such attacks? Explain.

  b. What security measures and controls would guard against Mitnick's tactics?

4. The chase:

  a. How was Mitnick caught?

  b. What was Shimomura's role in tracking and capturing Mitnick?

5. The punishment:

  a. What punishment does Mitnick face? Is this too servere for his crimes? Explain.

  b. How should Mitnick be punished? Defend your sentence.

6. The implications:

  a. What are the implications of this case for you as a business end user?

  b. What are the implications of this case for businesses who use the Internet or other online services?

B

Using Systems Development Tools

This appendix provides material on systems development tools that may be assigned at the option of your instructor. Read it if you want to know more about several types of tools used by information systems professionals during the systems development process.

Systems Development Tools

Many tools and techniques have been developed to help improve current information systems or develop new ones. Such tools help end users and systems analysts:

- Conceptualize, clarify, document, and communicate the activities and resources involved in an organization and its information systems.
- Analyze the present business operations, management decision making, and information processing activities of an organization.
- Propose and design new or improved information systems to solve business problems or pursue business opportunities that have been identified.

Many **systems development tools** take the form of diagrams and other graphic representations. That's because they are easier to understand than narrative descriptions of a system. Good graphic tools can also represent the major activities and resources of a system without a lot of detail and yet be able to show various levels and modules of detail when needed. They also can be modified during the course of analysis and design, as you specify more features of a present or proposed information system. Finally, graphics and other tools serve as documentation methods. For example, they document the results of the analysis stage for use in the design stage, then they document the results of the design stage to assist in the implementation and maintenance of a new system.

Overview of Systems Development Tools

Figure B.1 outlines some of the major types of tools used for systems development. Notice that the tools can be grouped into four categories based on the system features each typically documents: (1) the components and flows of a system, (2) the user interface, (3) data attributes and relationships, and (4) detailed system processes. We will briefly describe these tools now, and then show you examples of system flowcharts, data flow diagrams, and entity relationship diagrams.

Remember that such tools can be used in every stage of systems development as analytical tools, design tools, and documentation methods. For example, system flowcharts and data flow diagrams can be used to (1) analyze an existing system, (2) express the design of a new system, and (3) provide the documentation for the

FIGURE B.1
Examples of systems development tools. Note the four primary areas of use for these tools.

System Feature	Systems Development Tools Used
System components and flows	System flowcharts, presentation graphs, data flow diagrams, context diagrams, system component matrix
User interface	Input/output layout forms and screens, dialogue flow diagrams
Data attributes and relationships	Data dictionaries, entity relationship diagrams, file layout forms, grid charts
Detailed system processes	Decision trees and tables, structure charts, pseudocode, program flowcharts

implementation and maintenance of a newly developed system. You should also realize that software packages for computer-aided systems engineering (CASE) have computerized many of these tools. For example, many CASE packages will automatically draw and revise system flowcharts or data flow diagrams based on end user or analyst descriptions of a system, as well as create and maintain a data dictionary for the system.

System Components and Flows

These tools help you document the data flows among the major resources and activities of an information system. System flowcharts are used, typically, to show the flow of data media as they are processed by hardware devices and manual activities. Presentation charts are quite similar but use less-technical symbols. Data flow diagrams use a few simple symbols to illlustrate the flow of data among external entities (such as people or organizations), processing activities, and data storage elements. A context diagram is the highest-level data flow diagram. It defines the boundaries of a system by showing a single major process and the data inputs and outputs and external entities involved. A system component matrix provides a matrix framework to document the resources used, the activities performed, and the information products produced by an information system.

The User Interface

Designing the interface between end users and computer systems is a major consideration in developing new systems. Layout forms and video screens generated by a variety of software development packages are used to construct the formats and generic content of input-output media and methods. Dialogue flow diagrams analyze the flow of dialogue between computers and people. They document the flows among different display screens generated by alternative end user responses to menus and prompts.

Data Attributes and Relationships

As mentioned in Chapter 7, the data resources in information systems are defined, catalogued, and designed by this category of tools. A data dictionary catalogs the definitions (descriptions) of the attributes (characteristics) of all data elements and their relationships to each other, as well as to external systems. Entity relationship diagrams are used to document the number and type of relationships among the entities in a system. File layout forms document the type, size, and names of the data elements in a system. Grid charts help identify the use of each type of data element in the input, output, or storage media of a system.

Detailed System Processes

This final group of tools is used to help programmers develop the detailed procedures and processes required in the design of computer programs. Decision trees and decision tables use a network or tabular form to document the complex condi-

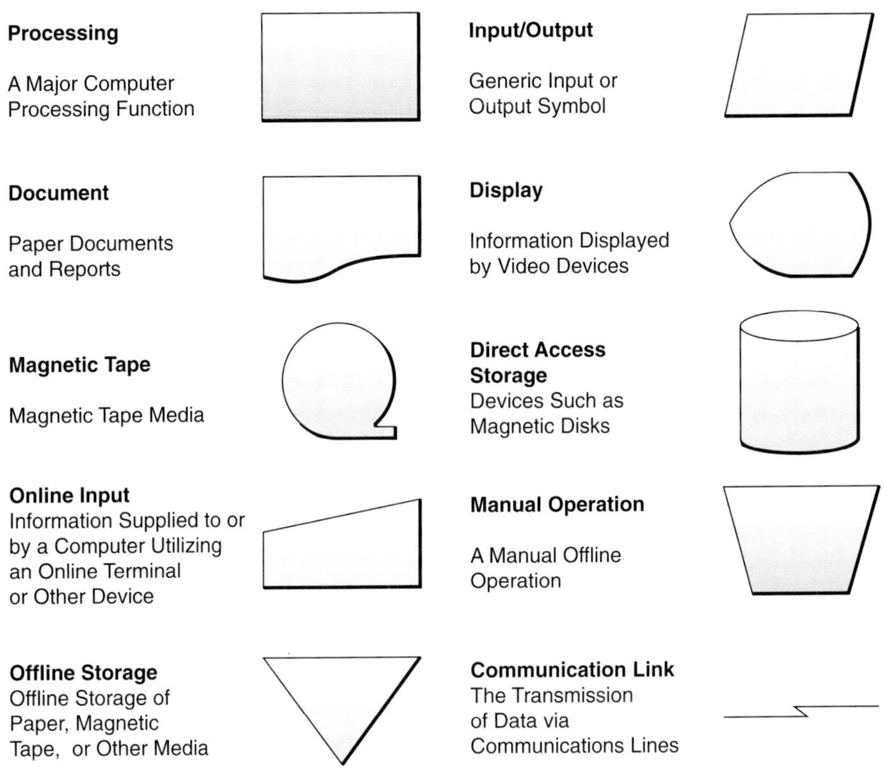

Processing

A Major Computer
Processing Function

Input/Output

Generic Input or
Output Symbol

Document

Paper Documents
and Reports

Display

Information Displayed
by Video Devices

Magnetic Tape

Magnetic Tape Media

**Direct Access
Storage**
Devices Such as
Magnetic Disks

Online Input
Information Supplied to or
by a Computer Utilizing
an Online Terminal
or Other Device

Manual Operation

A Manual Offline
Operation

Offline Storage
Offline Storage of
Paper, Magnetic
Tape, or Other Media

Communication Link
The Transmission
of Data via
Communications Lines

FIGURE B.2
Common system flowchart
symbols.

tional logic involved in choosing among the information processing alternatives in a system. Structure charts document the purpose, structure, and hierarchical relationships of the modules in a program. Pseudocode expresses the processing logic of a program module in a series of short phrases. Program flowcharts are used to illustrate the detailed sequence of processing steps required in a computer program.

System Flowcharts

A **system flowchart** is a graphic diagramming tool that documents and communicates the flow of data media and the information processing procedures taking place in an information system. This is accomplished by using a variety of labeled symbols connected by arrows to show the sequence of information processing activities. System flowcharts, typically, emphasize the media and hardware used and the processes that take place within an information system. They thus represent a graphic model of the *physical* information system that exists or is proposed. Figure B.2 illustrates some common system flowchart symbols.

    System flowcharts are widely used to communicate the overall structure and flows of a system to end users because they can offer a *physical view* that emphasizes the hardware and data media involved. However, in many cases, they have been displaced by data flow diagrams for use by professional systems analysts, and by presentation graphs for communicating with end users.

    Figure B.3(A) shows how a system flowchart is used as a tool for the analysis of the present sales processing system at Auto Shack Stores. It graphically portrays the flow of data media and the major information processing tasks taking place. Note how the flowchart symbols indicate the physical equipment and media used for input, output, and storage. For example, symbols and labels indicate the use of

FIGURE B.3
Flowcharts of a present and proposed sales transaction processing system.

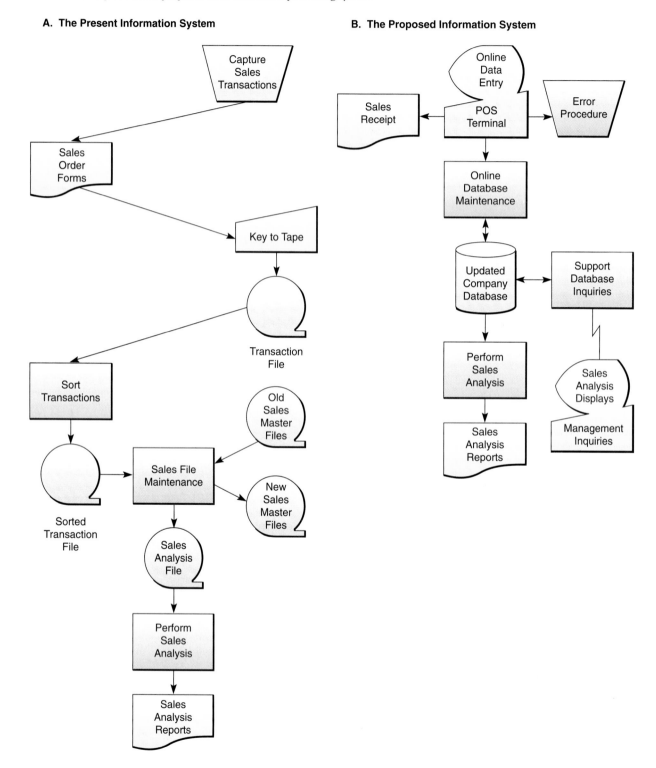

A. The Present Information System

B. The Proposed Information System

External Entities

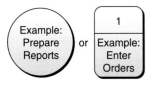

Example:
Customers

- Organizations, departments, persons, other systems
- Originate input or receive output
- May be duplicated

Processes

Example:
Prepare
Reports

or

1
Example:
Enter
Orders

- Transform inputs into outputs
- Represent manual or automated activities
- Must have at least one input and one output data flow
- May be numbered

Data Stores

Example:
Customer File

- Store data between processes
- Must be connected only to processes (by data flows)
- Must have at least one input and one output data flow
- May be duplicated

Data Flows

Example:
Payment

- Represent transfers of data among entities, processes, and stores
- Arrows represent direction of flows
- Must begin or end at a process
- Must be labeled to describe data being transferred

FIGURE B.4
Data flow diagram symbols.
Note how they should be used
when developing data flow diagrams.

many paper documents and reports, a key-to-tape data entry device, and magnetic tape storage.

Figure B.3(B) is also a system flowchart, but it is being used to illustrate the design of the proposed sales processing system for Auto Shack Stores. This is a new system that might replace the system illustrated in Figure B.3(A). Note how it shows an online data entry terminal, magnetic disk storage, and several printed reports. This is obviously a physical design, because the hardware devices and media that will be used in the new system are specified.

A **data flow diagram** (DFD) can help you identify the flow of data in a system without specifying the media or hardware involved. Data flow diagrams use a few simple symbols connected by arrows to represent such flows. Data flow diagrams can easily illustrate the *logical* relationships among data, flows, external entities (sources and destinations), and stores. Figure B.4 illustrates the four basic symbols used in data flow diagrams and summarizes some helpful information for their use.

This graphic tool is widely used for several reasons. It is simple to draw (mostly circles connected by arrows) and easily depicts the basic components and flows of a system. DFDs can also be drawn in increasing levels of detail, starting with a summary high-level view and proceeding to more detailed lower-level views. This supports a *modular, structured, top-down* view of system components and flows. For example, Figure B.5 illustrates the highest level of data flow diagram, called a *context diagram* or level-0 DFD.

Data Flow Diagrams

FIGURE B.5
A context diagram of a sales processing system. This level-0 DFD
is the highest-level view of this
system.

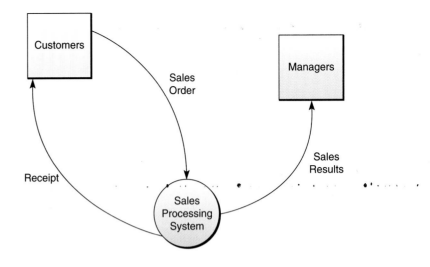

Figures B.6 and B.7 show the next level of detail in data flow diagrams used as a tool for both analysis and design. (These are level-1 DFDs.) Note that data flow diagrams can portray the *logical flow* of data in both the present and proposed sales processing system of Auto Shack Stores. That's because they do not specify the media and equipment involved. These DFDs illustrate only the logical relationships among the data flows, external entity sources and destinations, processes, and data stores in present and proposed sales processing systems similar to the ones portrayed by previous system flowcharts.

However, data flow diagrams can also be used to represent a physical view of a system. These *physical data flow diagrams* reveal the actual form of the data media used, the people and hardware involved in processing, and the devices in which data is stored. This is done simply by additional labeling of the symbols for the data flows, processing, and data stores in a logical data flow diagram. For example, adding labels such as "sales invoice" to a data flow arrow, "data entry by clerks using POS terminals" to a processing symbol, or "customer file on magnetic disk" to a data store symbol would begin to change a data flow diagram from a logical to a physical view.

Figure B.8 illustrates another level of system detail that data flow diagrams can represent. Figure B.8 is a portion of a *level-2* DFD for the sales processing system illustrated in the level-1 DFD in Figure B.6. Notice how process symbol 1.0 (Capture Sales Transactions) in Figure B.6 is *exploded* or *decomposed* in Figure B.8 into three distinct processes: 1.0 (Capture Sales Orders), 2.0 (Convert Source Documents), and 3.0 (Sort Transactions), as well as three different data stores and the many data flows between them. Thus, the DFD in Figure B.8 gives us more details on how data about sales transactions are captured and made ready for sales processing in the sales processing system.

Entity Relationship Diagrams

An entity relationship diagram (ERD) is a data modeling tool that reveals the associations among different categories of data within a business or information system. An ERD does *not* show how data is created, captured, processed, used, stored, transmitted, or deleted. There are various styles of ERDs. Figure B.9 illustrates an entity

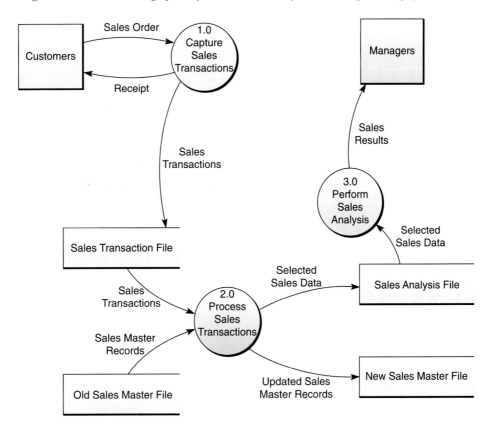

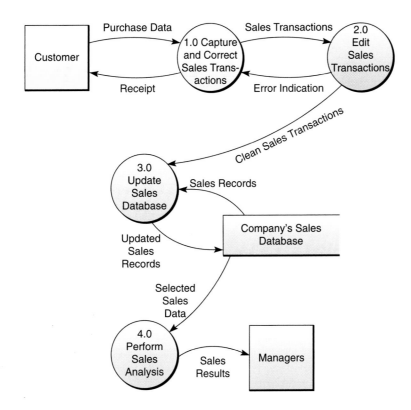

FIGURE B.7
This level-1 data flow diagram illustrates the design of a proposed sales processing system that uses online transaction processing database updates.

FIGURE B.8
A level-2 data flow diagram of the Capture Sales Transactions process (1.0) of Figure B.6.

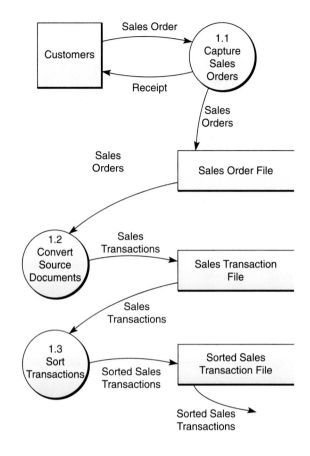

FIGURE B.9
An entity relationship diagram as a data model. One of the most popular data modeling tools is Peter Chen's entity relationship diagram. Entities (rectangles) are described by data attributes, which in this example are written inside the rectangles. Relationships are depicted by diamonds that are connected to the rectangles.

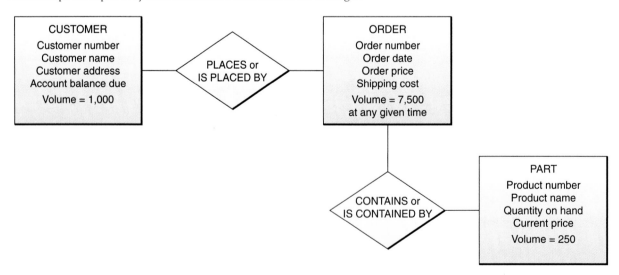

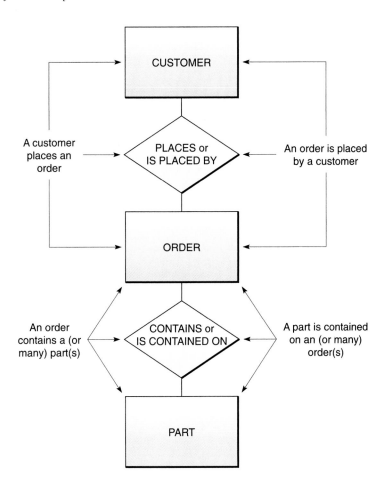

FIGURE B.10
How to read an entity relationship diagram. Reading an ERD is easy. If properly labeled, an ERD reads as a series of simple sentences that describe the relationships within the business. Notice that relationships can be interpreted in both directions.

relationship diagram using the popular Peter Chen style of ERD. Figure B.10 shows you how to read an ERD [2].

There are two other main symbols in an entity relationship diagram, one for an *entity,* the other for a *relationship.* An *entity* is anything about which we want to store data. Typically, an entity is a person, place, thing, or event. An entity is drawn as a rectangular box, which represents all occurrences of the entity. For example, the entity CUSTOMER would represent all customers. An entity box may also display typical attributes, such as customer name and number, that describe all or most occurrences of an entity. The number of instances of an entity (such as 1,000 customers) may also be recorded in an entity box.

A *relationship* is a natural association that exists between one or more entities. Typically, relationships are business activities or events (such as placing an order) that link two or more entities. In Peter Chen ERDs, a relationship is depicted by a diamond symbol that is connected to one or more entity boxes. In other ERD styles, the relationships between entities are shown by a variety of lines that connect entity boxes. Figure B.11 shows some of these relationship lines. Figure B.12 is an example of a James Martin style of entity relationship diagram that uses lines to show relationships between entities [2].

FIGURE B.11
Examples of relationship lines
that can be used in entity relationship diagrams.

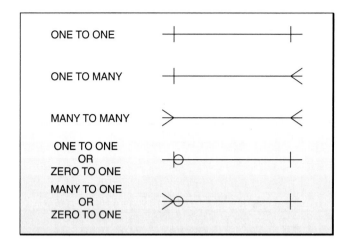

FIGURE B.12
An example of a James Martin style of entity relationship diagram for an order entry system.

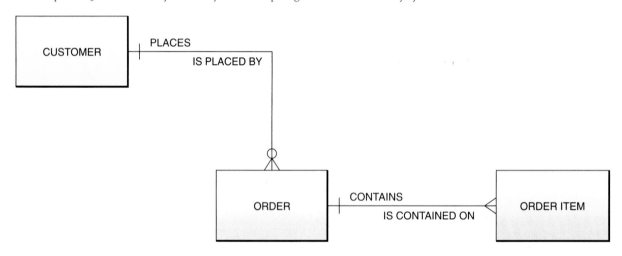

Application Exercises

1. Chevy Chase Bank: Mortgagevision Loan System

Chevy Chase Bank developed a Mortgagevision loan application service that is set in motion once field-based loan officers transmit loan information to the bank's mainframe using
their laptop computers. Then Mortgagevision notifies the
bank's mortgage underwriter, who integrates mainframe-
based data using a LAN micro workstation running the OS/2
operating system. This is done via IBM's Easel graphics package, which provides a graphical interface up front while deal-

ing with the mainframe in the background. The user just
points and shoots to select necessary data. Once the mortgage underwriter gets the credit and application data, it is
sent off in real time to the mortgage insurer via telecommunications links to their mainframe computer. Once the mortgage insurer has responded, Easel goes back into the
mainframe to grab additional applicant credit information
and then sends all collected and processed data over to a
mortgage expert system, which resides on a PS/2 server.

"We spend about a year training it," says IS Director Bob Spicer. "We took the problem of underwriting a loan and broke it into a number of problem sets and then trained the expert system to experience what we said were good and bad loans. Then we taught it how to render a final decision," Spicer explained. If the expert system encounters a decision it has not seen before, it logs it so that bank officers can study it to determine the proper reaction. The final decision is then relayed back to the field. Mortgagevision also utilizes a voice processing system from Syntellect Corp. Rather than chase loan officers with sometimes fruitless phone calls, users awaiting a loan decision can call into the host, punch in their applications numbers, and hear a computerized voice recite their current loan status.

a. What business problems and opportunities are being handled by the use of computer-based information systems at the Chevy Chase bank?

b. Use one or more tools of analysis and design (system flowchart, data flow diagram, entity relationship diagram, IS component matrix) to analyze the mortgage loan processing system at Chevy Chase Bank.

Source: Adapted from Patricia Keefe, "Taking OS/2 Benefits to the Bank," *Computerworld,* April 23, 1990, p. 37. Copyright 1990 by Computerland, Inc., Framingham, MA 01701—Reprinted from *Computerworld.*

2. University of California at Los Angeles: Student Registration System

UCLA uses a Touch-Tone telephone system for student registration. Each student is assigned two telephone registration appointments, with graduating seniors getting the first appointments. Each appointment is a 12-hour window during which a student can register for up to 10 credit hours. If a call is placed during the wrong window, the INFOBOT voice messaging computer checks the appointment schedule database, announces the correct appointment time, and hangs up. When students call at the appropriate time, they enter their student ID numbers and proceed to register. They can use the Touch-Tone phone to request courses, search for courses still open, register, and lock up their course schedules, from anywhere in the world. This has eliminated student registration lines, saved on mailing and clerical costs, and reduced transportation, traffic, and parking problems, since students do not have to come to campus to register.

a. Develop a context diagram (level-0 data flow diagram) for students enrolling in bachelor's degree programs at UCLA.

b. Draw a level-1 data flow diagram of the registration process at UCLA.

c. Draw a systems flowchart or entity relationship diagram, or develop an IS component matrix of the registration system at UCLA.

Source: Adapted from Leila Davis, "Phone Mail Gets Stamp of Approval," *Datamation,* April 1, 1989, p. 78. Reprinted with permission of *Datamation* magazine © 1989 by Cahners Publishing Company.

3. Jordan's Furniture: Computer-Based Receiving System

While thousands of furniture retailers go out of business in the United States each year, Jordan's Furniture has continued to grow. Why does Jordan's succeed where others fail? Information technology may be the answer. "Our computer system has allowed us to expand and grow in a controlled way. It has given us a real competitive advantage over other furniture stores," said Eliot Jordan, co-owner of the $70 million company. Jordan relies on a retail furniture software package and a Data General (DG) minicomputer and over 200 terminals in its main store and warehouse in Avon, Massachusetts, and two other stores in Waltham, Massachusetts, and Nashua, New Hampshire.

Jordan's premier application is a computerized receiving system that allows their store to make inventory available to customers just 20 minutes after it has been unloaded from delivery trucks. Since over 14 trucks and 1,500 pieces of furniture arrive each day, Jordan uses a bar-coding system where bar coded stickers are placed on furniture as soon as it arrives. When the furniture is stored in the warehouse, the bar-coding is scanned and transmitted to the DG mini, which updates their inventory database. Salespeople can then use their video terminals to check the availability of stock. The system has reduced inventory errors by 90 percent, and gives Jordan instant access to up to five years of customer data, giving it a vital edge in customer service.

a. What people, hardware, software, and data resources and information products do you see at Jordan's Furniture? What input processing, output, storage, and control activities do you recognize?

b. Use one or more tools of analysis and design (system flowchart, data flow diagram, IS component matrix, entity relationship diagram) to analyze the computer-based receiving system at Jordan's Furniture.

Source: Adapted from David Kelley, "From Truck to Customer in 20 minutes," *Computerworld,* January 11, 1993, p. 48. Copyright 1993 by Computerworld, Inc., Framingham, MA 01701—Reprinted from *Computerworld.*

4. United Airlines: Client/Server Menu

United Airlines' Catering Division handles 75 million in-flight meals a year. But until last June, the management of this giant inventory—including an annual allotment of 150 million swizzle sticks—was handled on stand-alone PCs running word processing software. "When we needed to make a change in a regulation or a menu, we had to find it and manually update it on thousands of pages," said Barbara Ibach, staff food and beverage planner at the Catering Division, which is based at United's Chicago headquarters. Changes had to be updated manually across United's own 17 kitchens and 250 food contractor locations worldwide. In addition, the 10- to 15-pound "Service Level" guides, which specify everything from the ingredients in a brownie to how many servings should be placed on each airplane, had to be printed and mailed out to these locations four or five times a year.

United Airlines now has a new telecommunications network and computer-based menu and procedures system. The menu and procedures tracking application software and its database were built with Borland International's Paradox for Windows relational database management package. Two 486-class local area network servers—one containing the software and database, the other acting as a communications server for remote users—are connected to five 486-based PCs at United's corporate headquarters in Chicago. Another 13 or so PCs at remote kitchen sites dial in to the database over dial-up lines. The division is also telecommunicating with one of its largest catering suppliers, Dobbs International in Memphis, Tennessee. Dobbs, in turn, passes along updated menus and schedules to its kitchens around the country. Savings in printing and distribution costs are a major benefit, but the biggest plus of the new system is in time savings and accuracy, according to United.

a. What people, hardware, software, and data resources and information products do you recognize in United Airlines' new system?

b. What examples of input, processing, output, storage, and control activities can you visualize in United's new system?

c. Use one or more tools of analysis and design (systems flowchart, data flow diagram, IS component matrix, entity relationship diagram) to analyze the menu and procedures system at United Airlines.

Source: Adapted from Ellis Booker, "United Airlines Adds Client/Server to Menu." *Computerworld*, January 17, 1994, p. 51. Copyright 1994 by Computerworld, Inc., Framingham, MA 01701. Reprinted from *Computerworld*.

Selected References

1. Flaatten, Per; Donald McCubbrey; P. Declan O'Riordan; and Keith Burgess. *Foundations of Business Systems*. 2nd ed. Fort Worth: The Dryden Press, 1992.

2. Whitten, Jeffrey; Lonnie Bentley; and Victor Barlow. *Systems Analysis & Design Methods*. 3rd ed. Burr Ridge, IL: Richard D. Irwin, 1994.

Glossary for Managerial End Users

Accounting Information Systems
Information systems that record and report business transactions, the flow of funds through an organization, and produce financial statements. This provides information for the planning and control of business operations, as well as for legal and historical record-keeping.

Active Data Dictionary
A data dictionary that automatically enforces standard data element definitions whenever end users and application programs use a DBMS to access an organization's databases.

Ada
A programming language named after Augusta Ada Byron, considered the world's first computer programmer. Developed for the U.S. Department of Defense as a standard high-order language.

Ad Hoc Inquiries
Unique, unscheduled, situation-specific information requests.

Agile Competition
The ability of a company to profitably operate in a competitive environment of continual and unpredictable changes in customer preferences, market conditions, and business opportunities.

Algorithm
A set of well-defined rules or processes for the solution of a problem in a finite number of steps.

Analog Computer
A computer that operates on data by measuring changes in continuous physical variables such as voltage, resistance, and rotation. Contrast with *Digital Computer*.

Analytical Database
A database of data extracted from oper-ational and external databases to provide data tailored to online analytical processing, decision support, and executive information systems.

Analytical Modeling
Interactive use of computer-based mathematical models to explore decision alternatives using what-if analysis, sensitivity analysis, goal-seeking analysis, and optimization analysis.

Application Development
See *Systems Development*.

Application Generator
A software package that supports the development of an application through an interactive terminal dialogue, where the programmer/analyst defines screens, reports, computations, and data structures.

Application Portfolio
A planning tool used to evaluate present and proposed information systems applications in terms of the amount of revenue or assets invested in information systems that support major business functions.

Application Software
Programs that specify the information processing activities required for the completion of specific tasks of computer users. Examples are electronic spreadsheet and word processing programs or inventory or payroll programs.

Application-Specific Programs
Application software packages that support specific applications of end users in business, science and engineering, and other areas.

Arithmetic-Logic Unit (ALU)
The unit of a computing system containing the circuits that perform arithmetic and logical operations.

Artificial Intelligence (AI)
A science and technology whose goal is to develop computers that can think, as well as see, hear, walk, talk, and feel. A major thrust is the development of computer functions normally associated with human intelligence, for example, reasoning, inference, learning, and problem solving.

ASCII: American Standard Code for Information Interchange
A standard code used for information interchange among data processing systems, communication systems, and associated equipment

Assembler
A computer program that translates an assembler language into machine language

Assembler Language
A programming language that utilizes symbols to represent operation codes and storage locations.

Asynchronous
Involving a sequence of operations without a regular or predictable time relationship. Thus operations do not happen at regular timed intervals, but an operation will begin only after a previous operation is completed. In data transmission, involves the use of start and stop bits with each character to indicate the beginning and end of the character being transmitted. Contrast with *Synchronous*.

Audio-Response Unit
An output device of a computer system whose output consists of the spoken word. Also called a voice synthesizer.

Audit Trail
The presence of media and procedures that allow a transaction to be traced through all stages of information pro-

cessing, beginning with its appearance on a source document and ending with its transformation into information on a final output document.

Automated Teller Machine (ATM)
A special-purpose transaction terminal used to provide remote banking services.

Automation
The automatic transfer and positioning of work by machines or the automatic operation and control of a work process by machines, that is, without significant human intervention or operation.

Auxiliary Storage
Storage that supplements the primary storage of the computer. Same as *Secondary Storage*.

Back-End Processor
Typically, a smaller general-purpose computer that is dedicated to database processing using a database management system (DBMS). Also called a database machine.

Background Processing
The automatic execution of lower-priority computer programs when higher-priority programs are not using the resources of the computer system. Contrast with *Foreground Processing*.

Backward-Chaining
An inference process that justifies a proposed conclusion by determining if it will result when rules are applied to the facts in a given situation.

Bar Codes
Vertical marks or bars placed on merchandise tags or packaging that can be sensed and read by optical character-reading devices. The width and combination of vertical lines are used to represent data.

Barriers to Entry
Technological, financial, or legal requirements that deter firms from entering an industry.

BASIC: Beginner's All-Purpose Symbolic Instruction Code
A programming language developed at Dartmouth College that is popular for microcomputer and time-sharing systems.

Batch Processing
A category of data processing in which data is accumulated into "batches" and processed periodically. Contrast with *Realtime Processing*.

Baud
A unit of measurement used to specify data transmission speeds. It is a unit of signaling speed equal to the number of discrete conditions or signal events per second. In many data communications applications it represents one bit per second.

Binary
Pertaining to a characteristic or property involving a selection, choice, or condition in which there are two possibilities, or pertaining to the number system that utilizes a base of 2.

Biometric Controls
Computer-based security methods that measure physical traits and characteristics such as fingerprints, voice prints, retina scans, and so on.

Bit
A contraction of "binary digit." It can have the value of either 0 or 1.

Block
A grouping of contiguous data records or other data elements that are handled as a unit.

Bootstrap
A technique in which the first few instructions of a program are sufficient to bring the rest of itself into the computer from an input device.

Branch
A transfer of control from one instruction to another in a computer program that is not part of the normal sequential execution of the instructions of the program.

Buffer
Temporary storage used to compensate for a difference in rate of flow of data, or time of occurrence of events, when transmitting data from one device to another.

Bug
A mistake or malfunction.

Bulletin Board System (BBS)
A service of personal computer networks in which electronic messages, data files, or programs can be stored for other subscribers to read or copy.

Bundling
The inclusion of software, maintenance, training, and other products or services in the price of a computer system.

Bus
A set of conducting paths for movement of data and instructions that interconnects the various components of the CPU.

Business Ethics
An area of philosophy concerned with developing ethical principles and promoting ethical behavior and practices in the accomplishment of business tasks and decision making.

Business Information System
Information systems within a business organization that support one of the traditional functions of business such as marketing, finance, or production. Business information systems can be either operations or management information systems.

Business Process Reengineering
Restructuring and transforming a business process by a fundamental rethinking and redesign to achieve dramatic improvements in cost, quality, speed, and so on.

Byte
A sequence of adjacent binary digits operated on as a unit and usually shorter than a computer word. In many computer systems, a byte is a grouping of eight bits that can represent one alphabetic or special character or can be "packed" with two decimal digits.

C
A low-level structured programming language developed by AT&T-Bell Laboratories. It resembles a machine-independent assembler language and is popular for software package development.

Cache Memory
A high-speed temporary storage area in the CPU for storing parts of a program or data during processing.

Capacity Management
The use of planning and control methods to forecast and control information processing job loads, hardware and software usage, and other computer system resource requirements.

Case-Based Reasoning
Representing knowledge in an expert system's knowledge base in the form of cases, that is, examples of past performance, occurrences, and experiences.

Cathode Ray Tube (CRT)
An electronic vacuum tube (television picture tube) that displays the output of a computer system.

CD-ROM
An optical disk technology for micro-computers featuring compact disks with a storage capacity of over 500 megabytes.

Cellular Radio
A radio communications technology that divides a metropolitan area into a honeycomb of cells to greatly increase the number of frequencies and thus the users that can take advantage of mobile phone service.

Central Processing Unit (CPU)
The unit of a computer system that includes the circuits that control the interpretation and execution of instructions. In many computer systems, the CPU includes the arithmetic-logic unit, the control unit, and primary storage unit.

Change Management
Managing the process of implementing major changes in information technology, business processes, organizational structures, and job assignments so as to reduce the risks and costs of change, and optimize its benefits.

Channel
A path along which signals can be sent. More specifically, a small special-purpose processor that controls the movement of data between the CPU and input/output devices.

Chargeback Systems
Methods of allocating costs to end user departments based on the information services rendered and information system resources utilized.

Check Bit
A binary check digit; for example, a parity bit.

Check Digit
A digit in a data field that is utilized to check for errors or loss of characters in the data field as a result of data transfer operations.

Checkpoint
A place in a program where a check or a recording of data for restart purposes is performed.

Chief Information Officer
A senior management position that oversees all information technology for a firm, concentrating on long-range information system planning and strategy.

Client/Server Network
A computing environment where end user workstations (clients) are connected to micro or mini LAN servers and possibly to mainframe super-servers.

Clock
A device that generates periodic signals utilized to control the timing of a computer. Also, a register whose contents change at regular intervals in such a way as to measure time.

Coaxial Cable
A sturdy copper or aluminum wire wrapped with spacers to insulate and protect it. Groups of coaxial cables may also be bundled together in a bigger cable for ease of installation.

COBOL: COmmon Business Oriented Language
A widely used business data processing programming language.

Code
Computer instructions.

Cognitive Science
An area of artificial intelligence that focuses on researching how the human brain works and how humans think and learn, in order to apply such findings to the design of computer-based systems.

Cognitive Styles
Basic patterns in how people handle information and confront problems.

Cognitive Theory
Theories about how the human brain works and how humans think and learn.

Common Carrier
An organization that supplies communications services to other organizations and to the public as authorized by government agencies.

Communications Satellite
Earth satellites placed in stationary orbits above the equator that serve as relay stations for communications signals transmitted from earth stations.

Competitive Advantage
Developing products, services, processes, or capabilities that give a company a superior business position relative to its competitors and other competitive forces.

Competitive Forces
A firm must confront (1) rivalry of competitors within its industry, (2) threats of new entrants, (3) threats of substitutes, (4) the bargaining power of customers, and (5) the bargaining power of suppliers.

Competitive Strategies
A firm can develop cost leadership, product differentiation, and business innovation strategies to confront its competitive forces.

Compiler
A program that translates a high-level programming language into a machine-language program.

Computer
A device that has the ability to accept data, internally store and execute a program of instructions, perform mathematical, logical, and manipulative operations on data, and report the results.

Computer-Aided Design (CAD)
The use of computers and advanced graphics hardware and software to provide interactive design assistance for engineering and architectural design.

Computer-Aided Engineering
The use of computers to simulate, analyze, and evaluate models of product designs and production processes developed using computer-aided design methods.

Computer-Aided Manufacturing (CAM)
The use of computers to automate the production process and operations of a manufacturing plant. Also called factory automation.

Computer-Aided Planning (CAP)
The use of software packages as tools to support the planning process.

Computer-Aided Software Engineering (CASE)
Same as *Computer-Aided Systems Engineering,* but emphasizing the importance of software development.

Computer-Aided Systems Engineering (CASE)
Using software packages to accomplish and automate many of the activities of information systems development, including software development or programming.

Computer Application
The use of a computer to solve a specific problem or to accomplish a particular job for an end user. For example, common business computer applications include sales order processing, inventory control, and payroll.

Computer-Assisted Instruction (CAI)
The use of computers to provide drills, practice exercises, and tutorial sequences to students.

Computer-Based Information System
An information system that uses computer hardware and software to perform its information processing activities.

Computer Crime
Criminal actions accomplished through the use of computer systems, especially with intent to defraud, destroy, or make unauthorized use of computer system resources.

Computer Ethics
A system of principles governing the legal, professional, social, and moral responsibilities of computer specialists and end users.

Computer Generations
Major stages in the historical development of computing.

Computer Graphics
Using computer-generated images to analyze and interpret data, present information, and do computer-aided design and art.

Computer Industry
The industry composed of firms that supply computer hardware, software, and services.

Computer-Integrated Manufacturing (CIM)
An overall concept that stresses that the goals of computer use in factory automation should be to simplify, automate, and integrate production processes and other aspects of manufacturing.

Computer Matching
Using computers to screen and match data about individual characteristics provided by a variety of computer-based information systems and databases in order to identify individuals for business, government, or other purposes.

Computer Monitoring
Using computers to monitor the behavior and productivity of workers on the job and in the workplace.

Computer Program
A series of instructions or statements, in a form acceptable to a computer, prepared in order to achieve a certain result.

Computer System
Computer hardware as a system of input, processing, output, storage, and control components. Thus a computer system consists of input and output devices, primary and secondary storage devices, the central processing unit, the control unit within the CPU, and other peripheral devices.

Computer Terminal
Any input/output device connected by telecommunications links to a computer.

Computer Virus or Worm
Program code that copies its destructive program routines into the computer systems of anyone who accesses computer systems that have used the program, or anyone who uses copies of data or programs taken from such computers. This spreads the destruction of data and programs among many computer users. Technically, a *virus* will not run unaided, but must be inserted into another program, while a *worm* is a distinct program that can run unaided.

Concentrator
A special-purpose computer that accepts information from many terminals using slow-speed lines and transmits data to a main computer system over a high-speed line.

Concurrent Processing
The generic term for the capability of computers to work on several tasks at the same time, that is, concurrently. This may involve specific capabilities such as overlapped processing, multiprocessing, multiprogramming, multitasking, parallel processing, and so on.

Connectivity
The degree to which hardware, software, and databases can be easily linked together in a telecommunications network.

Context Diagram
The highest level data flow diagram. It defines the boundaries of a system by showing a single major process and the data inputs and outputs and external entities involved.

Control
(1) The systems component that evaluates feedback to determine whether the system is moving toward the achievement of its goal and then makes any necessary adjustments to the input and processing components of the system to ensure that proper output is produced. (2) A management function that involves observing and measuring organizational performance and environmental activities and modifying the plans and activities of the organization when necessary.

Control Listing
A detailed report that describes each transaction occurring during a period.

Control Totals
Accumulating totals of data at multiple points in an information system to ensure correct information processing.

Control Unit
A subunit of the central processing unit that controls and directs the operations of the computer system. The control unit retrieves computer instructions in proper sequence, interprets each instruction, and then directs the other parts of the computer system in their implementation.

Conversion
The process in which the hardware, software, people, and data resources of an old information system must be converted to the requirements of a new information system. This usually involves a parallel, phased, pilot, or plunge conversion process from the old to the new system.

Cooperative Processing
Information processing that allows the computers in a distributed processing network to share the processing of parts of an end user's application.

Cost/Benefit Analysis
Identifying the advantages or benefits and the disadvantages or costs of a proposed solution.

Critical Success Factors
A small number of key factors that executives consider critical to the success of the enterprise. These are key areas where successful performance will assure the success of the organization and attainment of its goals.

Cross-Functional Information Systems
Information systems that are integrated combinations of business information systems, thus sharing information resources across the functional units of an organization.

Cursor
A movable point of light displayed on most video display screens to assist the user in the input of data.

Cybernetic System
A system that uses feedback and control components to achieve a self-monitoring and self-regulating capability.

Cylinder
An imaginary vertical cylinder consisting of the vertical alignment of data tracks on each surface of magnetic disks, which are accessed simultaneously by the read/write heads of a disk device.

Data
Facts or observations about physical phenomena or business transactions. More specifically, data are objective measurements of the attributes (characteristics) of entities such as people, places, things, and events.

Data Administration
A data resource management function that involves the establishment and enforcement of policies and procedures for managing data as a strategic corporate resource.

Data Bank
A comprehensive collection of libraries of data.

Database
A collection of logically related records or files. A database consolidates many records previously stored in separate files so that a common pool of data records serves many applications.

Database Administration
A data resource management function that includes responsibility for developing and maintaining the organization's data dictionary, designing and monitoring the performance of databases, and enforcing standards for database use and security.

Database Administrator
A specialist responsible for maintaining standards for the development, maintenance, and security of an organization's databases.

Database Management Approach
An approach to the storage and processing of data in which independent files are consolidated into a common pool, or database, of records available to different application programs and end users for processing and data retrieval.

Database Management System (DBMS)
A set of computer programs that controls the creation, maintenance, and utilization of the databases of an organization.

Data Center
An organizational unit that uses centralized computing resources to perform information processing activities for an organization. Also known as a computer center.

Data Communications
See *Telecommunications.*

Data Design
The design of the logical structure of databases and files to be used by a proposed information system. This produces detailed descriptions of the entities, relationships, data elements, and integrity rules for system files and databases.

Data Dictionary
A software module and database containing descriptions and definitions concerning the structure, data elements, interrelationships, and other characteristics of an organization's databases.

Data Entry
The process of converting data into a form suitable for entry into a computer system. Also called data capture or input preparation.

Data Flow Diagram
A graphic diagramming tool that uses a few simple symbols to illustrate the flow of data among external entities, processing activities, and data storage elements.

Data Management
Control program functions that provide access to data sets, enforce data storage conventions, and regulate the use of input/output devices.

Data Model
A conceptual framework that defines the logical relationships among the data elements needed to support a basic business or other process.

Data Modeling
A process where the relationships between data elements are identified and defined to develop data models.

Data Planning
A corporate planning and analysis function that focuses on data resource management. It includes the responsibility for developing an overall information policy and data architecture for the firm's data resources.

Data Processing
The execution of a systematic sequence of operations performed upon data to transform it into information.

Data Resource Management
A managerial activity that applies information systems technology and management tools to the task of managing an organization's data resources. Its three major components are database administration, data administration, and data planning.

Data Warehouse
A central source of data that has been extracted from various organizational databases and standardized and integrated for use throughout an organization.

Debug
To detect, locate, and remove errors from a program or malfunctions from a computer.

Decision-Making Process
A process of intelligence, design, and choice activities that result in the selection of a particular course of action.

Decision Support System (DSS)
An information system that utilizes decision models, a database, and a decision maker's own insights in an ad hoc, interactive analytical modeling process to reach a specific decision by a specific decision maker.

Demand Reports and Responses
Information provided whenever a manager or end user demands it.

Desktop Accessory Package
A software package that provides features such as a calculator, note page, alarm clock, phone directory, and appointment book that is available as a pop-up window on a computer display screen at the touch of a key.

Desktop Publishing
The use of microcomputers, laser printers, and page-makeup software to produce a variety of printed materials, formerly done only by professional printers.

Desktop Videoconferencing
The use of end user computer workstations to conduct two-way interactive
video conferences.

Development Centers
Systems development consultant groups
formed to serve as consultants to the
professional programmers and systems
analysts of an organization to improve
their application development efforts.

Digital Computer
A computer that operates on digital
data by performing arithmetic and logical operations on the data. Contrast
with *Analog Computer.*

Digitizer
A device that is used to convert drawings and other graphic images on paper
or other materials into digital data that
is entered into a computer system.

Direct Access
A method of storage where each storage
position has a unique address and can
be individually accessed in approximately the same period of time without
having to search through other storage
positions. Same as *Random Access.*
Contrast with *Sequential Access.*

**Direct Access Storage Device
(DASD)**
A storage device that can directly
access data to be stored or retrieved,
for example, a magnetic disk unit.

Direct Data Organization
A method of data organization in
which logical data elements are distributed randomly on or within the
physical data medium. For example,
logical data records distributed randomly on the surfaces of a magnetic
disk file. Also called direct organization.

Direct Input/Output
Devices such as terminals that allow
data to be input into a computer system or output from the computer system without the use of
machine-readable media.

Disaster Recovery
Methods for ensuring that an organization recovers from natural and human-
caused disasters that affect its
computer-based operations.

Disk Pack
A removable unit containing several
magnetic disks that can be mounted on
a magnetic disk storage unit.

Distributed Databases
The concept of distributing databases
or portions of a database at remote
sites where the data is most frequently
referenced. Sharing of data is made
possible through a network that interconnects the distributed databases.

Distributed Processing
A form of decentralization of information processing made possible by a network of computers dispersed
throughout an organization. Processing
of user applications is accomplished by
several computers interconnected by a
telecommunications network, rather
than relying on one large centralized
computer facility or on the decentralized operation of several independent
computers.

Document
(1) A medium on which data has been
recorded for human use, such as a
report or invoice. (2) In word processing, a generic term for text material
such as letters, memos, reports, and so
on.

Documentation
A collection of documents or information that describes a computer program, information system, or required
data processing operations.

Downsizing
Moving to smaller computing platforms, such as from mainframe systems
to networks of personal computers and
servers.

Downtime
The time interval during which a
device is malfunctioning or inopera-
tive.

DSS Generator
A software package for a decision support system that contains modules for
database, model, and dialogue management.

Duplex
In communications, pertaining to a
simultaneous two-way independent
transmission in both directions.

**EBCDIC: Extended Binary Coded
Decimal Interchange Code**
An eight-bit code that is widely used
by mainframe computers.

Echo Check
A method of checking the accuracy of
transmission of data in which the
received data are returned to the send-

ing device for comparison with the
original data.

Economic Feasibility
Whether expected cost savings,
increased revenue, increased profits,
and reductions in required investment
exceed the costs of developing and
operating a proposed system.

EDI: Electronic Data Interchange
The electronic transmission of source
documents between the computers of
different organizations.

Edit
To modify the form or format of data.
For example: to insert or delete characters such as page numbers or decimal
points.

Edit Report
A report that describes errors detected
during processing.

EFT: Electronic Funds Transfer
The development of banking and payment systems that transfer funds electronically instead of using cash or
paper documents such as checks.

Electronic Data Processing (EDP)
The use of electronic computers to process data automatically.

Electronic Document Management
An image processing technology in
which an electronic document may
consist of digitized voice notes and
electronic graphics images, as well as
digitized images of traditional documents.

Electronic Mail
The transmission, storage, and distribution of text material in electronic
form over communications networks.

Electronic Meeting Systems (EMS)
The use of video and audio communications to allow conferences and meetings to be held with participants who
may be geographically dispersed or
may be present in the same room. This
may take the form of group decision
support systems, teleconferencing, or
other methods.

Electronic Spreadsheet Package
An application program used as a computerized tool for analysis, planning,
and modeling that allows users to enter
and manipulate data into an electronic
worksheet of rows and columns.

Emulation
To imitate one system with another so
that the imitating system accepts the

same data, executes the same programs, and achieves the same results as the imitated system.

Encryption
To scramble data or convert it, prior to transmission, to a secret code that masks the meaning of the data to unauthorized recipients. Similar to enciphering.

End User
Anyone who uses an information system or the information it produces.

End User Collaboration
Using networked computers to share resources, communicate ideas, and coordinate work efforts among end user work groups.

End User Computing Systems
Computer-based information systems that directly support both the operational and managerial applications of end users. Also, the direct, hands-on use of computers by end users.

Enterprise Analysis
A planning process that emphasizes how computer-based information systems will improve the performance and competitive position of a business enterprise. This includes planning how information systems can support the basic business processes, functions, and organizational units of an organization.

Enterprise Model
A conceptual framework that defines the structures and relationships of business processes and data elements, as well as other planning structures, such as critical success factors, and organizational units.

Entity Relationship Diagram (ERD)
A data planning and systems development diagramming tool that models the relationships among the entities in a business process.

Entropy
The tendency of a system to lose a relatively stable state of equilibrium.

Ergonomics
The science and technology emphasizing the safety, comfort, and ease of use of human-operated machines such as computers. The goal of ergonomics is to produce systems that are user-friendly: safe, comfortable, and easy to use. Ergonomics is also called human factors engineering.

Evaluation Criteria
Key areas in which a proposed solution will be evaluated.

Exception Reports
Reports produced only when exceptional conditions occur, or reports produced periodically that contain information only about exceptional conditions.

Executive Information Systems
An information system that provides strategic information tailored to the needs of top management.

Executive Support System
An executive information system with additional capabilities, including data analysis, decision support, electronic mail, and personal productivity tools.

Expert System
A computer-based information system that uses its knowledge about a specific complex application area to act as an expert consultant to users. The system consists of a knowledge base and software modules that perform inferences on the knowledge and communicate answers to a user's questions.

Facilities Management
The use of an external service organization to operate and manage the information processing facilities of an organization.

Facsimile
The transmission of images and their reconstruction and duplication on some form of paper at a receiving station.

Fault Tolerant Systems
Computers that have multiple central processors, peripherals, and system software and that are able to continue operations even if there is a major hardware or software failure.

Feasibility Study
A preliminary study that investigates the information needs of end users and the objectives, constraints, basic resource requirements, cost/benefits, and feasibility of proposed projects.

Feedback
(1) Data or information concerning the components and operations of a system. (2) The use of part of the output of a system as input to the system.

Fiber Optics
The technology that uses cables consisting of very thin filaments of glass

fibers that can conduct the light generated by lasers at frequencies that approach the speed of light.

Field
A data element that consists of a grouping of characters that describe a particular attribute of an entity. For example: the name field or salary field of an employee.

Fifth Generation
The next generation of computing, which will provide computers that will be able to see, hear, talk, and think. This would depend on major advances in parallel processing, user input/output methods, and artificial intelligence.

File
A collection of related data records treated as a unit. Sometimes called a data set.

File Maintenance
The activity of keeping a file up-to-date by adding, changing, or deleting data.

File Management
Controlling the creation, deletion, access, and use of files of data and programs.

File Processing
Utilizing a file for data processing activities such as file maintenance, information retrieval, or report generation.

Financial Information Systems
Information systems that support financial managers in the financing of a business and the allocation and control of financial resources. Includes cash and securities management, capital budgeting, financial forecasting, and financial planning.

Fire Wall Computer
A computer that protects computer networks from intrusion by screening all network traffic and serving as a safe transfer point for access to and from other networks.

Firmware
The use of microprogrammed read only memory circuits in place of "hard-wired" logic circuitry. See also *Microprogramming*.

Floating Point
Pertaining to a number representation system in which each number is represented by two sets of digits. One set represents the significant digits or fixed-point "base" of the number, while

the other set of digits represents the "exponent," which indicates the precision of the number.

Floppy Disk
A small plastic disk coated with iron oxide that resembles a small phonograph record enclosed in a protective envelope. It is a widely used form of magnetic disk media that provides a direct access storage capability for microcomputer systems.

Flowchart
A graphical representation in which symbols are used to represent operations, data, flow, logic, equipment, and so on. A program flowchart illustrates the structure and sequence of operations of a program, while a system flowchart illustrates the components and flows of information systems.

Foreground Processing
The automatic execution of the computer programs that have been designed to preempt the use of computing facilities. Contrast with *Background Processing.*

Format
The arrangement of data on a medium.

FORTRAN: FORmula TRANslation
A high-level programming language widely utilized to develop computer programs that perform mathematical computations for scientific, engineering, and selected business applications.

Forward Chaining
An inference strategy that reaches a conclusion by applying rules to facts to determine if any facts satisfy a rule's conditions in a particular situation.

Fourth-Generation Languages (4GL)
Programming languages that are easier to use than high-level languages like BASIC, COBOL, or FORTRAN. They are also known as nonprocedural, natural, or very high-level languages.

Frame
A collection of knowledge about an entity or other concept consisting of a complex package of slots, that is, data values describing the characteristics or attributes of an entity.

Frame-Based Knowledge
Knowledge represented in the form of a hierarchy or network of frames.

Front-End Processor
Typically a smaller, general-purpose computer that is dedicated to handling data communications control functions in a communications network, thus relieving the host computer of these functions.

Functional Requirements
The information system capabilities required to meet the information needs of end users. Also called system requirements.

Fuzzy Logic Systems
Computer-based systems that can process data that are incomplete or only partially correct, that is, fuzzy data. Such systems can solve unstructured problems with incomplete knowledge, as humans do.

General-Purpose Application Programs
Programs that can perform information processing jobs for users from all application areas. For example, word processing programs, electronic spreadsheet programs, and graphics programs can be used by individuals for home, education, business, scientific, and many other purposes.

General-Purpose Computer
A computer that is designed to handle a wide variety of problems. Contrast with *Special-Purpose Computer.*

Generate
To produce a machine-language program for performing a specific data processing task based on parameters supplied by a programmer or user.

Generator
A computer program that performs a generating function.

Gigabyte
One billion bytes. More accurately, 2 to the 30th power, or 1,073,741,824 in decimal notation.

GIGO
A contraction of "Garbage In, Garbage Out," which emphasizes that information systems will produce erroneous and invalid output when provided with erroneous and invalid input data or instructions.

Global Company
A business that is driven by a global strategy so that all of its activities are planned and implemented in the context of a whole-world system.

Global Information Technology
The use of computer-based information systems and telecommunications networks using a variety of information technologies to support global business operations and management.

Globalization
Becoming a global enterprise by expanding into global markets, using global production facilities, forming alliances with global partners, and so on.

Goal-Seeking Analysis
Making repeated changes to selected variables until a chosen variable reaches a target value.

Graphical User Interface
A software interface that relies on icons, bars, buttons, boxes, and other images to initiate computer-based tasks for users.

Graphics
Pertaining to symbolic input or output from a computer system, such as lines, curves, and geometric shapes, using video display units or graphics plotters and printers.

Graphics Pen and Tablet
A device that allows an end user to draw or write on a pressure sensitive tablet and have their handwriting or graphics digitized by the computer and accepted as input.

Graphics Software
A program that helps users generate graphics displays.

Group Decision Making
Decisions made by groups of people coming to an agreement on a particular issue.

Group Decision Support System (GDSS)
A decision support system that provides support for decision making by groups of people.

Groupware
Software packages that support work activities by members of a work group whose workstations are interconnected by a local area network.

Hacking
(1) Obsessive use of a computer. (2) The unauthorized access and use of computer systems.

Handshaking
Exchange of predetermined signals when a connection is established between two communications terminals.

Hard Copy
A data medium or data record that has

a degree of permanence and that can be read by people or machines.

Hardware
(1) Machines and media. (2) Physical equipment, as opposed to computer programs or methods of use. (3) Mechanical, magnetic, electrical, electronic, or optical devices. Contrast with *Software.*

Hash Total
The sum of numbers in a data field that are not normally added, such as account numbers or other identification numbers. It is utilized as a control total, especially during input/output operations of batch processing systems.

Header Label
A machine-readable record at the beginning of a file containing data for file identification and control.

Heuristic
Pertaining to exploratory methods of problem solving in which solutions are discovered by evaluation of the progress made toward the final result. It is an exploratory trial-and-error approach guided by rules of thumb. Opposite of algorithmic.

Hexadecimal
Pertaining to the number system with a base of 16. Synonymous with sexadecimal.

Hierarchical Data Structure
A logical data structure in which the relationships between records form a hierarchy or tree structure. The relationships among records are one to-many, since each data element is related only to one element above it.

High-Level Language
A programming language that utilizes macro instructions and statements that closely resemble human language or mathematical notation to describe the problem to be solved or the procedure to be used. Also called a compiler language.

Homeostasis
A relatively stable state of equilibrium of a system.

Host Computer
Typically a larger central computer that performs the major data processing tasks in a computer network.

Human Factors
Hardware and software capabilities that can affect the comfort, safety, ease of use, and user customization of computer-based information systems.

Human Information Processing
A conceptual framework about the human cognitive process that uses an information processing context to explain how humans capture, process, and use information.

Human Resource Information Systems (HRIS)
Information systems that support human resource management activities such as recruitment, selection and hiring, job placement and performance appraisals, and training and development.

Hybrid AI Systems
Systems that integrate several AI technologies, such as expert systems and neural networks.

Hypermedia
Documents containing multiple forms of media, including text, graphics, video, and sound, that can be interactively searched, like *Hypertext.*

Hypertext
A methodology for the construction and interactive use of text material, in which a body of text in electronic form is indexed in a variety of ways so it can be quickly searched by a reader.

Icon
A small figure on a video display that looks like a familiar office or other device such as a file folder (for storing a file), a wastebasket (for deleting a file), or a calculator (for switching to a calculator mode).

Image Processing
A computer-based technology that allows end users to electronically capture, store, process, and retrieve images that may include numeric data, text, handwriting, graphics, documents, and photographs. Image processing makes heavy use of optical scanning and optical disk technologies.

Impact Printers
Printers that form images on paper through the pressing of a printing element and an inked ribbon or roller against the face of a sheet of paper.

Index
An ordered reference list of the contents of a file or document together with keys or reference notations for identification or location of those contents.

Index Sequential
A method of data organization in which records are organized in sequential order and also referenced by an index. When utilized with direct access file devices, it is known as index sequential access method, or ISAM.

Inference Engine
The software component of an expert system, which processes the rules and facts related to a specific problem and makes associations and inferences resulting in recommended courses of action.

Information
Information is data placed in a meaningful and useful context for an end user.

Information Architecture
A conceptual framework that defines the basic structure, content, and relationships of the organizational databases that provide the data needed to support the basic business processes of an organization.

Information Center
A support facility for the end users of an organization. It allows users to learn to develop their own application programs and to accomplish their own information processing tasks. End users are provided with hardware support, software support, and people support (trained user consultants).

Information Float
The time when a document is in transit between the sender and receiver, and thus unavailable for any action or response.

Information Processing
A concept that covers both the traditional concept of processing numeric and alphabetic data, and the processing of text, images, and voices. It emphasizes that the production of information products for users should be the focus of processing activities.

Information Quality
The degree to which information has content, form, and time characteristics which give it value to specific end users.

Information Resource Management (IRM)
A management concept that views data, information, and computer resources (computer hardware, software, and personnel) as valuable

organizational resources that should be efficiently, economically, and effectively managed for the benefit of the entire organization.

Information Retrieval
The methods and procedures for recovering specific information from stored data.

Information Superhighway
A proposed national network of networks that would connect individuals, households, businesses, government agencies, libraries, schools, universities, and other institutions with interactive voice, video, data, and multimedia communications.

Information System
A set of people, procedures, and resources that collects, transforms, and disseminates information in an organization. Or a system that accepts data resources as input and processes them into information products as output. Also, a system that uses the resources of hardware (machines and media), software (programs and procedures), and people (users and specialists) to perform input, processing, output, storage, and control activities that transform data resources into information products.

Information System Resources
People, hardware, software, and data are the resources of an information system.

Information Systems Development
See *Systems Development.*

Information System Specialist
A person whose occupation is related to the providing of information system services. For example: a systems analyst, programmer, or computer operator.

Information Systems Planning
A formal planning process that develops plans for developing and managing information systems that will support the goals of the organization. This includes strategic, tactical, and operational planning activities.

Information Technology (IT)
Hardware, software, telecommunications, database management, and other information processing technologies used in computer-based information systems.

Information Theory
The branch of learning concerned with

the likelihood of accurate transmission or communication of messages subject to transmission failure, distortion, and noise.

Input
Pertaining to a device, process, or channel involved in the insertion of data into a data processing system. Opposite of *Output.*

Input/Output (I/O)
Pertaining to either input or output, or both.

Input/Output Interface Hardware
Devices such as I/O ports, I/O busses, buffers, channels, and input/output control units, which assist the CPU in its input/output assignments. These devices make it possible for modern computer systems to perform input, output, and processing functions simultaneously.

Inquiry Processing
Computer processing that supports the realtime interrogation of online files and databases by end users.

Instruction
A grouping of characters that specifies the computer operation to be performed.

Intangible Benefits and Costs
The nonquantifiable benefits and costs of a proposed solution or system.

Integrated Circuit
A complex microelectronic circuit consisting of interconnected circuit elements that cannot be disassembled because they are placed on or within a "continuous substrate" such as a silicon chip.

Integrated Packages
Software that combines the ability to do several general-purpose applications (such as word processing, electronic spreadsheet, and graphics) into one program.

Integrative Information Systems
Information systems that combine the capabilities of several types of information systems.

Intelligent Agent
A special-purpose knowledge-based system that serves as a software surrogate to accomplish specific tasks for end users.

Intelligent Terminal
A terminal with the capabilities of a microcomputer that can thus perform

many data processing and other functions without accessing a larger computer.

Interactive Processing
A type of realtime processing in which users can interact with a computer on a realtime basis.

Interactive Video
Computer-based systems that integrate image processing with text, audio, and video processing technologies, which makes interactive multimedia presentations possible.

Interface
A shared boundary, such as the boundary between two systems. For example, the boundary between a computer and its peripheral devices.

Internet
The Internet is a rapidly growing network of thousands of business, educational, and research networks connecting millions of computers and their users in over 100 countries.

Internetwork Processor
Communications processors used by local area networks to interconnect them with other local area and wide area networks. Examples include bridges, routers, hubs, and gateways.

Internetworks
Interconnected local area and wide area networks.

Interoperability
Being able to accomplish end user applications using different types of computer systems, operating systems, and application software, interconnected by different types of local and wide area networks.

Interorganizational Information Systems
Information systems that interconnect an organization with other organizations, such as a business and its customers and suppliers.

Interpreter
A computer program that translates and executes each source language statement before translating and executing the next one.

Interrupt
A condition that causes an interruption in a processing operation during which another task is performed. At the conclusion of this new assignment, control may be transferred back to the point where the original processing operation

was interrupted or to other tasks with a higher priority.

Inverted File
A file that references entities by their attributes.

IS Component Matrix
A matrix that documents how hardware, software, people, and data resources support an information system's input, processing, output, storage, and control activities to produce information products for end users.

IT Architecture
A conceptual design for the implementation of information technology in an organization, including its hardware, software, and network technology platforms, data resources, application portfolio, and IS organization.

Iterative
Pertaining to the repeated execution of a series of steps.

Job
A specified group of tasks prescribed as a unit of work for a computer.

Job Control Language (JCL)
A language for communicating with the operating system of a computer to identify a job and describe its requirements.

Joystick
A small lever set in a box used to move the cursor on the computer's display screen.

K
An abbreviation for the prefix *kilo-*, which is 1,000 in decimal notation. When referring to storage capacity it is equivalent to 2 to the 10th power, or 1,024 in decimal notation.

Key
One or more fields within a data record that are used to identify it or control its use.

Keyboarding
Using the keyboard of a microcomputer or computer terminal.

Knowledge Base
A computer-accessible collection of knowledge about a subject in a variety of forms, such as facts and rules of inference, frames, and objects.

Knowledge-Based Information System
An information system that adds a knowledge base to the database and

other components found in other types of computer-based information systems.

Knowledge Engineer
A specialist who works with experts to capture the knowledge they possess in order to develop a knowledge base for expert systems and other knowledge-based systems.

Knowledge Workers
People whose primary work activities include creating, using, and distributing information.

Language Translator Program
A program that converts the programming language instructions in a computer program into machine language code. Major types include assemblers, compilers, and interpreters.

Large-Scale Integration (LSI)
A method of constructing electronic circuits in which thousands of circuits can be placed on a single semiconductor chip.

Layout Forms and Screens
Tools used to construct the formats and generic content of input/output media and methods for the user interface, such as display screens and reports.

Light Pen
A photoelectronic device that allows data to be entered or altered on the face of a video display terminal.

Line Printer
A device that prints all characters of a line as a unit.

Liquid Crystal Displays (LCDs)
Electronic visual displays that form characters by applying an electrical charge to selected silicon crystals.

List Organization
A method of data organization that uses indexes and pointers to allow for nonsequential retrieval.

List Processing
A method of processing data in the form of lists.

Local Area Network (LAN)
A communications network that typically connects computers, terminals, and other computerized devices within a limited physical area such as an office, building, manufacturing plant, or other worksite.

Locking In Customers and Suppliers
Building valuable relationships with customers and suppliers, which deters

them from abandoning a firm for its competitors or intimidating it into accepting less-profitable relationships.

Logical Data Elements
Data elements that are independent of the physical data media on which they are recorded.

Logical System Design
Developing general specifications for how basic information systems activities can meet end user requirements.

Loop
A sequence of instructions in a computer program that is executed repeatedly until a terminal condition prevails.

Machine Cycle
The timing of a basic CPU operation as determined by a fixed number of electrical pulses emitted by the CPU's timing circuitry or internal clock.

Machine Language
A programming language where instructions are expressed in the binary code of the computer.

Macro Instruction
An instruction in a source language that is equivalent to a specified sequence of machine instructions.

Magnetic Disk
A flat circular plate with a magnetic surface on which data can be stored by selective magnetization of portions of the curved surface.

Magnetic Drum
A circular cylinder with a magnetic surface on which data can be stored by selective magnetization of portions of the curved surface.

Magnetic Ink
An ink that contains particles of iron oxide that can be magnetized and detected by magnetic sensors.

Magnetic Ink Character Recognition (MICR)
The machine recognition of characters printed with magnetic ink. Primarily used for check processing by the banking industry.

Magnetic Tape
A plastic tape with a magnetic surface on which data can be stored by selective magnetization of portions of the surface.

Mag Stripe Card
A plastic wallet-size card with a strip of magnetic tape on one surface; widely used for credit/debit cards.

Mainframe
A larger-size computer system, typically with a separate central processing unit, as distinguished from microcomputer and minicomputer systems.

Management Functions
Management as a process of planning, organizing, staffing, directing, and controlling activities.

Management Information System
A management support system that produces prespecified reports, displays, and responses on a periodic, exception, or demand basis.

Management Levels
Management as the performance of planning and control activities at the strategic, tactical, and operational levels of an organization.

Management Support System (MSS)
An information system that provides information to support managerial decision making. More specifically, an information-reporting system, executive information system, or decision support system.

Managerial End User
A manager, entrepreneur, or managerial-level professional who personally uses information systems. Also, the manager of the department or other organizational unit that relies on information systems.

Managerial Roles
Management as the performance of a variety of interpersonal, information, and decision roles.

Manual Data Processing
(1) Data processing that requires continual human operation and intervention and that utilizes simple data processing tools such as paper forms, pencils, and filing cabinets. (2) All data processing that is not automatic, even if it utilizes machines such as typewriters and calculators.

Manufacturing Information Systems
Information systems that support the planning, control, and accomplishment of manufacturing processes. This includes concepts such as computer-integrated manufacturing (CIM) and technologies such as computer-aided manufacturing (CAM) or computer-aided design (CAD).

Marketing Information Systems
Information systems that support the planning, control, and transaction processing required for the accomplishment of marketing activities, such as sales management, advertising and promotion.

Mass Storage
Secondary storage devices with extra-large storage capacities such as magnetic or optical disks.

Master File
A data file containing relatively permanent information that is utilized as an authoritative reference and is usually updated periodically. Contrast with *Transaction File.*

Mathematical Model
A mathematical representation of a process, device, or concept.

Media
All tangible objects on which data are recorded.

Megabyte
One million bytes. More accurately, 2 to the 20th power, or 1,048,576 in decimal notation.

Memory
Same as *Storage.*

Menu
A displayed list of items (usually the names of alternative applications, files, or activities) from which an end user makes a selection.

Menu Driven
A characteristic of interactive computing systems that provides menu displays and operator prompting to assist an end user in performing a particular job.

Meta Data
Data about data; data describing the structure, data elements, interrelationships, and other characteristics of a database.

Microcomputer
A very small computer, ranging in size from a "computer on a chip" to a small typewriter-size unit.

Micrographics
The use of microfilm, microfiche, and other microforms to record data in greatly reduced form.

Microprocessor
A microcomputer central processing unit (CPU) on a chip. Without input/output or primary storage capabilities in most types.

Microprogram
A small set of elementary control instructions called microinstructions or microcode.

Microprogramming
The use of special software (microprograms) to perform the functions of special hardware (electronic control circuitry). Microprograms stored in a read-only storage module of the control unit interpret the machine language instructions of a computer program and decode them into elementary microinstructions, which are then executed.

Microsecond
A millionth of a second.

Middleware
Software that helps diverse networked computer systems work together, thus promoting their interoperability.

Midrange Computer
A computer category between microcomputers and mainframes. Examples include minicomputers, network servers, and technical workstations.

Millisecond
A thousandth of a second.

Minicomputer
A small (e.g., the size of a desk) electronic, digital, stored-program, general-purpose computer.

Model Base
An organized collection of conceptual, mathematical, and logical models that express business relationships, computational routines, or analytical techniques. Such models are stored in the form of programs and program subroutines, command files, and spreadsheets.

Modem
(MOdulator-DEModulator) A device that converts the digital signals from input/output devices into appropriate frequencies at a transmission terminal and converts them back into digital signals at a receiving terminal.

Monitor
Software or hardware that observes, supervises, controls, or verifies the operations of a system.

Mouse
A small device that is electronically connected to a computer and is moved by hand on a flat surface in order to move the cursor on a video screen in the same direction. Buttons on the mouse allow users to issue commands and make responses or selections.

Multidimensional Structure
A database model that uses multidimensional structures (such as cubes or cubes within cubes) to store data and relationships between data.

Multimedia Presentations
Providing information using a variety of media, including text and graphics displays, voice and other audio, photographs, and video segments.

Multiplex
To interleave or simultaneously transmit two or more messages on a single channel.

Multiplexer
An electronic device that allows a single communications channel to carry simultaneous data transmission from many terminals.

Multiprocessing
Pertaining to the simultaneous execution of two or more instructions by a computer or computer network.

Multiprocessor Computer Systems
Computer systems that use a multiprocessor architecture in the design of their central processing units. This includes the use of support microprocessors and multiple instruction processors, including parallel processor designs.

Multiprogramming
Pertaining to the concurrent execution of two or more programs by a computer by interleaving their execution.

Multitasking
The concurrent use of the same computer to accomplish several different information processing tasks. Each task may require the use of a different program, or the concurrent use of the same copy of a program by several users.

Nanosecond
One billionth of a second.

Natural Language
A programming language that is very close to human language. Also called very-high-level language.

Network
An interconnected system of computers, terminals, and communications channels and devices.

Network Architecture
A master plan designed to promote an open, simple, flexible, and efficient telecommunications environment

through the use of standard protocols, standard communications hardware and software interfaces, and the design of a standard multilevel telecommunications interface between end users and computer systems.

Network Data Structure
A logical data structure that allows many-to-many relationships among data records. It allows entry into a database at multiple points, because any data element or record can be related to many other data elements.

Neural Networks
Computer processors or software whose architecture is based on the human brain's meshlike neuron structure. Neural networks can process many pieces of information simultaneously and can learn to recognize patterns and programs themselves to solve related problems on their own.

Node
A terminal point in a communications network.

Nonimpact Printers
Printers that use specially treated paper and that form characters by laser, thermal (heat), electrostatic, or electrochemical processes.

Nonprocedural Languages
Programming languages that allow users and professional programmers to specify the results they want without specifying how to solve the problem.

Numerical Control
Automatic control of a machine process by a computer which makes use of numerical data, generally introduced as the operation is in process. Also called machine control.

Object
A data element that includes both data and the methods or processes that act on that data.

Object-Based Knowledge
Knowledge represented as a network of objects.

Object-Oriented Language
An object-oriented programming (OOP) language used to develop programs which create and use objects to perform information processing tasks.

Object Program
A compiled or assembled program composed of executable machine instructions. Contrast with *Source Program.*

Octal
Pertaining to the number representation system with a radix of 8.

OEM: Original Equipment Manufacturer
A firm that manufactures and sells computers by assembling components produced by other hardware manufacturers.

Office Automation (OA)
The use of computer-based information systems that collect, process, store, and transmit electronic messages, documents, and other forms of office communications among individuals, work groups, and organizations.

Office Management Systems
Office automation systems that integrate a variety of computer-based support services, including desktop accessories, electronic mail, and electronic task management.

Offline
Pertaining to equipment or devices not under control of the central processing unit.

Online
Pertaining to equipment or devices under control of the central processing unit.

Online Analytical Processing
A capability of some management, decision support, and executive information systems that supports interactive examination and manipulation of large amounts of data from many perspectives.

Online Transaction Processing (OLTP)
A realtime transaction processing system.

Open Systems
Information systems that use common standards for hardware, software, applications, and networking to create a computing environment that allows easy access by end users and their networked computer systems.

Operand
That which is operated upon. That part of a computer instruction that is identified by the address part of the instruction.

Operating Environment Package
Software packages or modules that add a graphics-based interface between end users, the operating system, and their application programs, and that

may also provide a multitasking capability.

Operating System
The main control program of a computer system. It is a system of programs that controls the execution of computer programs and may provide scheduling, debugging, input/output control, system accounting, compilation, storage assignment, data management, and related services.

Operational Feasibility
The willingness and ability of management, employees, customers, and suppliers to operate, use, and support a proposed system.

Operation Code
A code that represents specific operations to be performed upon the operands in a computer instruction.

Operation Support System
An information system that collects, processes, and stores data generated by the operations systems of an organization and produces data and information for input into a management information system or for the control of an operations system.

Operations System
A basic subsystem of the business firm that constitutes its input, processing, and output components. Also called a physical system.

Opportunity
A basic condition that presents the potential for desirable results in an organization or other system.

Optical Character Recognition (OCR)
The machine identification of printed characters through the use of light-sensitive devices.

Optical Disks
A secondary storage medium using laser technology to read tiny spots on a plastic disk. The disks are currently capable of storing billions of characters of information.

Optical Scanner
A device that optically scans characters or images and generates their digital representations.

Optimization Analysis
Finding an optimum value for selected variables in a mathematical model, given certain constraints.

Organizational Feasibility
How well a proposed information system supports the objectives of an organization's strategic plan for information systems.

Output
Pertaining to a device, process, or channel involved with the transfer of data or information out of an information processing system.

Packet
A group of data and control information in a specified format that is transmitted as an entity.

Packet Switching
A data transmission process that transmits addressed packets such that a channel is occupied only for the duration of transmission of the packet.

Page
A segment of a program or data, usually of fixed length.

Paging
A process that automatically and continually transfers pages of programs and data between primary storage and direct access storage devices. It provides computers with multiprogramming and virtual memory capabilities.

Parallel Processing
Executing many instructions at the same time, that is, in parallel. Performed by advanced computers using many instruction processors organized in clusters or networks.

Parity Bit
A check bit appended to an array of binary digits to make the sum of all the binary digits, including the check bit, always odd or always even.

Pascal
A high-level, general-purpose, structured programming language named after Blaise Pascal. It was developed by Niklaus Wirth of Zurich in 1968.

Pattern Recognition
The identification of shapes, forms, or configurations by automatic means.

PCM: Plug Compatible Manufacturer
A firm that manufactures computer equipment that can be plugged into existing computer systems without requiring additional hardware or software interfaces.

Pen-Based Computers
Tablet-style microcomputers that recognize handwriting and hand drawing done by a pen-shaped device on their pressure-sensitive display screens.

Performance Monitor
A software package that monitors the processing of computer system jobs, helps develop a planned schedule of computer operations that can optimize computer system peformance, and produces detailed statistics that are used for computer system capacity planning and control.

Periodic Reports
Providing information to managers using a prespecified format designed to provide information on a regularly scheduled basis.

Peripheral Devices
In a computer system, any unit of equipment, distinct from the central processing unit, that provides the system with input, output, or storage capabilities.

Personal Information Manager (PIM)
A software package that helps end users store, organize, and retrieve text and numerical data in the form of notes, lists, memos, and a variety of other forms.

Physical System Design
Design of the user interface methods and products, database structures, and processing and control procedures for a proposed information system, including hardware, software, and personnel specifications.

Picosecond
One trillionth of a second.

Plasma Display
Output devices that generate a visual display with electrically charged particles of gas trapped between glass plates.

Plotter
A hard-copy output device that produces drawings and graphical displays on paper or other materials.

Pointer
A data element associated with an index, a record, or other set of data that contains the address of a related record.

Pointing Devices
Devices that allow end users to issue commands or make choices by moving a cursor on the display screen.

Pointing Stick
A small buttonlike device on a keyboard which moves the cursor on the screen in the direction of the pressure placed upon it.

Point-of-Sale (POS) Terminal
A computer terminal used in retail stores that serves the function of a cash register as well as collecting sales data and performing other data processing functions.

Port
(1) Electronic circuitry that provides a connection point between the CPU and input/output devices. (2) A connection point for a communications line on a CPU or other front-end device.

Postimplementation Review
Monitoring and evaluating the results of an implemented solution or system.

Presentation Graphics
Using computer-generated graphics to enhance the information presented in reports and other types of presentations.

Prespecified Reports
Reports whose format is specified in advance to provide managers with information periodically, on an exception basis, or on demand.

Private Branch Exchange (PBX)
A switching device that serves as an interface between the many telephone lines within a work area and the local telephone company's main telephone lines or trunks. Computerized PBXs can handle the switching of both voice and data in the local area networks that are needed in such locations.

Problem
A basic condition that is causing undesirable results in an organization or other system.

Procedure-Oriented Language
A programming language designed for the convenient expression of procedures used in the solution of a wide class of problems.

Procedures
Sets of instructions used by people to complete a task.

Process Control
The use of a computer to control an ongoing physical process, such as petrochemical production.

Process Design
The design of the programs and procedures needed by a proposed information system, including detailed program specifications and procedures.

Processor
A hardware device or software system

capable of performing operations upon data.

Program
A set of instructions that cause a computer to perform a particular task.

Programmed Decision
A decision that can be automated by basing it on a decision rule that outlines the steps to take when confronted with the need for a specific decision.

Programmer
A person mainly involved in designing, writing, and testing computer programs.

Programming
The design, writing, and testing of a program.

Programming Language
A language used to develop the instructions in computer programs.

Programming Tools
Software packages or modules that provide editing and diagnostic capabilities and other support facilities to assist the programming process.

Project Management
Managing the accomplishment of an information system development project according to a specific project plan, in order that a project is completed on time, within its budget, and meets its design objectives.

Prompt
Messages that assist a user in performing a particular job. This would include error messages, correction suggestions, questions, and other messages that guide an end user.

Protocol
A set of rules and procedures for the control of communications in a communications network.

Prototype
A working model. In particular, a working model of an information system that includes tentative versions of user input and output, databases and files, control methods, and processing routines.

Prototyping
The rapid development and testing of working models, or prototypes, of new information system applications in an interactive, iterative process involving both systems analysts and end users.

Pseudocode
An informal design language of structured programming that expresses the

processing logic of a program module in ordinary human language phrases.

Public Information Networks
Networks provided by various organizations and companies to personal computer users that offer a variety of computing and other information services.

Quality Assurance
Methods for ensuring that information systems are free from errors and fraud and provide information products of high quality.

Query Language
A high-level, humanlike language provided by a database management system that enables users to easily extract data and information from a database.

Queue
(1) A waiting line formed by items in a system waiting for service. (2) To arrange in or form a queue.

RAID
Redundant arrays of independent disks. Magnetic disk units that house many interconnected microcomputer hard disk drives, thus providing large, fault tolerant storage capacities.

Random Access
Same as *Direct Access*. Contrast with *Sequential Access*.

Random Access Memory (RAM)
One of the basic types of semiconductor memory used for temporary storage of data or programs during processing. Each memory position can be directly sensed (read) or changed (write) in the same length of time, irrespective of its location on the storage medium.

Reach and Range Analysis
A planning framework that contrasts a firm's ability to use its IT platform to reach its stakeholders, with the range of information products and services that can be provided or shared through IT.

Read Only Memory (ROM)
A basic type of semiconductor memory used for permanent storage. Can only be read, not "written," that is, changed. Variations are Programmable Read Only Memory (PROM) and Erasable Programmable Read Only Memory (EPROM).

Realtime
Pertaining to the performance of data processing during the actual time a business or physical process transpires,

in order that results of the data processing can be used to support the completion of the process.

Realtime Processing
Data processing in which data is processed immediately rather than periodically. Also called online processing. Contrast with *Batch Processing*.

Record
A collection of related data fields treated as a unit.

Reduced Instruction Set Computer (RISC)
A CPU architecture that optimizes processing speed by the use of a smaller number of basic machine instructions than traditional CPU designs.

Redundancy
In information processing, the repetition of part or all of a message to increase the chance that the correct information will be understood by the recipient.

Register
A device capable of storing a specified amount of data such as one word.

Relational Data Structure
A logical data structure in which all data elements within the database are viewed as being stored in the form of simple tables. DBMS packages based on the relational model can link data elements from various tables as long as the tables share common data elements.

Remote Access
Pertaining to communication with the data processing facility by one or more stations that are distant from that facility.

Remote Job Entry (RJE)
Entering jobs into a batch processing system from a remote facility.

Report Generator
A feature of database management system packages which allows an end user to quickly specify a report format for the display of information retrieved from a database.

Reprographics
Copying and duplicating technology and methods.

Resource Management
An operating system function that controls the use of computer system resources such as primary storage, secondary storage, CPU processing time, and input/output devices by other sys-

tem software and application software packages.

Robotics
The technology of building machines (robots) with computer intelligence and humanlike physical capabilities.

Routine
An ordered set of instructions that may have some general or frequent use.

RPG: Report Program Generator
A problem-oriented language that utilizes a generator to construct programs that produce reports and perform other data processing tasks.

Rule
Statements that typically take the form of a premise and a conclusion such as If-Then rules: If (condition), Then (conclusion).

Rule-Based Knowledge
Knowledge represented in the form of rules and statements of fact.

Scenario Approach
A planning approach where managers, employees, and planners create scenarios of what an organization will be like three to five years or more into the future, and identify the role IT can play in those scenarios.

Schema
An overall conceptual or logical view of the relationships between the data in a database.

Scientific Method
An analytical methodology that involves (1) recognizing phenomena, (2) formulating a hypothesis about the causes or effects of the phenomena, (3) testing the hypothesis through experimentation, (4) evaluating the results of such experiments, and (5) drawing conclusions about the hypothesis.

Secondary Storage
Storage that supplements the primary storage of a computer. Synonymous with *Auxiliary Storage*.

Sector
A subdivision of a track on a magnetic disk surface.

Security Codes
Passwords, identification codes, account codes, and other codes that limit the access and use of computer-based system resources to authorized users.

Security Monitor
A software package that monitors the use of a computer system and protects

its resources from unauthorized use, fraud, and vandalism.

Semiconductor Memory
Microelectronic storage circuitry etched on tiny chips of silicon or other semiconducting material. The primary storage of most modern computers consists of microelectronic semiconductor storage chips for random access memory (RAM) and read only memory (ROM).

Semistructured Decisions
Decisions involving procedures that can be partially prespecified, but not enough to lead to a definite recommended decision.

Sensitivity Analysis
Observing how repeated changes to a single variable affect other variables in a mathematical model.

Sequential Access
A sequential method of storing and retrieving data from a file. Contrast with *Random Access* and *Direct Access*.

Sequential Data Organization
Organizing logical data elements according to a prescribed sequence.

Serial
Pertaining to the sequential or consecutive occurrence of two or more related activities in a single device or channel.

Server
A computer that supports telecommunications in a local area network, as well as the sharing of peripheral devices, software, and databases among the workstations in the network.

Service Bureau
A firm offering computer and data processing services. Also called a computer service center.

Smart Products
Industrial and consumer products, with "intelligence" provided by built-in microcomputers or microprocessors that significantly improve the performance and capabilities of such products.

Software
Computer programs and procedures concerned with the operation of an information system. Contrast with *Hardware*.

Software Package
A computer program supplied by computer manufacturers, independent software companies, or other computer users. Also known as canned programs,

proprietary software, or packaged programs.

Software Piracy
Unauthorized copying of software.

Software Suites
A combination of individual software packages that share a common graphical user interface and are designed for easy transfer of data between applications.

Solid State
Pertaining to devices such as transistors and diodes whose operation depends on the control of electric or magnetic phenomena in solid materials.

Source Data Automation
The use of automated methods of data entry that attempt to reduce or eliminate many of the activities, people, and data media required by traditional data entry methods.

Source Document
A document that is the original formal record of a transaction, such as a purchase order or sales invoice.

Source Program
A computer program written in a language that is subject to a translation process. Contrast with *Object Program*.

Special-Purpose Computer
A computer designed to handle a restricted class of problems. Contrast with *General-Purpose Computer*.

Spooling
Simultaneous peripheral operation online. Storing input data from low-speed devices temporarily on high-speed secondary storage units, which can be quickly accessed by the CPU. Also, writing output data at high speeds onto magnetic tape or disk units from which it can be transferred to slow-speed devices such as a printer.

Stage Analysis
A planning process in which the information system needs of an organization are based on an analysis of its current stage in the growth cycle of the organization and its use of information systems technology.

Standards
Measures of performance developed to evaluate the progress of a system towards its objectives.

Storage
Pertaining to a device into which data can be entered, in which it can be held, and from which it can be retrieved at a later time. Same as *Memory*.

Strategic Information Systems
Information systems that provide a firm with competitive products and services that give it a strategic advantage over its competitors in the marketplace. Also, information systems that promote business innovation, improve operational efficiency, and build strategic information resources for a firm.

Strategic Opportunities Matrix
A planning framework that uses a matrix to help identify opportunities with strategic business potential, as well as a firm's ability to exploit such opportunities with IT.

Structure Chart
A design and documentation technique to show the purpose and relationships of the various modules in a program.

Structured Decisions
Decisions that are structured by the decision procedures or decision rules developed for them. They involve situations where the procedures to follow when a decision is needed can be specified in advance.

Structured Programming
A programming methodology that uses a top-down program design and a limited number of control structures in a program to create highly structured modules of program code.

Structured Query Language (SQL)
A query language that is becoming a standard for advanced database management system packages. A query's basic form is SELECT. . . . FROM . . .WHERE.

Subroutine
A routine that can be part of another program routine.

Subschema
A subset or transformation of the logical view of the database schema that is required by a particular user application program.

Subsystem
A system that is a component of a larger system.

Supercomputer
A special category of large computer systems that are the most powerful available. They are designed to solve massive computational problems.

Superconductor
Materials that can conduct electricity with almost no resistance. This allows the development of extremely fast and small electronic circuits. Formerly only possible at super cold temperatures near absolute zero. Recent developments promise superconducting materials near room temperature.

Switch
(1) A device or programming technique for making a selection. (2) A computer that controls message switching among the computers and terminals in a telecommunications network.

Switching Costs
The costs in time, money, effort, and inconvenience that it would take a customer or supplier to switch its business to a firm's competitors.

Synchronous
A characteristic in which each event, or the performance of any basic operation, is constrained to start on, and usually to keep in step with, signals from a timing clock. Contrast with *Asynchronous*.

System
(1) A group of interrelated or interacting elements forming a unified whole. (2) A group of interrelated components working together toward a common goal by accepting inputs and producing outputs in an organized transformation process. (3) An assembly of methods, procedures, or techniques unified by regulated interaction to form an organized whole. (4) An organized collection of people, machines, and methods required to accomplish a set of specific functions.

System Flowchart
A graphic diagramming tool used to show the flow of information processing activities as data are processed by people and devices.

Systems Analysis
(1) Analyzing in detail the components and requirements of a system. (2) Analyzing in detail the information needs of an organization, the characteristics and components of presently utilized information systems, and the functional requirements of proposed information systems.

Systems Approach
A systematic process of problem solving that defines problems and opportunities in a systems context. Data is gathered describing the problem or opportunity, and alternative solutions

are identified and evaluated. Then the best solution is selected and implemented, and its success evaluated.

Systems Context
Recognizing systems, subsystems, and components of systems in a situation. Also called a systemic view.

Systems Design
Deciding how a proposed information system will meet the information needs of end users. Includes logical and physical design activities, and user interface, data, and process design activities which produce system specifications that satisfy the system requirements developed in the systems analysis stage.

Systems Development
(1) Conceiving, designing, and implementing a system. (2) Developing information systems by a process of investigation, analysis, design, implementation, and maintenance. Also called the systems development life cycle (SDLC), information systems development, or application development.

Systems Development Tools
Graphical, textual, and computer-aided tools and techniques used to help analyze, design, and document the development of an information system. Typically used to represent (1) the components and flows of a system, (2) the user interface, (3) data attributes and relationships, and (4) detailed system processes.

Systems Implementation
The stage of systems development in which hardware and software are acquired, developed, and installed, the system is tested and documented, people are trained to operate and use the system, and an organization converts to the use of a newly developed system.

Systems Investigation
The screening, selection, and preliminary study of a proposed information system solution to a business problem.

Systems Maintenance
The monitoring, evaluating, and modifying of a system to make desirable or necessary improvements.

System Software
Programs that control and support operations of a computer system.

System software includes a variety of programs, such as operating systems, database management systems, communications control programs, service and utility programs, and programming language translators.

System Specifications
The product of the systems design stage. It consists of specifications for the hardware, software, facilities, personnel, databases, and the user interface of a proposed information system.

System Support Programs
Programs that support the operations, management, and users of a computer system by providing a variety of support services. Examples are system utilities and performance monitors.

Tangible Benefits and Costs
The quantifiable benefits and costs of a proposed solution or system.

Task Management
A basic operating system function that manages the accomplishment of the computing tasks of users by a computer system.

Technical Feasibility
Whether reliable hardware and software capable of meeting the needs of a proposed system can be acquired or developed by an organization in the required time.

Technological Implementation
Formal programs of implementation-support activities to encourage user acceptance and productive use of reengineered business processes and new information technologies.

Technology Implementation
Methods for ensuring end user acceptance and productive use of newly installed information system technologies.

Technology Management
The establishment of organizational groups to identify, introduce, and monitor the assimilation of new information system technologies into organizations.

Telecommunications
Pertaining to the transmission of signals over long distances, including not only data communications but also the transmission of images and voices using radio, television, and other communications technologies.

Telecommunications Channel

The part of a telecommunications network that connects the message source with the message receiver. It includes the physical equipment used to connect one location to another for the purpose of transmitting and receiving information.

Telecommunications Controller
A data communications interface device (frequently a special-purpose mini- or microcomputer) that can control a telecommunications network containing many terminals.

Telecommunications Control Program
A computer program that controls and supports the communications between the computers and terminals in a telecommunications network.

Telecommunications Monitors
Computer programs that control and support the communications between the computers and terminals in a telecommunications network.

Telecommunications Processors
Multiplexers, concentrators, communications controllers, and cluster controllers that allow a communications channel to carry simultaneous data transmissions from many terminals. They may also perform error monitoring, diagnostics and correction, modulation-demodulation, data compression, data coding and decoding, message switching, port contention, buffer storage, and serve as an interface to satellite and other communications networks.

Telecommuting
The use of telecommunications to replace commuting to work from one's home.

Teleconferencing
The use of video communications to allow business conferences to be held with participants who are scattered across a country, continent, or the world.

Telephone Tag
The process that occurs when two people who wish to contact each other by telephone repeatedly miss each other's phone calls.

Teleprocessing
Using telecommunications for computer-based information processing.

Terabyte
One trillion bytes. More accurately, 2 to the 40th power, or 1,009,511,627,776 in decimal notation.

Text Data
Words, phrases, sentences, and paragraphs used in documents and other forms of communication.

Throughput
The total amount of useful work performed by a data processing system during a given period of time.

Time Sharing
Providing computer services to many users simultaneously while providing rapid responses to each.

Total Quality Management
Planning and implementing programs of continuous quality improvement, where quality is defined as meeting or exceeding the requirements and expectations of customers for a product or service.

Touch-Sensitive Screen
An input device that accepts data input by the placement of a finger on or close to the CRT screen.

Track
The portion of a moving storage medium, such as a drum, tape, or disk, that is accessible to a given reading head position.

Trackball
A rollerball device set in a case used to move the cursor on a computer's display screen.

Transaction
An event that occurs as part of doing business, such as a sale, purchase, deposit, withdrawal, refund, transfer, payment, and so on.

Transaction Document
A document produced as part of a business transaction. For instance: a purchase order, paycheck, sales receipt, or customer invoice.

Transaction File
A data file containing relatively transient data to be processed in combination with a master file. Contrast with *Master File.*

Transaction Processing Cycle
A cycle of basic transaction processing activities including data entry, transaction processing, database maintenance, document and report generation, and inquiry processing.

Transaction Processing System (TPS)
An information system that processes data arising from the occurrence of business transactions.

Transaction Terminal
Terminals used in banks, retail stores, factories, and other work sites that are used to capture transaction data at its point of origin. Examples are point-of-sale (POS) terminals and automated teller machines (ATMs).

Transborder Data Flows
The flow of business data over telecommunications networks across international borders.

Transform Algorithm
Performing an arithmetic computation on a record key and using the result of the calculation as an address for that record. Also known as key transformation or hashing.

Transnational Strategy
A management approach in which an organization integrates its global business activities through close cooperation and interdependence among its headquarters, operations, and international subsidiaries, and its use of appropriate global information technologies.

Turnaround Document
Output of a computer system (such as customer invoices and statements) that is designed to be returned to the organization as machine-readable input.

Turnaround Time
The elapsed time between submission of a job to a computing center and the return of the results.

Turnkey Systems
Computer systems where all of the hardware, software, and systems development needed by a user are provided.

Unbundling
The separate pricing of hardware, software, and other related services.

Universal Product Code (UPC)
A standard identification code using bar coding, printed on products that can be read by the optical supermarket scanners of the grocery industry.

Unstructured Decisions
Decisions that must be made in situations where it is not possible to specify in advance most of the decision procedures to follow.

User-Friendly
A characteristic of human-operated equipment and systems that makes them safe, comfortable, and easy to use.

User Interface
That part of an operating system or other program that allows users to communicate with it to load programs, access files, and accomplish other computing tasks.

User Interface Design
Designing the interactions between end users and computer systems, including input/output methods and the conversion of data between human-readable and machine-readable forms.

Utility Program
A standard set of routines that assists in the operation of a computer system by performing some frequently required process such as copying, sorting, or merging.

Value-Added Carriers
Third-party vendors who lease telecommunications lines from common carriers and offer a variety of telecommunications services to customers.

Value-Added Resellers (VARs)
Companies that provide industry-specific software for use with the computer systems of selected manufacturers.

Value Chain
Viewing a firm as a series or chain of basic activities that add value to its products and services and thus add a margin of value to the firm.

Videotex
An interactive information service provided over phone lines or cable TV channels.

Virtual Company
A form of organization that uses information technology to link the people, assets, and ideas of a variety of business partners, no matter where they may be located, in order to exploit a business opportunity.

Virtual Machine
Pertaining to the simulation of one type of computer system by another computer system.

Virtual Memory
The use of secondary storage devices as an extension of the primary storage of the computer, thus giving the appearance of a larger main memory than actually exists.

Virtual Reality
The use of multisensory human/computer interfaces that enable human users to experience computer-simulated objects, entities, spaces, and "worlds" as if they actually existed.

VLSI: Very-Large-Scale Integration
Semiconductor chips containing hundreds of thousands of circuits.

Voice Mail
A variation of electronic mail where digitized voice messages rather than electronic text are accepted, stored, and transmitted.

Voice Recognition
Direct conversion of spoken data into electronic form suitable for entry into a computer system. Also called voice data entry.

Volatile Memory
Memory (such as electronic semiconductor memory) that loses its contents when electrical power is interrupted.

Wand
A handheld optical character recognition device used for data entry by many transaction terminals.

What-If Analysis
Observing how changes to selected variables affect other variables in a mathematical model.

Wide Area Network (WAN)
A data communications network covering a large geographic area.

Window
One section of a computer's multiple-section display screen, each of which can have a different display.

Wireless LANs
Using radio or infrared transmissions to link devices in a local area network.

Word
(1) A string of characters considered as a unit. (2) An ordered set of bits (usually larger than a byte) handled as a unit by the central processing unit.

Word Processing
The automation of the transformation of ideas and information into a readable form of communication. It involves the use of computers to manipulate text data in order to produce office communications in the form of documents.

Work Group Computing
End user computing in a work group environment in which members of a work group may use a local area network to share hardware, software, and databases to accomplish group assignments.

Workstation
A computer terminal or micro- or minicomputer system designed to support the work of one person. Also, a high-powered computer to support the work of professionals in engineering, science, and other areas that require extensive computing power and graphics capabilities.

Name Index

Tansuk, David, 397
Tao, David K., 615
Tasker, Daniel, 261
Taucher, Fred, 45
Tayntor, Christine, 307
Te'eni, Dov, 398
Teitz, Jeff, 396
Teixeira, Kevin, 487
Teng, James, 243, 261, 440, 574
Terrell, Dale, 98
Tetzelli, Rick, 228, 441
Thompson, Don, A–15
Thro, Ellen, 487
Tobin, Bill, 345
Tonkel, J. Rock, 530
Torkzadeh, Gholamreza, 307
Townsend, Lucy, A–13 to A–14
Trachtenberg, Myles, 280
Trefts, Dorothy, 575
Trippi, Robert, 352
Trudell, George, 399
Turban, Efraim, 352, 398, 487
Turing, Alan, 446
Turoff, Murray, 398
Tuttle, Mark, 456

Underhill, Doug, 149

Valacich, Joseph, 307, 397
Valenzi, E., 487
VanLengen, Craig, 63
Van Slyke, Richard, 228

Vargo, Max, A–11, A–14
Venema, Wietse, A–36
Vessey, Iris, 102, 307
Vitello, Bonnie, A–31
Vogel, Douglas, 307, 397
Von Schilling, Peter, 228, 534

Waecker, Ann, A–5
Walker, Kent, 593, A–37
Wallaesa, Harry, 59
Wallich, Paul, 621
Walton, Richard, 575
Walton, Sam, 220
Wand, Yair, 63
Wang, Charles, 13, 28
Warga, Donald F., 301
Warkentin, Merrill, 574
Watson, Hugh, 102, 386, 387, 397, 398
Watson, Richard, 534
Watt, Peggy, 576
Weatherbe, James, 534
Weber, Ron, 63
Weinberg, Neal, 149, 224
Weiner, Norbert, 446, 458
Welch, Rich, 259
Wernsdorfer, Andy, 224
West, Paul, 395
Whipple, Jay N., III, 437
Whisler, T. L., 534
Whitesell, Joe, 97
Whitman, Gary, A–37

Whitten, Jeffrey, 102, B–12
Wilder, Clinton, 337, 352
Wilkes, Ronald B., 388, 397, A–25
Wilkinson, Joseph J., 326
Willbrock, Peter, 179
Williams, Deborah, 103
Williamson, Pat, 56, 349
Wilson, Linda, 262
Wimmer, Robert, 229
Winkler, Scott, 180
Winter, Richard, 258
Wiseman, Charles, 402
Wolinsky, Carol, 621
Wood, Elizabeth, 293, 295, 307
Wride, Evan, 531
Wrobel, Leo, 228
Wyatt, John, 573
Wylder, John, 261

Young, Greggry, 533
Young, Todd, A–34
Youngworth, Paul, 98

Zahedi, Fatemeh, 441, 575, 621
Zahra, Shaker, 574
Zedeh, Lotfi, 487
Zeigon, James, 309
Zigli, Ronald, 534
Zigurs, Ilze, 307
Ziswanathan, Ravi, 350
Zmud, Robert, 533

Organization Index

Subject Index